THE NATURE AND ELEMENTS OF SOCIOLOGY

THE NATURE AND
ELEMENTS *of* SOCIOLOGY

by MCQUILKIN DEGRANGE

Professor Emeritus of Sociology, Dartmouth College

GREENWOOD PRESS, PUBLISHERS
NEW YORK

PREFACE

To write any introductory comment to a sociological treatise is always difficult. The book is an illustration as well as a discussion. Everything that has gone to its making should, in a sense, be an occcasion for gratitude on the part of the author. So, too, everyone who has played a part in its making merits recognition.

Obviously personal mention in these cases is quite impossible. At the best it seems possible to make only such references as will show clearly the consciousness of indebtedness over a wide range of cooperation. In this sense, all who have contributed to the making of a text should be mentioned. On a narrower basis something can be done. There are, for example, all the long lines of students to whom through the years so much is due, even when it is unrecognized. There are the many colleagues with whom discussion has been continuously helpful. To both of these groups and all whom they represent, recognition is here offered.

There is another group to whom thanks are more specifically due. They can be mentioned by name because of the help they gave in the preparation of the manuscript. Notably, there was Miss Mary E. Wesbrook, who was careful to guard the accuracy of citation. And there was Mrs. David Horne, who gave to the final preparation of a long manuscript for the printer an unusual degree of care.

Finally, there are those to whom no thanks are adequate. All that I can do is to mention their names: Michael Choukas, Leonard W. Doob, Eugene Katz.

McQuilkin DeGrange

Hanover, N. H.

CONTENTS

vii

INTRODUCTION

In the second chapter of his *Cours de philosophie positive,* Auguste Comte remarks that in the exposition of any science two courses may be followed—other modes of exposition being but combinations of these two. These logically distinct courses are the historical and the dogmatic. To follow the first is to set forth in sequence the data regarded at a given moment as acquired by a science in the same order in which the mind attained them, retracing as far as possible the very routes that led to these original discoveries. To follow the second is to present the ideas composing the science in question as they might be synthesized by a single mind which, placed at the proper point of view and supplied with adequate information, should set itself to remake the science as a whole.

The first course demands only the study of the original works which contributed to the advance of the science; the second assumes that all these works have been fused into a general system and so can be presented in a more logical order than the original order of time is likely to have made possible. Obviously only for a science that has already arrived at a rather high degree of development is the dogmatic order practicable and even necessary, if and when later conceptions make it possible to present the earlier discoveries in a more synthetic and direct way. A geometer of antiquity, for example, had only to study in succession a few original treatises dealing with the various parts of geometry, whereas a modern geometer has seldom read an original work, the exceptions being those presenting the latest discoveries.

Thus every exposition is in fact and inevitably a combination of the two courses, with a tendency for the dogmatic constantly to assume a more and more dominant role. But the exposition can never be wholly dogmatic because for it to be so would require the fulfillment of an impossible condition, namely, the integration into the body of the science of the very latest discoveries. Hence

1

part, at least, of every such exposition is historical in method.

It need not be said that the foregoing considerations are at least as relevant to sociology as they are to any other discipline. It is especially clear that the reasons why the historical method of presentation is inevitable in reviewing the development of a science in its early stages are applicable in all respects to sociology. It is open to doubt indeed whether the science has yet passed the point where the education of the sociologist means anything more than the reading of certain original treatises. If it has, then the dogmatic order of presentation must be the end sought, but it is certain that the proportion of historical matter must be high. Only successive efforts like the present, integrating into a general body of doctrines the theoretical advances effected at successive periods, can reduce this proportion, thus ultimately freeing the sociologists of the future from the necessity of resorting to any but a very few original texts.

The present volume then must be a mixture of the two orders of exposition; it will be compelled to resort in many instances to the historical form despite the ideal which inspires it to make the dogmatic the essential framework of thought. It will be necessary, for example, to show how the concept of scientific knowledge rose gradually from the mathematical to the physical and then to the biological level, whence it became apparent that there were still other domains of knowledge of the utmost importance to men yet to be attained and traversed. The social world as a specific field of investigation came clearly into view only at this height of intellectual achievement.

It will be necessary as well to show how the rise of scientific inquiry from one domain to another made indispensable and inevitable a greater and greater concentration of attention upon the means whereby additions to knowledge can be made. What is scientific knowledge? How is it gained and increased? What, indeed, is a science? Only when questions such as these are given answers drawn from the entire record of man's accumulating experience can a motivated decision be reached upon the much debated issue: is sociology a science?

The first two sections of this volume, dealing in essence with the spirit and method of science, are therefore an integral part of the book and not merely an historical introduction. They are in no sense intended to be a sketch of the history of science, for which they would be inadequate; they are a part of the thought structure of the volume. Without them the book would not be, for they make it possible to state the requirements which sociology must fulfill to reach the dignity of science. At the same time, by virtue of the conclusions they reach they lay the groundwork for the remainder of the discussion.

The third part is intended to show the steps by which the general body of observation concerning what is still loosely called social gradually came to acquire the abstractness and precision which are the marks of approaching scientific maturity. Here the historical course of exposition is exclusively employed; and it continues until the point is reached where it becomes possible, in the fourth part, to formulate the conception, the abstract isolate, that does for sociology what analogous conceptions do for other domains of inquiry, namely, make a true science possible.

From this point on, the remainder of the volume, sections A and B of Part Five, adopts in principle the dogmatic manner of presentation. An attempt is made here to present the elements of sociological theory in a systematic and logical form, dividing and subdividing the field into appropriate sections and subsections.

The discussion ends with an epilogue in which the whole body of sociological thought is brought into relation with the other disciplines relating to the whole man, to whom all thought must in the last analysis be referred for meaning and significance.

The outcome, it is believed, is a substantial proof that the science of sociology may be said, in the terms of another of Comte's distinctions, to be effectively *instituted,* i.e., its basic phenomenon, its characteristic method, its essential subdivisions have been established; to *constitute* it, i.e., to develop it in all its implications, is a continuing task for the future.

PART ONE: THE RISE OF THE SCIENTIFIC SPIRIT

CHAPTER 1: *The Magical Mentality*

When men see how profoundly what is called science has transformed the world within the past twelve or fifteen generations, their first reaction is often one of surprise and incredulity. "Can it be that this world of ours, in all its characteristic features, has come into being since the days of Copernicus or even of Galileo?" And as these emotions subside under the accumulation of data, another question arises: "Why has man been so slow to gain this mastery over his world—why was science so long in appearing?"

The question is not without justification, but reflection will reveal that it is based upon two implications, each of which is unsound. First, it is not true that *all* science has been acquired and utilized in the past three or four centuries: in some form or other it goes back at least to the earlier Egyptians. Second, it is unjustifiable to assume even by inference that science exists so to speak *en bloc* and either is or is not. The more naive form of this assumption is that the only science is physical science, comprising the mechanical, physical, and chemical domains of knowledge with perhaps a province of biology.

But such an assumption is without adequate basis. Granted the advances and the triumphs in the physical fields, what of the greater part of biology and still more the social and mental fields in their entirety? Are they not the business of science as well as the others? Some, indeed, unaware of the conquests already achieved or disregarding them, are led by the courage of their ignorance to declare that never will man make scientific his knowledge of these higher levels of human concern. It is a curious attitude, this, which seeks to elevate one element of man's nature by seeking to discredit another, as if his nobility were bound up with his ignorance; and it deserves psychological analysis which cannot be given here. At any rate, it may here serve as a corrective for the too exuberant optimism of the original question: Why was science so slow to appear?

The simple fact of the matter is that the real cause for wonder is not why science was so late in coming but rather that it ever appeared at all.

Consider the facts from the point of view of time. The earliest moment of history to which even a nascent or embryonic science can be attributed is the third millennium B.C. Two thousand years B.C. and two thousand years more; four thousand years in all, less than a hundred and fifty human generations: throughout the entire remainder of man's days on earth there was no science and were few indications of its coming.

Or consider the matter from the point of view of numbers. Of the more than two billion human beings now alive how many comprehend even the spirit, and much less the method, of science, even in regard to the physical world? Whole continents must at once be omitted from the reckoning, whole populations from the continents remaining, great groups from the remaining populations; only small companies here and there remain to carry on scientific advance.

When this number, loosely and generally defined, is watched as it recedes into the perspective of time, historical, prehistorical, geological, what mathematical expression is sufficiently small to indicate its proportion to the whole mass of mankind?

Or finally, how many individuals are now in being for whom the spirit and method of science extend over the *entire* range of their thinking? No, the question of importance is not why science appeared so tardily upon the human scene but how it ever came to be there at all.

A glance at the situation of primitive man will give point to the reversal of the common attitude toward science which has just been suggested. True, this situation is not known from observation; primitive man, the chronological primitive, has long passed from the earth and a certain hesitancy is incumbent upon those who speak without knowledge based upon observation. Nevertheless, there is today no dogmatism in saying that the animal origin of man—or, if preferred, an animal stage in man's development—is as little a matter of personal opinion as the sphericity of the earth. Beside this main point all other questions are essentially insignificant: *at some time there was an animal Homo.*

What he was cannot certainly be known; what he was like is more ascertainable, for it is sure that he was to some extent like the contemporary, the "logical" primitives of the anthropologist—like them but inferior to them, for they have after all many millennia of social, i.e., human existence behind them which the "true" primitive had not. The knowledge now held in regard to the chronological primitive is no doubt not precise; that it is in its main lines certain, the logical primitive is a guarantee.

Behold, then, the animal Homo—not a being without culture but man before culture—emerging from among his fellows, about to become Man. His equipment is none too good: it is in fact so inferior as to justify the wonder that he managed to survive at all.

Survive however he did; he fed himself and protected himself; but here, from the beginning of this volume, a play on words must be guarded against. The "he" and the "himself" are words referring to "Man"—and Man in this sense is a collective noun. If man survived, it was that the members of his species were able to live to at least some extent vicariously, collectively, sociologically. He, they, lived not only with others but for others, if it was to begin with only the mother protecting against enemies of every kind the infant that developed so slowly through the months—and in every one of those months was just as toothsome a morsel for the enemies of man as their infants were (and are) for him. Survival, therefore, was something more than the continuous escape of individuals from personal danger; it involved the safety of others and to some extent the action and cooperation of others. To these ends something more than individual alertness was necessary; and loosely as the word must be used in reference to so far-off a time, this something can only be called learning.

If the animal Homo was to live as Man, he had to learn. Fortunately for him the one point of superiority he possessed over his rivals—and a small superiority indeed it must have been at the beginning—seems to have been an organic advantage making possible, and only just possible, communication in the large sense among individual members of the species. Man had to learn; he could learn, but more was required: to survive it would seem that he had to act collectively, in the accurate sense, i.e., not as a herd but as a unit or group. To do so he had to be able to learn collectively, to interlearn, and he could and did interlearn. Let the biologist explain the fact; for the sociologist, beginning where the biologist stops, it is enough to know and state it.

To learn, and to learn collectively: this was Man's first problem as he began to transcend the animal Homo. But at the very beginning a logical difficulty of a seemingly insuperable kind existed: What was Man to learn, and why? The logical problem involved may be put in the following form: to learn means to make a choice among facts, but making such a choice seems to imply a prior learning since a fact as such has no significance, no meaning, until brought into relations with other facts. In logical terminology, the circle without issue in which men were caught was this: without hypothesis, no observation; without observations, no hypothesis.

Now the circumstance which prevented Man from being eaten while he was endeavoring to find an issue from this logical trap—the circumstance which at the same time prevented him from knowing that he was in a trap at all—was very simple: it consists in the fact that for both the "what" and the "why," the animal Homo had provided him with a ready answer. What he was first to do and what he was first to think were decided for nascent Man by his animal heritage.

As Sumner (and others) has said, his first need is to live. And to live, the omnivorous nature of his ancestor bequeathed to him a something which must not be called an instinct but may be designated as x, which caused him to seize the first thing that seemed seizable and edible.

Why things were as they were is the second of Man's problems. It gave him, and the anthropologists who study him, greater difficulty than the first. Here too it is the animal Homo who provides the solution to the difficulty by bequeathing to Man a something which might be called a logic but will here be designated as y, which served to interpret, correlate, and unify such experiences as impressed themselves upon the attention of a quasi animal busily engaged in finding the wherewithal to live, in the strictly physical sense of the word.

An x, then, and a y: with these two legacies from his animal ancestor, Man, the descendant of the animal Homo, was able to escape the fate that would certainly have descended upon him if *as*

Man he had suddenly appeared and started to meditate upon the "what" and the "why" in the midst of forms uninhibited and untinted by the pale cast of thought. Two starting points they were from which to set out upon the road that was ever to lead away upward from the animal: one, deriving from action, giving a goal for collective activity; the other, essentially a matter of thought, the basis for correlating and synthesizing and interpreting and making collective the experiences of individuals. The two are from the beginning distinct. The needs and experiences resulting from x set y into action, provide materials for that activity, and in a general way prescribe the limits within which that activity shall be exercised; but that is all. X is not y; the nature of each activity is distinct and different, though they are always closely associated. They are two and not one; the point is worth stressing for important issues depend upon it, perhaps even the choice of a political party.

It is the second of these basic data for the understanding of Man's development that is the more difficult to grasp; it is also the member of the x and y combination which when clearly understood makes most evident the essential independence of the two from the very beginning on the animal level. It is therefore worthy of some further comment.

Order may or may not be Heaven's first law; it is certainly Man's first need. Imagine a world in which there is no recurrence of phenomena, in which nothing that once occurs will ever be seen again. No learning would be possible in such a world; no guidance from the past could arise. The only thing certain would be the fact that nothing that had been would ever be again. Learning would become mere recollection, erudition, without relation to life. What could Man do in such a world?

Fortunately for the offspring of Homo, his world is not the world just imagined. In it as it is events do recur, varied it may be and never in all respects exactly the same but recognizably alike for Man, nevertheless. There is an identifiable arrangement among phenomena; and in this sense there is an order in the world of Man.

In the world within him too there is an order. The existence of this inner order, this y, made it possible for Man in his departure from the animal to find a way to tie his experiences into meaning. His nature was emotional, affective, moral in the large sense, subjective. It provided a cause for things happening. The relation between feeling and action was direct and conscious, and to the extent to which this inner world *is* conscious it gave Man a way of coming into relation with the outer, since in each there was an order.

In terms that are much too precise, Man brought these two orders into harmony by assimilating one to the other—the world without to the world within—and so found himself in some degree "at home." This complexity in which he lived was in some way like himself, enough his kind in any case to enable him to live in it with a certain confidence. Storms there might be: well, Man knew storms too in his inner world; terrors of all kinds, but as long as they could be interpreted in human terms their ultimate awfulness was blunted. Calms, too, and peace—these had human meaning. Moreover, it is worth remarking, especially as regards the truly primitive period, that this interpretation, this translation of the outer world into terms of the inner, was particularly valid as regards the most active enemies and rivals of men, the higher carnivora.

In short, Man "hominized" the world—after first indeed having been made by that world—extending out into it the manifestations of his own mind, interpreting it as moved by human urges and impulses and feelings. No rational relation ensued, only an affective relation: Man was not trying to make the world intelligible; he was trying to make it so to speak sympathetic in the etymological sense. He knew so little about it; but he could feel with it, and that in the last analysis is the important thing. Without an affective bond, an emotional comprehension, what community is possible? To this day man's most coldly damning epithet implies the impossibility of mutual comprehension to any degree between himself and that other who by virtue of some train of conduct must be finally condemned as "not human."

"Human-like" then in the last analysis the world of nascent Man was held to be, and so Man could live in it and with it. And presently, because the world is immensely varied and it is hard to think of it and impossible to feel of it as one; and because there are many facets to Man's individuality, which successively dominate consciousness at various intervals; and because his activity brings him into relation with things as individuals and not *en masse,* the human-like takes on individuality of its own and becomes a kind of man, a superior man-kind, and the "hominoid" is born, springing from Man's heart by virtue of his needs and giving Man in return a world in which he can move with relative confidence and freedom.

It need scarcely be repeated that it was no construction of a calmly philosophical sort in which the primitive was engaged; he was striving with every means at his disposal to live. To live he had to learn: the whole difference between the primitive and the modern in the field of basic opinion lies in the difference as to what must be learned. Given his innocence of any but the most elementary and superficial knowledge comparable to that of the animals, of the nature of the world and the consequent necessity of seeing that world in terms of his own personality, there was but one direction in which man's thoughts could proceed: what was vital to Man at this stage of his development was a knowledge of "who" was behind phenomena. The hominoids was the answer, and so Man's chief concern became at once the discovery of how to influence those objective and powerful beings in a direction favorable to himself.

It must be obvious that the nature of those beings had to be of the most vague and indefinable kind. Powers, personalities, forces, spirits; formless, imprecise, fluent, amorphous, remote or near, small, fixed, sharply defined—in any case, the inhabitants of this new world came streaming from the scarcely developed personality of the primitive and reflected every aspect of his emotion and his experience. There can be no wonder then that the whole range of the imaginably possible was covered. It was a world of subjective creations and in this sense a moral world, a world therefore understandable by Man, and of course understandable by him because it was a reflection of him; but here again the "him" must be interpreted. The "him" is the collective Man embodying generations of experience; coming to any one individual it was overwhelming in its scope and unrecognizable as a human product, although essentially comprehensible; hence the power and the appeal, both, of the hominoid.

A world of order was the result; a world which could therefore be learned; a world in which therefore a man could live with some confidence; a world in which there was some arrangement on which one could rely. This arrangement rested finally upon an aspect of human personality which is now called the will; it was thus accessible to Man if he could reach the wills of the hominoids concerned.

It was they who ordered the world; and since their orders brought into existence the arrangement of that world, by their orders that arrangement could be altered. Knowledge, then, the knowledge that is of real worth, lies—and we are assured still lies—in learning more and more of the nature and working of the hominoid wills whence proceed the orders on which the arrangement of the world of Man depends.

If those wills reflect the sympathies of Man, his kindlier aspects, unfortunately so little in evidence under the harsh conditions of primitive life, then they can be revered and loved; if they are on the whole neutral and indifferent to Man, as men are to one another, they may be placated or influenced; if they are evil, embodiments of Man's own lower nature, so likely to manifest itself in the pressure of life at the subsistence level of primitive culture, they may be coerced or even terrified; but in any case the nature of the hominoids who peopled this subjective world was for primitive man the true cynosure of learning.

The disadvantages of the hominoid world for the primitive have been summarized in many anthropological treatises: how it blocks real learning, sanctions and sanctifies custom, narrows moral life to an almost personal range—these have been listed and detailed and criticized. The criticisms are all true and all unimportant.

The essential point is that the subjective system of thought and feeling out of which the hominoid world took shape made possible Man's first rise above the animal by giving his existence cohesion and significance. The basis of this system in feeling is the main source of its cohesive effect, for affective relations are more tenacious and profound than intellectual relations even if the latter had been possible at so early a stage of culture. Yet even on the intellectual side there is great adaptiveness in the system. Nothing in a world of hominoids can ever be difficult to explain, since everything happens in relation to them or by their agency. Nothing is inexplicable—even if events are momentarily astounding, they are never marvelous and much less miraculous; they can always be referred to powers different from or greater than those controlled by the persons astounded.

The outcome is a mental unity, a psychical integration more

complete than any other cultural period has ever manifested. No difficulty is too great to explain, no questions are unanswered, no problems resist analysis—there is nothing to fracture or endanger the unity of mind which a reliance upon the hominoid wills produces. In the worst cases the wills, being hominoid only and not strictly human, cannot be held to human standards and resignation becomes a necessary but laudable attitude.

Finally, what primitive man possessed was in effect a principle of explanation, applicable to the entire range of human interest and to social situations of the simplest or the most complicated nature. The necessary vagueness of the initial notions was an aid in extending them in all directions. They gave emotional satisfaction and resisted intellectual examination. The vast majority of men have held them in some form. They were inevitable because they were the direct issue of the psychical characteristics of the human animal; they were indispensable, for they alone under the circumstances could have enabled the animal Homo to transcend the animal level, to bind himself to his fellows, present, past, and future, and become Man.

For the mental attitude characteristic of this primitive development many terms have been devised. Basic to all of them is the ignoring or the ignorance of the logical relations which have slowly been brought to light through the centuries. In this primitive world view causes are personal. A thing is wanted; it is ordered to be; it is. All that is necessary for success in any activity is to have the right order issued by the right will; the right arrangement will necessarily follow. To this general attitude the word "magical" has more and more come to be applied. It is accordingly utilized here to summarize the present section, which has dealt in a general way with the magical mentality, the starting point of human thinking.

CHAPTER 2: *The Ancient Wisdom*

Can there be any doubt, in the presence of an all-embracing, soul-satisfying, magical synthesis, that another system based upon a non-magical foundation must have had the utmost difficulty in getting even a beginning? How indeed could it ever have come into being at all?

To this question there seems to be but one answer: the new system came into being because on the one hand the method of relying upon hominoid wills is too uncertain, too unstable to prevent recurrent disappointment and dissatisfaction; and on the other, the gradual accumulation, under the impact of experience in carrying on the basic activities upon which maintenance depends, of more definite, more sound, better verified, more positive knowledge provides an alternative method. The two factors of course worked in constant harmony; together they gave an increasing insight into the nature of the world, ever expanding in both extension and depth.

On the side of the strictly objective data it would seem that there were certain carry-overs from the animal stage in the form of a simple acceptance of conditions as they are, without even consciousness that any question need be asked. For example there has never been, it was remarked a century or more ago, any magical explanation for the differences in weight between objects, i.e., for the nature of gravity.

In other cases there was a curious paralleling of the magical and the positive, as if Man could never be quite certain of the efficacy of either alone. Here the skill and the spell run together to give the craft. The canoe is made by physical action upon a physical object; but it is not a canoe in the usable sense if its construction is not accomplished by the words which ensure that when finished it shall be a canoe psychically as well as physically. The smith, who wrought both iron and spells—a crafty man if ever there was one— is another example of the same parallelism between the objective

16

and the subjective. But finally skill and spell cease to be equals, the one advancing into science, the other receding into superstition.

Another line of mental evolution should be mentioned as pointing to an answer to the question how science came to be. It is far more subtle in operation than the two tendencies just indicated, but ultimately of profound influence. It is the tendency on the part of those who embody the magical mentality to render their magic more and more effective. To this end there goes on a continuous process of analysis ostensibly directed to the hominoid world but actually operating upon the objective world in which Man's activity is carried on. The nature of this analytical effort can best be shown by a question which at some moment had to be more or less conscious in the minds of those who wished to put their projects under the best possible auspices: "Which of the various wills is the best one to whom to appeal to ensure success to my plans?"

The question was inevitable, for it was very early seen that certain powers were more efficacious or benign or experienced in relation to a given form of activity than to another. Thus there proceeded a kind of division of labor among the hominoids, which followed or accompanied Man's growing familiarity with his environment. Interpreted in magical terms, the outcome was an inevitable specialization among the wills to whom results were attributed. Agriculture, for example, came to be understood as a process involving a series of steps, and as it was subdivided each step came under the jurisdiction of a member of the magical world. Childbirth, to take another familiar example, was the particular interest of a given power who took the trappings of a true personality.

Thus did advancing human knowledge reflect itself in the hominoid world; and so were slowly accumulated, analyzed, and classified the data that some day were to be the foundations of science: astronomical, physical, biological.

Sociological, too—for with the analysis of the external world there went a solidifying and integrating of the social world. It became organized; it became hierarchized, with differences between ruled and ruler, distinctions in function and authority. These distinctions too came to be reflected in the magical world, which thus became doubly hominoid, in the social as well as the psychological sense.

How long it took for Man to make such advances as the beginning of an analysis of the external world and an organization of the social world it is impossible to say. Down through all the stages of the Paleolithic era, which seems always to be receding further into the past; through the Neolithic, however defined or dated; into the ages of metal, Man's advance continued. Throughout this whole series of epochs the animal Homo grows more dim and his descendant stands forth more clearly. His life, material and spiritual, ameliorates; his society expands and is systematized; his religion becomes more synthetic; his government is centralized. Necessarily those who are in contact with the powers are in control of society; they become priesthoods and organize theocracies. In their hands through hundreds of generations is to accumulate "the ancient wisdom."

The disciplining of the animal Homo for human, i.e., super-animal purposes; the slow, persistent, patient gathering of the data upon which human effort through the centuries must rest: such seem to have been the essential services to mankind of the ancient theocracies. To these ends their multitudinous activities seem finally reducible. In this light their history must be judged and their shortcomings evaluated. Not the oppressors of a subdued and enslaved mass but the guides of nascent Man to a higher status: such in a word is the sociological verdict—more accurately, the statement of the sociological function of the theocracies in the making of humanity.

Consider the meaning of the phrase "the disciplining of mankind." The animal Homo, like any of the higher animals, is refractory to sustained effort. Primitives, even the contemporary primitives, notoriously will not work, as any colonial will affirm. Irregularity of application is one of his most striking characteristics. It is part of his heritage from the animal Homo.

The defect in character, if it is a defect, is not merely psychological. It is inevitable too because of the limitations of his knowledge. In a real sense he does not know enough to work. The nature of his environment, his hunting type of existence resulting in the finding of nourishment, make the thought of sustained, continuous, connected efforts impossible and even illogical. Besides, even when he has advanced beyond the hunting stage and may be envisaged as dependent upon his own energies as the grower of his

food supply, the sequence of relations, of a biological and particularly of a botanical, agricultural kind and their dependence upon
seasons, weather, soil, upon which his very life hangs, are not in his
own hands but in the hands of the hominoids.

Into these Edenic conditions comes the serpent of property relations, growing out of the sedentary agricultural cultures, with the
accompaniment of slavery. Even today the primitive is alive in the
judgment which connects work with slave; and the blessings of
work are still in need of constant buttressing from the hominoid
world, which itself is curiously like the primitive world from which
it sprang in showing a definite disinclination to engage in sustained
labor. In any case the animal Homo needed disciplining, no matter whence it came. Slavery seems to have been the original
form.

After slavery, and above it in human values, came caste. Fixity of
status, the very conception of a place to which an individual belongs and which belongs to him—this is a *human* conception. However disadvantageous it came to be in later days, it was at the beginning an advance. It begins to adumbrate some notion of rights
and right and the correlative duties and duty; something more than
caprice as regards individuals is in germ here; a conception of dignity is dawning.

Biologically, caste gave the possibility of increasing special adapt-
ability by selective mating. Since the same range of physical and
mental efforts is maintained through generations, discovery and
selection can be made of the particular type of capacity and personality needed for success in a particular occupation. In the absence of a knowledge of the laws of heredity, a way is opened toward
eugenic advance.

Intellectually too caste renders an indispensable service. It makes
possible the accumulation of knowledge concerning the objective
world without which human development would be impossible.
From father to son, through millennia, knowledge, information,
techniques, all the data now put in books and all the unwritable
but personally transmissible skills, knacks, rules of thumb were
passed on. Even if there had been no increase in the amount of
such information—and there is of course a limit to the purely empirical information gained from practice—the important point is
that the caste system ensures the transmission and so the preserva-

tion of the results of Man's increasingly intimate acquaintance with the world in which he lived and lives.

In still another way the theocratic phase of culture aided Man to be. It gave him stability and order, in the political sense. Both were needed; and if stability came in the form of fixity and order in the form of orders, those who object to either or both of the latter must show how either or both of the former could have otherwise been obtained, given the conditions and the nature of primitive man and the desirability of his becoming more human. In this matter the implications of the animal origin and nature of Man have seldom been clearly seen.

The animal then for higher ends had for a time to be *coerced*. But man is an animal with a difference, which difference makes him precisely the animal Homo and no other: given time he learns, individually and, more important, collectively. Because this is so, the coercion is but preparation and training and in time can be removed. Hence the historically relative point of view just stated is no apology for fatalism; on the contrary it makes real and righteous an indignation against those who seek to maintain for personal or group benefit institutions and usages which have rendered their full service in the making of Man and could be superseded by others more in consonance with his continuous growth.

It is no apology then for despots, rulers, kings, castes, classes to say that they have had their historical justification. So too have cannibalism and slavery, but they have disappeared all the same. To be human means to act and think collectively as the result of learning from the experience of others. At times men have had to be made to combine their efforts under the guidance or coercion of some individual or class. At other times the hominoids have had to be called in to give rulers support, either by aiding them directly or by including them in the ranks of the hominoids themselves. It is in such ways that human resource and power can be created and increased; only after it is created can it be controlled and utilized.

In the case of the theocracies, the control and direction of mankind was in the hands of a special class, the priesthood. It was normal that it should be so, given the mental status of Man at the time. When the ultimate control of the world is in the hands of the hominoids, it is inevitable that specialization should develop in carrying on the relations of men with the all-powerful wills; it is equally inevitable that they who come to possess the special knowledge whereby such mediation is brought to a successful conclusion should finally become the dominant forces in the community.

It would seem indispensable to Man's growth that this concentration of power in the priestly corporations should have occurred. They alone seem capable of the task of gathering, sorting, preserving, discovering, organizing, and transmitting the knowledge on which Man's future development was to depend. That they did these things in their own way, in their own time, and exacted full payment for their services is no doubt true but essentially unimportant. How else and by whom else could it have been done? The only other group possible was the warrior class; and certainly they would have been unequal to any but the initial stages of the accumulative process. Their function was the direction of activity, not the furtherance of thought. The priestly predominance, once a relatively well organized and internally peaceful society had developed, was a normal consequence.

The knowledge then accumulated need be neither overpraised nor overdisparaged. The task is to evaluate it in the light of cultural development as a whole. Judged in this light the theocratic cultures seem to mark the turn from Man's purely spontaneous accumulation of knowledge to his systematic gathering of it. As in all priesthoods, the shortcomings of the doctrines, based as they were on magical premises, had to be supplemented by the good sense of the membership; and for their guidance genuinely objective data were necessary. In the main the information gathered by the theocratic priesthoods seems to have been factual, directed to the satisfaction of needs, real or so believed to be, covering the entire range of human interest. The priesthoods seem to have been only slightly originative: long before their rise men had had to gather many disconnected bits of information in order to live. But the priestly caste organized and systematized these bits and carried some of them well on the way toward abstraction. All the arts seem to have been started on their way during the theocratic period, if not by the priesthoods proper then by the castes under their supervision and control. As F. A. Rey writes:

> Originally there can be no doubt that the theoretical sciences are the daughters of the arts. Not only is it almost impossible

to separate science from technique but it is by means of technique that we have been led toward science. The filiation of the two is not hypothetical; it can be followed historically.

Mathematics derives from practical calculation. Geometry from surveying; astronomy from the practical measurement of time and the efforts of men to orient themselves. . . . Mechanics is entirely derived from technical achievements, the first machines having existed long before—in the case of the lever, thousands of years before—the scientific principles had been even dimly seen. Physical science had its origin in the extension of mechanics and the use of apparatus for the making of sounds and the utilization of light. . . . If alchemy is the mother of chemistry, the latter is connected in its origin with the techniques of casting, engraving, painting, potterymaking, enameling and the pharmaceutical and medical techniques, whence in a similar way have arisen physiology and biology. Observations of a pedagogical kind as to the development of the human mind have in great part been, along with medicine, the sources of psychology: just as the techniques of law and economics have given rise to sociology.[1]

There is no necessary implication here that all these arts were initiated only during the theocratic period; all of them in germinal form at least are found among the primitives; the point is that they were encouraged, developed, utilized, and incorporated into the very basis of human life; given sanctions by being drawn into direct relations with the hominoid world; protected, sometimes monopolized, and systematically made a part of the growing heritage of mankind.

Clearly there is no point in saying that these arts were but slightly developed or that the knowledge on which they are based was only empirical. It is true that in the contemporary sense of the word "science" scientific achievements in the remote period of the theocracies were few and far between. But such remarks have no point. Looked at in retrospect these acquisitions are insignificant; but looked at in prospect they are the indispensable foundations for all that was to follow.

1. *La Science orientale*, Vol. *1* in *La Science dans l'antiquité* (5 vols. Paris, A. Michel, 1930–48), p. 50.

Still more in ultimate relation to science can be said: it was particularly during the theocratic period that the hominoid world
was organized. Human personality was studied and in all its conscious and many of its unconscious manifestations profoundly analyzed in an empirical way. Human society was developed and governmental and institutional hierarchies formed. Human needs were
increased and refined and the means of satisfying them investigated.
As the human world advanced, the hominoid world kept pace; and
much of what would today be called scientific analysis, classification, and arrangement was carried on in nonhuman, nonscientific
terms. There could have been no other procedure, given all the
conditions, including the animal origin of man's mind. Concealed
under a magical cover, a whole series of conclusions on which scientific inquiry was later to build was being reached. Analysis of
phenomena and their classification in the form of determining
the proper jurisdiction of this or that power, will, personality,
deity; the establishment of relations between classes of phenomena
through the formation of hierarchies among the hominoid wills
who controlled the various classes; finally the burgeoning of scientific law in the sense that natural arrangements were considered
to be guaranteed and fixed because they resulted from unchanging
orders issuing from magical sources: these are some of the ways in
which the materials of science were slowly accumulating and so effecting the filiation of science with the whole development of human thought.

An example of the development of scientific knowledge in the
theocratic epoch can be found in what is now called astronomy,
though it was then neither astronomy nor astrology but rather a
search for order, regularity, fixity in the regions where Man's little
influence could never penetrate and to which therefore he could
refer his ephemeral actions. The success of these early investigators begins an epoch in human history. It was the first successful
effort to mark and measure the flow of time. Something permanent
had been found—"given" is the humanoid term, *datum*, a date; and
Man could look before and after. What matter that the discovery
was interpreted in terms of magical powers, humanoid wills, divine
personalities?

The imagination must be sluggish that does not quicken at the
thought of the vigils kept in those brilliant planetariums of the

Eastern skies as night after night on their ziggurat towers the theocratic observers watched and recorded the movements of the heavenly bodies. With what enduring patience through the decades did they—no names can be given those far-off watchers of the skies—seek in the world above for some transcendent order to which the puny affairs of men might be related and fixed!

And with what successes were their labors rewarded! The recurrent mystery of the sun, departing and returning, with its reflection in the vegetal life so vital for Man; the existence of those wanderers, the planets, the perfect example of variety in the midst of constancy; the paths they followed, their relations to the sun and moon and earth; the mysteries of the dying and reviving moon; the recurrence after generations of familiar relations among the heavenly bodies; the statistical determination of eclipses; the establishment of those enormous cycles in which time seems to return upon itself; all the basic phenomena of the solar, the human, system, Man's own, on which all the astronomy of later centuries was to be based, on which indeed still essentially rests Man's assurance of an order far transcending his own.

Anonymous the epoch was as far as individuals are concerned, but out of it came geographical expressions which have become cultural expressions as well—such as in the East India and China and in the West Babylonia and Egypt. Slowly these cultures have come to the attention of modern man as the perspective of history has deepened. Gradually the past has become more and more detailed, bringing into light first dynasties and then individuals as the historical data have increased: the antiquity of Greece and Rome, the antiquity of Crete, the antiquity of Egypt and Babylonia. It has been said that we have outgrown the phase when all the arts were traced to Greece and Greece was thought to have sprung like Pallas full grown from the brain of the Olympian Zeus, and we have learned how that flower of genius drew its sap from Lydians and Hittites, from Phoenicia and Crete, from Babylon and Egypt. But the roots go further back: behind all these lies Sumer; and behind Sumer lie the Neolithic and the Paleolithic worlds, completing the continuity of mankind and bringing him back to his ancestor the animal Homo. All of them in their way contributed to the making of science, the first clear manifestations appearing in the theocratic cultures.

CHAPTER 3: *The Mediterranean Culture*

The main scene of the next stage in scientific development is the Mediterranean and its environing lands. Even in the theocratic period the eastern end of that sea had been the center of cultural expansion. Egypt and the Fertile Crescent had been the favored spots, for there the existence of fertile well-protected river valleys provided the milieu in which enduring cultures could take root. Moreover, these two had been favored above all other early culture centers by the fact of their geographical proximity, which made cultural contacts easy and inevitable. There had been subsidiary developments too, such as the Cretan and the Phoenician. The sea provided easy access to all these growing civilizations. Where the sea paths met was the central point of a culture area which was in time to comprise the entire Mediterranean. The history of this culture is divisible into three periods.

1. The Greco-Roman Synthesis

The effective agents of the cross fertilization of culture whence was to issue a new stage of advance were the Greeks. They were relatively new to the Mediterranean, and when they reached its shores they seem to have differed from all the other cultures facing onto that sea in that it was not the priestly classes who were predominant in their social organization but the warriors. Perhaps it was this fact of military or warrior dominance that prevented their unification; at any rate it prevented the stabilization, ending in immobility, which was the price of the theocratic control of society.

It was in Ionia, in fact, that marginal area between the mainland and the sea where the seaways crossed and the land ways terminated, that the gathering and correlating of facts entered upon a new phase. The century was the seventh B.C. The first name associated with the change in thought was that of that typical Greek the Phoenician-

25

sprung Thales. The new thought was this: the angles in a triangle, any triangle whatever, together always make a straight angle, or two right angles.

The significance of the statement is twofold. In a *general* sense it marks the beginning of the first conscious and deliberate attempt to comprehend, correlate, and synthesize an entire group of homogeneous phenomena without the utilization of any hominoid intermediaries whatever. Only when the facts are so viewed can any hint be had as to why the Egyptians, for example, seem never to have been able to advance to the level of Thales. Yet the required step seems such a small one. The only adequate answer seems to be that this small step led from their type of thought to a different one and so for them was impossible. The Egyptians, and more especially the Egyptian priesthood, were the possessors and the agents of a thoroughly integrated culture; they could not isolate even one geometrical abstraction from the matrix of the magical mentality in which for two hundred or more generations it had been embedded. Thales, representative of a people who had not been bred up for centuries in such a culture and coming moreover from a region where the comparison of different cultures had worked to produce a critical attitude of mind, was able to see a geometrical fact as a simple fact, completely separated from the culture of which it was a part.

In a *special* sense Thales marks the beginning of science in that he, or the Ionian school, was the first to develop an abstraction which was at the same time an isolate—consciously to develop, that is; for of course many abstractions and isolates had been spontaneously arrived at long before the period of Thales and the Ionians. They are to be found in all ranges of thought from the material to the spiritual: qualities, characteristics, virtues all give rise to abstract terms. Even in the special field of science, abstraction begins long before geometry.

The clearest case is the development of number concepts. Before the theocratic cultures, far back even on the primitive level, abstractions used for counting appear. One, unity, oneness; coexistence, duality, two, twoness; threeness; fourness, up to four nearly every human group seems to have been able to advance—beyond, it seems to have been the particular circumstances of the culture that permitted or dictated further development. For some peoples, for example, an abstract scale of six or seven degrees was reached:

one, two, three, four, a large-small number, a small-large number, and perhaps a very indefinite term for all beyond.

It must be remembered that it is *abstractions* that are here in question. The groups with the smallest abstract number series were capable of dealing with much larger numbers than their abstract terminology would seem to make possible: they did so *concretely,* that is, by relating each thing to be counted with some permanently accessible object such as the parts of the body, the fingers, hands, arms: "men as far as the left thumb," i.e., six if the counting is begun on the right hand; or, a little more abstractly, a hand and a thumb of men.

The advance toward mathematics is thus begun, but to have an abstraction is not enough; the abstraction must also be an *isolate,* that is to say, it must relate to a single quality or characteristic or property and no more. The concept of number is such an isolate. Nine for example conveys no notion of color or weight or quality or odor; it tells nothing as to whether men, horses, apples, or arrows are in question. It is so to speak pure number; it is an isolate, separated off from every other notion whatsoever than number; and just because it is so separated, it can on occasion be applied to any concept to which the notion of number is applicable.

In relation to the isolate, two remarks by way of further clarification are necessary. First, an abstraction, even an abstraction of number, is not necessarily an isolate. Three, seven, thirteen, for example, are often so surrounded with a magical aura as even to cease to convey notions of number at all; they may be merely symbols of good or bad luck. For the early mathematicians, such as the Pythagoreans, mathematical and magical or moral concepts were often fused and numbers became "perfect" or "golden"—and "odd" numbers, what are they? Second, the isolate may be a thing or an event, a being or a phenomenon. A city, an animal—these are isolates in the sense that they may be cut off in thought from all other things and regarded as existing in and for and by themselves. As such they may be dealt with descriptively, but the complexity of the many kinds of phenomena involved makes it necessary for the scientific investigator to analyze the complexity, classify the results, and study one set of happenings singly. One thing at a time; and for this reason the ideal subject of scientific investigation is an abstraction, an isolate, and a phenomenon.

The first such ideal subject for science was the mathematical concept of number. It was an abstract phenomenon and an isolate. In fact it was these things so perfectly that reflective thinking about number went on for centuries before there was any recognition of what was happening. In the main this thinking was of the positive type, i.e., free from any magical connotations or setting. As a result, when reflective thinking reached the point of dealing with such new abstract isolates as shape, a mathematical tool was already in existence to facilitate thinking on the new level.

The new subject was, and is, known as geometry and it was the Greeks particularly who developed it. They thus come back into focus at this point, with Thales at the center. He seems to have worked with angles, triangles, and circles, which means that he had reached the point where certain figures or shapes were conceived of as isolates with complete abstractness. *The* triangle, *the* circle were the material for his meditations. That is to say, he was occupied with special aspects of extension; it was not until Descartes that men were able to deal with extension in all its aspects.

Nevertheless, as far as they went the Greeks in their geometry attained the scientific ideal stated above, as the case of the circle will show. First, it was an abstract concept. A valuable ring of gold or silver, a fragile dish of clay, a great wheel of wood, a heavy ball of metal, even a hole in the ground—all of these manifested a single characteristic which could be separated in thought from all the other aspects they presented to the observer: they were round, they were circular and could be thought of as examples of *the* circle. Next, the abstraction was an isolate. The roundness was wholly independent of weight, value, use, sentiment, delicacy, or other qualities which might be associated with roundness. It did not even have to be physically tangible, as the case of the hole illustrates. Finally, *the* circle is not a composite of properties, a being separated for convenience from other beings such as *the* animal, *the* city; it is roundness, an abstract phenomenon, a mode of being.

In still other ways the circle illustrates the basic achievements of scientific thought. In it are to be discovered relations, and these relations are of an abstract kind. There are for example in the circle diameters, radii, circumferences. Among these phenomena of the circle are relations. Moreover, these relations are the same in all circles, large or small. That is to say, the circle illustrates the existence of constancy in the midst of variety, for which scientific investigation is ever in search. The relation between the diameter or the radius and the circumference is constant, i.e., it is the same in all circles. Then too this constant relation can be expressed in quantitative terms. True, this relation cannot be determined with absolute accuracy, but the accuracy can be estimated to a greater degree than is necessary in any particular case. Finally, not only is the relation between diameter and circumference constant and numerically expressible, it is of such a nature that a change in one of the two elements of the relation will bring a corresponding change in the other. Change the diameter or the radius and the circumference is changed; change the circumference and the diameter is changed, and to an accurately determinable degree. In other words the relation between the two is functional. Such knowledge gives power.

The Ionian Greeks of the seventh century B.C., then, under the leadership of Thales set to work on the new level of abstraction. They took the Egyptian attainments, usually of an empirical character, and carried them on systematically. They took the results of human experience in calculation—the number series, the basic processes, and certain axioms (really inductions) such as the halves of equals are equal, things equal to the same thing are equal to each other—which would seem to go back as far into history as the division of booty or the results of the hunt. With these they combined certain inductions reached it would seem on the basis of practical measurement, such as: the shortest distance between two points is a straight line; parallels do not meet. Developing all these data together, they came to use deduction as the characteristic mathematical method. With its use the mathematical thinkers from Thales to Euclid built up an imposing abstract construction. Free in the main from hominoid characteristics, it is one of the great achievements of Man.

On the arithmetical and geometrical basis thus provided the mathematical thinkers of the time proceeded to organize, correlate, and develop the inductions made by earlier generations in regard to celestial phenomena. Here the earlier achievements were perhaps not so striking; but in any case a new domain of order was added to Man's knowledge. Not only was this extension of the terrain of science made once for all but two distinct contributions of great theoretical importance were made at the same time. The first was the conception of a hierarchical relation between sciences, since the astronomical development was dependent upon the prior development of mathematics. The second was the addition to the scientist's tools of investigation of a new method, that of observation; for only through observation could the astronomical data be obtained which were afterwards utilized in deductive mathematical calculation.

The effect upon thought in general, then and after, was incalculably great. Two whole departments of knowledge had been raised to a new level. True, the hominoid influence was still in some form present; but even it had been changed from a purely magical to a metaphysical basis. It was weakened almost to the disappearing point in relation to mathematical conceptions; and in astronomy it was less and less the influence of feeling and will and more and more the working of a hominoid *intellect* that served to colligate phenomena.

Another general effect on the climate of opinion was a tremendous increase in Man's confidence in his own powers. To some extent at least the world was intelligible; it was tangible so to speak directly, or so it seemed, without any intermediaries between the thinker and the object of his thought. No doubt it was still necessary to think of the stability of the arrangement of the world as the result of an order from some nonhuman source; but it was a mind from which this order emanated, not a caprice. It was in this sense knowable, and Man could by his own efforts attain to a knowledge of it and the mind behind it.

Of course the conception gave men too great confidence considering the fact that they had traversed only the first of a long sequence of related and subordinated stages. At any rate the beginning had been made where it was both inevitable and indispensable it should be, namely, in the mathematical domain, where the accumulation of inductive data was easiest and the use, and so the exercise and disciplining, of the mind most necessary. At this stage of Man's ascent from the animal Homo the only confidence worth while was overconfidence. At any rate, whether for better or for worse, the result, as Burnet long ago made clear, was that a Greek Philosopher had no sooner learned half a dozen propositions of geometry and heard that the phenomena of the heavens recur periodically than he began to seek laws everywhere in nature and with a splendid audacity to construct a system of the universe.

He, or they, did even more. He set up the logical standards derived from geometrical reasoning as a test for adequate reasoning in all other fields, unaware of the inductive basis on which all human knowledge rests and exaggerating the part deduction should play in building up man's picture of the world. He spoke of axioms and such and believed them to be the products of the unaided mind. So the test of consistency became the touchstone of truth. All knowledge must be put in the form of a small number of incontrovertible statements upon which the intellect could then work deductively.

On this basis the Greek thinkers from the seventh to the fourth century set out to construct a system of the universe—in other words to make a synthesis of all knowledge. It was the first stock taking of man's mental equipment, made by men and for men, not an indirect and spontaneous classification such as went on when the various hominoid hierarchies had been elaborated in the different systems of polytheism.

Into the details of the syntheses of the period it is not necessary here to go. Three remarks only may be made in regard to them. First, the conception of order and regularity had by then extended up into the organic world, leaving only the phenomena essentially emanating from Man's social and psychic life in a separate category beyond science. Aristotle's division of philosophy into natural and moral, which in one or another form was to endure until the nineteenth century, illustrates and embodies the distinction. Second, in the natural world mathematics and astronomy were the only divisions into which the establishment of law had been extended on the basis of induction. In the region comprehensively called physics the order was dialectical and the science was descriptive. Finally, the very existence of a synthesis implies on the one hand the abandonment of the effort to see the world as one and on the other the existence of many special departments of investigation whose results can be correlated but not fused. The immediate logical result is the opening of a world of specialization.

This specialization on the basis of an encyclopedic view of Man's universe was effected by the generations following the Golden Age. The historical record is marked by the hellenization of the Mediterranean world, especially at first the eastern regions. By the fourth century B.C. the Greeks had assimilated and synthesized the results achieved by the theocracies and in their turn had become the center of cultural diffusion. The period that followed may be called the Hellenistic to distinguish it from the earlier Hellenic age. The full significance of the Mediterranean as the area of the new culture begins to be apparent, for all lands looking toward that sea were gradually being brought within the confines of a single civilization.

The first great agent of diffusion of the new cultural synthesis was Alexander, who carried it in one form or another as far as India and in the persons of his successors hellenized the near orient and brought the new synthesis back to the Egypt whence so many of its elements had come. The result was the saturation of the Near East world by the Hellenistic culture and the foundation of a new cultural center in Alexandria. The normal development of this new phase of human development was at first disturbed and then accelerated and solidified by the eastward spread of a new military and political power extending out from Rome. By the middle of the last century B.C. this power, already deeply influenced despite its Catos by the higher culture to the east, brought Alexandria under its domination, and the Greco-Roman period may be said to have begun. It endured until the great empire called Rome, faced with complete disintegration, abandoned its policies of conquest and consolidated what was left for purposes of defense around Byzantium, the new Rome.

The essential unity of this process has been obscured by the distortion of history at the hands first of Christian and then of classical advocates and special pleaders. The cultural fact is an uninterrupted continuity of development carried on for forty generations, i.e., from the period of Thales to the period of Byzantine resistance against encroaching barbarism. Such is the main fact in the time aspect just as the inclusion of the Mediterranean area as a unit is the main fact in the space aspect of the culture here in point. When these two elements of time and space are considered, the invalidity of certain commonly used terms becomes apparent. "Greek," for example, is practically devoid of meaning in a cultural sense; and "Roman" is no better. Who were the Romans? And what meaning is there in saying for example that the Romans had no scientific aptitude? Such terms are so to speak incommensurable with the culture they are used to refer to. "Greek" and "Roman" are pseudo-racial and at the best geographical terms; how can they serve to point intelligently to cultures?

No, regardless of the unsuitable names that an irrational use of history has bequeathed to the present day, throughout the time and space just defined there was a homogeneous evolution which *as a whole* laid the basis for the culture of later epochs. This is what both Bury and Tarn mean when they say that Hellenicism was the important factor for later European development. As Bury writes, "For anyone who is interested in exploring the history of European civilization and finding out how the past is stored in the present, this period of Hellenism may be said in a certain way to count more than the age of the independent city states; for it was through this period that the earlier age exerted its influence. It was in this period that the culture of Rome was semi-hellenized and it was through Rome that Greece leavened the civilization of Western Europe." [1] And Tarn: "The creative impulses evoked by Alexander's career forbade anything to be quite the same again as before, and after the Hellenistic world had finally gone down in the ruins of the Roman civil wars, with the Empire it began to be built up afresh on different lines; civilization became Greco-Roman." . . . "The Greece that taught Rome was not the older Greece but contemporary Hellenism, and so far as modern civilization is based on Greek, it is primarily on Hellenism that it is based." [2]

In short, it is for the sociologists to bring to an end the long ingrained intellectual habit of viewing the whole through its parts and to interpret the parts in the light of the whole, to cease looking at the players and study first the play, to take seriously their own doctrines in regard to the growth and influence of culture.

If they do so, it will become evident at once that there was another factor than the intellectual that went into the making of the

1. J. B. Bury, "The Hellenistic Age and the History of Civilization," in *The Hellenistic Age* (Cambridge, The University Press, 1923), pp. 2–3.

2. W. W. Tarn, *Hellenistic Civilization* (2d ed. London, E. Arnold, 1930), p. 1.

Mediterranean civilization. Men were engaged in action as well as thought. From this point of view the characteristic activity of the period was conquest: Alexander first, and then the expansion over all of Alexander's conquests of the power of Rome. Society was basically organized for war. And because this was so, the direction of intellectual activity was not unconditioned but was turned into definite channels. It is this fact which explains the mysterious aversion of the Roman mind, the Roman spirit, to scientific achievement in the theoretical sense. No magical or hominoid explanation is needed. Whatever science was needful or useful in the furtherance of the essential military purposes of society and the consolidation and administration of its results was favored and utilized. The rest was left to be the hobbies of genial gentlemen with curiosity and leisure, like Pliny. Fortunately for the leaders of the conquering armies, an adequate scientific basis for the satisfaction of their needs had been laid; it remained for them to utilize it.

This they did, with the utmost energy. "Never before and never since has any empire built so many, so splendid, and so enduring monuments for the service of its people. . . . Roman engineering is almost as distinguished as Roman law." [3] "A further development in technology corresponded more closely to their national needs, and in this field undoubtedly they came to surpass the Greeks." [4] But who were these surpassing engineers and technicians? On inquiry these "Romans" turn out to have been "Greeks" or at least Easterners: Byzantinians, Syrians, Egyptians, practically any nationality but Roman.

The thought need be labored no further. It is time to end once for all the treating of this or any other period as if society were composed of a mass of metaphysical egos, each working independently on stimuli arising from within and so exhibiting a mind attuned or not attuned to science or art or any other personified activity with no social significance or setting. Men and societies exist in space and time, which means that they have a definite relation to other men, present and, more important, past. Their energies, physical and intellectual, are exerted in the presence of these relations.

3. W. T. Sedgwick and H. W. Tyler, *Short History of Science* (New York, Macmillan, 1939), p. 158.

4. W. Libby, *An Introduction to the History of Science* (Boston & New York, Houghton Mifflin, 1917), p. 35.

In short men are relative to their particular culture, which itself is related to the whole sum of advances in feeling, thought, and action that form the increasing deposit on which Man arises above the animal Homo.

With this view then of culture as an integration of many elements, all of them existing in relation to one another and the whole of which they are a part, i.e., with a relative view of social development, it is possible now to return more intelligently to the main theme of this discussion and ask what were the summated results of the intellectual activities of the individuals who lived in and helped to make the Mediterranean culture, from its development in Ionia in the seventh century B.C. to its temporary suspension in Byzantium a millennium later—forty generations of men over a territory extending from the Indus to the Pillars of Hercules, from Britain and Germany to the Sahara, from the Black Sea to the Persian Gulf at its widest.

To begin with mathematics and astronomy as the most certainly included under the head of science, an immense and irreversible advance had been made when abstract relations of an unvarying kind had been found in numerous special cases of the isolate of extension and, on the basis of calculus, growing out of the isolate of number, had given rise to an imposing intellectual construction. In the calculus itself an advance in abstraction had resulted in algebra and the theory of numbers. In geometry, plane and solid, systematizations were made that endured after more than a thousand years and in the development of conic sections were reaching out for analytical geometry. Trigonometry was divorced from astronomy and made an independent branch of mathematics.

Astronomy, with the mathematical aids just enumerated, was able to incorporate the observations of the theocratic peoples into a body of doctrine which went on being supplemented until in the *Almagest* of Ptolemy it reached its definitive expression. It made use of such conceptions as cycles, epicycles, and eccentrics in a geocentric system to picture mentally the observed movements of the heavenly bodies.

In physics and chemistry—but was there any physics or chemistry? Was there indeed any science besides the mathematics and astronomy just mentioned? "Too much must not be made of Hellenistic science, exciting as it is," says Tarn, "since of the two sciences which today bulk so large, physics and chemistry, chemistry (except for alchemy) never got started and physics died with Strato." [5] In physics in the modern sense, then, some tentative advances, particularly in certain phenomena where mathematical concepts were easily applied, were made. These include some studies in movement and light. Williams sums up the development in these terms: Mechanics has been begun. Dynamics and hydrostatics, as well as optics have taken a place among the sciences; and thus physics may be said to have been differentiated, though not in the modern sense.

If therefore any further account of the scientific cumulations of the Mediterranean culture down to the Byzantine period is to be given here, it can be done only on the grounds that immense masses of data out of which future sciences were to be built had been and were continuing to be piled up. There is likely to be no objection to the position as thus generally stated; but there are certain implications in it that should not be left obscure. For example, what *are* these future sciences for which materials were being collected? Which disciplines of later epochs are to be included and which are to be excluded? As will at once be seen, the chemistry of today is no more to be discovered in the speculations of the early Mediterranean thinkers—or guessers—than is say a future psychology. If, then, the chemical speculations of the Greeks are to be included in this record, why must other types of speculation be rejected—on the ground that no other sciences than those now existing or recognized will ever come into being? or that the only true sciences are the physical sciences, or at any rate only the natural sciences? But where do the latter end? And what about the social sciences?

It should be clear by now that questions of the type just asked are essentially meaningless. At all times there have been spontaneously in process collections of data upon the whole range of human interests. From time to time one or another department of this accumulation emerges from the spontaneous stage, attains the dignity of recognition, and is added to systematically, first in an empirical and then in a positive, scientific, methodical fashion. One range

5. *Hellenistic Civilization,* p. 273.

after another of human knowledge has made an advance of this kind. It is a theological, not a scientific, attitude which presumes to say that no other ranges of interest than those that have already made this advance will ever accomplish it in the future.

Returning then to the stock taking of the Mediterranean accumulations to the Byzantine period, the record shows the existence beyond astronomy of a great mass of descriptive material to which can be applied Aristotle's phrase *Ta Phusika*. Into this group of natural phenomena, with its division into mineral, vegetable, animal kingdoms, fell a great multitude of more or less accurately described data out of which future abstractions and isolates were by observation, analysis, and classification to be made. In the meantime their essential nature and that of all material things was determined by arguing about them, i.e., by the use of the "dialectical" method.

The finest example of the use of this method is probably to be found in the dialectical analysis of the material world into its constituents. Thales seems to have started the process: water, said he, seemingly on the basis of Babylonian creation myths, is the source of all things. Then it was air, and so on until the constituents of the matter of the world were earth, air, fire, water—but not real earth, nor real fire, etc.; no, a dialectical earth, a logical air, fire, and water, forms of reality having behind them a dialectical substratum, "the formless." Such was the chemistry of the period which seems in Alexandria to have fused with the trade secrets of the Egyptian metalworkers to form what came to be known as alchemy. The fusion, with its deduction that a metal was a something on which a gold or silver or lead quality was imposed and that this quality could be detached from the something and another quality substituted, gave rise to generations of efforts to bring this change, this transmutation, of metals to pass. The fusion serves also to hint how there began to gather about the theories of alchemy that deposit of real knowledge about things, substances, in the objective world that was finally to lead men to a knowledge of the elements in the modern sense.

After chemistry came a wide range of descriptive data on subjects now classified generally under biology, particularly botany and zoology. Associated with this kind of inquiry was a mass of medical observation that had come down from the theocratic period and been added to frequently thereafter. Anatomy, physiology, diagnosis, prognosis, hygiene and therapeutics, materia medica, alchemy, and astrology—all these and more were elements in the makeup of the medical man of antiquity as he passed onward from the medicine man of the primitive world to the social psychiatrist of the future. His great compilation of data was known under the name of Galen, that famous Roman who was really a Greek and in fact was a Syrian.

Beyond natural philosophy and its practical offspring medicine lay the world of moral philosophy, where even the dimmest glimmer of science is wanting; and metaphysical or even purely hominoid explanations are in vogue throughout. Law and administration; philosophy and religion: is it credible that no enduring body of cumulated experience lies back of these activities of man? And what sciences are implied in these cumulations if not sociology and psychology? "Among the agencies that have done most to build up the collective force of man for the conquest of nature and the improvement of his lot, one of the highest places must be assigned to Roman law." [6] It could not have persisted as an active element in the lives of millions of men for a thousand years if it had not had sound experience and deep empirical knowledge of human relations underlying it. Sociologists and psychologists ought soon to be striving to formulate these empirical and implied doctrines into clear statements for incorporation into their science. They embody the experience of a whole culture for millennia, for of course they are not Roman but Mediterranean.

Much the same sort of statement can be made about the "psychology" of the period. It was even more saturated with, embedded in, and surrounded by magic than the law, but that fact is no enduring obstacle to the growth of knowledge or the accumulation of data. In the development of the theories of Aristotle and Plato in regard to the nature of Man, despite the dialectical method and the magical interpretation, new data are gathered and human nature is observed. The founder of a new world religion makes an epochal advance in the analysis of the human mind but necessarily conceals its positive import under the theological terms "nature" and "grace." World philosophies develop and base their principles

6. F. S. Marvin, *The Living Past* (4th ed. Oxford, Clarendon Press, 1923), pp. 115–116.

upon real or assumed doctrines concerning human nature. Neo-Aristotelianism and neo-Platonism develop the notions of men already twenty generations dead and introduce under old names new theories in regard to human mind and personality.

In the meantime the state, i.e., the current political form of the culture, militarily endangered, contracts its field of action, draws together for defense, tenses energies for self-protection, and hardens minds against new doctrines, which might serve to divide its forces. The culture of the Mediterranean area for a time seems completely static. Impetus to new developments must come, it would seem, from without. It does; and soon. Attention accordingly must now be turned to a new people and a new tongue.

2. *The Arabic Continuation*

By the middle of the first millennium the power and extent of the Roman Empire had become greatly reduced. In the west, Spain was in the hands of the West Goths, who were displacing the Suevi and Vandals; Gaul, in the hands of the Franks; the northern coast of Africa, especially the narrow strip of fertile land on the sea containing the cities and towns, under Byzantine authority; facing the region, Italy, nominally under the suzerainty of Byzantium. In the east Persia was under the Sassanids, who had been carrying on wars with the Byzantines for generations. To the north were the barbarians. In the center, weakened no doubt but still the dominant power, was the new Rome, including Greece, Byzantium, Asia Minor, Syria, Egypt.

"If," says Hitti, "someone in the first third of the seventh Christian century had had the audacity to prophesy that within a decade some unheralded, unforeseen power from the hitherto barbarous and little-known land of Arabia was to make its appearance, hurl itself against the only two world powers of the age, fall heir to the one—the Sāsānid—and strip the other—the Byzantine—of its fairest provinces, he would undoubtedly have been declared a lunatic. Yet that was exactly what happened." [7] The rapidity with which this

7. Philip K. Hitti, *History of the Arabs* (New York, Macmillan, 1937), p. 142. This section is based upon Hitti's book and in particular upon chaps. 19, 21, 24, 27, 40, and 42; the quotations following are from pp. 215, 240, 255, 240–241, 305, 306–307, 294, 309, 310, 311, 316, 368, 369–370, 370, 396, 400, 401, 380, 484, 486, 498, 510, 515, 509 (2), 578, 530, 543, 557, 565, 583, 606–607, 612.

new power spread is one of the marvels of history. "One hundred years after the death of the founder of Islam his followers were the masters of an empire . . . extending from the Bay of Biscay to the Indus and the confines of China and from the Aral sea to the upper cataracts of the Nile." To "Rome" was left Greece, Byzantium, and Asia Minor.

It is to Syria and the Mesopotamian lands, then, the ancient home of cultural development, that attention must now be turned. The story has two chapters. In the first is recorded the growth and consolidation of the Islamic conquest. The capital is Damascus. In the second is related the preservation and assimilation of the Mediterranean learning and its utilization and development. The center is Baghdad.

The first of these chapters must be brief. It recounts the rapid march of the conquerors east and west, the simplicity and austerity of the commanders of the new faith, their lack of culture, their military prowess, their devotion to the tenets of the Prophet, their nomadic mores and independence. Clearly these good things could not long survive the effects of conquest. Corruption naturally followed the softening effects of victory. Men intermarried and the Arabian stock dwindled. The rulers turned to the alluring aspects of conquest. They began to have drinking parties. They engaged in hunting, horse racing, dicing. They even encouraged poetry, music, and aesthetics. They cultivated oratory. Finally they turned to intellectual pursuits.

When they reached this point of decline from the mores of the desert, they found themselves in the presence of a considerable body of learning. "The invaders from the desert brought with them no tradition of learning, no heritage of culture." This they were to absorb from the conquered peoples over whom they ruled. Their beginnings were of course in the line of their own interests, such as the recording and developing of religious traditions; the writing of history as they understood it—genealogies, stories of the Prophet, deeds of heroes, etc.; theological arguments, of course; and some science, notably medicine. "A Jewish physician of Persian origin, . . . translated (683) into Arabic a Syriac treatise on medicine originally composed in Greek by a Christian priest in Alexandria, . . . and was thus responsible for the earliest scientific book in the language of Islam."

The fact was of course that all energies, within and without, were absorbed by the struggles which filled the century. Its first results were elsewhere than in the arts or science. They were in the expansion of the Arabic language, for example, which had to be subjected to a grammar so as to meet the needs of converts to the faith and indeed to raise and maintain standards for the Arabic itself, as it showed signs of being corrupted by contact with the various tongues and dialects of the conquered. There were great difficulties of administration, too, a field in which the Arabs themselves were never skilled. Almost from the beginning they had to utilize men trained in the old Roman, now Byzantine, methods of government. It was in all ways a period of absorption, assimilation, consolidation.

Out of the process emerged the cultural Arab, far removed indeed from the Bedouin who came out of Arabia in the first days of the conquest.

> As Persians, Syrians, Copts, Berbers and others flocked within the fold of Islam and intermarried with the Arabians . . . The nationality of the Moslem receded into the background. . . . An Arab henceforth became one who professed Islam and spoke and wrote the Arabic tongue, regardless of his racial affiliation. . . . When we therefore speak of 'Arab medicine' or 'Arab philosophy' or 'Arab mathematics' we do not mean . . . the product of the Arabian mind or . . . people living in the Arabian peninsula, but that body of knowledge enshrined in books written in the Arabic language by men who flourished chiefly during the caliphate and were themselves Persians, Syrians, Egyptians or Arabians, Christian, Jewish or Moslem, and who may have drawn some of their material from Greek, Aramaean, Indo-Persian or other sources.

In short, any writer or any product of the Arabic phase of the Mediterranean culture.

If, as Hitti states, Islam was originally a religion, then a government, and finally a culture, one chapter—its becoming a government—has just been glanced at. It is associated with the Umayyad caliphate which came to an end in 750. The next chapter deals with the Abbasid dynasty and the making of the Arabic culture.

The center of this development was Baghdad.

> Its advantageous position as a shipping centre made all parts of the then charted world accessible to it. Along its miles of wharves lay hundreds of vessels, including ships of war and pleasure craft and varying from Chinese junks to native rafts of inflated sheep-skins. . . . Into the bazaars of the city came porcelain, silk and musk from China; spices, minerals and dyes from India and the Malay Archipelago; rubies, lapis lazuli, fabrics and slaves from the lands of the Turks in Central Asia; honey, wax, furs and white slaves from Scandinavia and Russia; ivory, gold dust and black slaves from eastern Africa. Chinese wares had a special bazaar devoted to their sale. The provinces of the empire itself sent by caravan or sea their domestic products: rice, grain and linen from Egypt; glass, metal ware and fruits from Syria; bro-cade, pearls and weapons from Arabia; silks, perfumes and vege-tables from Persia. . . . From Baghdād and other export centres Arab merchants shipped to the Far East, Europe and Africa fabrics, jewellery, metal mirrors, glass beads, spices, etc. The hoards of Arab coins recently found in places as far north as Russia, Finland, Sweden and Germany testify to the world-wide commercial activity of the Moslems of this . . . period.

Within five generations this intense material activity had developed with the Moslem capital as its center. On this ascendant wave of invigorating achievement the peoples who had for a much longer time been depressed under the descendant powers of Byzantium and Persia showed an astonishing power of recuperation. The material basis of life enlarged and assured, they turned with energy to the revival of cultural interests.

> What has rendered this age especially illustrious in world annals is the fact that it witnessed the most momentous intellectual awakening in the history of Islam and one of the most significant in the whole history of thought and culture. The awakening was due in a large measure to foreign influences, partly Indo-Persian and Syrian but mainly Hellenic, and was marked by translations into Arabic from Persian, Sanskrit, Syriac and Greek. . . . In

three-quarters of a century after the establishment of Baghdād the Arabic-reading world was in possession of the chief philosophical works of Aristotle, of the leading Neo-Platonic commentators, and of most of the medical writings of Galen, as well as of Persian and Indian scientific works. . . . In absorbing the main features of both Hellenic and Persian cultures Islam, to be sure, lost most of its own original character, . . . but it thereby took an important place in the medieval culture unit which linked southern Europe with the Near East. This culture, it should be remembered, was fed by a single stream, a stream with sources in ancient Egypt, Babylonia, Phoenicia and Judaea, all flowing to Greece and now returning to the East in the form of Hellenism.

"Returning to the East"—the point is well taken, for there was in fact during several generations a displacement of center of gravity of the Mediterranean culture away from the eastern end of the sea to the Mesopotamian lands. It tended to turn its back for a time upon the West. The Caspian Sea because of its proximity to the Persian centers and prosperous cities of Samarquand and Bukhara with their timberland was the scene of active commercial intercourse. The result of this eastward movement was the addition to the Mediterranean culture base of many important new elements. They came from regions that had hitherto remained in large part outside the cultural area of the Mediterranean: Persia, India, China.

It was particularly Persia that was influential during the Abbasid period. "Arab Islam succumbed to Persian influence . . . Gradually Persian titles, Persian wines and wives, Persian mistresses, Persian songs, as well as Persian ideas and thoughts, won the day. . . . Persian influence . . . softened the rough edges of the primitive Arabian life and paved the way for a new era distinguished by the cultivation of science and scholarly pursuits." But from Persia no great contributions to scientific expansion were gained. Its influence was primarily aesthetic and literary. No close contact was established between the Arab mind and Greek drama, Greek poetry, and Greek history. In that field Persian influence remained paramount.

One new source of scientific knowledge was opened, namely, India, especially for mathematics with its numerals and its zero and for astronomy. But it was only secondary. "At the time of the Arab conquest of the Fertile Crescent the intellectual legacy of Greece was unquestionably the most precious treasure at hand. Hellenism consequently became the most vital of all foreign influences in Arab life." Edessa, Harran, Antioch, Alexandria were centers radiating Hellenistic stimuli. The various raids into "the land of the Romans," i.e., Asia Minor, resulted in the introduction, among other booty, of Greek manuscripts. Al-Mamun and al-Mansur received books from the Byzantine emperors direct, a Euclid among them. But the Arabians knew no Greek and had at first to depend upon translations made by their subjects, particularly Nestorian Christians, who translated first into Syriac and then from Syriac into Arabic.

> Before Hellenism could find access to the Arab mind, it had to pass through a Syriac version.
>
> The apogee of Greek influence was reached under al-Ma'mūn. The rationalistic tendency of this caliph and his espousal of the Mu'tazilite cause, which maintained the religious texts should agree with the judgments of reason, led him to seek justification for his position in the philosophical works of the Greeks. . . . In pursuance of his policy al-Ma'mūn in 830 established in Baghdād his famous Bayt al-Hikmah (house of wisdom), a combination library, academy and translation bureau . . . Down to this time sporadic translation work had been done independently by Christians, Jews and recent converts to Islam. Beginning with al-Ma'mūn and continuing under his immediate successors the work was centered mainly in the newly founded academy.

The Abbasid era of translation lasted about a century.

"It was first Greek medicine as represented by Galen . . . and Paul of Egina . . . Greek mathematics and allied sciences for which Euclid . . . and Ptolemy . . . stood, Greek philosophy as originated by Plato and Aristotle and expounded by later Neo-Platonists, that served as the starting-point of this voyage of intellectual discovery."

The result was that by the tenth century Arabic, surely one of the most remarkable languages ever spoken, "had become metamorphosed in a remarkable and unprecedented way into a pliant medium for expressing thought and conveying philosophic ideas of the highest order."

The age of transmission and assimilation once concluded, the Arabic scholars in the East proceeded to creative activity. In mathematics they carried on the work begun so many centuries before by composing standard treatises on arithmetic and algebra, which they did much to raise to a higher level, and by utilizing the geometry of the older period in the development of astronomy. They were, curiously enough, slow to adopt the Hindu numerals.

In astronomy they busied themselves with verification and extension of the earlier works such as the *Almagest,* new tables, observations and researches, extension and development of theory, discussion of new systems but no basic modification of the older ones. In the main the greatest contribution was revision and the collection of a vastly greater mass of data than had ever before been gathered. With astronomy might well be linked the achievements of the Arabic age in geography: descriptions of remote lands, determining of latitudes and longitudes, maps, great masses of concrete data and reliable information.

In the physical sciences they made notable studies in optics and the invention of the pendulum. It was in the alchemical field however that the most significant and original of the Arabic work was done. The principal operations of chemistry were developed and utilized. Many new substances were found and subjected to manipulation in the attempt to transmute them into gold. The basic principles governing the use of experiment were found and practiced. A departure from the dialectical constituents of matter as determined in Greek days was made in the direction of the more metaphysical three principles on which so much chemical attention was centered in a later time.

Above the physical sciences medicine was the great subject of attention. Materia medica was advanced, resulting in schools of pharmacy and apothecary shops, and hospitals after the Persian model were built in increasing numbers. Compendiums of medicine appeared and were composed throughout the period, reaching a final codification in the work of Avicenna, whose *Canon* remained "a medical bible for a longer period than any other work."

It is difficult to separate the medical men from the philosophers.

To the Arabs philosophy . . . was a knowledge of the true cause of things as they really are, in so far as it is possible to ascertain them by human faculties. In essence their philosophy was Greek, modified by the thought of the conquered peoples and by other Eastern influences, adapted to the mental proclivities of Islam and expressed through the medium of Arabic. These Arabs believed Aristotle's works to have represented a complete codification of Greek philosophical lore, as Galen's represented Greek medical lore. Greek philosophy and medicine meant then, of course, all that the West possessed.

But there was one excepted domain: as Moslems the Arabs believed that the Koran and Islamic theology were the summation of religious law and experience.

The result of the contact between the Hellenic and the Islamic heritages was a conflict which in the course of time gave rise to a fundamental distinction of great importance. "In course of time Arab authors came to apply the word *falāsifah* or *hukamā'* (philosophers or sages) to those philosophers among them whose speculations were not limited by religion, reserving the term *mutakallimūn* or *ahl al-kalām* (speech-makers, dialecticians) for those whose system was conditioned by subordination to revealed religion." Here evidently is the basis of the future distinction between the scientist and the theologian. Here also is implicit the intellectual movement later given the name of scholasticism, whose purpose is to bring knowledge and faith into harmony.

Obviously in philosophy much was included that concerned ethics and politics but was discussed in theological terms. Then too there was the wide field of law: "After the Romans the Arabs were the only medieval people who cultivated the science of jurisprudence and evolved therefrom an independent system." "Certain orientalists see Roman influence not only in particular regulations but also, and what is more important, in questions of principle and methodology."

In direct relation to the field of sociology may be mentioned as of this period al-Farabi, who in his *al-Siyasah al-Modeniyah* (political economy) presents his conception of a model city, which he conceives as a hierarchical organism analogous to the human body. The sovereign, who corresponds to the heart, is served by functionaries who are themselves served by others still lower. In his ideal city the object of association is the happiness of its citizens and the sovereign is morally and intellectually perfect.

In the field of psychology, mainly represented by the various schools of ethics or moral philosophy, "certain virtues such as resignation, contentment and endurance are admired; vices are treated as maladies of the soul with the moral philosopher as the physician; and the classification is founded on the analysis of the faculties of the soul, each faculty having its own virtue and its own vice."

Such in sum was the work in science, widely defined, of the Abbasid period of Arabic history: the conviction is inevitable that it was nothing but a continuation of the development of the Mediterranean culture conceived as a whole. To call it Arabic with any other purpose than to fix the place it occupied in a larger sequence of similar movements is to throw it into a false relief. In the matter of its relation to Hellenism, for example, it is pointless or misleading to speak of its having preserved the results of an earlier age, or conversely to say that the Hellenic period should be praised for having preserved the work of the theocracies.

In fact, each particular contribution to a continuing process may be thought of as having a special service to perform. In this regard the task of the Arabic epoch is clear enough. The Hellenic period had, on the basis of the empirical results of the theocracies, reduced to laws the mathematical and astronomical data cumulated up to the time of its activity. It had gone further and collected a mass of descriptive data under the general title of natural philosophy. It had in occasional investigations such as statics and optics even indicated the direction to be taken by future inquiry.

Thus the task of the Arabic culture was the continuation of its predecessor's achievements. The line of advance was clear: not only had the body of data logically next in order for scientific treatment been indicated, but the nature of the method with which, or the spirit in which, it was to be studied had been more than suggested. Not only was the physical world to be the main object of investigation, but investigation was to be carried on there with a greater regard for the facts and a greater care for accuracy than had been realized before, when the logical nature of the mathematical elaboration and the immutable nature of the astronomical phenomena were together a sufficient safeguard against excessive intellectual divagation on the part of the inquirer.

And whatever the theories on the subject, the fact as registered by all the historians is that it was in the physical fields, in the Aristotelian sense of the word, i.e., in the field of natural science, that the Arabic world made its most original discoveries and accumulated the greatest masses of material. Its greatest weakness was synthesis. "Accurate in the observation of phenomena and diligent in the accumulation of facts, the Arabs nevertheless found it difficult to project proper hypotheses and draw truly scientific conclusions. The final elaboration of a system was the weakest point in their intellectual armour."

Yet "the inability of the Arab"—a meaningless phrase—to make systems may easily be transmuted into a reluctance on the part of thinkers during the Arabic period to construct syntheses they felt to be premature. What they might have done, given a period of continued investigation as long say as the Greco-Roman, is wholly a matter for conjecture. The fact is that the golden age of Arabic science in the East closes with the tenth (Christian) century. "If anything parallels the astounding rapidity with which the sons of the Arabian desert conquered in the first Islamic century most of the civilized world, it is the swift decadence of their descendants' domination between the middle of the third and the middle of the fourth centuries." Too many factors, internal and external, administrative, racial, governmental, social, moral, and economic, went to the production of this catastrophe to be listed here. "National economic decay naturally resulted in the curtailment of intellectual development and in the stifling of creative thought."

It must also be added as regards the development of science that there was no very strong *social* motive for its continuance. The interest in Aristotle was the interest in defending or attacking theological doctrines: the interest in astronomy, the growth, description, mapping, administering of an empire. When the first was ended by the creation of a scholasticism and the second by the disintegration of the empire, the motives prompting continued scientific cumulation became mainly *personal:* the desire to find the philosopher's stone.

The Arabic power like the Roman was a military, conquering power. Unlike the Roman it spread over an enormous territory with extraordinary rapidity. It had no time, therefore, for the effecting of a true political consolidation. Its distinctive culture had no time to synthesize and unify. Hence with the disintegration of the empire in the tenth century Mediterranean culture closes its strictly Arabic phase. If any doubt exists that it was a Mediterranean culture, it should be removed on learning that the next cultural expansion occurs at the very opposite end of the inland sea, in Spain.

The capture of Spain by the Moslems had been one of the most rapid and dramatic victories in a conquest itself one of the most rapid in history. "Within the short space of seven years the conquest of the peninsula, one of the fairest and largest provinces of medieval Europe, was effected." The speed with which the country was reduced was the result of the disorganized political condition in which three centuries of invasions had left it. Upon the Roman inhabitants had descended the Germanic hordes, the Suevi and the Vandals. Following them in the fifth century came the Visigoths. The Gothic nobles developed into territorial lords who had begun to quarrel among themselves. According to tradition the ships in which the Arabic invaders crossed the strait separating Africa from Spain had been furnished by one of those lords, angered at Roderick the Visigothic King. There was a thoroughly dissatisfied native population, Catholic, unlike the Visigoth invaders, who were Arian. There was a considerable proportion of Jews, who had been persecuted by the Goths.

There was intermixture of blood from the beginning. The first governor of the conquered province married the widow of the deposed Gothic king. "Christian communities were left unmolested in the exercise of their faith and under their own ecclesiastical laws and native judges . . . In general, . . . the Moslem occupation of Spain entailed no new unbearable hardships to the natives. 'In some respects,' declares Dozy, 'the Arab conquest was even a benefit to Spain.' It broke the power of the privileged group, including the nobility and clergy, [and] ameliorated the condition of the servile class."

Toward the close of 'Abd-al-Raḥmān's reign the lure of the language, literature, religion and other institutions of the conquerors—including the harem system—had become so strong that a large number of urban Christians had become Arabicized though not actually Islamized. Dazzled by the glamour of Arab civilization and conscious of their own inferiority in art, poetry, philosophy and science, native Christians soon began to ape the

Arab way of living. . . . Spain, be it remembered, was one of
the last countries of Europe to be Christianized; some of its
country districts were still pagan at the time of the Moslem conquest and its Visigothic Arianism agreed in its Christology with
Moslem doctrine.

The mixing of blood continued. Abd-al-Rahman III, under
whom Moslem Spain reached its highest glory, was the son of a Christian slave. By the tenth century the intermingling of the two groups
was well on its way. From the beginning there were relatively few
real Arabians in the army of conquest and among the colonists,
limited to those in command and in high office. The number of
women accompanying the army and first immigrants was necessarily
small. Disease and fighting decimated the early conquerors and set-
tlers. After the fourth generation the Arabian blood must have become greatly diluted by intermarriage with native women. The researches of Ribera have shown that even the Moslems of Spain, the
so-called Moors, were overwhelmingly of Spanish blood.

In short, here is a perfect picture of an amalgamation both biological and sociological. As early as the 700's this fusion began: "In
various ways ['Abd-al-Raḥmān] diligently strove to fashion into a
national mould Arabians, Syrians, Berbers, Numidians, Hispano-
Arabs and Goths." He initiated that "intellectual movement which
made Islamic Spain from the ninth to the eleventh centuries one
of the two centres of world culture." Pagan, Jew, Moslem, and Christian, both Catholic and Arian; Roman, Suevian, Vandal, Gothic,
Berber, Arabian, Syrian; languages of many varieties; constant intermingling; constant exchange; constant competition and struggle:
into this chaotic fusion came the Mediterranean culture in its latest
form, the Arabic; from it was to arise a variant, the Arabico-Gothic.

"In the first centuries of Moslem domination in Spain, Eastern
culture flowed from a higher level into Andalusia, as can be seen
from al-Maqqari's list of Spanish savants who journeyed 'in quest
of learning' to Egypt, Syria, al-'Irāq, Persia and even Transoxiana
and China." But the direction of the cultural flow was to be reversed. The coming of learned men from abroad was encouraged,
professors from the East were brought into Spain, the bookshops
of Alexandria, Damascus, and Baghdad were ransacked for books,
libraries became common, universities were founded. Under al-

Hakam "the university of Cordova, founded in the principal
mosque by ʿAbd-al-Raḥmān III, rose to a place of pre-eminence
among the educational institutions of the world. It preceded both
al-Azhar of Cairo and the Niẓāmīyah of Baghdād and attracted students, Christian and Moslem, not only from Spain but from other
parts of Europe, Africa and Asia." At the same time "Cordova became the centre of a talmudic school whose foundation marks the
beginning of the flowering of Andalusian Jewish culture." The
importance of the Arabic culture was so well understood that in
Toledo a school of translators was founded to bring to those
Christians who were unable to read Arabic the treasures of the East.
To this school came scholars from Europe, but the school was primarily for the Spanish.

"Moslem Spain wrote one of the brightest chapters in the intellectual history of medieval Europe." What was the content of
this chapter? "In Spain Arabic philology, theology, historiography,
geography, astronomy and allied sciences had a comparatively late
development, since the Moslems there, unlike their co-religionists
of Syria and al-ʿIrāq, had but little to learn from the natives. Even
after their rise Spanish sciences lagged behind those of the Eastern
caliphate. It was mainly in such disciplines as botany, medicine,
philosophy and astronomical mathematics that Western Moslems
made their greatest mark." Advances in cartography, astronomical
tables, trigonometry; in botany, pure and applied, in agriculture;
in pharmacy, in surgery: such in detail are the debts due the
Spanish Moslems in science proper.

It is in philosophy that their work was perhaps most important.
In Spain was completed the work of reconciling Aristotle and the
Koran reason and religion. The work of ben-Gabirol (Avicebron),
a Jew, and Ibn-Bajjah (Avempace) and Ibn-Tufayl continuing the
work of reconciliation begun in the East culminated in Ibn-Rushd
and Ibn-Maymun (Averroes and Maimonides). The former particularly is a noteworthy figure. He stands almost alone. He had no
progeny in Islam. He is a transitional figure, belonging more to
Christian Europe than to Moslem Asia or Africa. "To the West he
became 'the commentator' just as Aristotle was 'the teacher.'
Though using in most instances a Latin translation of a Hebrew
rendition of an Arabic commentary upon an Arabic translation
of a Syriac translation of a Greek original, the minds of the Christian

schoolmen and scholars of medieval Europe were agitated by ibn-
Rushd's Aristotle as by no other author."

But here a new word appears: Europe. The end of the Arabic
phase of the Mediterranean culture is at hand. But before going on
to describe this end, it will be well to check the foregoing conclusions by reference to a similar case.

A similar feeling of fusion, preparation, culmination, and transition arises from a study of the case most like that of Spain: Sicily.
In this island in the city of Syracuse there had been an unbroken
occupation since at least the days of Magna Grecia. Through
Roman and Byzantine days the relations with the remainder of
the Mediterranean had been continuous. It was still in Byzantine
hands in the 800's when the widening boundaries of the Moslem
conquests encompassed it and made of it a base for attacks upon
Italy. For more than six generations the island remained in Moslem
hands, becoming a more or less independent and stable state with
a prosperous and cultured population, at least in the cities.

But Byzantine influence and civil disturbance opened the way
for the Normans to extend their power from southern Italy. By
1100 they were secure in their control. "Throughout the Arab
period of domination there streamed into the island, already rich
in memories of bygone civilizations, Eastern cultural currents
which, blending with the precious legacy of Greece and Rome,
took definite shape under Norman rule and gave the Norman
culture its distinctive character. Hitherto the Arabs had been too
engrossed in warfare and squabbles to develop the finer arts of
peace, but now their genius attained its full fruition in a rich
outburst of Arab-Norman art and culture."

Under Roger I and in particular under the glamorous Frederick
II, who maintained relations with the whole Mediterranean, Sicily
became for a time the most brilliant cultural center of the western
Mediterranean. "Its population comprised a Greek element which
used Greek, a Moslem element which spoke Arabic and a body of
scholars who knew Latin." The Jews too played a significant part.

This Arabico-Norman culture geographically was astride the
Tyrrhenian Sea; it is absurd to speak as if the culture of one part
of the Norman kingdom was transmitted to another; that culture
was a joint product, the result and the means of gaining and maintaining social homogeneity. The university of Naples was not a

center of transmission. It was an Arabico-Norman institution. Nevertheless, time was to give it an essentially European significance. It was to be integrated into a new cultural phase, for whose origin this narrative will have to retrace its steps for a thousand years.

3. The Teuto-Roman Assimilation

The line of cultural development in the Mediterranean runs from Thales to Averroes, from Ionia to Spain. In it there is but one notable break: that which is associated with the Fall of Rome in the fourth and fifth centuries A.D. At this period two events combined to give a new direction to Roman civilization. The first was the political disorganization and later the disintegration of the Empire, the second the replacement of polytheism by monotheism. The first was halted by the renunciation of conquest in favor of defense; the second renewed societal energies by coordinating them about a single deity instead of a dying pantheon. To make this fusion effective required the transference of the "capital" of the new structure to the east, where in fact the cultural center of gravity had always been. The outcome was Byzantium and a thousand years of continued existence.

Thus while a reorganization was taking place in the east which made the Greeks Romans and the Romans Greeks, in the west the disintegration continued. It was accompanied, occasioned, and accelerated by the migrations of the Germanic tribes. The process was at first a filtration of individuals and families, and then as the legions withdrew it became a mass movement involving whole tribes. It was a slow process extending over centuries. There was of course no "fall" of Rome in the dramatic sense. The Empire was disintegrating; at a certain stage of disintegration the fact was recognized; a deliberate reconstruction was undertaken; the result was a "new Rome." This Rome claimed suzerainty over the vacated territory and from time to time sought to make its authority felt. In some regions, as Sicily and Africa, the attempt was fairly successful. Only the arrival of the Saracens ended it. In other regions and notably the northwestern section of the Mediterranean area, the efforts were less successful and were abandoned at an earlier date. "The Roman world was won by the Germans gradually from within, by a peaceful penetration which went on for centuries, during which they absorbed its culture and even, to a considerable extent, took over its administration. . . . It is for this reason that the abolition of the western Roman Empire in 476 was not felt by contemporaries to be the fall of Rome, and indeed was hardly considered to be a really important event." [8]

The decline of Rome might well be interpreted in psychological terms. To begin with, in the third and fourth centuries men's sympathies, affection, and respect for the Empire began to weaken as is evidenced by the series of laws, edicts, etc., which were issued to hold Roman citizens of the higher classes to their civic responsibilities. Then slowly even men's ambitions could no longer be satisfied by action within the range of the political structure. It was worse to seek for and gain political preferment than to go without it. Finally even men's interests were imperiled. As is known, men actually fled from the Roman to the barbarian territories in search of tolerable conditions of living. When individuals could no longer satisfy even their basic needs within the framework of relationships that had held them together for centuries, then occurred the real Fall of Rome so far as the term has any psychological meaning.

What now were the Romans who were left in the vacated territories to do? How were they to live in the social disorder that followed the disappearance of constituted authority? The answer is clear from the record. The robe of political authority as it fell was seized by the religious authorities. The bishops—the word keeps appearing in the records—began to exercise more and more an administrative function. These men were the heirs of the experience of the Empire in the field of government and they turned it to the purpose of control. Success depended upon the spread of the Roman religion. The outcome was an immense missionary effort. The energies of the representatives of the older and superior culture were turned to the task of effecting a wholesale conversion.

The situation then in the northwestern section of the area was exceptional in the history of the Mediterranean world. For the first time in its record a superior culture was withdrawing through its own weakness in the face of an incoming group of a lower cultural

8. A. Dopsch, *The Economic and Social Foundations of European Civilization* (New York, Harcourt Brace, 1937), p. 386.

level. Only its religion retained vitality enough to make it a center of resistance.

The point of importance to cultural development is that the representatives of religion were gradually forced by external conditions and internal need to emphasize its magical aspects and neglect the intellectual aspects of the culture of which it had been a part. The traditions of the latter kind were lost more and more; the emphasis upon edification constantly increased; men tended more and more to think in magical terms. The ambitions of the representatives of the religion, as they came to be more strongly organized, worked in the same direction as their interests. They saw the advantages of independence, and by utilizing Latin as the Nestorians used Syriac they more and more divorced themselves from the more cultured east. At the same time the necessity of keeping their teachings on the level of the masses strengthened the same tendencies that isolation encouraged. Moreover and in a strictly material way, the growing ascendancy of the Saracens in the western end of the Mediterranean more and more brought about a physical isolation. The result was that by the tenth century the northwest portion of the Mediterranean lands had become a Dark Area.

A Dark Area and not a Dark Age: all that was said in section two of this chapter shows the absurdity of current historical phrases as descriptive of anything but a particular portion of the Mediterranean. In the east and in Spain the age was a brilliant one. Even in Byzantium, assailed on all sides, the cultural level was maintained if only at a level with the past. In only one region of the whole Mediterranean area had there been a reversion, a disintegration, a decline in the level of culture. It was not a Dark Age: there was no dark age in the whole of Mediterranean history, from the time of Thales to the time of Averroes. Always somewhere in the bounds of that sea a cultural advance was in more or less active progress. Only in the northwestern area after the withdrawal of the Roman power following upon the disintegration of the Roman Empire had there ever been so serious a cultural decline in so extensive a territory. It must therefore be repeated: there was no Dark Age, there was only a Dark Area.

In this declining culture, this submersion under invading barbarian populations, religion became the means of social control in the hands of the descendants of the Romans, but religion itself under the circumstances steadily became more and more debased and reverted to magical practices and doctrines. Its intellectual interests had never been wide—it is not in the west that the heresies grew—and now they centered more and more upon the one purpose of edification. Interest in science grew steadily less except insofar as it could be subordinated to edification, as astronomy was necessary for example for the fixing of dates of religious importance. The books that were still to be found were mainly liturgical, the authors from antiquity were the Fathers and the Platonistic writers. Aristotle and the scientific works of the Greco-Roman times were known only in fragments or not at all. From time to time a discussion on some religious issue, more accurately on some magical issue, would arise, but of genuine intellectual interest in a large or comprehensive sense there are few signs in what will later be called western Christendom from the sixth to the eleventh century.

An isolated group whose isolation had been fostered for purposes of institutional independence, a people of low culture characterized by an essentially magical mentality, occupying a region that for centuries had been on the outskirts of civilization: such was the Dark Area in the eleventh century. Into it a few rays of light from the outer world had by this time already begun to penetrate. It is obvious that the isolation had never been complete, that behind it lay in both space and time a cultural development from which some stimulus had been received. In the tenth century influences from without had already begun to percolate, mainly through isolated individuals.

However these sporadic influences may have operated, by the end of the tenth century direct evidences of more systematic interrelationship with the civilized world become numerous. Occasional individuals like Gerbert come into contact more directly with this outer world and attain prominence at home as a result. The movement known as the Crusades begins, touching the edges of the Moslem world and resulting in 1204 in the real Fall of Rome. The eastern cultural movement comes west and in Sicily and Spain develops at the very threshold of the Dark Area. In these two regions in particular, the achievements of the Mediterranean culture in its Moslem form are increasingly brought within the reach of those who are unable to deal directly with Arabic. Reymond of Toledo, Roger and Frederick of Sicily became active in furthering the translation of Arabic works—not, as is so often implied, for the sake of transmitting them to Europe but to enable their own people to stand on equal terms with their Moslem neighbors. In the case of the last two, those "baptized sultans," the direct result was the introduction of these works from one part of their realm to another, i.e., from Sicily to Italy. But even before this the new knowledge had begun to spread from the Christians of Spain to the Christians of the interior, and many individuals traveled across the Pyrenees drawn thither by intellectual curiosity and the ambition to exploit on their return the superiority that the new knowledge would give them. The age of transmission, so-called, had begun. In more accurate terms, the northwestern territories were about to become once more a part of the Mediterranean culture area.

Of the culture of that area as it existed in the twelfth century, what elements will be accepted in the European region by virtue of their compatibility with the thought and tendencies already existent there? The first and obvious answer is based on a priori grounds: it will be those parts of the newly arriving culture which best fit into the essentially edifying nature of the intellectual interests already there; that is, it will be the philosophical aspects, and the religious features of those aspects, which will be of most interest. Such was indeed the fact, but it need not have been foretold on a priori grounds alone. Precisely the same thing occurred when the Moslem teachers came into contact with the Hellenic learning in Syria and Persia.

There was one main difference, however. In the eastern case a new and magically minded people with an undeveloped religious doctrine expanded into a world whose soil was saturated with an earlier and more highly developed culture. The presence of this culture was a modifying and moderating factor in the entire series of events which followed. In the west, on the contrary, the culture so to speak moved in upon the people, with the result that it was their cultural level which conditioned the acceptance and selection of the incoming influences. In consequence, though the similarity between the two situations is real, the results are more extreme and striking in the west; and they were to influence the ulterior development of science in a marked fashion.

In the first place, the division of thought into two departments was a direct result. On the one hand were the theologians, on the other the men of science. This separation had its analogue in the Moslem world, with the difference that in the western world there was no countervailing influence to modify the theological attitude and so the domination of the sacerdotal group was complete. Theology became the queen of the sciences and remained so until its influence could be weakened by direct attack.

In the second place, the resort to authority in the determination of all doubtful questions was quite inevitable and understandable. Given the situation, what other result could have followed? From mathematics to philosophy through all the intervening stages, the translators had revealed works whose range of knowledge was so much greater than anything the western scholar could even hope to show that argumentation on a factual basis was impossible. Besides, of course, the whole tenor of edification is toward the acceptance, not the questioning, of statements; hence the regard for authority.

The most significant episode in the whole development was the debate and resulting action in regard to Aristotle. The tone of the earlier centuries was determined by the Fathers and by such neo-Platonic authors as survived. Plato served the purposes of edification admirably even at third or fourth hand. When Aristotelian arguments began to penetrate into the Dark Area, they were hostile in spirit to the existing opinion. In consequence their author was opposed and finally, in the University of Paris, he was condemned and his teaching forbidden. The action was in strict conformity with the general spirit of the age. Yet it had been felt from an early period of the penetration that the support of the theological doctrine by purely human means lay essentially in the Aristotelian direction. To exclude him was to give all the good arguments to the opposition. The problem had of course been discussed from every angle after the Arabic culture had passed its initial stage; the whole logical strategy involved had been worked out in the Arabic east.

What was obviously necessary was a reconciliation between faith and reason. This step too had been taken in the east, and the general lines of reconciliation were perfectly clear for any reader of the translations. Only one variation from the historical lines of thought was necessary. The Aristotelian system had to be brought into accord with the Christian variant of monotheism and particularly with the doctrines of the church of Rome. The requisite mental subtlety was found in Thomas Aquinas, who after his residence at the University of Naples proceeded to the creation of the philosophical synthesis which was to make him the official theologian of his church.

Such is the meaning of the scholasticism which in the minds of contemporaries was the great intellectual interest of the time. Considered in isolation, no doubt it deserves the attention it has received. It certainly set the tone and defined the field of discussion in the west for a number of generations. Considered historically and comparatively, however, it deserves no such emphasis. It was in fact the third such episode.

In substance the scholastic problem was a simple one; how can the hominoid will be harmonized with the hominoid intellect? What is the relation between the Allah of the Koran or the Jahveh of the Bible and the *theos* of Aristotle? How can one reconcile a god of magic with a god of law? All the scholasticisms centered about this basic question, from the dispersive and spontaneous discussions (the most normal of all because they arose along with the dogmas themselves) of the Greco-Roman world to the debates of the Arabic east—including by the way the Jewish development, which might be called another scholasticism—to the compromise reached in the Christian west. Of the three, or four, episodes the western, because of the cultural isolation which had influenced those who participated in it, presents the most extreme form mitigated least of all by being carried on in an atmosphere of high general culture.

Once this similarity with other periods of thought is grasped, together with the reason for the differences, the development of the western intellectual world for the six or eight succeeding generations becomes clear. First of all there was the sharpening of the common language of churchmen to enable it to serve as a medium for the discussions that were inevitable. It is true that this necessity gave rise to a highly refined logical vocabulary, which served well the ultimate outcome in making more subtle and more accurate minds; but after all it was only a logic of consistency and advanced science in the sense of knowledge not at all. It was a logic of signs, often without referents, and it is certainly arguable whether its effect in renewing a faith in dialectics as a means of increasing knowledge did not considerably overweigh its benefits in providing a more subtle means of expression.

Moreover the discussion made theology dominant over science. It did not, as is so tiresomely asserted, show itself hostile to science. On the contrary, as a part of the general debate and as a part of the reconciliation between caprice and order, it made a significant compromise which has prevailed in the world of intellect down to the present. It took the age-old distinction between natural philosophy and moral philosophy and kept only the latter strictly as a theological preserve in which grace and not law prevailed. The remaining human interests it turned over, not grudgingly but even overconfidently, to reason under the guidance of nature—more accurately indeed to reasoning and the reasoner. The dialectical processes were still dominant, but the inductive inquirer had a place. What he had to do to protect his position was to interpret his findings as laws in the sense of orders issued by a divine will. By doing so, he would not only aid man in gaining material advantages; he would also be aiding him in gaining a deeper comprehension into the depths and heights of the divine personality.

Of the intellectual interests lying outside the religious aspects of philosophy little need here be said. They mainly concerned medicine with its attachments astrology and alchemy. The church tolerated but did not foster these pursuits and forbade its personnel to concern themselves directly with them. In such fields as the alchemical the tendency was for its adepts to go underground, with the result that this type of inquiry became occult in a double sense. There seems little doubt that initiates in these studies were always more or less under suspicion. Certainly they had no such organic connection with the life of their day as to give them social significance; they remained individual seekers for such things as the philosopher's stone.

If in the organization of religious life that grew out of the era of conversion and isolation the best that could be done for science was to make it ancillary to theology, still less was done for it in the emerging political structure. Reason was necessary to build the scholastic framework of western catholicism; it played little formal part in the making of feudalism. Life based upon agrarian activity narrowed down to manorialism and devoted to hunting and fighting as its major concerns neither encouraged nor needed intellectual pursuits, scientific or other.

Nevertheless, despite these handicaps, whether feudal or catholic, two factors operated to maintain and then to intensify interests of a scientific kind. For one thing, there was an internal expansion reflected in the growth of towns and the beginning of commerce; for another, there was the continuation of the process of transmission now reaching beyond the Arabic to the Latin and the Greek. The two influences, working from within and from without, are closely related. An instance is the reviving of Roman law in connection with the development of the monarchies. The outcome, in summary, was a period of cultural assimilation.

The consequences can be seen for example in the enlargements of the curricula of the universities, in the rise in dignity of the library from a locked bookcase to an equally well locked and guarded room, in the rise of a class of legists, in the intensified attention given to the artistic achievements of antiquity, so that the intellectual renaissance of the twelfth century was followed by an aesthetic renaissance in the fifteenth. But these rebirths were in fact discoveries; and what was being discovered or revealed had to be mastered before men, having raised themselves to the level of earlier Mediterranean achievements and made them their own, could advance to the levels of initiation and origination and so become capable of adding to the sum of knowledge. If in the process the world of catholic feudalism gradually disintegrated, if scholasticism lost control of men's minds, if knights and castles were replaced by burghers and towns, if human activities tended to leave the Mediterranean and adventure out upon the oceans—all these are but evidences that a new phase of culture was developing. The fact was that the modern age was in process of formation.

An epoch of world history is about to begin, and so a retrospective view will not here be amiss. It will serve to bring the preceding pages into sharp focus. This view extends back to the era when the earth was dotted over with a great number of cultural centers, small in extent and population, with restricted culture bases, each in theory capable of becoming the center of a circle of expansion. Only a few of them were in fact destined to achieve such greatness, and around them were gradually incorporated the less fortunate groupings. Chief among these favored spots were the Fertile Crescent and the valley of the Nile. Here during millennia the slow development of culture proceeded. Never far removed from the Mediterranean, the civilization of those regions tended more and more to pass from the river valleys to the sea. At first the eastern end of the Mediterranean was the center of development, but the whole of that sea came with time to be the cultural unit. It was particularly with the expansion of Rome that the culture of the epoch tended to embrace all the lands looking toward the inland waters. Yet even the political predominance of Rome never caused the cultural predominance in the region to be transferred from the eastern to the western territories.

And so when the disintegration of the Roman power set in, it was to the east that the political center was moved, and Byzantium and Alexandria became the pivotal cities of the civilized western world. It was there that the continuity of culture was maintained and developed; it was there that was to be found the cultural deposit left from many millennia of human experiences; it was there that the starting point for future achievement would have to be found. It was there, in fact, that the resumption of cultural development took place. In Byzantium, in Persia, in Egypt the advancing conquerors from Arabia found the knowledge and refinement that were to conquer them and make them the agents whereby the achievements of earlier ages were preserved and increased. As this new power expanded its territory, the Mediterranean once more became the scene of activity. From Baghdad to the cities of Sicily and Spain the cultural network spread, bringing back into the Mediterranean circle all the shores of that sea.

The continuity of the Mediterranean culture: here is the key to the understanding of the cultural development of the two thousand years from Thales to Averroes. It alone makes sociological sense of the record.

In this continuous development during two millennia over a single culture area there is one anomaly. One part of the area, after

having been brought within the general influence of the development, fell away, lost immediate contact with it, and for nearly twenty
generations was isolated from it. The story of its separation and re-
incorporation can be succinctly told. It begins with the disintegration of the political aggregation called Rome. It is continued with
an increasing isolation of the abandoned region as it fills up with
representatives of lower cultures, who are brought only partially
into contact with a higher civilization by those whose chief object
is their conversion to a new religion. During this long period of
isolation and conversion life in the Dark Area goes on; it takes form
ultimately in a new social organization: catholic feudalism. No
sooner is this new cultural integration well on its way than there
begins a period of transmission during which the accumulated experience of the Mediterranean world is spread with relative sudden-
ness over the once isolated region. Necessarily a period of assimilation follows during which the process of diffusion operates with
slight impediment. Only when these six periods have ended can the
stage of initiation and origination begin and diffusion give way to
invention. Only then can the course be resumed which leads continuously from the animal Homo to Man.

CHAPTER 4: *The Modern Age*

Needless to say no comprehensive treatment of the modern world is intended here. Nothing less than an encyclopedic treatment of the development of thought since the disintegration of the medieval, i.e., Mediterranean culture would be implied by such a task. All that is sought is to place the purpose of the present volume in an historical perspective. To do so requires only an outline of the intellectual evolution of which the rise of sociology as a distinct domain of inquiry is a part. The starting point of such an outline is the work of Copernicus. It is by general agreement the most striking of the attainments that mark the beginning of modern times; and the judgment need not be questioned provided his work is regarded in the relative sense in which he himself would have considered it. It was not, that is to say, the dramatic and isolated achievement it was once thought to be but was on the other hand a development out of the astronomical study of the period.

Copernicus had attended the Italian universities, where he had heard the Ptolemaic system questioned, and so came to be interested in the problem of simplifying it by shifting the center of the system of heavenly bodies from the earth to the sun. He made no other alterations in the Ptolemaic system, retaining its cycles and epicycles but reducing the number from 79 to 34. He found ancient authority for the heliocentric system and so was able to shelter himself from immediate criticism; the evidence for such a heliocentric system was not at the time conclusive; to use it did but decrease the complexity and multiplicity of the movements which were thought necessary to enable the mind to picture the relations of all the members of the solar system. The theory found slow acceptance; its ultimate implications, resulting from the establishment of the double movement of the earth on its axis and round the sun, are not even today widely understood. Nevertheless, with Copernicus' theory and his book the older picture of the universe was ended.

Astronomy had become a matter of practical concern with the

increase of navigation, especially upon the oceans. The picture of Prince Henry the Navigator watching from his tower the departure of ships which by successive efforts were to round the Cape of Good Hope on their way to India gives point to the growing demand for more accurate tables based on better observations. Princes sought to gain fame by encouraging such observations, on condition that the tables were called by their name. It seems to have been in some such way that Tycho Brahe obtained royal support for his famous observatory Uraniborg, which he constructed with an equipment superior to any that the west had ever known. In it for twenty years he employed an unusual ability as observer for the collection of data of an astronomical type. Dying, he turned over this mass of material to Kepler, his assistant.

Kepler, intrigued by a discrepancy between the observed and the calculated movements of Mars that no error imputable to Brahe could account for, strove to find an orbit for the planet that would bring observation and calculation into accord. He tried many figures and at last hit upon an ellipse—a circle so to speak with two centers. With the sun at one of these centers Mars ceased to show discrepancy between the reality and the pictured movement. A new system, the accepted one today, was the result, for it was soon seen that the other planets too moved about the sun in elliptical orbits. So died the Ptolemaic epicycles, replaced by Keplerian ellipses.

In the course of his investigations leading to the selection of the ellipse and later, Kepler was able to find such order and regularity in the heavens as to be able to explain all the observed movements as manifestations of three uniformities. With them as the basis of calculation and elliptical movements around the sun as the mental image of their mutual relations, Kepler was able to show complete regularity in the heavens.

In the meantime mathematics and physics had been developing, in particular at the hands of Galileo, with the result that Newton was able to take the work of all his predecessors in the field of astronomy and show that all the movements they had observed in the heavens could be reduced to aspects of the isolate gravitation, itself capable of being reduced to a single basic and all pervading regularity formulated in a single statement: the law of the universe.

Enough eloquence has already been directed toward Newton for his worlds-embracing induction to dispense with any additional tribute here; in its place two remarks may be made. The first concerns the impression made upon his age by Newton's synthesis. In it he brought together and summarized the work of all the observers of the phenomena of the heavens back to and beyond the theocratic observers of six thousand years before. In Newton their work culminated; without them, he would have done nothing. The achievement was the summation of the collective effort of thousands of generations; it was the work of mankind; "the Heavens declare the glory of Man." It was this fact which gives significance to Newton's results and explains the profound and far-reaching effect they had and still have upon the imagination of modern man. Just as the thinkers of the Golden Age of Greece under the initiative of Thales had found order and regularity in number and extension with the result that geometry, mathematics, set the dominant note for their intellectual chorus and provided the ideal for their standards of thought, so did the Newtonian achievement serve as the ideal goal toward which his successors would strive. Law, once shown to be existent in the phenomena of the heavens, must be shown to be so in the phenomena of the earth; and the ambition to attain a similar goal in every department of man's investigations became and remained the driving force in science.

In the second place, the case of astronomy because of its completeness best illustrates a stage through which every homogeneous body of scientific phenomena, every isolated group of abstract data, must at some time pass. It may be indicated by several names: it is the passage into the strictly positive stage of investigation, the beginning of truly scientific study, the transition from magic to science —whatever the words the spirit behind them is the same, namely, the revision of the entire sum of cumulated data with the purpose of eliminating all hominoid influences and the determination "to see what is as it is." At some point in the history of each independent or separable body of data this revision will occur. It is the inevitable result of the continuous accumulation of data based on observation and experience.

Now the importance of the Newtonian synthesis of astronomical data lies precisely in the fact that it was the second and not the first such revision. As long as the mathematical was the only domain in which this revision had occurred, the achievement might be considered as unique, due only to the nature of the phenomena involved or to the nature of the human mind. Its occurrence and with such completeness in the domain of astronomy was proof that the first happening was not a unique phenomenon; it was on the contrary a precedent which might be repeated, should be repeated in every other science—which would be a science only when it had reached the same positive level. With impatient eagerness all the other sciences strove to accomplish for themselves the astronomical advance.

The first gains were in physics; but other fields of inquiry, thrown into obscurity by the brilliance of Newton's work, should not be forgotten. In the later 1400's, for instance, the advance of mathematical theory was systematically resumed and continuity with the work of the Arabic world became the basis of new mathematical developments. The work of Copernicus is partly the result of this renewed activity, and after 1500 the importance of the results obtained is no longer questionable. Without them the astronomical advances after Kepler would have been impossible.

Along with the work in mathematics and astronomy went speculation and discovery in what is today called physics. Here the most striking of the advances over the Mediterranean culture as respects science took place. It will be recalled that for Aristotle the natural world, *Ta Phusika*, was contained synthetically in natural philosophy. This natural philosophy, embracing the study of physical phenomena, was an essentially descriptive body of knowledge with its three kingdoms, mineral, vegetable, and animal. It contained little if any trace of the modern distinctions among physics, chemistry, and biology. In fact, looked at retrospectively, it was the task of establishing these distinctions which the Hellenic world bequeathed to its successors. To the accomplishment of this task the Arabic world contributed an enormous amount of factual information gathered loosely around the subject called alchemy and the clear beginnings of the appropriate method, the experimental, for advancing knowledge in this field. Both the knowledge and the method were improved during the latter part of the period of assimilation, and by the 1600's the beginnings of the modern point of view, involving the destruction of the older natural philosophy, were clearly under way.

These origins may be associated with Galileo. With him and roughly with the year 1600, the study of modern physics as opposed to the physics of the ancients may be said to have begun. This new physics, nontechnically defined, may be said to deal with the properties common to matter, the general properties of matter. Galileo dealt with movement abstractly defined and his discoveries in this field made possible the work of Newton. He also studied light and sound. Gilbert added to the general knowledge the properties of electricity and magnetism. Heat as a special subject of investigation was to come later; but the main lines of present day physics were slowly coming into existence, and the positive period of knowledge in this subject or series of subjects may be associated with the great experimenters of the 1600's and the growth of the scientific societies.

Of course the distinction between physics and chemistry was not clearly felt at first. Chemistry as the study of the special properties of the various substances was yet to arise, but it was clearly on its way after the iatro-chemical period. The great debate centering around the nature and existence of phlogiston marks the final transition in the science from the magical or hominoid influence to the positive. During this period the spirit of fire, fire as an essence or subtle something which was lost in the process of combustion, disappeared. Combustion itself was generalized to include burning, rusting, and breathing and the process was studied experimentally. During the same period also, the lesson the alchemists had been learning through centuries of effort to transmute metals, namely, that certain substances are specific and cannot be reduced beyond a certain point, was finally learned. It had been suspected as far back as the Arabic period; now "scepticall chymists" began to speak of "elements," and nothing was needed but the balance of Lavoisier to bring about a revolution in chemistry, i.e., to put it on a definitively positive level.

It is of course impossible here to give in detail the story of the gradual rise of biology and its detachment from the art of medicine. Perhaps it can be said to have begun with Vesalius. Certainly it extended down to the time of Lamarck and Bichat. With the latter comes the abstract definition of life which creates a general or pure biology as the study of a specific phenomenon, an isolate, which is not the subject matter of any other science. Such an advance in theory puts an end to the efforts of physics and chemistry to bring the phenomena called living under their control and establishes once for all the hierarchical conception that these other sciences are but the indispensable preliminary subjects needed as an introduction to the study of a higher phenomenon, independent, specific, and irreducible. Thus the "physics" of Aristotle is at last analyzed and his natural philosophy gives place to a series of sciences, astronomy, physics, chemistry, and biology.

The next step in this progression is regular in its direction and seemingly inevitable in its logic. It was taken by men among whom Cabanis was the most eminent. The aim of his effort was clear; it can be simply expressed. By the end of the 1700's science had come to include all the physical phenomena manifested by man. There was however one set of data as yet outside the scientific jurisdiction, namely, the moral. A continuation of the work of the century would require these moral phenomena to be studied just as the physical had been. Only so would they become "an essential part of the natural history of man." To link the moral with the physical was the purpose of Cabanis' two volumes: *Rapports du physique et du moral de l'homme.*

These volumes deserve momentary attention even in so summary a chapter as the present. "Nothing will be found in this book concerning what has long been called *metaphysics;* here are only simple investigations into *physiology,* directed toward the special study of a certain order of functions." [1] In these clear words did Cabanis indicate a fundamental change in attitude toward phenomena hitherto outside the range of scientific treatment. The results of his researches are presented in ten *mémoires,* the titles of which are sufficient to indicate their nature: the physiological history of sensation; the influence of age, sex, temperament, disease, regime, and climate upon the formation of ideas and of moral affections; considerations upon animal life, instinct, sympathy, sleep, and delirium; the influence or the reaction of the moral upon the physical.

The place of these considerations in the whole body of knowledge is for Cabanis quite clear. In the classification of the different fields of human interest they belong with those that "s'occupent specialement d'objets de philosophie et de morale." But it is easy

1. P. J. G. Cabanis, *Rapports du physique et du moral de l'homme* (nouvelle ed. Paris, Fortin Masson, 1843), p. 54. (Italics are Cabanis'.)

to see, he continues, "that the physical knowledge of man is their common basis; that here is the point from which they must all set out, if they are to avoid raising a vain scaffolding strange to the eternal laws of nature." Hence it is that Cabanis deals with "the relations between the physical study of man and the workings of his intellect; between the systematic development of his organs and the analogous development of his sentiments and his passions: relations whence it can clearly be seen that physiology, the analysis of ideas and moral phenomena, are but the three branches of one and the same science, which can justifiably be called *the science of man.*" [2]

The special significance of Cabanis' work then is clear. After his time it is forever impossible to draw a sharp line of demarcation between the moral life of man and his biological life. The two are indissolubly connected, and the fact that the study of physiological phenomena is once and for all a part of the domain of scientific inquiry implies that the moral world is included in the same territory, subject to like laws and to be studied by analogous methods.

Thus the connection between the biological and the psychological became a permanent achievement of scientific efforts and the terrain of positive knowledge was greatly extended. There was, however, a question that remained unanswered. What is the place of the new doctrines with relation to those already existing? What in a word was their hierarchical position in the scientific synthesis? The intimate connection established by Cabanis between the biological and the psychological seemed to supply the correct answer. Physiological phenomena were individual manifestations; moral phenomena, indissolubly connected with them, would likewise be individual. Both categories would in logic precede the study of data gained by the observation of individuals in their relations with one another.

This apparently unchallengeable position was further fortified by the work of still another group of thinkers who came into prominence during the 1700's and especially in the second half of that period. These men had been devoting their attention to the analysis of phenomena that were at first called political in the large sense of that word and then as the 1800's drew near began to be termed

2. Cabanis, p. 59. (Italics are Cabanis'.)

social. Thus there seemed to be a direct route, a logical progression from the physiological to the moral to the social.

The men who were engaged in the study of the political, or the social, were contemporaries and friends of those who were working in the other lines just mentioned. Hence the objectives and criteria of all of them were similar. The thinking of all of them had as its background and even as its basis the conception of universal law. They all had a regard for science as the one source of reliable knowledge on a strictly human basis. The agreement that experiential and where possible experimental processes are the best source for data upon which conclusions are to rest was nearly universal among those who concerned themselves at all with such matters. The notions of a hierarchical arrangement of positive sciences developed. They are to be found in those words in the manifesto of the intellectuals of the period: the Introduction by D'Alembert to Diderot's *La Grande Encyclopédie*. The same work confirms the conclusions reached on logical grounds as to the nature of the next stage of scientific inquiry. The social life of man, after the physiological and the moral, is clearly in the line of advance. It had as a matter of fact already begun to be analyzed. Vico, a Baconian, in Italy for example had written a *Scienza Nuova;* Montesquieu in France, trained in the science of his time, extended the conception of law to social phenomena. Impressed by the needs of his country Quesnay, a physician, sought to bring to society the scientific regime that biology was learning to apply to the individual and planned a physiocracy. Turgot and Condorcet were soon to follow.

Obviously the time for a science of social phenomena is at hand; its rise will of course be the subject of extended treatment later in these pages. But here the important matter is that after six thousand years of effort, after the passage of culture from the theocracies to the Mediterranean and thither to Europe, after the summated intellectual efforts of two hundred generations of men, it had at last been clearly seen that the spirit of science is the determination to subordinate all ambitions and interests to one great aim: to see what is as it is. On that foundation alone can a society of men, descendants of the animal Homo, securely rest. To bring that spirit into the study of society came toward the end of the 1700's to be the ambition of a group of men whose efforts laid the foundations of sociology.

PART TWO: THE DEVELOPMENT
OF SCIENTIFIC METHOD

CHAPTER 5: *The Making of Method*

The course of cultural development from the remotest past to the present has now been traced down to the end of the 1700's, when the conception of a science of society was coming into being. From this cooperation of human generations had come, in one domain of human concern after another, organized bodies of knowledge serving to guide the actions of men. Mankind in a word *learned* and so became able to guide conduct by knowledge. In terms of the individual man, his acts were performed under the guidance of the experience of the race. From this accumulated learning came not only direction for particular acts but a general doctrine as well— what may be called the spirit of science. Briefly expressed, it is the teaching that inquirers, whatever personal desires or ambitions they may have, must subordinate such motives to the aim of gaining an understanding of the world in which they live, uncolored and unaffected by any secondary considerations whatever. Expressed in general terms, imagination in any of its thousand forms must be subordinated to observation. Men must strive to know what is as it is. In these words lies the spirit of science.

It is not enough, however, for the scientific inquirer to be imbued with the spirit of science. Before he is equipped to become a contributor to the sum of human achievement, he must have some knowledge of scientific method. For mankind in its accumulation of experience has not only acquired learning and come to feel the spirit in which learning must be sought, it has also gained some knowledge of the collective processes by which learning is increased. *Man, that is, has not only learned, he has learned how to learn.*

It has not been an easy thing, this making of method. Consider for a moment the first descendants of the animal Homo on the upward path to Man. In what a complexity did they find themselves! Surrounded by an infinity of changing details, submerged beneath the vastness of the unknown, what were they to learn and how? Even when it seemed that something had been gained, how were they to be sure? The days go by, the seasons change, growth and decay transform the environment—what is there constant in this ceaseless variety and how is it to be found?

It was not a willed nor even a willing process, this learning. The animal Homo was and still is strong within his descendants. He was not patient, industrious, slow to decide—he could not be. His sons preferred the easier path which leads to the direct control of things by an exercise of the will. They were by nature disinclined to thought; they were and are designed for action and for emotion. Hence they were condemned, on leaving the animal plane, to try by instinct the wrong ways and to arrive at the right ones only after having tried the others.

It was, however, a necessary process. No matter how tempting the other ways, in the long run they fail. To achieve through the utterance of a bold "Be done," however satisfying to the spirit, is yet an inadequate recourse for the obtaining of food. To determine the nature of things by arguing about them, by dialectical processes, is a noble and stimulating procedure. By it a heaven may be constructed; it is no way to build a house. The house must be lived in, it must stand erect and resist the winds and the rains. And because these tests had to be met, when a first trial resulted in failure a second had to be made, and so on until the right way was found.

It is finally a continuing process. Not yet has the last experience been had, the final and perfect method found. Hitherto the path of science has led through the material world to the world of life in the biological sense. There yet remain the immense territories— to men the most important of all—which lie within the domains of culture and personality. Only when these have been studied will the construction of scientific method be complete. But even now the nature and aim of that method are clear. In the course of learning how to learn, men have amassed an armory of means whereby to assure themselves of the validity and dependability of their facts and the conclusions they draw from them. By a study of what has already been accomplished, some insight can be had as to what yet remains to accomplish and how to effect it.

But can the discussion of method be of avail in the advancement of science? The answer depends upon the nature and purpose of the discussion. For example, certain aspects of method need no special attention. The logical bases of thought are in this category.

The thought processes by which science is built up may be subject to a severer discipline than those of everyday existence, but fundamentally the two are the same and are to be studied together. Again, that phase of method which includes special techniques may also be excluded here. They are too closely associated with the nature of the matters studied to be extended by generalization to other fields. Nevertheless even when all the exceptions have been made, just as the history of science was useful in revealing the spirit in which further study should be carried on, so certain general conclusions may emerge from a review of the experience that men have gained from the making of the sciences that already exist.

To begin with, then, sciences are not made; they grow. The search for beginnings is as futile here as in any other instance of cultural phenomena. At all times men have been accumulating data which have later been classified under one or another head; but the result was never in the minds of those who made the early accumulations. Men in the first stages of human existence were busy with meeting the needs of daily existence. They could not, even if they had wished to, have departmentalized their life. They lived—as a single process involving man and the world. The whole range of phenomena, from the psychical down to the mathematical, was included.

At all times and in relation to all subjects of knowledge, the cumulative process has been in operation. The needs and conditions of life make it inevitable that it should be so. Relations with other human beings, as individuals and as members of the group, relations with things outside, plants, animals, the earth, the winds and weather, the sun, moon, and stars—all these in their complexity and in their isolatedness impinge upon man's senses and his mind and leave their trace. He must attend to them, too, for they condition his existence. There is seemingly no order in which they occur; they happen as they happen; man has no control over them. But as they affect him directly he is compelled to remember them, to store them up in his mind, i.e., in the thing with which he "minds": the motives and conduct of his fellow beings, the habits of animals, the edibility of vegetables and fruits, the signs of storms, the recurrence of the moon, an unceasing stream of impressions which for him have meaning. Because they are in relation with him he must give heed to them; but because he can at first exercise no deliberate choice, make no selection, this first learning is wholly spontaneous.

At what point the spontaneous process becomes systematic it is impossible to say. It seems certain, however, that there are two stages in the systematic gathering of knowledge: the empirical and the scientific. The first of these terms applies to man's knowledge when he has reached the stage of discovering fixed relations between phenomena or beings that seem unconnected with any general scheme of things, relations which are therefore unexplained. They are *so* and can be relied upon for guiding action but only in a particular set of circumstances. Discovery of such relations began early in the history of man. Many of them go back to the primitives, as for example the properties of quinine. They are found in every department of science from the mathematical on. The area of a rectangle, the use of the lever, the effect of vinegar upon certain metals, the rise in the price of goods when they are scarce, the psychical effect of fasting—these are simple illustrations of man's early successes in discovering relations of similarity and sequence in the mass of otherwise disparate phenomena with which he was at first surrounded.

It seems likely too that as early at least as the theocratic period man deliberately sought to increase this kind of knowledge. It is particularly the outcome of the application of individuals and castes to certain lines of occupation exclusively. Artisans, craftsmen, workers were bound to make discoveries of this limited sort, and so they handed on from generation to generation a respectable mass of detailed but unsynthesized knowledge which became the foundations later of a more systematic knowledge. The combination of the recipes of the metalworkers in Egypt with the speculations of the Greeks to make alchemy is a case in point.

It was probably the theocratic priesthoods who first began to further this empirical type of knowledge and seek to correlate it. Their influence in the community, the need for whatever knowledge there was whereby they could guide or if need be dominate the societies in which they were the directive caste—these were incentives for gathering and utilizing data. In arithmetic, geometry, and astronomy at least and no doubt in the sociological and psychological fields they made real advances.

In no case, however, unless it was in elementary mathematics do the theocrats seem to have risen above the empirical plane. Perhaps it was the influence of their religion that prevented advance. The attribution of phenomena to hominoid agency tends certainly to inhibit the search for relations among the phenomena themselves. At any rate a new tendency begins to show itself in the eastern Mediterranean. The first clear manifestation of a systematic search for new data and their correlation into a synthesis solely on the basis of an analytical study of their nature and relations seems to date from the efforts of the Ionian Greeks of the seventh century. From them it spread over the Hellenic and Greco-Roman world and became a part of the cultural heritage of mankind. From geometry it expanded into astronomy and then slowly but certainly came to dominate the investigation of the physical world until now it is the ideal toward which all investigators strive. To obtain as extensive a knowledge in a given field as possible, to colligate the data acquired by discovering fundamental relationships among them, and to express these relationships in an all-embracing theory— such is the outcome of the spontaneous efforts of early man to learn enough of the nature of the world to enable him to live.

It is important to emphasize the first two of these stages, the spontaneous and the empirical, with respect to all the sciences and particularly those which have not yet been able to attain fully to the ideal set forth above. The point is that *at all times there have been accumulations of data on all the subjects of interest or concern to men.* Physical phenomena did not begin only when physics as a science came to be. Sociological and psychological data come down to the present from the earliest days, sometimes by implication, often by direct record. Laws, constitutions, codes, sacred texts, rituals, proverbs, mythology, literature, language are repositories of the experience of men in dealing with their fellows. If these classes of facts seem late in reaching the scientific stage, it is only that though they were among the first to be collected they are among the last to which the scientific method has come to be applied. The point is that variations in rate of advance are in no wise to be interpreted as differences in capacity for reaching the goal. The earliest entrants may be the slowest, but they may finish the course for all that.

The variation in the rate of speed with which certain classes of data pass through the progression from spontaneous to scientific seems to be related to a similar variation in regard to the formation of abstractions; and since the formation of abstractions is at the very foundation of scientific knowledge, a consideration of the process by which they come into being will be the second general aspect under which scientific method will here be envisaged.

The importance of abstraction in the growth of science has already been illustrated in connection with the rise of geometry; its nature and effect must be discussed more fully at this point. To begin with, then, since man would be helpless if he had to deal with each single phenomenon in all its uniqueness, the only way, given the limitations of his psychical equipment, for him to come into effective relation with the environment is to base action upon what is common to a whole range of experience, presenting at least some obvious points of likeness. Each animal hunted for example is unlike every other, as any hunter well knows; nevertheless a number of them unlike in every other respect may be hard to catch because they are so swift in running. All other differences may be lost sight of in contemplation of the one common characteristic: their swiftness. In this simple case there has obviously been first a purely spontaneous analysis involving the separate consideration of the various characteristics the animals in question manifest, and then an abstraction from among them of the one they present in common, upon which attention is centered. Thus the contemplation of a red flower, a red sky, blood, a glowing fire gives rise to the abstraction redness. A number of similar abstractions allows the process to go further and result in the abstraction color, which may vary in intensity, and so on.

An analogous mental operation instead of resulting in abstract phenomena, i.e., qualities or properties may give abstract types, as happens when the characteristics which separate a given class of animals from all other classes are kept in mind and the differences which distinguish each animal within the class are forgotten. Thus arises the concept of *the* lion, *the* lamb. Iron, water, air, gas, matter are examples of such types in the inorganic world; animal, mammal, dog, man in the world of life; the animal, that abstract being "the definition of which can fit all the representatives of animality, without designating any of them; the mammal, a term which expresses the fundamental nature of the tiger or the lion as well as that of the whale or the rat; the dog, which is no dog, but whose constituent parts are common to all the species; . . . the man, whose characters are found wherever a man is met, to whatever race he belongs." [1]

Such are the two forms of abstraction: abstract phenomena and abstract beings. Without them science, learning, would be literally impossible. Every event, every being is in the final sense unique. Nothing quite the same ever recurs; no two beings are ever entirely alike. It is only because they can be thought of abstractly that their differences can be lost from sight and their points of likeness held in mind. "Abstraction, in proportion as it has grown, has reacted upon civilization by giving men a greater and greater number of common points which have allowed them to act in concert. The knowledge of only *special* objects or beings would not in a fact suffice to determine a common understanding since this knowledge evidently cannot be common to all; it is only with the aid of abstractions that men communicate, and the more the abstractions grow in number, the more do their relations extend." [2]

It is particularly in the field of science that abstraction has played a fundamental role. The cases of geometry and astronomy have already been cited. In physics the same procedure has given the same results. An admirable example is to be found in the case of Galileo establishing the parallelogram of forces. To the objection that events do not occur in the real world as his law represents them, he replies: "I admit that the laws so well demonstrated *in abstracto,* cease to be true *in concreto,*" [3] and in a passage too long to be quoted here he goes into detail to show how the complicating factors of the real world have to be set aside in establishing the law, and that later when the law is applied these factors *then* must be taken into consideration.

Another example from the field of physics affords a perfect instance of the development of a scientific abstraction. It is the case of Gilbert beginning the study of electricity. Attracted by the

1. P. Laffitte, *Cours de philosophie première* (2 vols. Paris, Société Positiviste, 1928), *1,* 53.

2. Laffitte, *1,* 54.

3. Galileo, *Discorsi et dimostrazioni matematiche,* pp. 243–247, quoted in Laffitte, *2,* 62. (Italics are Galileo's.)

medieval stories in relation to amber and the lodestone, Gilbert set out to increase the sum of knowledge as opposed to folklore on these subjects. In particular he gave attention to amber, the material called *elektron* by the Greeks. The most striking characteristic of this substance was, according to the stories, that when rubbed it attracted to itself small particles of matter. Here then was a property, a characteristic way of behaving, that deserved attention. Was it really true or only a matter of legend? The only way of deciding, unless the dialectical method was to be relied upon, was to try and see. On trial the alleged fact was found to be exact. The next question was whether amber—elektron—was the only substance to act so under the same circumstances, i.e., whether other substances possessed the same property. Were they, in other words, "amberish," electrical? Gilbert assembled a variety of substances and put them to the test. Some revealed amberishness and others not. He therefore divided them into two groups: the amberish and the nonamberish, the electrics and the nonelectrics, using these words as substantives. There Gilbert, not knowing of insulation, stopped with his abstraction incomplete. Once a hint in the matter was obtained, however, Gilbert's successors, insulating their materials, were quick to show that all substances were electrics; that is to say, though they possessed distinctive characteristics by virtue of being gold or glass or wood, the fact did not prevent them from being alike in one single aspect, from being amber-like; and thus the way was opened to the establishment of a new abstraction or property, electricity.

Other examples of abstractions that have come to summarize centuries of work could be given. The most notable would no doubt be the highly refined abstraction upon which the science of biology rests in the general or pure conception of that science. Here it is the very existence of the science that is at stake, for unless biologists could produce an abstraction demonstrably their own their science would be in danger of being absorbed in one of the other sciences, physics or chemistry, or divided between them. But when Bichat, summarizing centuries of investigation, defined life as the sum of the forces which resist death and Blainville carried the analysis further so as to enable Comte to reduce the phenomenon to its essential phase, namely, the continuous renewal of material substance, they were working to determine once for all the essential independence of biology by seizing upon the one phenomenon which characterizes all living forms whatever and no inert existences at all.

It is clearly implicit in what has already been said that of the two forms of abstraction, the phenomenon and the type, it is the phenomenon which has the greater scientific significance. This superior significance is due not only to the fact that the type can be analyzed into a combination of properties; it grows also out of the fact that on the basis of phenomena a still more refined but also still more valuable abstraction can be made, namely, the abstract relation, i.e., a precise relation established between abstract phenomena.

> Abstract properties constitute that mass of common ideas without which there can exist only narrowly extended feelings of community between men; they furnish materials and a basis for the construction of abstract relations. . . . The importance of the latter is very different from that of the former. By the strict dependence that it establishes between two phenomena of the same or of different nature, the discovery of an abstract relation makes possible the prevision and the modification of one of them. If the relation between the circumference and the radius has been discovered, it becomes easy to determine the circumference for a given radius, or reciprocally what must be the radius of a given circumference. All the industry of the modern world is based upon this knowledge.[4]

"The relations between the volume of a pyramid or a cylinder and its base and height; between the idea of the time and that of the space traversed by a falling body; between the ideas of volume and compression in the case of gases: these are instances of abstraction of the higher sort, which is indeed the pure domain of science." [5]

The scientific usefulness of abstraction does not stop here; it goes still further. It gives, when so extended, the possibility of dividing the world of observation into a number of distinct categories. When for example an abstract phenomenon has been discovered, further analysis may show that it is essentially independent of all the other manifestations with which it is found to be associated.

4. Laffitte, *1,* 55.
5. Laffitte, *1,* 67–68.

That is to say, certain properties may not only be abstracted; they may be isolated.

Laffitte sets forth this conception as follows:

> It is evident that the world presents itself as a whole in which all parts are bound together by constant relations. But the complete representation of this whole and above all the determination of the reaction upon the whole of each special modification are certainly above the power of the genius of man, however great it may be supposed to be. . . . It has therefore been necessary to find a way to fill the gap in thought created by the impossibility of determining the laws which bind together all the particular constituents of the whole. It has been done as follows: It has been shown that *there exist separable parts which form partial wholes.* Evidently they exist in no absolute fashion; but the relations which connect them with other such divisions of the entire mass of things are so slight that they can be neglected. These partial wholes are in effect composed of such constituent parts of the whole sum of things as are found to be connected together in such a way that they act one upon another in an appreciable fashion; whereas those parts that are considered as separate undergo from them only inappreciable modifications. Thus when a man pushes an object, the object, the man and the earth form a whole; but the reaction of the man upon the earth being infinitely slight can be neglected, and the man and the object can be considered as two separable elements. This relative separation of different beings is the basis of all science.[6]

Levy puts the same thought in more recent words: "Science, like common sense, sets out in the first instance to search for systems that can be imagined as isolated from their setting in the universe without appreciably disturbing their structure and the process they present." "There are no absolutely isolated systems unless it be the whole universe. Science does, in fact, find circumstances in which they can be delimited with great precision. Scientific laws and scientific facts are all statements concerning such systems, perfected, idealized." "Scientific truth is not an idealized truth to which the universe closely approximates, it is a first step in the process of finding out the truth about the universe by examining it in chips."

6. 2, 12. (Italics are Laffitte's.)

"The method of isolation is itself characteristic of the scientific method. It is once more the search for permanence in a fluctuating and changing environment. Science attempts to attain that permanence by isolating aspects of the behavior that can be regarded as unchanging and fastening them as properties on the object." "We have begun with the universe of common sense, the universe we apprehend, and we have seen scientific development as the search for isolates in this world process." [7]

It is thus a vital part of scientific method in the wide sense, this search for partial wholes, for isolates, for abstract phenomena connected so closely by abstract relations that compared with these connecting relations all others seem trivial and of so slight account that they can be neglected. Practically every important abstraction hitherto presented in these pages could serve as illustrations of isolates as well, for they were the basic abstractions upon which great divisions of science depend: the circle, i.e., roundness, isolated from every other property with which it is found associated and shown to possess qualities in no essential sense dependent upon or related to these other properties; the deeper abstractions of extension and movement; the isolates of gravitation, heat, light, sound, electricity—all independent of one another and of associated properties; finally in the world of living things, the creation of abstract types and the discovery in these types of an abstract phenomenon, the phenomenon of life, completely independent so far as man's ability to analyze can discover of any appreciable connection with all the characteristics such as weight, complexity, form, type of structure, etc., etc., of which the various abstract types are composed. When such an isolate is known a science exists; when a new abstract phenomenon is recognized and isolated, a new science comes into being.

Finally, one further consideration in regard to the dependence of science upon abstract isolates may be presented. The order in which the various fundamental sciences have come into the intellectual world seems to be related to the ease with which their respective isolates have been discovered, or in other terms, to the relative isolation or isolability in the whole scheme of things of a particular class of abstract phenomena. Number, for example,

7. H. Levy, *The Universe of Science* (London, Watts, 1932), pp. 45, 52, 53–54, 57, 72–73.

seems to be nearly an absolute isolate; extension, less nearly so; but how easy it seems to be after all to isolate shapes from any associated or accompanying qualities whatever. Hence the special nature of the geometry of the ancients. Extension is an abstraction of a higher order; it was reached and isolated only with Descartes. So with the other isolates here discussed, directly or indirectly. As the accumulation of data proceeds, spontaneously, empirically, scientifically, there goes on—and indeed this accumulation in part consists in—a gradual analysis on the basis of which abstractions slowly arise. Not every class of abstract phenomena is so unrelated to other and accompanying phenomena as to be obviously an isolate in the midst of the system of things which is the universe. The more obvious the isolability the more easily the class of phenomena of which it is true rises to the level of science; the greater the complexity of relationship between associated properties, the more difficult the isolation of any one of them; hence the sequential differences in the establishment of the various sciences, some appearing early in man's cultural development, others later. Such differences as these are however a secondary matter. Whether old or young, what determines the potential existence of a science is the recognition of a clearly demonstrated abstract isolate. When the fact that there is a body of homogeneous abstract phenomena, separable as a class from the whole system of things, is brought to the level of demonstration and abstract relations are discovered among them, a science begins to be.

At this point the discussion comes closer to the question of method, for at once upon the definition of an isolate arises the problem of how the existence of isolates is established and how the phenomena subsumed under them are to be developed into an organized science.

On the first of these points experience in a double sense leaves no doubt. In the first place the summated teaching of generations is that every effort must be made to clear away all obstacles that might intervene between the investigator and the phenomena investigated. All preconceptions, magical interpretations, hominoid intermediaries, etc., etc., must be scrupulously and ruthlessly set aside. All other aspirations must be subordinated to the purpose of seeing what is as it is. From the second point of view, that of the investigator himself, the same conclusion emerges. Unless his efforts to learn and use the relations that exist among the phenomena he is occupied with are carried on in an objective spirit, the conclusions will flow not from the facts themselves but from stereotypes or prejudices or ignorance; there will be a discrepancy between the data and the derived doctrines which will betray itself and the investigator at some point in his attempt to utilize his conclusions.

Of course both kinds of experience are summarized in the statement that in scientific research the imagination must be subordinated to observation; and this in turn is only another way of saying that before the treatment of facts can reach a scientific level all hominoid influences must be removed. Such a thought was no doubt in the background of Descartes' recommendation that at some time in their intellectual life men should empty out their minds, inspect the contents with the greatest care, and replace only those items which withstand the most rigorous inspection. At any rate, every body of organized knowledge that has with time become a science has passed through just such an inspection. At some point in the history of every science the hominoids must be expelled. How strongly they are entrenched is seldom realized even after the expulsion has been begun. Only when the subjective and hominoid elements have been excluded does the scientific epoch for the given discipline begin.

Obviously the recognition of isolates is involved in the process of purifying the data of science. As foreign influences are recognized and set aside, the homogeneity of the remaining elements becomes clearer. The work of analysis and abstraction becomes easier. Relationships and the absence of relations are more certainly established. Finally the work of analysis and classification comes to an end. Certain phenomena are declared to be specific; they cannot be reduced to combinations of simpler phenomena. They are *irreducible*. They stand not absolutely alone in the midst of the sum of things but so relatively independent of the remainder that they may be considered without regard to the rest. Such a class of phenomena will be by definition abstract; when viewed in its relative independence as the outcome of many generations of experience, it is an isolate.

So much for the general spirit of method in the usual sense. But what is to be inferred from the fact that each isolate, by virtue of the circumstance that it is an isolate, is distinct from all the others: what are the implications of *this* fact as to method? Here again both universal experience and individual investigation agree. They accord in saying that for each basic isolate (for each class of abstract phenomena, that is, which analysis can reduce no further and which therefore remains a specific class in a positive point of view) and so *for each of the fundamental sciences, there is a best*—not an only, but a best—*way of dealing with its materials.*

This best method can be discovered not by discussion beforehand but only by actual dealing with the phenomena in the attempt to systematize them and discover similarities and sequences in them. As the scientific inquirer advances from isolate to isolate, he gradually finds himself utilizing a number of distinctive methods. When the phrase "scientific method" is used without qualifying terms, it is these methods as a whole which are usually meant. Each of them may be of some use in relation to each isolate, but the fact does not invalidate, it only emphasizes the related fact that for each isolate there is a characteristic, a best method. That this best method cannot be predetermined in a dialectical manner is the basis for the frequent dismissal of discussion in this connection as futile.

The general validity of the position just stated can best be shown by a rapid review of the fundamental sciences with an eye to the methods they employ. To begin with, there is mathematics. Because of essential likeness among the isolates involved, number, extension, and movement (giving rise to calculus in the broad and inclusive sense, geometry, and mechanics) are usually grouped together. That the grouping is logically sound can be seen from the fact that the same general method is applicable to them all.

That this method is the method of deduction and that it arises from the nature of the isolates grouped under the head of mathematics will scarcely be contested. For its existence mathematics depends upon a body of inductively determined facts. For its development into the imposing intellectual structure which it now presents, induction is not responsible. Given a very small number of starting points arising out of experience in counting and measuring, geometry, say, has been made by intellectual processes alone. That is to say, the utilization, ordering, combining of the original data, which have hardly been increased since the emergence of the subject in Ionia, are all the outcome of those operations of the mind to which the word "deductive" is applied.

In the light of this fact, the question as to whether mathematics is a science or not has little point. In any case it was the very simplicity of its data and the spontaneous ease with which they were obtained that made possible the establishment of the first isolates. Because it was so slightly dependent upon systematic factual accumulation mathematics gave the first scientific thinkers the relatively easy task of building up by purely human means a body of knowledge free of hominoid undercurrents. Thereby confidence in their own powers and certitude as to the results of their exercise were for the first time obtained—an outcome of such transcendent value to man that even today the paradoxical and humorous aspects of attributing the governance of the universe to a mathematical hominoid pass unremarked. So clearly were these results due to the deductive method, so obviously was it the way by which its isolates should be developed to bring out the abstract relations inherent in them, that mathematics in its latest form has worked free of its natural foundations and come to be a discipline involving symbols and the consistency of their relations and designated as logic.

If even in mathematics the increasing importance of inductive data begins to show itself in mechanics, in the case of astronomy their indispensability is beyond doubt. There is no doubt either as to the way in which these data must be gained and utilized. They call for observation in its simplest and most characteristic form. Recourse to it indeed is almost as naive and instinctive as the use of deduction in mathematics. The theocratic priest watching from the summit of his ziggurat the movements of the heavenly bodies had already grasped the essentials of the method that was best adapted to the study of the phenomena of astronomy. His successors have only refined upon his procedures. From the gnomon to the 200-inch reflecting telescope, the one purpose of the whole series of inventions which connects the two has been the increase in accuracy of observation. Deduction no doubt can be carried over from mathematics to the next science above it, but its use there is secondary and subject to constant check by observation. When it takes the lead over the latter, as it does in astrology, the results are misleading and dangerous.

If the examples just given do not remove doubt that the appropriate method for dealing with the abstract phenomena of an isolate must be the result not of dialectical discussions engaged in beforehand but of actual working with the phenomena, the case of the physical sciences should be conclusive. The length of time required to perfect the appropriate way is evidence of the principle involved. From the time of the *Physics* of Aristotle down to the resumption of the scientific movement in the 1600's, the search for the proper method to deal with the enormous body of physical phenomena was under way spontaneously and empirically. The necessity of some form of observation was felt from the beginning. The acceptance of a traveler's tale may show credulity, but it also witnesses to a reliance upon observation. But just what form was the observation to take, and why was it so long in being taken?

Leaving aside completely that aspect of the explanation which consists in showing the absence of any compelling pressure from the active aspect of social evolution and confining the thought to the logical or intellectual aspect, it seems obvious that one of the factors causing the delay was the difficulty in so vast a field of forming the abstractions on which isolates could be established. Confusedly mingled in the physical world were phenomena that a later analysis was to apportion among three sciences. Even when the initial disentanglement had been effected, many groups of data required generations to be recognized as homogeneous and isolated. In physics, for example, heat and electricity were slow to become subjects of investigation. In the chemical domain there were some ninety elements, each irreducible and having its own special properties. There is no wonder that in dealing with such complicated data abstractions such as "metallicity" should arise to balk investigation.

Again, even when it was clear that the properties of a substance could be determined only by taking it into a laboratory and subjecting it to tests, there was a logical difficulty to be removed arising from the difference between an experience and an experiment. The two, though related in the sense of a reliance upon observed phenomena, are yet worlds apart as regards the instructive qualities they possess. Men had to learn not only to submit to experience; they had to learn to ask questions which the experience could answer. Even today the distinction is often lost sight of, especially when medieval investigators are given praise they do not deserve. To control the conditions under which an experience is undergone: such is the essence of the experiment. And the control of conditions implies a considerable knowledge beforehand, enough at least to base a plausible guess upon or even to allow the framing of a complicated hypothesis.

Nevertheless, despite the difficulties the analyses proceeded, the abstractions were made, the isolates gradually separated out; and the one best method of dealing with them and disclosing the abstract relations that connect their phenomena was recognized. The armory of scientific method was enlarged by one of the most powerful instruments of investigation man ever developed, namely, the method of experiment. Yet it did not for that reason become the sole instrument of science. *There is no one scientific method.* There are methods, as many as there are fundamental sciences built upon irreducible isolates. As long as any important division of human interest remains outside science, the number of methods and therefore scientific method itself is incomplete. The case of biology will point the moral.

The hunter, the agriculturalist, the stock breeder, the butcher, the haruspex, the priest, the medicine man, the medical man—all these and countless others have cooperated in accumulating material bearing upon life. They needed no theoretical considerations to prove that neither deduction nor simple observation nor experimentation was the key to its comprehension. True, all of them might be used, might in certain cases become indispensable; but neither all nor one could apply universally to the myriad forms in which the isolate called life is to be observed. Here once more the use of observation is inevitable, but here again also the other methods of observation are inadequate; a new method, adapted to the nature of the phenomena to be investigated, is needed. In time it was found. In essence it was simple enough; it must have begun in the earliest days of primitive man. In brief it was the observation of similarities and differences between living forms, and their comparison. By the use of this device it was possible to group and classify the infinity of living forms and bring them to some extent within the grasp of the intellect. Even where the resemblances were superficial and the comparisons faulty, something had been done to bring order into the realm of disorder, to find constants in the midst of variation, and so to permit of true learning on man's part.

Nor were the resources of the new method so limited as might at first appear. There are so many ways of utilizing comparison: comparisons between groups, between the members of the same group, the young and the old, the male and the female, the healthy and the diseased. There are comparisons of a more subtle kind: structure with structure; function with function. Despite the use of the experimental method in certain divisions of biology, upon the comparative method the whole of the great structure of biological knowledge is ultimately based.

The moral then should be clear. Each distinct and basic isolate, each of the fundamental sciences has, will have, must have its appropriate method arising out of constant dealing with the phenomena within its domain. It may utilize other methods secondarily, but to compel it to utilize them exclusively on the pretext that they alone are scientific is historically unjustifiable and logically pernicious.

The making of method is thus a continuing cultural phenomenon. It has gone on in the past as the various isolates have been distinguished. It will go on in the future as masses of phenomena still unanalyzed are reduced to distinct classes. As new isolates are discovered new methods will arise as the result of the efforts to discover abstract relations within the bounds of the isolate. Only when the whole mass of phenomena observable by man has been analyzed into specific classes will the making of new methods cease. Only then will the scientific method be complete.

A final question will return this chapter to the broader ground of scientific method in the large sense and bring the discussion of method to a close. Once an isolate has been recognized, the establishment of abstract relations within its confines should begin. What is the best procedure? Evidently there is no best procedure. Scientific men have gone to work in all sorts of ways to make their addition to the knowledge which elevates man above his animal progenitor. Among these ways, useful particularly because of its synthetic tendencies, is the method of successive approximations. This intellectual procedure consists in the accumulation of a number of facts, the formation of a logical structure holding the facts intelligibly together, the accumulation of new facts on the basis of inquiries suggested by the theory. When the sum of facts so acquired renders it untenable, it is amended so as to allow the new facts as well as the old to be colligated in a second theory. In its light still more facts are gathered which are held together by a new theory, and so on, each theory being a closer approximation to the reality and bringing men's minds nearer to a perfect picture of the world without, until mental operations on the basis of this reflection make it possible to anticipate the changes in that world.

An example of the working of this method is the growth of the theory which now prevails in astronomy. By successive stages men have built up a mental representation of the solar system so perfect that it now is possible by calculation to foresee the positions of the members of that system for hundreds of years in advance. This intellectual structure seems to have begun with the notion that the heavens are a sort of inverted cup over a flat earth. Over the internal surface of the cup pass the heavenly bodies, the sun and moon particularly, under hominoid guidance. In the course of time, after how many observations and modifications in the original representation it is impossible to tell, there comes a relative equilibrium between facts and picture in the theory of Aristotle, according to which the universe consisted of a number of crystalline spheres centering at the earth and revolving about it. With each sphere moved one of the planets, directed by an intelligence. On the outer sphere were the fixed stars. Relative differences in the direction of revolution and speed of movement of the spheres accounted for the observed differences in the positions and movement of the heavenly bodies.

Under the impulsion of an increasing mass of astronomical data, accelerated by the development of arithmetic and geometry, a revision of the Aristotelian scheme became necessary. Out of it came the Ptolemaic picture of the universe, in which the crystal spheres of revolution gave place to a more complicated system of eccentrics, cycles, and epicycles—the earth still the center of reference—which after some further amendments enabled men to foresee the movements of the heavenly bodies with sufficient accuracy to guide their movements on land and sea during some fifty generations.

Again the accumulation of data raised questions as to the validity and particularly the complexity of the mental picture; and Copernicus, changing the center of reference from the earth to the sun, cut in half the complexities of the Ptolemaic system. But still the data, especially the discrepancy between observation and calculation in regard to the movements of Mars, made clear the existence of some fundamental weakness in the system as pictured. Hitherto all the movements had been thought to be circular. Must they be so? Kepler with infinite labor calculated the positions of the members of the solar system on the hypothesis that their movements were other than circular. One type of movement, the elliptical, satisfied all the requirements, and elliptical orbits once for all replaced the circular. With the aid of Galileo's advances in dynamic mechanics Newton was able to reduce all movements in the solar system to special cases of a single general law. The increase of knowledge continued; presently it was seen that Newton's law was valid only within the solar system, and astronomers set out under the guidance of Einstein to create a faithful picture of the sidereal universe.

As the example illustrates, the method of successive approximations permits of the formation of a tentative theory embracing the known facts and provides, as essential to the operation of the method, for the continuous modification and correction of existent theories. In this way a steady advance is made possible in science and constant encouragement is offered for improvement. At the same time, such facts as exist are utilized to the full and become both a stimulus and an aid in increasing the cumulations of experience. Here then is a general method, applicable within the entire range of science. It seems particularly useful in the early stages of development of a given abstract phenomenon once it is isolated, for it allows of a combination of boldness and caution otherwise difficult to attain. Once the existence of an isolated class of abstract phenomena has been established, the method of successive approximations affords immediate guidance in its development.

CHAPTER 6: *The Making of Sciences*

For the purposes of this volume the making of scientific method need be followed no further. Only the larger aspects of method are relevant here and they are now clear enough to make it possible to inquire what general conditions must be satisfied before a science may be said to exist. The question is especially in point with reference to those disciplines that are still in transit toward full positivity, particularly those that deal with data lying beyond the biological, such as the social. The record of scientific advance brings such an inquiry well within the reach of answer.

But before it is possible to proceed to the primary business of this chapter, two obstacles should be removed. The two are connected in that both raise by implication the problem of the essential nature of scientific knowledge. Both seem to raise a priori objections to the possibility of science as an all-inclusive category. They do so by drawing a line through the field of knowledge on one side of which sciences can be made or found, on the other of which they cannot.

The first of these objections can be put in the scholastic form: science is ancillary to theology, the queen of the sciences; or in more recent terms, science is one thing and religion another and the two can never overlap or conflict. Despite certain divergences, these formulations amount to saying that there are several sorts of knowledge, hierarchically ordered. The one is in some way higher than the other. Only the lower is material for science. In whatever words the objection is phrased, the answer is the same. It consists simply in a denial of the validity of the asserted distinction on the ground that its existence can be explained historically.

The fact is that there are two elements in the making of mind; they always coexist but are none the less separable for all that. One is what may be called the emotional or affective and the other the intellectual. Both are the outcome of the organic evolution which produced the higher mammals. In the case of the animal Homo one of the two elements reaches a degree of independence in operation above that attained in analogous forms: that is to say, on the affective side the animal Homo is on a like plane with his congeners, but on the intellectual side he has over them a slight but real superiority in being able to transmit to his kind the results of his individual experiences.

Thus there are two factors of mind, the affective and the intellectual, one of them practically constant, the other variable and in effect increasing in influence as the results of experience grow. That is to say that the feelings are aroused by and attached to the results of experience. As the latter accumulate and change, the incidence of the feelings undergoes corresponding modification. The normal outcome of such a relation is a steady expansion of the intellectual and a gradual correlative modification of the affective elements of the mind. The point is that there could never be any conflict between the two so long as the original evolutionary process of development of the intellect continued without break or discontinuity. Man, that is to say, would pass from one belief to another without ever being aware of serious mental dislocation. The feelings would be slowly reoriented about the gradually changing views which experience provided as the ground for thought. Hence there could never be any notion of a double standard of knowledge and of course no conception of a hierarchical relation between two presumably opposed constituents. The cultural record seems to validate this position by revealing a long series of modifications in beliefs without any indication of awareness that a transformation was going on. As experience revealed new horizons, emotions were adjusted to them as a matter of course.

But what would be the consequence if the development and correlation of the two elements were to go on at different rates of speed in different localities and the end products of the two evolutions were suddenly to be juxtaposed? An extreme case in point occurs when the primitive and the civilized are in presence of each other. Here, where the differences are so great that adjustment is impossible, the only solution is rejection by each side of the other's position. The primitive solves the problem simply by setting the "white man's magic" outside his own cultural complex. The civilized on his part disdains the primitive views which are for him mere survivals, superstitions. Only a knowledge of the fact that the civilized is a later stage in a development of which the primitive represents an earlier stage prevents a dismissal of the whole problem on the ground that two quite different kinds of thought are in contrast.

What will be the situation, however, when a given line of thought, developing uniformly out of the past, happens for historical reasons to bifurcate and each branch proceeding from the common point of departure at different rates of speed produces different end results? And what if these end results are not in complete contrast but allow because of their common point of departure a certain, though limited, compatibility to exist between them?

A situation in point is to be found in the so-called medieval world. When the time finally came for the Dark Area to be reunited with the Mediterranean world, the hitherto isolated region found itself at a disadvantage in relation to the thought of the remainder. It had so long been concerned with conversion that other intellectual interests had declined. Yet the differences were neither sharp nor deep enough to necessitate a rejection on either side. The common historical source precluded so easy a solution. The outcome was a distinction in value between two kinds of knowledge: the kind that had been fostered in the Dark Area, based upon edification—and a real need for it, too—and the kind that had developed in other regions where the need for edification had been far less compelling. A parallel position was reached in the Arabic world, in circumstances however which had not made its acceptance so mandatory. In any case the point is clear: the erection of a wall between two domains, one devoted to edification, the other to investigation, one divine, the other human, was the outcome of a sociological situation, having nothing whatever to do with the nature of knowledge.

The gradual accumulation of experience has gone on regularly and passed from one level of opinion to another. In the normal case, the adjustment of emotional attitudes to acquired facts has proceeded without excessive jar. Only where the cultural process has gone on at different rates of speed in different milieus and the end products are suddenly contrasted is the situation favorable to an interpretation of the facts in a way that denies the homogeneity of knowledge. There are only historical grounds for the distinction in value between theology or religion and science.

Logically quite distinct from the one just discussed is the question whether the data comprised in certain domains of investigation are or are not in fact susceptible of scientific analysis. The customary form of phrasing this objection to scientific advance runs somewhat as follows. The field of knowledge is divisible into two, natural philosophy and moral philosophy. The first of these is susceptible of scientific examination; its phenomena can be analyzed and classified; regularities and uniformities can be discovered there. The second, because of the nature of its data, is forever closed to scientific inquiry.

The answer is simpler than that required for the first objection. The problem of making science in the field of moral phenomena is in principle solved when it is shown that there is no break in the range of phenomena extending from modest numerical data to exalted spiritual manifestations. In other words, the distinction between physical and moral was but an expression of the state of scientific inquiry at the time of its formulation. Now that the summation of experience has enabled men to make further advances, it is no longer tenable.

The point of critical change in the mental transition leading to the disappearance of the distinction just mentioned came in the 1700's when the advance of thought made possible the elevation of biology to the level of an independent science. Once in possession of an isolate of its own, what had been physiology became biology and was permanently freed from its dependence upon medicine. For the old division of natural philosophy into three kingdoms, mineral, vegetable, animal, there came to be substituted the three domains of natural science, physical, chemical, biological, with a basis in mathematics and astronomy.

In the light of this development in the 1700's the general problem as to the nature of knowledge could from this time on be stated as follows: is there no connection whatever between the biological domain, say, and the moral? That is, must science, having reached a certain point in its development, stop once for all? But is no analysis of the moral world possible? If it were attempted, would the result necessarily be failure? Is the moral, that is, different in kind from the natural? And indeed what particular significance did the latter term possess once the biological had been established as a specific category of phenomena? Could moral life really be cut off completely from life in the general sense?

Answer to these questions was made by men of whom Cabanis was the best representative. It rested squarely upon a wide and deep foundation of facts. It was simply this: there is a basic and unbreakable connection between the biological and the moral. No distinction of kind can be envisaged as separating the two. If the one is a subject of scientific inquiry so is the other, since the relation between the two is intimate and reciprocal.

How much this position was to be strengthened by the elaboration of the evolutionary point of view need not be emphasized. Whence indeed could the animal Homo have come into possession of such transcendent characteristics as are accredited to his descendants by pre-evolutionary theorists? Man as he rose above his origins must hesitantly have accumulated materials from the world about him and developed ideas to correlate them. No doubt the new domain of science thus opened to view would be slow to develop; to analyze, classify, and isolate its data would be a long process. It *had* been a long process, and the reason was now obvious: the data involved are among the most complicated with which man has had to deal. But the discovery and organization of the biological domain removed the chief obstacle to the delimitation and ordering of the data lying beyond.

One point only need be emphasized for the purposes of this discussion. What was in process here as elsewhere in the making of science was the analysis and classification of phenomena and their isolation. It is no objection to the general conclusion reached above to speak for example of moral phenomena as physiological because the brain, their source, is a part of the organism. At the best such a position would negate the possibility of placing moral phenomena in an isolated category. It would not remove them from the jurisdiction of science.

What is in point here however is something quite different. It is the study of *all* the phenomena manifested by the organism and the answering of the question whether these phenomena do not belong in specifically different categories. The point is vital in this discussion; much confusion results from a failure to grasp it firmly. Thus a certain view of biology makes it include all phenomena whatever manifested by living beings. But so inclusive a definition fails altogether to consider the ultimate objective of analysis and classification, which is to establish specific categories of homogeneous phenomena essentially isolated. Cabanis made the first step in this direction in a new field by distinguishing between the physical and the moral at the same time that he showed them to be intimately related. His work did but begin a long course of development which was to end by showing that all the phenomena above the physical and the chemical were susceptible of scientific treatment. He omitted for example a large mass of data with which many of his contemporaries were concerned, namely, the social. But his work was critical in importance. In principle the distinction in kind between natural and moral was destroyed: both lay on the line of scientific advance; the second was situated further along that line. Exactly where and how much further along were questions susceptible of answer. A whole new domain was opened to scientific occupation.

Science then is homogeneous, covering the entire field of human observation and interest. Both theoretical considerations and factual achievements combine to demonstrate the validity of the position which deduction on the basis of the animal origin of man makes plausible to begin with. And since the nature of knowledge is uniform, then *it becomes possible to utilize the results of an inductive study of the history of the sciences already in existence for facilitating the progress of sciences still in process of formation.* This chapter is thus brought to a focus on the questions: What are the prerequisites for the existence of a science? What are the conclusions to be drawn from a review of the history of science?

In a somewhat condensed form the essential historical process can be described as follows. In the normal course of scientific development the first stage is the collection of masses of data roughly of a homogeneous kind. The gathering of such information is almost entirely spontaneous under the pressure of the events of life. Later, of course, a more systematic procedure becomes possible and greater attention can be given to the nature of the facts collected.

Obviously, even in the earliest phase of the first stage a process of analysis is tacitly in operation, though its operations seldom reach the conscious level. Evidence of the existence of the analytical tendencies is to be found in such unsystematic manifestations as language, where the need to symbolize the various aspects of daily experience gives rise to more or less clearly specialized vocabularies. Often too the existence of certain empirical discoveries, relating phenomena within closely circumscribed limits, is revealed in literature, traditions, codes of custom, etc.

When the stage of formal analysis is reached—a stage which is shown by the record to have been reached at different rates of speed for different subject matters—the classification of data into independent categories goes on in a systematic fashion. The result is a growing and ultimately complete realization of the fact that the external world is a complex of many constituents related in too intricate a way for it to be dealt with as a whole. It must be broken up so that the component factors may be dealt with singly.

No doubt the first and most important agency in thus bringing the world within the power of human interference was the process of abstraction. It alone could make possible the conceiving of the world as something other than an infinite sum of entirely individual existences. It made possible too the treating of the constituents of the nonhuman mass of things from the human point of view, i.e., they were grouped, like was put with like, and so a generalized type of knowledge finally came to be.

The analytical process once formally begun continues to operate. It advances in several directions. It is particularly the advance in the direction of phenomena that is important because only in them can be discovered the complete generality that gives rules without exception for the guidance of conduct. The implication is that for the study of beings the study of what goes on in them is substituted. "Phenomena to be manifested must be attached to matter; substances are cognizable only through their properties. The twofold connection does not prevent the process of abstraction from habitually distinguishing events from beings, looking now to the attributes many bodies possess in common, now to the sum of the qualities which constitute any given existence." [1] It is in the former direction that science in the abstract sense lies.

In that direction too lies the advantage that comes from the establishment of abstract relations among abstract phenomena whereby man provides himself with guidance in circumstances that as yet

1. A. Comte, *Système de politique positive* (4 vols. Paris, Carilian-Goeury & Vor Dalmont, 1851–54), *4*, 170–171. (All editions are identical.)

exist only in mind. Here is the field of science, itself abstractly defined.

> With the study of abstract relations we penetrate into the world of science, the world of true and high abstractions. . . . Here is no longer found the arbitrary, the fantastic, the capricious, the personal. An abstract relation is, or it is not. To establish it, there is needed a rigorous and consequently difficult demonstration, which requires the intervention of the highest human faculties. But once demonstrated, the relation imposes itself by its own weight; it is permitted to no one not to believe in it and not to accept its consequences. The sum of known abstract relations constitutes *science,* divided into as many parts as there are abstract phenomena of different order.[2]

Not, of course, that the process of analysis and classification of experiences may not continue in other directions; in the case for example of the gradual recognition of abstract beings, i.e., types, much can be done. Such types conceived of as a sum of qualities present many difficulties to the investigator. It may be that the sum is so great, i.e., there are so many qualities involved that it is beyond possibility to deduce all the consequences of the combination. That is to say, the mental reflection of the reality is too confused or inadequate to allow meditation to take the place of observation. It may even be that the nature and working of some of the properties involved are quite unknown.

In such conditions, where the relations between abstract phenomena cannot be ascertained or where the number and natures of the variables involved are too great to allow of deductive conclusions, the next best expedient is to await the outcome and deal with it on a statistical basis. Regularities and correlations may thus be discovered even if the single event escapes analysis. Thus it is possible to obtain very significant data of a regular, i.e., constant kind in regard say to suicide, even though it is quite impossible to deal with the complication of factors involved in such a way as to make precise the particular persons who will die by their own hands. The social phenomena in question are evidently true of an aggregate, but of what is the aggregate aggregated? Not until the

2. Laffitte, *Cours de philosophie première, 1,* 57–58. (Italics are Laffitte's.)

aggregate is adequately analyzed can each series of related phenomena be traced to its individual outcome.

Evidently, then, the sciences which deal with the abstract being will sooner or later be superseded by those which deal with the attribute or property. The normal course of scientific development is bent in this direction by the isolating tendency. The being, the type is the first object of attention, for the reasons made clear in the following words: "There is involved in every act of awareness an act of selective attention—an act of isolation by which the occurrent is taken out of its structural setting and held up for consideration." "The actual locus of this selective act cannot be determined in advance with any high degree of certainty. . . . All that we can say is that description represents the beginning stage of knowledge and man naturally begins with man-sized objects. . . . We do not talk about the extremely great or the extremely small. . . . Similarly, we are first concerned with occurrents of moderate complexity—with things rather than with properties of things." [3]

Once however the analytical process has distinguished between the thing and the property and found the thing to be a complex of properties, the next stage in the making of a science is to deal with properties; and in so doing the object will be to isolate the property in question as completely as possible, if only to simplify the task of examining it for uniformities. The tendency is obviously strong, given the motivation; how far can it be carried?

The answer would seem to depend upon the nature of the isolated property undergoing analysis. As long as it can be shown to be analyzable, i.e., essentially composite or reducible despite its relative isolation to a combination of properties no matter how complex the combination may be, the isolating analytical process continues. But finally it would seem it can be carried on no longer. The phenomena on which the property rests can be broken up no further. They are specific; they are irreducible. They are the *proprium quid* of a science, whose *"quidditas"* is undeniable precisely because the fact reached by continuing abstraction can be analyzed no further. When such a fact is attained a science exists, basic and abstract in nature.

3. A. C. Benjamin, *Logical Structure of Science* (London, Kegan Paul, 1936), pp. 272–273, 274.

The massing of experiences into a body of data; the analysis of these data; the creation of homogeneous classes within them; the distinguishing between concrete and abstract, i.e., between things and properties; the isolation of basic attributes—with such a series of achievements a fundamental science begins to be. The course of its development continues with the determination of the appropriate way of dealing with the abstract phenomena recognized as specific and irreducible. What is now sought is the discovery of abstract relations between the phenomena in question. No theoretical discussion of method will avail at this stage of normal scientific advance. Only the manipulation or the handling or the use of the body of data that analysis, classification, abstraction, and isolation have given will serve to determine the best way in which the given material can be brought into mental relationships.

It will distinctly not do at this point to employ methods developed out of the experiences gained in dealing with other classes of abstract phenomena. By definition each specific class is unique; it is not reducible by analysis to a complex of properties belonging to other classes. For this reason if for no other a unique method is called for. The next stage in the development of a given science is thus the discovery of a method peculiarly applicable to the establishment of relations within the specific class.

Methods developed elsewhere in the domain of science will be of service no doubt but only in a subordinate capacity. If the same method were applicable throughout two classes considered to be distinct, the fact would be symptomatic of a defect in analysis. Particularly is the use of mathematical aids in a newly recognized abstract isolate to be regarded with suspicion. Nothing goes into a formula or equation that was not already clarified and defined before going there; if a phenomenon was in fact composite before undergoing mathematical manipulation, it will emerge as a composite—not of course that recourse to mathematics is to be frowned upon. The point is that the use to which mathematical aids are to be put should be dictated by the nature of the data to be mathematicized; such a procedure should mark the maturity rather than the infancy of a discipline. It may even be that a new science will call upon mathematics for new expedients adapted to the nature of its new fact and never before conceived of even by mathematicians.

The rise of a new method engendered from the spontaneous utilization and systematic investigation of the new material should be manifested by the discovery of uniformities of similitude and succession, bringing order into confusion, discovering the constant in the midst of hitherto unchallenged variety. New abstract relations among new abstract phenomena: such will be the signs of the advent of a new science.

The generally accepted test of the final validity of the relations established by a science as it reaches toward maturity is its power to achieve prevision. But here a word of explanation and caution is necessary. What is meant by "prevision" must be well understood. The term is in this case used as a synonym of neither prophecy nor forecast nor prediction; in fact it does not by any necessity even refer to the future. It is only man's preoccupation with what will be that gives it this prospective sense. All that it means is that the unseen shall be perceived by a mental process instead of a physical one; the reality, that is, can be replaced by the mentality. In this procedure there is no time element necessarily involved. What gives prevision its value in scientific effort is the evidence it provides that the inner world has become so complete a reflection of the outer that the processes of the mind can dispense man from the necessity of turning his observation upon the world in order to ascertain what is the consequence of a given train of events. Thus the future is no more involved than the past.

What happens to the circumference of a circle when its diameter is doubled? Time is not at issue in this case. An interested individual might want to know the result before it occurs; it might be that the diameter was actually doubled a generation or a millennium ago and a disinterested observer might still be unaware of the result and desire to know it. In short, prevision is a test of the completeness with which a knowledge of the abstract relations discoverable within a given set of abstract phenomena has been mastered. If they have been established, then the working of the phenomenon is known and calculations in regard to it are practicable, regardless of time. Forward or backward, the words have little meaning in this case; the question is rather whether, given the conditions, the outcome can be calculated or must still be awaited and observed.

Moreover, the nature of prevision should be safeguarded from misconception arising from another source. The procedure it involves is strictly deductive and can never be made to replace induction. Thus one might conceivably have an exhaustive knowledge of the relations among phenomena classified as sociological and be able to work out the consequences of their continued operation without for that reason having any inkling of the discoveries that might be made in the field, say, of psychology. At the best, one could only point to certain acquired data of a sociological kind and ask the psychologist to find a basis for them; but what the psychological theories and explanations will be is not a subject of prevision. The same must be said of any other body of irreducible phenomena, the biological for example, with reference to sociology. For each such specific category methods must be evolved in harmony with the nature of the facts to be reduced to law. Prevision operates only when these laws are known and only in relation to the data they cover. In short, prevision is a means of testing the validity of inductive conclusions; it can never serve as a means of scientific discovery in new fields.

A mass of homogeneous data, a body of abstract phenomena arising therefrom, the isolation of these phenomena, the working out of a method to deal with them, the discovery of abstract relations among them, the multiplication of these abstract relations until the point is reached where a knowledge of relations can effectively replace observation: such is what might be called the normal course of development in the making of sciences. A knowledge of the sequence of steps should make possible the avoidance of all those spontaneous difficulties and indirections that the making of a new road in the wilderness of things has hitherto involved. Why here or elsewhere regard as inevitable the procedures or the expedients that grew out of inexperience?

The growth and multiplication of abstract sciences as here described has as its ultimate consequence two results worth bringing into light as a conclusion of this chapter. In the first place, continued abstraction and isolation may conceivably end with the establishment of a series of isolates covering the entire range of human concern. It is strictly permissible, in fact logically inevitable to

hold that the whole sum of phenomena may be analyzed and classified, abstract relations being discovered in each specific class and
prevision becoming possible and usual in each of them and for all
of them together once their laws are known.

But once the abstract series is in existence, then the position of
the concrete sciences, i.e., composites of the various abstract isolates
in varying proportions, changes. The alteration in the intellectual
light in which they now stand will make it possible to see them as
dissolving and disappearing insofar as they seem now, simply for
historical reasons, to be fixed combinations. Indeed they will disappear more and more as permanent complexes of inquiry and reappear as shifting compounds of data brought together for special
purposes. "The immense field of the concrete sciences will finally
disappear; some of the researches connected with them being abandoned as useless; others incorporated with the corresponding arts.
The true purpose of these special studies is to create the various
orders of conceptions which stand half way between theory and
practice, and which are at present in so imperfect a state, requiring
as they do the combination of all the primitive elements belonging
to the sphere of abstract science." [4]

But to combine these elements is essentially the task of practical
men. Once the abstract advances have been made, "the only scientific specialists will be practicians, with functions more or less
resembling those of engineers in the present day." "There will be
no pure theorists except philosophers in the true sense of the word,
whose life will be devoted to the construction and application of
the general synthesis. From this universal source, practical men will
draw the rational basis of each special synthesis, which they alone
are competent to construct, from being thoroughly conversant with
its nature and object." [5] In other words, the extension of the process
of isolating abstractions tends toward two sets of consequences: the
establishment of a small number of basic, component, irreducible
classes of abstract phenomena or fundamental attributes, truly isolated; and the immense multiplication, but only for particular purposes and by qualified practitioners, of concrete, special, composite
intellectual tools of construction.

To further both of these aims by the development of a new ab-

4. Comte, *1*, 434–435.
5. Comte, *1*, 433, 434.

stract isolate and to demonstrate that it *is* the basis for a new science by showing how it meets the requirements conditioning the rise of a new science: such is the purpose in the remainder of this volume, with reference in particular to social phenomena and a science of sociology.

PART THREE: THE APPLICATION TO
SOCIAL PHENOMENA OF THE
SPIRIT AND METHOD OF SCIENCE

CHAPTER 7: *The Passage of Social Observation*
from the Spontaneous to the Systematic

The collection of the materials of which sciences are ultimately constructed is, it has been said, first spontaneous and then systematic: empirical, then scientific. Sociology followed this general rule. For centuries, for millennia indeed, the accumulation of data which would serve for later abstraction went on in a purely incidental and spontaneous fashion. Whenever there was any need for the directing of human conduct or the control of human action, experiences resulted which served as the basis for observation and precept. That this position is no dialectical or deductive conclusion is proved by the existence of great numbers of proverbs, maxims, wise saws, etc., among practically all peoples and in particular among primitives. Wherever there were women who had in any way to control children and influence men; wherever the old had to guide and counsel the young; wherever there were leaders, however temporary, who had to direct followers—wherever, in short, pure force was impractical as the sole method of social control— there the accumulation of experience in analyzing human behavior and finding ways to direct it must have been in operation, providing the materials for a future sociology or psychology.

Of course this period antedates all records. That such accumulation must have been in spontaneous operation for ages and even reached the systematic level is evident from the appearance in the record of codes, laws, books, tables, etc., associated with the names of individuals: Hammurabi, Manu, and so many others. Shall these be listed and considered more or less in detail as an introduction to the advent of sociology?

The whole question of the selection of writers for admission to pages such as these is raised at this point. The answer is easy. This volume deals not with that amorphous something called social thought; it deals with sociology the science. All that it needs to show for its purposes is that there was always in process a collection of observations in regard to this or that society or to society in general which could serve in later times for the purposes of abstraction. This fact is of course undeniable; the manuals and encyclopedias put the matter beyond doubt.

But what of the hundreds of writers who in later times in one way or another touch upon matters that now would be termed social or even sociological? On this point this volume stands squarely on the position taken long ago by Small.

> There are two tendencies among sociologists with reference to classification of social theorists. One section of the sociologists prefer to call everybody a sociologist who has ever rationalized about social relations, and to rate as sociology the whole menagerie of opinions that have ever been held about different phases of the human lot. Of course, with this type of sociologist, Plato is exhibit A in the sociological museum. On the other hand, some of the sociologists say that the line should be drawn between dialecticians, whether ancient or modern, and social scientists. That is, they insist that the thing which matters among people who are thinking about human affairs is not that they are all thinking about the same human affairs, but the *way* in which they are trying to pry into human affairs. There is the subjective way, and there is the objective way, the way of the speculator and the way of the scientist. The second sort of sociologist maintains that the line should be drawn between dialectical social philosophers and sociologists, so as to leave in the former category all those thinkers about human affairs whose method is primarily subjective, and so as to advertise as the finding mark of sociologists the adoption of a genuinely objective method of research into human relations.[1]

By the time of the Greeks of the Golden Age, then, the observation of the complex life of men had led to the rise of a more or less systematic discussion of the phenomena now called social. The records are singularly bare of any account of the introduction into Greece during these centuries of anything that could today be called sociological. They are bare, it would seem, because of the simple

1. A. Small, "Sociology and Plato's Republic," *American Journal of Sociology*, *30* (1924-25), 515.

fact that there were no such theories then extant. Just as what are now physical and chemical were then fused into a common category called natural, *Ta Phusika*, so what is today gradually coming to be thought of as sociological and psychological were then completely merged into a common category, the moral, moral philosophy, dealing with ethics and politics, the individual and the social. What the Greeks were dealing with was a mass of phenomena into which can be read with little accuracy the terminology developed by the last five or six generations as they have come with such difficulty to carry the spirit of science into the highest ranges of man's interest.

There will therefore be no reference here to Plato as one of the precursors. Not only is Small right in regard to Plato's method; he could have made his case even stronger if he had chosen to refer to Plato's doctrines. The simple fact is that Plato was as completely ignorant of either sociology or psychology as he was of physics or chemistry. The words mean just what they say, no more and no less. Millions of men today are in exactly the same case. They live an active life in constant contact with things and men and are highly intelligent in relation to their tasks, but what physical scientist would give a moment's time to hearing their views on the nature of electricity or the number of elements? In precisely the same way, despite their experience with people and knowledge of human nature, what are their ideas worth concerning the origin of the mores or the influence of the unconscious? No doubt whatever, Plato had many insights into social and other phenomena, but so had Shakespeare, and so on occasion has the man in the street: none of them are for that reason authorities in psychology or sociology or biology or chemistry. They simply aid in amassing the stores of material from which some day is to come science. At the best Plato, assuming as true all his devotees say of him, is but an amateur social psychologist; and continued reliance upon his thought is evidence not of his authority but of the backwardness of social theory.

But—but—Aristotle? In him at least are to be found the beginnings of sounder views on the nature of society? Such at least is the accepted view. It is probably little better justified than the "correct" views about Plato. It is hard to see how the few years' difference in age between the two men could have changed the whole nature of Greek culture, which is what is here in point. What is evident in Aristotle is a stronger personal interest in factual data than in Plato, and the dim awareness that the personal impressions of one individual should be kept open to correction, since the approach to truth is not purely personal but follows a "way." Men should study *methodos*—the implication being perhaps that learning is essentially a collective process.

As regards Aristotle's views on social phenomena, it is so difficult to know just what Aristotle thought that it seems best to say little about the matter; not that there is any difficulty in putting meanings into his words. True, he collected and studied a large number of constitutions of city-states; but even if we knew what the constitution of a city-state was, the fact would make him only the first political theorist and would carry no implications at all concerning sociology any more than the fact of having collected and arranged the data about the constituents of matter make him the first chemist.

Comte, it is true, gives Aristotle high praise when he says that twenty-two centuries ago "the incomparable Aristotle discovered the essential character of every collective organization, when he made it consist of the separation of functions and the combination of efforts" [2] and so attributed to him a service in sociology akin to that of Archimedes in mechanics, i.e., the founding of statics. But with all deference to Comte, who was always most generous in attributing ideas to others when they really were his, it would seem that he does Aristotle too much honor. In the first place the idea, at least in the precise formulation of Comte, is not to be found in Aristotle. In the second place, whatever Aristotle did say is probably derived from Plato. And finally the idea in neither of them was anything more than elaboration of the fable of "The Belly and the Members" as told by Aesop, who probably got it from Pilpay, thereby revealing a very respectable antiquity for the biological analogy in sociological theorizing.

But did not Aristotle say "man is a social animal"? Definitely, no; he did not say with the eighteenth-century translators that man is a political animal, nor with Marx that man is by nature a town dweller, nor with Sumner and Keller that he is a being of urban characteristics. What he actually said is that man is a *zōon politikon*.[3]

2. Comte, *Système de politique positive, 2,* 158.

3. " 'Man,' said Aristotle, 'is a political creature.' That is to say a member of a polis or city state. With this, contrast the Stoic definition, coined perhaps

Now there are two ways of approaching the translation of the phrase. One is the way of the classicists. Genuflecting after the fashion of Maimonides and the other scholastics, declaring that everything Aristotle teaches of sublunary matters is the unconditioned truth, and carrying the aura of revelation into the scientific world, they conclude that any idea developed by later peoples or times—of necessity inferior to the great times of revelation—must be contained in the words of the antique sage. No matter what idea may be worked out in later days, *that* was what Aristotle meant.

The other way is that of the anthropologists. For them the words used by an author must have referents determined by the cultural conditions of the time. In order to translate Aristotle's phrase it would be necessary to know what the cultural complex was, especially the zoological and political elements, out of which the phrase came. And when this investigation was made it would be found that even if the word *zōon* had now a true equivalent, the word *polis* has none; and the best translation could do, with some knowledge of Aristotle's general ideas plus a study of his culture, would probably be: "Man is a living form whose 'end' or 'destination' is to live in a *polis*."

The fact is of course that for every science there comes a time when it must liberate itself from the influence of Aristotle. That time usually seems to coincide with the moment when the particular science is ready consciously to begin divesting itself of hominoid influences. If Aristotle could not do without hominoids in astronomy it is highly unlikely he had freed his thought of them in sociology. For men engaged in the construction of that science, Aristotle's views become ever more quaint or amusing and untenable. What is the origin of the family? Aristotle at the beginning of the *Politics* says that in common with other plants and animals mankind has a natural desire to leave behind them an image of themselves. Plants have a desire . . . ? What conception of biological phenomena lies behind those words? The family, continues Aristotle, is the association established by nature for the supply of man's everyday wants; when several families are united and the associa-

----

by Chrysippus, that man is a *koinōnikon zōon*, i.e., a member of the universe, Epictetus, *Disc.* ii, 10, 4." [The adjective is related in root origin to *koinos* "sharing, held in common."] W. R. Halladay, *The Pagan Background of Early Christianity* (London, Hodder & Stoughton, 1925), p. 151.

tion aims at something more than the supply of daily needs, then comes into existence the village; and when several villages are united into a single community, perfect and large enough to be nearly or quite self-sufficing, the state comes into existence. "Established by nature": nature = *phusis*. But *phusis* is quite as untranslatable a word with as magical a content as, say, *mana*—and imagine *any* Hellenic word of the fifth century being translated by the modern word "state." All this and more is on the first pages of the *Politics*. Insofar as this material represents the collection of data for ulterior classification and abstraction, it can be found in the pages of the manuals and the mistranslations. It is far indeed, however, from a science of sociology.

It would be more to the point here to turn from attempts to make a sociology on the basis of dialectic to an analysis of the efforts of men who were closer to the facts, even though they interpreted them theologically or metaphysically. Here for example is the case of a new religion: its growth and persistence are proof of the structural soundness of its sociological bases, however they may have been expressed. "Ye are members, one of another," said Paul. Is the statement merely another case of the organic analogy, or is it the outcome of the growing awareness of social solidarity? Men are saved by vicarious suffering; purgatory, the communion of saints, the church militant and the church triumphant; here are concepts that contain elements of sociology and social psychology as truly as the doctrine that Nature abhors a vacuum contains a physical fact.

Here is the same religion building up an organization: in the hands of men imbued with the spirit of the Roman system of government and administration it extends and specializes, works out a hierarchy, concentrates and delegates authority, meets crises with flexibility and utilizes them to perfect its organization, discusses and answers questions of franchise and election, representation, and legislation, and evolves a system which has endured through thirty generations or more. Such structures provide for analysis masses of facts on which a sociology may be built, just as chemistry was built upon the data which the alchemists collected through generations of crude experiment upon substances of all kinds.

Here are two great philosophies, the stoic and the epicurean; here is one of the most imposing systems of law ever developed by man; but the doctrines contained in these and similar constructions, however sound they empirically are, have yet to be examined in a critical way. Such work is for the future; it is not a part of the historical introduction to the science of sociology.

The same must be said concerning the debates that arose from time to time between the agencies active in the government of man. Such for example was the great controversy over the relations between the pope and the emperor, the church and the state, the *sacerdotium* and the *imperium*. What *is* the relation between the temporal and the spiritual? The issue was never decided; but it is not dead. What was concealed under the theological arguments and the metaphysical language of the writers of the time?

Here once more a question was raised at a time when it could be discussed only in dialectical fashion and with theological and metaphysical interpretations of the data. In the language of today the issue was, and is, what is the nature of social phenomena? Are they a true isolate, or are there under the term "social" two classes of data, the sociological and the psychological? And if so, what is the relation between the two? Solutions to such questions are not to be found in the past; it is only the scientific approach that can provide them.

The discussion over the two powers was the nearest the medieval period came to bringing into the light the profounder sociological problems; the period of assimilation was to pass without any renewal of the discussion. Besides, the intellectual energy of the time was channeled into the development of the data on which the physical sciences were so soon to arise. Politically the rise of the monarchies is the distinctive feature; and intellectually the "discovery" of Rome as a historical unit was most influential. Down to the very end of the 1700's the Roman record remained the most impressive historical event to which men could turn. Two men particularly made use of this new body of data in a way that brings them within at least the margins of this volume. They were Machiavelli and Bodin. The first turned to it to secure generalizations on the art of governing men, the second to find justifications for the growing power of the monarchies.

Strictly speaking, an analysis of the work of the two men with a view to ascertaining their direct contributions to sociology reveals rather little. Of the first it may be said that it is decidedly his method rather than his conclusions that entitle him to admission into the select company of the precursors. Both *The Prince* and the more important *Discourses* are based upon history, and Roman history especially. The interest of them both for the sociologist lies in the spirit and method of the approach to that history. Machiavelli is himself quite conscious of his departure from the customary way of making such studies. He states clearly his wish to know the facts of government. He wants, that is, to know what is as it is.

The outcome of his efforts was startling for moralists. What he did was to reveal the animal Homo underneath the man. The picture is far from flattering. The animal has neither dignity nor courage. If ever conditions arise or can be contrived which overwhelm the man, the animal can be controlled by appeals to his basic needs and drives or coercions of them. Most of the sensational or startling pronouncements of the Italian observer are simply statements of the contrast between the animal and the cultural human being. Machiavelli is in effect saying that Man is as yet but slightly superposed upon the animal Homo; therefore an ambitious ruler will be wise to make his appeal to the second rather than to the first.

From the point of view of method, then, Machiavelli is a point of real interest along the route leading to the scientific study of the data on which a sociology is to be founded. To go straight to the facts, to study them without prejudice or prepossessions with an eye only to the conclusions they indicate: here is the achievement and the example of Machiavelli. An objective method, free from the magical or other presuppositions\ ready to see in the behavior of men only the behavior of men and nothing more, on the basis of which general conclusions can be drawn concerning the nature and conduct of men, particularly their political conduct: such was the aim of the writer who in his time and since has caused so much pain to well-meaning souls.

Perhaps it is unfair to say that Machiavelli belongs on the periphery of sociology and that only by virtue of his method, for his work does mark an advance in the analysis which is finally to end in a complete separation between the cultural and the psychological. This outcome was only implicit in Machiavelli's time, but it has since become more and more clearly recognized.

His works are of great importance in the history of the development of human thought, but his importance lies entirely in the system followed by the author. Before him many had imagined republics or kingdoms that have never been known or existed. He was the first to observe that our mode of life differs greatly from that in which we ought to live, and he abandoned the paths trodden by others, finding it more convenient to follow truth than the flights of imagination. He thus founded the positive school of statecraft, which caused in politics the same revolution that Bacon and Galileo produced in the science of nature. The method followed by Machiavelli in the analysis of human deeds is the very same that these two geniuses followed in the study of nature. For the statesman, as well as for Bacon and Galileo, the true science and the true philosophy is that which *dictante mundo scripta est,* or at least that which is the image and the reflection of the world. . . .

The stateman does not reject ethical principles; on the contrary he would like to make use of them, but he cannot do so, because they are not deeply rooted in the life and conscience of the nations.[5]

Machiavelli's view on the origin and nature of morality is a product of his observation of phenomena. He did not attempt to introduce into his discussion an abstractly formulated moral theory. His views on morality are free from preconceived notions. His discussion is not burdened with artificial constructions and imaginary scholastic formulas, but was derived directly from life. No wonder then that his views on morality were overlooked by his contemporaries, or that he was abused by later scholars on that score. As a matter of fact, he was the first modern writer who expounded the idea that moral principles are not inherent in human nature and that they are simply a necessary condition and a result of social life.[6]

No doubt Machiavelli failed to obtain quite the unclouded vision of the *Id* that the critics occasionally assert or imply; but he did show, on a moderately objective basis, that in certain cases it was

5. Ernesto Grillo, *Machiavelli and Modern Political Science* (London, Blackie, 1928), pp. 19–20, 21–22.

6. C. D. Kojouharoff, *Niccolo Machiavelli* (Washington, D. C., 1930), p. 39.

wiser for those who wish to control men to do so through an appeal to the animal Homo than to Man; and in doing so he took a place among those who opened the way to driving a distinction between cultural and psychical phenomena.

Quite another factor in the movement toward sociology is represented by Bodin, whose life overlaps Machiavelli's and brings this record down into the 1600's. It is likely that Bodin's importance has been overrated. For a long time he was the only name representative of the period to be found in the manuals. At present he takes a place in the ranks of those who were busied at the time with the defense of the monarchies. In this action he shows little originality and even less in the utilization of numerology, astrology, and magic in general to throw light upon the course of history, even if in the midst of the discussion some reference to the geographical conditioning of society is introduced. Perhaps more important is the indication that the period of assimilation is ending to be found in the rejection of the book of Daniel as the basis for the division of history into stages, and the use of history itself as it then existed for the purpose. The result was a threefold division: two thousand years of predominance by the southeastern peoples, two thousand years of Mediterranean history, and the period of northern civilization since the Fall of Rome—a version of the record which is uncomfortably like Hegel's. Whatever its defects, it shows a growing reliance upon the information gathered by the scholars of his own time and the conclusions as to the value of the modern period that it seems to support.

It may be that the most significant of the tendencies shown in Bodin is his inclination to reject the old doctrines of human degeneration from a golden age of some sort. He begins to see that human abilities have been more or less the same at all times; that men make history; that they change, rising and falling, from one epoch to another, and yet there has been "a gradual ascent from the period in which men lived like wild beasts to the social order of sixteenth-century Europe." [7] So does Bodin take his stand cautiously on the side of progress in the great quarrel between the ancients and the moderns, along with Perrault and Fontenelle. But his arguments are not beyond suspicion, since they are used to de-

7. S. B. Fay, quoted in S. A. Rice, *Methods in Social Science* (Chicago, University of Chicago Press, 1931), p. 291.

fend the monarchial power in its ascendancy. In any case he represents the growth of doctrines rather than the development of method
and so is less significant than Machiavelli.

The famous quarrel between the ancients and the moderns has
just been referred to. It would be a mistake not to give this celebrated historical episode at least a brief glance in passing; for it not
only illustrates the nature of the cultural change taking place in
the 1600's, it throws light upon the way in which the change came
to be, and finally it brings into prominence a basic problem in relation to the distinction between sociological and psychological phenomena. Happily for these points, the classical study of Rigault is
adequate. The section, then, rests upon the pages of the French
critic.

The quarrel, he insists, is no mere frivolous question of *préséance*.
On the contrary in it was concealed a very great philosophical idea,
namely, the idea of the intellectual progress of mankind. Correla-
tively there was the idea of the independence of the taste and the
emancipation of the spirit of the modern, freed at last of the need
to imitate the ancient. The two ideas are not at first on the surface
and are often lost from sight entirely for the moment, "but the
spectacle of these vicissitudes is informing. It shows how slowly ideas
advance in the world, the obstacles they find in routine and in human passions, the irregularity of their itinerary, their lively advances, their brusque retreats. In a word, this history of the philosophical idea of progress, making its way, so to speak, *incognito*,
under cover of a literary discussion until it came out into the open
where it could freely go forward," [8] is itself an illuminating instance
of human progress.

The first stage of the episode began in France. It was due in particular to the introduction into France in the first half of the 1600's
of the work of Tassoni, where what had begun as a quarrel over the
relative merits of Tasso and Ariosto was raised to the level of a discussion over a question of taste interesting all who were acquainted
with the ancient literature of Greece. Once begun in France, men
took sides as the debate spread. Boisrobert first, then Desmorets,

8. H. Rigault, *Histoire de la querelle des anciens et des modernes*, Vol. *1* in
Oeuvres complètes (4 vols. Paris, L. Hachette, 1859), pp. xxx–xxxi.

and so on to Fontenelle and the brothers Perrault the discussion extended. Saint-Evremond introduced it into England at the end of the century. At Will's coffeehouse was a faction for Perrault and the moderns, another for Boileau and the ancients. Temple and Wotton wrote *Essays* and *Reflections*. By way of Bentley and Boyle the *Battle of the Books* was reached. The discussion swung back to France where by a curious detour it becomes a quarrel over the merits of Homer. Fenelon mediates for the ancients but in vain. In 1715 the abbé Terrasson in his *Dissertation sur Homère* raises the question to the philosophical level of the problem of progress. The debate returned to Italy. "It is the eternal honor of Vico to have been the first to take from the hands of Bacon and of Pascal, of Perrault, of Fontenelle and of Terrasson the idea of the progress of the human spirit, to undertake to make use of it as a philosophical explanation of history, and to seek in the centuries past the manifest proofs of this progress and the secrets of its laws." [9] The simple controversy over taste had ended in a discussion over one of the most important problems of history and philosophy.

In conclusion, says Rigault, it is regrettable that the question of the ancients and the moderns should so long have been so badly put. The human mind is not methodical; it advances, retreats, side-steps, detours. It would have been better if a systematic discussion could have decided whether there are human productions which need time to attain perfection and others which do not. What is certain is that some sciences, based upon observations transmitted from age to age, have had to advance in proportion as these observations become more numerous and exact. Medicine and psychology are instances. A fortiori is progress evident in the natural sciences, mathematics, and astronomy, which have a new theorem every day and people the skies with stars unknown to the ancients.

But there is another order of labors, that of the arts, composites so to speak of matter and thought, like sculpture, painting, music. These arts, comprising an intellectual part necessarily destined to progress, are both perfect and imperfect at once.

Finally there are other arts more purely emotional, like eloquence and poetry, which have need only of vigorous thoughts and lively feelings to reach perfection, geniuses to utter them, and a language capable of expressing them. All these the ancients had, plus the

9. Rigault, p. 479.

youth of the world, "when the genius of man was more fresh and free, taste more natural and simple, languages more harmonious and pure." [10] Consequently poesy and eloquence and in general ancient literature by necessity reached perfection.

Yet the problem is a most difficult one. "It calls for a profound knowledge of the arts and sciences, industries and inventions; . . . it would demand not only a history of the route the human mind has followed, . . . but a description of the path it must yet follow. . . . It will be long before such a book is written." [11]

But no man will ever write such a book, of course. Such an inquiry is a collective task calling for the cooperation of generations. Rigault missed this point and so failed to see in his critics and historians, in Vico particularly, the first steps leading toward the analysis and explanation that he was calling for. To Vico, then, attention must next be turned.

If in Machiavelli and Bodin the beginnings of methods and doctrines which were to receive recognition in later generations can be seen, in Vico the first step in the direction of a general analysis of human history on a nonmagical basis can be found. Vico's life began in the 1600's and at the halfway mark passed into the 1700's. He then felt the glow of confidence that was raised in men of his time by the realization that the ancients had at last been surpassed and that mankind was ready once more to resume its cultural advance. New sciences were being called for and constructed. Tartaglia had already written one, a *Nuova Scienza*, 1537, dealing with physics. A new tool, the *Novum Organum*, for investigation had been found. Kepler provided an *Astronomia Nova*. Galileo wrote on *Two New Sciences*. Leibnitz made *A New Physical Synthesis*. Vico would write his own *Scienza Nuova*, carrying into the field of social phenomena the new spirit and the new method. Baconian then with all the word implies was the underlying influence in Vico's attempt to reach what was in essence a social-psychological explanation of the development of mankind.

The history of Rome and in particular the law of Rome were the most important factual sources of Vico's thought; but his mind

10. Rigault, p. 493.
11. Rigault, pp. 493–494.

ranged much further. He has trouble in getting his ideas clearly expressed. He uses words in a sense not that of the common usage of his day. His first edition of the *Scienza Nuova*, despite its brevity and simplicity of arrangement, has been said to be scarcely translatable. Not only is the Italian two centuries old; it is Vico's language, strained from the ordinary sense to fit his efforts to make it hold new thoughts. No sooner is the first edition published than its author hurries on to the elaboration of his thought in a second and a third, which are for him the definitive form of his work.

The central and guiding conception of this work is clear: "He grasped with extraordinary vigor the conception that amidst all the diversities of customs, language, and events of different nations, there were underlying uniformities; and that by disengaging these it was possible to form an ideal eternal history, representing the laws of evolution of the human race. To find these general laws guiding the destiny of nations was the object of his work." [12] The principles of human development must be sought in language, basic institutions, and poetry. The early development of man was purely spontaneous; the free play of natural tendencies resulted in achievements that were entirely unplanned. The outcome was a kind of language common to all men; hence Vico's constant preoccupation with a kind of philosophical philology. When men are ignorant of the causes of phenomena they attribute them to the passions of their own nature, "as the common people, for example, say that the magnet is *in love* with iron." [13] "The sublimest work of poetry is to give sense and feeling to inanimate things. This children do; and in the childhood of the world, men were all poets in this way." [14] The psychological basis of Vico's position is clear. "Uniform ideas, arising among nations widely separated in space and time and cut off from all contact with each other, must have some common groundwork of truth." [15] An inductive study of nations and tribes shows the soundness of the psychological conclusion. Thus every-

12. J. H. Bridges, "Vico," in *The New Calendar of Great Men*, F. Harrison, ed. (London, Macmillan, 1920), p. 564.

13. V. F. Calverton, *The Making of Society* (New York, Modern Library, 1937), p. 82.

14. Bridges, "Vico," p. 564.

15. P. 564.

where are found three institutions: religion, marriage, burial. But the argument is really more deductive than inductive: if there were no marriage, how would men know their own offspring?

With time the primitive nations evolve: "The three great theorists of the doctrine of the natural law of nations (Grotius, Selden, and Puffendorf) unanimously went astray in establishing their systems. They thought that natural equity in its perfect idea must have been grasped by the Heathen nations as far back as their beginnings, without noticing the fact that almost two thousand years were needed in order that philosophers might arise in one or the other nation." [16] In their early life, nations are incapable of abstractions. Hence there is a *development* of civilization and an historical *sequence* in the records of a nation. Vico sees the point clearly. Every civilization starting *de novo* and proceeding independently (the idea is not expressed but it is clearly implicit in his thought) must pass through the three ages into which "the Egyptians divided all time preceding their own": [17] the age of gods, of heroes, and of men. In the first, when the gods, feared by men, rule and discipline them by terror, the basic institutions of society such as the family are founded. In the age of heroes, the agency of the gods is reduced to the activity of heroes such as are pictured in Homer and the early annals of Rome, and social organization advances to the formation of powerful aristocracies. In the age of men, the causes and motives of action are recognized for the human phenomena they are and men become the conscious agents of their own destinies. The aristocracies pass into popular commonwealths and these become imperial monarchies, destined at last to decay and disappear.

Probably Vico deserves the attention he has received. His work was assuredly a work of power and originality in its time. It is hardly a forerunner of the conception of progress; but the *ricorsi* do not always have to end at the same point, and so progress in a spiral fashion is possible. More important is the general thought of the volume. Underlying the whole of human society, past and present, are certain fundamental forces of a psychological nature which make it possible to think of the whole record in terms of human causation. So understood, it becomes rationally comprehensible. There

16. Calverton, p. 93.
17. Calverton, p. 81.

are reasons, says Vico, for things having come to be what they are. The hominoids in other words are being eliminated from one more field of human inquiry.

Whether the relation in thought between Vico and Montesquieu is direct or indirect seems never to have been determined; for the purpose of this account it is unimportant. The notion of order in the world of man, comparable to that in the world of nature, was definitely in the line of intellectual advance. Where Vico avows his indebtedness to Bacon and his philosophy, Montesquieu is a descendant of the whole scientific movement culminating in Newton and extending beyond him. "Between two bodies in movement the relations of mass and velocity determine the increase or diminution of movement; throughout every variation there is uniformity and constancy. Similar relations are to be found in human affairs." [18] Nothing could be clearer than the bond of thought which joins Montesquieu to Galileo and to the whole intellectual development which was giving the 1700's the confidence to assert once for all their superiority over the ancients.

The significance of Montesquieu for the development of sociological thought is apparent from the first sentences of his main work *L'Esprit des lois:* "Laws are the necessary relations following from the nature of things. . . . Such relations are to be found in human affairs." Montesquieu's argument grows partly out of the double meaning of the word "law." It may represent the utterance of the lawgiver or the relations between things to which that utterance is related, i.e., it may represent legislation or order.

What, in the case of human society, is the relation between the two? A social situation may be regularized, sets of relationships between men sanctioned or penalized, new relationships initiated— is there nothing the legislator or the legislature may not do? Nothing, Montesquieu implies, that he may not strive to do, no whim he may not seek to realize; but the moment legislation is regarded as something more than the effort to satisfy a whim, the moment it is considered as a serious effort to deal with human affairs as they exist, then it must be thought of as the outcome of a societal situation which pre-exists and conditions it. There is then a *law* deeper and more fundamental than the *laws:* to find the spirit or nature

18. J. H. Bridges, "Montesquieu," in *The New Calendar of Great Men,* p. 568.

of this law underlying the laws of a particular group or age is Montesquieu's ambition. In other words, what are the factors that condition and limit the powers of legislatures?

The first and immediate answer is that the legislature is a direct outgrowth of the particular form of government in which it exists and operates; the second and more fundamental answer is that this form of government is itself the outcome of a determinate set of causes, physical and social: hence the distinction between kinds of laws. What kinds are there? There are two main classes: positive laws, i.e., those established by the legislator, and natural laws. Of the latter there are two subdivisions, psychological and mechanical. The nature of the difference which serves to subdivide the group of natural laws is worth noticing. Montesquieu is well aware that man has certain innate propensities—laws of human nature, as the phrase goes—but with them he is not concerned. Acts of legislation are not passed merely to satisfy the innate drives. What the legislator is concerned with is something else, namely,

the *mechanical, necessary* relations which, despite the will of men and legislators, regulate the nature of societies, their mores, their political institutions, their legislation. It is evidently the existence of the latter that must be established if material for science is to be seen in social facts. . . .

Now that there are laws of this kind [Alengry's able exposition continues] is a thing that cannot be in doubt, since, according to Montesquieu, all beings, all phenomena have their laws —i.e. the necessary relations growing out of the nature of things. Thus, all the radii of a circumference are equal, as the result of the definition of the circumference. In the same way, the positive laws of a country grow out of the form of the government, but the latter necessarily grows out of the number of citizens living in society, the volume of this society, the nature of the soil which supports it and the climate which environs it. In all these factors are so many mechanical causes, in regard to which human will can do nothing; for it must submit to them as to other natural fatalities, astronomical or physical for example. Familiar, thanks to his physical and physiological studies, with the mechanist explanation of the world as Descartes conceived it, Montesquieu opens to mechanism the domain, up to that moment closed, of social facts.

He goes one step further: "If positive laws depend upon necessary causes and are relative to a host of circumstances which vary with peoples, climates, terrains, they can evidently not be known *a priori;* it is indispensable to begin by observing them." [19] Here then is a new field for induction.

Implied in such an effort are certain positions to be taken and held once for all in sociological investigation, namely, the abandonment of any future recourse for the explanation of man's social life to hominoid fingers, hands, or wills and the acceptance in this new field of research of the same idea of seeing what is as it is, that animated the sciences already in existence. True, behind all phenomena lies still the *theos* of Aristotle, whence the necessity of the relations between things; but relegation of primary causation to a hominoid intellect leaves entirely free any and all examination into secondary causes.

In working out his position Montesquieu carried still further Vico's initial analysis of the general features of society. In the first eight of 31 subdivisions Montesquieu discusses the relations between forms of government and legislative enactments. He next asks what is the principle of stability in such types of government as republics, monarchies, and despotisms and finds a psychological answer: it is respectively virtue, honor, and fear. In books 9 and 10 he deals with war, offensive and defensive. In three succeeding books the conditions of political liberty and their connection with taxation are explained. Then follows the famous section devoted to climate and its effect upon national character; its bearing upon the institution of slavery; and the effect upon civilization of the fertility or sterility of the soil. The 19th book considers the bearing of national character upon legislation. Three sections set forth the relations between commerce and law. The book on the population question sounds a modern note. Religion is given three sections, and the effects upon legislation of various systems of inheritance of property, one. The treatise concludes with a review in four books of the course of French legislation, beginning with its rise out of its feudal origins.

What clearer picture could be asked for of what are now called social phenomena and regarded as consisting of a vast number of

19. F. Alengry, *Essai historique et critique sur la sociologie de Auguste Comte* (Paris, F. Alcan, 1899), pp. 392, 395.

related human activities, conditioning one another and conditioned by such general phenomena as climate or soil and underlying the acts of legislation intended to sanction or condemn particular lines of conduct with reference to those activities? The analytical study of society in all its phases, even to some extent the evolutionary aspect, is begun. How inevitable that a Beccaria should, avowedly under Montesquieu's inspiration, turn from the study of law to the study of crime and begin the development of a positive criminology; how evident too the ancestry in Montesquieu of the great variety of special studies which are later to illustrate the range of social theory.

With Montesquieu both the spontaneous and the empirical collection of social data are definitely at an end and the scientific begun; sociology exists. Given his basic conceptions, the observation and consequent analysis of sociological phenomena were certain to go on until the level of abstractions and isolates was reached. The movement in this direction was hastened by the school centering about Quesnay, to whom the name physiocrats was given.

In Quesnay the filiation between sociology and the physical sciences is clear; but more than other men Quesnay brings the nascent discipline into relation with the relatively new doctrines of biology. In physics, Harvey had found the support he needed for his theories regarding the circulation of the blood. The biological concept was extended by Quesnay to the political organism. The circulation of the blood was a physical phenomenon with biological conditions and consequences. It was a part of the natural order which could be studied and the conditions of its efficient operation learned. If so much could be done for the physical body, why could not the like be done for the body politic? The phenomena were similar; what the circulation of the blood is for the one, the circulation of wealth is for the other. Whatever the facts, the comparison was plausible enough to bring a phrase into modern speech and keep it there, and under the influence of the thought Quesnay brought his command over the sciences of the time to the creation of a new one the nature of which is not quite clear. Using distinctions developed in later years to describe his efforts, one may say that what he sought was a sociological economics, or an economic sociology, in which were to be fused such other elements as the psychological and the moral.

If however the ultimate nature of the new science is not easily defined, the concept upon which it was to be built left nothing to be desired in respect to clarity. The idea was built into the very name of the new doctrine. There are natural laws, laws of nature, that govern: such is the thought behind physiocracy. "Let the nation be instructed in the general laws of the natural order, which constitute the government that is obviously the most perfect." [20] "Quesnay strove to depict the social movement of wealth, all the phases of which movement follow one another according to invariable laws. A *natural order*, the principle of which is *within* society, thus took the place of *artificial arrangements*, whose principle is *without*. Before this great spectacle, he experienced the same divine emotion that Galileo and Newton had felt." [21]

The identification of law in the scientific sense with law in the ordained sense, as emanating from a hominoid will, is so clear in Quesnay's theories as to constitute regression rather than advance as compared, say, with Montesquieu's version of law. The conception is a dangerous one, too, in that it renders easy the projection of the desires of an individual or class, which then become the will of the higher power. "Less concerned with describing what is, than with seeking what should be, for the greater good of society, the founder of the new science rose to the conception that nature, the interpreter of the Supreme Legislator, had outlined a code of laws as inflexible and immutable as herself, thus providing for human wills, in the economic order, the guidance best fitted to assure the general welfare. The law of nature once recognized and proclaimed, the social world could be abandoned and left to itself, for it obeyed the laws laid down by providence." [22] "Man," said Quesnay, "can no more bring the natural order into existence than he can create himself. The laws that result in the constitution of society are not of human institution. . . . Legislatures have no power over the basic laws on which societies depend, for that power belongs only to the All Powerful, who has regulated everything and foreseen everything in the general order of the universe." [23]

20. Quesnay, *Maximes générales*, quoted in J. Rambaud, *Histoires des doctrines economiques* (Paris, Larose, 1899), p. 94.

21. H. Denis, *Histoire des systèmes economiques et socialistes* (2 vols. Paris, Giard & Briere, 1904), *1*, 8.

22. Denis, *1*, 8.

23. Quoted in Rambaud, p. 95.

If however the physiocrats did little more for the advance of a social science than to argue that the economic life of men lay within the domain of law, certain other intellectual activities of the period of the mid-1700's aided considerably in the advent of sociology as regards both doctrine and method. Notable among these influences was the increased attention being drawn toward what are now called the primitives. As information regarding them seeped slowly into Europe after 1492 from priests and travelers, explorers and traders, the consciousness of an earlier stage of culture quite distinct from any known to Europe began to affect the historical thinking of the age. This discovery of the primitive was to play a very real part in the formation of opinion from Vico, at least, down through Rousseau. Montesquieu for example was considerably influenced by data of this sort. The awareness of other cultures, both primitive and advanced—the Chinese, for example—was widening and deepening. Men were beginning to ask the question, always so difficult to answer, How can one be a Persian? Anthropology, in short, was on its way with an answer to such questions by bringing to Europe a more and more detailed knowledge of other lands and peoples.

In many of the writers of the period, the odd bits of information concerning savages—*sauvages,* i.e., not *policés*—served as in Montaigne's case earlier as the basis for meditations upon man and his *ondoyant* nature. For others more detailed information became the basis for a new method of inquiry into social phenomena. Among the latter, Charles DeBrosses deserves more than a passing reference. Of him Maunier speaks as follows, and with no exaggeration: "If DeBrosses had had in view the whole range of the life of societies, instead of confining himself to religion only, he would without any doubt have been the founder of the comparative study of society." [24] As it was, DeBrosses, besides introducing a word that was to have so great a use, strove to throw light upon an ancient religion by comparing it with the religion of certain contemporary primitive tribes. The full title of his book is *Concerning the Cult of the Fetish Gods, or Parallel between the Ancient Religion of Egypt and the Present Religion of Nigritia.* In it he compares the Egyptians of old with certain Negro groups of his own time and draws conclusions from the comparison, with reference notably to

24. R. Maunier, *Introduction à la sociologie* (Paris, F. Alcan, 1929), p. 81.

the cult of animals found in both societies. DeBrosses "is one of the first to reach the conception that 'the same actions have the same principle'; he confidently affirms the validity of the ideas of causality and necessity; he lays down the rule that it is wrong to imagine what man *might* have done instead of 'observing what he does.' And comparison leads him straight to explanation." [25]

Perhaps it is unfair to deny DeBrosses the praise for being the first to bring the method of comparison into use in the study of society: to have made a general instead of a special study at the beginning would have laid him open to the charge of hasty and premature work; in any case it was not long before others were supplying the generality which DeBrosses lacked. Chief among these writers were the members of the Scottish school of philosophical writers, such as Ferguson, Robertson, Smith, Hume, all of whom dealt with historical and social phenomena in the large sense. With all of these men it is impossible to deal in detail. Clearly the time has arrived when the accumulated mass of data in regard to social life has reached the point where synthesis is becoming necessary. Doctrines and methods both are developing. To each of them Ferguson for example made significant contributions.

To him Maunier gives the praise for the achievement which he denied DeBrosses; the honor of founding the comparative study of society, he says, should go to Adam Ferguson. Going beyond Montesquieu, by whom he was greatly influenced, he did not stop with asserting principles, he put them to use. On them he constructed his *Essay on the History of Civil Society*, in which he reconstructs types of society and forms of institutions on the basis of the data of ethnography and history.

> The "savages" of today revive the past; the Iroquois have their Amphictyonies, as did the ancient Greeks. And if this is so, it is because man is dependent upon climate and mode of life. Henceforward, therefore, there are no excuses for "romances" regarding a state of nature. Civilization, quite as much as savagery, is "natural." And it is the part of wisdom, in the absence of sure information, to renounce the hope of learning the true origins of mankind. We can only reconstruct them imaginatively, by looking at the life of the "savages" of today. Such is

25. Maunier, p. 80. (Italics are Maunier's.)

the basic principle of all positive work in this field; and De-Brosses had already grasped the fact. In order to write the history of society and distinguish its characteristic types, it is necessary to observe, i.e. "to collect facts instead of putting forward conjectures." This is what Ferguson set out to do in his work. Before DeBrosses and Ferguson, these truths have been suspected; with them they are actually applied; descriptions become the basis of comparisons and so give rise to explanations.[26]

Robertson as a philosophical historian belongs here. Similarity of mores, he points out in *The History of America,* is the necessary product of similar states of sociability. Here too would come Adam Smith and Hume if they were not elsewhere in this volume given consideration. The fact is that under the thought of such men was a fundamental structure of synthesis, to which a moment's attention should be given.

First among the materials for the building of the new view of the world was the scientific activity of the age. Working itself out in special cases here and there, often implicit rather than explicit, it finally came to expression in Bacon. In him the inductive spirit characteristic of the period of origination came to consciousness, as opposed to the deductive and dialectical spirit of the periods of transmission and assimilation. The whole cultural movement on its intellectual side called for the extension of inquiry into the physical world as a continuation and completion of the efforts carried on in the Arabic period; the achievement of progress in this direction could come only through the wider and more systematic use of the method of experimentation as a means of seeing what the world is really like. Bacon felt this necessity; and his expression of it, not any personal use of it, is his real service to modern thought. Buckley has some judicious opinions in regard to him which put the case for him clearly: "Though his system has not proved of the assistance he anticipated, nor are there any discoveries to which he can lay claim, Bacon really played a very important part in the history of science. This is because he expressed so well and so elo-

26. Maunier, pp. 81–82.

quently ideas which were, so to speak, waiting for expression at the time, and because above all he provided a motive for the study of science." [27] "In direct opposition to the opinions of Greek philosophers, Bacon maintained that the value of knowledge depended solely on its utility. . . . To Bacon the aim of science was not only to search for and to contemplate Truth, but 'to endow the condition and life of man with new powers or works,' and 'to extend more widely the limits of the power and greatness of man.' " [28]

But not only was the power of man to be extended by a new and inductive procedure; the very content of men's minds needed a basic reorganization. During the period of transmission and assimilation ideas had been accepted more or less passively and juxtaposed to those already in men's possession; but now came the realization that such an uncritical mental attitude was no longer compatible with truly original work in the direction clearly indicated by the pioneer investigators of the time. It was necessary at some period in the individual's acquisition of knowledge to review the items that had been acquired, to examine them all from first to last so as to be sure none were spurious. What was desired can be expressed in terms of the cultural movement of the age: see that no items of knowledge, so-called, persisting in the mind from pretransmission days and pretransmission methods shall unwittingly be allowed to impair the strength of the conceptions now being originated. Naturally, Descartes put the thought otherwise.

The sense of evidence (or *lumen naturale*) must be trained, and a keener sense of responsibility in making scientific assertions must be implanted. This can be effected only by means of methodical training, and the best method is to collect experience of the facts of the universe, since every intellectual inaccuracy and every faulty syllogism is punished most quickly and severely in the events of practical life. For this reason Descartes himself undertook long journeys, took part in campaigns, and practised diverse crafts—all in order to gather experience; and it was not until he had completed this training that he withdrew into solitude in order to elaborate the theories which in part had already taken shape. . . .

27. H. Buckley, *A Short History of Physics* (London, Methuen, 1927), p. 14.
28. P. 12.

He proposes to sweep away the whole of the world of concepts and beliefs, in so far as these are traditional or have been reached by non-logical processes, unless they succeed in satisfying his demand for the most rigorous demonstration. To this end he introduces scepticism as a method. By proceeding in this manner he throws light on the defects of the accepted systems, and in this way renders more acute the sense of evidence and the feeling of responsibility in scientific matters.[29]

Only when all these precautions have been taken, i.e., when none but unquestionable data are present in a given mind does Descartes permit of a free use of the deductive method in building up a logical structure in which none but the most unexceptionable materials can ever find a place. "The deductive method is a certain guide only for a limited distance; and in order to obtain a deeper knowledge of the more complex facts of nature, Descartes proposes the inductive method. This demands a careful observation of the facts of nature, and a method by which the conditions under which a given phenomenon occurs are systematically brought about and altered." [30]

Still other men might be mentioned: Leibnitz for example with his conception that the present is pregnant with the future, which so easily suggests prevision in social science; Hume, who as a philosopher had seen the vices of metaphysics and rejected the illusory search for final causes, substituting for them the phenomenal and relative points of view: there are only facts and laws, the mind can know nothing beyond them; the ultimate always eludes it.

What these men were saying is clear enough; Bacon leaves no doubt: his Idols are nothing but warnings to Man against the animal Homo; both he and the others keep insisting that Man shall rely only upon himself and watch that the hominoids do not enter into his studies of the world in which he lives. Long tested observations based on generations of study and bound together by relations not imposed from without but discovered within the various groups of phenomena: on this firm basis all the triumphs of Man had been founded, on it alone could be raised structures of knowl-

29. L. Fischer, *The Structure of Thought* (London, Allen & Unwin, 1931), pp. 213–214.
30. Pp. 213–214.

edge overtowering the products of the past. And triumphs there
had been, since the 1500's, silencing one after another the defenders
of the Ancients against the Moderns. These triumphs had become
so numerous as finally to necessitate their collection and presentation in a great system of organized and ordered knowledge—*La
Grande Encyclopédie*—where Diderot and his associates opened to
their own and succeeding generations the achievements of the Moderns.

The *Encyclopédie* was intended in the first place to be a balance
sheet of human knowledge, of not only the physical but the social
sciences as well, says Hubert.

> The labors of the erudite scholars of the 1700's was in fact con-
> siderable. The methodical exploration of the literature of an-
> tiquity, the researches of exegesis, provoked by the passions of
> religion, made more and more clear the character of the pre-
> Christian civilizations. The jurists set themselves to study the
> origin of national institutions. The religious orders and the
> learned academies rivaled one another in activity. From their
> efforts soon grew highly detailed memoirs on particular prob-
> lems, sometimes vast compilations of criticism, sometimes even
> broad syntheses that were a prelude to future universal his-
> tories. The related sciences, such as epigraphy, numismatics,
> paleography, diplomacy, were constituted and cultivated with
> great success, while a general theory of historical method was
> slowly elaborated.[31]

D'Alembert was conscious of this aspect of the encyclopedia and
wrote in the *Discours préliminaire:* "The first step we have to take
in our task is the examination into the genealogy and filiation of
the elements that compose our knowledge, the causes that have
given rise to them, and the characters that distinguish them; in a
word, to go back to the origin and generation of our ideas." [32]

"To go back to the origin"—the words are a reminder that the
writers hitherto included here have in the main been analytical
rather than historical. They have sought to know the relations be-

31. R. Hubert, *Les Sciences sociales dans l'encyclopédie* (Paris, F. Alcan,
1923), pp. 24–25.
32. J. L. D'Alembert, *Discours préliminaire de l'encyclopédie* (Paris, Li-
brairie Armand Colin, 1929), p. 13.

tween the various elements of society and their conditioning effects upon one another, as well as the nature of their relations to the environment. Montesquieu is of course the typical example. But there was no lack of historical interest, to which attention must now be turned.

From the historical point of view, the chief question which points the way to a sociology can be phrased as follows: Is there a meaning in history? Men for reasons already made clear were discovering a certain continuity between themselves and the past. The record had been pushed further and further back beyond the Greeks and Romans; now it was becoming necessary to see how all these periods were related. The primitive, the prehistoric, the stone age, the age of metals, Babylonians, Egyptians, Greeks, Romans, Dark Ages, Goths—how were they, were they indeed, related? Has history a meaning?

The reader is at last face to face with the philosophy of history. It is clear to begin with that the attempt to interpret the historical sequence may be made in two ways: the key to the meaning may be found elsewhere and brought to the task of explaining the record; or the key may be sought in an inductive study of the facts, so that the meaning emerges from the record itself. In other words meaning may be put into history or found there. It goes without saying that the philosophy of history in the usual sense is essentially an effort of the first kind just mentioned. Typical instances abound among the theological writers. For them it is easy to project a will into the universe and so to show how all things are designed and ordered to a given end. In a particularly difficult case, like that of the martyred virgins of St. Augustine, a final answer can be imposed: that divine Providence which admirably conducts all things governs the course of human generations from Adam to the end of the ages. In the words of Delvaille: "For St. Augustine, all human events can be classed according to a law of Providence which supplies their meaning and their guidance. That law is the following: Everything is subject to the secret direction of God, whose judgments are just and incomprehensible. . . . If things develop in a certain order, it is because God, letting us remain in ignorance of this order, rules it as he pleases." [33]

33. J. Delvaille, *Histoire de l'idée de progrès* (Paris, F. Alcan, 1910), pp. 31–32.

Such a doctrine is manifestly impossible in an age when Bacon and Descartes are dominating men's minds; and Bossuet, coming to the writing of a *Discours sur l'histoire universelle* for his Dauphin pupil, modifies it to the point where only a slight further change is required to bring the volume into conformity with the then current scientific doctrines. The Greek and Roman periods, of course, obtain meaning from the fact that they are preparations for the advent of Christianity; but aside from that deviation, Bossuet presents a practically universal picture of cause and effect in history.

> This view of universal history is to the histories of each country and people what a general map is to special maps. . . . God, who created and organized the universe, appointing for the establishing of order that all parts of this grand whole shall be mutually connected, hath also appointed that the course of human affairs should have its due stages and proportions—I mean that men and nations have had qualities commensurate to the height they were destined to attain; and that excepting certain extraordinary strokes where God would have His Hand appear alone, *no great change has ever taken place without having its causes in the ages antecedent.*[34]

For the more metaphysical type of philosopher, the task of synthesizing history is identical with that performed by the theological type and even easier. Instead of a will, an intellect is projected into the reality and the way is opened to a rational interpretation such as Kant, for example, presents in his *Idea for a Universal History on a Cosmopolitical Plan.* Being a philosopher he is of course already in possession of certain universal principles which, being universal, are therefore operative in history; for example, "Nature —the wisdom of whose arrangements must in all cases be assumed as a fundamental postulate—does nothing superfluously; and in the use of means to her ends does not play the prodigal." The case of man in history is not difficult to interpret. "The means which nature employs to bring about the development of all the tendencies she has laid in man is the antagonism of these tendencies in the social state." "Whatever difference there may be in our notions of

34. Bossuet, *Discours sur l'histoire universelle,* quoted in Vernon Lushington, "Bossuet," *The New Calendar of Great Men,* p. 272.

the freedom of the will metaphysically considered, it is evident that the manifestations of this will, viz. human actions, are as much under the control of universal laws of nature as any other physical phenomena." [35]

With this basis to start with,

> Kant goes on to explain with extreme precision that the play of man's passions, private and social, tends toward an ultimate state, not consciously perceived by any one generation, in which the self-seeking propensities of individuals, and the ambitious tendencies of nations subordinate themselves without self-extinction, to a state of social harmony. For arrival at this final state, egoism no less than altruism is necessary. The struggle to improve personal wellbeing has stirred man's energies to the creation of new ideals which, once arisen, have knit men together by free-will, and have thus diminished the need of compulsory union.[36]

Here is the clue to a universal history; nature may produce a man to execute it, "just as she produced a Kepler who unexpectedly brought the eccentric courses of the planets under determinate laws; and afterward a Newton who explained these laws out of a universal ground in Nature." [37]

There could scarcely be a clearer call for a sociology; and others than Kant had been working in the same direction, but with the determination to find the guidance for their efforts in the historical record itself rather than to bring to it principles already formed. Chief among men of this type was Turgot. The native bent of his mind, so clearly sociological, the immediacy with which he caught the significance of the kind of inquiries called for by the cultural situation in which he lived, are shown by the list of treatises the writing of which he projected, as his biographers have constructed it. Some of these works he never even began; none were completed. Only once did he give free rein to his power in the field of social science. It was his valedictory to the clergy, of whom he had up to the time been a potential member; it was also his farewell in all

35. I. Kant, *Idea for a Universal History on a Cosmopolitical Plan* (Hanover, N. H., Sociological Press, 1927), *passim.*

36. J. H. Bridges, "Kant," in *The New Calendar of Great Men,* p. 579.

37. Kant, *passim.*

essential respects to the field of sociology, which he was soon to leave
for administrative activities in the king's thankless service.

The oration *On the Progress of the Human Mind,* delivered in
the Sorbonne in 1750, was a sweeping, brilliantly colored review
of the whole past of mankind from the primitive beginnings down
to his own times, in which the keynote and the burden is the concept of human continuity. Nor is the idea present only by implication. It is expressed very vividly at the beginning: "The succession of men offers from century to century, an ever varied spectacle.
Reason, passions, liberty, give rise unceasingly to new events. All
the ages of mankind are enchained, one with another, by a sequence
of causes and effects that binds the present to the whole preceding
past." [38]

In it is also to be found the idea of a social accumulation, the
gradual building up of a social heritage:

> Societies are established and nations formed. They become domi-
> nant one after another and yield to other nations. Empires rise
> and fall. Laws and forms of government succeed one another.
> Arts and sciences are discovered and perfected one after an-
> other; and one after another, as they are hastened or delayed in
> their progress, they pass from climate to climate. Interest, ambi-
> tion, and vainglory at every instant change the face of the world
> and inundate the earth with blood. In the midst of their ravages,
> manners grow refined, the mind of man becomes enlightened,
> nations leave their isolation to draw nearer one another; com-
> merce and politics unite at last all the parts of the globe; and
> the total mass of human kind, through alternations of calm and
> agitation, of evil days and good, ever advances, though with drag-
> ging pace, towards a higher degree of perfection. [39]

In still another place Turgot, reflecting upon the history of the
sciences, sees that there seems to be a recurring sequence in their
development:

> Before the relation between physical facts was known, there
> was nothing more natural than to suppose that they were pro-

38. A. R. J. Turgot, *On the Progress of the Human Mind* (Hanover, N. H.,
Sociological Press, 1929), p. 5.

39. Turgot, p. 5.

duced by intelligent beings, invisible and like ourselves; for what else would they have resembled? . . . When philosophers had recognized the absurdity of these fables [about the gods], without having, however, acquired true light upon natural history, they imagined they could explain the causes of phenomena by means of abstract expressions such as *essences* or *faculties*. . . . It was only later, when the mechanical action of bodies upon one another was observed, that from this mechanical relation were drawn other hypotheses that mathematicians could develop and experience verify.[40]

Finally, in the surviving half of the *Mémoire on Tolerance* Turgot anticipates the application to human betterment of the knowledge of social phenomena. He proposes to deal with—but never does—the measures that prudence may require in adapting to varied circumstances principles that are recognized to be true, in order to prepare and bring to pass without disturbance the changes that very justice and wisdom render necessary. A science with true principles which are the source of applications—what more is needed but the name to make Turgot the first sociologist?

The work of Turgot leads straight to the work of Condorcet. In the latter, the conceptions more or less implicit in the thought of men from Vico onward become explicit. In them the bond of continuity was more and more clearly being seen as the source of a certain unity in the whole passage from the animal Homo up through the various stages of Manhood. In Condorcet the tracing of this continuity becomes a conscious method whereby meaning can be found in history. It is at this point that Condorcet and the sociologists, Turgot in the lead, pass out of the group of philosophers of history. The departure is effected as it should be if the outcome is to aid in the development of science, namely, through the channel of method. Condorcet, unlike Kant, will find a meaning in history, not put it there.

In consequence of this methodological difference, the most important section of Condorcet's work *The Progress of the Mind* is the introduction, where the method to be utilized is outlined. Obviously he is not free from the presuppositions of earlier periods—and later—when for example he begins by distinguishing between

40. Turgot, p. 23. (Italics are Turgot's.)

the study of the individual and that of societies. He is still thinking
in terms of moral philosophy and its division into ethics and politics. But he is well on the way to a new position when he states that
the study of societies deals first with the phenomena of reaction
between individuals and secondly with the phenomena involved
in the succession of generations. He advances to sure ground when
he lays emphasis upon the procedure of abstracting from the concrete descriptions of observers and historians the broad facts common to each particular case. He rises still further in the degree of
abstraction when he asserts that we must choose and combine these
general facts from the history of different peoples so as to construct
the hypothetical case of a single nation continuously progressing
from the beginning of time. With these directive ideas he proceeds
to make a first approximation of such an abstract picture of human
development, the one effective means whereby the method and the
doctrine may in time receive elaboration as the first effort, continued and refined, gives place to another, and so on.

In this *Sketch of an Historical Picture of the Advances of the
Human Mind*—a "sketch" for it is only the prospectus of a work
later, never, to be written—Condorcet divides the life of his hypothetical nation into nine periods:

> Passing from the tribe living by the chase (1) to the nomad peo-
> ples, (2) and thence to the sedentary stage of tillage, in which
> finally alphabetic writing is discovered (3), he reaches Greek
> civilization, saved from destruction by the battle of Salamis (4).
> He describes the rise of Greek philosophy and art, the begin-
> ning of the Positive sciences of mathematics, biology and ethic
> (5). . . . [Next he passes to the] Roman conquest, and its pre-
> cious legacy of jurisprudence; the rise of Christianity from the
> decay of Rome: the obscurantism which followed: the culture
> of positive Sciences by the Arabs (6): the renascence of Science
> in Europe with the Crusades; the discovery of the compass, and
> the invention of printing (7); and the stimulus to free thought
> given by the Reformation (8). The title of his Ninth Period is
> remarkable as showing his firm grasp of the correlation of social
> and intellectual changes: 'From Descartes to the formation of
> the French Republic.' He concludes with an impressive picture

of the 'Future Advances of the Human Mind,' (10) and of the social renovation which will follow from it.[41]

What the general method was on which he worked can best be expressed in his own words:

> This picture is historical, since, subjected to perpetual variations, it is formed by the successive observation of human societies at the different epochs they have traversed. It must present the order of the changes, show the influence which each moment exercises upon the moment which succeeds it, and thus show, in the modifications the human species has received as it ceaselessly renews itself in the midst of the immensity of the ages, the course it has followed, the steps it has taken toward truth or happiness. These observations upon what man has been, upon what he is today, then lead to the means of assuring and accelerating the new advances that his nature allows him to hope for still.[42]

Is there any point, any intelligence even, in saying that Condorcet's work has striking defects, that for instance it is deficient to say the least in its appreciation of the Middle Ages, or that it is colored by prejudices against priests and religions, or that it has an intellectual bias and is not sufficiently economic in its interpretations? Set over against such weaknesses the conception underlying the tenth epoch, and they fade into nothingness. Here is the first specific and conscious effort to introduce into the study of Man's record the possibility of foreseeing the general direction of future development on the basis of an understanding of the past. With this concept, the entire range of thought implicit in the notion of natural order and natural law is incorporated once for all into the study of social phenomena. Sociology is begun once more.

The eighteenth century, during which lived most of the men dealt with above, was a revolutionary period in the political sense. Some of these men, like Condorcet, were active revolutionists; all

41. J. H. Bridges, "Condorcet," *The New Calendar of Great Men*, p. 581.
42. M. J. A. N. Condorcet, *Esquisse d'un tableau historique des progrès de l'esprit humain* (Paris, Masson & fils, 1822), p. 3.

wrote in a revolutionary atmosphere. The fact is not important as an implied criticism of their theories. Theories are not necessarily wrong because they are revolutionary in nature or inspiration. Indeed they are often subversive merely because they result from the discovery and use of newly discovered data. It is not as a test of their validity that their subversiveness is mentioned; it is not the correctness of the theories that is in point, it is their completeness, their inclusiveness, that is put in doubt.

Most if not all of the men in point were primarily interested in reform of a wider or narrower scope; they were seeking to improve society; they advocated social advance; in short they were advocates of social change. That was what made them revolutionary. In order to make any theoretical case for their proposals, they had to emphasize the unceasing course of historical variation. And since they believed the changes they proposed or found necessary to be changes for the better, they logically interpreted the course of history as progressive and regarded themselves as standing for progress.

But there were those whose interests, ambitions, or sympathies were gravely affected by a subversion of society. Consequently they vigorously reacted against the words and deeds of the progressive groups. They required a respectable logical basis for their position as opponents of change or proposed changes; and so they insisted that history, to whom all parties appealed, made clear the fact that beneath all social variations were certain permanent elements, no matter what the outward appearances might be. With these permanent institutions of society the opponents of revolution identified themselves; and when their adversaries, striving to modify these foundations of society, inevitably produced at least temporary disturbances and often long continued disorder, they distinguished themselves from such subversive acts and thoughts by referring to themselves as the party of order.

Now the arguments which they developed to fortify their position were no less valid because they were used by conservatives than were the opposing views because they were held by radicals. The validity of theories is not decided by the motivation of the theorist. Nevertheless, for a long time the arguments for order went unheeded. The forces of change were too powerful; they went on to reshape the institutions of society. Their agents concentrated men's attention upon the theories by which the new social policies were defended. The thought of the conservatives was no less and no more valid than before; it was simply disregarded. It went underground, so to speak, there to remain until the time should come for it to reappear. Then by another of history's ironies it became subversive in its turn.

The foregoing remarks can be summarized in the statement that the revolutionary movement of the eighteenth century generated a counterrevolutionary opposition. The first was in its theoretical aspects mainly concerned with demonstrating the reality and accelerating the rate of social change; the latter was mainly confined to the defense of social stability. Each of these parties in their clashes of opinion adduced certain facts. Because they are facts, regardless of their provenance, they must be wrought into the structure of sociology. Thus will be built up a science which, rising above parties, will provide something other than partisan advantage for the guidance of political policies. The progressive group has already been briefly considered; it is now the turn of the conservative.

By common consent, the ablest representatives of the party of order are de Maistre and de Bonald. Of the two the former is the more powerful mind, but as regards theory the two men may be considered as one. Indeed de Maistre declared in a letter to de Bonald, "I have never thought anything you have not written; I have never written anything you have not thought," and the compliment is something more than conventional courtesy. Their views are therefore here considered together, with only a casual effort to keep the two men separate. It is regrettable but unavoidable that the lack, in the existing handbooks of sociological theory, of summaries of the work of the counterrevolutionists will tend to make the present treatment of their work seem inadequate.

Their general position arose out of and was wholly antagonistic to the French Revolution. For de Maistre there was even something *satanic* about that social upheaval. "What distinguishes the French Revolution and makes of it a unique *event* in history is that it is *bad* radically; no element of good in it soothes the eye of the observer; it is the highest degree of corruption known; it is pure impurity." [43] It is so because it is based upon a completely false principle, namely, that a constitution, i.e., *the fundamental basis*

43. J. M. de Maistre, *Considérations sur la France* (Paris, J. B. Pelagaud, 1863), p. 60. (Italics are de Maistre's.)

of a society, can be made by men. "One of the greatest errors of a century which committed them all, was to believe that a political constitution could be written and created *a priori,* whereas reason and experience unite to prove that a constitution is a divine work and that it is precisely what is most fundamental and essentially constitutional in the laws of a nation that cannot be written." [44] "It is a truth as certain in its kind as a proposition of mathematics, that *no great institution results from a deliberation,* that human constructions are weak in proportion to the number of men who are concerned in their making and to the machinery of science and reasoning that is employed in it *a priori.*" [45]

Nothing great has great beginnings; hence "no great and real institution can be founded on written law, since the men themselves, successive instruments by which it is to be established, do not know what it ought to become, and since an insensible growth is the true sign of duration, in all possible orders of things." [46] "No nation can give itself a government; only, when this or that right *exists* in its (natural) constitution, and when this right is misunderstood or restricted, some men, aided by certain circumstances, can set aside the obstacles and cause the rights of the people to be *recognized:* human power can go no further." [47] "Not only does creation not belong to man, but it does not appear that our power, *unassisted,* extends to the changing of established institutions for the better. . . . Hence this mechanical aversion of all good minds for innovations. The word *reform* in itself and before any examination will always be suspect to wisdom, and the experience of all the centuries justifies this quasi-instinct." [48]

"An assemblage of men taken at random cannot constitute a nation." "The people will always accept its masters and will never choose them." "Every sovereign family reigns because it has been chosen by a higher power." [49] "Monarchy by the very nature of things becomes more necessary in proportion as association becomes

44. J. M. de Maistre, *Essai sur le principe générateur des constitutions politiques* (Paris, J. B. Pelagaud, 1864), p. 1.

45. *Considérations,* p. 96. (Italics are de Maistre's, here and in the following quotations.)

46. *Principe générateur,* p. 31.

47. *Considérations,* p. 141.

48. *Principe générateur,* pp. 53–54.

49. *Considérations,* pp. 85, 127.

more numerous." There can be no society without government; "no institution whatever can last if it is not founded upon religion." [50] "Whether religious ideas are laughed at or venerated is unimportant; whether true or false, they form the sole basis of all durable institutions." [51] Such are the teachings of history, which is "experimental politics." It shows too that there is more than human guidance in politics, that "thorniest of the sciences, with its ever renewed difficulty of discerning between what is stable and what is unstable in its elements." [52]

> Is it credible that the political world goes by chance, that it is not organized, directed, animated by the same wisdom that shines in the physical world? . . .
>
> The guilty hands that overturn a state necessarily inflict grievous wounds; for no free agent can go contrary to the plans of the creator without bringing down in the sphere of his activity evils proportionate to the greatness of the attempt; . . . but when man works to re-establish order, he associates himself with the author of order, he is favored by *nature*, i.e. the whole of secondary things, which are the ministers of the divinity. His action has something of the divine.[53]

"All the pieces of the political machine having a tendency toward the place which is assigned them, this tendency, which is divine, will favor all the efforts of the king [when the king returns to France]; and order being the natural element of man, you will find in it the happiness you seek vainly in disorder." [54] Such were the basic and directive ideas of the two men; they were in accord as well in regard to many secondary aspects of political doctrine, i.e., social theory. The family for example holds a high place in their regard. It results from marriage, the sacred basis of public happiness. It is the primitive society and the social unit. It is the type so to speak of the state. Father, mother, children; cause, means, effect; king, minister, subjects: so does de Bonald in his own way draw the parallel. Only one other of these secondary

50. *Principe générateur*, pp. 23, 41.
51. *Considérations*, p. 68.
52. *Principe générateur*, p. iv.
53. *Considérations*, p. 145.
54. *Considérations*, p. 147.

points emphasized by the two men can here be mentioned: they both saw the social significance of language. "Every language of man is learned and never invented. No imaginable hypothesis in the circle of human power can explain with the slightest appearance of probability, either the formation or the diversity of tongues." [55] "We might ask the atheist where he learned to speak, and so by this consideration alone, we would rise to the *necessity* of a being other than man, from whom man received the art of speech." [56]

Into these secondary matters there is here no space and no occasion to go. The main point is clear. The unchanging aspects of society have been brought clearly into the light; they serve to complement the views which regard social phenomena as subject wholly to man's will. It is true that the method and the language of both writers and particularly de Bonald are essentially theological and dialectic; but the fact should not obscure an even more important fact, namely, that by the end of the 1700's a considerable mass of observations from history—that "experimental politics"—had been assembled in relation to social order. The conclusions from these increasing bodies of data were expressed in various forms, often far from scientific; they are none the less often worthy of consideration. In an earlier age men said that Nature abhors a vacuum; so indeed she does, within what limits was later discovered. To attribute political phenomena to divine wisdom is in a way to recognize their basis in law; to argue that they are organized and directed by the same wisdom that shines in the physical world is clearly to point toward a new science, of a nonphysical kind. At this point both progressives and conservatives meet.

With the men of the end of the revolutionary period, the time of general preparation for a true science of society may be said to have ended. All the elements that are needed for the beginning of a new science are in existence, no matter how greatly they may need ultimate development and correlation. The existence of an intellectual environment, a climate of opinion, is evident. After Condorcet the making of other like efforts is not to be doubted. Turgot had

55. De Maistre, *Considérations*, p. 147.
56. L. G. A. de Bonald, *Legislation primitive* (Paris, Le Clère, 1857), p. 254. (Italics are de Bonald's.)

been drawn into the field of administration; Condorcet died in the shadow of the Revolution. Other men were certain to take their places and did take them. Had their work been done by still other thinkers in other days and in more favorable conditions, the vocabulary now utilized might be different but the essentials would be the same: can there be any doubt that the general doctrines of sociology in regard to invention are strictly applicable to its own advent?

Consider in conclusion of this section the factors working toward the creation, the invention, of a new science to deal with the phenomena first called political in the large sense, then social, and now sociological:

the general development of the sciences, culminating for a time in Newton and then moving forward from the field of physics to that of biology;

the growth of a scientific hierarchy and the expansion of a scientific method;

the widening conviction that a natural order of society existed, which men could learn and be guided by;

the growing importance of scientific applications, working for a shift in emphasis from agricultural to industrial interests;

the extension of history back into the Egyptian, Babylonian, and other past;

the increase in knowledge after 1492 of uncivilized or early or primitive man and in general other than European cultures;

the greater interest in the philosophy of history and especially in such concepts as the unity and continuity of the human record;

the new regard for problems of national economy and economics in general as with the physiocrats and Adam Smith;

the closer analysis of political phenomena in the larger sense, with emphasis on the concept of social conditioning and causation, as in Montesquieu;

the search for causal sequences in human history, making the prevision of the future a possibility, as in Condorcet;

the challenging of authority, religious and political, past and present;

the outbreak of a violent revolution, seeking to modify or re-make every element in the cultural pattern;

the rise of a counterrevolutionary school of thinkers, empha-sizing the need and nature of social stability.

Juxtapose these elements in a single head and subject it to the synthesizing influence of a consciousness of social needs, made clear by a profound social crisis, and a science of society is a certain out-come. The crisis was the French Revolution; there were as a matter of fact several heads in which synthesis was being effected or essayed; by common consent, the best of these was Auguste Comte's.

CHAPTER 8 : *Auguste Comte: Point of Arrival and Point of Departure in Sociological Theory*

It is in the *Positive Philosophy*, Comte's first great treatise, that the intellectual achievements of the 1700's are fused into a uniform body of thought around a single center and with a single objective. Comte himself knew the significance of his efforts and expressed it clearly: "I have devoted my life to the organization of an ensemble of conceptions," he wrote to Mrs. Austin in 1844. The originality of discovery, of moving into distinctly new territory, was Comte's only in his later, not in his earlier, years. It is this very fact which largely accounts for the acceptance of the earlier work and the obscurity into which his later work fell. The former was accessible to his contemporaries; the latter was beyond them.

A synthesis, then, was the primary object of Comte's first efforts; but the nature and purpose of this synthesis should be clearly understood. That they are not always comprehended is no doubt partly due to the very title which Comte gave his treatise: *Cours de philosophie positive*. It was a *cours* because the work was first planned and delivered as a course of lectures, which were then expanded into written form. It was a *philosophie* because Comte used the word in the Aristotelian sense as a synthesis of knowledge.

Immediate stress, however, should be placed on the fact that Comte was in no sense a "professional" philosopher whose whole life is centered in an intellectual construction. From the beginning of his career Comte never deviated from the straight road leading to the accomplishment of his ultimate purpose. What he aimed at from the first was a re-formation, a renovation, a renewal of men's social life, a change of basic purpose and direction in politics defined in the broadest sense, the need for which had been shown so tragically by the Revolution. Before such a re-formation was possible a new science—a science of "politics," a science of society —would be required. But such a science could be properly envisaged only in the light of knowledge as a whole. Such a synthetic view

151

would show the place of the proposed construction in the whole scheme of things as well as determine its scope in relation to that of the other departments of learning. Once the preliminary task of synthesizing was completed, the ultimate object, i.e., the construction of the new science could be undertaken intelligently.

On what basis could such a theoretical construction be erected? Solely upon a basis of knowledge. Hence the *philosophie*, i.e., the synthesis, had to be *positive*. By this word Comte indicated his rejection of all philosophers in the theological or metaphysical sense. He saw from history how from an ascending series of logically determined classes of phenomena—i.e., the sciences—hominoid influences, whether in their theological or metaphysical form, had successively been excluded. The same exclusion would have to be effected in the domain of politics. So and so only would men come to see what is as it is in social phenomena and so would they at last be in a position where it would be possible for them to guide their social life systematically on a basis of scientific knowledge.

In accordance with these conceptions and aspirations, then, Comte began his temporary and incidental career as a philosopher. His lectures as expanded into chapters begin with a definition of "positive," based upon the empirical discovery dating back to Turgot that our principal conceptions—i.e., each branch of our knowledge—pass in succession through three different theoretical states: the theological or fictitious state, the metaphysical or abstract state, and the scientific or positive state. Of this discovery, which was later to be raised from its empirical level and made into a law and an integral part of the science of sociology, the definition of the positive is the point of main interest here: "In the positive state, the human mind, recognizing the impossibility of obtaining absolute truth, gives up the search after the origin and destination of the universe and a knowledge of the final causes of phenomena. It only endeavors now to discover, by a well combined use of reasoning and observation, the effective *laws* of phenomena, that is to say their invariable relations of succession and likeness." [1]

1. This chapter is based on A. Comte, *Cours de philosophie positive* (5th ed. 6 vols. Paris, Société Positiviste, 1892), *4*, and all quotations are from this volume.

The statement just given implies a knowledge of the various branches of knowledge. What are they, and how are they defined and delimited? Here is the second stage of Comte's initial inquiry. Whatever the names or number of the sciences, they have all been obtained first by an analysis and second by a subsequent classification of the phenomena observable by men. With analysis and classification goes abstraction: "We must distinguish, with reference to all kinds of phenomena, two classes of natural science. The first consists of the Abstract or General sciences, whose object is the discovery of the laws regulating the different class of phenomena in all conceivable cases. The other group comprises the Concrete, Special, or Descriptive sciences, whose function consists in applying these laws to the actual history of the different existing beings. The abstract sciences are therefore the fundamental ones, and our studies in this *cours* are concerned with them alone." The distinction is well illustrated by general physiology on the one hand and zoology and botany on the other. The first of these studies the laws of life in general; the others determine the mode of existence of each living being. The relations between chemistry and mineralogy afford another illustration of the principle stated above, without which the positive philosophy would never have come into being.

How, finally, are the results of the classification to be arranged? The order of arrangement is not arbitrary. There is an order of history, a chronological order in which the abstract or general sciences have appeared. There is a logical order as well. "We must begin with the study of the most general or simple phenomena, and proceed from them successively to the most special or complex." These two orders, of time and thought, essentially coincide; and when the various classes of phenomena are arranged chronologically and logically, the result is the following: mathematics, astronomy, physics, chemistry, physiology, and social physics. To the last two members of the sequence other names were given later: physiology became biology and social physics became sociology; but the substitution of these new names for the older ones implied no other change in Comte's arrangement.

Since the six general sciences just named cover the whole range of human interests, they compose an encyclopedia; since they are logically ordered, they form a hierarchy. When the members of this encyclopedic hierarchy or hierarchical encyclopedia are decomposed into their constituent divisions, the result is a series of easy transitions from the simplest to the most complicated phenomena. The hierarchy is therefore a true *scala intellectus,* as Bacon foreshadowed it, and so it provides not only the basis for a thoroughly self-consistent and homogeneous education but it makes clear the fact that the logical approach to the more complicated sciences is by way of the simpler ones.

Comte proceeded to use this approach, this ladder of the intellect. Hence a good half of the *Philosophie* is devoted to a study of the lower degrees of the hierarchy. As Comte passes from one level to another, his concern is to make an accurate delimitation of each science, to determine the particular method that has grown up within each as a result of the study of its special data, and to subdivide the content of each science, i.e., apply the general principle of classification on which the whole hierarchy is built to the task of ordering the content of each particular science so as to show how it grows out of its predecessor and leads directly to its successor in the hierarchy. Thus biology for example begins with the study of vegetal life which is so slightly separated in its lowest forms from the highest level of chemistry, the organic, goes on to animal life, and ends with the study of intellectual and moral life. Beyond, but not far beyond, lies the domain of social phenomena, the data for the science of social physics, or sociology.

It may be wise to pause here a moment to notice some of the advances in theory that Comte has made at this point in his thinking, as well as to see some of the elements of weakness carried over from earlier thinkers. In the first place, in his clear recognition of the importance of the social domain, the significance of the cultural development of mankind with its outgrowth in science was firmly grasped. Next, the importance of abstraction as the basis of scientific thinking was well understood. That each class of abstract phenomena should be specific and irreducible was his closest approach at the moment to the conception of the isolate. That each group of phenomena has a best method; that this method grows out of actual dealing with the particular class of phenomena; and that these methods, resting upon observation in the widest sense, are when taken together the basis of the scientific method: these points are acquired once for all.

That beyond the biological lies the sociological seems clear enough; but in the position as stated lies concealed an implicit difficulty that was to cause Comte and all his successors an immense labor of analysis and reclassification. This obstacle in the path of sociologists to come consists in the equating of biological and individual, sociological and social. Stated in other words, it is the belief that to study society adequately, the individual must first be known. Behind this equating of individual (i.e., men) with biological, and social (i.e., society) with sociological stands the age-old division of knowledge into natural and moral philosophy, the second particularly obstructive with its division of data into ethics and politics.

Of the logical difficulty concealed in this ancient assumption Comte like everyone else was at the time completely unaware. He gave it no thought as he proceeded to the institution of his new science of social physics. Such a science, he declares by way of introduction to his elaboration of the idea, is today both necessary and opportune. "The theological and metaphysical philosophies have failed to secure permanent social welfare, while the positive philosophy has uniformly succeeded—and conspicuously for the last three centuries—in reorganizing to the unanimous satisfaction of the intellectual world, all the anterior orders of human conceptions, which had till then been in the same chaotic state that we now deplore in regard to social science."

Contemporary opinion regarded the state of each of those sciences as hopeless until the positive philosophy brought them out of it. There is no reason why it should fail in the latest application, after having succeeded in all the earlier. Advancing from the less complex categories to the more complex—and final—one; and comparing this regularity of advance with the picture given in this chapter of our present social condition, we cannot fail to see that both political and scientific analysis concur in demonstrating that the positive philosophy, carried on to its completion, is the only possible agent in the reorganization of modern society. I wish to establish this principle first, apart from all considerations regarding my way of proving my point, so that, if my attempt should hereafter be condemned, no unfavorable inference may be drawn in regard to a method which alone can save society, and public reason should have nothing to do but require from happier successors more effectual endeavors in the same direction. In all cases, and especially in this one, the method is of even more importance than the doctrine.

So then only the scientific spirit and method can avail in the present crisis of society: are there any thinkers who have already moved in the desired and defined direction? The second introductory chapter deals with such historical preparations as have been made for the advent of a science of social phenomena. The inevitable remarks about Aristotle precede more meaningful comments upon Montesquieu and Condorcet, who are Comte's effective predecessors—in particular Condorcet, whom Comte ever regarded as his spiritual godfather.

Once his acknowledgements of intellectual indebtedness have been made, Comte proceeds to a more vital part of his effort, namely, the problem of method. "In every real science, conceptions regarding method in the exact sense are by their nature essentially inseparable from those directly connected with the doctrine itself," and the more complex and special the phenomena—such as those of sociology—the less is it possible to make the separation. Some clear conception then of the content of the new science must therefore precede the determination of the precise method most suited to its development. Granting this logical position to be sound, it is nevertheless possible to make certain general preliminary statements as to the nature of the method to be selected. Since the new science is to *be* a science, it will have to possess certain characteristics common to all sciences.

Thus, being a science, the science of society will be distinguished as regards its method first by a necessary and permanent subordination of imagination to observation, since such a subordination marks off the scientific spirit and approach from all theological or metaphysical principles and procedures. In the second place, an essential character of the conceptions of the new science, as of all sciences, must be their relative nature. It is this contrast between the relative and the absolute and the acceptance of the first which is the decisive difference between ancient and modern thinking. In the third place, as in all other sciences, the notion of an unlimited control over phenomena, so characteristic of ordinary political thinking, must be given up once for all. True, the more complex phenomena are the more modifiable they are, but that is not the same as saying they are indefinitely and arbitrarily controllable. There are regularities in social phenomena as elsewhere. Finally, the general spirit of science, and therefore of the new science, demands that social phenomena be conceived of as inevitably subjected to true natural laws, and therefore rational prevision in regard to those phenomena is possible, always however within the limits of precision compatible with their greater complexity.

So much for the general spirit and method of the new science. What of its content? There are to be laws: but laws of what? What is to be the precise subject and true character of these laws? To answer this question, says Comte, it is necessary to extend to the whole body of social phenomena "a truly fundamental scientific distinction which I have established and utilized in all the parts of this treatise and principally in the philosophy of biology. This principle is by its nature radically applicable to all phenomena whatever and especially to all those that can be presented by living bodies. It consists in considering in separation but always with a view to exact systematic coordination the *statical* and the *dynamical* state of every subject of positive study."

At this point Comte seems to be about to give a general, i.e., abstract definition of the basic data with which sociology will deal. He does not do so, however. Moving cautiously, he is satisfied to define them by exclusion. All the phenomena above the biological will be comprised within the new science, and these phenomena are social. Social phenomena is as far as he goes at the moment; and as a matter of fact he does not, either here or in the *Philosophie* as a whole, define an appropriate and distinctive isolate. It was to come only very much later in his career. Instead, he goes on at this point to justify his distinction between "static" and "dynamic" as follows: "In simple biology, i.e. for the general study of individual life only, this indispensable decomposition gives rise to . . . a rational distinction between the purely anatomical point of view relative to ideas of organization and the physiological point of view proper, directly relative to ideas of life."

In sociology, the decomposition should be operated in a quite analogous and not less pronounced manner, by a radical distinction, in regard to each subject of political meditation, between the fundamental study of the conditions of existence of society and that of the laws of its continuous movement. This difference seems to me from this moment to be sufficiently well characterized to allow me to foresee that in the future its spontaneous development will be able to give rise to the habitual decomposition of social physics into two principal sciences, under the names, for example, of social statics and social dynamics, as essentially distinct from one another as individual anatomy and physiology are today.

But it would certainly be premature today to attach any grave importance to this methodical distribution at the very moment of the first institution of the science. . . . Besides it might be feared that such a clear-cut division of social science should today introduce the capital inconvenience, all too much in conformity with the dispersive tendencies of contemporary minds, of causing a vicious neglect of the permanent and indispensable combination of the two points of view. . . . In any case, any scission whatever of the work of sociology would evidently be inopportune, and even irrational, so long as the science as a whole shall not have been conceived of adequately.

Before passing to the further exposition of the bearing of "this indispensable elementary decomposition" upon his general thought, Comte pauses to note how this

scientific dualism corresponds, with perfect exactness, in the political sense proper, to the double notion of order and progress, which can henceforward be regarded as spontaneously introduced into the general domain of the public reason. For it is evident that the statical study of the social organism should coincide at bottom with the positive theory of order, which can in fact consist only in an exact permanent harmony between the diverse conditions of existence of human societies. It is in the same way even more evident that the dynamical study of the collective life of mankind necessarily constitutes the positive theory of social progress, which, when all vain thoughts of an absolute and unlimited perfectibility are set aside, must naturally be reduced to the simple notion of this fundamental development.

It is evident in all the foregoing statements that Comte is proceeding in an essentially dialectical rather than an inductive manner. He is of course simply feeling his way. He has certain directive ideas, based upon his own studies and those of his predecessors, but he has not as yet carried them to the point at which a final decision, on an inductive basis, as to the subdivisioning of the new science can be made. He therefore utilizes as a guide a general idea, the division between statics and dynamics, which arose in mathematics and has been applicable elsewhere, especially in biology. In substance, then, he is proceeding by way of analogy and in particular by way of an analogy between the biological and the social organisms. Thus the definitions of statics and dynamics are taken word for word from his earlier discussions of biology; but he is quite aware of what he is doing and so proceeds cautiously and tentatively.

In any case, whatever the nature of the reasoning, Comte has established a logical division in the subject matter of sociology and he at once uses it to advance his progress in the direction of finding a method which shall be distinctive of the new science. Such a method, it will be recalled, could in Comte's view be developed only by dealing with the data. It was necessary therefore to decide what the data were, and it was for this purpose that Comte sought to subdivide the new science. It consisted of a statical and a dynamical division. What did each of these divisions deal with? What was the general nature of the data contained in each of them? The answer to this question gives the content of sociology as Comte conceived of it at the time.

First, then, what does the statical section of sociology include? With what will the laws of social statics be concerned? Of what will they be the laws?

The true philosophical principle which is theirs seems to me directly to consist in the general notion of the universal con-

sensus which characterizes all the phenomena whatever of living bodies, and which social life manifests in the highest degree.
Thus conceived of, this sort of social anatomy which constitutes
statical sociology must have for permanent object the positive
study, at once experimental and rational, of the mutual actions
and re-actions which are continually exercised one upon the
other by all the different parts whatever of the social system,
while provisional abstraction is made as scientifically as possible of the fundamental movement which is always gradually
modifying them. . . . From this first point of view, the previsions of sociology, based upon the exact general knowledge of
these necessary relations, will have as their characteristic purpose to draw conclusions—in ulterior conformity with direct
observation—in regard to the various statical indications relative to each mode of social existence, by studying their mutual
influences. . . . This preliminary aspect of political science
evidently presupposes, then, of all necessity, that contrary to
the philosophical habits of today, each of the numerous social
elements, ceasing to be envisaged in an absolute and independent manner, shall always be exclusively conceived of as relative
to all the others, with which a fundamental solidarity should
always intimately combine it.

Already, remarks Comte at this point, one of the characteristics
which will mark the future sociological method becomes apparent.
It grows out of the very conception of social consensus; and out of
the same conception will come that aspect of the sociological method
which is its most distinctive contribution to scientific method as
a whole. The point is the synthetic nature of the study that is required by statical investigations.

Since social phenomena are so profoundly connected, their real
study can never be rationally split into parts; whence results
the permanent obligation always to consider simultaneously
the various social aspects, whether in statics or in dynamics.
Each of them no doubt can become in isolation the preliminary
subject of appropriate observations; it is quite necessary that
such should be the case to a certain degree in order to aliment
the science with suitable materials. But this preliminary necessity is in strictness applicable only to the present time, when the

first sketch of the science is being made—a sketch which must employ, with the indispensable precautions, the incoherent observations that were made with quite different intentions, by the irrational researches of earlier days. When the formation of the science shall have been sufficiently advanced the fundamental correlation of phenomena will doubtless serve as the habitual guide in their direct exploration.

No doubt social science will one day be able to a certain degree to be subdivided rationally and usefully; but we can in no wise know today in what this ulterior division will consist, since its true principle should result only from the gradual development of the science, which can now certainly be founded only in the light of a synthetic study of the whole subject. There would even be a true philosophical danger in wishing at this time to make final, on the ground that it was a permanent decomposition of labor, the indispensable distinction between the static and the dynamic states, despite its evident rationality and its continuous usage. At any age whatever of the science, the partial researches which may become necessary for it will be able to be pointed out and envisaged properly only in the light of its entire development as a unit. Only such a synthetic view will be able spontaneously to see the special points on which enlightenment will be useful in aiding the direct improvement of the subject. *Following any other path, there will essentially be obtained only a sterile encumbrance of irrational special discussions, badly instituted and worse carried out,* much rather destined radically to hinder the formation of the true philosophy than to prepare for it useful materials.

The very nature of the statical section of sociology brought into the foreground another question in regard to method which Comte disposed of before at last reaching the dynamical division. The point of the question is made clear by the quotation:

An essentially empirical aphorism, transformed with little insight into an absolute dogma by modern metaphysicians, prescribes the constant proceeding on every possible subject from the simple to the composite; but at bottom there is no other solid reason for the advice than that such a path is in fact suited to the inorganic sciences. The latter, by virtue of their simpler and more rapid development and their higher perfection, have inevitably had to serve hitherto as the essential type for precepts of universal logic. Nevertheless, it is impossible in reality to conceive in this regard of any other logical necessity truly common to all speculations than the evident necessity of always going from the known to the unknown. . . . Now it is clear that this spontaneous rule prescribes the going from the composite to the simple as well as from the simple to the composite, according as, in the light of the nature of the subject, the one is better known or more accessible than the other.

From the point of view just stated there is a fundamental and inescapable difference between the whole of the inorganic philosophy and that of the organic.

For in the first, where the solidarity is very slightly pronounced and has a very slight effect upon the study of the subject, it is a matter of exploring a system whose elements are almost always better known than the whole and are ordinarily even the only aspects directly appreciable. Such a situation in effect makes necessary to proceed from the less composite to the more composite case. But in the contrary situation, where man or society constitutes the principal object, the only rational procedure, by another consequence of the same logical principle, is the opposite approach, since the whole of the subject is certainly much better known and more immediately accessible than the diverse parts that will ultimately be distinguished in it.

Having made it clear that sociology need not begin its researches by minute analyses of small societies or small parts of the entire social development but could proceed from the study of the whole social development to the various parts of which it is composed, Comte was ready to turn from statics to dynamics in his quest for the nature of the phenomena which was to decide the method of the new science. Of the two basic ideas or seed thoughts or *idées mères* on which sociology is founded, the first—universal social solidarity—is less capable at the moment, Comte thinks, of giving the new science a philosophical character than the second—con-

tinuous progress or rather the gradual development of mankind.
It is of course the latter which is the elementary conception of social
dynamics.

Dynamics then is the study of the continuous succession observable in the whole development of mankind. In making this study
Comte follows Condorcet's indispensable scientific abstraction,
namely, the hypothesis of "a single people to whom would ideally
be transported all the consecutive social modifications effectively
observed among the various populations. This rational fiction is
much less distant from the reality than is customarily supposed; for
from the political point of view, the true successors of this or that
people are certainly those who, utilizing and pursuing their predecessors' primitive efforts, have prolonged their social progress, whatever the territory these successors inhabit or the race to which they
belong."

Leaving aside then by way of abstraction the influences of what
would today be called diffusion and considering only the ideal case
of a single people accomplishing all the stages of progress, Comte
proceeds:

> the true general spirit of dynamic sociology consists in conceiv-
> ing of each of these consecutive social stages as the necessary
> result of the preceding and the indispensable motor of the suc-
> ceeding, according to the luminous axiom of the great Leibnitz:
> the present is big with the future. The science henceforward
> has for its object to discover the constant laws which regulate
> this continuity, laws which as a whole determine the funda-
> mental course of human development. . . . In a word, social
> dynamics studies the laws of succession, while social statics seeks
> those of co-existence: so that the general application of the first
> should be to furnish to political practice the true theory of prog-
> ress at the same time that the second spontaneously forms that
> of order.

The scientific character of the concept of dynamics is now clear,
for it deals only with the question of successive stages of development without raising any questions as to values or relative ranking.
It also ends the controversy about human perfectibility, since the
whole problem of dynamics could be discussed without once using
the words "perfection" or "perfecting." They could always be re-

placed by "the simple scientific expression of *development*, which without any moral appreciation designates a generally incontestable fact."

At this point in his exposition, Comte at great length goes into the defense of the concept of dynamic sociological laws. The details of this defense need not be given here. Comte was so insistent upon the matter because the establishment of regularity and law in the domain of sociological phenomena would drive the theological and metaphysical philosophies from the last domains in which they were influential and so the triumph of the positive philosophy would be complete and final.

> Without admiring or blaming political facts, and seeing them, as in every other science, essentially as simple subjects for observations, social physics considers every phenomenon from the double elementary point of view of its harmony with co-existing phenomena, and its enchainment with the anterior and posterior state of human development. It strives in both of these respects to discover, as far as possible, the true general relations which bind social facts together. It considers each of them to be explained, in the scientific sense of the word, when it has been suitably connected, either with the whole of the corresponding situation, or with the whole of the preceding movement, always setting carefully aside all vain and inaccessible searching for the intimate nature and the essential mode of production of all phenomena whatever.

This new science sees "the mass of the human species, whether past, present, or even future, as constituting in all regards, and more and more, either in the order of places or in that of times, an immense and eternal social unit, whose different organs, individual or national, ceaselessly united by an intimate and universal solidarity, inevitably co-operate, each according to a determinate mode and degree, in the fundamental evolution of mankind—a truly capital and wholly modern conception."

The general nature of the new science thus clearly determined and eloquently stated, Comte was finally able to turn to the question which had been in his mind throughout the whole of the preceding discussion in regard to the content of statics and dynamics, namely, the question of method. What, given the nature of the phenomena of sociology, is the one most suitable and characteristic method?

There are, says Comte, two kinds of methodological resources: the direct, consisting in the various means of intellectual exploration which belong properly to a given discipline; and the indirect, though not less indispensable, which result from the necessary relations of a science with the whole system of sciences that precede it in hierarchical order. Of these two classes sociology is primarily concerned only with the first. Like every other general or abstract science, sociology must develop its appropriate *new* method; the second class of methods available for its use consists only of adaptations to its own data of methods first developed elsewhere and in relation to abstractions of a different order of complexity.

The final solution of the first of these questions is to be had only from actual dealing with the phenomena of sociology in the course of constructing the science. Obviously no definitive pronouncement was possible in this regard at the initial stage of development in which sociology at the moment was. Comte therefore sought suggestion elsewhere: first, in a review of the basic scientific methods already developed. These are pure observation, experimentation proper, and comparison. Now sociological phenomena are closest to biological, for which the comparative method is the appropriate means of discovery. Some form or modification of comparison seems therefore to be indicated.

Looking over the sociological field in a general way, then, Comte reviews certain types of comparison that might be of value in dealing with it. Human societies might be compared with animal societies; different coexisting states of human society in different parts of the world might be compared, especially when the populations are entirely independent of one another. The employment of comparative observation in the way last mentioned would give useful results but only on one condition, namely, that there was already in existence some generally accepted rational conception of the fundamental development of mankind as a whole.

Now a first indispensable sketch of general social development must itself result from the primitive employment of a new method of observation, more rational in character, better adapted to the nature of the phenomena, and exempt from the defects of the other procedures. Comte at this point was sure of his argument, for as a matter of fact this better use of comparison was already in existence. It had grown up spontaneously, just as experimentation had in its less elaborate forms always been utilized in the study of the physical world. It was the direct outcome of the study of the human record, carried on in the simple naive way. Men that is to say in dealing with human affairs had spontaneously, long before science had arisen, worked out the essentials of the way by which to connect human achievements. It needed only to be developed systematically. It was in short the historical method, "the one fundamental basis on which the system of political logic can really rest."

The historical comparison of the various consecutive states of mankind not only constitutes the principal scientific artifice of the new political philosophy: its rational development will form the very foundation of the science, in all its most characteristic aspects. It is above all in this way that sociological science must first be profoundly distinguished from biological science proper. *The positive principle of this indispensable philosophical separation results from the necessary influence of the various human generations upon the generations following, which, gradually accumulated in a continuous manner, soon ends by being the preponderant consideration of the direct study of social development.* So long as this preponderance is not immediately recognized, this positive study of mankind must rationally appear to be a simple spontaneous prolongation of the *natural history* of man. But this scientific character, quite suitable when the first generations are considered, is necessarily more and more effaced in proportion as *social evolution* begins to become more manifest, and must finally be transformed, when once the human movement is established, into an entirely new character, directly suited to sociological science, in which historical considerations must immediately prevail.

When the effective application of this new means of investigation shall have been sufficiently developed for its characteristic properties to have been able to become, in all eyes, sufficiently pronounced, it will be recognized, I presume, as a sufficiently clear-cut modification of the fundamental way of positive exploration for it to be classed, finally, after pure observation, experimentation and comparison proper as a fourth and last essential mode of observation, destined, under the special name of *the historical method,* for the analysis of the most complicated phenomena, and having its philosophical source in the immediately preceding mode, by way of the biological comparison of ages.

So Comte ends his preliminary survey of the problem of method in relation to the new science. It would be difficult to find a more revealing instance of a science in the making, a more convincing example of the dependence of method upon data, a clearer proof of the reciprocal relationship between method and doctrine, or a better illustration of the way in which science grows out of common usage and good sense, merely refining, elaborating, and extending the concepts and usages that have come spontaneously into existence.

The difficulties inherent in such an undertaking as Comte was engaged in can be felt to some degree in following his thought up to the present point. Method depends upon and grows out of data; data are gathered by method. Comte meets the difficulty by stopping in the midst of his chapter on method to discuss the data sufficiently to enable him to proceed with his discussion of method. The chapter thus achieves a first approximation of both data and method and allows Comte to proceed logically with the subdivisioning of the phenomena.

Needless to say, the first of these logical subdivisions is social statics. Comte admits that a methodical and special treatise on political philosophy would contain a developed analysis of the conditions of existence common to all human societies and the corresponding laws of harmony before it proceeded to the study of the laws of succession. However, in the *Philosophie,* since it is but a first survey of the field, he thinks that the chief attention should be given to dynamics rather than statics, not only because of the greater interest inherent in the dynamical aspect of the subject but also because of the greater aptitude of the phenomena of movement to manifest the laws of fundamental solidarity.

Nowhere is it made more clear than in this chapter that Comte is still under the handicap of the old conception dating back to the Greeks that the individual must precede the social in the movement of sociological theory. Statical phenomena are divided into three classes, relative to the individual first, then the family, and finally to society itself. The problem of the individual and his relation to social phenomena is evidently a troublesome one, for no sooner does Comte list the individual as above than he eliminates the subject from his list on logical grounds, as follows: "Any system whatever has necessarily to be formed of elements which are essentially homogeneous to it, and so the scientific spirit does not allow of regarding human society as being really composed of individuals." "The true social unit is certainly the family, at least reduced to the elementary couple which constitutes its principal basis, for the family spontaneously presents the true necessary germ of the various essential dispositions which characterize the social organism."

The chapter comes to an end with a discussion of society in general, envisaged as composed of families and not of individuals and always examined from the point of view of what its fundamental structure manifests as necessarily common to all times and all places, namely, an invariable conciliation between the separation of labors and the cooperation of efforts. On this conciliation social life finally depends, "for there can be no true society without the permanent concurrence in a general operation, pursued by distinct means, suitably subordinated one to another." On this inductive ground the chapter closes, leaving for the future a more acute analysis of social phenomena and the whole problem of the relation between the individual and the social. The germ of all Comte's later work on the subject is to be found in the chapter but only by implication; and the implications are profoundly hidden.

The way was thus finally cleared for Comte to proceed without interruption to the discussion, analysis, and construction of social dynamics, the culmination of the *Philosophie*. Of the many long chapters devoted to the general elaboration of dynamics, only the first, chapter 51, is here in point; and of it there are directly germane to the present chapter—concerned only with the basis on which a science of sociology must be constructed—only two items, namely, the definition of dynamics and the proposed laws of dynamic development.

On the first of these points no great direct advance over the *idée mère* of the gradual development of mankind is made. Nevertheless the precision with which the concept is envisaged is sharpened by the elimination from the central thought of a number of factors which are shown to be only secondary in importance because they affect only the speed and intensity of the dynamic movement. Among these secondary or conditioning factors are climate, race, ennui, the length of human life, and the natural increase of population. None of these essentially modify the necessary direction of human evolution as a whole, which emerges from the analysis more clearly conceived than ever. Their elimination shows how Comte was advancing toward a sociological isolate.

Finally, Comte proposes two laws which an examination of the gradual development of mankind reveals. The first of these is the law of the three states, which now ceases to be an empirical statement based upon the history of the sciences and becomes one of the two fundamental conceptions on which social dynamics is based. Its inductive foundation is the general history of the human mind, with a predominant attention to the most general and most abstract conceptions. In other words, the law results from "the successive appreciation of the fundamental system of human opinions relative to all phenomena whatever considered as a whole, in a word, to the general history of philosophy."

The law itself states that there is "a constant and indispensable succession of three general states, primitively theological, transitorily metaphysical, and finally positive, through which our intelligence always passes, in any kind of speculation whatever."

The second law revealed by an inductive study of social progression concerns the material development of mankind. "This supplementary study being today much better conceived of than the principal theory," Comte gives it only a rapid appreciation. "All the various general means of rational exploration applicable to political researches, have already concurred in showing in a decisive manner, the inevitable primitive tendency of mankind toward a mainly military life, and its not less irresistible final destination in an essentially industrial existence." Between the two is a phase necessarily equivocal and fluctuating in character which essentially consists in the habitual substitution of a defensive for the originally offensive military organization and the involuntary general subordination, more and more pronounced, of the spirit of the warrior to the instinct of production.

These two laws, the intellectual and the material, are fundamentally connected, each main state of the one being associated with the corresponding state of the other; they form a triple successive dualism, the necessary basis of a sound historical philosophy. Equipped with them, Comte proceeds in the remainder of the *Philosophie* to the task of explaining the past as a guarantee of his ability to deal with the future; and for the time being his thought ceases to be the center of interest of this volume.

Had he at this point created a sociology? The question may be left to those who specialize in beginnings. What is certain is that for the first time in history a science of social phenomena had been clearly envisaged, its essential data provisionally defined, an appropriate method suggested, a tentative division of the field proposed, several basic laws formulated, and the whole apparatus utilized for the explanation of the past with a view to the prevision of the future. The mirage, if it was no more, was never to be lost from the sight of men. In Comte's own language, sociology, the new science, was instituted; it remained to constitute it.

CHAPTER 9: *The Expansion of Sociological Theory*

To regard Comte as a point of arrival and a point of departure in social theory and to describe sociology from Comte's time on as the application of the spirit and method of science to the study of social phenomena is not to assert nor even to imply that all the men who followed him derive directly from his efforts. All those indeed who strove to bring their work within the scope of the description above, regardless of their source or ultimate success, may be regarded as sociologists. To some of these men attention is now to be turned. Even their failures will be instructive, either as warning to others against certain lines of investigation or as showing the existence of difficulties unsuspected before their efforts. If not wholly unsuccessful, their work can point to new researches and the results incorporated into new structures of knowledge.

Moreover, in these analyses there is no attempt to decide whether a given author is right or wrong. Such a position would be presumptuous, to say the least. All the men whose work is reviewed were men of ability, often of the very first grade. They were all engaged in like tasks. They were all looking at the same thing. If they looked at it from different angles, as they did, they were bound to see different aspects of it. If their training in early life had given them distinct points of view, they found different elements of interest in the material they were examining. And they did of course have different points of view. Not one of them had been trained as a sociologist; such training was impossible until almost the present generation. They were trying to create a new science. So they came as philosophers, engineers, paleobotanists, jurists, judges, military men, political scientists, revolutionists, clergymen, teachers—each with his special interest and training. They were not really rivals, despite occasional personal rivalries. They were cooperating in a single enterprise. Actually they were the agents of mankind in a great intellectual operation, and as such they are now to be examined.

Finally a remark should be added here in relation to the sociologists selected for comment in the present chapter. That a dozen were included is of no significance. Six or twenty could have been chosen. What is important is to emphasize the fact that the work these men were engaged upon is of the nature of the sociological achievement now called invention. This new science like any of the older was not an individual product. What is of importance and interest is the way in which *all* these men gave rise to a collective product, to which other men have made and will continue to make additions. The outcome will be a cumulative result, to which many men will have contributed. Hence it is pointless and of no significance to remark that this or that man did not "make" sociology. Who "made" chemistry? What is of interest here is the way a new scientific effort took shape and to what successive efforts it will in turn give rise.

1. LePlay

Earliest in the period of expansion of sociological theory came a man who was slow to be recognized as a contributor to the nascent science. Yet he seems to belong in the list of early sociologists by virtue of his reliance upon a scientific method in constructing his theories of social organization. The man was Francis LePlay (1806–81).

LePlay was in his early life securely sheltered from the revolutionary influences dominant in France during the first quarter of the century. The biographical details, told with a curious mixture of naivete and complacency, can be found in the first section of *Les Ouvriers Européens*. The essence of the matter is that under the tutelage of priests, conservatives, and returned *émigrés* LePlay very early in life reached the central positions he was thereafter to maintain. "Returning to Honfleur in 1815, I noticed at once [at the age of nine!] the exactness of the teaching which the wisest of my Parisian masters had brought back from the emigration. I saw that the principal factors of happiness were religion, peace and national custom." [1] In brief, LePlay from the beginning, under the

1. Quotations in this section on LePlay are from his autobiography, the first 10 vols. of *La Réforme sociale* (Paris, 1881–85), and E. Demolins, *LePlay et son oeuvre* (Paris, Bureau de la Réforme Sociale, 1882).

EXPANSION OF SOCIOLOGICAL THEORY

influence of the church of which he was always a faithful member, was inclined to discount the part played by material conditions in bringing about social contentment and to emphasize moral influences; and this inclination was fixed by contacts with émigrés who agreed that the French Revolution was due to the moral lapses of the dominant and ruling classes before 1789.

These and similar notions were already fixed in LePlay's mind before he entered upon his engineering and mining studies, and they continued throughout them. He remained "indifferent to political passions"; "from taste and duty avoided the company" of students animated with revolutionary aspirations; "did not allow himself to be dazzled" by the lectures in the *Collège de France*. When the time came for him as a student of mining to make a tour of inspection, he persuaded his friend Jean Reynaud to select northern Germany as the region to be visited, for he "had not forgotten the accounts of the émigré who *in 1814* had pointed out Northern Germany" to him as "the home of wisdom," "the country of sensible social arrangements" (*la patrie de la sagesse*).

The pair returned after a tour of 6,800 kilometers in 200 days. They had not reached agreement upon "the social question." "We only understood that it was much more complicated than we had at first thought. I was strengthened in the idea that the solution would be found in the customs of the past. My friend, on the contrary, retained his convictions upon the doctrine of 'continuous progress,' and in general upon the help which the spirit of novelty and invention could give in this matter as in every other."

In 1830 came the frightful accident which all but deprived LePlay of his hands. "This hard apprenticeship of pain, complemented by a forced meditation, came to me as one of the decisive events of my career; it was then in fact that I formed the resolution to remedy as much as possible *the curses loosed in my country*. I vowed to devote six months of each year to traveling not only to study metallurgy but to investigate families and societies." "By reciting the story of my youth, I wish to prove that the method, the principal object of this volume, does not derive from a preconceived idea of my own. The fundamental impulse was of course an interest in understanding *the disasters which seemed widespread* in my own country."

LePlay seems quite unaware that his basic doctrines antedated his method. Demolins puts the matter somewhat more objectively when he says: "LePlay found the revelation of the method of monographs in a fact that his numerous observations *put in evidence,* namely, the true constitution of a people is in the ideas, the mores, and the institutions of private life rather than in written laws, private impressing its character on public life; the family being the principle of the State."

"From this point on, the manner of proceeding was quite naturally indicated. It was a matter of observing, in the least details, a certain number of families *to discover there* in their deepest source the causes of strength or weakness, of prosperity or decadence of nations. Thus limited to the family, the work of observation which would have been vague, indefinite, without possible conclusions, if it had been extended either to isolated individuals or to the mass of social facts, became precise and conclusive."

Only at the point reached in the two paragraphs preceding, which is obviously that occupied by de Maistre and de Bonald and a faithful reflection of the dependency of politics upon ethics, did the influence of LePlay's scientific training begin to operate.

> There must be, he thought, a criterion which permits the recognition, with all scientific evidence, of the causes of the prosperity or decadence of societies. This criterion cannot consist in theoretical and arbitrary inventions but in social facts methodically observed. Indeed, since there are laws for the society of bees and ants, there must be laws for the higher and more perfect society of men, and these laws cannot vary with place and times; they must be immutable and be recognizable by the sign that they always give rise to peace and stability. So then the problem is not to withdraw into the study but to traverse the world in order to gather facts, many facts, which when coordinated will have to give up the secret of human societies and the fundamental laws that peoples cannot infringe without falling into decadence and decomposition.

Here then was a need for a method; its source was no less clear than the need: "it was the one that thousands of savants had long been applying to the study of chemistry, physics and the various sciences of observation. The difficulty was to adapt it to the study of social

facts so varied and so complex that they seem to escape all scientific
analysis and methodical observation."

LePlay then, in accordance with his basic conceptions, developed
in the course of his professional activity, which led him often repeatedly into practically every country in Europe and once at least
into Asiatic Russia, a variant of observation so distinct as to have
gained a special name: the method of monographs. The basis of
this mode of inquiry is the conviction that the family is the true
social unit and the reasoned position that among families the worker's family is the truly significant one. The workers are not only
the most numerous element of the population, they are the most
important as being the great source of population; they are the most
revealing, for it is for them that finally the industry of society is carried on, and so they give the greatest insight into the truly capital
conditions of a community. The family is the place in which men
are born, fed, trained, i.e., the place where men are made.) Once a
typical worker's family in any agricultural or industrial region has
been selected, a minute investigation of its circumstances is undertaken.

The man, the worker, lives with his family in the place where
he works; from his labor, from the resources furnished by the
soil or by his *patron* or some other authority, he draws his means
of existence; this wage earned by labor, these resources *due to
the generosity of his master,* he spends for his daily needs, for
the upkeep of his family. His family exists not only in the present; however humble it may be it has a past and a future, a future which often depends upon his qualities, his energy, his labor, upon the protection accorded him. Besides, the family does
not live isolated in an inaccessible sphere, it is on the contrary
closely bound up with the locality where it is, it undergoes the
influence of the institutions which govern it, it shows pointedly
by its situation, the good or the bad side of these institutions.
Finally, all its life absorbed in the earning of daily bread is reflected at once in its receipts and its expenses.

Such is the natural scope of the monograph. It springs from
the very observation of facts and is in reality very simple, but
its simplicity is not of the sort which would have allowed it to

be reached, from the beginning, by the force of thought alone. One of the fundamental points of the method is the way in which it allows the study of the worker to be controlled and checked, i.e. by the budget, with its two parts, income and outgo. It contains a statistic of the life of the worker; it measures the phenomena of that life, and it makes possible complete confidence in the assertions contained in the other part of the monograph.

Upon the results acquired through many years' use of this monograph method, LePlay supported the generalizations which served him as the basis for his proposals for securing human welfare. Those general principles are condensed by LePlay's follower Demolins as follows:

When LePlay had applied the method of monographs to a great number of families, the social problem which had at the beginning of his travels seemed very complicated, took a very simple form. It had been demonstrated to him that peoples must provide for two essential and primordial needs, the satisfaction of which is for them an absolute necessity: *the teaching of moral law,* which represses in the individual the tendencies toward evil, and *the possession of daily bread,* which allows the needs of existence to be satisfied. Societies that fill these conditions are happy and prosperous; those that do not are unhappy and unfortunate.

Next, he saw that these two needs were satisfied by a series of uniform institutions always in operation among prosperous peoples. He designated these institutions by the term *essential constitution,* to indicate that there was no society possible without them, and he divided them into three groups under the names of *foundations, bonds,* and *materials.*

The two *foundations,* so-called because they form the base and substructure of the entire edifice, are the Decalogue, which complements the imperfect nature of man, by regulating the use of his free will; and *paternal authority* which imposes on the younger generations the practice of this moral law and performs the function of the domestic power.

These two fundamental institutions are solidified and protected by two other institutions which serve as *bonds.* These are the *clergy* and the *sovereign power;* the clergy having as its mission to teach the Decalogue and religion; the sovereign power, charged with the responsibility of complementing, in the larger world of public life, the authority of the father in private life.

But these elements concur only to maintain moral and material order, they do not satisfy the second need of men, the possession of daily bread. This is the role of the institutions that LePlay called the *materials* of the social edifice. They are: *primitive communism, individual property,* and *patronage.*

The latter are three forms of social organization, roughly chronological in order of appearance, the third the form especially suited to the present time.

Brief as it is, the foregoing summary is lengthy enough to show the fundamental bases of LePlay's position and the intellectual materials of which they are built. Clearly the monograph is an excellent instrument for gathering knowledge concerning the concrete, actual, practical conditions of everyday human life. Just as clearly however it is, as contrasted with the methods of Comte, a means of gathering the facts upon which generalizations and abstractions may later be built rather than of reaching those similitudes and sequences called laws. No *observational* process alone is adequate to the task of classifying, abstracting, isolating, and by induction reaching abstract relations among abstract phenomena. Such a method as LePlay's seems best suited for use in the presence of general doctrines already accepted rather than for discovering unknown ones. It is probably for this reason that for few sociological thinkers is it easier to make the distinction between doctrine and method.

Essentially, his sociology consists of a statical section based upon traditional doctrines and an observational method suited primarily for discovering to what extent the tradition has been departed from. LePlay's "great discovery" is that in social science "there is nothing to invent"; what is needed is merely observation, or at most a rediscovery of forgotten truths. There is no dynamics, then, in Comte's sense; the foundations of social existence lie too deep for change. "In all times and in all places, there are, beneath the changing forms of institutions and mores, certain conditions, immutable and permanent, like the very nature of mankind, to which is bound the maintenance of social peace."

Add to this doctrine the method and LePlay's sociology is complete. It is interested primarily in concrete details and analytical processes. The method particularly is intended to reveal the intimate secrets of daily life especially as they are reflected in monetary transactions of an inclusive kind. As a method of observation, presumably similar to that employed in the physical sciences, certain reservations might be made as regards its scientific genuineness. When it is strictly applied, two points at once become apparent: the doctrine may not be a consequence of the method; the method itself may be inadequate. On both these points divergence was to be produced among LePlay's followers.

Even while LePlay was still alive there was a tendency for his work to split apart, and it actually did so shortly after his death. On the one hand was the group which held to the doctrines of Le-Play and his church, for whom the monograph method revealed evil conditions to be destroyed or ameliorated, who thought therefore in terms of social reform and moved in the direction of the Encyclical *De Rerum Novarum* and similar pronouncements. This group centered about the periodical *La Réforme sociale* which Le-Play had founded; and the identification thereby made between LePlay and a particular doctrine, and theological at that, has been the probable cause of the hesitancy on the part of the sociological world to give LePlay greater attention than he has received.

At the same time there has always been a curious air of hesitancy on the side of the theological group in giving LePlay the hearty acceptance he would seem to deserve from them. The fact is of course that LePlay is not above suspicion. His wholehearted acceptance of the scientific point of view and his fashioning of a scientific tool for investigation into social phenomena give him a distinctly untheological aura, despite his constant use of the language of religion. His eager desire to lead communities to a happy existence is certainly harmless on the face of it; but his method has hidden dangers. The use of a tool is determined not by those who make it but by those who use it, and a method is in precisely the same case. The monograph method often leads into unexpected regions and to surprising conclusions. Science is quite impersonal; its conclusions can never be monopolized by any one school.

For these reasons there are contradictory elements in LePlay's work. There is the evident conviction of LePlay that the Christian family life of the mid-nineteenth century has a sort of static permanence; there is the conviction of the reader that such is not necessarily the case. The general formula of foundations, bonds, materials interpreted by LePlay in quite Christian, if not Catholic, terms has the air of a general condition which might be satisfied by any other well-knit and logically developed ethic. It might be applied to a Mohammedan or Buddhist or even communist society. The question at once arises which of these possible ways of satisfying the requirements of the formula is best; and the decision would have to be given on quite other than religious grounds.

No wonder then that there has always been a second tendency in LePlay's work which has attracted the attention of men not primarily interested in reform. For them the interest of LePlay was essentially in the method and the data it gave rise to, and the way in which generalizations of a far-reaching kind might be attained. Under the leadership of de Tourville and Demolins a group separated from the original founders of *La Réforme sociale* and only a few years after the death of LePlay founded *La Science sociale*. The point of difference from the first group is made clear in the very title of the new publication. In order to accent the scientific aspect of LePlay's work, the monograph was greatly enlarged; its insistence upon budgetary data was modified; a series of inquiries covering every aspect of a community was gradually built up and under the name of *The Nomenclature* was made into an admirable tool for investigation into the concrete aspects of the life of man in society.

Toward the end of the century, Patrick Geddes saw the possibility of uniting the abstract and general spirit of Comte with the practical and concrete interests of LePlay and worked out a series of correlations between work, place, and folk, the obvious consequence of the monograph method pushed to its logical limits. In this way and others the work of LePlay, nearly three generations after it had been begun, ceased to stand distinctly apart from the general line of sociological inquiry. Its concrete and analytical emphasis is a useful supplement and often a needed corrective to excessively theoretical and generalizing tendencies elsewhere. Just so is his insistence upon the static aspects of societal phenomena a useful counterpoise to excessive emphasis on the dynamic. But sociology cannot be made to consist of statics alone.

2. *Spencer*

What keeps the men of this chapter together is but one thing: the conviction that a science of society is possible, i.e., that the spirit and method of science can be applied to the study of social phenomena. Other than this, it is seemingly impossible to find any general classification that can be applied to the multitude of men who set out, each in his own way, to expand the theoretical boundaries of social science. Attempts have been made, of course, to classify them. Such efforts proceed seemingly on the assumption that classification of authors can precede an adequate analysis and classification of the material. It is as if the makers of these lists of theories sought an analysis of the subject by way of a study of the investigators. The attempt has not been successful; the method is doubtless defective. Here nothing of the kind is tried. The order of presentation is mainly chronological, with arbitrary variations.

Herbert Spencer (1820–1903), then, is the next in time and in order of treatment. In him the avowed, the professional philosopher appears upon the sociological scene, a philosopher who proposed to write a synthetic philosophy. The adjective seems unhappily chosen, for it is of the nature of philosophy to be synthetic; what Spencer sought to do was to make a synthesis of the results of scientific inquiry; his philosophy in this sense was to be quite as positive as Comte's. Now the first condition for a synthesis is some correlating principle. Where was Spencer to find such a scientific principle for correlating all knowledge when one part of it, the sociological, as Comte had shown, had not yet been raised to a scientific level? There was no such principle—none at least which could be shown to have arisen inductively out of the whole range of science.

Consequently Spencer, in all that concerns sociology, is in the position of the theological or metaphysical thinker in that he approaches the data—or more exactly in Spencer's case, the collection of the data—with a principle not derived from the inductive study of those data but drawn from the results of study in other fields and therefore, so far as sociology is concerned, with a synthesizing principle which is to be applied to it as truly as a metaphysical principle would have had to be applied. Spencer's contribution to the general development of scientific method, in Comte's sense, is therefore nil: he has but one all-inclusive method, applicable to all sciences indifferently. What he is concerned with in sociology is merely to show how a certain something called evolution which operates everywhere else also operates there.

But why *must* it operate there? To find the answer, it is necessary only to go back to the history of science for a moment. In 1750 when the need or possibility of a science of social phenomena was beginning to be seen, physiology was already on its way to biology, a general abstract science of all the phenomena of life, which it became around 1800. This new science had inherited a highly developed animal series which arranged the forms of life in an ascending scale. The original and purely logical relationship of the series was rapidly becoming a chronological sequence and then a genealogical evolution in the theories that developed on the one hand from Buffon through Lamarck and Erasmus Darwin and from the geologists on the other. The earth, the latter showed, had evolved and was still evolving; life too in all its forms was evolving, this evolution having finally produced Man, who in his turn had produced society. The thought, in a deistic interpretation, was well known before Darwin. Evolution was rapidly becoming the key word, the master concept in the first half of the 1800's; its operation was universal, from the making of worlds and the world to the making of Man, his mind and society.

Here then was the approach to knowledge which Spencer had been maturing for years, even before his essay of 1856 on *Progress: Its Law and Cause.* This development hypothesis, as he termed it, went on developing in his mind until it became a truly universal principle covering the entire range of phenomena accessible to man. Hence the only matter of interest in a methodological aspect to a reader of Spencer as the reader passes from one level of the synthesis to another is the question, How will the theory of evolution be applied next?

Actually the answer to this question as it is found in the three volumes of the *Philosophy* which are devoted to sociology is very simple, as are the arguments on which it rests: "Those who have been brought up in the belief that there is one law for the rest of

the Universe and another law for mankind, will doubtless be aston-
ished by the proposal to include aggregates of man" in any generalization which puts man along with the rest, even the general
truth that "the character of the aggregate is determined by the characters of the units." "And yet that the properties of the units determine the properties of the whole they make up, evidently holds of
societies as of other things. A general survey of tribes and nations,
past and present, shows clearly enough that it is so." [2]

"Setting out with this general principle that the properties of
the units determine the properties of the aggregate, we conclude
that there must be a Social Science expressing the relations between
the two, with as much definiteness as the natures of the phenomena
permit." Such a science "in every case . . . has for its subject-matter the growth, development, structure, and functions of the social
aggregate." "We cannot fail to see that the phenomena of *incorporated human nature* form the subject-matter of a science." [3] That
is to say, the nature of the strictly individual, unincorporated human being is known from biology and psychology; the aggregated,
incorporated resultants arising when individuals are combined in
societies will be the domain of sociology.

So does Spencer express himself in *The Study of Sociology* of
1872, the volume which in the English-speaking world has probably done more than any other to draw men's minds to the study
of sociology—more even, it may be, than the three volumes on
Sociology themselves. But there is a curiously metaphysical ring
about "one law for the universe" and therefore one law, the same
law, for man. It seems to justify the opinion that in Spencer the
metaphysical type of philosophy meets its ultimate reduction. Beyond it lies only the positive type exemplified in Comte.

Given then a general or, more accurately, a universal principle
of evolution, Spencer enters upon his sociology with a systematization of the facts which account for social life, the data of sociology.
"Be it rudimentary or be it advanced, every society displays phenomena that are ascribable to the characters of its units and to the

---

2. H. Spencer, *The Study of Sociology* (New York, Appleton, 1924), pp. 45,
43, 45.
3. Spencer, *The Study of Sociology,* pp. 47, 53.

conditions under which they exist." [4] First, the *extrinsic* factors of social evolution must be known. They are several, variously operative: climate, surface and configuration of surface, flora and fauna. "On these sets of conditions, inorganic and organic, characterizing the environment, primarily depends the possibility of social evolution." [5]

What then are the *intrinsic* factors of social evolution? They are the characteristics of the individual men and women of which the society in the last analysis is composed. "When we turn to the intrinsic factors we have to note first, that, considered as a social unit, the individual man has physical traits, such as degrees of strength, activity, endurance, which affect the growth and structure of the society. He is in every case distinguished by emotional traits which aid, or hinder, or modify, the activities of the society and its developments. Always, too, his degree of intelligence and the tendencies of thought peculiar to him, become cooperating causes of social quiescence or social change." [6] In other words, the physical and psychical characteristics of the individuals who are to make up the future society must be known.

Sociology, that is, is still in the realm of moral philosophy, moving from the individual—biological and psychical—to the social. When the intrinsic factors have been duly ascertained, then the units will be sure to be found in possession of certain elementary ideas and be moved by the feelings aroused by them. It would seem that Spencer was arguing directly from psychical characteristics to the existence of certain elementary cultural phenomena. At any rate he gives the greater part of Book I to such phenomena, notably the ghost basis of religion. When these elementary ideas have been described at length, Spencer concludes his *Data* with the words: "Setting out with social units as thus conditioned, as thus constituted physically, emotionally, and intellectually, and as thus possessed of certain early acquired notions and correlative feelings, the Science of Sociology has to give an account of all the phenomena that result from their combined actions." [7] The words form a some-

4. H. Spencer, *Principles of Sociology* (3 vols. New York, Appleton, 1892), *1*, 18–19.

5. Spencer, *Principles of Sociology*, *1*, 9.

6. Spencer, *Principles of Sociology*, *1*, 9.

7. *Principles of Sociology*, *1*, 437.

what surprising conclusion. They certainly seem to say that sociology is to be not an inductive but a deductive science.

In any case, the data upon which sociology is to operate are clear. The next question is whether there are any directive principles in operation among sociological phenomena and if so how they have been found. Here, then, would seem to be the place for an inductive study establishing the operation of evolution in society and societies. It is the place for such a study and Spencer goes at it, but with an unexpected twist. The reader's surprise is due to Spencer's lapse from the rigor of scientific reasoning. He does not go directly to societal phenomena to demonstrate by inductive procedures that evolution is operative there; he knows that it must be, since evolution is universal; his reasoning at this point follows a different path.

Yet there is still fidelity on his part to inductive procedures. He subordinates the "if" of social evolution to the "how" of it and in the answer to the latter finds adequate support for his position. How, he asks, does evolution work in societies? Induction will supply the answer, which is: just as it does in organisms, with only such differences as are to be detected between the organism, the biological being, and the superorganism, the social being. The reasoning is as follows: if the social aggregate composed of biological units could be shown by induction to be essentially an organism, then induction would have served its purpose, for all the knowledge already possessed as to the evolution of organisms could be used as a guide in studying the evolution of societies. In this way it would seem does Spencer avoid, or evade, the necessity of building a sociology on its own inductive basis. It is enough for him that inductive evidence shows that societies are essentially organic in nature; therefore biological doctrines of evolution can be carried over, with modifications, to the domain of sociology.

"Let us now sum up the reasons for regarding society as an organism." And at this point Spencer's ever vigorous insistence upon the inductive basis of his thought can be understood. These reasons have all been inductively established.

It undergoes continuous growth. As it grows, its parts become unlike; it exhibits increase of structure. The unlike parts simultaneously assume activities of unlike kinds. These activities are not simply different, but their differences are so related as to make one another possible. The reciprocal aid thus given causes mutual dependence of the parts. And the mutually dependent parts, living by and for one another, form an aggregate constituted on the same general principle as is an individual organism. . . . Though the two are contrasted as respectively discrete and concrete, and though there results a difference in the ends subserved by the organization, *there does not result a difference in the laws of the organization:* the required mutual influence of the parts, not transmissible in a direct way, being, in a society, transmitted in an indirect way.[8]

The lines italicized above are the key to Spencer's position: his induction, based upon a study of "the entire assemblage of societies," shows there are not sufficient differences between the biological organism, or organism proper, and the sociological organism, the superorganism, to negate the possibility of using the knowledge of evolution gained in the one as a proof and guide to the understanding of the evolution of the other. All that is required is an adequate checking by reference to sociological facts to prevent the analogy from being slavishly followed. "But let us now drop this alleged parallelism between individual organizations and social organizations. I have used the analogies elaborated, but as a scaffolding to help in building up a coherent body of sociological inductions. Let us take away the scaffolding: the inductions will stand by themselves." And in conclusion Spencer clears away the doubt as to method raised a few paragraphs above: "The inductions arrived at . . . show that in social phenomena there is a general order of co-existence and of sequence; and that therefore social phenomena form the subject matter of a science reducible, in some measure at least, to the *deductive* form." [9]

The conclusion is at first surprising, it is so much at variance with the notions of the proper method of sociology explicit or implicit in the work of almost the whole range of sociologists. Yet the conclusion should not be unexpected by anyone who remembers that Spencer's method is one: no matter what the body of phenomena in point may be, evolution—as defined by Spencer—is

8. *Principles of Sociology, 1,* 462.
9. *Principles of Sociology, 1,* 592–593, 597.

the master key. In sociology, then, given the extrinsic conditions, the intrinsic conditions, the elementary ideas of man, and the general laws of evolution as they are found in the organic and therefore in the superorganic world—given these, the task of giving an account of all of the phenomena that result from their combined actions *is* deductive in method and social in content.

From this point of view Spencer goes on to analyze the life of the superorganism and then to follow the evolution of the domestic and other institutions of which social life is composed. His work is thus rather a sociogeny than a sociology.

Considered as a whole, the influence of Spencer's work in sociology has been great; scarcely a writer of the generation following his own was not affected by one or more aspects of his work. This influence, though greatest in the English-speaking world, especially outside England, was not limited to that world, as the example of Worms in France makes evident. Yet the Spencerian period in sociological development seems definitely over. The notion of a deductive sociology has found no wide acceptance; the biological parallelism is rejected; the universal evolution defined by Spencer is gone. Even so, he marks a distinct epoch in the development of the science. His reliance upon anthropological data to an unprecedented degree is evidence alone of his importance. More than one writer has found stimulus and support in his massing of facts. Perhaps his very deficiences were aids in his time to ready acceptance. The absence of theoretical discussion, the neglect of methodological refinements, the reliance upon an evolutionary theory generally accepted, even if not in his special sense, all helped to gain acceptance for the general notion of a science of societies, of social phenomena.

3. Ward

Influenced greatly by both Comte and Spencer was Lester Frank Ward (1841–1913), the American paleobotanist, last of the synthetic minds characteristic of the early period of sociological thought. Ward was one of those who most strongly emphasized the possibility of applying the results of sociological research to the improvement of society. Obviously this position implies a preliminary study of social phenomena inspired by a single-minded desire to make secure the theoretical foundations on which ameliorative efforts can be based. There were therefore for Ward two aspects of sociological thought: the pure, which is exclusively devoted to securing data and inferences of an unchallengeable kind; and the applied, which utilizes the results of the pure science for social modification. The systematic presentation of this distinction is found in Ward's two volumes, *Pure Sociology* and *Applied Sociology*.

The *Pure Sociology* deals with a distinction between two kinds of social development, the genetic and the telic.

> There are two ways in which the social energy has been controlled, the one an unconscious process comparable to that of organic evolution, . . . the other conscious, and wholly unlike the first. . . . [The latter] is the telic method or social telesis. Through the unconscious or genetic method—social genesis—all the fundamental social structures or human institutions were formed or constructed, and under the operations [of the principles already considered], these structures were enabled to change and social progress was made possible. Moreover, . . . a certain degree of socialization was achieved and civilization was carried forward to a certain stage. It only required the addition of the telic or directive agent to make possible all the higher steps that have been taken practically in the same direction.[10]

"Just as pure sociology aims to answer the questions What, Why, and How; so applied sociology aims to answer the question What for? The former deals with facts, causes, and principles, the latter with the object, end, or purpose. The one treats the subject-matter of sociology; the other, its use." [11]

But what then *is* the subject matter of the science?

> My thesis is that the subject-matter of sociology is human *achievement*. It is not what men are, but what they do. . . . To be less technical, but really to repeat the same thing, sociology is concerned with social *activities*. It is a study of action, *i.e.*, of *phenomena*. It is not a descriptive science in the naturalist's sense—a science that describes objects looked upon as finished products. It is rather a study of how the various social products

10. L. F. Ward, *Pure Sociology* (New York, Macmillan, 1925), p. 463.
11. L. F. Ward, *Applied Sociology* (Boston & New York, Ginn, 1906), p. 5.

have been created. These products once formed become permanent. They are never lost. They may be slowly modified and perfected, but they constitute the basis for new products, and so on indefinitely.[12]

In these and other passages found in the opening sections of the *Pure Sociology,* Ward seems to have caught sight once for all of a true abstract datum for sociology, if not a genuine isolate. The reader of the opening chapters is undoubtedly led to expect a full consideration of achievement in the remainder of the volume. Of what would a treatise on sociology treat if not of its subject matter? Curiously enough, however, nothing of the kind occurs. Instead, the matter of achievement receives almost incidental treatment in the succeeding chapters of the volume. What is the explanation for what is surely a singular deviation from the straight path of logical development? The best answer is found in the following quotation: "Feeling is a true cosmic force and constitutes the propelling agent in animals and in man. In the associated state of man it is the social force, and with it the sociologist must deal. Under this agency social phenomena take place according to uniform laws which may be studied in the same way that the laws of any other domain of phenomena are studied. Sociology is thus a true science, answering to the definition of a science, viz., a field of phenomena produced by true natural forces and conforming to uniform laws." And this position is complemented as follows: "By pure sociology . . . is meant a treatment of the phenomena and laws of society as it is, an explanation of the processes by which social phenomena take place, a search for the antecedent conditions by which the observed facts have been brought into existence, and an aetiological diagnosis that shall reach back as far as the state of human knowledge will permit into the psychologic, biologic, and cosmic causes of the existing social state of man." [13]

There seems to be a confusion of thought here. Thus after having caught sight of an essential aspect of sociological phenomena suggested of course by Comte's insistence upon the cumulative effect of the succession of generations, Ward, instead of making this phenomenon the basis of his study as he seems to the reader to be

12. Ward, *Pure Sociology,* pp. 15–16. (Italics are Ward's.)
13. Ward, *Pure Sociology,* pp. 99, 4.

about to do, turns aside to explain *why* it is that man is an achieve-
ment-making animal. He deals therefore in the greater part of the
volume with what he calls the social forces, the psychic factors lying
behind the actions which result in achievements. Thus the avowed
subject matter of sociology—a subject matter which is clearly not
a psychological phenomenon at all—is set aside for the discussion
of the basic drives of human nature, a matter which is clearly within
the scope of psychology. It is as if a chemist should say that the basic
subject matter of his science is the elements and the affinities between them and the results of their combinations and should then
devote the remainder of his treatise to explaining why these affinities exist.

In the second place, and to complicate matters still more, Ward
after having caught sight of one of Comte's basic conceptions is then
influenced by Spencer's conception of the task that sociology should
perform. "An aetiological diagnosis that shall reach back as far as
the state of human knowledge will permit into the psychologic,
biologic, and cosmic causes of the existing social state of man"—
such a statement of the objective of sociology is thoroughly in the
spirit of Spencer and his conception of sociology as a deductive science. It would seem that Ward never made a genuine synthesis of his
two predecessors in his own mind. In fact, it is impossible to do so.
Comte is primarily interested in seizing upon an isolated class of
abstract phenomena and discovering the abstract relations and uniformities they present; Spencer, in explaining the existence of a
group of concrete facts and following their development in combination. Ward varies between the two.

It is unlikely that anyone at the time could have avoided the confusion which Ward seems to reveal; the fact is that even today the
analysis upon which a demarcation between such closely related
domains as the sociological and the psychological is still incomplete.
It is pointless to criticize Ward for a failure to see what has not yet
become clearly visible. It is by dealing with such difficulties as are
implicit in his work that advances in science, sociological or other,
are made. It seems to be a fact that the most complete explanation
of the urges which lie behind human achievement would never explain the essential nature of achievement nor show the ways in
which it grows nor reveal the uniformities, if any, in its growth.
That Ward was nevertheless so entirely convinced of the necessity

of showing that sociology is a science because it has a field of phenomena produced by true natural forces is only an illustration of the defensive attitude forced upon sociologists only a few decades ago.

Whatever Ward failed to do, he certainly did arouse men to an interest in sociology by showing its possibilities and stimulating their emotions with a vision of mankind where each individual participated to the extent of his ability in the whole heritage of the race. "The socialization of achievement" is still one of the most expressive formulations of the aims of sociology once it passes from the pure to the applied stage, and society instead of undergoing a spontaneous genesis can actively enter upon a state of systematic telesis.

4. Gumplowicz

By Ward's time—his *Dynamic Sociology* dates from 1883—the number of those who see the new science in a comprehensive fashion is increasing. Among such men is Ludwig Gumplowicz (1838–1909). In his work the expansion of sociological theory is well exemplified, despite or even because of the fact that he makes no strikingly original addition to it.

He illustrates to begin with the widening of the intellectual basis on which sociology is to rest. His *Grundriss der Sociologie* in its introductory pages names Comte and Spencer first, of course. To them he adds as minor influences Quetelet, Holbach, Schaeffle, de Roberty and as major influences Bastian and Lippert. Then come such contributory sources as political science and national economy, for example, with men like Stein, Mohl and Gneist, Manger, Carey, and the socialists, all with a certain emphasis upon economic factors in social causation; the philosophy of history, with Rocholl; the history of civilization, "agent of the transition from the philosophy of history to sociology," with Kolb, Henne am Rhyn, and Hellwald; the study of prehistory, with Lubbock, Tyler, and Caspari; anthropology and ethnography, with Waitz-Gerland, Perty, and Peschel: with such growing sources of information sociology, says Gumplowicz rightly, is not lacking in materials; what is needed is untiring work.

He illustrates too the increase in the precision of basic definitions. The *Grundriss* begins with the conventional classification of phenomena: the inorganic, the organic, the psychic. But where, it asks, do *social* phenomena fit into this scheme? They cannot be ranked among the first or the second, since they have the characters of neither the inanimate nor the animate; besides, society can no longer be considered as an organism. They do not emanate from the individual soul and so it is difficult to see how social phenomena are a subdivision of the psychic. They have differentiating characters; they are never produced except through a collaboration of a plurality of men, whereas the phenomena properly called psychical (*schlechtweg geistige genannten*) cleave to the mind (*geist*) of the individual, where they have their point of departure and their sole terrain.

Social phenomena, as distinguished from the psychical, are all the relations of men with one another: political, juridical, and economic. Their distinguishing characteristic is that *a plurality of men* is their indispensable preliminary condition. Without this plurality there can be no social phenomena.

> In truth and to go to the bottom of things, the world about us is one. Every divisioning of its phenomena is only a means for getting to know it: thus there is in principle only *one* science, proposing to discover the laws of these phenomena (the discovery of the laws by which are regulated the succession and development of phenomena being the essential business of science). But along with the distinguishing of phenomena into several groups and the need for a division of labor in the domain of knowledge, a corresponding division of science into several classes, which would each take as its object a special kind of phenomena, was at an early period recognized as desirable, and undertaken.[14]

The notion of a scientific isolate is implicit, but not more, in Gumplowicz's thought.

The recognition of a new class of phenomena is thus only an extension of a process long in operation. Social is the characteristic quality of the new class. But are there laws in this newly recognized domain? Are there, that is, phenomena within its scope which succeed one another or which coexist always in the same form with the

14. L. Gumplowicz, *Grundriss der Sociologie* (Vienna, 1885), p. 56.

result that they can be attributed to a higher fictitious will? "Without social laws, no social science." [15]

The answer is yes. There are, decidedly, recurring social uniformities. "The relation of social groups with one another, the formation of social communities, their development and decline, incontestably present a series of such uniformities. We can therefore justifiably undertake the task, in the social domain, of drawing up the simplest formulas of these uniformities, of discovering, that is, social laws." [16]

For Gumplowicz, then, "social phenomena are the relations which come to be by virtue of the operation of human groups and communities upon one another. These groups and communities constitute the social *elements* of these relationships. The earliest and simplest social elements must have been the primitive human hordes, which once, in early days, must have existed in great numbers." [17] Gumplowicz is here evidently thinking of precultural, prehuman beings living in bands on a purely biological level like the higher apes.

"All the later and more extended combinations and complications of these simplest social elements into larger communities, tribes, clans, peoples, states and nations are just so many social phenomena." There are, besides,

the socialpsychical phenomena, which occur in consequence of social co-operations and of their influence upon the individual mind, such for example as Speech, Mores, Law, Religion, etc. The territory of sociology extends over all these phenomena; it has . . . to show the working of social laws in their development.

All the various groups of phenomena have been taken as the objects of independent sciences; the fact will not prevent sociology from studying them from the social science point of view. The majority of them, up to the present have been studied only from an exclusively individualistic point of view. It is precisely the task of sociology to study the *social* origin of these groups

15. Gumplowicz, p. 57.
16. Gumplowicz, p. 57.
17. Pp. 71–72.

of phenomena, to bring into the light the social fashion of their production and the social laws of their development.[18]

People naively believe that the human race is a genealogical unit and consider this unit, i.e., mankind to develop spontaneously like a vegetal or animal organism. They speak easily of transitions from hunting to pastoral life, from cattle raising to agriculture, to war and so on to industrialism and imagine a single social group traversing the different stages of civilization in accordance with an inner law of development and by virtue of an immanent tendency toward development. They are in error; they forget one fact: there is a law of inertia operative in social groups as in all natural beings and objects; and so when these groups find themselves immobile in a certain social state, they cannot pass to another state except as the effect of adequate social causes and influences.

"In other words, no change in the state of a social group can be effected without a *sufficient social cause* and this cause is always an action exercised by another social group. History and observation furnish us with sufficient proofs of this law: whence results a rule important for the *method* of sociological investigation: every time a change in the state of a social group is shown, the question arises by what intervention of another group has the change been produced." [19]

Thus does Gumplowicz arrive at the essence and the nature of a social process. Such process is always evident when two or more heterogeneous social groups come into contact and penetrate into one another's sphere of action. A homogeneous social group remains in its original animal state so long as it is not reached by the influence of another group and cannot itself exercise action upon another group. Hence it comes about that in some isolated corners of the globe hordes are still met with in the primitive state of their ancestors millions of years ago. There is to be seen in such cases an elementary, primitive, social phenomenon or, better, a social element but not a social process nor therefore a social development.

The play of the natural forces which constitutes the social process begins from the moment when a social group is sub-

18. Gumplowicz, p. 72.
19. Gumplowicz, p. 73.

jected to the action of another, from the moment when the first enters into the sphere of action of the second. What everywhere and always gives the first impulsion to this process is the natural tendency of each of them to exploit the other—a tendency so inherent in every human group, so natural and irrepressible that it is absolutely unthinkable that two social groups should ever meet without its coming into evidence and, consequently, without the social process beginning.[20]

But no question of beginnings in the sense of first appearance is here involved. Sociology starts with mankind as it is, composed, as can be irrefutably shown, of an extremely great number of heterogeneous social groups. How this state came to be is not within sociological competence. "The discovery of Copernicus concerns only the laws of the natural course of the planets, their movements of deplacement; it is not concerned with their appearance; the discovery of the circulation of blood by Harvey is limited to a process which goes on under one's eyes; it is not encumbered with the creation of man." [21]

Into the details of Gumplowicz's sociological doctrines there is no need here to go. The essential point is that the Austrian theorist had a subject matter and a method and so the basis for a science. Sociology, in his conception, gives up the effort to embrace the whole of the history of mankind. It contents itself with studying the process whereby are elaborated human associations. "It is *therefore* not occupied with the significance of the general course of history, which it does not know; it is content with establishing the regularity of this course, with studying the fashion whereby social development is effected, and so, in brief, to set forth the regular processes which, arising from a given contact between human societies, develop in virtue of these reciprocal contacts and reactions." [22]

There is no development of mankind. There is only a social development within the ranks of the human race. Always this develop-

20. Gumplowicz, p. 74.
21. Gumplowicz, p. 75.
22. Gumplowicz, pp. 217–219.

ment begins wherever are found or are established the necessary and adequate social conditions. It operates regularly up to the final point where, finding no longer the requisite conditions, it slows up and stops. In its operations it gives rise to groups, circles, classes, professional bodies, societies, and states. The term "society" has served its time and may be dropped. There are only societies, i.e., the numerous groups, circles, classes, etc., in their reciprocal actions or reactions, the word applying not only to the various social groups within the state but also to circles having interests and relations beyond.

Finally certain implications of sociological theory are made explicit once for all, for example the profound influence of the social upon the individual. "The greatest error of the individualist psychology," says Gumplowicz, "is to admit that *man* thinks. From this error there results the unceasing search in the individual for the source of thought and the causes for his thinking as he does and not otherwise. But *what thinks in man is not the man but the social community;* the source of his thoughts is not in him, it is in the milieu where he lives, in the social atmosphere he breathes; he can think only in the light of and by virtue of the influences of his social milieu, such as his brain concentrates them." "The intellect of man is always the same; it moves within a sphere whose surface is fixed and inexpansible. . . . Later generations work, not with superior or more perfect intellects, but with the more considerable resources accumulated by the preceding generations; having better tools, so to speak, they obtain greater successes." [23]

5. Small and Ratzenhofer

It was no doubt worth while giving Gumplowicz a perhaps disproportionate space if only to show how far the development of sociological thought had proceeded by the beginning of the last quarter of the 1800's. Especially noteworthy is the continuous expansion of the factual and conceptual basis upon which the growing science might rest. Gumplowicz in the introductory section of his *Grundriss* makes the matter clear; another sociologist, this time an American, goes even farther in the same direction. Not only does he name the authors who were gradually building up a social view-

23. Pp. 167, 223.

point in historical and related studies, he also goes on to show that the emergence of a sociological science was only a matter of time. The author of course is Albion Woodbury Small (1854–1926) and the volume in which the emergence of sociology is recounted is his *Origins of Sociology*.

What Small did in his volume was a sociological rather than an historical achievement. He planned to give, and did give, not an account of the men who actually strove to realize a sociology but a statement of the influences which were turning men's minds inevitably in the direction of sociological inquiry. It was in other words a sociological explanation of the rise of sociology, with particular reference to American conditions. His purpose was to show "the vital connections between sociology and the whole modern unfolding of social science," to make clear to sociologists that "their specialty came into existence as an organic part of this maturing of social science as a whole." [24]

The line of thought is clear: "during the nineteenth century, the social sciences were half-consciously engaged in a drive from relatively irresponsible discursiveness toward 'positivity' or 'objectivity.' . . . the initiation of the American Sociological Movement was as truly a lineal continuance from the previous tradition of social interpretation as was any other of the tendencies which varied the technique of historiography, or economics, or political science." "The most easily authenticated line of descent, between pre-scientific social rationalizings and the sociological branch of positivistic social science, is through the German historians, and economists, and political scientists." Hence Small's volume traced "almost exclusively that succession of antecedents and consequents." [25]

Yet the fact that the links are more easily traced there than elsewhere does not mean that the movement was a strictly German one; it is merely that "the relations of the rapid developments in different divisions of social science to one another are more obvious in German scholarship than elsewhere, and they accordingly are most available for exposition of an evolution which followed parallel or converging courses throughout the Western World." [26] In other

24. A. W. Small, *The Origins of Sociology* (Chicago, University of Chicago Press, 1924), pp. 13, 14.
25. Small, pp. v, v–vi, vi.
26. Small, p. 15.

words, the development of sociology in some form was a certainty. As the cultural sociologist would put it, the elements of the invention were present in the culture base and they were certain to be combined in one or several ways.

What then were the intellectual developments occurring in Germany between 1800 and 1880 which produced a climate of opinion favorable to the growth of social science? First in order was the awakening of the historical spirit or, more accurately, the rise of a critical spirit in relation to what was called history and its outcome in historical criticism. Of the historians moving in the direction of a greater objectivity Small cites four: Savigny, with whom is associated the idea of continuity in human experience; Eichhorn and the insistence upon the complexity of social life; Niebuhr with his demand for subjecting alleged evidence to the severest scrutiny; von Ranke and the demand for verification of historical data by reference to documentary evidence.

After the historians came the political scientists. "With the exception of history, the social sciences in the modern sense have their origin in Germany in the theory of government." [27] Here the beginnings of objectivity come in the body of social theory known as cameralism, raising the question, How may states secure a sufficient supply of ready means, i.e., money? Out of the discussions aroused by the combining of Adam Smith with the older theorists came the economic development exemplified by Roscher, exponent of the historical method; Menger, founder of the Austrian school with its emphasis on psychology; Knies, emphasizing the moral aspects of social relations; on the political side von Mohl, distinguishing between society and state; and others.

"Few historical facts are better attested than that the tradition which we have sketched was at once transmitted to the United States." [28] There the influence of Spencer was direct and Comte's example through Ward's writings was indirect, but both of the earlier writers aided in giving a definite form to the new tendencies. Nevertheless, even without them nothing in Small's opinion was more certain than the rise in America of a *general* social science. "Not as patterns, but more as tonics, these ideas actually entered into the formation of a distinct tendency in social science which

27. Small, p. 110.
28. Small, p. 325.

German professors presently, partly in ridicule, partly in admiration, referred to as the 'American Science.' If there had been no other impulse to innovation, the stimuli which we have described would have been enough." [29]

Of course there were other impulses, as Small himself most clearly reveals. They can best be discovered by an analysis of his work. The theories that Small's name recalls to the mind of the historical student of sociology are to be found in continued and coherent expression mainly in his volume of 1905 entitled *General Sociology*.

To begin with, then, what is the special significance of the title *General Sociology*? By emphasizing this aspect of the nature of sociology Small raises a question which must at some time be faced by sociologists, namely, the relation between their discipline and those historically accredited to such other types of inquiry into social phenomena as economics, political economy, history, etc., all of which were earlier to develop than sociology. Small's position on this much discussed question is clear: economics, politics, linguistics, ethics, religion, history are all *special* social sciences, special in that they occupy themselves only with specific aspects of culture or the life process of society, whereas sociology seeks to explain the process insofar as in its wide outlines it is capable of a general explanation.

What then is the basis for such a general explanation? At this point Small draws upon a number of his predecessors for an answer. Among them Spencer, Schaeffle, and Ratzenhofer are the most important. Of the three Small finds the last mentioned to be most suggestive. Thus a new name is brought into the record.

Gustav Ratzenhofer (1842–1904) presents a problem to the historian of sociology. How important is he in the development of the science? And what were his theories? No one is more in need of original firsthand study. For the present volume the Ratzenhofer dealt with is the Ratzenhofer of Small, for it is this sociologist, however he may differ from the original, who has been influential in relation to sociological theory, especially in the United States.

For Small's Ratzenhofer, then, "sociology is 'the science of the reciprocal relationships of human beings.' It is these human reciprocal relations that constitute its phenomena and [they are capable of being treated scientifically because] they are [subject to] 'a

29. P. 328.

regularity which is immediately contained in no other order of regularity.' " [30] Human beings are brought together for the satisfaction of interests, and so upon interests Ratzenhofer builds his science. Back of all the structural or even functional relations of society there stand the interests of the individuals who compose the group, and these when analyzed in turn will explain all structure and function. "Social life is a huge mass or bundle of interests, and society is formed through the constant conflict, adaptation, and reciprocal interplay of the interests of individuals." [31]

From this logical starting point Small proceeds, first revising Ratzenhofer's analysis of interests: "The individual accepted by the sociologist as his working unit is the human person endowed with interests which manifest themselves as desires for health, wealth, sociability, knowledge, beauty and rightness." [32] Because of their variations of interests, people are drawn into innumerable varieties of arrangements. These arrangements bring about such close relations between numbers of people that the individuals so related must be thought of together as one. Under such circumstances they form a group, which thus becomes the center of sociological interest.

> Whatever social problem we confront, whatever persons come into our field of view, the first questions involved will always be: To what groups do these persons belong? What are the interests of these groups? What sort of means do the groups use to promote their interests? How strong are these groups as compared with groups that have conflicting interests? These questions go to the tap-root of all social interpretation, whether in the case of historical events in the past, or of the most practical problems of our own neighborhood. We have to understand the whole tangle of group-interests in which the persons are involved, in order to deal with the rudiments of the problem which the group presents.[33]

It is in the light of such a paragraph as the foregoing that the general drift of Small's thinking in later years becomes apparent. Be-

30. J. P. Lichtenberger, *Development of Social Theory* (New York & London, Century, 1925), p. 443.

31. Lichtenberger, pp. 457–458.

32. A. W. Small, *General Sociology* (Chicago, University of Chicago Press, 1905), p. 447.

33. Small, *General Sociology*, p. 497.

ginning with an emphasis upon the group as a key to the understanding of society, he came gradually to see that society was not a "thing" at all. "It has gradually resolved itself into a near-infinity of group relationships and processes. Accordingly, the procedure, the technique, which sociologists have found themselves obliged to invent, has turned out to be mental tools for detecting and interpreting all sorts of group phenomena." [34] And so he was able to declare with approval after twenty-five years of reflection: "The American sociological movement has become an assemblage of techniques for investigating the part which the group factor has played, the part which the group factor is playing, in different areas of human experience." [35] It was still a general science, however, for it covers in its own way the whole ground covered by all the various sciences devoted each to some one aspect of the whole mass of human relationships.

6. Sumner

Another American who studied in Germany and brought back with him a distinct influence is William Graham Sumner (1840–1910). Trained as a clergyman of the Episcopal church, his deeper interests finally carried him into the professorate. He gave most attention to economics and politics at the beginning of his professorial career. His study in Germany, however, had given him still another and even deeper interest, which the work of Spencer served to stimulate. The immediate source of this interest was the work of Lippert on the subject then known in Germany as *Kulturgeschichte,* with its basis in anthropology.

The influence of anthropological investigation has already been mentioned several times in this narrative. It began at least as early as Montesquieu and in DeBrosses Comte found in the word *fétichisme* the name for the first of his three states. As a systematic study it came to organized form in Tyler in the middle of the 1800's and was of course the basis of much of Spencer's sociological work. In its initial phases anthropology was mainly physical, devoting itself to descriptions of the more or less primitive peoples brought to the

34. *Origins,* p. 337.
35. *Origins,* p. v.

notice of the European world during and after the period of exploration and colonization. The study of physical characteristics, traits of a purely physical kind, shows that they are often associated with and even caused by equally characteristic traits of the social life of the community. It was logically inevitable, then, that the study of the physical characteristics of a group should finally involve the entire life of the community.

Under the term "culture" the sum total of the traits of a given group, its entire response to the life situation began to be the center of interest. The various cultures of ethnically different peoples, especially those that had no history in the usual sense, came more and more to hold the attention of observers. The study and analysis of specific cases gave rise as always to generalizations, and the word "culture" came to be used in a general and increasingly abstract sense. It was soon seen that many if not all of the most characteristic phases of this generalized culture had come into being in the most primitive groups and were only developed more fully in their successors; hence the conclusion that these cultural developments, being basic to social life, were more important than the more obvious changes in rulers, dynasties, empires. The word thus gradually grew to include the entire sum of adjustments, material and mental, that had been developed by man in all times and places, so that the phrase "the culture of mankind" finally arose to mark the ultimate extension of an idea that had begun with reference only to a particular tribe at a particular place and time.

Obviously it is possible to take an historical interest relative to the development of culture as a whole; and this the culture historians did. It was in Germany that this development was most marked, and it was there that Sumner began his attention to the subject, under the influence of Lippert. The addition of a great and growing mass of information concerning the earlier developments of the historical civilization to the increasing sum of data concerning the primitives made possible the conception that the best source of knowledge regarding social phenomena lay in the field of culture, especially in its earlier phases. Not only was this position sound as regards the mass of data, it was justified also by the relative ease with which the investigator of long past or faraway societies could avoid the emotional toils in which an observer of contemporary events is likely to be caught.. Struck by these advantages, Sumner began to utilize the data of anthropology and culture history in the composition of *The Science of Society*.

It is to be noted in passing that Sumner refused to employ the word "sociology," for reasons that are quite understandable. As a result of the indetermination of the word in the post-Comte, post-*Philosophie* period, it had fallen into the hands of all sorts of intellectual adventurers, careless thinkers, well-meaning philanthropists, and hard-working scholars each of whom used the term in accordance with his own interests, wishes, charities, or discoveries. It came to have no fixed meaning and so both name and subject came to be open to severe criticism, and rightly. Sumner sought to dissociate himself from it and its connotations by using the term "science of society."

Nevertheless, with all his efforts Sumner was unable to find a more satisfactory term and was never able to dispense with the adjective "sociological." Both noun and adjective are in fact indispensable. No doubt they are still open to criticism, but the fact is irrelevant. Their content will be determined by the development of the subject. A case in point is the word "psychology," which, discredited in the middle of the last century as the name for a metaphysical account of the ego, has now come to have a definitive place in the scientific vocabulary. Sumner's *The Science of Society*, then, is a sociology: a sociology based upon the abstract phenomenon termed "culture," itself the result of the long-continued study of particular cultures.

It was while Sumner was engaged upon *The Science of Society* that he found himself confronted with a concept that was to throw him completely off his course, to which as a matter of fact he never returned. What had happened was that in his meditations upon the nature of culture, his analyses of the phenomena involved therein had carried him to a degree.of abstraction he had never before attained. Underneath the growth of culture was a phenomenon which was not only an abstraction, it was in the language of this volume an isolate as well. The impact upon his mind of the new idea was so great that he turned aside from the longer work to give form to the new thought. The result was *Folkways*.

Despite the essentially monographic nature of the work, its first two chapters present the main lines of a new departure in sociological thought of great promise. The concept is familiar today; a single paragraph may be quoted for the sake of precision:

In the present work the proposition to be maintained is that the folkways are the widest, most fundamental, and most important operation by which the interests of men in groups are served, and that the process by which folkways are made is the chief one to which the elementary societal or group phenomena are due. The life of society consists in making folkways and applying them. The science of society might be construed as the study of them. The relations of men to each other, when they are carrying on the struggle for existence near each other, consist in mutual reactions (antagonisms, rivalries, alliances, coercions, and coöperations), from which result societal concatenations and concretions, that is, more or less fixed positions of individuals and subgroups towards each other, and more or less established sequences and methods of interaction between them, by which the interests of all members of the group are served. . . . The societal concretions are due to the folkways in this way—that the men, each struggling to carry on existence, unconsciously coöperate to build up associations, organization, customs, and institutions which, after a time, appear full grown and actual, although no one intended, or planned, or understood them in advance. They stand there as produced by 'ancestors.' These concretions of relation and act in war, labor, religion, amusement, family life, and civil institutions are attended by faiths, doctrines of philosophy (myths, folklore), and by precepts of right conduct and duty (taboos). The making of folkways is not trivial, although the acts are minute. Every act of each man fixes an atom in a structure, both fulfilling a duty derived from what preceded and conditioning what is to come afterwards by the authority of traditional custom. *The structure thus built up is not physical, but societal and institutional, that is to say, it belongs to a category which must be defined and studied by itself.*[36]

Here is clearly a basic, synthesizing concept of great power. Its consequences are still to be worked out. In Sumner's case the result was immediate. The existence of a great central principle like that

36. W. G. Sumner, *Folkways* (New York, Ginn, 1906), pp. 34-35.

of folkways is totally incompatible with the mere gathering of data in orderly arrangement around a few psychological drives, much on the plan of Spencer's study of institutions. Even if the drives themselves—the famous love, hunger, fear, vanity—resisted analysis better than they do, they would not fit into the folkways structure. They do not of course resist analysis. Fear, for example, is not really fear—granting fear to be a basic drive—but only a special case, i.e., ghost-fear, which is obviously when so defined not an innate drive. Vanity when thought of as self-gratification is in an even worse case.

But far more important than such details is the fact of far-reaching significance that *the concept of folkways relieves the sociologist once for all of the necessity of resorting to psychological data at all.* If instead of the four drives listed above any other four were operative, the making of folkways would go on all the same. And even more to the point, the process of making and developing them and the study of the process would go on just as well if there were no knowledge of psychology at all and drives had never been heard of. No wonder that Sumner, broken in health, declared "that all he had written on the general treatise must now be done all over again in the light of *Folkways* and that he could never rise to the task." [37]

Not only is the way opened to the elimination of the psychological from the attention of the sociologist, but also, and because of it, the beginning of a technical vocabulary for the sociologist receives a sound basis. It is no mere accident that Sumner's words "folkways" and "mores" have become along with "sociology" a part of the current vocabulary. They all represent a real thing; they have referents, for which signs were needed. Not only these three but the adjective "societal" is needed, for it makes possible the setting aside of the equivocal and indeterminate "social"—the parallel of Aristotle's "physical"—in favor of a term descriptive of the phenomena with which the sociologist is essentially concerned. "Societal" equals social minus psychological, and its use indicates the approach to the isolate which is the goal of all the sciences.

37. W. G. Sumner and A. G. Keller, *The Science of Society* (4 vols. New Haven, Yale University Press, 1927), *1*, xxiv.

7. Giddings

Whether these advances in theory were all clearly conscious in Sumner's mind it is of course impossible to say. In any case, while he was turning away in implication at least from psychology as an aid to sociology, others were doing almost exactly the reverse. Among these was the American Franklin Henry Giddings (1855–1931). The explanation of his position is to be found in a distinction which he drew between two kinds of sociology. There are, said he in a passage not often cited, two ways of looking at society: the objective and the subjective. The objective is the way of Spencer, for example, who follows the development of society from the outside so to speak, observing and recording the phenomena of differentiation, etc., which occur in its evolution. The subjective approach follows a different line. It is interested in the inner forces which hold the members of the society together while the objective evolution is proceeding. How can this fact of social cohesion be explained?

The key to the solution of this problem Giddings found in the work of Adam Smith, who is thus drawn into the general current of sociological theory. Smith (the fact is known but too often disregarded) was a professor of moral philosophy before he became known to the world as the author of *The Wealth of Nations* and as such was interested in the general problem of human nature, as indeed were all the members of the Scottish school, Hutcheson, Reid, Browne, and Hume. One of their problems was to account for man's actions as the result of his emotions. One of the strongest of these emotions is that of the fellow-feeling aroused within men by the consciousness of the emotions of others. "Sympathy" was the term used by Smith in his *Theory of the Moral Sentiments* to apply to this fellow-feeling.

This concept Giddings seized upon and translated into one of the most successful phrases in sociological literature, "the consciousness of kind," and out of it he developed a theory which has thus been summarized:

> [The] most important similarities [in life-organisms] will be found in their behavior. The primary activity of the living organism is to adapt the environment to itself in order to satisfy

thereby its primary needs of safety and of food. In the human being these adaptations are the basis of appreciation, that is, a change in consciousness describable as the attaching of more interest or value to one thing than to another. Appreciation arises out of those reactions, which are, first, instinctive, then habitual, and later on are rationalized. When, at length, man finds the limits which restrict the adaptation of the environment to himself, he begins the reverse process of the adjustment of himself to the environment. His interest is attached to the behavior of his fellows who, by reason of their biological relationship and the pressure of a common environment, are at the same time interested in his behavior. His reactions and those of his fellows tend to be alike, and there arises a perception of the likeness of external stimuli to self-stimuli. This is co-ordinated with the adjustment of one organism to the like behavior of similar organisms, a process furthered by imitation and reflective sympathy. . . . Out of [language and collective behavior] arises a consciousness of kind compounded of "organic sympathy, the perception of resemblance, conscious or reflective sympathy, affection, and the desire for recognition." There is a distinct stimulus in 'kind' and a direct reaction to it, and presently a discriminating awareness of it. Natural selection works upon this; and, since competition and the struggle for survival lead to co-operation and preferential associations, there is produced that collective behavior with which social organization begins." [38]

The influence of many factors of contemporary scientific thought is obvious in such a theory, notably that of Darwinian evolution and the psychology of the period. Behind it is to be seen the working of the same motives that sent Ward to the study of the social forces and Sumner to the four drives. From it clearly emerges the conception of sociology as the science of social behavior. Nevertheless, insists Giddings, all these elements are but the instruments for creating a new science, which is still sociology and never becomes psychology. "Psychology is the science of the association of ideas. Sociology is

38. C. H. Northcott, "The Sociological Theories of Franklin Henry Giddings," in H. E. Barnes, *Introduction to the History of Sociology* (Chicago, University of Chicago Press, 1948), pp. 746–747. Opportunity has been taken to refer the interested reader to a few alterations that Northcott saw fit to make in his earlier version of Giddings' theory as here printed.

the science of the association of minds." [39] As minds become associated the range within which the consciousness of kind can operate widens also; and so the way is opened to a consideration of the development of society—to which *The Principles of Sociology* is for the most part devoted.

Ingenious as Giddings' theory undoubtedly is and accurately as it responds to certain well observed facts, it was nevertheless not as resistant as, say, Small's idea of the group to continued analysis. The consciousness of kind is so evidently a result rather than an original operative factor—as after all Smith's sympathy was in theory intended to be—that the phrase has come to be recognized as a useful summarizing and descriptive term rather than an instrument of scientific explanation. Giddings himself seems to have recognized something of this weakness, for in later years he turned in the direction of a different psychology, behaviorism, and an emphasis upon pluralistic doctrines. It seems not unjust to question whether the later theories were ever thoroughly integrated with the earlier ones; and in any case his work raises and leaves the question whether the words "a science of collective behavior" are not more accurately descriptive of social psychology than of sociology.

8. Tarde

While Giddings in the United States was developing his theory of a consciousness of kind, an analogous attempt was being made by Gabriel Tarde (1843–1904) in France. Tarde was by profession a judge in the criminal courts. There he had had occasion to observe the curious fact that a serious or even horrible crime was often followed in the very same locality by another, the second being very similar to or even exactly like the first, as if the perpetrator of the second had sought to imitate the perpetrator of the first. This train of thought, followed through some years, led to the celebrated theory of imitation as the basis of social cohesion. The gist of the matter is easily stated, with no more violence to the original thought than is usual in such summaries. "Like many other sociologists, Tarde . . . sought the quintessence of society, that single aspect or process of our complex common life which makes it what it is by

39. F. H. Giddings, *The Principles of Sociology* (New York, Macmillan, 1928), p. 25.

distinguishing it from everything else under the sun. He finds this to be imitation. Invention is an individual product, belief and desire are individual, and logical conflicts are at bottom conflicts in individual minds. The social stage appears in the *passage* of an invention from one individual to another, in a *relation between* two individuals, and so far as this relation is social, says Tarde, it is an imitative relation. Whether it be a one-sided copying as that of parent and child or a mutual one as in a democratic society, the essential social act, the sociological starting point, the social datum is thus an act of imitation. Such is the core and the key of Tarde's Sociology. The process of socialization is a growth of similarity through the method of imitation. Every social similarity has imitation for its cause. A group of beings is a social group, a society 'insofar as its members . . . , without actual imitation, ... resemble one another and possess common characteristics which are the ultimate copies of one original model.' "

The theory in its day had great vogue. Like Giddings', it is a faithful picture of certain facts of society, and they will always have to be taken into consideration in any theory of the social whole. Nevertheless, again like Giddings' theory, it was unable to resist critical analysis; it was not a representation of the fundamental social phenomenon.

Moreover it involved certain perplexities of its own as a theory in addition to the perplexities of society. What, for example, is the invention which when imitated becomes possessed of unique sociological merits? It is obvious that the elements of the invention exist outside the individual: in what sense then is an invention an original individual act? And what are the inventor's relations to society? And besides, what is an individual? And what are his relations to society? Nothing could more clearly reveal the difficulties which lay all unsuspected in the old division of moral philosophy into ethics and politics.

Besides, even within the limits proper of the theory there were difficulties. What is imitation? When Tarde carried his definition to the point of including such phenomena as hypnotism, he was no doubt on a suggestive line of thought but not one ending in sociology. And what of the social actions prompted by a desire to be as different from others as possible rather than as like? When Tarde, in the effort to enclose these evident facts within the net of his theory, developed the concept of counterimitation, he was no doubt growing in stature as a thinker with respect to the complexity of the data with which he was concerned, but what remains of the original point of departure? In all fairness to a great contributor to the study of social phenomena, it would seem that he no less than Giddings was dealing with what would now be called social psychology, the appearance of which as an important field of study is certainly one of the stages in the creation of an accurately defined sociology.

9. Durkheim

Tarde's rival in his own country was Émile Durkheim (1858–1917), with whom sociology entered formally into the University of France. Hailed by many, though with doubtful justification, as the continuator of Comte, Durkheim became the head of the most influential school of sociologists in France. His works, such as *The Division of Social Labor* and *The Elementary Forms of Religious Beliefs,* are applications to the study of social phenomena of principles formulated most systematically in his *Les Règles de la méthode sociologique.* In this little volume Durkheim strives earnestly to show that sociology is not concerned with the whole range of facts called social. "There is," says Gehlke, "a decided limitation of the scope of social phenomena, as usually defined. It does not admit, as do so many definitions, that everything in society is 'social.' Durkheim thinks that to define 'social' in the latter [all-inclusive] way takes away from 'society' all the individuality that it may possess as a separate field of scientific investigation. . . . Consistently throughout all of his writings, 'exteriority' and 'constraint' are emphasized as the criteria par excellence of social phenomena." [40]

Clearly, then, Durkheim was working toward an isolate as the object of sociological investigation, and in so doing he defines as follows the facts he considers proper to sociology: social facts "consist in ways of acting, thinking, and feeling (1) exterior to the individual and (2) endowed with a power of coercion or constraint, by reason of which they impose themselves upon him. Consequently they should not be confused with organic phenomena, since they

40. C. E. Gehlke, *Émile Durkheim's Contribution to Sociological Theory* (New York, Columbia University Press, 1915), pp. 59–60.

consist of representations and actions; nor with psychical phenomena, which have existence only in the individual consciousness and through it. *They constitute thus a new variety of phenomena,* and it is to them that ought to be given and for them reserved the epithet 'social.' " [41]

What then is the essential nature of the "things," as Durkheim calls them, which have the properties just described?

> The thing that characterizes Durkheim and his followers is their insistence upon the fact that all cultural materials, and expressions, including language, science, religion, public opinion, and law, since they are the products of social intercourse and social interaction, are bound to have an objective, public, and social character such as no product of an individual mind either has or can have. Durkheim speaks of these mental products, individual and social, as representations. The characteristic product of the individual mind is the percept, or, as Durkheim describes it, the "individual representation." . . .
>
> The characteristic product of a group of individuals, in their efforts to communicate is, on the other hand, something objective and understood, that is, a gesture, a sign, a symbol, a word, or a concept in which an experience or purpose that was private becomes public. This gesture, sign, symbol, concept, or representation in which a common object is not merely indicated, but in a sense created, Durkheim calls "a collective representation." [42]

It is a social fact, because it is the sum of many different individual percepts, which are all collected, corrected, and cumulated in a representation of the reality which is superior to that which any individual would make for himself.

In Durkheim's theory there is a considerable reliance upon psychological theory for the construction of sociological concepts; nevertheless the fact and the explanation are not interdependent. Whether the explanation of what happens is the one given by Durkheim or not, the fact remains that it is collective life which gives

41. Émile Durkheim, *Les Règles de la methode sociologique* (7th ed. Paris, F. Alcan, 1919), p. 8.

42. R. E. Park and E. W. Burgess, *Introduction to the Science of Sociology* (Chicago, University of Chicago Press, 1921), pp. 37–38.

meaning to signs, etc., and changes that meaning with changes in collective life. This point is essential in Durkheim's theory; and it can stand solidly as a fact of observation, be the explanation what it may. Thus there is here an approach to the condition requisite for the construction of a truly homogeneous and independent science, viz., an abstract phenomenon which, especially in its rejection of the psychological, tends toward an isolate.

10. Simmel

Among the German writers on sociology it is difficult to make a choice for purposes of inclusion in a list like this. It is likely however that there would be some agreement on the position that if the test for selection is the authorship of works that have pointed out distinctions of general validity in the field, then two men, Ferdinand Tönnies and Georg Simmel, would be the first choices. The first of these men has to his credit one of the classics in the field, *Gemeinschaft und Gesellschaft;* the second was the originator, the source, of a type of sociological theory which has become the center of the work of a school. To Simmel (1858–1918), then, for the circumstance just stated, some attention will be given here. The basis of the summary will be Spykman's analysis.

The foundation of Simmel's position is the doctrine that each science has its own abstraction. It sees in each object a thing which is an actual totality. This totality cannot be grasped as such, i.e., as a unity by any science but can only be regarded from the viewpoint of some specific concept. Each science is thus the result of a decomposition of the unity of things and a corresponding division of labor. As a result of both, the given object is resolved into a number of specific qualities and functions. There must be some central and specific concept if a number of factors and functions abstracted from a variety of different objects or things are to be coordinated into a single subject matter. Thus in the presence of the highly complex facts of historical society, which cannot be interpreted from a single point of view, the concepts politics, economics, and culture have been the centralizing and specific ideas about which sciences have been constructed. Such categories of cognition may be utilized in two ways: they may combine certain parts of the facts into a unique historical sequence, eliminating other parts or using them in a merely accidental fashion; or they may combine different parts into groupings of elements which contain a timeless correlation.

Sociology, then, might become a special science in the same way. It might find its subject matter by drawing a new line through facts which have already had many lines drawn through them and which are therefore well known. All that is needed is a unifying concept adequate to the task of coordinating into a synthesis the similar aspects lying along the new line. The new concept therefore means that the sociohistorical data have been subjected to an abstraction followed by a coordination, whence comes the possibility of observing together certain peculiarities that have hitherto been seen only in other relations. This new grouping will be the subject of a new science. Now the concept of society as the external aggregate of social phenomena cannot serve as the requisite concept for a new science. For that purpose it becomes necessary to distinguish between the *content* and the *form* of the society and use the latter as the unifying viewpoint. This concept of society as form, or rather this concept of the form of socialization, makes possible the formation and the delimitation of the new science and is therefore the category of cognition which is required as the central concept of a science.

Society in the wider and larger sense consists of both form and content. But if the subject matter of sociology is to be society and nothing else, it can investigate only the processes of association, the kinds and the forms of socialization. Everything else found within society and realized by means of it and within its framework is not socialization itself but merely content. A special science of society as such can be founded only when these two elements, inseparably united in actuality, are separated in scientific abstraction. But can this separation be shown to be legitimate? Only if two conditions are fulfilled: similar forms of socialization must occur having quite dissimilar content and similar social interests must be found in quite dissimilar forms of socialization.

That this is the case cannot be denied. There are similar forms of relationship between individuals in groups which are wholly dissimilar in aim and purpose. Superiority and subordination, competition, imitation are found in civic groups and they are found as well for example in religious communities. However diverse the interests from which the socializations arise, the forms in which they occur may nevertheless be similar. On the other hand, the same content can be realized in very different forms of socialization. Thus, the interests which lie at the foundation of the relation between the sexes are satisfied in a greater variety of family formations than can be enumerated. So it is, then, that in one aspect the forms in which the most divergent contents are realized may be identical, and in another the substance may remain while the socialization that carries it may change into a variety of forms. Hence it is that there can be a sociology, a special science not encroaching upon the domains of other disciplines. It is true that in their objective reality and concreteness, substance and form are inseparable and form an indissoluble unity. But that concreteness *by abstraction* can give a special subject matter: the identification, systematic arrangement, psychological explanation, and historical development of the pure forms of socialization.

11. Marx

The names of two other men should be added to those already given, even though they represent a less direct approach to sociology than do the others. The first is that of a man in whose work a sociology is contained by implication: Karl Marx. The second is that of a man for whom a sociology was the outcome of an effort to supplement a lifework in other lines: Vilfredo Pareto.

In the case of Marx (1818–83) there are, it is universally agreed, three general sources whence came the materials of his theoretical constructions. The first of these is the French writers, such as Saint Simon; the second is the philosophical work of Hegel; and the third is the classical economists, especially the English group. It is of course quite impossible to determine the part of each of these influences in the ultimate thought of Marx. In any case, he made them his own; but the general lines as stated are clear. The French group seems to have turned Marx' attention in the direction of economic phenomena as the basis for social reform and reconstruction. Upon them as a group, however, Marx' judgment was not unlike Comte's upon Saint Simon. In Marx' language they were utopian, not scientific. Before their various plans, proposals, and expedients could become of use they would all have to be analyzed and the thought behind them incorporated into a systematic body of doctrines on sounder bases than any of them had been able to reach. Their utopianism would have to become science.

The intellectual framework into which their and all similar thought could be integrated was supplied by Hegel, but a Hegel transformed. History, Hegel showed, could have a meaning; but could that meaning not be based upon something more solid than the metaphysical playing with the "idea," regarded as emanating ultimately from a divine source? Marx' answer was an inversion of the Hegelian position. The one way to lay the basis for a sound interpretation of history was to see in its records the operation not of metaphysical but of real factors, i.e., to rest the interpretation not upon mere reasoning but upon observation; in other words the meaning must be found there. So, in opposition to Hegel's idealism, Marx based his historical explanations upon materialism.

As a matter of fact, then, Marx' real purposes are the same as those of any sociologist whatever who deals with history. The fact is obscured by the choice of a term, "material," which is so inevitably bound up with the whole history of metaphysical philosophy. What was in Marx' mind is clear enough: he was trying to put his doctrines upon a basis of observed reality. "The mind of man appears to him as a social product and as part of the reality which he contrasts as material with the purely ideal reality of the Hegelians. Much of the prejudice against his doctrine comes from a failure to understand this. Marx' materialism is not materialistic in the sense that it excludes the action of mind, but only that it seeks its reality in this world of men and things, and not in any universe of ideas transcending this world and its limitations." [43]

In the terms of this volume Marx was striving to exclude the hominoid influences from the field of history. That his thought came to more and more clear understanding of his original position is obvious from, and is an explanation of, the varying meanings ascribed by him and Engels and others after them to the word "material." Comte had had to do very much the same thing, and in his word "positive" can be found an exact parallel to Marx' "material." If freedom from metaphysical connotation is a title to superiority, Comte's is the better word.

43. G. D. H. Cole, Introduction to Karl Marx, *Capital* (2 vols. London, Everyman's Library, Dent, 1934), *1*, xvii.

Whatever the secondary considerations, the main point is clear: Marx was looking for a meaning in history, not smuggling it in via philosophy. At this point the influence of the economists begins to show. Into what factor of the historical reality should one look in order to find that which is most potent in bringing about the changes that history records? But first, what is the essence of historical change? Marx on this point is at one with most of the sociologists in seeing society as a structure of relations between men. What he was in search of, then, was the factor most potent in bringing about changes in human relations. The economic answer was the simplest. Men must live: it is the one basic and inescapable necessity. Those relations, therefore, that are made necessary by the furnishing of the means of subsistence are the determinant ones.

The organization, in any particular mode, of the means of production tends to stabilize and even petrify the structure of human relations and to build up forces strongly resistant to change. When translated into terms of human psychology these forces become ideological, and the result is a stabilizing of society on a class basis. The logically obvious result would be for the historical movement to cease. However, as a matter of fact it has not ceased; why not? At this point the Hegelian method as opposed to or at least distinct from the Hegelian doctrine provides the answer—an answer, it should be observed, that was all the more attractive in that there was during Marx' formative years no vocabulary of evolutionary terms in existence to facilitate reference to the phenomena of change. Now according to the Hegelian method, change comes about through the confrontation of opposites—thesis versus antithesis—and their merging into a third form, neither the first nor the second—a synthesis.

This dialectical—in the Hegelian technical sense—becoming provided the hint needed for answering the problem of history. The means of supplying human needs vary with time. To each set of means corresponds a structure of relationships manifesting themselves as classes. Under a given structure of human relations grows up slowly a variant in the means of production. The new means imply a new structure of relationships, and when this structure begins to take clear form it comes into conflict with the older structure and finally replaces it. Thus one class replaces another and history be-

comes a meaningful record of the supplanting of one class by another—a history of class struggles. In this way, historical materialism is the key to history.

Each class as it comes to dominance controls for its own benefit
all the means of production that have been developed by earlier
classes and so obtains all the advantages due to them. As these means
can be made productive only through the labor of individuals, those
who control them gain for themselves all the values that are produced, over and above the amounts necessary for the maintenance
of the laborers, and so the doctrine of surplus value emerges, via
the teachings of the classical economists in regard to the labor origin
of value, from the larger theory of historical development. But at
this point the Marxian theory goes off into economic considerations
of too technical a nature to be in point in a discussion of sociological doctrines.

Regardless, then, of the economic superstructure or the revolutionary animus of the Marxian theories, they clearly contain the
essentials of a sociology. There is a positive view of historical causation, an abstract phenomenon, a method, and a statement of regularity and sequence based upon the use of the method. The method
is essentially dialectical and the view of history partial, excluding in
theory the period anterior to the formation of economic classes and
the (hypothetical) period after their extinction; the emphasis on
economic data is exaggerated; but these defects, admitting them to
be such, are no more serious objections to Marx' claim to sociological consideration than the shortcomings of sociologists already mentioned. It may even be, considering the development of economic
theory since Marx' time, that his importance as a sociologist is
greater than as an economic theorist. In any case, his insistence upon
the positive or material nature of social phenomena and his clear
acceptance of a responsibility resting upon students of social phenomena to push their conclusions to the point where prevision becomes possible are ample titles to consideration as a sociologist.

12. Pareto

The case of Vilfredo Pareto (1848–1923) is still more interesting
than that of Marx. Pareto had passed the greater part of his life
dealing with a more and more abstract conception of economic

phenomena. As he worked on he became convinced that to deal with only the economic factor in social life was inadequate for any complete explanation of that life; that the economic was only one of the abstract factors that go to make up the social reality. He therefore set himself to make such an inclusive study as his deepening understanding of that reality made more and more necessary. The analyses he had made earlier into the nature of *Les Systèmes socialistes* had put him on the track of the fact that the reasons men give for their actions are not at all the real reasons. They simply find good reasons for doing what they want to do, often for motives that are not avowable. The realization of the fact started Pareto on his extra-economic search for other real forces, i.e., constant social factors at work in history.

In order to get close to the bases of human action, Pareto subjected the data offered by history to the scrutiny of a method which was intended to be strictly objective. He called it the logicoexperimental method, its essence being to make certain that sociological reasoning and conclusions should rest only upon those data which were found by the use of a rigorous logic operating upon the results of experience, excluding all theological or metaphysical or emotional elements.

Once his point of view is taken, Pareto goes to work in a way which can perhaps best be illustrated by a suppositious case. Assume a geologist who has been devoting his life to the study of the physical factors in geological causation. Suddenly he finds that his geological phenomena are due in some degree to the action of nonphysical forces. For a time he abandons his physical investigations and concentrates upon the discovery and study of the newly recognized forces. This he does without reference to the existence of a possible new science, say chemistry; he simply discovers the existence and effects of a number of what a chemist would call chemical elements and chemical compounds. That the new data might find a place in a distinct science is of no immediate concern. They serve to throw light upon geological phenomena, and that is the one point of importance. They are constants with reference to geology. With them in hand he returns to his geological studies and devotes himself to the analysis and explanation of a large number of geological formations, often of the most concrete and specific type.

Very much like the imaginary geologist is Pareto in relation to social phenomena. Having found that economic explanations were inadequate to the task of accounting fully for the facts with which he was dealing, Pareto threw himself into the task of discovering other data which would serve to supplement the economic factors. From an inductive study of history he found certain general facts, certain recurrent kinds of social behavior, certain constant psychical forces to which he gave the name "residues" because they remained after his analysis of historical data had been carried as far as he could carry it. Rising around the residues and concealing them are verbalizations and doctrines—a fact which is historically demonstrable. This second class of constant social phenomena, not based primarily on either logic or experience but prompted by the feelings which underlie the residues, Pareto calls "derivations." By the aid of these two classes of constant social phenomena he was able to approach the reality of social life far more closely than he had before been able to do. Now he could deal with the *real* reasons for human actions and not the ascribed ones. That a certain other science called psychology might throw light upon these constants was irrelevant. Whatever it might do, it could not alter the fact that they *were* constants in the field of social phenomena.

Still another constant in the same field was social heterogeneity and circulation. Human society is not a homogeneous thing; individuals are physically, morally, and intellectually different; social classes are not entirely distinct even in countries where a caste system prevails, and in modern civilized countries social circulation, i.e., movements of individuals from one class to another, is exceedingly rapid. From the viewpoint of social heterogeneity, society is divisible into at least two strata: "a higher stratum, which usually contains the rulers, and a lower stratum, which usually contains the ruled." [44]

But because of constant social circulation, "the governing *élite* is always in a state of slow and continuous transformation" [45] as the abler individuals from below rise to the higher stratum; and the less able members of the ruling group tend to sink to lower levels. When the circulation is free in both directions, the society is normal; when it is obstructed, difficulties arise which may lead

44. V. Pareto, *The Mind and Society* (4 vols. New York, Harcourt Brace, 1935), *3*, par. 2047.
45. Pareto, *3*, par. 2056.

even to revolutions. "Revolutions come about through accumulations in the higher strata of society—either because of a slowing down in class-circulation, or from other causes—of decadent elements no longer possessing the residues suitable for keeping them in power, and shrinking from the use of force; while meantime in the lower strata of society elements of superior quality are coming to the fore, possessing residues suitable for exercising the functions of government and willing enough to use force." [46]

Such were the new elements of social existence that Pareto found as the result of his inductive studies. They were not the only ones, of course. Many had been known long before. Taking the new and the old together,

> the following groups may be distinguished: 1. Soil, climate, flora, fauna, geological, mineralogical, and other like conditions; 2. elements external to a given society at a given time, such as the influences of other societies upon it—external therefore in space; and the effects of the previous situation within it—external, therefore, in time; then 3. internal elements, chief among which, race, residues (or better, the sentiments manifested by them), proclivities, interests, aptitudes for thought and observation, state of knowledge, and so on. Derivations also are to be counted among these latter. [47]

Knowing all these factors, a sociologist should be able to work out for a given society all the details of the structural relationships which would hold individuals together and so account for its form. The difficulty however of bringing to a successful conclusion a deductive enterprise of such complexity is evident.

It is not impossible, however, to make a first approximation by limiting the number of factors in play to the more important and the better known. The effects of the interplay of a small number of factors of fundamental importance having been worked out by deduction, other and secondary influences could then be added and the outcome of their addition would be a second approximation; and so on, each step bringing the inquirer closer to the reality.

Such a first approximation Pareto proceeds to attempt, selecting as the main elements involved the following: residues, interests,

46. Pareto, 3, par. 2057.
47. Pareto, 4, par. 2060.

derivations, and social circulation. Thus Pareto's range of discussion includes the various types of recurring social behavior, the economic factors, the types of reasoning which bring otherwise unaffected persons to the support of this or that interested individual or group, and the degree of social circulation existent at the moment. Out of the interaction of these four elements results the form of the society, at least in major part. "In order thoroughly to grasp the form of a society in its every detail it would be necessary first to know what all the very numerous elements are, and then to know how they function—and that in quantitative terms" [48]—an evidently utopian requirement, to which however successive approximations may ultimately lead.

In any case, all these interdependent elements constitute in their functioning a social system, the essential characteristics of which are (1) that it is what it is because of the conditions in which it exists and (2) that its elements are in equilibrium. Hence any attempt artificially to change the relations of the elements will at once produce a reaction. But it will do no more, so long as the elements retain their initial vigor. So long as the relations only of the elements in equilibrium are affected there will be no permanent change, since the original equilibrium of the system will tend to be restored. Permanent modification of the system could be successful only if it affected the conditions of the elements directly, thereby bringing about indirectly a new equilibrium which in turn would tend to persist.

Clearly Pareto's sociology is a deductive construction, resembling in some respects the sociology of Spencer. Indeed, it would be pushing coincidence too far not to see in the wording of Pareto's list of social elements the direct influence of the English philosopher. In Comte's words, which Pareto knew well, the Italian was working at the construction of a concrete rather than an abstract science. Nothing could make the point more evident, in all probability, than the passages toward the end of Pareto's work where he shows how certain sociological situations work toward the selection of given types of residues, i.e., the dominance in society under certain conditions of individuals or groups who will—whatever the psychological reasons for their actions, which may conceivably be different in every individual—act in a particular way or take a pre-

48. Pareto, *4*, par. 2062.

dictable position, i.e., embody certain social constants. For this reason, and others, it is not an injustice to rank Pareto with the social psychologists rather than the sociologists.

To the foregoing group of sociologists others might well have been added if the honoring of individuals had been the purpose of this chapter. Such recognition is here and now irrelevant. It is rather the influential concepts than the influential names that are here in point. It is believed that no basic position in relation to the defining and delimiting of the new science has been omitted. Everything secondary, however, has been systematically thrown into the background that the central concepts might be the more clearly perceived. Certainly the procedure adopted cannot be criticized on the grounds of minimizing the differences among the various theories. On the contrary it seems to accentuate them. There is nothing to gain from hiding the divergencies that exist among the men analyzed above. If their efforts are in fact totally irreconcilable the fact should be known. Are they really so?

One encouraging circumstance colors the whole situation favorably. All the men involved are looking at the same general body of phenomena, the social. They are most unlikely, therefore, to be revealed by analysis as completely contradictory or even divergent. It may well be found that their ideas differ materially in hierarchical or proportional value with relation to the task of setting sociology upon a sound theoretical basis; it is unlikely that in any case the concepts developed will be found to have *no* value. The next task then is to see how far they do help to achieve for sociology the objective that the history of science sets as the goal for any science.

PART FOUR: THE SOCIETAL ISOLATE
AND ITS IMPLICATIONS

CHAPTER 10: *The Societal Fact: Abstract and Isolate*

At the basis of each of the sciences of the encyclopedia is an abstract phenomenon, an isolate. Sociology can be no exception. Realization of the fact transforms the task of evaluating the men grouped together in the preceding chapter from an uncertain comparison of individuals into a review conducted upon a reasoned and uniform criterion. How far does each of them aid in the discovery or attainment of a specific class of abstract phenomena? Such is the question that must now be asked. How far did each advance toward an isolate?

Moreover, the attainment of such an isolate would go far toward converting what has been a spontaneous and individual search for the basis of a new science into a collective and systematic effort to reach a rational conclusion generally accepted. It would besides supply a rallying point where new inquirers could join their efforts to those already exerted. It would be more than a school, with the particularity the word connotes; it would be the center of an integrated movement toward the isolation of a class of abstract phenomena—the requisite for a sociology without qualifying or restrictive adjectives.

If, however, the notion of a societal isolate is to be made a kind of touchstone of sociological science, then another name must be added to those contained in the preceding chapter. The name is that of a man who from the beginning of his career was stimulated by the thought of applying to the construction of a new science dealing with the social life of man the spirit and method of the sciences that had already come to maturity and whose whole career centered about the construction of a sociology. Even more to the point, his work was marked by a steady advance in theory, the stages of which have never received the attention they merit. In it, taken as a whole, can be found the requisites for the collective and systematic develop-

ment of sociology as a basic abstract science. The man, of course, is
Auguste Comte.

The inclusion of Comte a second time among pioneer sociologists
is motivated by the fact that for him, quite as much as for every one
of his successors and emulators in the field of sociology, the *Philosophie* was a point of departure. The great difference between him
and them in respect to that treatise is that for them it was rather the
formulation of a goal which they strove to attain each in his own
way, whereas for him it was but *the first stage* of an intellectual development, to which all his later thought was organically related.
What for them was the statement of an ideal was for him the beginning of an evolution in thought which was to endure through his
entire life. In the course of this development he refined and expanded his original ideas, gave them greater precision, and finally
succeeded in reaching a conception of the subject matter of sociology which is in substance the isolate on which a science can be built.
These achievements were effected in Comte's second great treatise,
Système de politique positive.

To the *Politique,* then, attention must now be turned. In its pages
is to be found the record of the successive advances of Comte's
thought as he cleared away one obstacle after another to the attainment of a rigorously logical position in regard to his new science.
This record must now be examined. In the course of the examination Comte's work will be treated exactly as was treated the work
of the men summarized in the preceding chapter, i.e., with regard
solely to the central problem of the nature of sociology. Such questions therefore as the unity of Comte's work, the nature of his religious construction, etc., will here be rigorously set aside. Only one
question will be dealt with, namely, the nature of sociology as it is
found in his later work, particularly as represented by the *Politique.*

An even sharper focus of the central point of interest in Comte's
later work can be made. Sociologists may or may not be concerned
with the development of Comte's general theories; they must be
concerned with his approach to an accurately defined isolate which
would put their subject upon a sound scientific basis. Such a concentration of interest has nothing to do with Comte as an individual. To deal with him in this way is merely a recognition of the
simple fact that he lived and worked nearly a score of years after
writing the *Philosophie.* The one novel aspect of the matter is that

for reasons not here in point Comte's strictly sociological thought in the *Politique* has never been incorporated into the general body of sociological doctrine.

Enough has been said in the chapter devoted to the sociology of the *Philosophie* to make evident Comte's concern with the relation between sociological data and data of other kinds. In one long section he makes clear how environmental, biological, and other conditions affect the operation of sociological phenomena. From the conditioning influence of these and other factors upon social life taken as whole, Comte was able to isolate the sociological facts with sufficient sharpness to make impossible, after his work, any real confusion between them. But there was one point to which in his first outline of sociology practically no attention was given, in regard to which indeed there is little evidence of any awareness on Comte's part that it needed attention.

Expressed in the language of today, the problem to which little if indeed any attention is given in the sociology of the *Philosophie* is that involved in the relations between sociology and psychology or, more accurately, between sociological and psychological phenomena. As is sometimes said, Comte in his earlier work had no psychology. The statement is as true in form as it is completely false in substance. The position of the *Philosophie* is simply that what are now called psychological data form *the highest level of biology.* If, however, the question of the nature of these two classes of phenomena and the relations between them is practically ignored in the *Philosophie* because it seemed not to be a difficulty at all, in the *Politique* on the contrary it permeates the whole thought of the treatise. It was raised early in the second volume and reappeared from time to time throughout the treatise until finally in the last (fourth) volume the basis of a solution was found.

The working out of a solution to the perplexing problem of the relation between sociology and psychology gave to Comte's work as a whole a logical completeness it had hitherto not possessed; its importance to scientific thought can scarcely be exaggerated. Both motives combine here to make essential a presentation of Comte's final position. Its significance for the purposes of this volume needs no stressing.

In the first place then—and to put Comte's conclusion in the fewest possible words—there is *no* connection between sociology and psychology. They are two distinct sciences, dealing each with an isolate of its own as definitely and as clearly as do physics and chemistry. The basis of each of these four sciences, on either the inorganic or the organic level, is a homogeneous group of abstract phenomena susceptible of complete isolation.

In other terms, Comte after many years saw that his analysis of the phenomena on the organic level of the encyclopedia into two classes, the biological and the sociological, was incomplete. A more accurate analysis of the phenomena loosely called living revealed the existence of three levels and not two: the biological, the sociological, and the psychological. This is to say the social category, with which he had begun his work and which was the basis for the sociology of the *Philosophie,* proved to be a combination of phenomena and not a single homogeneous class. Hence there should be, there were, seven fundamental sciences and not six as Comte had thought at the time of writing the *Philosophie.*

The reason he had been so long discovering the error of analysis and classification was simply that he had been so convinced of the validity of the age-old division of moral philosophy into ethics and politics that he never even suspected its inaccuracy. It had been generally accepted by mankind ever since the time of Aristotle. The individual first, and then the society: such was the universally accepted order of intellectual precedence and such it had been for two thousand years. Nevertheless it was wrong; it rested upon a metaphysical, not a scientific, view of the individual. Comte finally began to see that he did not have to deal with individuals and societies as such. They both merely present to him and to all observers great masses of phenomena which have to be analyzed and classified. The old strife between individual and society ceased once the new point of view became tenable. The two are not opposites but correlatives, and underneath both are three levels or classes of phenomena: the organic, the collective, and the psychical. Men that is to say are concrete realities manifesting properties which, as analysis demonstrates, belong to three categories, the vital, the societal, and the personal, the bases respectively of biological, sociological, and psychological science, having as their respective fields of concrete data life, culture, and personality. When this fact becomes evident, the old category of moral philosophy disappears as completely as did the category of natural philosophy after the coming of physics, chemistry, and biology. Moreover the old contrast between the two philosophies disappears as well. In the place of the old division— mineral, vegetable, animal; ethical or individual, political or social —there is now an unbroken series of sciences from mathematics, astronomy, physics, and chemistry on through biology, sociology to psychology.

Moreover, as Comte worked more and more from the new position he began to see that all the matters of most intimate concern to men in the full sense, i.e., persons, individuals, moral beings were concentrated in the higher levels of the hierarchy and he began to use a new criterion for deciding the rank of a given class of homogeneous phenomena. These classes were to be ranked not only according to the decreasing generality they manifested but also according to their increasing dignity. In other words, the hierarchical arrangement reflected not only an intellectual judgment but a moral judgment; that is to say, the scale of sciences was also a scale of values. Man as an organism is conditioned by the operation of all the phenomena of the exterior world, i.e., by the milieu in which he lives; as a member of society, he is conditioned by the culture into which he is born; only when all these conditioning factors have been isolated is it possible to consider him in his psychical aspects, which are therefore the ultimate reality.

It is this fact which condemns the Spencerian position inserting a psychology between biology and sociology. This view of the matter is only a reflection of the old moral philosophy. It differs in no essential respect from Comte's original position in the *Philosophie*, where the intellectual and moral aspects of existence were placed at the summit of biology and so came immediately before sociology. Comte's position as finally worked out in the *Politique* is quite different. Here the psychological, the individual, the moral are placed above and beyond the sociological and the biological. These phenomena are least general because they require the presence of all the other levels of phenomena in order to become manifest; their manifestations are the most complex because they are conditioned by the operation of the laws of all the other classes of phenomena; they are at the same time the highest values because it is they which make men men in the fullest sense, i.e., of personality.

It will perhaps facilitate the comprehension of Comte's position if the encyclopedic scale be traversed in the descending direction. At the top is the psychological, the potential person, with possibilities of feeling, thought, and action. These potentialities are exercised, developed, made real in a given sociological setting, a culture, which will favor some of them and subordinate others, afford a basis for thought, and direct the activity. These potentialities will be still further conditioned by the state of the organism which is the basis of the psychical qualities, and the organism in turn is conditioned by the whole sum of environmental influences. The effect of the last set of conditioning factors is today in theory quite clear; the effect of the organic factors too is well enough understood in the theoretical sense. It is the nature and relation of the remaining two which are today in question.

For Comte in the *Politique* the answer is that there are two homogeneous classes of phenomena: the sociological or collective and the psychological or individual. The latter is not a part of the organic group though based upon it. Neither is it a part of the sociological class; sociological conditions do not account for psychical activities. They do however canalize, direct, modify, and condition them in countless ways. But that is all. These psychical activities are essentially independent; they are a category by themselves with their own regularities of similitude and succession, their own laws, that is, which it is the business of the psychologist to discover.

The conception, it may frankly be admitted, is difficult at first to fit into the mind. The reason is not the inherent complexity of the idea, which is quite simple considered in itself. It is rather the fact that the new conception runs counter to notions which have been embedded in the cultural heritage for so long as to seem beyond question: moral philosophy, a domain into which the entry of scientific law is by definition impossible; the necessity of knowing the individual as a preparation for the study of society. These are the chief obstacles. The others are minor ones and deductions from the first two, such as the necessity of having a science of psychology as a prolegomenon to the science of sociology. This relation is reversed by the new intellectual position. The conditioning effects of culture must be understood before the complexities of the personality can be reduced to order. Then the psychologist will be free to deal with the real mysteries which confront him. What is feeling? What is thought? Feeling, thought, and action are purely descriptive terms. Will the future show them to be as little related to the psychical actuality as the *tria prima*—salt, sulphur, and mercury—of the alchemist were to the elements of the chemist?

Such speculations as these are not for the sociologist, and far less are they the material for this chapter. What it must now do is to facilitate and accelerate the entrance of the new conception into the body of current thought by showing the steps whereby Comte reached it.

The story in the main is that of Comte's gradual disentangling of the isolates upon which the sciences of the hierarchy must rest. The first and in many ways the most important discovery was that of the isolate distinctive of biology. It came at the end of the second volume of the *Politique*. Up to that time Comte had thought of biology as the general science of living things, divisible into three levels: vegetal, animal, and intellectual and moral. Sociology was the general science of the social, the next level in the hierarchy and the highest. "Before beginning the final science [sociology] it is necessary to have sketched the abstract theory of the exterior world, and of individual life." [1] Such were his words in 1851, beginning the *Politique*. They are but a repetition of his statement made twenty-five years before: "Social phenomena, being manifested by human beings, are doubtless comprised among the phenomena of physiology. But although for this reason social physics must of necessity take its point of departure in individual physiology, and be kept in relation with it, it should none the less be conceived of and cultivated as an entirely distinct science." [2]

The position is perfectly clear; it is the position of moral philosophy so often referred to. It is still commonly held and is the reason why nearly all the sociologists have felt an imperative need of dealing with the social forces, interests, drives, and psychical factors in general before entering upon sociology proper. To see that no such introduction to the science is needed is difficult, because it requires reorientation of thought, and not merely their own thought but that of many, many generations. Such a reorientation Comte was

1. Comte, *Système de politique positive, 1, 42.*
2. *Politique, 4,* Appendix, 150, n.

to make during the writing of the *Politique*. It began in the second volume.

Up to the time of composing this second volume of the *Politique* Comte had considered biology to be the abstract study of the individual life, of individual physiology, starting with the vegetal level and including as its terminus the study of the intellectual and moral phenomena, i.e., feeling, thought, and action. During the writing of the volume the inclusion in biology of the intellectual and moral level of the living being became more and more doubtful, until at the end of it Comte was saying: "A too vague conception of biology leads to the representation of the study of our individual existence as already comprised in the general theory of vitality." In fact, "True biology has in no wise for its object the individual knowledge of man, but only the general study of life, envisaged above all in the whole of the beings who enjoy it." [3] This "fundamental vitality alone common to all organized beings," he said, "consists in their continual material renovation, the only attribute which universally separates them from inert bodies, where the composition is always fixed." [4]

Here then at last was a true isolate, the basis of an abstract science, biology, which thus became the general study of the process of continual renewal of material substance in all the forms in which it is to be observed. This process is an abstract phenomenon and it is a true isolate because the process is separable from all the other characteristics which living forms may manifest.

At the same time Comte was working in another direction. Since feeling, thought, and action were not to be comprised in the definition of vitality as given above but only rested upon that vitality as a basis, what science or sciences were to deal with them? An answer at once suggested itself, based upon his previous work in sociology. In that science as he had worked out its details in the *Philosophie* there were two great classes of phenomena each with a special dynamic law: the law of intellectual development and the law of material development resulting from man's activity. Hence the answer to the question above was simple: thought and action would be the domain of sociology, while feeling, the ultimate source of human existence, would go into a separate science. This science

3. *2*, 436, 437.
4. *1*, 586.

would be superior to sociology, since the manifestations of feeling were the most complicated of all the phenomena man could study.

This is precisely the position taken in the third volume of the *Politique.* Comte is quite aware of the significance of the change. The *Philosophie,* he says, "represented sociology as the universal point of arrival, while here this supremacy belongs only to *la morale* [positive psychology], which alone constitutes the terminus of science and the source of art. There is really no contradiction between these two successive appreciations, since my sociology at first included *la morale* [psychology] although in a confused manner." [5] In order to remedy this confusion, Comte proceeds to define sociology in accordance with the new position. "Sociology considers in man mainly intelligence and activity. . . . This study of collective development especially brings into relief our theoretical and practical progress. Our feelings figure in sociology only for the stimulation they give to the common life or the modifications they receive from it. Their own laws, to be properly studied, must be studied in moral science [positive psychology] where they acquire the preponderance due to their higher rank in the system of human nature." [6] Sociology "should indeed besides the intellect embrace also the activity, leaving to [psychology] the proper and direct study of the feeling, as the supreme motor of human existence." [7]

Here then is a distinct advance in theory. Biology, once for all, has been defined on the basis of a true isolate; the existence of a domain of science beyond sociology has been established. But the definition of sociology as consisting essentially in the total study of the human intelligence complemented by the study of the activity is far from giving it either an abstract phenomenon or an isolate. Besides it involves a glaringly false view of human nature, as Comte was presently to see, during the composition of the fourth volume of the *Politique.* In the early chapters of this volume he was particularly concerned with the problem of human unity, especially in the aspect of that conception which would today be called the integration of the personality. The elements of that unity are feeling, thought, and action; but if these elements are so distinct from one

5. *Politique, 3,* 5.
6. A. Comte, *Catechism of Positivism,* R. Congreve, tr. (3d ed. London, Kegan Paul, 1891), p. 172.
7. *Politique, 3,* 48.

another as to be the bases for entirely different sciences, how is the unity ever to be achieved?

The fact is of course they cannot be so separated. Comte finally saw the error and the way to remedy it. Sociology does not provide materials for understanding the unity of the personality. Sociology "opens the way to the systematic study of the soul, by the appreciation of collective existence, statical and dynamical. In it we feel that since the special study of intellect and activity are separated from that of feeling, it allows only of *the appreciation of RESULTS*, the source and destination of which belong to the following science. If this false position of the mind is not manifest in the treatise I am completing, that is due solely to the fact that the elaboration of [psychology] is therein spontaneously mingled with the construction of sociology." And so Comte continues: "Despite the systematic superiority of my religious construction [*La Politique*] over my philosophical foundation [*La Philosophie*], the treatise I am finishing [*La Politique*] cannot allow of the complete rationality to which I always aspired, since the normal separation between sociology and [psychology], alone decisive from the synthetic point of view, arose while I was executing an elaboration that it should have dominated." [8]

In these two statements Comte avows his failure to make the completely rational treatise he had hoped and puts future sociologists on the path to the desired success. He tells them what to look for and how to look for it. The method is to make a complete separation between sociology and psychology. In addition he gives a hint as to what sociology will deal with when this separation shall have been effected. The study of feeling, thought, and action in their essential nature is the business of psychology. Sociology does but study the results of the collective exercise of the last two of these elements of psychical unity: not thought in itself nor intellect nor intelligence, not activity nor action, only the collective results of the operation of those psychical aptitudes to which the loosely descriptive terms "thinking" and "acting" are given.

Implicit in the words of Comte is a sociological isolate; but it will require the aid of several of the later sociologists to make the definition explicit. At the moment Comte has done three things: he has established a definitive isolate for biology; he has given more than

8. *Politique, 4,* 232–233.

a hint of the true nature of the sociological datum; and he has suggested a method whereby this hint may be acted upon.

The key to the future sociology is in the word "results." Whatever thinking and acting may turn out to be in the hands of future psychologists is of no interest to the sociologist. He knows that when these psychical aptitudes are exercised collectively, there will be results; with them is his real concern. So far does the guidance of Comte extend, but no further. On his own admission he never wrote the completely rational sociology to which he had always aspired. There is therefore no "Comtian" or "Comtist" sociology, and so one of the many differentiating and limiting adjectives for sociology disappears. In any case Comte had never thought of a personal construction; his whole ambition was to add another to the list of basic sciences; what he strove to construct was a positive, i.e., scientific sociology. Such a creation is by definition a collective product. All that any man however great can do is initiate the process and serve for a time as the rallying point for other investigators. Out of their combined labors may with time emerge a sociology—without adjectives.

What this volume then has next to do is strive to effect just such a combination as that described. The materials are the work of the men already mentioned; the rallying point is the work of Comte, especially in his latest phase; the objective is the discovery and establishment of an abstract phenomenon which is at the same time an isolate on which a science can be built; the guide is no one man but the general experience of thinkers embodied in the history of sciences. The task should not be too difficult in view of what has just been said, for it is in effect the statement of a general rule whereby to determine the relative availability of the various major sociologists with respect to the creation of a sociology as defined.

The immediate result of putting this rule to work is the exclusion from the field of sociology as here defined of those efforts which plainly and unmistakably contain or are even built upon psychological data. Such an elimination, it should be emphasized, is no dogmatic or arbitrary exclusion of the work of able men from the consideration of sociologists, present and to come. On the exact contrary, it is an effort to facilitate the strictly sociological process of combining their efforts into a collective result which will be the product of no one of them but the outcome of their separate efforts centered about a concept which meets the requirements that an inductive study of science in general shows must be met if a new science is to be created. Neither is any denial involved of the essential validity of the views of such men as are rejected from the sociological field. Often indeed it is the very soundness of their doctrines which motivates their exclusion from the domain of sociology defined as an isolate. Moreover, their conclusions in regard to special questions are often of the utmost interest and value and must be incorporated into the sciences of the future; all that is meant is that their work is not a basis for sociology as here defined.

The first application then of the proposed standard is to divide the sociologists listed here, and by implication all others, into two general groups: those who by their basic conceptions essentially meet the requirements of an isolate and those who do not. Tarde, for example, so clearly incorporates a large and even basic element of the psychological into his theories as to eliminate him from further consideration; and Giddings is almost certainly in the same case. Spencer and Pareto, despite their differences, are yet curiously alike in their efforts to deal with societies as wholes, with reference to either their evolution or their form, and so cannot be thought of as dealing with either an abstract phenomenon or an isolate. LePlay can be envisaged from two points of view. If he is regarded as carrying his analyses into the remote regions where they deal with place, work, and folk, i.e., the sum of the formative elements in the making of a people, then he may be placed alongside Spencer and Pareto. If he is considered as the observer of but a single form of association, the family, then he is concerned with but a variant of the group, which in its formation is dealt with in various ways by Small along with Ratzenhofer and in a special way by Simmel and the formal school. All of these men, especially those just named, provide rich stores of material which can be incorporated into the body of sociology once the implications which underlie their thought are made explicit by being viewed in the light of the isolate to be defined.

Of the sociologists that remain it may be said with fair accuracy and definiteness that they do tend to deal not with society or societies or with groups or motivations but with the abstract phenomena which underlie them. Their terms differ: Comte speaks of results,

Ward of achievements, Sumner of folkways, Durkheim of collective representations. The first two terms are general and inclusive; the third throws emphasis on action, the fourth on thought; but they all are alike in having as referent not individuals or groups or collectivities but consequences, i.e., phenomena.

The point is put concisely enough in *The Science of Society:* "Any real science of society will obviously study what it professes to study, namely, a society. In so doing it must watch what really happens, that is, *consequences* as distinguished from purposes or motives." [9] All four agree that there is a distinctive science with a distinctive subject matter; and Sumner, finding the current technical vocabulary of his time too vague or too loose to refer with accuracy to the phenomena with which he is concerned, makes a beginning of a special terminology with the term "societal." "The structure thus built up is not physical, but societal and institutional, that is to say, it belongs to *a category which must be defined and studied by itself.*" [10] All that would seem to be needed as the basis of a science is a sufficient analysis of the various concepts in question to reduce them to a common level of abstraction.

To carry out such a reduction requires only a brief review of the thought of the sociologists in question. Comte, as a result of a lifetime of meditation upon the general content of the science which he was the first consciously to propose, came at last to see that he had, in consequence of ideas as old as Aristotle, been thinking in terms that were in part psychological; hence his avowal that he had never achieved in his sociology the complete rationality to which he had ever aspired. Ward coming later is able to get free to some extent of the psychological and to frame a definition that gives sociology a datum, an isolate, of its own; yet he is sufficiently under the sway of the ideas flowing from moral philosophy to turn squarely away from the data he had just declared to be the subject matter of his science and enter upon a discussion of their psychological sources. Sumner and Durkheim carry the analysis further. For each of them there are sociological phenomena, not reducible by analysis to any simpler form, composing a category that must be studied in and for and by itself. As Durkheim put it, sociological phenomena are things. A societal or sociological fact is of course to be explained

9. Sumner and Keller, *The Science of Society,* 3, 2175.
10. *Folkways,* p. 35.

by another societal or sociological fact. By what else would it or could it be explained? Gumplowicz, without adding any essentially new elements to the concept, sees and expresses clearly the implications of the general idea. In Marx the problem is obscured, but the idea at the basis of changes in the means of production is certainly not in contradiction with the general concept here in point.

What then is the abstract phenomenon which is at the same time an isolate capable of supporting the structure of a science of sociology? The answer is to be had from a fusion of the ideas presented by the four men here in point, supplemented by some others. The first common aspect of the four theories is that the societal phenomenon is collective in nature. It is not and cannot be produced by a single being acting alone. The best that can be done in the case of the isolated individual is to say with Comte that a single organism can improve upon its own previous efforts and so create a condition that ameliorates; but unless these ameliorations or improvements are in some way transmitted to others they never become of sociological interest. There must be a convergence of efforts if sociology is to be concerned. All the men here in question from Comte down agree in emphasizing the fact that *the result of interaction* but not the individual is the center of interest: not what men are but what they do; the individuals pass, the facts remain; the individual representation is of interest only when by being fused with another it becomes collective.

The members of a given species, evolved by biological processes to the point where they can learn from others, find themselves in the presence of the problems that the maintenance of life entails. They meet these problems as animals, urged by the biological drives to live. Then they join efforts, at first very crudely and slowly, as the imperfections of the biological equipment make inevitable, and then more rapidly and effectively as the growing fund of collective results makes possible new achievements. These collective results are combined, contrasted, compared, corrected, expanded. They are due not to individuals separately but to groups or collectivities. It is not even necessary that the individuals concerned should belong to the same species, as the association between Homo, Canis, and Equus makes clear. The individuals are lost from sight and only the results remain, for the sociologist to study as abstractions.

But the collective nature of the societal fact is only one of its essential characteristics. There is another of equal importance. Where a number of individuals engage in collective activity, new results flow from their cooperation; effective as regards the past, they are also starting points as regards the future. In other words, collective activities do not have to begin always at the same zero point of departure. On the contrary the point of arrival of the first collective effort is the point of departure for the next such effort. Something has been achieved in the first cooperation; it is the basis for a new achievement. That is to say, a single collective effort is not a true societal phenomenon but bears to it only the relation of a crystal to a living organism. Collective results must be built so to speak into a continuing sum of results; they must be cumulated if the societal phenomenon is to be seen in its fullness.

Hence the facts on which a sociological science operates are both collective and cumulative. They are doubly abstract in that individuals and generations both are lost from view in the presence of a constantly recurring phenomenon. The process by which the facts in point make possible the life of societies is a process of continuous cumulation of collective results. The abstract societal isolate, basis for a sociological science, may be defined as a collective cumulation. Just as biology studies the continuous renewal of material substance so does sociology study the continuous cumulation of collective experience.

With the spirit of this definition all the writers named are in accord; and Sumner and Durkheim go even further in the sense that taken together they illustrate certain complementary aspects of the phenomena underlying all culture and the social heritage as a whole. Sumner, to begin with, emphasizes the aspect of sociological data which reveals them as the result of men (individuals, that is) acting, doing, living in the sense of physical activity. The folkways are primarily ways of doing things and result in mental cumulations only at a second remove so to speak. Durkheim enters at this point with the complementary conception of representations. The emphasis here is on the inner aspect of societal phenomena. A picture of reality or of a given part of it is to begin with an individual product, but it is only the reality as seen by one being among all the countless ones who contemplate it. When seen, however, by a being with the power of communication and the capacity of learning, the picture as existent in one mind soon comes to be a composite of all the pictures existent in all the minds of the intercommunicating group. In other words, the representation is collective and because it is collective is soon cumulative as well, enabling a new individual to see the reality as all the old ones together have succeeded in seeing it. In a very real sense, he sees it through their eyes. And in an equally real sense, this cumulative representation is an external thing with regard to the new member of the intercommunicating group. In short, Sumner and Durkheim show that sociological data, results, may grow out of either action or thought.

It need not be said that the validity of the concept defined above is not dependent upon the authority of Comte or Ward or Sumner or Durkheim, that it is not limited to the scope of results or achievements or ways or representations. These men and their formulations are but parts of a great process, itself collective and cumulative, whereby men have sought to gain greater knowledge of their world and greater control over it. They are but the latest and most conscious stages in a vast and almost timeless induction, which preceded them and survives them and which by its multiform immensity makes quite impossible the presentation of its results in any inductive fashion.

But if these thinkers and their thoughts are only the movements and the moments of an enduring process, then it is an inescapable inference that the essence, the basis, the characteristics of the thought they all express must have been recognized in some form or other earlier than their efforts or outside of them. Too great originality in the results of analyzing so basic an element of human existence would in other words be a symptom of hasty analysis rather than a sign of sure penetration. It has been said that originality is the least of recommendations for fundamental conceptions.

Of course—and it is easy to show that an awareness of the essential societal idea has long existed; but the seeker for the evidence must know where to look; it is not always on the surface. Here at least it is not possible, for example, to start with a quotation, more or less accurately translated, from Aristotle. Yet with no desire to overpraise the Greeks, it would be surprising if they had not had some surmise at least of the existence and influence of so vital an element in the making of Man.

They did, too; but it is not in the direction of Greek science that attention must be turned if the evidence is to be found. It must be remembered that science had for the Greeks passed only through the mathematical and lower astronomical levels. It was far from the physical or biological plane; and as for the moral and political life of man, no serious effort of a scientific kind was at the time even conceivable. No, the evidence that thought on these levels was moving is to be found in religious or philosophical doctrines; it is among the hominoids, especially the so-called metaphysical concepts, that it is to be found.

It goes without saying that here is not the place for the discussion of ideas that would lead down from Anaxagoras through Aristotle to the neo-Aristotelians and so on to the Arabs and medieval scholastics, but the path can be pointed out. Bussell makes it possible to delineate it with extreme concision. Before Anaxagoras, when motion was postulated, the Greeks were content to refer it to some immanent force or inner impulse of the world mass. With Anaxagoras appeared another solution—the hypothesis of *nous*—upon which later Greek philosophy was little more than one long commentary. "An extraneous power, *nous,* once visited our world and imparted a *motion* which could never otherwise have arisen. When this was called *mind,* it is clear that we are beginning the long period of *dualism;* between object and subject, present and future world, earth and heaven, the true function and the secondary duties of our soul." [11]

The almost infinite variations on this theme cannot be even hinted at; but one of them is pertinent here, namely, the distinction between the active and the passive intellect. For Aristotle "there is that in man which cannot be explained by natural causes

11. This passage, pp. 241–242, is based on F. W. Bussell, *Religious Thought and Heresy in the Middle Ages* (London, Robert Scott, Roxburghe House, 1918), pp. 469–501, 509–527. The words quoted are to be found on pp. 510, 489–490, 490 (2), 491 (3). (Italics are Bussell's.)

and enters his nature from another sphere. Man's mind, bound to the senses as the sole vehicles or avenues through which knowledge can reach him, is at first a *tabula rasa*. His intellect may be divine but it cannot manifest itself in this lower world without the stimulants of sense-impressions. But this dormant or *virtual* faculty becomes *active* by a gradual union with a divine power, also regarded as entering from without."

"The Active Intellect (superior to the passive) is separate, impassible and immortal. *We cannot then look for the Active Intellect in the individual.* It is therefore a gift or grace coming to us from without; . . . *it is, and yet it is not, the human faculty of reason at its highest point.*" That is, there is a double view of the nous, which makes it "a man's truest personality, and yet a power intruding (as it were) from elsewhere."

The later Peripatetics developed the thought. Aphrodisias speaks of the passive intellect as "a transparent crystal, formless and colorless in itself," which "thus has aptness to mirror what passes; it is *pure receptivity*." "The act of knowledge is due to God's intervention: He uses our faculty as an instrument: Active Intellect is then God himself who for a short space enters into relation with our soul; it is but a transient theophany and the mortal element soon relapses into its nothingness." "Themistius followed the same mystical view: intellect, one in its source (God), is manifold in those who partake of it, as infinite rays come from a central sun. Our dormant intellect (conceived by him more substantively than in some other Peripatetics) desires to perfect itself and aspires to complete union with that Being, in which it both achieves its final development and as the price ceases to be itself." "Philoponus brings in a realistic element (in the medieval, not the modern, meaning) by speaking of mankind as *a collective thinker who is always thinking.* Units of the human family may be asleep or abstain from thought in any true sense, but there are always some who keep the sacred fire burning, and maintain the electric current between heaven and earth."

It requires little penetration to get beneath the mysticism of such passages and discover the modern problems of the relation between the societal and the psychological, between the collective and cumulative and the individual, to see the animal Homo being made Man, and that by a power not his own. Sumner saw the point clearly and gives the clue to its understanding: "Often in the mythologies, this ultimate rational element in the folkways was ascribed to the teaching of a god or a culture hero." [12]

Once the collective and cumulative principle is clearly grasped, the road between Philoponus and Pascal is direct. "By a special prerogative, not only does each man advance in the sciences from day to day, but all men together make a continual progress in them, as the world grows older, because the same thing happens in the succession of men that happens in the varying ages of an individual. Whence it follows that the whole succession of men, during the course of so many centuries, must be considered as a single individual, ever living and ever learning." [13] Or between Pascal and Ferguson: "In the human kind, the species has a progress as well as the individual; they build in every subsequent age on foundations formerly laid; and, in a succession of years, tend to a perfection in the application of their faculties, to which the aid of long experience is required, and to which many generations must have combined their endeavors." [14] And so on to the cultural concepts of today.

Other men than sociologists have come to a realization of the thought here in point, often long after it had been clearly expressed. A case in point is that of Korzybski, and his discovery was put in words that have had a certain renown:

Like the animals, human beings do indeed possess the *space-binding* capacity but, over and above that, human beings possess a most remarkable capacity which is peculiar to them—I mean the capacity to summarize, digest and appropriate the labors and experiences of the past; I mean the capacity to use the fruits of past labors and the experiences as intellectual or spiritual capital for developments in the present; I mean the capacity to employ as instruments of increasing power the accumulated achievements of the all-precious lives of the past generations spent in trial and error, trial and success; I mean the capacity of human beings to conduct their lives in the ever-increasing light of inherited wisdom; I mean the capacity in virtue of which man is at once the heritor of by-gone ages and the trustee of posterity. And because humanity is just this mag-

12. *Folkways*, p. 28.
13. B. Pascal, *Pensées de Blaise Pascal* (Paris, Dufour & Cie., 1828), p. 28.
14. Adam Ferguson, *An Essay on the History of Civil Society* (London, 1768), p. 7.

nificent natural agency by which the past lives in the present and the present for the future, I define *Humanity*, in the universal tongue of mathematics and mechanics to be the *time-binding class of life*.[15]

Still another writer, Spiller, approaching the subject from the ethical point of departure, arrived at the same destination. Seeking some explanation for the fact of man's close affiliation to the higher apes and his almost infinite potential superiority over them, for the difficulty of harmonizing human experience, human history, and human hopes with current biological appreciations of man's place in animate nature, Spiller undertook to analyze and summarize the differences which separate men from animals and the characters common to them both, and so to define the distinctive nature of man, and complemented his work with a very extensive canvassing of opinion on the subject.

His conclusions are as follows: "All animals without exception are *incapable* of learning freely from others and even under ideally favorable conditions they never manifest as much as a trace of this capacity," whereas "all human beings without exception, leaving aside pathological cases, are *capable* of learning freely from others." That is to say, "just as all animals are by nature unmistakably *individuo-psychic,* so all men are by nature unmistakably *specio-psychic*—by which we mean that, broadly, all men are by nature alike dependent on and capable of learning freely from their fellows, alike capable (unaided) of the equivalent of slightly improving a primitive tool or idea during a lifetime, and alike responsible therefore for the high culture which develops in the course of the ages as the result of species-wide mental cooperation." [16]

Between individuopsychism and speciopsychism no gradations are conceivable "save in so far as growth in the mental powers of animals naturally and inevitably culminated in a mentality just sufficiently developed to allow of collective thought." [17] The case is an admirable example, though Spiller does not say so, of the de-

15. A. Korzybski, *Manhood and Humanity* (New York, Dutton, 1921), pp. 59–60. (Italics are Korzybski's.)

16. G. Spiller, *The Origin and Nature of Man* (London, Williams & Norgate, 1931), pp. 116, 98. (Italics are Spiller's.)

17. Spiller, p. 137.

pendence of quality upon quantity. A slight increase in the mental powers gives rise to a quite new capacity. A quantitative modification of the brain is thus the source of a qualitative alteration of the possessor's existence. But the strictly individual change is slight. And so Spiller's inference is difficult to refute: "So low do we therefore rate the individual's native intelligence that we regard the variations to be found in man's innate mental powers as for all intents completely negligible when discussing the method of man's progress. What the individual is able to add to the common stock should be hence considered as microscopic in dimension, although none the less invaluable from the viewpoint of there being a measureless number of such increments." [18] It is almost as if one were hearing Aphrodisias or Themistius speak in modern language.

The writers just cited were in a real sense off the direct route of sociological advance; it will be well therefore to bring this section of the chapter to an end by a return to the direct line of thought followed by the anthropologists. Here again it is quite impossible to cover the field. It is possible however to make a selection, and choice under the circumstances must almost inevitably fall upon the classical treatment of the subject in Kroeber's essay upon *The Superorganic*. It not only has the merit of clearly conceiving of the nature of the societal phenomenon but its title brings into view an implication of Spencer's work which the philosopher himself did little to bring out. Kroeber's point of departure is the distinction between the organic and the cultural.

> The line between the social and the organic may not be randomly or hastily drawn. The threshold between the endowment that renders the flow and continuance of civilization possible and that which prohibits even its inception, is the demarcation —doubtful enough once, in all probability, but gaping for a longer period than our knowledge covers—between man and animal. The separation between the social itself, however, the entity that we call civilization, and the non-social, the pre-social or organic, is the diversity of quality or order or nature which

18. P. 272.

exists between animal and man conjointly on the one hand, *and the products of the interactions of human beings on the other*.[19]

Social evolution is without antecedents in the beginnings of organic evolution. It commences late in the development of life. . . . With the unknown bearers of the primeval and gradually manifesting beginnings of civilization, there took place a profound alteration rather than an improved passing on of the existing. A new factor had arisen which was to work out its own independent consequences, slowly and of little apparent import at first, but gathering weight and dignity and influence; a factor that had passed beyond natural selection, that was no longer wholly dependent on any agency of organic evolution, and that, however rocked and swayed by the oscillations of the heredity that underlay it, nevertheless floated unimmersibly upon it.

"The dawn of the social is thus not a link in any chain, not a step in a path, but a leap to another plane." "The point is, there was an addition of something new in kind, an initiation of that which was to run a course of its own."

All the evidence known directs us to the conviction that in recent periods civilization has raced at a speed so far outstripping the pace of hereditary evolution that the latter has, if not actually standing still, afforded all the seeming, relatively, of making no progress. There are a hundred elements of civilization where there was one in the time when the Neanderthal skull enclosed a living brain; and not only the content of civilization but the complexity of its organization has increased a hundredfold. But the body and the associated mind of that early man have not, by any scale that can be applied, attained a point a hundred times, nor even twice, as fine, as efficient, as delicate, or as strong, as they were then; it is doubtful if they have improved by a fifth.

And so Kroeber begins a sketch of the curve of societal development, parting from the line of organic evolution at the point where there arises on it the first human precursor—the first animal that carried and accumulated tradition—and ascending even further above it as the two movements proceed each on its own course.

19. In this section, pp. 245–246, the quotations are from A. L. Kroeber, *The Superorganic* (Hanover, N. H., Sociological Press, 1927), *passim*.

One point raised by implication in the foregoing theory is important enough to demand discussion. The difficulty may be put in the form of a question: Is the sociological phenomenon as defined above an objective phenomenon? The answer here given is an unconditional affirmative. Both Sumner and Durkheim accord in the answer, the latter clearly, the former by implication. The only objection to the affirmative answer would seem to be that the societal fact is essentially psychical. So it is of course in most cases; what else would, say, the result of a communication be? But why must *all* the phenomena termed psychical be subjective? The whole encyclopedia of the sciences, as it develops from mathematics onward, is a movement of thought from the objective toward the subjective. At one time the movement seemed to end with sociology, as with the Comte of the *Philosophie*. It was precisely because Comte finally saw that there is beyond the sociological a level of phenomena where true subjectivity lies that in the *Politique* he extended the encyclopedia to seven members, of which the seventh and last was a positive *psychology*. Only when the thinker has reached this level has he finally come to the subjective; and in reaching it he passes through and goes beyond the sociological.

The thought seems perhaps subtle and scholastic. It is not really so. Seeing physics and chemistry where once was but the mineral kingdom, and understanding why chemistry as the science of the special qualities of the elements must occupy a level of abstraction above physics, the science of the general properties of matter, is essentially all that is implied; the only difficulty is to extend the thought beyond the inorganic to the organic levels.

The real obstacle to such an elevation to the higher levels of a classifying conception easily comprehensible on the lower is the enduring influence of the moral philosophy of old. The newer analysis disposes completely of the earlier conception, just as the creation of physics, chemistry, and biology forever ended the natural philosophy of the Greeks and Aristotle. Where there was once moral philosophy, a domain closed to science, within which ethics and politics were manifested by the individual and society, now is to be found a biological level of phenomena on the upper reaches of which appear forms capable of intercommunication. At this point a sociological level of phenomena appears, characterized by a collective and cumulative quality, giving rise to a culture and a social heritage. Conditioned by both the biological and the sociological but beyond and superior to them is the psychological, where lies the truly subjective, the inner series of reality, manifesting itself under the influence of the conditioning factors as personality. There is no longer a break in the continuity of thought or data; there are no longer two philosophies, natural and moral; there is one science, passing with unbroken gradations from the simplest phenomena of number to the most complicated manifestations of the human psyche.

There, in the data of the psychologist abstracted from the manifestations of personality, lies the subjective. Sociology lies just this side. It is or may be in part psychical; it is not for that reason subjective. The psychoanalyst of the present makes the distinction more understandable than it was in earlier days. On it in fact his whole position is based.

> Above all, psychoanalysis . . . considers mental life as the manifestation and intricate interplay of tendencies and strivings which ultimately express themselves in motor behavior. Apart from this dynamic feature, psychoanalysis has introduced into psychology two fundamental aspects, a sociological and a biological aspect. . . . The biological orientation consists in considering all the dynamic forces as biologically conditioned, as manifestations of those energy-consuming processes that constitute the biological phenomenon, "life." . . . The sociological orientation can be briefly formulated as follows: The development of personality can be considered and understood, at least partially, as a process of adjustment of the original inherited phylogenetically predetermined instinctive cravings to the requirements of collective life as they are represented by any given culture. . . . The problem which the individual has to solve during his development [is] the adjustment of the original inherited strivings to the social setting into which the individual happens to be born.[20]

From these statements emerge clearly the isolates that are the foundations of the three sciences distinctive of the modern era: the energy-consuming processes that constitute the biological phenom-

20. F. Alexander, *The Medical Value of Psychoanalysis* (New York, Norton, 1936), pp. 132–133, 137.

enon life; the cumulative results of collective life as they are represented by any given culture and by culture in general; the phylogenetically predetermined instinctive cravings, biology, sociology,
and psychology, the first and the second being conditioning, i.e.,
objective factors as regards the last.

The continuous renewal of material substance, the cumulation
of collective efforts, the interplay of instinctive cravings and strivings; three levels of phenomena, three abstract isolates: such are
the three sciences that compose the organic portion of the hierarchy.
Sociology is the intermediate member, and by virtue of its position
it has in earlier days inevitably drawn within its range data that
in strict logic belonged elsewhere, above and below. Not that such
combinations are in any sense to be condemned; the reality is infinitely complex and it must be studied in every way possible. But
now that the analysis is achieved in the abstract sense, a certain intellectual clarity results which may be utilized to throw light upon
some conceptions of sociology other than the strictly abstract one
and to reveal them as combinations of the various isolates just defined. In entirely different words, the same thought may be expressed in this question: What sciences are there other than the
strictly abstract ones? Or, again, what happens when several isolates
are studied in combination?

From the first moments when sociology was being outlined, an
answer to the foregoing questions was set forth. Comte in the opening chapters of the *Philosophie* distinguished between the abstract
and the concrete sciences. The distinction was elaborated by de
Roberty. There are, says the latter, three kinds of sciences: descriptive, abstract, and concrete. The first is but a systematic collection
of classified aspects or examples of real things which serve as the
source whence materials for the other sciences may be drawn. An
abstract science studies certain natural aggregates which it chooses
as best exemplifying the manifestations of an irreducible property
of matter; its ultimate purpose is to arrive at a distinct knowledge
of this property. A concrete science is one which studies aggregates
of aggregates—already studied by the different abstract sciences—
in order to reach an analysis of these complex aggregates, but with
this inevitable difference in the result: it never attains to the knowl-

edge of a new irreducible property, since the aggregates which it studies are composed of only the properties already studied by the abstract sciences; nor does it gain any new knowledge of the irreducible properties themselves, for it would then be encroaching upon the ground of the abstract sciences.

An abstract science analyzes the particular object it studies into certain elements or properties; a concrete science studies the combinations in nature of the aggregates already analyzed. But such a combination of objects, such an aggregate of aggregates can evidently contain no new factors which were not contained originally in the particular aggregates of which it is itself composed, whence it follows that a concrete science is in reality only a combination of abstract sciences united for a special end. The combinations may be of two kinds also: those which deal with beings in all their complexity and those which include only certain features or manifestations. For greater logical clarity, the sciences listed above may be renamed as follows:

Descriptive (or strictly concrete) sciences, providing materials:

Component (or abstract) sciences studying isolates of abstract phenomena;

Composite (or concrete) sciences studying combinations of the isolates already studied by the abstract group, the combinations being made with regard to wholes (or beings) or with regard to parts (or aspects).

Considered in relation to the above list, it is possible to classify the various sociologies represented by the authors whose theories have been summarized earlier in this volume. To begin with, the descriptive sciences on which the sociologist primarily depends for materials are those which deal with the cultures that lie at the foundation of societies. What zoology and botany are to biology (i.e., pure biology) anthropology and history are to sociology.

As to sociology regarded as a component or abstract science, Comte avowedly from the first was aiming for it, as was Ward. Sumner and Durkheim were working in the same direction, perhaps not so consciously; so too were Gumplowicz and Marx in his capacity of sociologist. The work of Giddings and Tarde was obviously composite, based upon sociological and psychological isolates—a combination for which the usual name of "social psychology" is evidently appropriate and logical. The cases of Spencer and Pareto are equally clear. They belong in the class of composite sciences dealing with wholes. The object of their attention was societies in their concrete reality, to the study of which they brought to bear the whole range of knowledge—Spencer to explain their evolution, Pareto their form. That Pareto was aware of the nature of his efforts is put beyond question by his own words: "When economic and social phenomena are considered together, *as we are considering them here* [i.e., in the *Treatise*], the development is in the concrete direction." [21] An additional proof is the deductive nature of their efforts, Spencer avowedly and Pareto obviously working deductively.

In the case of LePlay dealing with the family, Small with the group, and Simmel with the association, the effort is still in the composite field with special attention to aspects; and as the aspects chosen for attention become narrower but tend to involve extraneous conditions, as in urban or rural sociology, the result is even more clearly composite and concrete. In any case, there is one criterion for deciding whether a given effort does or does not fall within the general category of sociological. It is this: Does the argument *in the last analysis* rest upon societal data? Is it ultimately concerned with facts and inferences resting upon an analysis of the cumulated experiences of collective life?

Finally, one other question remains. With the nature of the societal isolate defined, what is the appropriate method for dealing with it? What was said on this subject in an earlier discussion of method still remains decisive: the one best method for dealing with a particular class of abstractions can be determined only by actual handling of the material. In this case enough has been done to show that Comte was on the right track when he proposed the historical method, a variant of the comparative method, as the one most appropriate for the nature of the data of the new science. In his later stage Comte generalized upon the historical method and gave it a

21. Pareto, *The Mind and Society, 3,* par. 1731.

new name, filiation. The cumulative nature of societal phenomena seems to give complete approval to this development on Comte's part. It is in fact the actual method used by Sumner, for example.

The nature of the method is in a real sense indicated, as in other cases, by the phrase used to denote it. Filiation (even though the word sounds biological it is not), "son-ship"—this term describes not biological but sociological relationship. Moreover, Spencer and others used the term "historical method" in a way quite distinct from Comte's use of it to apply to a naive comparison of sequential social stages. Not only does the term "filiation" serve to distinguish Comte's conception from later ones; it is more accurate too than the phrase "the historical method," for the latter almost inevitably points to the past and a connection with a long distant epoch. But the societal isolate does not necessarily have any such connection. The process of collective cumulation may begin at any time; it may relate to any kind of action or thought; it is certainly in operation as actively now as at any period, perhaps more intensely now than ever. A new invention or a borrowing of an old one from elsewhere may set it in motion in a new direction or field. Past and present and future are all within its scope; none of them is more important than the other; they are, or their societal phenomena are, all filiated together. It is in fact because the sociologist is dealing with a continuing process with no necessary restriction to the past that he can consider reasonably the prevision of the future. And because no other discipline utilizes or can so characteristically utilize this method, he may feel all the more confident in the reality of the isolate which determines the extent of his domain.

Thus the science of sociology has its history, its isolate, and its method: what more is needed for the institution of the science? Many have of course striven to accomplish this institution; mostly they have been more or less independent or even isolated in their efforts. The present differs from them only in that it believes the time has come to incorporate all their doctrines in a fresh collective effort. It in turn may become the starting point of new efforts; and so the progress of the science becomes one of the best illustrations of the process upon the study of which it is founded.

CHAPTER 11: *The Nature of Society*

If collective cumulations are the components of culture and the nature of their relations makes the method of filiation the most suitable for their investigation, the possibility of following the development of the societal phenomenon from its initial stages on to the formation of what is called a cultural heritage comes at once within the range of possibility. Since the formation of a cultural heritage is the product of a society, to trace the growth of the one will be to penetrate to the underlying conditions of development of the other. And since the process of societal development is an abstract phenomenon, emerging from an inductive study of the cultural development underlying all societal growth, the outcome will be the comprehension of society in the abstract. To discover and reveal the stages in this process, whereby all societies grow and in growing bring into relationship greater and greater numbers of men, past, present, and future, is the purpose of this chapter. It will show how a time binding, speciopsychic form of life rises to a superorganic, social, cultural, societal level of existence by virtue of the filiation that springs from the cumulating of collective experience and so will make clear how sociology at a certain stage of its development came to be defined as the science of society.

To start with, then, the animal form that was to rise to a new level of existence had from the beginning to live in an environment which had long pre-existed its emergence. It was in the presence of this milieu and with reference to its constituent elements that the members of the biologically favored species had to act. Its acts had to conform to the nature of the milieu if the species was to survive, and survival was at once the test and the evidence of the effectiveness with which the conditions of the environment were met. In other words, the animal Homo in the initial stages of his advance toward the level of Man had to meet the varied conditions which were presented to him by the inorganic world and the biological forms in which and with which he had to live. That is to say, nascent Man was confronted by a vast mass of facts, to which his behavior had to be adjusted if he was to live.

Adjustment to these facts was in the initial stages of human existence an individual necessity. The biological requirements of the species left no choice to the individual beings involved; they had to meet imperative needs and to do so were compelled to act. In this respect they were in a situation no different from that in which other animals found themselves. But unlike these other animals, the potential men possessed the power of learning from others and so were not dependent solely upon their individual experiences. Thus the acts by which individuals satisfied their needs by coming into adjustment to the facts which conditioned their existence tended to assume in increasing degree a collective nature.

The increasingly collective nature of acts was due primarily of course to the initial capacity for interlearning, but certainly the original weakness of this capacity would have precluded any significant results had it not been for the fact that the original range of human activity was severely restricted to the satisfaction of the biological needs common to all the members of the species. Thus, the original weakness of the capacity for interlearning was compensated for by being concentrated upon a narrow range of acts necessarily performed by all individuals. Individual acts thus tended to be guided by collective experience; and acts in the strictly personal sense came slowly to be replaced by action in the group sense. But from this change in the nature of man's actions no mitigation resulted in the necessity for the acts to be in strict conformity with the facts. The two were so related that no essential change in the first could occur in the absence of any important change in the second. That is to say, the basic sequence in the societal process is the adjustment of action to facts.

The third level in the sequence begun by the relationship between facts and action results from the increasing influence of the collective element in the makeup of the animal Homo as its continued operation works to produce cumulative results. Acts, dealing at first with isolated instances, tend when the instances themselves are related to become related in turn; one act, that is, depending upon, or being meaningful only when performed in connection with, another. The outcome, with time and the cumulation of collective experience with reference to a related set of facts, is a course of action, i.e., a sequence of acts performed with reference to a given end.

Here once more it is no digression to emphasize the dependence of the acts upon the facts which is the very basis of the societal sequence here in point. If the dependence is not direct, if the bond between the two is not effective, then the original need is not satisfied and the ultimate objective is not attained. If the objective aimed at is critical for the existence of the group, the failure to attain it jeopardizes or even ends the existence of those concerned; if it is not critical, then at least the effectiveness of the action is weakened and the group's energy impaired or wasted. Assuming for the normal case, however, a close relation between facts and acts and a consequent maintenance or increase of social welfare, the advisability of certain courses of action will tend to become evident as the result of the cumulation of collective experience in adapting or adjusting acts to facts. To such generalities favoring or rejecting given courses of action may be applied the term "policies," and they become the third stage in the societal sequence which now reads facts, action, policy.

The societal process continuing, a still more advanced position is the outcome, clearly in evidence in developed societies and existing in germ in the simpler ones. It is of course the result of the working of the same forces that produced the earlier members of the sequence. As general conclusions concerning the advisability, or the reverse, of related courses of action are themselves in turn made the subject of collective cumulation, the resulting analysis even though quite spontaneous eventuates in the adoption of general doctrines concerning the ultimate purposes of the group in relation to the policies followed. The final outcome is the recognition of basic general rules for guiding the group activities of the individuals whose permanent relationships are the essential reality of the society. To these fundamental, i.e., all-embracing generalities as to the choice of policies correlating the courses of action which bring adjustment to the facts of existence the term "principles" may be applied.

With this term, and with this stage, the societal sequence marking the essentially indivisible societal process may be said to end; other phenomena there are in the reality of a given society, but they will be found to contain other than strictly sociological elements. Within the societal isolate the sequence is as just analyzed: facts, action, policy, principles. These four are the characteristic and hierarchical resultants of the societal process in the abstract. They serve in every society to bring the behavior of individuals into the permanent relationships which issue in the formation and the continued existence of the group.

Facts → action → policies → principles: such then is the abstract process by virtue of which societies, i.e., aggregates of men in permanent relationship with one another are built up. This abstract societal process may be put in simple diagram form. When so pictured it shows the way in which societies develop when nothing is in operation but societal factors alone. Viewed in this uncomplicated perspective, the diagram shows also how society "ought" to develop and be developed. The "oughtness" in this case and the "rightness" of the ensuing societal growth is not a matter of moral judgment; it is the ought and right that are used when it is said that men ought to eat if they are to live and do right to partake of food in the circumstances. From still another point of view, the diagram presents a view of the stages by which aggregates of men become societies in the typical, average, characteristic instance. The diagram thus becomes a picture of the normal case—the abstract process underlying the normal course of societal growth.

The diagram which represents the normal societal growth, based on an abstract process which integrates generations of collective cumulation, is the following:

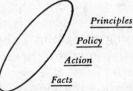

Principles
Policy
Action
Facts

Not only is the normal growth of a society represented by the diagram, but the normal state of a society is graphically pictured by it as well. The oval containing the related stages of growth may be thought of as excluding every nonsocietal influence from the factors on the working of which the normal growth depends. The oval is thus expressive of an integration completely covering the life of the society, i.e., the enduring network of relationships which holds together in essential harmony the aggregate of individuals constituting the biological basis of the society, and makes possible the continuous cumulation of collective products. This integration begins with the facts and extends on upward to directive principles. Thus there would not only be a complete integration once full adjustment to the facts is effected, but there would be no motive for modifying the integration so long as the facts are unchanged, for by definition such modification would result in something less than the best possible adjustment.

The integration figured in the diagram is applicable to any aggregate whatever of cooperating individuals. It may be the tiny society of paleolithic man or the earth-wide unicultural society of the hypothetical future. In either of these societies or in any others, the essential phenomena pictured by the diagram will be found. That is to say, beneath the diagram lies a completely abstract conception.

That the foregoing conception of a process of societal relationing which establishes more or less fixed constellations of individuals could have been derived directly and deductively from the concept and study of the societal isolate is evident. It was not so derived, however. On the contrary it is the outcome of the work of many sociologists; some, like Comte, contributing directive ideas; others, like Ward, generalizing earlier conceptions; still others, like Durkheim and Sumner, advancing to more and more detailed analysis.

Of these later and more detailed accounts of the formation of societies none is so significant in the present context as that elaborated by Sumner on the basis of his theory of the folkways. Since the essential importance of Sumner from the standpoint of these pages consists in his having done more than any sociologist since Comte to discover and analyze the phenomena circumscribed by the societal isolate, it will here be necessary to set forth Sumner's theory in its main lines with reference to the position of this chapter.

Such a summary will give a view of Sumner's work quite different from that taken in the stereotyped form into which his theory has fallen. Following Sumner, it begins with the evident fact that the struggle for existence must be carried on under life conditions. Among these conditions are "variable elements of the environment, the supply of materials necessary to support life, the difficulty of exploiting them, the state of the arts, and the circumstances of physiography, climate, meteorology, etc., which favor life or the contrary." [1] Between the two elements of the situation there is an intimate connection. They may be thought of as variables, one dependent, the other independent. When the conditions change the efforts to satisfy needs must change also.

Now the struggle to maintain existence in the human case presents a distinctive feature. Though it is in the last analysis individual, yet the individuals involved live in groups. Each can and does profit by the other's experience, and so there is concurrence towards what proves to be most expedient. When all at last adopt the same way for the same purpose, the ways that were to begin with individual habits turn into customs and so become group or mass phenomena. The ways, that is, of meeting the conditions of life from being at first individual become collective; and to mark this aspect of their nature Sumner calls them folkways.

The operation by which folkways are produced is simple. It consists in "the frequent repetition of petty acts," often by numbers acting either in concert or in the same way when faced with the same need. Of the first petty acts by which men try to satisfy needs, each stands by itself and looks no further than immediate satisfaction. "From recurrent needs arise habits for the individual and customs for the group, but *these results are consequences which were never conscious, and never foreseen or intended.* They are not noticed

1. Sumner, *Folkways*, p. 16, par. 21. The date of *Folkways,* it should be noted, was 1906 and of course the concepts which it introduces were still earlier in date. The point of the remark is that the terms "folkways" and "mores" were, and are, *societal* in contexture. Both words antedate the purely individual meanings which have since been given them. Such a transformation of meaning is also a transformation of the concepts which Sumner made the basis of his theories. It is this change, made in the past fifty years, which denatured Sumner's original ideas and probably accounts for the decline in his reputation.

This section, pp. 258–268, is based on *Folkways* and the quotations are from pp. 3 (2), 35 (italics are Sumner's), 5, 64, 119, 27–28, 28, 29, 35, 38, 30 (2), 36, 38 (4), 475, 476, 477, 70, 74 (italics are Sumner's), 80, 79, 79–80, 84 (2), 85, 86 (2), 117, 64, 57, 184, 32, 261, 307.

until they have long existed, and it is still longer before they are appreciated. . . . *The folkways, therefore, are not creations of human purpose and wit."*

Not only are folkways made unconsciously, they are being made continuously; they are coming into existence *now* all the time. The process of making them is never superseded or changed. It goes on now just as it did at the beginning. "The range of societal activity may be greatly enlarged, interests may be extended and multiplied, the materials by which needs can be supplied may become far more numerous, the processes of societal cooperation may become more complicated, and contract or artifice may take the place of custom for many interests; but, if the case is one which touches the ways or interests of the masses, folkways will develop on and around it by the same process as that which has been described as taking place from the beginning of civilization."

Moreover these unconscious and persistent phenomena are characterized by a strain of improvement. The folkways, being ways of satisfying needs, succeed more or less well. "If they were imperfectly adapted and unsuccessful, they produced pain, which drove men on to learn better. The folkways are, therefore, subject to a strain of improvement towards better adaptation of means to ends, as long as the adaptation is so imperfect that pain is produced." It is with this thought of improvement in mind that Sumner defined folkways as "expedient devices, developed in experience to meet the exigencies of life." "The processes and the artifacts which are connected with food supply offer us the purest and simplest illustrations of the development of folkways."

Certain other characteristics of these collective ways may be noted. Notably they are the source of the notions of right and truth. "If a savage . . . wants to catch an animal for food, he must study its habits and prepare a device adjusted to those habits. If it fails, he must try again, until his observation is 'true' and his device is 'right.'" These right ways to satisfy interests become traditional. "The 'right' way is the way which the ancestors used and which has been handed down. The tradition is its own warrant. It is not held subject to verification by experience. The notion of right is *in* the folkways. It is not outside of them, of independent origin, and brought to them to test them. In the folkways, whatever is, is right.

. . . When we come to the folkways we are at the end of our analysis."

Hence the folkways are the ultimate source of such phenomena as morality and its related manifestations. " 'Rights' are the rules of mutual give and take in the competition of life which are imposed on comrades in the in-group, in order that the peace may prevail there which is essential to the group-strength. Therefore rights can never be 'natural' or 'God-given,' or absolute in any sense. The morality of a group at a time is the sum of the taboos and prescriptions in the folkways by which right conduct is defined. Therefore morals can never be intuitive. They are historical, institutional, and empirical."

Finally, the folkways are in their nature collective and cumulative.

> The making of folkways is not trivial, although the acts are minute. Every act of each man fixes an atom in a structure, both fulfilling a duty derived from what preceded and conditioning what is to come afterwards by the authority of traditional custom. The structure thus built up is not physical but societal and institutional. . . . It is a category in which custom produces continuity, coherence, and consistency, so that the word "structure" may properly be applied to the fabric of relations and prescribed positions with which societal functions are permanently connected.

That folkways are the product of the abstract societal process defined in the preceding chapter has an important consequence, namely, that they are but the first stage in a sequence which leads from them to higher levels. Sumner of course saw the point involved here and extended his theory in accordance with it. Folkways come to have the force of ritual; they become coercive. "All are forced to conform, and the folkways dominate the societal life. Then they seem true and right, and arise into mores as the norm of welfare." In other words, here is the third stage in Sumner's sequence: individual ways, folkways, mores. What are they, then, and how do they arise?

The point of origin seems to lie at the juncture where judgments of expediency cease to operate in isolation and are combined with inferences as to societal welfare.

It is quite impossible for us to disentangle the elements of philosophy and custom, so as to determine priority and the causative position of either. Our best judgment is that *the mystic philosophy is regulative, not creative, in its relation to the folkways.* They reacted upon each other. The faith in the world philosophy drew lines outside of which the folkways must not go. Crude and vague notions of societal welfare were formed from the notion of pleasing the ghosts and from such notions of expediency as the opinion that, if there were not children enough, there would not be warriors enough. . . . The notion of welfare was an inference and resultant from these mystic and utilitarian generalizations.

The conclusion is that "when the elements of truth and right are developed into doctrines of welfare, the folkways are raised to another plane. They then become capable of producing inferences, developing into new forms, and extending their constructive influence over men and society. Then we call them the mores." Hence the mores are composites of two elements, folkways and notions of welfare. If the first of these elements are thought of as expedients and if for the second the term, unused by Sumner but now current, "values" is utilized, then the mores may be defined as expedients plus values. When so defined it is evident why they become norms of welfare.

It is of course impossible here to follow Sumner in his detailed examination into the characteristics of the mores. Of these characteristics, certainly the one most significant in the present context is the critical position the mores hold with relation to the subsequent members of Sumner's sequence. The ultimate explanation for any societal phenomenon "is that it conforms to the mores of the time and place. Historians have always recognized incidentally the operation of such a determining force. What is now maintained is that it is not incidental or subordinate. It is supreme and controlling. Therefore the scientific discussion of a usage, custom, or institution consists in tracing its relation to the mores, and the discussion of societal crises and changes consists in showing their connection with changes in the life conditions, or with the readjustment of the mores to changes in those conditions." The relation in point here is clearly a relation of filiation.

Above the mores then but filiated with them come societal products of greater complexity, such as institutions and acts of legislation. On a still higher level, i.e., at a further stage of removal from the folkways come systems of ethics, life policies, and world philosophies.

With regard to the preceding and all similar phenomena the basic question raised by Sumner's theory is the relation between them and the mores. On this point Sumner leaves no doubt: they are late members of the sequence which leads from individual ways through folkways to mores. Philosophy and ethics do not furnish creative and determining forces in society and history. "That view comes down to us from the Greek philosophy and it has now prevailed so long that all current discussion conforms to it." On the contrary, *"Philosophy and ethics are products of the folkways; . . . They are . . . never original and creative; they are secondary and derived."* "The real process in great bodies of men is not one of deduction from any great principle of philosophy or ethics. It is one of minute efforts to live well under existing conditions, which efforts are repeated indefinitely by great numbers, getting strength from habit and from the fellowship of united action." Out of the resulting folkways and mores come "faiths, ideas, doctrines, religions, and philosophies, according to the stage of civilization and the fashions of reflection and generalization."

On the whole problem involved here, the critical passage is to be found in the chapter of *Folkways* entitled "The Social Codes":

A recent German writer on the history of public morality says of the moral development of the German people that one cannot bear to contemplate it, because the people face the facts with absolute indifference. There is not a trace of moral initiative or of moral consciousness. Existing morality presents itself to us as a purely accidental product of forces which act without sense or intelligence. We can find all kinds of forces in history except ethical forces. These are entirely wanting. There is no development, for development means the unfolding and growth of a germ according to the elements which it contains. The people allow all kinds of mores to be forced on them by the work of their own hands, that is, by the economic and political arrangements which they have adopted . . .

On these conclusions Sumner comments at length, and since his position is essential to the construction of a scientific sociology, his words should be quoted:

> Rudeck's book is really a chapter in the history of the mores. The above are the conclusions which seem to be forced upon him, but he recoils from them in dismay. The conclusions are unquestionably correct. They are exactly what the history teaches. They ought to be accepted and used for profit. The fact that people are indifferent to the history of their own mores is a primary fact. We can only accept it and learn from it. It shows us the immense error of that current social discussion which consists in bringing "ethical" notions to the criticism of facts. The ethical notions are figments of speculation. . . . "Existing morality does present itself as a purely accidental [i.e., not to be investigated] product of forces which act without sense or intelligence," but the product is in no true sense accidental. It is true that *there are no ethical forces in history*. Let us recognize the fact and its consequences. Some philosophers make great efforts to interpret ethical forces into history, but they play with words.
>
> There is no development of the mores along any lines of logical or other sequence. The mores shift in endless readjustment of the modes of behavior, effort and thinking, so as to reach the greatest advantage under the conditions. "The people allow all kinds of mores to be forced on them by the work of their own hands," that is, by the economic and political arrangements which have been unconsciously forced on them by their instinctive efforts to live well. That is just what they do, and that is the way in which mores come to be. . . . All ethics grow out of the mores and are a part of them. That is why the ethics can never be antecedent to the mores, and cannot be in a causal or productive relation to them. . . . The mores grow as they must grow under the conditions. They are products of the effort of each to live as well as he can, and they are coercions which hold and control each in his efforts to live well.

" 'Our age presents us the incredible spectacle that the dependence of the higher social culture on the economic development is not only clearly recognized by social science, but is proclaimed as the ideal.' Social science does not proclaim this as an ideal. It does not deal in ideals. It accepts the dependence of culture on economic development as a fact."

Finally, as the last stage in the working of the societal process comes the making "of the group character which the Greeks called the ethos, that is, the totality of characteristic traits by which a group is individualized and differentiated from others." Japan, China, and India are cases in point, as well as Europe, despite local variations. "The ethos of any group deserves close study and criticism. It is an overruling power for good or ill. Modern scholars have made the mistake of attributing to race much which belongs to the ethos. . . . Others have sought a 'soul of the people' and have tried to construct a 'collective psychology,' repeating for groups processes which are now abandoned for individuals. Historians, groping for the ethos, have tried to write the history of 'the people' of such and such a state. *The ethos individualizes groups and keeps them apart.*" The stage at which an ethos is produced is the culmination of the societal process which begins with folkways.

If now attention be turned from the stages in the societal sequence to the characteristics of the mores which are the central phenomena of that sequence, certain comments of Sumner are in point. To begin with, the mores are always characterized by the element of persistency. "They are elastic and tough, but when once established in familiar and continued use they resist change. They give stability to the social order when they are well understood, regular, and undisputed." "They coerce and restrict the newborn generation. They do not stimulate to thought, but the contrary. The thinking is already done and is embodied in the mores. They never contain any provision for their own amendment. They are not questions, but answers, to the problem of life. They present themselves as final and unchangeable, because they present answers which are offered as 'the truth.'" "Some barbarian peoples have brought their mores into true adjustment to their life conditions and have gone on for centuries without change."

But persistence may harden into inertia and complete rigidity.

Ghost fear and ancestor worship tend to establish the persistency of the mores by dogmatic authority, strict taboo, and weighty sanctions. The mores then lose their naturalness and vitality. They are stereotyped. They lose all relation to expediency. They become an end in themselves. They are imposed by imperative authority without regard to interests or conditions. . . . When any society falls under the dominion of this disease in the mores it must disintegrate before it can live again. In that diseased state of the mores all learning consists in committing to memory the words of the sages of the past who established the formulae of the mores.

Fortunately such moral diseases are rare; "no less remarkable than the persistency of the mores is their changeableness and variation." The mores change because conditions and interests change. "It is found that dogmas and maxims which have been current do not verify; that established taboos are useless or mischievous restraints; that usages which are suitable for a village or a colony are not suitable for a great city or state; that many things are fitting when the community is rich which were not so when it was poor; that new inventions have made new ways of living more economical and healthful." Thus when the life conditions, the economic conjuncture, and the competition of life vary, the interests vary with them. "The mores all conform, unless they have been fixed by dogma with mystic sanctions so that they are ritual obligations. . . . The rights of the parties, and the right and wrong of conduct, after the mores have conformed to new life conditions, are new deductions. The philosophers follow with their systems."

The combination in the mores of persistency and variability raises the question as to the extent to which they may be changed by purposive action. The need of an answer to the question becomes acute when it is seen that "in higher civilizations crises produced by the persistency of old mores after conditions have changed are solved by revolution or reform." In a revolution, the mores are broken up. The outburst of a revolution is followed by a period in which there are no mores. "Revolutionary leaders expect to carry the people over to new mores by the might of two or three dogmas of political or social philosophy. The history of every such attempt shows that dogmas do not make mores." Reform (to which missionary effort may be assimilated) is the alternative to revolution. In essence, agitation is the substitute for violence.

"It is not to be inferred that reform and correction are hopeless. . . . The inference is that intelligent art can be introduced here as elsewhere, but that it is necessary to understand the mores and to be able to discern the elements in them, just as it is always necessary for good art to understand the facts of nature with which it will have to deal." Such understanding of the mores reveals two lines of attack upon the problem.

The first is the spontaneous method hitherto utilized. It consists in an arbitrary and direct attack upon the mores. Nothing sudden nor big can follow. It is not possible "to change the mores by any artifice or device to a great extent, or suddenly, or in any essential element; it is possible to modify them by slow and long continued effort if the ritual is changed by minute variations"—and even so only if the mores are ready for change.

The second is the systematic and scientific method of the future. Far more effective than attempts directly to modify the mores is the effort to affect them indirectly by alteration of the life conditions whence come the folkways that lie beneath them. The techniques of such alteration remain to be developed. "The statesman might well be appalled if he should realize that he probably never can lay a tax without effects on industry, health, education, morals and religion which he cannot foresee and cannot control . . . for, through the mores, they will enter into the web of life which the people are weaving and must endure."

Such in epitome is Sumner's theory. On it two comments are particularly pertinent here. In the first place, it is built upon a study of human action rather than human thought. That is to say, the element of expediency, the question of adequate satisfaction of need, is kept constantly in the foreground, to the point where the intellectual aspects of culture growth are often entirely out of sight.

Now this omission, serious as it is in relation to Sumner's development of his own idea, is much less so when that idea is given a setting in a wider perspective. In fact it is easy to strengthen the concept materially by bringing Durkheim to complete Sumner. Not only are there collective ways growing out of individual efforts to satisfy needs, but there are collective representations growing out of individual efforts to picture the reality. If the individual's visions of reality are called pictures, then there is a progression from pictures to representations to ideologies. In short, what has been said here and elsewhere in regard to Durkheim makes it possible to complement Sumner and bring the intellectual phase of human existence into the cultural domain where the collective and cumulative process operates.

In the second place—and far more important since the criticism goes to the validity of the intellectual construction outlined above —the theory presented accords imperfectly with the facts, especially in its stress upon the element of experience and expediency and in consequence the logical nature of ways and folkways. Society does not in fact develop in such a fashion.

The answer is simply an admission that Sumner never reached the end of the line of thought along which he was advancing and that his failure to do so blurs and dims the outlines of his thought. Thus for example even in regard to folkways, conceived of as expedient devices, Sumner wavers. Certain folkways are harmful; others have been formed by accident; there is always a large element of force in the folkways. "It constitutes another modification of the theory of folkways as expedient devices." His treatment of the mores too is wavering and uncertain, reaching direct contradiction on at least one occasion. "Fashions, fads, affectations, poses . . . must be included in the mores." "There are a number of mass phenomena which are on a lower grade than the mores. . . . These are fashion, poses, fads, and affectations."

Now Sumner was not unaware of the mixed nature of the data with which he was dealing, nor was he oblivious to the weak points of his theory. On the first topic he speaks at some length:

> The correct apprehension of facts and events by the mind, and the correct inferences as to the relations between them, constitute knowledge, and it is chiefly by knowledge that men have become better able to live well on earth. Therefore the alternation between experience or observation and the intellectual processes by which the sense, sequence, interdependence, and rational consequences of facts are ascertained, is undoubtedly the most important process for winning increased power to live well. Yet we find that this process has been liable to most pernicious errors. The imagination has interfered with the reason and fur-

nished objects of pursuit to men, which have wasted and dissipated their energies. Especially the alternations of observation and deduction have been traversed by vanity and superstition which have introduced delusions. As a consequence, men have turned their backs on welfare and reality, in order to pursue beauty, glory, poetry, and dithyrambic rhetoric, pleasure, fame, adventure, and phantasms. Every group, in every age, has had its "ideals" for which it has striven, as if men had blown bubbles into the air, and then, entranced by their beautiful colors, had leaped to catch them.

On the weaknesses in the theory Sumner was able to speak candidly. "Slavery is a thing in the mores which is not well covered by our definition. Slavery does not arise in the folkways from the unconscious experimentation of individuals who have the same need which they desire to satisfy, and who try in separate acts to do it as well as they can. It is rather due to ill feeling towards members of an out-group, to desire to get something for nothing, to the love of dominion which belongs to vanity, and to hatred of labor." "Inasmuch as slavery springs from greed and vanity, it appeals to primary motives and is at once intertwined with selfishness and other fundamental vices. It is not, therefore, a cause which gradually produces and molds the mores, nor is it an ethical product of folkways and mores. It is characteral."

The last quotation is the most revealing of all. It reveals Sumner in the search for what Comte would have called complete rationality. The two elements involved in such cases as the above are to-day clear. In the language of this volume, they are the societal and the psychical; in Sumner's words they are the societal and the characteral; in terms of science, the sociological and the psychological; in Comte's language, *la morale* is spontaneously intermingled with sociology. The two have to be separated. Comte saw the nature of the problem; Sumner very considerably advanced its solution; it was Pareto who finally opened to sociologists the road to the desired goal. To him then attention must be turned.

Pareto, it will be recalled, was an economist who found that the economic was only one of the factors operating to produce a given social situation. His *Treatise* was an effort to discover (the) other factors and combine them with the economic so as to determine the

form of society that would result from their interdependent operation. In his analysis of the factors accounting for the form of a society he was forced to make the distinction already adverted to between residues and derivations. It is in the discussion by Pareto of
the facts leading to this distinction that the corrective complement
of Sumner's theory is to be found. Very briefly, the essential point
is that there are two ways which men follow in reaching conclusions
as to the validity of the principles which they adopt with reference
to their actions. These two are the logicoexperimental and the nonlogicoexperimental.

Of the first class Pareto says: ". . . a person stating a logicoexperimental proposition or theory asks [proofs] of observation, experience, and logical inferences from observation and experience.
But the person asserting a proposition or theory that is not logicoexperimental can rely only on the spontaneous assent of other
minds and on the more or less logical inferences he can draw from
what is assented to. At bottom he is exhorting rather than proving." [2] Of the second class he says: "We see that there are many subjective, sentimental considerations of great potency which prompt
people to evolve and accept theories independently of their logicoexperimental validity." "Those considerations carry us into the
field of the *logic of sentiments*. . . . In ordinary logic . . . the
conclusion follows from the premises. In the logic of sentiment the
premises follow from the conclusion." [3]

What is involved here is no question of exalting logic and experience to a greater power and majesty than dogmas accepted by sentiment, nor even of passing judgment on their relative merits and
virtues, but simply of keeping the two sorts of thinking distinct. "In
both logico-experimental and non-logico-experimental theories,
one gets certain general propositions called 'principles,' logically
deducible from which are inferences constituting theories. Such
principles differ entirely in character in the two kinds of theories
mentioned." [4]

In logico-experimental theories, principles are nothing but abstract propositions summarizing the traits common to many different facts. The principles depend on the facts, not the facts on

2. *The Mind and Society, 1,* par. 42.
3. *1,* pars. 516, 514. (Italics are Pareto's.)
4. *1,* par. 54.

the principles. They are governed by the facts, not the facts by them. They are accepted hypothetically only so long and so far as they are in agreement with the facts; and they are rejected as soon as there is disagreement. . . . But scattered through non-logico-experimental theories one finds principles that are accepted *a priori,* independently of experience, dictating to experience. They do not depend upon the facts; the facts depend upon them. They govern the facts; they are not governed by them. They are accepted without regard to the facts, which must of necessity accord with the inferences deducible from the principles; and if they seem to disagree, one argument after another is tried until one is found that successfully re-establishes the accord, which can never under any circumstances fail.[5]

Now Pareto's purpose in making a contrast between the two kinds of principles was to separate them completely, so that he might eliminate one of the two classes from his data. Hence he was satisfied to define the excluded class in a negative fashion. They were *non*-logicoexperimental. But what would they be called by an inquirer who *included* them in his discussion? How could they be defined in a positive fashion?

With this question Pareto was not concerned. He had discovered certain psychical constants in the data he was analyzing, and beyond that fact he had no need to go. He was not interested in the ultimate nature of these constants. Nevertheless he knew that they were essentially psychological, and his statement to that effect is unequivocal: "Logical actions are at least in large part results of processes of reasoning. Non-logical actions originate chiefly in definite psychic states, sentiments, subconscious feelings and the like. It is the province of psychology to investigate such psychic states. Here we start with them as data of fact."[6]

In these words is implicit the idea whence will come the positive term desired. If nonlogical actions originate in definite psychic states, it must be that these states are not neutral but are already of such a nature as to be more inclined toward certain courses of action or lines of appeal than others. If derivations, for example typical nonlogicoexperimental phenomena, are persuasive, it must be that

5. *1,* pars. 55–56.
6. *1,* par. 161.

they meet the inclinations of the individuals persuaded. In other words, these states, i.e., those in whom these states exist, prefer one sort of excitant to another—an excitant becoming a true stimulus only when it accords with the preference inherent in the state to be affected. If this line of reasoning is sound, then the negative term "nonlogicoexperimental" can be replaced by the positive term "psychopreferential."

Thus there are two classes of collective cumulations, the logico-experimental and the psychopreferential. So far, doubtless, so good. But still a question remains, expressed by Pareto:

> Concrete theories in social connexions are made up of residues and derivations. The residues are manifestations of sentiments. The derivations comprise logical reasonings, unsound reasonings, and manifestations of sentiments used for purposes of derivation: they are manifestations of the human being's hunger for thinking. If that hunger were satisfied by logico-experimental reasonings only, there would be no derivations, instead of them we should get logico-experimental theories. But the human hunger for thinking is satisfied in any number of ways: by pseudo-experimental reasonings, by words that stir the sentiments, by fatuous, inconclusive "talk." So derivations come into being. They do not figure at the two extreme ends of the line, that is to say, in conduct that is purely instinctive and in strictly logico-experimental science; they figure in the intermediate cases.[7]

Pareto, it seems, is no more free of difficulties than Sumner. In this instance they seem to center in the term "logical," and the clue to their removal lies in the last sentence quoted: "[Derivations] do not figure at the two extreme ends of the line"; they are intermediate cases. That is to say, at one end of the line of thought is the animal Homo, going like any other animal straight from desire to act. At the other end is Man, directing his activities solely by logicoexperimental science (and writing a huge volume to defend the procedure).

But how did the animal Homo become Man? Only by the operation of the process of collective cumulation. Once this element hitherto concealed is brought into the light, the situation is clarified. The main difficulty lies in the term "logic." Logic is a societal

7. *3,* par. 1401.

product; it is still in the making. Pareto seems not to have envisioned this fact. There is no evidence whatever that the animal Homo had any hunger for thinking. Such evidence as there is points in the opposite direction. His descendants then could not have inherited it. What nascent Man felt was a hunger of a very different kind. It was a need for support and reassurance. It was not an intellectual but an affective need. As Man became more human he felt an increasing urge to show the congruity of his personal views with the cumulated experience of the collectivities to which he was becoming more and more closely bound. It was the collectivity which thought, and individual men needed to be identified with it. His derivations are at once a cry for help, an assurance of identity with his group, and an assertion of confidence. They show the passive intellect yearning and striving to be merged with the active intellect.

The logical then is really the social, and in the same line of thought the experimental implies a relatively high level of inquiry consciously systematized and utilized. As such, it is too portentous a word to be applied to the essential fact of man's reliance upon experience. And since the experience is that of the race, the term "logicoexperimental" can be replaced by the less imposing but more generically accurate term "socioexperiential."

In this fashion the factor of logic disappears, as it should, as a means of distinguishing between the two kinds of thinking with which Pareto is concerned. What really is important is the source of the materials for thought. Since neither kind can be dealt with logically, the point of Pareto's remark that a belief in logic has nothing to do with logicoexperimental science needs no laboring. What is involved is the source of the notions with which men busy themselves. Do they result from the cumulation of collective experience or are they prompted by psychic states, sentiments, and the like?

This division of the materials of thought into socio-experiential and psychopreferential on the basis of their intimate sources explains why Sumner had so much trouble with such deviations from expediency as arose from the aleatory element, the influence of force, the effects of error and superstition, and the characteral factor in general. It also opens the way to fusing the complementary theories of the two men into a synthetic and highly collective representation of society. To this end the statement in conclusion of this section of one more important point on which the two men agree will contribute.

The point is that the psychic states of Pareto may be thought of as active as well as passive. Sumner's comments on slavery clearly imply the possibility. Pareto states it plainly, as in the following passage: "It is obvious that the causes of such things [as virginity as a requisite for a Vestal, or 'perfectness' in objects or persons serving or offered to the Gods] are not to be sought in logical explanations of this kind, and that we shall find them only as we turn our attention to certain sentiments which *account both for the things* and *for the explanations given of them.*" [8] Since these states then may be active or passive, their power to color and tone the folkways and break the normal relation between interests and mores is accounted for as well as their influence in the making of derivations, whether logical or illogical. In either case it should be emphasized that the collective and cumulative nature of societal phenomena remains unaffected, whether they are classed among the socioexperiential or among the psychopreferential. It is only results that are societal phenomena, their source and ultimate purpose remaining elsewhere, i.e., outside the domain of sociology.

With the two classes of societal phenomena now established—the socioexperiential, which in its advanced and systematic stage becomes the logicoexperimental, on the one hand, and the psychopreferential on the other—it is possible to return to Sumner, put his theory in order, and combine it with Pareto's and others such as Durkheim's as well. The outcome should be a first approximation of a complete picture of the process, now entirely abstract, by which all societies, and so society, are brought into existence and maintained.

Thus to begin with, the conditions of life can be given a broader definition than before. All the circumstances which give rise to the reactions of individuals in the task of maintaining existence are included. The phrase really means all those things which create interests as Sumner defines them, i.e., the relations of the needs to the conditions. Thus the physical milieu to begin with, then the competition of life, then the state of the arts, then the amount of knowledge—all these things in all their implications make up the conditions of life.

The responses to these conditions come by two ways: ways of

8. *I,* par. 753.

doing, i.e., of satisfying need; and ways of judging, i.e., of satisfying desire. The first give rise to usages of various kinds, ways in which expediency can be served, any of which may become a custom if and when it is followed by all. Above this level come the ways which rise to the level of technique; beyond them are the expedients which embody conclusions based on collective experience as to the efficiency of devices in the satisfaction of needs. Thus there is here a succession: individual ways of satisfying needs and collective ways, the latter taking the forms of usages, techniques, and expedients.

Ways of judging are individual ways prompted by or satisfying to the psychic preferences of the individual. They have, in Sumner's words, characteral qualities and characteral effect. As these become collective they give rise to rituals, which on the psychic level are comparable to usages on the experiential level; they are fixed ways of affording psychical satisfaction to the members of the collectivity and intensifying though not altering sentiments. Above them come fashions, which since they are only temporary, changeable, momentarily gratifying, are never raised to the level of decisions as to ultimate societal worth. At a higher level arise ideals—combinations of sensations into more or less stably organized systems of images and pictures held together by feelings. Finally on this side of the development arise values—preferences which are based upon profound sentiments common to the members of the collectivity. Here too there is a succession, individual ways of responding to desire and collective ways, the latter rising from rituals and fashions through ideals to values.

When the expedients and the values meet, uniting the experiences and preferences of the collectivity, the mores arise, coming out of all that has preceded and becoming the starting point for all that is to follow and thus being according to the point of view the central point, the culmination, or the foundation of the collective life, for they determine the entire network of relationships which hold together the individuals and establish them in a society.

From expedients and values and serving to give stability to both arise interests in the Paretan, i.e., economic sense, and ideals. They merge and fuse and in so doing produce the mores whence, by way of determinations as to welfare, proceed those results of the abstract societal process which widen out into structures and doctrines. Of the first, giving rise to legislation and institutions, what Sumner has been quoted in an earlier passage as saying is sufficient for present purposes. On the matter of doctrines however including philosophies and mythologies, a few comments are needed.

Of philosophies as deliberately constructed syntheses of general principles little need be said. Of mythologies, it may be observed that they seem to stem from representations. One point in regard to the latter is particularly worthy of mention. It is that these mental pictures, whether individual or collective, may be the result not merely of observation, when the psychic constants behind the psychopreferential may be thought of as passive; they may be the result of imagination, when the constants may be thought of as active, impelling the intellectual faculties toward combinations of sense impressions that have never as combinations occurred in real life. And these combinations, once made, may have such appeal to the sentiments of the members of the society as to be accepted by them and made the subject of the collective process, whereby the ultimate representation becomes a truly collective product.

This fact and the consequences that follow it were the point of Pareto's observation: "The capacity for influencing human conduct that is possessed by sentiments expressed in the form of derivations that overstep experience and reality throws light upon a phenomenon that has been well observed and analyzed by Georges Sorel, the fact namely, that if a social doctrine (it would be more exact to say the sentiments manifested by a social doctrine) is to have any influence, it has to take the form of a 'myth.' " [9]

What seems to happen in the case of the myth is first the rise of a collective representation of a relatively restricted kind. As it becomes more and more the subject of the societal process, it inevitably comes into contact and in some cases at least into harmony with other representations. What results from the combination may be termed a view. It too undergoes transformation by being incorporated into a still larger unit which has as its purpose the picturing of the society as a whole in some one of its essential operations. Thus myths arise, being syntheses made from fusions of views, themselves integrated from representations which have their source in the collective transformation of pictures in individual minds.

No society exists without some picture of the world in which the

9. *The Mind and Society*, 3, par. 1868.

individuals composing it live and with relation to which they are coworkers. As this picture grows or as it declines in affective power, so the society grows or declines in cohesive strength. If it loses its power, i.e., if the experience of the collectivity makes it impossible for the old and familiar association of views to continue, the myth dies and the society tends to dissolve, i.e., the individuals become simply an aggregation once more. With its disappearance goes the culture which modified and even created by selection the type of man which was identified with it.

Much the same can be said in regard to the disappearance of the philosophies that rise out of the generalizations which condense on ever more abstract levels the experience of the community. Not that the myth is causally connected with the principles: the two grow out of the same set of basic conditions, the same body of mores; and when the basis changes, all the superstructure changes also. They are all interdependent, and there is constantly at work to bring them into greater harmony what Sumner calls a strain of consistency. It operates because they all answer their several purposes with less friction and antagonism when they cooperate and support one another. So with the structures which maintain the society. They too as well as the doctrines are, as regards one another, simply interdependent; they all have their foundations in the mores and, below them, in the folkways; and as these basic phenomena extend and are consolidated, the framework of structure and doctrine comes into being.

Thus the development of a society, when all the foregoing factors are envisaged as operating interdependently, is revealed as nothing but the gradual integration of hitherto merely aggregated individuals as they are bound more closely together by societal relationships whereby they become socii, members of a community, and so enter into a new state.

The final outcome of the societal process, rising from folkways to mores and thence to doctrines and structures, institutions and legislation on the one side and mythologies and philosophies on the other, is a distinct and unique morality, characteristic of the new state. When individual lives are lived in this new and unique societal state, an essential outcome on the structural side is a new government, holding individuals together in a relatively fixed network of temporal relationships, whereby their ultimate activities are kept from being conflicting and reciprocally destructive. On the doctrinal side, it is a new religion in which the socioexperiential and the psychopreferential are fused into a unity which binds together past, future, and present individuals into a network of spiritual relationships, producing a solidarity which makes possible a true communion among all the members, living, dead, or unborn. Thus every society has, i.e., is built upon a government, a morality, and a religion.

When, finally, a societal foundation for a social union of the kind just delineated has existed sufficiently long for its constituent elements to have become established, it influences the individuals who are newly inducted into its network of relationships in every aspect of their developing personalities. Their daily and even momentary actions, their thoughts, their feelings—the whole range of their existence is colored, shaped, moulded, patterned, unified, stamped with the mark of the culture, given its character, until at last is produced the effect which Sumner calls the ethos. No matter what the initial psychical differences of individuality, the influences under which it becomes personality are so uniform and general as to impress each member in the society with qualities or defects, characteristics, that are recognizably alike; that is to say, the societal arrangements are so inescapable as to produce tendencies toward homogeneity in the minds and even bodies of the descendants of the animal Homo who live within the network of relationships those arrangements in any given case imply.

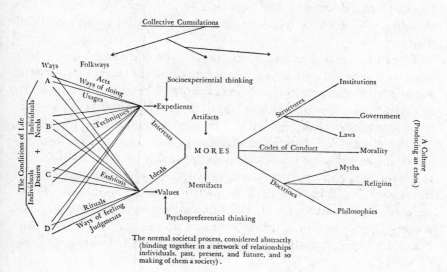

The normal societal process, considered abstractly (binding together in a network of relationships individuals, past, present, and future, and so making of them a society).

In conclusion, the recognition of a societal isolate comprising the phenomena of collective cumulation makes it possible to envisage in complete abstractness the making of societies and so of society. It makes possible the discussion of society without reference to any particular form of life. All animals, including the animal Homo, capable of carrying on the societal process can found societies, i.e., enter into societal relationships and so become socii. Moreover they can do so in proportion to their capacities. In short, society can be discussed in a strictly abstract way. There ceases to be an animal society; there is a new kind of existence to the level of which all beings with the requisite endowments can rise.

Another consequence of the isolating of societal phenomena is that the possibility of systematic intervention in the making of society becomes something more than theoretical. The modification, the creation, and ominously the destruction of a particular form of society all come within the range of the practical. To change the conditions of life, to impede or stop the cumulation of collective experience, to destroy societal relationships and reduce socii to so many specimens of the animal Homo: such procedures have already passed the empirical stage and approach the scientific level.

From the special point of view of this volume, however, the most important consequence of the establishment of the new isolate is its effect upon the conceptions so long dominant under the doctrines of moral philosophy. In one word, the notions of "individual" and "society" are destroyed and replaced by conceptions which show the old problem of the relations between the two to be only a pseudo problem.

The individual does not make society; the individual in the old sense of a rational and independent ego does not exist. What exists are animal organisms more or less capable of entering into societal relationships whereby they can expand, develop, *mettre en valeur* their psychic potentialities and so become personalities. That is to say, there are three levels of abstraction involved in the situation instead of two kinds of beings. Society from this point of view is the resultant of the interplay of essentially independent influences, i.e., influences which have each their own uniformities or laws. They act interdependently; out of their interplay comes a state of society. Society then is no force in itself; it can do nothing. It cannot, for example, make criminals; it cannot govern itself. It ensues when the necessary conditions exist. It is a term descriptive of the results of the operation of uniformities, known and unknown. It is a hominoid like nature who makes the grass grow. "Says Darwin [*Origin of Species*, 75] . . . 'It is difficult to avoid personifying the word Nature'; and he goes on to state that by nature he means 'only the aggregate action and product of many natural laws, and by laws the sequence of events as ascertained by us.' " [10]

Today it is even harder to avoid personifying society but it means no more on its own level than nature means on its. No one would now think of writing a science of nature. Even if the will to do so were strong it would be impossible, for the very first task would be to classify the phenomena of nature, and the outcome would be the various sciences in the lower half of the abstract encyclopedia. Then after nature had been resolved into its constituents, these would be studied in their relations with one another and nature thus be reconstituted.

What is true for nature is true also for society. The individual and the society, in the old usage, are simply correlatives; they can no more be separated than hills and valleys. They must both be analyzed. The result is the discovery of three levels of organization. Society cannot be studied scientifically otherwise. So inevitable is this requirement that the very beginnings of the scientific efforts to deal with the social produced a division between the organic and the superorganic. Comte did not use the latter term; he invented another, "sociological"; but both his term and Spencer's had, to begin with, the same referent.

But the superorganic itself proved to be descriptive of a composite phenomenon which had in its turn to be broken down. To effect this decomposition was the work of the last half of the 1800's. It began with Comte's *Politique;* it was in effect consummated by Freud. Hence it is no longer possible to write a science of society, or if it is, then it can consist only in a study of the organic, the societal, and the psychical isolates for the purpose of seeing how they operate and what happens when they come into relations of interdependence and equilibrium.

In consequence, the sociologist is finally free of the last obstacle which has prevented him from coming into possession of a distinc-

10. Darwin, *The Origin of Species*, quoted in Sumner and Keller, *The Science of Society, 1,* 654–655.

tive and unique subject matter. He studies only the societal isolate, not the thing called society. This isolate is a class of abstract phenomena, definable as collective cumulations. To deal with this specific property, this irreducible phenomenon, is the next task of this volume. It requires a segregation of the data into two divisions: that which defines the essential nature of the phenomena, regardless of time, and that which reveals the sequential phases of their development.

PART FIVE: THE DIVISIONING OF THE SOCIETAL DOMAIN

A. Societal Statics: Structure and Pattern

CHAPTER 12: *The Universal Culture Pattern*

To subdivide the phenomena proper to the abstract, component science of sociology is the purpose of the present chapter. The task is but the continuation and extension of a process which has been in operation spontaneously or systematically from the first moments when men set out to learn enough about their world to guide their activities in it. Against this historical background only does the effort to analyze and classify the cumulative results of collective experience assume its just significance.

The record opens with the animal Homo, an organic form which biological processes had raised to the stage of evolution where communication on a conceptual level becomes possible. With this initially meager differential equipment, nascent men set out upon the course which was to develop their potentialities and transform them into the social being Man. The road was the road of interlearning, collective activity, cumulative achievement. It was to lead far; but it began at the animal level, where knowledge, if comparative psychology is trustworthy, is zero.

With time, however, i.e., with experience, it was seen that certain phenomena were so easily separated from the whole complex of circumstance that they came slowly to occupy a special position. In this class of data the characteristics of the phenomena themselves as they came to be known after generations of observation served as the principle of synthesis, and so certain constant elements were found amidst what had at first seemed nothing but pure variety and variation. The ultimate outcome of these early discoveries in the more easily isolated domains was the encouraging of an ever-intensified search for analogous regularities, for those unvarying similarities and sequences often called laws but now more and more referred to more simply and precisely as uniformities.

The search for uniformities, for that knowledge by which on account of its unvarying nature human action can be guided, for science, in short, moved from one level to another. Certain classes of phenomena by virtue of their generality and independence were more easily abstracted and isolated than others. Mathematics was the first striking result. Its elaboration gave Man a tool for facilitating further investigation. The physical world came next after the mathematical to be subjected to the abstracting and isolating process, whereby astronomy and then physics and chemistry came slowly into being. That is to say, the more general and less complicated phenomena were the first to be isolated.

As the inorganic world was gradually analyzed and its uniformities discovered, the relations between it and the organic world became clearer at the same time that the essential independence of the two became evident. The outcome was the recognition of the necessity of analyzing the phenomena called organic in the same fashion that had been followed in the case of the inorganic. The first subdivision of the phenomena above the inorganic came when a completely abstract definition of life was attained. Biology as an abstract science was the consequence. Its very existence made it clear, however, that there were many phenomena not inorganic outside its scope.

Thus was the fact made evident that the organic was not a specific class of phenomena but a general group contrasting with another general group termed inorganic. The latter had been subdivided; the former would in its turn have to be analyzed and ordered. The phenomena called vegetal were evidently the most general and least complicated, being closest to the highest levels of the inorganic. Above them came the animal; but where were the still more complicated phenomena observable in the organic group to go?

It was the effort to effect this analysis and classification of the higher phenomena that gave special significance to the scientific thought of the 1800's. The first simplification of the problem had been the isolation of the biological phenomenon. When this factor had been set aside it seemed that but one other, at first called the social, remained. Sociology arose at once to deal with it; but the efforts of the thinkers who dealt with the general task of analysis, down even to the end of the century, made clear the fact that the complication was greater than had at first been thought. The rise or, more accurately, the elevation of a previously quite metaphysical subject called psychology to the level of science marks the point at which the complication of what had been at first considered a relatively simple problem was clearly recognized.

The recognition of a new factor was tentative and hesitant but continued attention gave rise to systematic efforts to deal with it. Early efforts had produced new terms, such as ideology in the case of Maine de Biran or *la morale* in the case of Comte. These terms were suggested because a new word was needed and the term "psychology" was at the time so identified with theology and metaphysics as to seem useless. Psychology, nevertheless, by the accidents of language came for better or worse to be the accepted term for a new field of inquiry. Thus it is that the main difficulty for nineteenth-century intellectual effort to understand all the facts of human life was to determine whether the social, i.e., the body of facts lying above the biological level was in fact a specific or a composite phenomenon.

Now the sociologist in playing his part in the general effort has always had in either the foreground or the background of his thought what has come by general consent to be called the cultural heritage. The essential idea in this concept is the cumulative influence of one generation upon another in the sequence of Man. To understand how this heritage was formed no refined psychological information is needed. Biology presents the inquirer with an almost infinite variety of forms in which the process called living is carried on. Some of these forms obviously, i.e., observably present the characteristic that the second generation is able to enter upon the tasks of life where the first left off, the third with the equipment provided by the first and second, and so on. They can in other words learn from another and thereby create an increasing sum of achievements, which is the social heritage. Nothing more in the way of an intimate understanding of men's minds is required to grasp the sociological thesis.

None of the words just used involve any psychological knowledge in the accurate use of the word. To learn is only a descriptive term masking an inner process, not an analytical term revealing it. What the process called learning in the human sense, i.e., interlearning, involves for the individuals concerned, that is to say, what are the psychic factors that make achievements possible—these are inquiries for the psychologist to answer, not the sociologist. What seems to be certain is that the former is dealing with a less general and more complicated body of data than the latter.

If the conclusion just reached is valid, then an answer is forthcoming to the question: What is the relative position of these inquiries in the scientific hierarchy? Does psychology precede or follow sociology? Spencer, for example, places his psychology between biology and sociology. He has until lately been generally followed; but there are three reasons at least for dissenting and placing psychology at the summit of the scientific series. The first is that *as a fact* the advent of sociology as a science antedates the rise of psychology. The implication is that the isolate dealt with by the first is more general than that constituting the second. Secondly, Spencer's arrangement, essentially that of Comte in his first phase of thought, does but reflect the age-old arrangement of moral philosophy, placing the study of the individual and his improvement before the study of society and its modification. Finally, the shifting of the ground of psychology in the direction of the study of personality and the coming of what has been called psychoanalysis seems to place the order of the two sciences beyond further debate.

Thus the body of phenomena above the inorganic is divisible into three domains, each with its constitutive and characteristic isolate. Sociology becomes the sixth member of the scientific hierarchy, between biology and psychology. It has as its definitive and differentiating isolate the phenomenon which has been variously termed the social heritage, the cultural heritage, achievement, collective representations, folkways, results, and is here defined in what is believed to be a completely abstract manner as collective cumulation.

Involved in the foregoing reallocation of the positions of the sciences in the abstract encyclopedia is obviously a redefinition of terms. What changes will follow in the terminology of the other sciences is not here in point, but the possibility of a stricter use of terms in the field of sociology should be indicated. Thus the loose, ambiguous, and equivocal term "social" disappears from the sociologist's vocabulary when he is restricting his discussions to sociological data precisely defined. In its place appears the term "cultural" and the still more precise term "societal." Just as the biologist may use the words "vital," "organic," "biological" to refer to his data envisaged from different points of view, so the sociologist may utilize the terms "cultural," "societal," "sociological": cultural when he is thinking of the general field whence his isolate is immediately derived, societal when he is thinking of the essential nature of his data, sociological when the results of applying scientific methods to his phenomena are in question.

It goes without saying that the analytical and classifying process which built up the hierarchy of the sciences on the basis of a distinction between classes of phenomena more or less general, more or less complicated, is not restricted in its operation to the effecting of that construction. It has in fact always been at work, determining not only the nature and place of particular isolates with reference to others but also establishing divisions within the field of each isolate and the relations between these divisions. Sociology, it need scarcely be said, was no exception to the general rule. Both spontaneous and systematic efforts have been made to answer the question: Is the content of sociology divisible, and if so, into what divisions?

The normal procedure at this point would be to present the purely spontaneous answers to the question just asked and then advance to the systematic. But an exception to the rule will be permissible here in view of Comte's argument that the making of sciences had reached the point where it was possible consciously to undertake the task of facilitating and expediting the advent of a new science. Sociology was this new science. It will be interesting then to look first at Comte's efforts to subdivide it and then turn to the spontaneous *tatonnements* observable elsewhere.

It was in 1839, it will be remembered, that Comte summarized his thought on the possibility of subdividing his newly named science. Running through all the sciences, he said, there is a more or less explicit distinction which first presents itself in mathematics, where in mechanics there is a division into statics and dynamics. In biology there is an established distinction between structure and function. In politics a contrast exists between order and progress. A comparable division, he suggested, could be effected in the domain of sociology. It would serve at least as a point of departure; but he was careful to add that the final divisions and subdivisions of the science would not be the result of any logical discussion in advance of research. They would be the outcome only of the work done on the data of the science by those actively engaged with them. Such was the formulation of the position a hundred years ago. How far does Comte's tentative separation of societal data into "statics" and "dynamics" accord with the results of other efforts to classify them?

One of the directions which would undoubtedly be followed by an inquirer seeking outside the domain of sociology for hints that would lead to a logical subdivision of its data is that afforded by anthropology. Here is a field of investigation which in theory covers the whole range of Man's life. It is true that the meaning of the term suffers from the indetermination inevitably characterizing the disciplines which have grown up in modern days as a result of the very same urge to understand human life that gave rise to sociology itself. The existence of such related or overlapping fields as ethnography and ethnology gives point to the observation. Without, however, complicating the present effort by trying to elucidate the interrelations of the various specializations that have arisen in the anthropological field, it will suffice here to adopt the description of anthropology which makes it the study of cultures.

The definition may be criticized as being too restricted since it omits the physical aspects of the science; the point is not relevant here; the essence of the matter is that as anthropologists went from one people to another, observing their life in detail, recording their habits, customs, ways in general, they found it necessary to establish a unit of observation to render their work more accurate. This unit was the trait. As the number of traits increased through more intimate acquaintance with a given people or with a number of peoples or both, it became evident that only a few categories were necessary for listing all the traits observed. Continued research did but confirm the possibility of establishing a small number of cadres which would be applicable to any culture whatever. In a word the categories that emerged from anthropological observation seemed to be universally valid. Here then was a genuinely inductive result based upon an analysis of a wide variety of instances, more or less complex and more or less remote in time and space.

Moreover, as time elapsed, another characteristic of cultures began to be remarked. In each culture the elements of which it was composed, though found in all other cultures, were nevertheless present in proportions characteristic of that culture only. Thus each culture was unique and yet to some degree like all others. Hence there arose the concept of pattern in relation to a culture; and soon these notions were generalized, since they were applicable to all cases. That is to say, still another example had been found of the constant in the midst of the varying, and so a new field for scientific cultivation. The passage from concrete cultures to the abstract conception of culture was thus achieved, and the concept pattern became established in anthropological investigation.

Now there is another point of view which anthropology might have taken could it have been the all-inclusive science of social phenomena its name implies. Patterns are not fixed; they do not remain the same from one moment of time to another; they are modified; in short, they change. Here then in the study of the alteration of patterns, in the study of cultural change, was a possible opportunity for the science of Man. The possibility is but suppositional, however; in fact, long before anthropology was even dreamed of as an organized body of data, the interest in social change had given rise to the type of intellectual activity known as history.

Always Man has been interested in his past; it gives him something more than individual significance to feel a relationship with the earlier members of his particular in-group. It gives him more: it gives him guidance as well. The record of the past not only binds men together in unity and gives them pride in collective achievement; it points to the future. Why know the past unless in the last analysis it has some relation to the future? Why learn, if not for guidance? Or rather, is it true learning if guidance does not, cannot result? If no such result follows, then nothing but erudition or complacency is in point.

Hence the problem: Has history significance? The question is bound to come to any thoughtful follower of the historical record once it has reached any considerable length. Besides, it is an essential inquiry for any individual or group upon whom falls the responsibility for social direction. What will the future be? Theological and metaphysical thinkers have long been absorbed, in certain aspects of their thought, in finding an answer. And not they alone; in other ways, on what are believed to be sounder methods, men have asked what is the direction in which they or their society are going. Given the record of the past and the sequence of changes there established, what is the trend of events?

Pattern and trend: here are the two lines of inquiry which a general study of Man, interested primarily in culture, might have followed if the way had been open. But it was not, and so there occured a more or less conscious division of intellectual labor. Anthropology restricted its activities mainly to societies or peoples without history, i.e., with no records of their past. Then by a gradual modification it became the study of all cultures, with or without a history, but only insofar as the pattern of social life was concerned. History continued to be a record of social change, interpreted more and more broadly as the scope of the concept pattern widened out beyond political and related phenomena; and it became even more concerned than before with the drift, the direction of events.

Both of these disciplines began by dealing with strictly concrete materials: the particular trait, the actual event. But it is simply not possible for men to restrict their minds to concrete materials. Sooner or later the fieldworker comes back to his armchair, the annalist exhausts his documents; they both begin to think. That is to say, they begin to analyze and classify, to abstract, and ultimately to isolate. As they do so the nature of their pronouncements slowly changes, as do the methods they utilize. Anthropology becomes less and less physical; it becomes cultural, social. History becomes cultural too; it becomes philosophical. Both begin to utilize special methods, comparative and historical.

Both are now on their way to the domain of the sociologist, whose very existence is often unsuspected by them. In a sense no harm is done; for those to whom sociology is a horrid word it is nice that another term is available, and for those for whom the word savors too much of conjecture and philosophy it is well that other terms more to their taste exist. But nothing seems to be gained by such indirection and something is lost. The anthropologist restricts his attention too narrowly to the primitive and the pattern; the historian can certainly not develop the requisite new methods. It would seem on the whole wise to allow sociology to be developed by the sociologists.

Thus both spontaneously and empirically the division of the world of the social goes on and has long gone on: from anecdotes, *histoires,* and annals to history, to comparative history; from travelers' tales to physical traits and cultural traits, to patterns, to cultural and social anthropology, the analysis and classification of social phenomena has advanced. It is now clear that what men working in the field of social phenomena have always sought is the analysis and classification in their main lines of phenomena upon which societies ultimately rest. Concretely, these phenomena compose cultures, beneath which lie the abstractions here called collective cumulations. In the task of making a basic division of these societal products two agencies have been spontaneously at work: anthropology and history.

Under the auspices of the first, even before it became a recognized field of science, the essential differences which separate culture from culture were recognized and the identification begun of the elements basic to the life of a society. Continued observation, more systematically pursued, developed in effect into an analytical and abstract study of society with the object of discovering what constants it presents in all times and places. It gradually became evident that if there is to be a society at all, i.e., if men are to live in permanent societal relationship, certain phenomena must exist, classifiable in a small number of categories and integrated in such a way that a recognizable pattern results. No movement is involved here; the phenomena are at rest. If the word "statics" is ever to be applied outside the mathematical subdivision called mechanics, here would seem to be a likely and a suitable place.

Under the guise of history a number of activities have been carried on, since the concrete materials it gathers are the subject matter for many abstractions. Thus for example until very recently in the development of thought, history was the only anthropology. Men of the 1600's and 1700's—not to mention Pareto—had little but the history of antiquity and Rome in particular to base their analyses of society upon. But these analytical results were only secondary and unintended. What history was primarily concerned with was the record of the social changes produced by the societal process. In these changes historians, once they ceased to be merely recorders, sought to find guidance, lessons; hence the discredit history has often suffered from, since it seemed to be simply a source of arguments for doing what men wished to do or thought other men should do.

But this change is not a valid one, however great the seeming justification at any given time. As the scope of history widens, it ceases to be concerned with this or that time or people and comes to embrace them all. As it does so, it ceases to be a mass of examples and becomes more and more a series of connected preparations for a future the outlines of which can be perceived. It tends, that is to say, to pass from lessons and examples to the determination of the nature and direction of trends. The word "dynamics" would seem to be applicable here.

Thus the sociologist, pushing to the end of the generalizing and abstracting tendencies in both of the foregoing disciplines, seeks to isolate the phenomena they are concerned with. Thus they become descriptive sciences, and sociology becomes the abstract science utilizing the materials they provide. The division of labor inherent in the two descriptive efforts provides sociology with its main divisions: statics, the study of patterns, and dynamics, the study of trends. Comte's provisional division of the field seems therefore to be essentially justified, even if his terms are rejected; and with the modifications that are implicit in viewing the data now in a more abstract way than Comte could in his day, his are the divisions of sociology that will be utilized here.

What now are the relations of sequence between the two constituent parts of sociology? Recourse to the principle already utilized provides the answer. The division called statics is more general than that called dynamics. The first deals with the elements of the pattern which constitutes culture in the generic sense. It may thus be envisaged as defining the conditions of a superanimal level of being; that is to say, statics is the division of sociology closest to biology. As the statical elements develop and become more interdependent, they move in the direction of the more complicated phenomena of personality; that is to say, dynamics is the division of sociology closest to psychology. Statics then precedes dynamics in hierarchical order; hence the order of treatment in this volume, which now turns to an analysis of the cultural pattern as the basis for the detailed discussion of societal statics that follows.

No one approaching the task of breaking up culture patterns either in particular cases or in general for the purpose of classifying the collective cumulations of which they are composed can do so without being impressed by the fact that what is to be done is essentially a logical performance, that the phenomena in question cannot in fact be divided. From Comte to Sumner and Pareto, all the writers stress the intimate relationship among societal data. In fact the subdivision of the field of statics, i.e., the establishment of subisolates of a sociological nature is only an incidental or at best a secondary aim. The pattern is to be broken up only that its constituent elements may be the more effectively studied. The breaking up is only a logical process in the domain of abstraction, the continuous interplay of the isolated elements never ceasing for a moment in the concrete reality.

Thus Comte says that statics will be concerned with "the mutual actions and reactions continually exercised one upon the other by all the various parts whatever of the social system," [1] marking in this way even in his first phase the essentially coordinating and synthetic nature of the new science. "A society," say Sumner and Keller, "is not composed of sets of institutions that have been analyzed out and separately examined; it is the whole of them acting together," but "there is no way to portray at once the whole intricacy of society and societal life. . . . If we take society and societal life down into its components, we must put them together again and try to see them in their involved interaction." [2]

This involved interaction had from the beginning been stressed by Comte under the term "consensus." Utilizing a biological parallel—and Spencer was to do the same, using the same word—he says that the principle of statical laws is "the inevitable universal consensus which characterizes all phenomena whatever of living bodies, and which is manifested to the highest degree in social life." [3] Other men have used other terms for a similar idea. Sumner, for example, speaks of a strain of consistency among the folkways. Pareto points out that all the factors which go to the making of the form of society are interdependent and normally in equilibrium. Certain other terms have been used, notably by the anthropologists, for example "integration" and "configuration." The historians have long been using the word "system" to describe a pattern of historical development.

Whatever the term used, the fact of the intimate relationship among the collective cumulations which combine to produce a given societal situation is recognized by all of them. Indeed so close

1. *Cours de philosophie positive, 4*, 259.
2. *The Science of Society, 1*, 87.
3. Comte, *Philosophie, 4*, 258.

is the connection that some writers question the advantage or even the possibility of separating or isolating them, especially in the case of lower cultures. Thus Rivers says: "The constituent elements of such cultures as those of the Melanesian, Australian or African are so closely interwoven with one another, it is so difficult or impossible to disentangle these elements, that the work of the specialist in social organization, religion, language or technology must be unfruitful and soulless." [4]

Thus the task of dividing the indivisible, of isolating the constituent elements of cultures, would seem to be impossible. Certainly it would be beyond the power of any single sociologist, but what an individual starting *de novo* could never do has in fact been initiated and carried on by the very process of collective cumulation which sociology studies. Here as everywhere else there has always been going on that purely spontaneous isolating and analytical process which gives results that are for any science whatever its starting point. In the social domain, for example, it has always been seen that the activities of human beings are varied and that it is possible to make a rough classification of them. Language, growing in a quite unconscious fashion, testifies to these spontaneous distinctions at the same time that it perpetuates them.

Any casual reference to politics, for example, demonstrates the existence of spontaneous inductions within the domain of social phenomena and even shows by the etymology of the word how these categories have come to be. So long ago was the distinction between political and other cultural phenomena made that the antiquity of the subject as a specialized study makes difficult the recognition today of the societal reality underlying the term. A later but still essentially spontaneous classification of cultural achievements gave rise to the term "economic." Here once more the task of the sociologist striving to subdivide the field of statics has been simplified, to the extent that another category of social phenomena has been given the sanction of long use. The term "religious" is still another instance of the recognition—and the expression by language—of a distinct category of social phenomena. What remains for the sociologist is to penetrate beneath conceptions growing out of societal

4. W. H. Rivers, *The History of Melanesian Society*, quoted in Sumner and Keller, *1*, 88.

situations often of a high level of development to the general concepts underlying them and having a universal application.

The approach to the task of finding societal subisolates was mainly
spontaneous and always indirect until a few generations ago. Somewhere, however—say in the 1500's—the mass of observations made
by traders, travelers, missionaries, explorers, colonizers, pioneers,
etc., began to increase and assume something like a systematic form.
The anthropologist presently appeared upon the scene to do deliberately and methodically what had been before the work of
chance or curiosity. The outcome was the concept of configuration
or pattern already described and the making of a system of categories applicable to all cultures and so able to serve as an instrument
of systematic observation.

It will be well to illustrate the outcome of this analysis and classification of cultural phenomena at the hands of the anthropologists
by citing a few representative lists. Morgan in his *Ancient Society*
has three major divisions: government, the family, and property.
Tylor uses mythology, philosophy, religion, language, art, custom.
Lubbock in his *Origins of Civilization* has seven subdivisions: art
and ornaments, marriage and relationship, relationships, religion,
character and morals, language, and laws.

Later anthropologists follow the road of their predecessors. Thus
Goldenweiser lists all of the aspects that characterize human civilization as religion, art, social and political organization, industries,
economic pursuits and ideas. Wissler, carrying the idea to its logical
conclusion, works out the elements of a universal pattern of culture
as follows: speech, material traits, art, mythology and scientific
knowledge, religious practices, family and social systems, property,
government and, dubiously, war. Whatever criticisms may be made
of the entries taken singly, the point of the construction is its universal applicability. It is in intention an entirely abstract point of
arrival for all the efforts of anthropologists. As such, it gains a prominent position in sociology as at the very least an objective at which
to aim.

Of course the anthropologists have not been the only ones to
draw up such lists. The sociologists have always been busy with a
like effort. Spencer for example uses institutions as the basis for
his classification: domestic, ceremonial, political, ecclesiastical, pro-

fessional, and industrial. Fairbanks deals with the essential activities: economic, social, political, and psychical. Tarde divides the separate elements of a society into six groups: languages, religions, governments, legislations, usages and wants (political economy), morals and arts. De Greef divides social phenomena into seven classes: economic, genetic, artistic, moral, juridical, political, and phenomena of belief. Giddings divides the social mind into four sections: cultural, economic, moral and juristic, and political. The followers of Durkheim study general sociology and domestic, political, moral and juridical, economic, and ideological sociologies. Sumner and Keller base their classification upon interests and the satisfaction of them through institutions: societal self-maintenance, including the industrial and the regulative organization and religion; societal self-perpetuation, including marriage and the family; and self-gratification.

Hankins develops the analyses of earlier writers into language and communication, practical knowledge and industrial arts, genetic groups and mores, ideas and practices regarding the nature of the world and man, ideas and practices governing private relations of individuals, ideas and practices governing public relations of individuals, art and decoration, war and diplomacy. Spiller goes into detail, as follows: language and transport; buildings and furniture; implements, methods, and processes; domesticated animals and plants, energies and raw materials; work and play and inner life; trading, travel, and diffusion of information, practices, ideas and sentiments; nutrition and care of health; dress and education; morals and religion, customs and philosophy; science and art; the family and other civil groupings, civic groupings and government and law; and miscellaneous.

From an examination of the analyses just presented a conclusion and a possibility emerge. The conclusion is that while both anthropologists and sociologists are dealing with the same phenomena, the relation among them is that of the zoologist or botanist to the pure biologist, the relation that is of the concrete to the abstract. Anthropology provides the material for the abstracting and isolating procedures of sociology, but since it has to classify that material, the classifications are a guide to sociologists. For the latter all these materials are the outcome of collective cumulation; and so all the items in all the lists may be considered as results to be classified on some uniform basis which when determined will apply throughout the range of cultural phenomena; it will provide the basic constituents of a truly universal pattern.

Two ways suggest themselves for realizing the possibility thus made clear. One is by way of logic, i.e., to analyze all the entries in all the lists to see which are the more inclusive entries and which the less inclusive, to reduce the number of major divisions by subordinating the latter to the former—in short by a delicate and simplifying disentangling of complicated ideas to arrive at last at an improved classification, one which would stand the logical tests for determining the validity of such constructions. The temptation to essay the logical enterprise just described is great and becomes greater when it is realized that an opportunity would be given at the same time to seek for what Comte called complete rationality by carefully dissecting the psychological from the social so as to obtain the societal—that is, to distinguish results on the one hand from their source or destination on the other.

Tempting though the intellectual game just suggested is, it suffers even when taken seriously from a notable defect. Its outcome would in fact be only the last stage in the spontaneous and empirical gathering of stores of material, not the first step in their scientific utilization. What is meant can best be shown by two illustrations.

The first is taken from the world of color. Benedict says:

> The commonest difficulty in color tests in other societies is that the categories of color differ so widely. The spectrum is a color continuum with no sharp breaks anywhere; the English language draws a line at one point and we see "yellow" on one side of that line and "green" on the other. Another language decrees a dividing line at another point, somewhere, let us say, between light green and dark green, and it calls the light green *and certain yellows* both "young leaves color," and the dark greens *and certain blues* both "shaded water color." [5]

The second illustration could certainly be chosen from the world of sound; but it is perhaps more interesting to take it from the treatment of time. "Take the verb, for instance. . . . Principal parts of verbs exist so that we can discriminate time relations. The notions

5. R. Benedict, *Race: Science and Politics* (New York, Modern Age, 1940), pp. 112–113.

of temporality and verbality are inextricably connected in our heads. We who speak English assume that the question of paramount importance in verbal inflections is the determination of the time of an action in relation to other times of action, present, past, and so on. But this is not necessarily so. Intricate verbal inflections can exist which ignore or subordinate the notions of present, past, future, and perfect." Some languages "are much more elaborately explicit than anything we are accustomed to." [6] That is to say, in the continuum of time many lines may be drawn, one culture dividing it in ways quite different from those developed by another.

Now if this general concept of cultural relativity, which is after all an anthropological commonplace, were to be applied to the categories utilized by the anthropologists themselves for the classification of cultural traits, it would be evident that the terms used are in practically every case drawn from a single cultural source. Without conscious purpose *the investigators have all used the terminology that came to them from the Mediterranean development* that had its beginnings in the Greece of Athens and in the works mainly of Aristotle. Thus the term "political" could only have arisen in a culture where the *polis* was the significant form of social organization. "Economic" betrays its origin in the same way. "Religious" arises out of a particular culture with distinctive valuations. Much of the confusion and uncertainty surrounding the term "art" is certainly due to its development as a category under special and perhaps very exceptional cultural conditions.

What is wanted, then, is something more than a logical analysis and reshuffling of accepted terms; it is rather an analysis of an inductive kind going to the very nature of collective cumulations and drawing lines in the continuum they constitute in a way which would cease to be identified with one particular culture but would indifferently apply to all cultures. The outcome would be a classification of social phenomena equivalent to that effected for natural phenomena when the kingdoms mineral, vegetable, animal were replaced by the sciences physical, chemical, biological.

It is clear that neither of the two revisions of the culture pattern and its elements that have just been outlined can be undertaken here. The first would not justify the space required, since its results

6. Margaret Schlauch, *Gift of Tongues* (New York, Modern Age, 1942), pp. 155–156.

would be superior to the existent classifications only in logical precision if at all. The second would be justified by its disengagement from conventional cultural concepts but it would be involved, lengthy, and perhaps in certain categories immature. There seems but one way out of the difficulty. It is to make a choice of one of the analyses already in existence and use it as the basis for a first approximation of the desired result.

The arbitrariness of the course indicated can be defended or excused if the choice made meets certain standards. It can serve as a point of departure if it has in its favor the facts that it is the work of a sociologist, substantially agrees with the conclusions reached by others, both anthropologists and sociologists, and seems to initiate the scientific type of classification just described. Such a point of departure exists. It is in fact the work of Comte and is to be found in his volume devoted to social statics, the second volume of the *Politique.*

That one of the earliest efforts, if not the first, to analyze social phenomena into a small number of categories has gone unnoticed by the commentators seems due to the neglect into which the *Politique,* as compared with the *Philosophie,* has been allowed to fall. Nevertheless, there it is; and so it enjoys whatever prestige is due its priority and the reputation of its author.

That Comte's analysis conflicts with none of the latter attempts is evident. The *Social Statics* is built upon a foundation consisting of five basic elements: religion, material property, the family, language, and society. All of these items in one form or another appear in the lists drawn up by later writers. That they are the only categories is not asserted; that they are indispensable in any classification seems beyond debate.

That Comte was working toward a functional analysis of cultural phenomena, though not in all probability in a deliberate fashion, seems evident from his text, which generalizes the concepts listed above. Thus the theory of property includes the discussion of the accumulation of material products, which language has qualified as capital. The family is the least extended and most spontaneous association, where the natural laws of all human association may first be studied. Language includes the general system of intellectual and affective communication. The last category points to the force of social cohesion and direction everywhere designated by the word government. Such, says Comte, are the elements of the human order studied as if it were timeless and immobile and so revealing what is common to all times and places, whether primitive or highly developed. Together these elements form a true system. That they are conceived of functionally is evident from the statement that whenever property, the family, and language, developing upon a suitable territory, lead any population whatever to a government, even if only spiritual, there exists a nucleus, a *cité* whence might come with time the whole of mankind, even if there were but one such nucleus.

It will be noticed that from Comte's original list of societal elements as given above, religion has in the preceding paragraph been omitted. The omission is deliberate; it is indeed the work of Comte himself. The fact when explained strengthens the belief that Comte was working toward a truly scientific analysis of cultural phenomena. There is some evidence to the same purpose in the chapters of the *Social Statics* devoted to the generalization of the ideas conveyed by the terms "property, family, language." The case of religion is different. Continued meditation on the subject had resulted in its elimination from the list entirely.

The elimination occurred in the third chapter of the fourth volume of the *Politique* where Comte for the last time reviewed and revised his sociological thought. What had happened in the interval between the second and fourth volumes of the *Politique* seems to be that Comte had given much attention to the nature of religion and come to see that it is not a basic and elemental societal phenomenon. It is in fact a composite made up of a societal and a psychological constituent. For individuals the elements of personality must, in current psychological terms, be integrated; personalities must be united in common understanding. Religion is the name given to the social influence which unites and integrates. But the two functions however intimately they may be combined belong nevertheless in quite distinct categories.

Comte seems to have been applying, more or less consciously, his own rule: to reach complete rationality in sociology, separate the individual element from the collective, the psychical from the societal. When this separation is affected, religion as a basic classification of cultural phenomena disappears; one of its functions, being assumed by association in its highest form, thus remains in the domain of sociology, the other is transferred to a different science, psychology. Such a conclusion is obviously at variance with present day thought, but it is just as obvious that conclusions based upon a universal and abstract view of societal phenomena will differ greatly from those reached during only one phase of cultural development.

Here an effort is to be made to approach a strictly sociological analysis of the data. Hence the discussion to follow will be based upon what is believed to be a functional classification of the products of collective cumulation. In it there will be four main categories: material accumulation, association, communication, and direction. That but four major categories are used is not an assertion that four is the definitive number. What future investigators will do remains to be seen. It is asserted with some confidence, however, that the four here discussed will appear in any ulterior analysis. They will certainly be among the elements that compose the system whose consensus, pattern, configuration, or equilibrium will be studied in the future.

One other question may be asked in this preliminary chapter: Is the order in which the elements of the universal culture pattern are here presented anything more than an order of convenience? The answer to this question makes inevitable a return to the general principle with which the chapter opened and on which it is based. The order of treatment of the elements of statics is determined by the application of the same general principle on which the scientific hierarchy itself rests, on which the subdivision of sociology depends, as well as the relative position of the subdivisions, namely, the decrease of generality in the classes of phenomena. In the list as given, the items are arranged in the order of increasing distance from the biological, or if preferred, in the order of approach to the strictly human.

Sumner and Keller seem to be approving when they say that the rest of the mores take their tone from the maintenance mores, that the latter are closest to life conditions and so form the foundation lines to which the mores further removed from the ground of natural conditions must conform. The Marxian analysis gives weight to the conclusion here reached, but only insofar as it is not understood to mean that changes on the economic level are the direct cause of changes above it.

It must always be remembered that the various subisolates, as the name indicates, are in the relation of interdependence, not of causal dependence. Thus for example the reproduction mores no doubt are affected by economic change, but they have their ultimate root in a bisexuality which no economic influence can shake. Within the radius of that biological fact changes from whatever source must move. In short and in conclusion, the four factors of cultural existence form a system. That one class of factors may be more sensitive than another to conditions external to the system does not alter that essential fact. It only makes possible an arrangement of the factors in an order of decreasing generality.

The chapters to follow will take up in turn the basic classes of cultural phenomena—phenomena which are classified functionally with relation to the societal isolate, the cumulation of collective efforts: first, those that comprise material accumulations, giving rise to property and resulting in capital; then those related to human groupings which rise from the family to the higher ranges of association; next the phenomena of communication, beginning with language and including art and science; finally, the class which derives from the necessity of securing a certain cohesion and correlation of individual efforts in the societal process whence ultimately issues government. In all these cases an abstractive procedure is involved which destroys temporarily the intimate relationship of interdependence that binds all the elements together in a functional unity. It will be necessary then to discuss the nature of this functional relationship which, whether it be called consensus, integration, configuration, equilibrium, or strain of consistency, results in a particular pattern for a given culture and so, in the last analysis, results in the identification of the pattern with the very existence of the society. Thus in concluding the statical portion of the present discussion, the whole problem of societal order will be raised.

CHAPTER 13: *The Societal Subisolates: Material Accumulation*

To begin the discussion of the societal subisolates by the consideration of the class here called material accumulations is not only to grant a certain predominance in the field of collective cumulations to what are usually called economic phenomena, it is also by implication to take a position regarding the relation between sociology and economics. On the first point, the classification of collective cumulations on the principle of decreasing generality provides an adequate explanation and justification. It seems certain that the animal and the human have along the economic line their contiguous territories. Moving away from it, Man widens the distance between himself and the animal Homo.

On the second point, considerable amplification is necessary to make explicit the position of the two sciences with relation to each other. In the first place, then, practically all the anthropologies have an entry "economic" for the listing of traits, and practically all the systems of sociology have a place reserved for the discussion of economic data. In the Durkheim school, for a characteristic example, the divisions of the science are general and special, the latter including such subdivisions as domestic, political, economic, etc. Small in his *General Sociology* takes the same line and defines his position by saying that culture, or the life process of society, is what sociology seeks to explain insofar as that process in its wide outlines is capable of a general explanation that applies to all of its subdivisions, economic, political, linguistic, etc. The very title of his volume indeed arises out of a distinction between general and special studies of cultural phenomena. Giddings says practically the same thing. Sumner and Keller are of essentially the same opinion: "Modern economics we regard as a branch of the science of society that has, by reason of long and intensive cultivation, become independent." [1] In what sense, however, can a special science become independent of a general science?

1. *The Science of Society, I,* 109.

This question is answered by Pareto, whose competence to give judgments on economic matters will scarcely be challenged. In speaking of the nature of the data that go to the making of the social equilibrium as a whole, he says: "The equations that determine the equilibrium can be divided into groups in such *a way that inter-dependences with other groups can be disregarded.* There are good examples of that situation in pure economics where there may be equations of only two variables." [2] In the words italicized lies the principle whereby the respective domains of the general and the special sciences may be delimited. It is the familiar principle of isolation, operating here inside the boundaries of a given abstract phenomenon to discover subisolates.

Sociology as the general science deals with the relations among all the factors of the culture pattern, economic and other, regarded each as a subisolate. The special science, in this case economics, strives to discover uniformities within the boundaries of a single cultural element. In Pareto's words, wherever the variables relate to different elements of the entire cultural unit, there sociology is concerned; where they lie within the boundaries of a single cultural element, the special science is in control.

If, now, it is easy to define the relation between sociology and economics insofar as it is a relation between a general and a special science, it is less easy to reach conclusions when the functional problems raised in the preceding chapter are in question. Just what *is* economics? Hence the necessity of a second and more analytical consideration of the matter; from this second point of view, the difficulty of fixing the place of economics in relation to sociology has several sources. The first of these is historical, the second theoretical. From the historical point of view, the economics of today stems from the physiocratic movement. For the physiocrats, the subject of their meditations was natural or political economy, and the use of either or both of these modifying terms indicates clearly how wide a range of social phenomena was included within the scope of their thought. "Political economy" is surely a case of "young-leaves" color in a different context. Moreover economists are deeply knit into the whole western cultural symplegma.[3] It was the Greeks,

2. *The Mind and Society, 4,* 1455, par. 2100.

3. This useful word is due to Professor Michael Choukas. See "The Concept of Cultural Lag Re-examined," *American Sociological Review, 1* (October, 1936), 756.

indeed, who gave them both the word "economic" and its associations with the household.

On the theoretical side the difficulty is greater and more deep seated. In a word, the economist perhaps even more decidedly than the sociologist has failed, in Comte's words, to attain to the complete rationality desirable in a science. Both classes of theorists have so far been unmindful of the need to separate and to dissect out the psychical from the societal. Some economists have gone so far as to make their science essentially psychological. Many of them too have failed to note the existence of other societal subisolates than the economic; hence the tendency to make economics comprise the whole of sociology and much of psychology and also the impulsion to pronounce value judgments. Nevertheless, whatever the case in the past, the greater scientific sensitiveness of today makes it desirable to distinguish, if not yet to separate, the various constituent factors of a general social complex. There is no longer a need for economists to suffer from an irresistible urge to do the work of sociologists. The various disciplines should in theory at least be kept distinct.

It is not too difficult to effect the separation. It requires the drawing of two sets of lines, one horizontal, the other vertical. The horizontal lines separate the societal from the organic below and the psychical above. The vertical lines divide the continuum of collective cumulations on functional principles.

When these lines are drawn, there results a certain simplification of the complex problem. In a given social situation there are two main factors. On the one hand is a societal element consisting of a given set of collective cumulations, divisible into distinct classes; on the other is a number of individual urges, drives, propensities, instincts—psychic realities and constants, whatever they are called. The latter have to operate in the environment created for them by the former; i.e., the societal conditions the psychological; yet each has its own regularities and uniformities. To consider both factors in their interplay is to engage in a composite or concrete science, whatever its name, and work deductively.

Pareto is probably the greatest of the theorists who have recognized in the social situation the interplay of distinct factors. Indeed it was because he had first dealt with the strictly abstract economic factor and found it inadequate as an instrument of social explanation that he was compelled to recognize the existence of other factors and strive to take them into account. In so doing, he became a sociologist in his definition of the term. Indeed he went even further and revealed the selective influence of the economic upon the psychological; he pointed out how a given type of personality, characterized by definite and definable residues, is encouraged by an existent economic situation and how another and different economic conjunction will favor residues and personalities of another kind. It was the very recognition of these two correlatives that made it possible for Pareto to keep them separate and insist with all the greater force upon the duty of the economist to confine his attention to working out the consequences of the operation of economic forces alone.

So much then for the first stage in the present analysis. Sociology is a general science, economics a special one. Neither is concerned with the psychical. What, now, of the result of drawing vertical lines *within* the societal "spectrum"? The difficulty here is quite parallel with that already pointed out in the discrimination and naming of colors. Where once certain yellows and greens were combined under the term "young-leaves" color, the establishment of the spectrum made it possible to separate the green from the yellow and to see how the combination had come to be made. In the analogous case of the economic, combinations of various elements have been made in various cultures, all prior to any scientific analysis of the data involved. The western world was no exception, and it has continued to use the terms that grew out of its cultural experience without subjecting them to analysis.

The present attempt is a first approximation in the effort to divide the phenomena of culture on a strictly functional basis. Success in the attempt would result in giving to the special science, still called economic, a field of inquiry which would be detachable not only from the psychical but also from all the other special fields comprised under the general title of sociology. In this way a true intellectual cooperation would be furthered, the economist working out the regularities observable within his subisolate and supplying them to the sociologist for coordination with the results reached by other special inquirers in the societal domain.

What class of data then would be included in the area delimited by the vertical lines suggested? In other words what societal phenomena constitute the economic subisolate? No final answer can yet be made, of course; it will require a long collective effort. But a beginning is possible by virtue of the exclusion of the psychical from the social. A definition of the economic limited to the societal only can start with a universally recognized fact, namely, that the accumulation of material things is certainly the aspect of the societal process most clearly in evidence in the class of cultural phenomena called economic. Indeed, a new light is thrown upon the economic concept of wealth when it is envisaged as the result of the process of collective cumulation operating through the centuries upon the material world.

In the work of Comte, who was one of the first to regard the economic as a societal subisolate, the societal nature and material basis of the phenomena in question are made clear. It is a fact of observation, he says, not necessarily inherent in the nature of the world in which men live, that each man can produce more than he consumes. True for some of the animals, who collect and keep useful substances without submitting them to any preparation, it is all the more certain for even the crudest human groups. In the human case, the efficacy of man's intervention is sometimes reduced by the necessity of exerting effort, i.e., labor upon a more or less profound modification of the materials, and so although the final amount accumulated is often small, the utility and stability of the results are thereby guaranteed. Nevertheless, on the lowest levels of mankind "each head of a family can produce considerably beyond what is needed for the subsistence of himself and his." [4]

Here already is a point on which the sociologist should be able to consult the economist with advantage. Beginning with the simplest and smallest populations and the most elementary forms of production, what is the relation between the two? And what changes in the relation arise as both parties to it evolve? In other words, what is the economic uniformity which might guide the sociologist to a decision as to what proportion of the total members of a society must engage in productive activity to satisfy, say, the physical needs of the whole? Obviously, the proportion must be greater in the simpler types of society and decrease as the state of the arts improves; but there should be some positive guide of an economic nature as to the number of individuals or the proportion of energies to be

4. Comte, *Politique*, 2, 151.

engaged in, say, the primary industries or even in agriculture alone, in a given society.

The second basis for material accumulation is given in Comte's words as follows: "The materials obtained can be conserved beyond the time needed for their replacement." [5] This second material condition of existence evidently assumes the first without being a consequence of it. This statement, like the first, is a fact of observation. It would be easy to conceive of a world so constituted as to render all human productions so alterable that they would go bad before they could be replaced, in which case no cultures would ever have been possible. But the most unfavorable localities are far from being so destructive, even with regard to those agricultural products the least susceptible of conservation. And this second economic law, like the first, is more clearly observable as material industry rises in the scale of human needs and its elaboration becomes more concentrated, as the arts of clothing and still more of housing demonstrate.

Such are the two elementary conditions which, when existing in their normal combination, permit at once of the accumulation of temporal riches, i.e., economic wealth. Even if the excess products were much fewer and kept for a shorter time than is usually the case, it would suffice that the surplus should exist and persist beyond the time needed for its reproduction to render possible the formation of material treasures. Once begun, they grow with each new generation, domestic or political, especially when the fundamental institution of money allows of exchanging almost at will the less durable productions for those that pass easily to succeeding generations. It is the natural combination of these two general facts which constitutes the basis of the positive theory of accumulations—the foundation of material existence and progress. "It is for this reason that the admirable spontaneous wisdom which directs the gradual institution of language has everywhere qualified as *capital* each durable group of material products." [6] So was it able the better to indicate the fundamental importance of material accumulation for the whole of human existence.

Such, then, is the first consequence of extending the concept of

5. *Politique,* 2, 150–154.
6. Comte, *Politique,* 2, 150–154.

collective cumulation to the phenomena of economics. It makes of them a subisolate of societal phenomena basically concerned with the cumulation of collective results in the material world. It is in one sense an elaboration of the doctrine that the origin of capital is saving; but the whole spirit of Comte's context, as well as the implications of the definition of the societal fact, carry the thought far beyond the notion of thrift. What Comte had in mind and what the process of collective cumulation makes clear is something much more fundamental and far-reaching. It is not merely the result but the process that is in point. It is not so much that savings are possible and are in fact made; it is that they are the result of the accumulations produced by the collective efforts of both individuals and generations. They are in other words societal phenomena, and because of this basic sociological fact wealth is a social product.

That the whole process of the accumulation of wealth is social, or in the narrower sense societal, seems undeniable. It is difficult even to present systematic proof of the fact without entering on the humorless emission of solemn commonplaces.

> Wealth has been created by the whole series of preceding generations. The entire sequence of historical ages has contributed to the formation of the instruments, materials, and provisions which serve to nourish the present and permit it to work for the future. The wealth thus founded by our predecessors is conserved and augmented by the labor of our contemporaries. There is more to be said; in proportion as society extends in space and time, the part of "predecessors" in the formation and conservation of wealth constantly grows; and the influence of each successive individual in the total production becomes a continually decreasing fraction of the production of our ancestors taken as a whole. Thus, however great may be the intervention of an individual in the production of the wealth he possesses, that intervention is insignificant compared with the labor of anterior generations. In consequence, it is incontestable that wealth is collective in its source.[7]

7. P. Laffitte, "Discours d'ouverture," in *Cours philosophique sur l'histoire générale de l'humanité* (Paris, Dalmont & Dunod, 1859), pp. 105–106.

It is in contributions of the foregoing type, resulting from the study and analysis of societal phenomena taken as a whole, that sociology, the general science, can repay the various special sciences for the details they supply concerning their respective subdivisions of the domain of culture. In the particular case of economics, for example, sociology can certainly be of service in revising the conception of man that underlies so much economic theory. Reference is made not so much to the famous *homo economicus* as to the metaphysical and individualistic conception of man in general. Pareto has shown the validity of the concept of economic man as an abstraction deliberately made for purposes of pure economic theory, and no objection can be made to the abstraction as such; but when, as is so often the case, it is forgotten that the abstraction is a scientific artifice deliberately made for special purposes, then the societal aspect of Man the descendant of the animal Homo must be emphasized. It is not *homo economicus* who does the damage; it is rather *homo metaphysicus*. The man who makes money, who is the architect of his own fortune, the producer of wealth, the fleeting ghosts and apparitions of the self-made man—all of these must be confronted by the societal reality in which successive generations coöperate in the production of wealth and individuals are but agents in a continuous societal process.

A single case of the limitations in economic theory resulting from a failure to recognize the societal nature of Man may be cited. It is probably because of the individualistic, metaphysical conception of man as an ego that there has never been any generally acceptable economic theory of wages. All of those proposed are essentially attempting an insoluble problem—insoluble because it is based upon a premise untenable in the light of the sociological analysis of the process whence arises the accumulation of wealth. This process is a never ending cumulation of collective efforts in which, as Sumner so clearly points out, the act survives the individual participation; how then is it possible to determine the rightful wage due the individual? The problem as ordinarily put conceals two irreconcilable conceptions; it is in effect asking: How determine on the principles of a metaphysically conceived individualism the share of a cooperator in a societally produced wealth? There is obviously no answer possible.

A rational doctrine of wages must be based on the position that economic facts are but a subdivision of sociological or societal facts. Once this viewpoint is taken the problem becomes soluble, but at the expense of the elimination of the older individualism. The first result of this transformation of the problem is the destruction of the distinction between private and public functions, since all participate in the formation of material wealth. Clearly in a sociological sense there are no private functions. The second consequence is the recognition of the fact that the essence of the productive function, i.e., the cooperation with the past and present cannot be paid for at all; all that can be done is to make certain the welfare of the individual cooperating by providing him with the means for maintaining himself and those dependent upon him in a state assuring his continued efficiency as a societal agent. It is true that the economic theories here indicated are being approached by way of a living wage and a standard of living on the one hand and by the provision of security and a fixed annual salary on the other; but only the understanding of the societal nature of economic factors can provide the general theory underlying these hitherto empirical proposals.

There is still another aspect in which the sociological viewpoint can be of service in perfecting economic theory. Sociology, it may be recalled, is built upon a study of culture, past, present, and future. Its concepts therefore are intended to be general and succeed in being so by virtue of the universal range of phenomena from which its abstractions are drawn. It strives to be relative and historical. At this point the economist might well take advantage of the range of data studied by the sociologist. The world of the preliterate and the primitive, the neolithic civilizations and the theocratic regimes, as well as the entire course of history are open to his examination.

An inductive study of the economic phenomena thus open to observation would go far toward removing the deductive appearance which economic argument often seems to take. It would also preclude the possibility of the economist's speaking as if economics were a science limited to the present, i.e., the so-called capitalistic, period. It need not be said that such is not the case; economic phenomena are a part of any culture pattern and would exist in a communistic culture just as they existed in a theocratic; the fact is often obscured in economic texts. It is nevertheless beyond doubt. To some of these permanent aspects attention must now be turned. The central region of the economic band of the societal spectrum having been fixed, the band can now be widened with advantage.

To begin with, the production of wealth, as already said, must be a function of every culture. The point needs no elaboration and has always been in the forefront of economic discussion. The inclusion of economic facts among societal phenomena leads to certain refinements, however. Among them is the establishment of the fact that the initial source of wealth, whether private or public, is labor, i.e., man's real and useful action upon the exterior world, since all the materials of nature always need some artificial intervention before they can be used, even if it is limited to picking them up from the place where they lie in order to transport them to their destination. The point just made emphasizes the necessity of regarding wealth as things, not tokens or symbols; and partly because this is the case and partly because of the nature of the societal process as a continuous cumulation of collective results, there follows the necessity of giving adequate attention to the stages in the accumulation of wealth that lie beyond production.

It is the continuity of the process that leads to giving the function of conservation in material accumulation the importance it deserves. It is only in the simplest cultures that the maintaining of a store of provisions, the formation of reserves, and the treasuring of materials are not characteristic features of the economy. In fact it is this aspect of the accumulation of wealth, rather than its production, which the social mind that makes language seized upon when it identified economy with conservation. And as societies grow and develop in space and time the importance and necessity of the conservation of the resources natural and other whence only true wealth can be drawn comes more and more into the forefront of the consciousness of those concerned with societal welfare. From the societal viewpoint, the conservation of wealth is a rubric quite as important as production.

It is in strict theory possible that in quite special circumstances the successive products of a single individual should be accumulated and conserved; but the result would of course fail to be a societal phenomenon. It would simply be a hoard, such as some animals seem to make. Such is not the case when the third phase of the economic process comes into play, namely, transmission. It is through transmission that the societal character is definitively impressed upon material wealth, which thereby becomes both collective and cumulative, and the participators in the process become societal agents. Moreover, the usefulness and efficacy of accumulations become really notable only when they reach a degree of concentration superior to that which ordinarily results from the simple accumulations of the successive products of a single individual laborer. It is then only that begins the effective formation of the various capitals that play so great a part in collective development. It is therefore essential to see how these transmissions occur, since they are at least as important as the production or the conservation which make them possible.

It is here in particular that an inductive study on the basis of anthropological data will be of service in the future. Already much interesting information has been collected throwing light upon primitive economic activities and the practices from which they grew. Much more remains to be done. Comte, whose general plan has been followed down to the present point, arrived at an enumeration of the varieties of transmission deductively as well as inductively:

> Our material riches can change hands either freely or by force. In the first case, the transmission is sometimes gratuitous and sometimes interested. Likewise, the involuntary transfer can be either violent or legal. In the light of their decreasing dignity and efficacy, our four general modes of material transmission should be ranked as follows: gift, exchange, heritage and conquest, this being also the order of their historical introduction. The second and third modes are the only ones generally used among modern peoples, as best adapted to the industrial existence which was fated to prevail among them. But the two extremes cooperated more in the initial formation of great capitals. Although the last is destined ultimately to fall out of use, it will never be so with the first,[8]

8. *Politique*, 2, 155.

which has been relegated to an inferior position only because of the present predominance in the industrial regime of an egoistic character.

That the transmission of wealth voluntarily, by gift, has been historically important can be shown inductively. The social utility of the concentration of wealth is so undeniable that from the most ancient times a spontaneous impulse led numerous populations involuntarily to endow their worthy chiefs, to the extent that in the theocratic regimes this source of wealth became the source of immense fortunes too often attributed to conquest. "Among the polytheists of Oceania, several tribes still offer us admirable examples of the real power that is inherent in such a mode of transmission." [9] Comte's anthropology is no doubt weak and his inductions imperfect. Nevertheless his essential point is beyond attack, namely, that the formation of capitals has never been due alone to the egoistic urges of the metaphysical man of the economists.

Moreover the sociologist studying results is not concerned with motivations. For him the point of this discussion is that the formation of capitals is the condition of truly human advances. To concentrate wealth is to increase the power to advance human development. As the needs of Man increase, the necessity for the formation of great material accumulations increases also; they have in fact increased. Thus the very nature of the societal process underlies and justifies the generalization that human industry becomes more and more concentrated in proportion as the ultimate purposes for which it is to be used requires a more and more elaborate preparation.

One consequence of the general fact just formulated may in passing be pointed out. With the development of capitals came the possibility of a differentiation of effort among men. The division of labor in the economic sense is a different thing and was only a later development. The first specializations were not economic, as the case of the shaman, the medicine man in general, makes clear. But obviously any specialized function, particularly one that withdraws its organs from wealth-producing activities, must have an economic basis and indeed presupposes it. Moreover the very division of labor itself is understandable only in a relatively advanced culture. In order for each individual to limit himself to the production of a single one of the varied materials indispensable to a de-

9. Comte, *Politique*, 2, 156.

veloped cultural existence, it is necessary in fact that the other requisite products be first accumulated elsewhere so as to permit, by way of gift or exchange, the simultaneous satisfaction of all personal needs.

The point of the preceding paragraph can be strengthened by the consideration of a distinction between the two main purposes for which capitals can be used. One of these uses is to maintain the individual worker in his physical strength, the other to facilitate his labors by supplying him with adequate tools. This division of capitals into provisions and instruments varies in relative importance with time. In the earlier ages materials were required rather for the support of the worker than for supplying him with means for making his work more productive. Only in later periods, in a developed civilization, is the individual producer more dependent upon others for his instruments than for his provisions. The contrast between provisions and instruments with regard to possible variability and the consequent influence upon human differentiation need not be labored.

The elements, then, of the economic process are thus clearly established and their essentially societal nature put beyond doubt. The production of wealth; its conservation; its transmission by way of gift, exchange, heritage, or conquest; the consequent formation of capitals, whereby human advances become possible through the differentiation of individual efforts: such are the conditions so to speak of the economic process. It is to the process itself that attention must next be turned. It was in fact through striving to analyze the nature of this process that economics in the modern sense came to be, for in it were discovered certain sequences and uniformities that attracted the attention of the philosophical minds of the 1700's. Out of this study were to come the physiocrats and the economists in general. It was to have a real part to play in the development of sociology as well.

The analysis of society on its economic side may be said to have begun with Hume. More precisely this beginning may be found in the essay on "Commerce" which opens his volume of *Political Discourses* of 1752. In this essay Hume says:

The bulk of every state may be divided into *husbandmen* and *manufacturers*. The former are employ'd in the culture of the land. The latter work up the materials furnish'd by the former, into all the commodities, which are necessary or ornamental to human life. As soon as men quit their savage state, where they live chiefly by hunting and fishing, they must fall into these two classes; tho' the arts of agriculture employ *at first* the most numerous part of the society. Time and experience improve so much these arts, that the land may easily maintain a much greater number of men, than those who are immediately employ'd in its cultivation, or who furnish the more necessary manufactures to such as are so employ'd.

And again, "land furnishes a great deal more of the necessaries of life, than what suffices for those who cultivate it. In times of peace and tranquillity, this superfluity goes to the maintenance of manufacturers and the improvers of liberal arts." [10]

The thought of the passage, which was given so much development in succeeding decades, is clear. All other classes of society live upon the excess of the production of the agricultural class over its needs of consumption. It is this excess which provides for the material existence of those who carry on other economic functions, and all other functions whatever. It is upon the existence of this excess in an adequate amount that the life of society as a whole depends, and indeed all the advances of civilization, for without it there could be no devotion to those theoretical activities on which culture depends. It is of course this thought which is also the basis of the doctrine of the physiocrats, dividing the whole of the industrial hierarchy into two classes: the "agriculteurs" and the "salariat," the latter including all men from cobblers to kings, all of them conceived of as being paid and fed by the agricultural class, the only one truly productive.

For Hume, in addition to the direct influence of agriculture upon industry, there was a definite reaction of the manufacturing class upon the agricultural; and out of the actions and reactions of the two great elements of the hierarchy came the notion of an economic order: one group forming its basis, furnishing food and raw materials; the other, dependent upon the first, transforming and transporting its products. Here was an important modification of the original thought. Instead of a "host" class and a "parasite" class,

10. D. Hume, *Political Discourses* (Edinburgh, Fleming, 1752), pp. 4, 12.

the two classes came to be envisaged as factors—not necessarily equal factors—in the making of a joint product. Each of them stands in a determinate relation to the other. They are partly independent and partly interdependent. They make adjustments to each other. The outcome is an equilibrium revealed particularly in the distribution of the joint product. So arises the notion of a system, an economic order.

It was upon the general principle of the differentiation of human activities, manifested by the division of society into economic classes and made possible by the accumulation of capitals, that Adam Smith seized when he made so much of the economic principle of division of labor, placing it at the foundation of the decomposition of industry and explaining it as due to the power of exchanging prompted by the propensity to truck and barter. The attribution to psychological causes of phenomena due to sociological development is worth noting, but the point is a minor one here; what is important is the decomposition into increasingly minute functions of the class Hume dealt with as a whole as the manufacturing class. It contains elements that came to sharp distinction with the growing specialization and condensation of capitals: those that dealt with the production, elaboration, or transportation of materials for the satisfaction of human needs. The three were finally to be topped by the most concentrated group of all, in which capitals were most highly condensed, namely, that concerned with the circulation of securities and the expansion and extension of credit. Thus the economic order came to consist of a hierarchical arrangement of agriculture, manufacture, commerce, and banking, each group functionally divisible into "directives" and "operatives."

In this hierarchy the operation of the principle of the division of labor can be clearly observed, for industrial life from top to bottom is founded upon it, i.e., upon a decomposition into economic functions executed by distinct agents. Once in being, too, it continues to operate, in the fashion of Smith's makers of pins, so that the subdivisions constantly multiply and become more minute. The result is a greater and greater diversification of the economic order, and so the increasing importance of the question as to the relations between the various subdivisions. That industrial life is divided into a number of distinct but related economic functions is only a preliminary analysis. A true order requires a much more definite conception of the conditions according to which these different functions work together.

Here again Hume was one of the first to deal with the problem. He demonstrated that notwithstanding all artificial obstacles whatever a monetary level always tended to be established, for, said he, despite the artificial obstacles of politics, money always remains at the end of a certain time in a determinate relation with the development of the agriculture and manufacture of a population. There is then, as regards the role of money, an equilibrium or a natural economic order, which always tends to establish itself despite the artificial obstacles opposed to it. The French economists proved the same theorem with regard to wheat. They showed the constant tendency toward the establishment between the production and distribution of wheat and the other economic functions of a society of an equilibrium or natural order. Going in opposition to this order was to be avoided on penalty of the most serious danger.

> The money value of products, the revenue, the rate of wages, the population, are bound together by a reciprocal dependence, and come into an equilibrium, following a natural proportion, and this proportion is always maintained when commerce and competition are entirely free. The thing is evident in theory; for it is not by chance that prices are fixed; their determination is *a necessary effect of the relation which exists between each particular need of men and their needs as a whole, between their needs and the means of satisfying them.* It must be that the man who works should gain his subsistence, for that is the only motive which puts him to work. It must be that he who sets him to work should give this subsistence and in this way buy the work of the wage, since without this work he could have neither revenue nor the enjoyment of it.[11]

On this capital point the ideas of Quesnay and of Turgot met; they were clearly expressed by Condorcet in his *Du commerce du blé*. This conception of a spontaneous order in the economic world lies somewhat cloudily beneath Quesnay's *Tableau économique;* and the thought becomes more than implied, it is clearly expressed even, in the title of Mercier de la Rivière's volume: *L'ordre naturel*

11. Turgot, *Lettres à l'abbé Ternay*, quoted in "La Politique positive," *Revue occidentale, I* (1872), 115.

et essential des sociétés humaines. It was in ways like this that the thinkers of the period arrived at a general conclusion, implicit rather than explicit in their works, but certainly the logical outcome of their thoughts: "the various functions, necessarily distinct, of industrial activity, left to themselves, tend at the end of a certain time, spontaneously to reach a certain equilibrium, which constitutes a natural economic order." [12] The conception is obviously but a part of the general tendency of thought from Vico's time and earlier down to Montesquieu and his successors to find in social phenomena uniformities of similitude and succession; and as such it is clearly one phase of the movement which in the 1800's was to arrive at the science of sociology.

Thus there is an economic order, a system of relationships among all the elements that go to make up the world of human industry. From the basic operations of agriculture, in all its ramifications, through manufacturing in the widest sense and commerce in all its activities, including transportation, to the most abstract and remote transactions of banking, including in all cases both the directive decisions of the entrepreneur as well as the operative exertions of the worker, there runs a subtle connection holding them all in the network of relationship and forming a true system.

It was the vision of this all-inclusive web of activity which prompted Comte's passage to the effect that it is impossible to conceive, in the whole range of natural phenomena, of a more marvelous spectacle than this regular and continuous convergence of an immensity of individuals, each endowed with an existence fully distinct and to a certain degree independent, and yet all of them ceaselessly disposed, despite the more or less discordant differences of their talents and still more of their characters, to concur spontaneously by a multitude of different means in the same general development without being ordinarily in any wise concerted in their actions, and most often without the greater part of them being aware of what they are doing and believing that they are obeying only their personal impulsions. It is understandable that the contemplation of such a coordinated activity could throw certain minds into an ecstasy whence they emerged as economic mystics. It is much more to the point of this chapter to ask what proof could be more

12. Laffitte, quoted in "La Politique positive," *Revue occidentale, 1* (1872), 128; see also Aug.–Sept., 1872, Nos. 8, 9, 10, pp. 113–115, 129–133, 145–150.

eloquent of the societal nature of economic phenomena than the sight of this immense cumulation of collective efforts extending over vast distances in space and even over generations in time.

The mechanism whereby the relations were effected was a simple one, at least for the economic theorists of the time: exchange. The equilibrium was established by a vast system of exchanges; and of course no such far-reaching system could have resulted from direct barter of products. A means was necessary for facilitating the economic relationship. It was found of course in what is called money and defined as the medium of exchange. But Hume was at least one of the first to see in money something other than a medium of exchange. It was a means for facilitating the establishment of an equilibrium among the elements of the economic order. From the sociological point of view, it is a means for facilitating the collective efforts whereby material cumulations are made by bringing into adjustment all the specialized activities whence wealth results.

It would seem therefore that its efficiency in this regard would depend to a very considerable degree upon its being neutral to the system, that is to say, the means for facilitating the establishment of an economic equilibrium should stand in no effective relation to the elements of the system. If the means of exchange is itself subject to alterations by the process of exchange, the establishment of an equilibrium by means of such a medium would be made difficult and its maintenance jeopardized. It would seem that the first goal of an applied economics would be the discovery or invention of such a neutral means; but at this point the discussion enters upon that recondite domain where all the variables lie strictly within the economic field and so are outside the jurisdiction of the sociologist.

The representative of the general science can, however, at this point envisage as a whole the theoretical structure erected by the workers within the field of the special science and consider it with relation to his own syntheses. In return, he can ask of them to be informed of the effect of any proposed or effected change in the economic system in all its ramifications. The synthetic and the analytical as always are here once more complementary. The sociologist and the economist, each remaining strictly within his own domain, can work together toward the goal of providing the knowledge of the phenomena of societies and the uniformities observable therein which will provide guidance for the statesman.

The first consideration that comes to the mind of the sociologist as he contemplates the material order worked out by the economists is the realization that the data used in building up the admirable structure of economic equilibrium are in fact abstractions. They are, that is, only parts of the whole mass of societal phenomena. The economic element is but one of the constituents of the pattern of cultural existence. Inevitably, then, conclusions as to practical consequences based upon deductions from the ideal construction are highly dangerous as guides to action when unaccompanied by deductions based upon the study of other aspects of the societal reality. This weakness of exclusively economic conclusions has in recent years become so generally understood as to need no further mention.

Moreover, the sociologist may point out that if the economic structure be allowed complete freedom of development, the inevitable result will be a continuous operation of the principle of differentiation of function with the result of so fractionalizing and specializing the elements of economic order that an equilibrium among them becomes ever more difficult to effect and more delicate to preserve when secured. The result is that the oscillations about a center which, because of inevitable spontaneous variations within the boundaries of each element, characterize even the normal working of the system become more rapid and more easily produced when the system is allowed complete freedom of differentiation and expansion. They may even come to have a rhythmical recurrence.

It is of course a threat to the societal pattern as a whole that its most general element should be subject to recurrent crises. It is no doubt true that as the economic system expands, the importance of any one disturbing influence *within* the system diminishes and disturbed relations tend to be reestablished automatically. But reliance upon this *vis medicatrix naturae* is dangerous, because the expanded system offers so many points at which factors *external* to it may unfavorably affect the operations of any one of its highly specialized elements—farm, factory, business, or bank—to the detriment of them all.

Moreover, when the two factors coincide, internal and external, the system itself may be endangered. The ensuing consequences are many. For example, important enterprises may seek to make their positions more firm by the formation of monopolies or other combinations relatively undisturbed by shifts of economic equilibrium. The result is to intensify the tendencies already present to secure or devise some particularly advantageous position with relation to the circulation of goods within the system in order to maximize profits. Individuals or groups may in this way be materially injured or handicapped so that they will begin to consider how to destroy the system. Inevitably the demand will arise for the instability of the system and the extent of its oscillations to be prevented or the consequences to be remedied by action on the part of other elements of the societal pattern, notably the governmental.

Envisaging economic phenomena as purely abstract and as constituting in themselves an isolate instead of a subisolate gives rise to certain consequences which because of their social implications are noteworthy. Thus the worker, i.e., the socius engaged solely in the production of material accumulations tends to lose contact with the societal process as a whole and thus become only a purveyor of a commodity—his labor. The consumer, under pressure to maintain and as the economic system expands to increase his consumption in order that the normal equilibrium of the system may be preserved, tends to be regarded in the ideal case as a suggestible simpleton with insatiable wants. And as the economic phenomena become more and more abstract, the tendency grows to replace the personal responsibility of individuals by the impersonal anonymity of corporations.

Not only has the economic domain been regarded as abstract and independent; it has usually been considered only from the point of view of statics. The results are therefore subject to the weaknesses of a purely statical analysis. The point is that statical concepts are reached by abstracting the element of time and considering the particular phenomena in their ideal development. The economic equilibrium tends to establish itself "at the end of a certain time," to reestablish itself, when disturbed, "in the long run." Such statical considerations assume that time need not be considered.

For all concerned in the reality, however, time is essential. It may be individuals displaced by a new process; it may be communities economically backward forced into free trade relations with more advanced societies. In either case, whether the use of a new process or the extension of the idea of economic equilibrium to the whole world, each part having its own division of labor, the result is disastrous for those who are thus compelled to subordinate their own welfare to long-run societal gain. In both cases the result is due to the application of a statical theory without regard to the time conditions of its application. The transference from the abstract to the concrete cannot be made so cavalierly. The stage in dynamical development reached by a collectivity must be known before statical judgments can be intelligently reached concerning it.

The sociologist, on the basis of his own studies, can make another suggestion to the economist, this time concerning the nature of scientific laws. Societal laws, like any other kind, are nothing more than statements of observed uniformities of similitude or succession. Ordinarily they can be expressed in terms of a functional relation between two variables. Whether they can be so expressed or not, however, there is nothing immutable or in-the-nature-of-things in their ultimate foundations. The almost devotional attitude toward economic laws which lends an air of quaintness to some of the older economic writers is only a survival of the eighteenth-century spirit which led Quesnay to say: "Legislatures have no power over the basic laws on which societies depend, for that power belongs only to the All-Powerful, who has regulated everything and foreseen everything in the general order of the universe." [13] On the contrary of the older idea, a fixed relation between two variables need foster an attitude of resignation only if neither of them can be influenced; otherwise a law is a means of interposition, not a subject for pious meditation. The knowledge of a uniformity should be in economics as elsewhere the starting point for a fruitful series of inventions, allowing of many societal modifications.

Finally, the sociologist, urging the utilization of a knowledge of uniformities for purposes of interposition, is guarded against utopianism in economic matters, whether of the optimistic or the pessimistic variety, for he knows that abstract economic laws never in fact operate in ideal, i.e., unconditioned circumstances. They are but one set of laws among the number that control the whole mass of societal phenomena, and their operation will always be limited by the simultaneous operation of the uniformities manifested by other classes of facts within and without the sociological domain.

13. Quoted in Rambaud, *Histoires des doctrines économiques,* p. 95.

To bring this chapter to an end and throw into relief its central thought, it is enough to point to the analytical efforts which have been in process through five generations. They have at last reduced the social to its elements and given one of them, the societal, a place in the hierarchy of abstract isolates. The outcome must have repercussions upon all the fields of investigation hitherto called social. Economics can be no exception. In the past it has on the vertical plane embraced all sorts of phenomena from the biological to the psychical; on the horizontal level it has ranged from the household to the nation. It has been what was called in an earlier chapter a concrete, i.e., a composite science. With no solid central core of theory, it has in its various schools emphasized now one factor, now another of the composite.

For this reason economics has at one time seemed to be hardening into a kind of scholasticism and at another to be in full deliquescence; hence the "lament for economics." But no lamentation is called for. To give it a definitive place as a societal subisolate concerned with material accumulation is to give it a sound theoretical basis and open the way to the discovery of new uniformities and sequences. At the same time the systematic combination of its doctrines with the uniformities discovered by other sciences will be promoted, and to a degree hitherto not possible. Moreover the expansion of the economic within the societal range will become more discriminating as the existence of other factors of the cultural pattern is recognized. For there *are* other factors than the economic, as will be seen.

CHAPTER 14: *The Societal Subisolates: Association*

O ff the east end of New Guinea, on a closed circuit comprising a ring of islands, Malinowski found a curious cultural phenomenon called the *kula*. Along this circuit articles of two kinds were constantly traveling in opposite directions. In one direction moved necklaces of red shell, in the other bracelets or arm bands of white shell. In every island village a more or less restricted number of men took part in the kula—that is, they received the goods, held them for a short time, and then passed them on. Thus every man in the kula periodically though not regularly received one or several arm shells or a necklace and then had to pass it on to one of his partners from whom he received in exchange the commodity traveling in the opposite direction. No man ever kept any of the articles for any length of time, nor did he ever stop with one exchange. The rule was, once in the kula, always in the kula. A partner relation between two men was a permanent affair. In the main, the fundamental aspect of the transaction was a ceremonial exchange, interminably repeated, of articles intended for ornamentation but little used for that purpose and so from any utilitarian standpoint useless.

But accompanying the exchange or under its cover were many secondary activities. Thus side by side with the ritual exchange of arm shells and necklaces the natives carried on ordinary trade, bartering from one island to another a great number of utilities. Further, there were other societal phenomena preliminary to the kula or associated with it, such as the building of canoes, certain forms of mortuary ceremonies, and preparatory taboos. The kula was thus an extremely big and complex institution. It welded together a considerable number of tribes and embraced a complex of activities, interconnected and playing into one another so as to form one organic whole.

Now suppose the kula to be subjected to the sort of analytical examination exemplified in the preceding chapter. Where would the lines be drawn? The horizontal lines are fairly clear: there is little of primarily biological concern to be found, much evidently of a psychological nature, and a core of societal phenomena. But in this societal residuum where are the vertical lines to be drawn? And what would they enclose? Would there be any content, for example, for the category of economic as defined in the preceding chapter? Certainly there seems to be very little addition to the mass of material accumulations, despite the expectations aroused by the terms "exchange" or "trade" applied to the kula. In the societal spectrum the characteristic phenomena of the kula fall far away or at least distinctly apart from the economic. It would be hard to find a case better illustrative of the young-leaves principle of the preceding chapter.

Economic phenomena, of course, are not the only ones whose study is in logical confusion; other long established categories seem equally in need of critical redefinition. Thus for example the family among the Bantu corresponds to the western family in some of its essential functions but has others to which the western family will not lay a general claim, more particularly in that it is a much more comprehensive economic unit among the Bantu. Western concepts simply do not fit the results attained in cultures where the vertical lines have been drawn otherwise than in the West. The point is that today *all* the concepts of the past require scrutiny; in the kula case the question arises, as it does in the Bantu case, where shall the data go which do *not* belong in the category of economic?

Even if the anthropologists did not suggest the answer to the question just asked, it would be easy to find all the same. Both the kula and the family, Bantu or other, are phenomena of association. As such they fall within a classification which under various terms has long been recognized and by a variety of observers. Even so, the phenomena of association were slower than the economic, say, in being withdrawn from the theological and philosophical domain in which they had so long been confined and set on the path leading to scientific consideration. It was not until about the middle of the last century that sociologists began to analyze the phenomena termed social and find there several classes of occurrents, the association forming one such class.

An enlightening example of the way in which the analysis proceeded is to be found in the work of Comte, where, as the pioneer work in the subject, so many beginnings are to be found. In the

Philosophie, in the chapter instituting social statics, Comte outlines the contents of his new and tentative subdivision of sociology. Statics in this chapter is said to include three principal orders of sociological considerations: the general conditions of social existence relative first to the individual, then to the family, and finally to society proper. Comte, it is plain, is still thinking at this point in terms of individual and society. But he is beginning to move away from moral philosophy. The separation between the two orders is too wide to be bridged; that, Comte already sees; soon he will see they are not commensurable.

As to the first item, the individual, it would be superfluous, Comte says, to give any formal demonstration of the fundamental sociability of man. But Comte does not feel relieved from the necessity of presenting certain other considerations in regard to the *psychology* of man. Yet even after he has done so he is not ready to discuss society in the large sense, for there is too great a separation in logic between the idea of the individual and that of the species or society. Between the two there is too great a gap; it must be filled by an intermediate association, the family. Comte is not repudiating the individual; he is only insisting that the larger association is made up not of individuals directly but of smaller associations, that only through them and as formed by them do individuals come into relation in larger associations.

When Comte comes in the volume on *Social Statics,* however, to review the same material, he has advanced to the point at which he sees that the individual, i.e., the human being, the animal Homo made Man, cannot be the starting point of the study of association. It is the family, i.e., *the least extended and most spontaneous association* which is the starting point. The decomposition of humanity into individuals in the proper sense constitutes only an anarchical analysis which tends to dissolve social existence instead of explaining it since it becomes applicable only when the association ceases. Any system whatever can be formed only by elements similar to itself and differing from it only in being smaller. A society then is no more decomposable into individuals than a geometrical surface is decomposable into lines or a line into points. The smallest society, namely, the family, sometimes reduced to its fundamental couple, constitutes the true sociological element. The natural laws of all human association must be explained first with reference to the lowest degree. From it are derived the more composite groups, such as classes and *cités*.

The importance of the topic is so evident that from the beginning of theorizing in regard to the general phenomena of social life there has always been reserved a distinct place for the discussion of association. No filiation with Comte is in any way required to explain the circumstance. Men, however defined, do not as a simple matter of elementary observation live in isolation. They always present themselves to the observer as *socii*, who are associated, i.e., related to one another in a special way, for which the Latin word meaning "aid" or "ally" has been found most accurately descriptive by the general mind which analyzes facts and finds words to fit them. Men in the sense of *human* beings are always in some network of relationships with other human beings; they live with their fellows in such relations that they form recognizable units, to which the general word "group" has come to be applied.

There is nothing then to demand complicated explanation in the fact that the study of groups has always been one of the characteristic activities of sociologists, nor that it has held the first place in the theoretical conclusions of many of them. In the case of Small, for example, under the partial guidance of Ratzenhofer, sociology came to be the study of groups. But even here distinctions had to be made. A group, said Small in his earlier work, is "any number of people, larger or smaller, between whom such relations are discovered that *they must be thought of together*." [1] As the words here italicized for the purpose show, Small was then thinking of the group as an entity, a thing. Another American sociologist, Ross, is thinking in the same way when he says: "Whatever marks off certain persons from others, or establishes among them a community of interests" [2] tends to create a group. From this position there was an advance which can best be marked in the words of Small, writing some nineteen years later: "This supposed thing, 'society,' has steadily resisted expression as a thing at all. It has gradually resolved itself into a near-infinity of group *relationships and processes*. Accordingly, the procedure, the technique, which sociologists have found themselves obliged to invent, has turned out to be mental tools for

1. Small, *General Sociology*, p. 495.
2. E. A. Ross, *Principles of Sociology* (New York & London, Century, 1924), p. 515.

detecting and interpreting all sorts of group *phenomena*." [3] In the words here italicized—*relationships, processes, phenomena*—as contrasted with the words italicized in the older work of Small— *they must be thought of together*—is a convincing proof in a special case of the general thesis of this volume: sociology, by a process of continued analysis, has ceased to be the study of society conceived of as a unit or whole and become the study of a phenomenon, an abstraction, an isolate.

Now it was inevitable under any circumstances that the phenomenon of association should become the object of special study on the part of those interested in society in general. It presents characteristics quite as marked as those which caused the study of material accumulation to take the special form of economics. What was not inevitable or even likely beforehand was that such special study should come to be considered the whole of sociology. Nevertheless such a development forms a distinct phase in the history of the science. Only a particular set of cultural conditions can account for the development in this direction.

It is therefore to Germany and to Simmel in particular that attention must be turned, for there it was that the conditions and the man were found which had the result just mentioned. Becker writing of the extreme academic specialization which characterized Germany declares "that even under relatively favorable circumstances a very halting development of the subject [of sociology] could hardly have been avoided in countries where academic lines are so sharply marked" [4] and in a paragraph of details gives specifications. It was a stroke of genius when Simmel, studying the forms of association, noted that a large number of social units, despite the sometimes diametrically opposed purposes they furthered, were nevertheless structurally similar. Here was an untrodden field; and the sociologist was free to occupy it, provided he agreed to stay within it.

The idea was adopted by two men of ability: Alfred Vierkandt and Leopold von Wiese. The former seems to have deviated from Simmel's direction by way of an examination into the field of psychology in order to go beneath the forms of association. Von Wiese, on the other hand, stayed strictly within the lines laid down by

3. *The Origins of Sociology*, p. 337.
4. H. E. Barnes and H. Becker, *Social Thought from Lore to Science* (Boston, Heath, 1938), p. 879.

Simmel and in so doing produced the most exhaustive study of the nature of association yet achieved. It is because the work of the "formal" school of sociologists seems for the present to be the summation of the studies in this section of sociological theory that it can be the basis—but the basis only—of the present section.

In utilizing the work of this school as the main source of material for the present chapter, only one reservation need be made. The naive claim that formal sociology, however disguised, is the *only* sociology may be dismissed with the comment that the mountain of sociological theory raised by Montesquieu, Turgot, Condorcet, and Comte, not to mention a single one of the great men who succeeded them, cannot be made to produce a mouse simply because nothing larger can be inserted between two *Fachmänner*. In fact it is advisable, in order to prevent any possibility of confusing a special aspect of the science of sociology with the general science, to have a name for the smaller domain. For this reason the term "socionomics" is presented for the consideration of those who believe that advances in the precision with which the divisions of a science are formulated should be reflected in the growth of a corresponding terminology. To use such a term would serve to acknowledge the unquestioned place which the study of association holds in the science of sociology and at the same time reject the claim that such study is the whole of the science.

Such a socionomics would have for its special domain the study of the conditions, formation, integration, maintenance, and dissolution of association and the forms to which it gives rise. It would be interested in these phenomena as a specially isolated body of data, but in the background would always be the fact of the process of collective cumulation. It would set aside all discussion of motive, etc., as being strictly outside the domain of sociology as the study of the societal isolate. It would be based ultimately upon the cultural phenomenon already so often referred to, namely, the making of the cultural heritage; and in the consciousness that such a heritage could not exist and therefore no society could exist without relations being formed between individuals who thereby become socii, it would devote itself to the study of one of the essential elements of the cultural pattern, thereby becoming what it is here asserted to be, namely, a strictly special science comparable to economics as described in the preceding chapter or either of the other special studies to follow. Like them, it will be independent in the sense that it will have uniformities whose variables will lie wholly within its own boundaries; like them, it will have to work out all the implications of its own subisolate and thus play its part in enabling the general science to deal with societies as integrations of relationships whence societal phenomena arise.

To begin with, then, the conditions of the operation of the socionomic, or associative, process are simple. All that is required is the biological organism, raised by strictly evolutionary forces to the point where it has become sociable. That certain animal forms are so is a fact of observation dependent upon no notions whatever of a theoretical kind. Observation in presenting this datum to the sociologist makes the point that mere aggregation or herding is not the essence of sociableness. What is in question is the ability of certain animal forms to learn from others, to help them and be helped by them. The difference was long ago seen by the general mind and expressed in the verbs "aggregate" and "associate."

There might be said to be two bases on which rests the whole possibility of association, just as there were two supports for the accumulation of material products. In the first place, certain animal forms find it tolerable and normal to live in the presence of one another. All their lives are passed in the companionship of their kind, simply feeding together. Nothing more is necessarily involved, as the existence of herds makes clear. The needs of each are answered in a strictly individual fashion. In the second place, animal evolution has produced forms which can aid others in meeting the conditions of life. There is no necessary connection with the first fact just stated. Indeed observation might be said to show an inverse relation between the two animal characteristics. But when the two meet in a given animal form, new possibilities begin to present themselves. Relations of a new kind come into existence. Individuals now do more than exist in one another's presence; they aid one another and so become associates.

With such simple data of observation the sociologist begins his study of a new subisolate. He takes the animal Homo, watches him in his associating, and strives to find just what is involved in the process. He knows nothing of the higher, i.e., psychological nature of the animal; it may be that such knowledge will emerge from the observation of the associating process. Where else would he find it? Does the biologist know anything of ambition, say, or veneration? It is only by seeing what the animal Homo does in his associative existence that his psychical capacities and potentialities can be inferred. Comte's early error in this matter should be a guide to others; it should not be repeated endlessly. Sociology precedes psychology. The capacities of the sociable animal must be known in the light of his achievements, his results, not his achievements in the light of a prior knowledge of his personality.

The sociologist, then, approaches the study of association with only a biological knowledge of the form he is to observe and thus meagerly equipped begins to study the formation of associations. The starting point is the purely methodological one of an inferred condition of isolation. As is said in Sumner and Keller's paragraph on primitive atomism, "If, as we go back over the course of evolution, we encounter less and less perfect types of association, the inference is that beyond the range of our information, . . . the measure of association approaches zero." [5] There is no reason however to suppose that it actually does so; long before the point of zero is reached the counteracting principle, "Association started, like all other social habitudes, with action in response to need," [6] must have prevented the arrival at the geometrical beginning of the process. Moreover, the idea of isolation is only a relative one. Complete isolation would involve the destruction of the very association which is the thing to be explained. The only importance of the concept is that it throws into relief the necessity of sustained relations with other beings if a human life is to result.

Isolation, in the foregoing abstract and relative sense, is broken by *contacts* of various sorts, which are therefore the points at which sociological interest begins. They are the initial stages in the formation of associations. Park and Burgess expand the notion of contact to include the following senses: "Three popular meanings of contact emphasize (1) the intimacy of sensory responses, (2) the extension of contact through devices of communication based upon sight and hearing, (3) the solidarity and interdependence created and maintained by the fabric of social life, woven as it is from the intri-

5. *The Science of Society, 1,* 16.
6. *1,* 19.

cate and invisible strands of human interests in the process of a world-wide competition and co-operation. The use of the term 'contact' in sociology is not a departure from, but a development of, its customary significance." [7]

Little can be said here of the various classifications of contacts; the one most to the point in these pages is the distinction between primary and secondary, or direct and indirect. "The former are directly mediated by the senses; persons in primary contact must also be in relative spatial proximity. . . . The secondary variety is indirectly mediated and usually involves greater spatial separation." [8] The extreme importance of the latter to the process of collective cumulation is well described in the following paragraph:

> the greater part of the history of material culture may be regarded as a lengthy contribution to the discussion of secondary contacts, for they are primarily long-range contacts which have been facilitated by diminution of time-cost distance. Persons and places formerly far apart have been brought into such close connection that time and distance seem almost annihilated. Means of communication, from the horse and wheeled vehicle to the airplane, postal service, telegraph, telephone, radio, press, cinema, water-borne traffic, writing, printing, photography, money, and credit are exceedingly effective devices of secondary contact. . . . So far as technical means are concerned, it is now possible to place all the human beings on the planet "in touch" with each other, as well as to effect an external union of past, present, and future. [9]

After contact comes the formation of association, facilitated says the formal school by the satisfying of certain prerequisites such as sufferance and compromise, which result from a preliminary lowering of guards. "The stage where incipient association is possible has now been reached—isolation has been disrupted by the intrusive factor, contact; this in turn makes eventual sufferance necessary, and sufferance slowly generates compromise." [10] Associations may

7. Park and Burgess, *Introduction to the Science of Sociology*, pp. 281–282.
8. L. v. Wiese, *Systematic Sociology*, H. Becker, tr. (New York, John Wiley, 1932), p. 155.
9. Wiese-Becker, p. 162.
10. Wiese-Becker, p. 194.

now be formed. There are four stages in the abstract process of forming them: advance, adjustment, accordance, and amalgamation.

Under advance the first tentative stages of association may be included. It sometimes has features that place it among the prerequisites of association rather than among the genuinely associative processes. In advance there always remains some feeling of hesitation; the incipient association is still regarded as a more or less doubtful experiment. Usually one of the participants manifests greater reserve and is less desirous of closer approach than the other. The conscious or unconscious resolve to break the spell holding them apart falls to the latter, who then carries out an act of advance or as it were makes advances or overtures.

When the stage of adjustment is reached, however, association is clearly manifest, although the connotations of the term indicate that the beings associating retain many of their differences. Adjustment implies similarity but by no means identity. When the great differences prevailing among human beings are recalled, it is evident that a very large proportion of all associative processes are classifiable under the category of adjustment. Every such process emphasizes and utilizes whatever similarity may be present, but in order to do this attention must be paid to points of difference as well. Many phenomena of culture contact may be considered from this point of view, and often the adjustment is made at the expense of the physically or militarily stronger power.

Even at the stage of adjustment certain requirements of association are already fulfilled. There arises a more or less orderly and regulated system of social intercourse; and in some instances nothing more than processes of adjustment are necessary even when individuals are associated for relatively long periods. All adjustment makes greater efficiency possible and advantageous adjustment alone frequently results in a marked increase in efficiency. Nevertheless mere adjustment does not wipe out feelings of difference; the latter persist, although they are usually somewhat less intense. Profound emotional and intellectual participation is of course out of the question. When once the stage of accordance is reached, however, mutual participation in emotions and habitual attitudes ensues; behavior becomes more and more in accord, grows more and more similar. There is a large store of shared experience both de-

riving from and issuing in common cultural traits and culture patterns that play a large part in the culture complexes concerned.
Such accordance falls short of amalgamation, the final phase, only
because it has not yet reached the stage when it is taken for granted,
when it is automatic and unconscious, when accumulated conver-
gences have brought about virtual uniformity and hence one inclusive culture complex. Accordance does no more than bring about
similarity; it does not achieve identity: hence though in many respects close to amalgamation, it is still distinct enough to be treated
separately.

Once the association has been consummated, there begin certain
processes which may be considered as complementary and coexist-
ent. They have the same ultimate objectives as well, the consolidation of the association. Among the differentiating factors are the
rise and perpetuation of disparities, on the basis of which the differentiating processes proper operate. Chief of them are the processes
of domination and submission. Says Ross: "In the life of societies no
phenomenon is more persistent, recurrent, or frequent than *domination*. Not only has each social group brought adjacent social
groups under its will so far as it could be dared, but each element
within the group rides other elements so far as it can." [11]

Large associations offer so great a contrast to their individual
members that the latter seem but tiny atoms within the larger structure. The only way in which these minute fragments can be effectively joined into a large cooperative structure is through the formation of more intimate and less extensive intermediate groupings;
hence such processes as gradation, stratification, and selection. The
first two of these establish different levels of association on which
each "atom" can find its place. As to selection and the development
of *élites* it is difficult to speak with confidence. Extensive studies
have not been made in this field; biological and societal selection
have often been confused. It is likely that several decades of analysis
will be required before the special sociologist is able to bring to the
solution of this problem the finality already attained in other regions. It will therefore be more advantageous to turn to the processes of integration.

These are three in number: uniformation, ordination, socialization. Of these the first requires little comment. Obviously the uni-

11. *Principles of Sociology*, p. 117.

formity of the members aids in the integration of the association, even when authoritative representatives of the group formulate the results of their experience into binding rules which are then impressed or imposed upon the other members. More important perhaps is the fact that every human being is enclosed in a network of group affiliations; men are almost always occupants of some niche in the social order and are bound to others in definite although widely varying ways. In other words they are subject to ordination, i.e., they are ordered, arranged, disposed, placed, located, or established in definite positions within a social system. Finally, there is the process which develops the we-feeling in associates, their growth in capacity and will to act together, and the establishment of ethical sanctions for this harmonious interaction. This process by which ethically sanctioned intragroup and intergroup bonds are established is socialization: with it the process of association reached its fullness.

At this point there is a notable gap in the formal framework. Surely there are processes by which associations are maintained. The nearest the formal specialists come to the treatment of such an important aspect of association seems to be the establishment of a class of processes which are called constructive. The reasons for this curious lapse seem to be two: first, the necessity of strict adherence to a purely formal classification of relationships—those which bind or loose or do both. The classification is not, however, the result of an exhaustive analysis of all the phenomena of association; it was an empirical generalization before the formal school came into existence. Now the maintenance of association cannot be fitted into the binding-loosing-or-both formula at all. It is as inapplicable to the phenomena as would be the effort to explain the rising and falling of a boat on the swells of the surf by reference to the fact that the boatman was dominated by a desire (a) to get into the water or (b) to get out of it or (c) to get in and get out of it. There is probably another cause of the omission, too. The sociology called formal is the study of social processes *as such,* i.e., in relation to nothing. The maintenance of association is obviously a minor matter when nothing is in point. But when, as in this chapter, the process of association is of interest only because it is one of the indispensable requisites for the basic societal phenomenon of collective cumulation, then the matter of associative maintenance becomes of very real concern. As MacLeod rightly says: "Too often, social scientists have spoken of human groups as growing through the *coming* together or aggregation of individuals or families. As a matter of fact, the typical growth phenomenon has been merely the result of the *staying* together of progeny." [12]

It would seem then that there is a need in the systematics of association for the entry continuation, which would imply not the forming of bonds, for they already exist, nor the strengthening of bonds, for they are already strong, but simply the maintenance of relations already in existence. Such continuation is effected by a variety of means. "Some types of unity can be maintained only through silence," [13] where silence is really a positive, not a negative, factor. It may take a more active form, such as consideration, in which the members of the association use tactful methods in relation to the other members. It may remain on the level of complacence or rise to compliance. It may be passive as in acquiescence or active as in concurrence. All of these words, by their very etymology, imply a "togetherness" the existence of which is to be neither initiated nor strengthened but maintained.

Stabilization may follow continuation, utilizing many devices. Chief among them perhaps is the officializing of certain relationships by the recognition of the fact that they are of special interest and worthy of fixed or at least definite remuneration. Institutionalization is the word often employed in this connection, but professionalization would seem to express the essence of the thought in a more realistic way, since it may lead more directly to formalization and ultimately to ossification.

Associations pass, however, and so there is need to consider the ways by which their dissolution is effected. These are in general three: competition, contravention, and conflict. Competition arises when several members of an association strive to attain an identical objective. In this respect associative processes themselves may arouse competitive endeavor and the immediate result may be useful for the association. In consequence, competition is a process of dissociation of the lowest power. Contravention is the next more serious danger to the life of the association. It is marked by doubt as to the

12. W. C. MacLeod, *The Origin and History of Politics* (New York, John Wiley, 1931), p. 100. (Italics are MacLeod's.)

13. E. E. Eubank, *The Concepts of Sociology* (New York, Heath, 1932), p. 163.

necessity, utility, or value of continued association, as to whether conflict should be entered upon, as to scope and mode of antagonism. When these and similar doubts disappear, conflict reaching its ultimate stage in combat ensues, leading to deterioration, which points to a diminution of the unity, strength, and efficacy of an association and when extreme leads to its total collapse.

In this way then associations live and die; and in the study of the processes *as such* whereby the result is attained, a perfect example of a special science may be seen. Here is an explanation of the charge of emptiness sometimes brought against the formal school, which it would seem to deserve when it asserts for example that style is a virtually inexhaustible theme for sociological study or finds in secrecy a wide scope for inquiry. But it is precisely in such investigations that the special science finds its justification. They are no more empty than the esoteric mysteries of pure economics to which they are a parallel. When socionomics, having arrived at maturity, begins to find uniformities expressible in terms of dependent and independent variables, it will be of real service to sociology. Already it is clear that the formal school in pursuing the processes of association into the remotest pigeonholes of specialization is throwing light upon the formation of the groups which are the results of the cumulation of collective experience and its most effective agents. To them attention must now be turned.

What now are the associations to which the abstract societal process gives rise? To begin with, it is clear from the work of the special sociologists that there is a purely general, if not completely abstract, process underlying the formation of all associations. It is only an easy deduction from this position to ask whether there is an equally abstract association underlying all associations. In other words, is there a general form of association of which all special associations would be but variants? Or simply is there a word embodying a general concept applicable to all associations?

Fortunately there is such a term, so widely accepted and used as to be completely free from all taint of the deductive device by which it has here been approached. From the time of Comte, who used the word only incidentally, to the work of Small, who made the concept the center of his sociology, the word "group" has been a general term, applicable to all sorts of associations and inclusive of them. The group in general, the outcome of the process of association in general, thus becomes the center of the second half of this chapter. After the study of relations comes the study of structures. What then is a group? What is this common denominator by which to define every sort of human association?

The starting point of the discussion may well be the summary which Eubank makes of the conclusions to which the more recent analyses of an old conception seem to lead. From the work done in this regard it would seem that the elemental conception of the group comprises a plurality of units, in such physical interaction as to be envisaged or at least envisageable as a whole, an entity. In expanded terms, "a group is two or more persons in a relationship of psychic interaction, whose relationship with one another may be abstracted and distinguished from their relationship with all others so that they must be thought of as an entity." [14] The essential point in the existence of such an entity is its intermindedness, which is the chief and distinguishing characteristic of the group.

Notable also are certain conclusions regarding the importance of group life which emerge from the whole mass of discussion. Thus it may be regarded as a definite acquisition of sociological theory that human life is necessarily group life. "The preservation of the individual and the fulfillment of his major needs and desires, both physical and psychic, require a life of group association. From infancy to old age, one can live as a human being only by being a member of various groups to which he is bound by ties of varying degrees of necessity and interest." Moreover, "it is from the groups of which one is a part that he mainly derives his attitudes toward life. The culture, standards, ideals, patterns of thought which exist in the group become a part of the life of its members just as inevitably as do its language and manners." [14]

The essential validity of this definition and its consequences seems beyond question. All that can be said of it critically seems to be that it could be advanced still further in the direction in which discussion has already carried it. Thus the nature of persons and of intermindedness may profitably be subjected to further analysis. At precisely this point the basic definition of the societal fact on which this volume is based comes into play, as well as the general method

14. Eubank, pp. 163, 167.

by which the definition was reached. Both positions were the outcome of Comte's experience. In the light of his lifework it became necessary to give sociology a complete rationality by separating the psychological from the sociological, i.e., results from sources or destination. Such a separation gave rise to a definition of sociological results as collective cumulations, the societal isolate, on which sociology as a member of the encyclopedic hierarchy solidly rests.

In the light of this delimitation of the domain of sociology, what modifications in current theory profitable to sociological theory may be made? Is it possible, always respecting the continuity and filiation of sociological discussion, to push the conception of the group to a still further and perhaps final degree of abstraction? Thus a far-reaching question may be asked: Do groups really consist of persons, and if so, in what sense? Wiese-Becker raise this question by implication when they say with justice: "Let us be plain upon one point: never under any circumstances is the *whole* human being, with *all* his psychical capacities, incorporated in the group. His entire ability for devotion, hatred, or revulsion is never completely absorbed in the life of the group. Each separate emotion and the total capacity for emotion never reaches full manifestation in the group member as group member." [15] The distinction is sound, even though the emphasis is placed on the wrong grounds. In what sense, then, does the person become a group member? The conception of the societal process as a cumulation of collective efforts gives the ready clue to the answer: A person is a group member only as he participates in the process of collective cumulation; i.e., he is a member of a group *only as a socius* and not as a complete person.

The problem of intermindedness receives an analogous solution. What the word means in the group sense is that the participators in a common process are directing their efforts as similar, interlocking parts toward a whole emerging result which alone gives meaning to their separate, partial achievements and *know that they are participating in the common process*. It is by what they are doing and thinking that human beings become group members, not by what they are feeling or experiencing emotionally. The two elements are entirely separable in theory, and present day theory is making the separation more and more a commonplace of thought. From mem-

15. P. 535. (Italics are Becker's.)

bership in associations, i.e., socii working together, men mainly derive their attitudes toward life.

Comte once again seems to have caught sight of the idea and been the first to express it as a general concept when he said that it is sociological phenomena which determine the fundamental direction of all our tendencies whatever and so generalized an earlier statement to the effect that "the exterior world radically modifies the affections, without having any direct relations with them. It stimulates some of them and represses others *according to the opinions and acts that are provoked by our theoretical and practical situation.*" [16] Does the following quotation, already used in another connection summarizing the latest psychological research, do more than give a certain precision to the general idea? "The development of personality can be considered and understood, at least partially, as a process of adjustment of the original inherited phylogenetically predetermined instinctive cravings to the requirements of collective life as they are represented by any given culture." [17] In other words, there is a clear separation possible between the psychological and the sociological. The likemindedness is the result of the societal acting upon the individual, the influence of the socius upon or in the person.

It would seem then that the concept group could be still further analyzed than it has yet been, and even broken up. The aspect of the matter that particularly interests the sociologist is the cooperation of socii, not the manifestations of personality. A person may be a socius in many different regards; the concept of pattern, underlying the statical division of sociology, seems particularly applicable here. A person may be grouped with others in many different associations; it would seem therefore advisable for sociologists to consider the possibility of dropping the word "group" when they are thinking strictly in regard to their own isolate and yet to retain all of its useful significance by utilizing the word "groupings" for those associations, those cooperations of socii upon which in the last analysis depends that process of collective cumulation which has made Man. The advantage of the substitution is that it throws the emphasis away from the relatively permanent entity and places it upon the changing pattern of relationships.

16. *Politique*, 2, 256.
17. Alexander, *The Medical Value of Psychoanalysis*, pp. 132–133.

It might be well too to point out, while possible new terms are under consideration, how useful it would be if a purely neutral word could be found to apply on any level of culture to the entire network of associations which taken as a whole characterize a given society. Such a general structure of relationships might well be referred to as a "socionomy." There would thus be a term quite parallel to the word "economy" so useful for summarizing general conditions of an economic kind. At any rate, for the present purposes the phrase "societal groupings" is entirely adequate for the purposes of the present chapter. The phrase will probably meet other requirements as well; for the idea of a group entity is clearly dependent upon the possibility of identifying individuals as socii engaged in a societal, i.e., collective and cumulative task regardless of the time or space by which they may be separated.

An illustration of the foregoing conclusions, as well as a welcome relief from their aridity, may be found in the marvelous vision of the Divine Rose which Dante pictures in the Paradise. Here all the souls of the redeemed are gathered row on row in mystic union with God. There it is their felicity to remain forever. They do nothing; they have no needs. They think not at all; they have transcended thought. They simply are, eternally. They can be of no aid to one another; they can have no relations with one another—the very word implies incompleteness and imperfection. Here reigns the absolute. They have no memories, for they have drunk of the water of oblivion and passed beyond its shores. They are souls, *soli*, alone, each in perfection. If by a profane imagination scientific investigators were to be admitted to Paradise temporarily for purposes of making observations relative to their particular science, only one group of them would find material for their inductions. Physical and biological phenomena by definition no longer exist. Physicist and biologist would find no reason for admission. The sociologist would be in the same case. There are no socii among the eternally blessed; the process of collective cumulation is forever at an end. There is no association; the souls are simply in presence of one another. They constitute one vast assemblage. There is no group and no grouping; the patterns are identical. There are no sociological interests; there is neither economy nor socionomy. Of all the scientists in the hierarchy, the psychologist alone would find material for observation; for it is the essence of Dante's Heaven that the sublimest urges of the essential personality there find timeless satisfaction. "One can tire of acting; one can even tire of thinking; one can never tire of loving."

But enough to occupy the sociologist can be found on earth among men. In particular, and in connection with the preceding definition of association, what are the societal groupings that are of chief interest to him? And in what order can he arrange them? On this point, fortunately, there is no difficulty except the difficulty of choosing. Thus there is the distinction between the we-group and the they-group. Sumner has made the difference so clear and so familiar as to dispense with its discussion here.

It will be more to the purpose of classifying socionomic phenomena to examine into societal groupings from other points of view: for example, the distinction so often found between primary and other groups. What lies behind this word "primary"?

In American sociology at least, the classical presentation of the primary group with its intimate, face-to-face relationships is in the work of Cooley, *Social Organization*. Many other writers, however, from Comte's time to the present have considered essentially the same body of data. Thus there is a series of distinctions—embodying the facts Cooley so clearly presented and serving to establish a classification of societal groupings—which may be said to be the generally accepted results of an analysis carried on through a number of decades. On the basis of this analysis it may be said that there is a twofold classification of associations: the first class arises from primary, direct contact, spontaneous, independent, nonoptional, unauthorized, and instinctive. It would seem to be the community of Tönnies. It is characterized by what the formal school not very happily terms common-human relationships, which it describes as follows:

There are basic types of interhuman behavior which are only superficially altered by changes in existing plurality patterns. Social processes and relationships called forth by love, hatred, envy, hunger, thirst, lust for power and similar elemental forces are always influenced, modified, diverted, weakened, or strengthened by the forms of the existing folkways and mores, church, state, economic organization, class stratification, law and so on, but they can never be created or destroyed thereby. It should be noted, however, that these common-human processes are not evident in all spheres of social life; the great majority are found only in the dyadic or pair relationship.[18]

If from this account be eliminated all but the biological data, which alone the sociologist has the right to utilize in beginning the study of societal phenomena, the residue will explain why it is that the basic distinction on which the present discussion rests has come to be so generally recognized and incorporated into sociological theory.

The second division of associations is of course based upon derivative, secondary, indirect contact, predetermined, dependent, optional at least in part, and rational. It is the society of Tönnies. "The earliest and all the 'natural' groupings of men, are of the purely fortuitous type found in *Gemeinschaft*. Later, man begins to discriminate, and to form his associations upon the basis of mutual and sympathetic interests, thus establishing *Gesellschaft*. The latter are rational, purposive, and founded upon commutuality, hence represent constructive advances in the direction of socialization." [19] The relationships obtaining in this type of associations are termed circumscribed by the formal school, an unfortunate adjective in that it suggests precisely the opposite of what it means, for the range in which the processes operate is by far the least restricted of all.

There is no need, however, of going deeply into the discussions centering about the main point here in question. What is involved is quite simple. Human beings come into relations with one another in an infinity of ways. Where they take part in collective efforts aimed at the cumulation of results, they are of interest to sociology, otherwise not. Such cooperations of socii, such societal groupings are divisible into two great classes: the simple or primary and the composite or derivative. They might well be classified as psychopreferential and socioexperiential. In the first case, the groupings are more strongly influenced by biological factors than by all others combined. They are necessary for the existence of the animal Homo. But human beings associate to pool their efforts in other ways necessary for the existence of Man. These associations are composite

18. Wiese-Becker, pp. 169–170.
19. Eubank, p. 151.

or derivative in that they are entered into by socii already deeply influenced by their first having been acted upon by the spontaneous type of association. The results are thus composite in the sense that the agents, the socii, were not wholly unconditioned in their activities but brought to the second type of association elements deriving from the first. That families make societies is one way of putting the fact. That a smaller plurality pattern is a component of a larger is still another.

That the first class is essentially identifiable with the family is practically agreed upon by the authors already quoted from. By the term is meant the domestic grouping, however it may be defined in any particular culture. Ellwood points out three ways in which it influences the members who are part of it: it socializes them; it carries custom and tradition; it is the source of primary social ideals. And of course LePlay had long ago called attention to the same or analogous facts. Spencer places the domestic relations at the beginning of his analysis and treatment of basic sociological institutions.

The attributions may and do vary, but in general the psycho-preferential grouping that first arises out of biological conditions and then becomes a cooperation in the making of collective cumulations is the associative phenomenon to be found in all cultures. Above it may be found a certain number of other associations; they must of course be studied; but the basic, essential grouping is that which comes out of the biological necessities and then goes on to perform a collective task as well. If, then, the sociologist says that the family is the foundation of society, he is not in effect recommending that people marry and behave themselves; he is saying that as a fact the association which lies at the foundation of Man's societal existence is the primary association, of which the simplest form is the family, sometimes reduced to the fundamental couple. Here is the unit of society, the true sociological element.

Once the nature of association as a subject of sociological interest has been established and the basic societal grouping recognized, it becomes possible to carry on investigation in two directions. First, what of the relations among individuals which do not satisfy the minimum requirements of association? Second, what of the groupings which rise above and pass beyond the simplest forms?

Subsocietal phenomena offer much valuable material for sociological research and have as a matter of fact been given considerable attention. Here there is no possibility however of going into the refinements of association. It cannot be asked what are nascent or potential associations nor explained why the accomplishment of a single given act by a concerted effort does not make the participants true socii. What lies below the level of association—the multitude, the crowd, abstract or concrete—must be omitted, though it is no doubt an introductory part of the socionomic study of sociological phenomena. What is in point in all these distinctions is basically the fact that the individuals involved do not become true socii, although tending more and more to reach that societal level. Wiese-Becker are in sight of the essential point when they say that crowd members, in others words, do not complement one another. From their activities, that is, no collective cumulations result.

Of the societal groupings which rise on the foundations of the primary associations to impressive heights, here is the appropriate place to speak. Unfortunately adequate space is lacking; fortunately the formal treatises supply the lack. Besides, the general thought underlying the development of the topic is simple. As men aid one another or combine their efforts they become socii; as socii they enter into more or less permanent relationships, which may be called in general societal groupings or patterns of socii. Some of these groupings become permanent and abstract. Here the word "group" has usually been employed to designate the results. Since the word has however been identified customarily with the full range of social phenomena, it may be that another term, exclusively societal in its implications, would be useful. If so, the element of fixity implied by the word "set" would seem to point to it as the desired term. Then the societal ascent from crowds would reach the level of sets and pass on to abstract collectivities.

Of these highest types of societal groupings which so far transcend the individual socius in space and time as to seem completely to absorb him, a few may here be given brief attention. Thus among the elementary associations, somewhat above the family or domestic grouping is the folk. By virtue of the source of its formation it belongs among the sacred, i.e., the psychopreferential patterns of socii. Stripped of its mystical and political trappings, the concept pictures a reality. "The difficulties of existence confronting human beings living in association cannot be overcome by the family structure alone. Much larger social units are also required. Just as in the family, the most readily acceptable basis for such units is blood relationship. In periods when human beings are united by relationships that are relatively crude, predominantly irrational, and with little conscious purpose, the biological link between those of common ancestry is taken for granted as the source of social unity capable of overcoming life's difficulties." [20]

Vastly more important than the sacred, especially with the passing of time and the lengthening of the societal radius, are the secular, i.e., socioexperiential associations. Among them for example is the class, i.e., more or less permanent groupings, sets which are composed of socii in whom "approximately equivalent financial status, education, and degree of political power bring about a close connection between ideologies and interests." [21]

Still more abstract is the city, cité. It is based primarily upon activity and is predominant in the material sphere. It harmonizes the results of inferior groupings such as families or classes for the advancement of the common welfare. It utilizes the diversities of families and individuals and by organizing them about a central purpose brings into being a true separation of offices and functions in the place of chaotic differences. Although the city "is necessarily composed of many domestic associations, it alone determines the whole of the existence proper to each of the latter, since the general distribution of human labors everywhere decides men's respective occupations. This fact, unmistakable since the first rise of civilization, grows more marked as our solidarity and our continuity are extended. Universal feeling essentially confirms this view of the matter by tending everywhere to cause men to be habitually regarded as citizens." [22]

If the city is an organization of socii with regard to activity, the church is a still more abstract collectivity centered about the spiritual. "It unites Cities in a free union just as each City unites various families, first grouping them in classes according to their social functions." [23] It does so by providing an intellectual bond for all the socii cooperating in the maintenance of the collectivity, past, present, and future, thus ensuring the voluntary nature of their cooperative

20. Wiese-Becker, p. 579.
21. Wiese-Becker, p. 581.
22. Comte, Politique, 2, 341–342.
23. Comte, Politique, 2, 305.

activities. It affords the structure whereby are held together the dead, the living, and the unborn. It thus serves especially to emphasize and strengthen the continuity of the association, just as the city emphasizes its solidarity.

Last of all may be mentioned the most abstract as well as the most inclusive collectivity: humanity. "This is not a mere ideological construct but a genuine abstract collectivity—a fact that is frequently denied at the present time. . . . Such denial, however, cannot overcome the overpowering weight of the data to the contrary—all the more compelling because of their utter naturalness and self-evident character." [24] Such data are the fundamental physical and psychical sameness of human beings; the relative similarity of needs and urges; the common ignorance of the "whence and whither" of earthly existence; the knowledge that death comes to all men alike; the vague wishes for supernatural aid in which all human beings sometimes indulge; the common capacities for joy and sorrow.

So much can be said on the evidence open to all; the societal viewpoint makes possible a confirmation of the general fact at the same time that it reveals that humanity, in its double sense, is not a term applicable to all the descendants of the animal Homo indifferently agglomerated. Humanity, said Comte,

is the sum total of the beings, past, future, and present *who freely work together* in perfecting the universal order. Every sociable species naturally tends toward such a convergence. But collective unity can be realized, on each planet, only in the preponderant race, whose very expansion would necessarily prevent that of animals of less high rank. That is why the systematic definition of the composite being has no need of mentioning its specific nature. So too, the spontaneity of the co-operation and its external objective are evidently indispensable for its consistency and its perpetuity. If then everything is set aside that can be implied without confusion,

including the societal core of the phenomenon, the definition of humanity can be formulated as follows: "The whole continuing sum of convergent beings." [25]

24. Wiese-Becker, p. 580.
25. *Politique, 4,* 26.

In conclusion, the study of association emerges from the work of the sociologists as the first special science in the field of social theory to be developed on its own, free within the limits of the historically possible from the influences and probable handicaps of spontaneous and empirical efforts of earlier times. It has been unusually free, too, from the workings and inversions so often consequent upon theological and philosophical methods. It needs no doubt to refine its conclusions still further, especially in the direction of the separation of the societal from the psychical. But it still remains in the control of a highly important subdivision of sociological phenomena. All that need be denied it is its claim to absorb the whole domain of sociology. That there are other societal subisolates demanding attention the chapters to follow will show.

CHAPTER 15:

The Societal Subisolates: Communication

It is curious that so evident a social necessity as language should have received so little formal attention from sociologists. True, they have practically all bowed in its general direction as they passed, but few of them have thought it worth while tarrying long over its analysis. "Society begins where communication begins," says Eubank in a typical passage, "and ends where communication ends. . . . The question of efficient communication, therefore, becomes the starting point of a consideration of the problem of human development." [1] But after so promising a beginning the discussion of the subject dwindles into a brief chapter. Bernard is more prescient but no more lavish when he says that tomorrow we may expect the sociological analysis of language to become dominant; it may even become one of the major divisions of sociology.

As a matter of fact, however, the study of language has always been one of the major subdivisions of the science. It was put in that position by Comte in his analysis of social statics in the second volume of the *Politique,* chapter 4. The reasons for his action are clear. Nowhere else is there to be found a better example of the results which sociology is to make its subject matter. No data better show the effect or the working of the cumulation of collective efforts. Language might indeed be thought of as *the* example of societal phenomena, as the most characteristic of the occurrents on which a sociological science must be built.

Because of Comte's early regard for communication as an essential societal function, then, the present chapter will begin with a brief exposition of his theory. To do so will serve not merely to emphasize Comte's position as a pioneer in sociological territory; it will also vindicate the sociologist's right to bring it within his jurisdiction. It is as well a necessary course. What other sociologist has a theory of language to offer?

1. *The Concepts of Sociology,* p. 4.

In his chapter Comte follows the hierarchical order of the sciences. Sociology is the science above biology in the scale; what aid then can biology give to sociology in the construction of a theory of communication? This question Comte asked, and it brought him straight to the construction of an *animal* theory of language upon which to erect his sociological conclusions. Both lines of inquiry have as their point of departure a general definition of *signs*.

Any language whatever is composed of signs. Every sign results from habitual connection, voluntary or involuntary, between a movement and a sensation. By virtue of this connection, each movement objectively reproduces the corresponding sensation; or the cerebral revival of the sensation may subjectively represent the movement whence it emanated to begin with. In this way the brain translates to the world without its various internal impressions, its power to do so arising from the mutual relations of the two apparatuses of nerves, sensory and motor, which are exterior to it. Communication follows essentially the same course, in any case, whether the motor apparatus and the sensory apparatus belong to one and the same being or two distinct beings. Every movement which recalls a sensation is essentially objective, even when it emanates from an organism which addresses to itself the sign thus produced. Hence a sign may be defined abstractly and precisely as the "constant connection between an objective influence and a subjective impression," [2] the essential point being that the connection should be constant.

To adapt this definition to the distinction between the biological and the sociological requires a line between involuntary and voluntary signs. In the first case, the various acts which animals accomplish are themselves the necessary signs of the propensities which prompted them or the projects they realize. This involuntary language is found in pure form only among the lower animals, but it can be understood in essentials by all animals having a common or comparable basis of organization. Important as this language of action may be in itself, it is important here only because it serves as the natural basis of the higher, voluntary system of signs. The making of these signs can never become completely arbitrary. If it did they would fail to achieve their main purpose, which is to effect communication within the group, domestic or other. The fixity nec-

2. Comte, *Système de politique positive*, 2, 222.

essary for mutual comprehension is secured by basing the voluntary signs upon the natural, biological, involuntary signs which accompany and are in fact a part of the accomplishing of the various organic functions and which are gradually decomposed and simplified without ceasing to be intelligible.

Here then is the transition from the biological to the sociological and the bond between them. Voluntary signs acquire the requisite fixity from their having arisen out of involuntary signs; but they are always true social institutions since they were originally intended for mutual communications. They are not limited to Man. Each species has its own natural language. Man's superiority lies elsewhere, namely, in his superior sociality.

Voluntary language is the only kind that allows of significant progress, since it alone can be made to keep step with the complication and extension of society. "When more complicated and more frequent relations between beings reveal the inadequacy of natural signs, a more or less artificial language is added to them, the first elements of which result from the decomposition of spontaneous cries or movements. Among the sociable species, this institution is extended and consolidated, in proportion as notions and relations are developed. Language thus becomes the continuous depository of collective wisdom." [3]

Having thus established a positive foundation for the study of language, Comte next turned to the task of tracing the gradual growth and formation of voluntary signs from their involuntary roots. His first recourse was to the method of comparison, on a biological basis. All artificial signs are originally derived, even in the human species, from a simple voluntary imitation of the different signs which involuntarily result from the corresponding existence. Only this spontaneous origin can explain both their formation and their interpretation. "The fundamental condition for any true language is the sufficiently facultative reproduction of its natural elements by virtue of the movements originally bound up with the passions communicated." [4]

It is evident from the principle just stated that the higher animals

3. Comte, *Politique*, *1*, 721.
4. *Politique*, 2, 226–227.

can use only two systems of exterior signs: one addressed to the eye, the other to the ear. Each of them has its own advantages and so they are both used concurrently. Applied in characteristic fashion to the expression of the most powerful emotions, they everywhere give rise to a certain spontaneous foreshadowing of aesthetic expansion in that they initiate the two fundamental arts, the mimetic and the phonetic. From these two spontaneous sources come all artificial signs, multiplying in proportion as the communication of feeling is weakened by the extension of social relations, whereby intellectual transmission comes more and more to prevail.

But biological comparison prevents any misconception as to the influence of intellectual transmission in the creation of language. The whole animal kingdom bears witness to the fact that movements and cries are used much more to communicate feelings than to transmit notions or even to concert projects. A like contrast is observable among men when their social relations are limited to domestic or weak political groupings. It is the development of man's activity and the corresponding extension of his society that make it possible for the intellectual part of human language, theoretical and practical, to hide gradually from sight the affective and consequently the aesthetic source whence it always arises and whose traces it never loses. *Language, that is to say, is always in the last analysis the outcome of affective impulsion,* even in man and in his most intellectual products.

At this point, i.e., where human development becomes the center of interest, Comte turns from biology to sociology and has recourse to the method of filiation. With respect to the expression of feeling and aesthetic manifestations in general, the two senses susceptible of ulterior development do not stand at first upon equal terms. At the beginning of all human evolution, individual or collective, the mimetic long prevails over the phonetic, as in the majority of the animals, since the movements which produce visual signs are both easier to renew and more closely connected with the corresponding feelings than sounds.

Nevertheless the natural transiency and impermanence of mimetic expression soon lead to a profound modification of the fundamental art. Permanence is sought even at the cost of diminishing aesthetic power. So the mimetic gradually falls into disuse when it has sufficiently fostered the two principal arts of form, sculpture first and then painting. The visual part of human language comes at last to be derived from the forms just mentioned and particularly from the second. If all writing has its original source in a true design, every design was intended at first to perpetuate an expressive attitude.

It is easy to explain the preference that phonetic expression soon acquired and then developed over mimetic. Its greater independence of time and place renders it more apt than mimetic for communications even at short distances between all who are adequately skilled in the voluntary formation of sounds. But the phonetic means of transmitting states of mind, though capable of widening cerebral existence by its power of reproducing the finest nuances of mutual communications, is yet deficient in spontaneity and so is dependent upon collective expansion for its improvement; but in compensation it can grow with the growth of society.

Not only has phonetic expression greater potentialities for collective development than mimetic; the vocal apparatus is dependent upon the brain more intimately than any other part of the muscular system. It is thus the part most fit for furnishing signs capable of expressing emotions and thoughts, even the most delicate. Add to these advantages the fact that phonetic expression far more than mimetic allows of a true monologue in which beings can address themselves, and the sum of characteristics is complete which explain why in all the higher animals the phonetic system of signs gains an almost universal preponderance and why other modes of communication are called language, i.e., tongue-age, only by metaphor.

Such, says Comte, was the evolution which among all human populations transformed visual and mimetic language into a simple auxiliary of auditive and phonetic language. The latter was destined to be the normal system of expression the best adapted to an existence like that of man's, in which, despite the fact that the affection always dominates the intellect, the signs that most suit the latter were destined to take precedence over those that are preferred by the former. Comte's argument affords a striking illustration of the way in which the animal Homo was transformed by societal influences.

After the inversion of the relative positions held by the two pos-

sible human systems of signs, i.e., after the ascendancy of the phonetic over the mimetic, there was, continues Comte, a second transformation of language, the outcome of a gradual decomposition of
the phonetic system.

The second modification of language was due to sociological
causes, as was the first. In proportion as man's social evolution developed his mind on either the theoretical or the practical side and
diminished the initial preponderance of affection, visual influences
tended to modify the language of sound. Collective existence, that
is, tended constantly to increase the number of relations joining
man to the world and so to multiply the number of *images*. Hence
even the primitive mimetic language became more analytical and
less aesthetic in order that it might embrace the notions which concern the exterior order and man's constant reaction upon it. Now a
purely phonetic language could not directly, i.e., without modification spread over the vast field of expression which comprises images,
properly so called, linked at first as they always are with purely visual impressions. This too synthetic language had therefore to be
decomposed to allow of auditive distinctions susceptible of being
associated suitably with such increasingly numerous visual sensations. The necessity became still greater when imagination, by
uniting visual impressions in novel ways, came to supplement observation.

The first profound modification experienced by both art and
language in virtue of this growing reaction of visual images upon
vocal signs consists in the decomposition of the original phonetic
into two distinct branches. Whereas the more affective receives the
name *music,* the more intellectual constitutes *poesy.* This new coordination became more and more widespread in proportion as
intellectual expansion, theoretical and practical, made men more
conscious of the need of a less synthetic language in which *notions
and enterprises* could be better formulated.

This separation between poesy and music and the inversion of
the original relation between them must be regarded as the principal characters which distinguish true human language from all the
other animal tongues. The analogous reversal which first raised the
phonetic over the mimetic is not peculiar to man; the majority of
the higher animals reach it in the same manner as he does. But none
of their races could attain to the more delicate decomposition which

separates simple poetical language from pure musical language, the latter alone being suited to natures whose intelligence is too little developed.

With all the more reason must the new modification be considered as exclusive to mankind, since under the growing impulsion of the same motives the language of poesy was decomposed in its turn. From this third transformation finally resulted the full constitution of human language, when *prose* proper alone allows a free development of *the active and speculative objectives of language*.

Such are the three great revolutions which produced successively the normal constitution of human language, the phonetic prevailing first over the mimetic, then poesy over music, and finally prose over poesy. Each of these essential modifications of the natural order was compatible with that universal communication which is the principal purpose of language; each step was likewise indispensable and inevitable to *the most important of man's special developments, namely, the practical and theoretical growth of intelligence for the direction of the activity which always dominates human existence*.

Comte's account of the way in which the impermanence of the language of sound was remedied by recourse to the language of form—that is to say, how the phonetic and the mimetic were finally combined to give *writing,* first in its hieroglyphic and then in its syllabic and alphabetic modes—need not here be summarized. It does but show how far the system of communication has been extended under the urge of collective existence.

Language thus comprises, when given its full philosophical extension, all the means for transmitting to the without the various and varied inner impressions of men. Such a system forms in fact an indivisible whole in which the more usual and less expressive part, constituting language proper, is really inseparable dogmatically as well as historically from that which specially bears the name of art. The latter, considered not only in its general source, poesy, but also in its four essential special branches, music, painting, sculpture, and architecture, forms the necessary complement of language with respect to our profoundest impressions. Besides, art constitutes the only truly universal part of it, understood at once by all the human species and even in different degrees among all the higher animals. Finally, since the more pronounced part of the communication system is the true source of the more customary part, the separation of the two would for this reason alone be arbitrary and irrational.

Nothing, in conclusion, is more clear than the fully social nature of the institution of language. It is so relative to the sociability of Man that purely personal impressions can never be suitably formulated in it, as is shown by daily experience with sickness and disease. Its slightest elaboration always implies a collective influence, in which the cooperation of generations quickly becomes not less indispensable than that of individuals. The greatest efforts of the most systematic geniuses could never attain to the personal construction of any real language.

The preceding conclusions as to the nature and elements of language were the product of Comte's seeking a solution to his problems first by way of beginning with animal, i.e., biological data and second by taking the animal Homo as the starting point and proceeding under the guidance of the conception of Man as a cultural product and not a metaphysical ego. These methods made clear the whole system of communication and the place of language therein. They did more. They revealed that communication is based upon feeling and operates by means of images and signs. They established on a positive basis of induction the fact that mental life is developed and manifested by a combination of feelings, images, and signs, voluntary and involuntary. It follows that there are three processes, three "logics," which together guide the mind of Man.

The first of these is the logic of feeling, i.e.,

the art of assisting the combination of notions by resorting to the connection between the corresponding emotions. No artificial method can be so powerful as this instinctive one, whence in reality spring all the great inspirations of our intellect, notwithstanding the shallow disdain it meets in the majority of modern thinkers. Its efficacy rests directly upon the cerebral law that the affective organs are more energetic than the speculative. But this basic logic has two serious natural imperfections: its exercise is not adequately under control; its elements are much too imprecise. We are unable at will to reproduce the emotions most fit to aid our various thoughts. Besides, since our conceptions are necessarily much more multiple than our feelings, a mutual correspondence between them cannot become adequately established.[5]

These imperfections of the logic of feeling find their first spontaneous compensation

when the logic of images is sufficiently developed to be an habitual aid to that of the emotions. The reproduction of images is much more under control than that of feelings, and besides they can be multiplied to a far greater degree. Hence we are able much more easily to connect each notion with an image than with a feeling, and so the better to aid the natural combination of our thoughts. But this second logic, though more available and more precise, is less potent than the first. Besides, images are far from being reproducible or multipliable in such measure as to meet all our needs, especially the intellectual ones.[6]

What is lacking at this point is an easier method of making mental combinations. What is needed is a way of converting into a practical instrument of reasoning the easily controlled and highly variable impressions that give rise to images. At this point the logical services of language become clear and the second spontaneous compensation for the weakness of the logic of feeling appears. Language is composed of voluntary, artificial signs. These signs are "bound up with our thought in a far less intimate and spontaneous fashion than feelings or even images are. But when the artificial connection is adequately established by exercise, the facility with which they can be reproduced and multiplied makes the work of speculation more rapid and more precise." [7] That is, there is a logic of signs.

One word of warning, says Comte in concluding this section of his chapter. The normal service of voluntary signs ought never be conceived of apart from the general theory which holds them together with the other divisions of logic. "This was the irrational course of all the ontological schools, except during the Middle Ages; they failed to do justice to the two natural logics. Despite these doctrinal aberrations, which tend to reduce human reason to mere language,

5. Comte, *Politique*, 2, 239.
6. Comte, *Politique*, 2, 239–240.
7. Comte, *Politique*, 2, 240.

the very nature of Man has ever made the logic of feelings and of images take spontaneous precedence over that of signs." [8]

The main use of the third element of logic consists in assisting the second to facilitate the combination of images as the second aids the first to establish connections between the feelings. Yet the bond between voluntary signs and feelings, singly or in combination, *can* become direct and often should be so, especially with regard to abstract notions.

> Then is our interior world bound up by artifice with the exterior world. But this immediate relation has much less consistency than that which is established for the involuntary interplay of images and feelings. Our logical perfection then, hardly more than sketchily envisaged hitherto, must be regarded as consisting above all in an adequately happy combination of these three general processes to the end that each word shall recall as far as possible an image and each image a feeling. We shall then have applied the exterior order to the perfecting of our interior elaboration, by connecting our emotions, essentially subjective, with signs principally objective, by the intermediation of images, objective in their source and subjective in their seat. [9]

Such was Comte's analysis of communication and of language in particular, reached in 1853 and essentially unchanged thereafter. In the course of reading it two things become evident. First, Comte was still distant from the point he was later to reach, where results were clearly distinguishable from sources and ends. Second, and partly as a consequence of incomplete analysis, Comte had failed to reach the distinctions, later made clear by others, between signal, sign, and symbol. That he was moving in this direction is evident from the indications marked by italics in the passages above; but his words do not clearly show the wide difference that exists between the signific and the symbolic.

Exactly where this distinction begins is difficult to determine; but it seems that the divergent paths of each element of meaning

8. *Politique,* 2, 240.
9. Comte, *Politique,* 2, 240–241.

can be traced backward until they meet at the point where a given movement or cry is at once the sign that an image has taken form and a revelation of the nature of the form taken. A hypothetical illustration may be hazarded here. A small group has in its environment the usual sources of fear and one supreme source of terror, say a tiger. Sight of the tiger arouses a cry of acute fear, distinctive in pitch and timbre. A member of the group hearing this distinctive cry is not only alarmed; the image of the source of terror is raised as well. His mind is "informed" of the presence of the tiger. The cry is thus not only a sign of terror; it is also the symbol of a tiger. And because the cry and the image are common to the group the symbol makes conceptual communication possible and actual. That there is such a meeting place, where the same sign, phonetic or mimetic, expresses to the outer world both the synthesizing of an image—i.e., the making of a concept—and its form as well, is not open to doubt. From it the paths diverge. The development of the signific follows one course, that of the symbolic another.

The recognition of the distinction just drawn leads to a fourth reversal of initial importance between elements of communication, to be added to the three pointed out by Comte. This time it is the predominance in the system of communication of the symbolic over the signific. As the life of men in society grows more complicated, the inaptness of the sign to keep pace with the rapid multiplication of social relationships and the respective images makes more and more necessary the expansion of the symbol. Finally the latter becomes the chief means of communication. And because the phonetic type of communication is so much more flexible than the mimetic and lends itself so much more easily to the making of distinguishable signs, the symbolic becomes more and more identified with the phonetic. Man, that is, becomes able to talk, and of course he talks prose.

It is probable that at this point the natural history of language ceases and its cultural development begins. At some point such an origin must be found for there is nothing whatever on the organic level which corresponds to the cultural. Once the process of collective cumulation begins to operate, signs as such cease to be adequate. The latter meet the needs of all expression of an organic nature; but societal results are not produced by the evolutionary processes of biology. Yet these results must be expressed by the use of the bodily

—sensory and motor—systems evolved on an organic basis. Biology has nothing to say about group loyalty, for example. Hence the limitations of the signific as compared with the symbolic.

To make a cleavage between the organic and the societal does not mean that the development of the signific must cease when that of the symbolic has begun. Images can be enacted, acted out, as well as symbolized; but the sign thus enacted is much less facultative than the symbol. Men may dance, in the primitive sense, even when they cannot talk; but once they can talk, the range of expression is vastly extended. In other terms, at the point just determined there begins a growing distinction between the representational and the symbolic. But because of its greater ease of production and repetition, the second lends itself to communication in a way that the first does not; discourse ensues. Hence the difference between the two kinds of expression takes a still more advanced form, expressible in the terms "representational" and "discursive."

Analysis of the representational leads to a still further advance in the theoretical consideration of the elements of communication. It leads to the inclusion of art in its varying forms in the system of communication. Comte saw this fact clearly and made place for it in his discussion. What he seems not to have seen, and what is still obscure, is the inclusion in the same system of what is broadly known as ritual, extending out into magic. No survey of the human record, especially in its earlier stages, no review even of the present can fail to reveal the immense part played in the transmission of the social heritage and in the strengthening of social relations among individual beings by the sum of procedures to which the word "ritualistic" is applicable. Obviously the mimetic can become symbolic as well as the phonetic; but the essential distinction between the representational and the symbolic is not therefore done away with. Hence a final distinction can here be drawn between the ritualistic and the discursive modes of communication, the latter increasing in importance with the expansion of the societal.

Continued use of biological comparison and sociological filiation have given Comte's conclusions an amplitude they did not originally possess. It is now certain that the animal Homo, like all other animals, is activated, moved, motivated by affective forces.

Various terms have been found for these forces: instincts, urges, drives, hungers, orexis.[10] Comte's name for them, though little known, still seems the best because it clearly indicates their double function. He called them affective motors to show that they may be either passive, giving rise to feelings, or active, setting the organism into operation. He took the hint for this distinction from Gall's observation that certain senses alternated between active and passive states: looking and seeing, listening and hearing, for examples. The observation has been generalized; now there is for the orectic constants a sequence from unconsciousness, subconsciousness, awareness, feeling on the passive side to desire, propensity, passion, mania on the active. In whatever degree of intensity, they are the *source* and their satisfaction the *destination* of that process of collective cumulation which produces the results with which sociology is concerned.

Whether active or passive, these affective motors come into relation with the world without solely by virtue of the sensory and motor systems, the first giving an awareness of the exterior world and the second allowing of coming into relations with it. The sensory system receives and registers the impressions made through the senses. Its essential quality for this discussion is its capacity for reviving and combining impressions once made and its facility in doing so. Because the operation of the sensory system and its controlling centers gives form to images, it may be described as eidomorphic and its action as a whole termed the faculty of ideation. The motor system is the means whereby the affective impulsions and their consequences are exteriorized. In order to distinguish between impulsion and exteriorization, the term "exergy" will be employed, to apply to the results of the promptings of orexis. These outcomes appear whether the orectic constants are stimulated by the impressions made on the sensory system or are spontaneously active.

The point is there are three systems involved—orexis, ideation, and exergy—each characterized by a distinct type of functioning within the organism. Consequently each being on the requisite

10. "Here and elsewhere I propose to follow a number of modern writers in using the convenient Aristotelian term 'orexis' (with the adjective 'orectic') to describe the feeling, striving and wishing aspects of the mind." J. C. Flügel, *Man, Morals and Society* (London, Duckworth, 1945), p. 14, n. 2.

level of organization has the capacity for expression which ultimately makes communication possible. Moreover the simple early expressions were exteriorizations of inner impulsion, i.e., they were affective in nature; they remain so. The relation between affective impulsion and action—i.e., between orexis and exergy—is often so immediate and direct that the action is the sign of the inner state. A crude sort of communication is the outcome, perhaps not the least effective. Even in man the deepest, most satisfying relationships rest upon a basis of common feelings. Finally, the three systems despite their intimate interdependence are capable each of independent activity. Hence each can be abstracted and isolated. When so regarded, each has its own constituent elements with determinate relations between them. Each, that is to say, has its own way of working, its own logic.

In regard to the logic of the oretic constants it is difficult today to be specific, especially as to the name and nature of each. There is to begin with the difficulty of finding a generic name for an orectic force which varies in intensity from subconsciousness to mania. Each of these characteristic mental states has in the past received a distinctive appellation. There is the difficulty of disentangling the constituent constants that have been combined to produce states of mind regarded hitherto as indivisible. There is the difficulty of recognizing the elemental urges, hungers, and drives under the disguises which varying cultural conditions tend to impose upon them. The phenomena in question here are clearly the most complicated with which men are called upon to deal. Reducing societal phenomena to the degree of regularity where they can be isolated and cancelled from the general problem is certainly an essential precondition to its positive study and solution.

Nevertheless despite the difficulties sociological induction, on the basis of the whole available cultural record, reveals certain facts. First of all, the animal Homo is no exception to the rule which puts affective drive at the basis of animal existence. Second, there are distinctive affective motors, i.e., orectic constants with determinate relations between them. That the number of these basic drives is not great the animal world in its entirety makes clear. That they have a possible spontaneity of their own, separable from the general activity of the organism, the data of psychopathology demonstrate. That they may be distinguished in a generalized form under cul-

tural variations is the implication of the assertion that human nature cannot be changed. What is meant of course is that the set of
orectic constants bequeathed by the animal Homo to his descendants has not been essentially altered by cultural evolution. All
of these points together give a solid foundation for an affective
logic.

The working of the affective motors in the mind may be envisaged
as either passive or active. In the first case, a low degree of intensity
due seemingly to simple reaction to circumstance within or without
is indicated by certain psychical stirrings, often rising from the un-
or subconscious level to that of awareness. In some cases the consequences are suffused feelings, apparently unaccompanied by any
sensory or motor activity, describable as for example terror or awe
or doom or exaltation or ecstasy. In still other cases the functioning
of the orectic constants on the subconscious level ultimately takes
form in mental constructions whose origin or cause or occasion is
completely obscure. The consequence, as in all analogous instances,
is the attribution of the form, image, or vision to some hominoid
power or being working from without.

Men in whom these purely subjective operations occur with unusual vividness or regularity are said to be inspired; they are the
recipients of revelations. Once they were said to "have" a genius;
gradually possession became identification; they are now said to
"be" geniuses. Once the external source of these visitations is dismissed, however, it becomes evident that all men manifest like
phenomena in some degree. The hunch, the presentiment, the inspired guess, the prophecy gradually assume their relative positions
together with like phenomena in a synthesis describable as the
logic of intuition.

Increase in the intensity of the functioning of the same constants
leads to a change in the quality of the manifestations. From passive
they become active; feeling rises to desire, and beyond. At this level,
passive reaction to circumstance ceases; the organism tends to modify the milieu for the satisfaction of desire. Attention and tension
follow. Both the sensory and the motor systems are aroused at this
point. The image of the desired object is revived; new images, presumably of objects that would give more intense satisfactions, may
be synthesized from the sense impressions of an earlier moment;
images may be brought together in new configurations, hitherto

unexperienced or unrealized. To make them real, the motor system sets to work. New, artificial arrangements of the constituents of the world without result. Men, that is to say, originate. Their originations are the exteriorizations of their imagination. Roused by desire man thus becomes a maker; new combinations of desires in varied degrees of intensity produce—bring forward—new projects; on the level of imagination, man becomes a poet, on the level of reality an artificer. Here are the elements of a *logic of creation.*

Zoological comparison makes evident the existence of various urges, of which the primary one is no doubt the hunger that reaches the level of desire under the stimulus of organic need. It shows also that these hungers are "blind"—notoriously they are not under the control of the will. In fact, as Comte was led by Gall to see, they *are* the will, i.e., "the ultimate condition of desire, when after the deliberative mental process the appropriateness of some dominant impulse has been recognized." [11] Thus the will ceases to be an entity. The orectic forces have to be guided; food has to be found, to be known when found, to be found again and recognized. The senses— sight, taste, smell—work to satisfy the needs of the organism, the stomach particularly. Because of the connection between these quite different functions, the organism can come into contact with the outer world and lead the life of relation which defines animal existence.

By virtue of the sensory system impressions are registered and immagazined, in the central sensory ganglia if that is where they are stored up. Stored up somewhere or somehow they are; and so they can be renewed, revived, brought together again, i.e., remembered after the initial impressions. Not only is this power of recall—by voices, active and passive—a reality; there is also the capacity of combining and recombining elemental sense impressions into shapes, forms, images that were never experienced in the outer world at all. These products of the imagination can be reproduced too. In the original experience, the object that impressed the senses may be said to have been present; when the impressions are subjectively revived the object is re-presented, and these representations are images. Because they *are* images, they must be dealt with in a particular way. The sense impressions and their combinations may be compared, contrasted, broken up, recombined, analyzed, abstracted, iso-

11. Comte, *Politique, 1,* 711.

lated, brought into unprecedented relations—in short there is a *logic of images.*

Midway between the inner world of orexis and the outer world of reality where exergy operates the representative function has its place. The affective constants are purely subjective. They come into contact with the outer world only by means of the sensory and motor systems. The latter are thus objective as regards the orectic constants within and subjective as regards the without. Ideation may thus be passive or active with relation to either the urgings from within or the sensations from without. To the sensory system falls the task of making accurate and discriminating images of the aspects of the world without so that wise choice may be made among them and conduct be modified to adapt it to situation. Societal experience has seized upon this discriminatory function as the chief business of the picturizing faculty of the mind and has given it an apposite name, the intellect, which thus ceases to be an entity along with the will.

Whether the intellectual faculties are capable of spontaneous exercise is open to doubt; the observable reluctance of mankind to engage in thought when any alternative is possible leads to a negative answer. In any case, cause or occasion of activity is never lacking: it may come as the result either of the stimulus of circumstance or of the impulsion of orexis, i.e., through activation or motivation. In the first of these cases, the impressions and their combinations are objective as regards the affective motors; they reflect the conditions under which desires in accordance with their own logic must unite if possible to energize the organism. In the second case, the ideation may be controlled by orexis and so see the external world in a special way or even reject it in favor of an inner vision. Here it is the subjective which dominates.

The function of the intellectual faculties is to deal with the impressions made upon the organism through the senses. This they do with no discrimination between the various senses, giving form to sense impressions by combining them in endless ways. These eidomorphic faculties may be active or passive, as just said. When they are passive the results are either contemplation or reverie, i.e., a simple flow of images relating to the without or the within. When they are stirred to activity, ideation if prompted from without becomes observation, if from within, imagination.

Valid as these distinctions are, they do not lead to true logics because they do not rest upon basic differences between images and the uses to which they are put. To make the required advance, two levels of ideational functioning must be established, with two kinds of result on each level.

The first level is that on which impressions are given form. On this level ideas are produced. They arise in two ways. Impressions may be formed into combinations or syntheses, issuing in representations or presentations of beings, things, seen or never seen; the mental power of concretion ensues. Impressions may on the other hand be revived, classified, set apart from their original contexture, i.e., analyzed, and regarded as occurrents, happenings, repeated or unique; the power of abstraction is the resultant.

If on the first level ideas, i.e., combinations of images are produced, on the second arise thoughts and thought, i.e., combinations of ideas; and so at this point the existence of different logics becomes evident. Here as elsewhere there is an active and a passive phase, meditation and rumination; but these differences are unimportant compared with the differences in the ways in which ideas are formed into thoughts.

There are two such ways. The first works by way of the comparison of images, disclosing by virtue of a kind of metaphor the existence of similarities between images and thus advancing to the establishment of uniformities. Continued use of this method results in the expansion of original concepts to include characteristics at first not noticed or not properly evaluated. It gradually expands an original representation to include or incorporate within an encompassing conception a gradually extended range of phenomena. In this way the mind is led to comprehend similarities and uniformities in the world without. Hence it is appropriately called the logic of induction; it is in fact the *logic of discovery*. The second logic works by way of bringing order into the representations that ideation produces. Whereas the first generalizes, the second systematizes. Instead of finding similarity, it finds (or does not find) congruence, thus disclosing compatibility or incompatibility among concepts. The mind is thus led from one position to another as the coordination of ideas becomes clear. Appropriately this way is called the way of deduction; it is the *logic of consistency*.

Essential to animal existence on any higher level is evidently the complication of image that comes from reaction to circumstance. For societal existence, however, and its changing conditions and situations passive reflection of the outer world no longer suffices. Societal life provides new stimuli for the orectic constants; under this activation the eidomorphic faculties tend more and more to respond to sensory impressions and even to seek for new ones and bring them together in concepts that would never be formed in the normal experience of animals. Indeed at this point the imagination of individuals, having no adequate check in observation, might become dominant and fantasy take the place of fact; hence the need for the various processes of reasoning, i.e., measuring means against end or end against end as pictured by the imagination, of finding ratios between them and so discovering reasons for the adoption of one as against another.

In either of its aspects the logic of images advances the arrival of communication and widens its scope. Experience supplements motivation and tends to direct it. Inductive thinking begins with the comparison of images; metaphor is its foundation. The first similarity was the first regularity. Animals must know what is like what they like and how to tell it. Multiplied similarities are the bases of laws. As larger numbers of men come to live under similar conditions they tend to find similar pleasures and have common feelings, whence the deductive broadening of the basis of agreement and consent. Up to this point the psychopreferential is in control. When the image as well as the emotion is transmissible, the socioexperiential begins to condition the exercise of the orectic constants. Inductive thought is collective and cumulative in nature; hence all the characteristics of inductive logic, particularly its lack of finality. It must always be in course of revision and change with the growth of experience. It does not impart the certitude so dear to the animal Homo; deductive processes, operating mainly within, give him much greater confidence. Induction, following the processes of societal change, denies him the security of immobility. It certainly renders communication more difficult insofar as new images and configurations are constantly being synthesized.

Hence a third logic is required if communication is to include within its scope notions and projects as well as feelings and desires. Here the motor system comes into functional exercise. It may well be that the motor system has with the orectic system a far more direct relationship than is pictured in the metaphysical view of man as reasoning ego, that the logic growing out of its existence should be second in order and importance rather than third. On certain levels of organic evolution the relation between desire and act seems to be direct despite high functional and organic differentiation. It may be that man's difficulty of sympathetic comprehension of such animals is due to this very fact. In any case, on the higher levels—Man's, of course—there is a clear interposition of image between act and desire. It may even be that the position of an organism in the scale of superiority is to be defined by the degree to which ideation intervenes between orexis and exergy.

Nevertheless, the fact that there are image-making, picturizing, eidomorphic functions must not throw into obscurity the fundamentally important organic elements to which is due the exteriorization of the orectic constants. To these exergetic functions is due the very existence of the signs which are the basis of communication. To begin with they are signals rather than signs, but this distinction is not important here. What is necessary is to emphasize, after Comte, the natural, organic fixity of relation between orexis and exergy, whence results meaning for all beings of similar organization, even for an isolated individual being. When now the organism reaches the ideational level, the sign acquires a new importance. The image, the product of the sensory system as a whole under the urging of oretic forces in a state of activity, may be exteriorized, enacted, acted out. Even in man it often occurs that profound emotions cannot be verbalized but must be expressed in action. This action does not stand for the image; it *is* the image. It may even be an entire configuration, as has already been said; it may be a cry, a dance, a rite. Thus it gives rise to a *logic of representation*.

Such logic may be very effective, but it is deficient in one essential requirement. It is not adequately facultative. It is particularly unequal to the task of expressing delicate distinctions or bringing order into a mass of observations. For these and similar ends symbols are indispensable. They are highly facultative; they may be mimetic or phonetic. They respond readily to the controls general to the motor system, i.e., they are easily initiated, maintained, or inhibited. Morever they are so potent in arousing desire and image and action that the magic of the word is easily comprehended. Finally, as symbols they must be employed in certain ways if contradic-

tions and inconsistencies are to be avoided; hence such constructions as syntactic systems, truth tables, etc. In short, there is a *logic
of discourse.*

On the basis thus laid it would be possible to proceed straight to
the problem of communication. It would be advisable to do so but
for the fact that certain inferences so important to the general position of this volume can be drawn from what has just been said that
a digression must here be opened to allow of their being made explicit.

The first of these implications concerns the separation of results
from sources and destination and the consequent distinction between the societal and the psychical. To distinguish between the
two requires no profound penetration into psychological phenomena. In what has been said no depths have been plummeted, no
seals broken. All that has been done is to arrange in a more or less
consistent sequence the language in which men of the Occident
have signalized, signified, and symbolized such aspects of communication as they have been conscious of in themselves or have observed
in others. These inner and outer observations are collective and
cumulative; they will some day be widened and deepened by the
addition of evidence drawn from all available languages. But even
then no answers of a psychological nature will be obtained; at the
best the framing of intelligent questions will be advanced. The
problem of the nature and working of orexis will remain; men will
still have to inquire as to the very existence, the making, the duration of images and configurations. The true task of psychology lies
in this domain.

Meanwhile the sociologist can continue his work. There may be
no images; it does not matter. What is certain is that in some way
men can and do combine their actions in the outer world with their
sense impressions in the inner. The consequences are clear: a new
set of conditions comes into being to which later generations must
increasingly respond. It is these results of psychic functioning, whatever it may one day be revealed to be, which can be abstracted from
their psychical connections and isolated. To study them by the use
of an appropriate method is the sociologist's concern.

A second inference of importance carries thought back to the quarrel between the ancients and the moderns. At that time the question was asked whether there was progress in the arts. In the sciences, yes; but in the arts? In the light of the foregoing section the definitive answer is no. In the sense that Ptolemy was an advance over Aristotle and Kepler over both there is no progress in the arts. The fact is due to the differences in nature and functioning between the orectic system on the one hand and the sensory and motor systems on the other. *Feeling and desire do not cumulate;* they are individual and not collective; *they vary in intensity only.* Images and acts are combinable; it is precisely because they are that a cultural heritage can be built up.

Impulsion is one thing, instrumentation another; creativity and originality differ in kind from intelligence and activity. The latter doubtless account for improvements in techniques and so introduce into the arts a societal element; but techniques and such give only facility, they do not give power. It is the feelings, the drives, the orectic constants that set the imagination to work constructing new forms; it is the intellectual faculties that work together in successive individuals to refine the means whereby impulsion can be more effectively expressed. Late comers are thus spared the difficulties of creating new techniques; but rarely do they manifest the depth of feeling that characterizes the innovators, who are seldom distinguished by technical perfection.

Still other factors complicate the problem. Orectic forces—all of them—may differ in intensity; they differ also specifically. There are interests, ambitions, sympathies. They combine too in different ways and different proportions, often in response to the images and configurations that the eidomorphic faculties construct. Around these varying pictures gather constellations of feelings, shifting and changing with societal developments. The word "sentiment" by its very derivation points to such impermanent combinations or adhesions where feeling and configuration temporarily unite—temporarily in most cases because the societal situation disintegrates and the feelings then combine in new ways around new objectives. Moreover the very forms of art, though they may and do converge, have different sources. Thus the show—pantomime, puppet, pageant, drama—where action is of the essence—seems to point back to the logic of sign and representation, whereas the poem in all its forms—lyric, elegy, epic, etc.—is clearly governed by the logic of symbol and discourse.

For all of these reasons, the word "progress" if it is to be applied to art at all must be given a special definition. Insofar as collective and cumulative factors are directly in play, the arts progress; but these factors are seldom prominent and never dominant. What gives art its special importance is the way it serves as the outlet and embodiment of emotion. It may even be that the techniques developed for the expression of sentiments corresponding to a societal situation of the past may become obstacles to the expression of new sentiments growing out of a developing situation in the present. In such a case creative minds, sensitive to the new influences, may reject the old techniques and strive for new forms of expression. But will the new sentiments be an advance? Not until the growth of science, reaching the psychical domain, has systematically dealt with the orectic constants, evaluated them, and arranged them in a hierarchical order of importance, that is, not until a scale of values has been scientifically determined will it be possible to speak intelligently of progress in the arts.

No one today doubts that the arts are social in origin; but what is not clearly seen is that "social" is a composite term, applicable to a union or fusion of societal and psychical. The first of these two factors provides means, i.e., it is the cumulation of individual effort and experience in the effective exteriorizing of images synthesized under the impulsion of desire. Only the second deals with ends, i.e., it concerns the ultimate orectic forces which impel expression. They are purely subjective. They drive the exergetic faculties to modify the material world for their satisfaction; their own realm is the spiritual. Not until hominoid concepts and terms have been eliminated will a positive analysis and evaluation in these matters be possible. Only then will the question of progress in the arts be closed.

Continuation of the line of thought connecting the two inferences just drawn leads to a third, namely, a conclusion as to the essential nature of man. That men do possess some quality by virtue of which they are superior among living beings seems incontrovertible. Biological induction however has failed to reveal their possession of any distinctive difference in kind elevating them above comparable and related forms. Their superiority must therefore be based upon some quantitative advantage in respect to capacities which all the higher forms possess to some degree.

Search for such a quantitative difference, resulting in a qualitative superiority, has tended gradually to move in the direction of the mental rather than the physical characteristics. Even here the higher animals possess at least in germ all the capacities distinctive of men; and men's initial advantage could not have been very great; why otherwise the millennia of the paleolithic? Some slowly developing character there must have been, it would seem, which gradually opened to men a new mode of being.

Review of the mental characteristics revealed by a survey of the groundwork of communication makes it possible to narrow the search for the operative factor. It is evident that the orectics do not satisfy the requirements. Not only is Man but one of the forms in whom drives are observable, it is even arguable that they are stronger in other forms than in the animal Homo. The exergetic faculties are more promising, but left to themselves alone they are too greatly limited by the nature of the world without, a judgment which is reflected in the commentary that such agents of modification are too material. It is only when the ideational faculties come into operation that a new horizon begins to be visible.

Man can join man in activity, it is true, and so ameliorate conditions for their successors as well as for themselves. But where the relation between orexis and exergy is direct, the blindness of the former must greatly limit the effectiveness of the latter. Only when the picturizing faculties come into operation does a directive influence begin to guide both desire and action. It serves to begin with as a means of reflecting the without; it registers the sense impressions and synthesizes them into representations of the outer world. It stores up these impressions and combines them in abstractions and isolates. In this way it builds up a treasure of experience which *nous*, the active intelligence, brings to the aid of the passive intelligence of the individual. This image-making faculty does more. It makes possible the picturing of a limitless number of nonexistent, imaginable, impossible situations to which the term "fantasies" may well be applied. Their importance to Man is a simple induction from all the myths, religions, arts with which his record is filled.

Man then *is* one of the forms of life complacently called higher by him because he is one of them. But in one essential point he differs from his fellows, namely, in the possession of a superior apparatus for the registration and revival of sensory impressions, their elaboration into new forms, and the analysis, comparison, and ordering of these representations. Most important of those capacities, perhaps because of its illimitable nature, is that which enables him to reorganize sense impressions into new forms, for here is the source of infinite variation, origination, and creation. Here is the distinctive human quality. Man has been defined in many ways: he is the rational animal; he is *Homo sapiens;* he is the religious animal; he is the speciopsychic organism; he is the time binder; he is *Homo faber,* the maker of tools. All these he is; but Man is these things because he is to begin with and fundamentally *the maker of fantasies.*

For an animal whose differential characteristic is an unusual if not unique capacity, first in the storing of sense impressions, then in their analysis and synthesis, and finally in the comparing and ordering of the resulting mental pictures—a form that is which is gifted with an unusual potential of conceptual thinking—the problem of communication is particularly formidable and momentous. It is formidable because of the difficulty of transmitting notions; it is momentous because it is precisely in the transmitting of notions that its future lies. The implication is that such a being will long remain on a level with its original compeers and even run great danger of failing to survive but will, when once the critical point where its superiorities can be realized has been passed, very rapidly come to dominance over related forms.

By virtue of a basis of organization common to animal existence all forms of life on this level possess the characteristics requisite for communication in the first degree. That is to say, they act in order to satisfy need, and the act is a sign of the need. Action thus makes it possible for the existence of a world within to be indicated to the world without. *Expressibility,* the first requirement for communication, is the result.

Of course expressibility, making possible a connection between the two worlds, is only a first condition. A second requirement is some degree of *stability* in the source and means of expression. Particularly is this necessity urgent for animals at the stage where the image intervenes between the urge and the act. Below this level biological limitations leave little scope for variations. But at and above it, the very existence of images seems to jeopardize stability at the moment when it is most necessary. If no factors of stabilization existed, then men could not be understood by other men; they could not even understand themselves. "I do not know how I came to act in such a way; I was not myself." Clearly the source of the difficulty of obtaining stability on this high level is the nature of fantasy. How does fantasy become fixity?

It would seem that the stability requisite for some degree of self and mutual comprehension is a consequence of the fact that fantasies are not completely uncontrolled. There are some, even definite, limitations to the picturing in which the intellectual faculties engage. These limitations are divisible into two classes: those that are due to conditions within the organism and those that exist in the world without.

Of the first of these classes, implying the existence of an orectic logic, little can now be said with confidence. Even that little is likely to be colored if not distorted by such hominoids as will or intelligence which the older doctrines utilized to synthesize observed results. In the case of the affective motors there is disagreement as to their existence, their number, their nature, their relations. Yet the spontaneous observation of Man's behavior through the ages has given rise to expressions which seem to point to the existence of well-differentiated impulsions and permanent relations between them. "To understand the workings of human nature" is a phrase in point, more than hinting at stability in the inner world. It implies that some affective regularities exist, that there are orectic constants, and that a knowledge of them can serve to guide the conduct of men in relation with their fellows. Mill's idea of an ethology is here in point.

Relations between affective motors would seem to imply relations between the images they arouse or are roused by; but no results going much beyond the general acknowledgement of the primacy of the drives in mental activity seem to have been attained. Whether any particular kinds of thought are fathered by any particular kinds of wish is yet to be ascertained; the practices of the ascetics and the mystics might be taken to indicate that such relations exist.

It is not even clear whether the intellectual functions are capable of independent exercise, i.e., without the urge from within; nor is the making of images well understood. Nevertheless the reduction of the intellect to an image-making and relating procedure opens the way to new scientific terrain. Comte, pioneering here, formulated certain inductive conclusions as to the operations of the intellect and thus advanced the concept of stability in regard to it. Normal thought, he said, presents three characteristics, or in an operational sense should follow three rules. First, subjective constructions are or should be subordinated to objective materials. Second, interior images are or should be less vivid than exterior impressions. Third, one image predominates or should predominate over all the others to which cerebral agitation gives rise at the same time. Manifesting these characteristics, thought is normal and to that extent understandable by others than the thinker; obeying these rules the thinker arrives at normal results and to that extent makes them communicable. In other words, fantasy is not illimitable; there are conditions which when observed give it fixity. Insofar as sanity is a requisite for communication, these conditions provide it, and from this viewpoint sanity is but an aspect of stability.

It is clear that Comte in the formulations above was proceeding on the theory that thinking is a process of making and relating images. Following the same line of thought, it is logical to ask the source of the materials of which images are constructed. To do so leads to the establishment of a third requisite for communication. The general answer to the question just raised is that all the materials derive from the world without. But there are two classes into which these objective sources are divisible: the environmental, in the inclusive physical sense, and the cultural. Between these two there is in relation to communication a vital difference. The first class of sources whence impressions derive implies in strictness only one individual who could in complete solitude experience the sensations aroused by the outer world. The second class could not exist in the absence of individual beings related to one another in the sense that they form a society. Not only does the societal relation multiply and intensify the impressions made by the outer physical world, it is the source as well of impressions that would never be made at all did the social relation not exist.

In relation to communication, the importance of the physical

SOCIETAL SUBISOLATES: COMMUNICATION

world is that the sensations it produces and the impressions it makes are essentially alike for all those who experience them. That world changes, no doubt, but the rate of change, even on the biological level and still more on the geological, is so slow compared with the rate of change in the individual that the world seems permanent as contrasted with the impermanence of the being. Hence the impressions of the without, while not identical in two individuals, are yet comparable even when the individuals belong to successive generations. A tree does not make an identical impression, no doubt, upon two minds; but the impressions are sufficiently alike to be compared. The same may be said of the impressions made by two trees on a single mind. The central image, i.e., the preponderant one, is the same; the subordinate impressions may differ, but the ultimate concepts are uniform. Because this uniformity exists there is *comparability of image*, and communication advances a step toward realization.

But it is not yet a reality. There is a fourth requirement. Even at this stage it is still true, as Goldberg says, that "there are far more languages than we realize; in a sense everyone's language has its individuality, and no two persons speak precisely the same tongue." [12] Communication reaches a culmination only when in addition to comparability of image, which is strictly possible with relation to one being, there is *mutuality of experience*. Here at last two beings enter upon the scene and communication justifies its derivation. It is also here that sociological considerations come to complement the biological and the psychological.

Societal existence by producing a mutuality of experience turns the comparability of images to advantage in two ways. The first is simple and leads no further from what has been said than the fact that two or more individuals living in the same environment ultimately come to possess like images of it and its constituent elements, and so they gain a certain homogeneity of thought. Two men see the same tree. For one its shape is predominant in the mental picture, for the other its color. The subordinate elements of the picture identify the tree as the same object. Having the same tree in mind the two men can, by transmitting their concepts, proceed to revise—i.e., by looking at the tree again—and to re-present the

12. I. Goldberg, *The Wonder of Words* (New York & London, Appleton-Century, 1938), p. 156.

mental picture in such a way as to include within it the particular aspects which each had failed to observe when he first looked at the tree. The resulting image is thus in a true sense a collective representation. A third individual may add another detail and so on until the image attains a completeness of representation which was at first absent from all minds. It may now be transmitted to a fourth individual and to others who have never seen the tree but will recognize it when for the first time they do see it.

In the second place, the societal milieu gives rise to collective representations of a more special kind than the preceding. As the relations among individuals grow, in a given case, more complicated than the biological needs of the animal Homo require for their satisfaction, a network of relationships comes into existence holding individuals together in superorganic ways. A collectivity is in process of formation. A new feature is added to the world outside, which now comes to include not only nature but society as well. The societal conditions and manifestations are even more imperatively in need of representation than the natural ones; hence the necessity of the collective picturing of the collectivity.

The exteriorization of the mental representations at this primitive stage of superorganic existence can no doubt be affected by configurational means to a high degree, especially since the emotional intensity of the inner life is proportionate to the narrowness of the range within which affective life is confined. But emotional release and satisfaction are increasingly inadequate for the conducting of societal existence. Projects for example have increasingly to be concerted. Notions multiply with the growth of fantasy under superorganic prompting. Symbols, in short, and discourse become dominant as images grow in importance and complexity. How they originate, even if the question could adequately be answered, is at this point logically irrelevant. Suffice it to say that any single explanation is out of court. There are too many small collectivities, each with its particular environment and characteristic fantasies, to allow of any one operative cause. The whole range of experience in each case must have been called on to supply external indications of internal images. That such was the case the great variety of languages by means of which men attained to communication seems to demonstrate. These languages also show that on the superorganic level all individuals are controlled by factors which have been accurately described as external and coercive. Because they are so controlled, communication between them can be effected.

The analysis of communication is thus brought to an effective conclusion and tied in with the entire body of sociological theory, since it began with Comte and ends (for the time) with Durkheim. All that need be done to underline the nature of the results attained is to glance at the consequences which ensue when the elements that make effective communication possible cease to exist in combination. Laffitte pictures the outcome in a vigorous passage. It is bad enough, he says, when the instability of the exterior world in the case, say, of an earthquake shakes not only the ground beneath man's feet but the grounds as well of his thought. Still more terrible is the effect of social instability, for the latter releases man's passions.

> The continual abrupt disturbances of social relations, incessant changes in forms of government, the habitual spectacle of so many extraordinary upturns of fortune and so many sudden catastrophes, all of them occurring without apparent reason— must not all that drive the mass of men to believe that there is nothing but arbitrariness in social phenomena? That everything is possible to the man with a strong enough will? That from the wretched state in which he struggles today it is possible to rise tomorrow to the top of the social scale, with only a little luck? That in the end everything in the world is a lottery, with the big prizes going to no one? And then how many insensate ambitions in all heads! How many inconsiderate hopes! How many deceptions! At this point madness lies in wait for man; he will not, he cannot, abandon at one stroke the images which he has for months or years cherished in the visions that ambition or cupidity aroused.[13]

In such crises, when communication ceases to be easy or even possible, fantasy comes into control. Men create for themselves private worlds in which all dreams come true. Or if their dynamism takes an exterior form, still more tragic results ensue, for then fantasy demands as indispensable complement the exhilarating use of force.

Evidently then communication is no simple phenomenon just to be taken for granted. Research into the facts is not greatly more advanced today than was the study of respiration before the air was

13. *Cours de philosophie première, 1,* 298–299.

analyzed. In the efforts to gain a further understanding of this vital element of cultural existence sociology will have an important part. Here the investigation can be pushed no further. It remains to summarize what has been said, draw some evident conclusions, and bring this chapter to a close.

The animal Homo like all other animals is animated, activated, energized by orectic or affective drives, i.e., by affective motors. They are both the source and the ultimate goal of animal action, providing stimulus to begin with and requiring to be satisfied at last. The activities which they urge have in the final analysis no other goal; and this fact is as true of the animal Homo and his descendants as of any other animal form.

Now there is one notable characteristic of the activities which serve to satisfy the affective drives. Men and animals have organic needs, and these hungers can be fed only by contacts with the world without. But not all the constituents of the outer world are equally suited to satisfy animal needs. Animals are therefore under the necessity of discriminating among the constituents of that outer world. Besides the driving functions, then, discriminating functions are required if animals—who live by definition a life of relation—are to exist. If they could not find, i.e., know a supply of proper materials, food, they could not even live in the elementary sense, i.e., maintain the continuous renewal of material substance which is the characteristic of all life.

The senses are the avenues through which the without comes into relation with the within. Where these relations are few and simple, the sensory system need not be complicated; but where the needs are many and particularly when they are intermittent, the necessity of recognition, with its corollary discrimination, becomes imperative and the organic requirements become greater and more complex. The animal organism must not only be aware of what will satisfy its needs; it must not only have the capacity, that is, to present to the within what is without; it must also be able to re-present it. Thereby the outer satisfacients can be recognized when they are present or reproduced mentally when they are absent.

This indispensable animal function is the affair of the image-making faculties, which picture the world without to the within.

Beginning with the production and reproduction of the image, these eidomorphic faculties expand and develop in capacity until they seem able to become active independently of the initial subjective impulsion or the objective impression. The animal Homo seems to possess this power to the point where two superiorities— (a) the making of complicated images out of sense impressions and then (b) the utilizing of the same impressions to construct images that have no parallel in the world without—produce a qualitative distinction between him and other related forms. He thus becomes potentially a maker of fantasies; and this capacity, with its ulterior consequences, sets him off from all other animal forms.

Evidently these two functions, the energizing and the picturizing, are so distinct that they cannot be thought of as coincident in the same organic seat; evidently also they are so intimately related that they must be in the closest proximity. But if they do not coincide organically, the centers of the respective functions must be distinct; and if so, one is objective as regards the other. The relation would be mutual but for the fact that the energizing centers set the picturizing functions in operation. Moreover, these centers come into no direct relations with the exterior world which affects them, i.e., sets off their characteristic energies—only indirectly, by way of the intellectual functions. Thus the affective motors are the only truly subjective element of the organism. With respect to them the picturizing and the exteriorizing systems are objective. But with regard to the outer world the picturizing centers are subjective, since they are set in operation by influences emanating from it. Thus the terms "subjective" and "objective" receive an extended and at the same time a positive meaning. The organism as a whole is subjective in its relations with an objective world; but in regard to the constituent parts of the organism itself some of them, and notably the image-making faculty, are objective to other parts. Chief, or unique, among these are the sources of the energies, the drives that ultimately set in operation the organism as a whole. They are the seat and source of the psychopreferential; in them the ultimate subjectivity resides.

The foregoing remarks are intended to emphasize the double relationship which characterizes the presentational functions: first, they are roused to exercise by urges from within; second, they are stimulated to activity by sensations from without. They may work, that is, under the stress of impulsion or of impression. They are, from different viewpoints of course, both objective and subjective. They direct the energies to appropriate objects; they are directed toward them by the tendencies characteristic of the various affections.

The position of the image-building faculties is therefore crucial in the problem of communication. On them falls a double task: they must guide the energies supplied by the drives, by presenting a faithful picture of the situation in which action to satisfy the drives must take place; they must also submit to the impulsions emanating from the affective motors, sometimes even to the point of misrepresenting the reality when the impulsion is imperative. Finally, in addition to this subjective service, they may become in a given case objectively active and stir the affections from passivity to activity by the construction of unreal images designed to appeal strongly to one or more of them.

To complete the series of psychical capacities involved in communication a third function is necessary, one which ensures the action that is required as an outlet for the energies arising when once a pictured situation has been presented, i.e., what has here been termed exergy. Indispensable as this third element is, it is nevertheless subordinate to the other two in the effecting of communication. Its basis and seat is the motor system, by which the life of relation is perfected and perpetuated. It provides signs and the material for symbols. But since these, and particularly the latter, are subordinate to the pictured world of the image, they will not be given detailed attention here.

Images, then—and by image it is important to remember is meant the revival of all or any of the sense impressions and not those of sight only—may do two things in addition to responding to the impulsions emanating from the energizers: they may guide them and they may arouse them. Where the impulse is single, the situation simple, and the appropriate act uncomplicated, the action itself may be a sign, transmitting to the world without a clear and unmistakable indication of the state of mind within. To transmit a state of mind in this primitive way is a first stage of advance toward communication, but a first stage only. Even in the case of a simple feeling the transmission may be only partial or even quite inadequate; and certainly the sign is inadequate on the level of projects or notions. Even when intentions rather than purposes are disclosed, notions are not transmitted at all.

Something more than signs, tied up and identified as they are with the relations among the members of the organism, is needed at this point. Two paths open here: one is more directly connected with action and so may be thought of as a development of the sign; the other leads through the finding of a substitute for the image. The outcome is configurations on the one hand and symbols on the other. From this point of departure the lines of development diverge, one moving in the direction of art, the other in the direction of science.

In the case of art and artistic evolution it is clear that certain complicated states of mind, affective in nature, cannot be expressed otherwise than by action of a particular kind. The statement is true even of a highly developed culture. Since these feelings are the outcome of completely subjective states, they are the source of action *in* the environment but not necessarily related to it. The series of movements—actions, that is—which serve to discharge the energies of the affective motors are in effect *one act;* that is to say, they are configurations, any one movement having meaning only in relation to all the others. The primitive dance is a typical, if not the only, instance. What are called rites, and ritual in general, is another. In these cases there may be an improvement in the configuration in the sense that more effective means of releasing the energies may with time and experience be found; but these improvements are not the essence of the matter. What really moves the participants is the drive beneath the action. Should these driving forces fail, the dance or the ritual does not degenerate; it simply ceases. In extreme cases, when the emotional set is abruptly broken say by sudden contact with a different culture, the energies have no outlet and the individuals affected may even cease to desire to live, so empty, i.e., devoid of emotional significance does their life become.

From this configurational source, involving the whole range of the senses—sound in particular as well as sight—there flows a whole sequence of manifestations to which the word "art" has usually been applied. It is an essentially psychopreferential phenomenon and is aided by the cumulation of collective experience only to the extent that the latter may provide more effective means of expression, technical or instrumental. On this level there may be progress; but on the affective level, the societal process has no direct influence; the essential phenomenon escapes into the higher domain, the psychological, the individual, the personal, the moral, where are studied the nature, working, interrelationships, complications, and integrations of the driving forces, the affective motors.

In these psychopreferential manifestations, the affections are in complete control over the picturizing functions, and so any variant in the picture is immediately detected. Since the picture as a whole is to be enacted, should any small part—otherwise insignificant but essential as completing the entire configuration—be omitted, the whole ceases to have value. It may only be the mispronunciation of a word. If so, the ritual is valueless. Nothing can be changed; only the original form, the ancient language, say, remains potent no matter how the cultural situation may have been altered or even transformed. Ritual embalms and immobilizes. Rituals are *gestalten*, configurations. They are not symbols, they are enactments; they *are* the pictures formed by the imagination, not substitutes for them. And if language is to be thought of as symbols only, there is no reason why ritual may not long have preceded it.

The symbol, the substitute for the image, the means used to recall the configuration to mind—these may have their potency too, but only in a secondary fashion, only by their power to revive the image. It is the image which intensifies the feelings which at first impelled the imagination to become active.

Thus a whole range of phenomena of the utmost importance to man, from dreams through reveries on to ceremonies, ritual, and art, have their ultimate source in the subjective life. They are distinctive of Man in that they are observable throughout his history and hardly to be seen elsewhere at all, and in that they seem to be closely correlated with a quantitative differential in his organic structure as compared with that of the other higher animals. For these reasons the play of fantasy is for Man not a play at all but a necessity. It is what makes him Man.

But man cannot live by fantasy alone. He must act and so come into relation with fact. At this point the second function of the figurationing faculties operates, with far-reaching consequences. The forebrain not only presents, it re-presents; it goes still further and creates. The images that result may be compared, contrasted, ordered, fused even when only one brain is their seat. When the process results in an increasingly faithful, accurate picture of experienced situations, learning is the outcome. Moreover, the existence and form of these images may be indicated to the world by the use of symbols. By their means, as the whole history of mankind shows, the pictures in one brain may be compared, contrasted, fused with those in another. In short, the animal Homo by virtue of his cerebral differential can lead a collective existence to a degree impossible in any other form.

The fantasy nature of this collective life is constricted by Man's organic necessities. He must come into effective relations with his milieu. This too he pictures, but these images are not under the complete control of his wishes. Feeding on honeydew will not keep him alive; he must have carbohydrates, proteins, and fats. Hence there is always an ultimate corrective of fantasy. Where there are no actively opposing feelings, the picture of the without can become a more and more faithful image; fortunately there are conditions in which the orectic constants, especially on the level of hungers, intensify the interest in the without and so impel the imagination to become subordinate to observation and thus impel the mind to remain strictly within the realm of the real. The ideal in this kind is to make the within so complete and accurate a picture of the without that mental operations will be able to replace its actual workings and so, by making man capable of prevision, ensure an adequate supply of provisions.

At no point in this mental development is there a severance of the bonds which connect the higher intellectual phenomena with the primordial play of the imagination under the impulsion of the affective motors. "Thinking is the final refinement of the reverie processes by which we meet life." From sensation to sensations, from sense impressions to constructs, from concepts to conceptions, from images to configurations, the line of development is continuous. In the case of the animal Homo as he advances toward Man, the individual processes become collective as images are communicated. Thinking is the result, and thought. Comparison between means and ends gives rise to reason and reasoning. In this sense Man is a rational being; but only in the collective sense does he deserve the compliment, for his guide in this progress is the socioexperiential. To reason is to be guided by the experience of the race.

Still further advance gives knowledge and ultimately science;

and the intellectual goal of communication is reached. The domains of knowledge are surveyed and apportioned as successive levels of organization are discovered. The methods of investigation are discovered and refined. Man comes to utilize them to dismiss at last the hominoids from his own brain. The imagination is not thereby inhibited; it is only harnessed and directed.

The thought of the chapter need be carried no further. Its main task was to analyze the statical societal element called communication and ascertain its part in the whole sum of sociological phenomena. The analysis had to be somewhat detailed, for no statical element is more deeply influenced by the persistence of the notion of the metaphysical ego, with its domestics the will and the intelligence. The outcome of the analysis is however to put the phenomena of communication on a par with those already discovered in the domains of material accumulation and of association.

From fantasy to fact, from reverie to reason, mankind has slowly advanced, gradually subordinating imagination to observation. His progress in this domain has been marked by gradually expanding circles of understanding; within the extending radius of each circle is to be found an ever increasing number of increasingly human beings with a common basis of understanding. These circles tend to overlap and finally to merge in one all-embracing communion in which all the means of communication will unite to make all men communicants.

From another and more prosaic point of view, the problem of communication is a problem of culture. It is the cultural influence which tends with time to move men from their private, tribal, national worlds into a universal relationship. This tendency in communication is precisely the same as in the other societal elements already studied. It could not be otherwise, for such is the nature of the collective cumulation of which they are subdivisions. A common culture implies a common language. In that culture the language finds the referents which give it meaning. That is why in the last analysis one of the main subdivisions of societal statics is semantics.

CHAPTER 16: *The Societal Subisolates: Direction*

$\mathbf{A}$t this point the familiar figure of the animal Homo reappears, now equipped for achieving the status of Man with material accumulations, a variety of associational connections, and a language. All of these acquisitions make it easy for individual differences to be developed to an extent otherwise impossible. The sources of these differences are two: the organic and the psychic. On the first level are the variations of a strictly physical kind, such as bodily strength or capacity for sustained exertion. On the second are such factors as the variations of the affective motors in intensity and of the picturizing faculties in readiness of response to sensation. The end product of both sets of characteristics in isolation and in combination is human variability, but not variability without limits. There is a common basis of existence since the forms involved belong to a single species. Hence there are both constancy and variety: they characterize the descendants of the animal Homo.

Thus the inevitability of a certain interdependence and correlation among the various and varying propensities and activities manifested by the similarly organized members of a human group is clear. Complete atomism would have made impossible, or if it occurred would terminate the operation of, the societal process. The fact is obvious enough in the case of adults; it is even less disputable in regard to the young. In some form, no matter how spontaneous, the mutuality of relationship which holds biological units together in a group (and is indeed its essential characteristic) must be incessantly operative with respect to the immature. The influence of generation upon generation, which is the distinguishing aspect of sociological phenomena, could not otherwise be exerted or even exist.

Implicit, then, in the nature of nascent Man is the appearance of activities which become meaningful only when they are performed in concert and in relation, i.e., when they are collective. The results of these related actions are distinguishable from other consequences of individual exertions in that they would not have existed if only unrelated energies had been in operation. It may be on occasion that an act is performed by an individual in complete isolation, but in such cases the distinctive quality in question may be detected by the circumstance that the given act becomes significant—i.e., is not merely idle—because it bears definable relation to some other act or acts already performed or to be performed. That is, it is defined by being either the initial or the consequent stage in a related series leading to an objective. In other words, the energies of the individual are not aimless or for purely personal ends but are directed toward some extra-personal goal. And in such cases the individual in question may be said to be controlled; that is, he is geared into a mechanism the relation of whose parts determines his role.

The somewhat labored form just given to a seemingly simple fact may be excused on the ground that under the simplicity lies a problem only less needful of examination than was the case in regard to communication. "Of course people work together; how else would they get things done?" But the relative rarity with which collective acts are to be observed in animal forms other than man and the relative preponderance of such actions in his case seem to raise a question that must be answered. Control is as frequent among men as it is rare among animals. The fact points straight to the fourth of the constituents which are requisite for societal phenomena. Its analysis and discussion are the affair of the final division of societal statics. Animals are free, men are not: how does this transformation occur?

The initial conditions for the change no doubt are biological. Group existence is a direct consequence of the immaturity of the young; in the case of the animal Homo four or more years of his life are passed in such complete dependence upon others as to make unthinkable the continued existence of the species without group action. In this respect man, no doubt, is only an extreme case of a common phenomenon. But here as elsewhere a quantitative difference produces a qualitative result. The one condition for reaching a higher level is a sufficient difference in some potentiality which can be developed by group existence at the same time that it reciprocally facilitates the development of the group.

This potential superiority is the faculty which is at the same time the source of fantasies. It is the picturizing faculty. The affective motors need not be, probably are not, inherently more vigorous in men than in other animals; but group life, extending and enduring over a period of years, for this very reason energizes to a unique degree the representational faculties, already possessed by man to a higher degree than by other forms. Group life, that is, by strengthening the affections intensifies the activity of the imagination. At the same time it tends to concentrate the exercise upon a restricted number of beings: the family, the domestic association, to begin with.

This biological unit easily becomes the nucleus for the sociological development. It is in the first instance a collecting agency whereby the needs of existence are supplied and where the individuals work together, at first only being in the presence of one another and then coming to the assistance of one another; the collecting units become a collective unity. At this low level of achievement, the relation of act to act whereby a collective result is obtained seems to be secured only by purely configurational means. Things are seen in relation to the satisfaction of common needs, calling at once for relatively or nearly identical actions. The picture prompts the activity, and the adjustments required to pattern the activities of all the beings involved are very small. Such configurations may well precede and be the source of ritualistic procedures intended to stabilize conditions and so ensure success in the group activities.

Now on the configurational level, the wholly spontaneous collaboration of individuals can evidently not advance to great lengths. Increasing complexity of the things to be patterned makes it less and less likely that these things will be patterned so similarly in different minds as to secure practical identity of action. Projects, i.e., individual patterns of actions to be effected tend to be formed under the impulsion of the individual's drives and so become individualized. As soon as this stage of separate projects is reached, some sort of adjustment or arrangement will have to be made among individual action patterns. The normal solution to the problem is the recognition of the necessity of having a "head"—i.e., one head—to decide upon the nature and sequence of actions and, as a corollary, to assign to individuals particular shares in the combined action. The latter when completed is a collective result, needing only to be combined with succeeding efforts of a like kind to become cumulative.

If this tendency to supplant what might be called group configurations with individual action patterns, with its increased emphasis upon a chief, is already visible in the domestic association as the collective element in the actions of its members grows more marked, the same tendency will be all the more evident when the domestic association tends to be enlarged. The increase in size is both a condition and an outcome of the greater efficiency of action that ensues when it is made increasingly collective. No head or chief may yet be required as a *permanent* feature of the societal organization, but the existence of temporary or limited heads for special purposes is clearly a stage of advance toward the time when a permanent over-all head will characterize the socionomic organization.

The foregoing remarks have the air of deductive conclusions and might therefore be suspected. As a matter of fact they are nothing but generalizations from facts long in process of assembling. Moreover, the phenomena in question are statical in nature. They are not limited in time, that is, but are valid whenever human beings tend to gather into groups. Here, for a single example, is an observation made in regard to two boys' gangs formed quite spontaneously. There was "no sense of community between the boys, no feeling of a common end dominating or animating the group as such. . . . What held them together, on close examination, was the fact that each one of them needed some form of psychological outlet which could only be found through the temporary aggregation. Furthermore, it was discovered that there was always in both groups at some time or another a 'master-mind,' who would either from time to time take command of operations, or would instigate the others to carry out these operations." [1] In this case the beginnings were of yesterday; in another case they may be of tomorrow. They are in short the outcome of the constant influences with which statics is concerned.

1. J. D. W. Pearce, "Certain Aspects of Juvenile Delinquency," in *Mental Abnormality and Crime*, P. H. Winfield, ed. (London, Macmillan, 1944), p. 221.

If these constant forces manifest themselves even in the domestic groups as they rise above the biological, it will be no surprise to find them even more strongly operative at the societal stage above the domestic. In the cité as already defined, the relationship among the members becomes more and more extensive at the same time that its intensity diminishes, but the collective nature of the co-operation loses none of its importance. If the cité is to be preserved, the necessity of strengthening the solidarity of the network of extended relationships is basic. Otherwise the larger unity would be dissolved into the original primary units whose amalgamation produced it. Obviously the decrease in the intensity of the relationships which characterizes the larger unity tends to increase the facility with which divergent activities, whether deliberate or unintentional, are entered upon. Evidently then these tendencies toward divergence must be kept within limits.

Of course these tendencies and their significance for societal theory have long been observed, especially on the level above the domestic, i.e., civil stage of cultural development. Sumner and Keller put the gist of the matter very clearly. They say: "Regulation is one of the very life-necessities of society." And they are equally clear as to the circumstances whence the need for regulation arises: "To secure the co-ordination it is not sufficient . . . to rely upon the natural impulses of group-members, for there is too much variation in them and too many antagonisms between them; *the vision of the constituent individuals and groups must be surmounted by a super-vision over them all.* Cooperation is too strongly tinged by the element of antagonism to pursue its course in the absence of a co-ordinating agency. While individuals can see their own interests, or what they take to be such, plainly enough, they do not readily appreciate those of others, much less the interests of society as a whole." [2]

Comte, generalizing the idea as always, expressed it as follows: "The regime of active co-operation proper to civil society becomes for it a continuous source of divergences, mental and moral, which would tend to destroy such an association, if its conservation was not suitably assured by *an apparatus of systematisation.*" [3] And he

2. *The Science of Society, 1,* 459–460.
3. *Système de politique positive, 2,* 350–351.

elaborates upon the idea by saying that there are two general conditions between which every collective organization must institute an adequate conciliation, independence and cooperation.

> On the one hand, without a separation of offices, there would not exist, among the different families, a true association, but a simple agglomeration. . . . It is this principle which directly defines the fundamental character [of a super-organism] as composed of beings susceptible of existing apart, but concurring more or less voluntarily in a common end. . . . As soon as sedentary existence allows this fundamental principle adequately to manifest its social efficacy, it tends to cause the rise of the bonds of solidarity and continuity, which multiply and extend more and more.[4]

But these ultimate and desirable results of the operation of the principle definable as the differentiation of function could never be realized if it were not complemented by the application, spontaneous or systematic, of another principle, that of the coordination of efforts. The tendency toward separation could "easily become a continuous source of grave dissidences, in the light of the opposition of habits, opinions, and even of propensities that it would tend to arouse between different families. The need of co-operation, inseparable from that of independence, demands then its own permanent satisfaction too, through a fundamental institution suitably adapted to this necessary end. . . . Now such is the general destination proper to the force of social cohesion everywhere designated under the name of *government*, which should at once *contenir* and *diriger*," [5] i.e., hold within bounds and supply direction.

The general nature of the fourth necessary constituent of societal statics is now clear. The animal Homo, maker of fantasies, once supplied with material wealth, held to his fellows by increasingly tenuous but numerous bonds of association, and in possession of language, art, and science tends only too readily to multiply his fantasies and so stands in imperative need of an agency which shall hold him in that relationship with other men which, by resulting

4. Comte, *Politique*, 2, 293–294.
5. Comte, *Politique*, 2, 294–295. (Italics are Comte's.)

in collective and cumulative products, makes possible and permanent his elevation to an increasingly human height. A double task is implied: certain fantasies and the consequent actions must be discouraged and prevented, others should be encouraged and facilitated.

Once more the thought of the volume traverses a new sector of the societal spectrum. It has already passed from collective satisfaction of material needs to the grouping of individuals by virtue of their collective functions, to the making of collective representations and the expressing of these visions by signs and symbols. It now reaches the point where supervision is required to maintain and further collective existence. The need is clear, and its double aspect, negative and positive, as well. What term shall be applied to the whole sector? Control, supervision, regulation, restraint, coercion: all of these terms have a certain validity. Still another exists and will be used here. The fact is English has no neutral term applicable throughout the sector. In this contingency, the word "direction" will be utilized mainly because it explicitly conveys such positive meanings as control, guidance, straightness, rightness, immediacy and implicitly contains such negative ones as constraint and coercion.

Analysis of the inclusive image symbolized by direction brings into view certain less comprehensive concepts. The primary aspect of the phenomena here in point is that they are produced by the collaboration of individual beings. From this collective point of view even an individual working in solitude may be considered as effectively engaged in collaboration. First, the very performance of a given task, even if it calls for only one worker, may be due to the societal situation as a whole, which may call for the initiation, continuance, or completion of labors involving or implying others. Second, and especially where intermittent efforts are practicable, it is quite indifferent as regards the accomplishment of the work, whether it be carried on after a break by the same individual who was before occupied on it or by a comparable successor. The point is that individuals are not in question; what is involved are tasks and results.

From a different point of view, all the manifestations of a single human being or of all of them may be divided into three classes: the organic, the societal, the personal. He and they are organisms socii, persons. He and they exist so to speak on three levels of organization, each of which manifests phenomena studied by different methods: hence the three sciences biology, sociology, and psychology. Individuals, that is, do not cease to be when they are not collaborating; they simply cease to be socii. They may be satisfying organic needs; they may be enjoying personal pleasures while they bridge the intervals between societal, i.e., more significant activities. It is only as the animal Homo develops into a socius that he begins to produce results of interest to sociology.

When, then, the activities of several beings or the several activities of one are correlated—i.e., when they are given significance by being combined, when they all aim at a single end or goal—there is not only a collaboration, there is a concentering as well. For this reason the working together of socii may accurately be termed a societal concentration. The notion of a center of aim implies the concept of direction; it implies also a singleness of objective. Where neither of these conditions any longer exists nor can be brought back into being, the concentration is destroyed and the socii revert either to the organic or to the personal plane of existence—usually to the first, for the maintenance of the second is dependent upon the continuance of the societal.

Now where desirable or desired ends are attained by collective action, i.e., where the energies of socii are focused upon an objective, the effectiveness of the results will ensure the continuance for a longer or shorter period of the combining of exertions. Where the concentration advances only temporary aims, the concentration may endure for a brief time only and leave no easily apprehended starting point for ulterior continuation in a determinate direction. But where the needs or desires served tend to be permanent because they are general and recurrent, i.e., when a basic interest is involved, there arises a societal structure. To this type of societal concentration the word "institution" has come to be applied.

The germ of this societal phenomenon is to be found in the earliest manifestations of the animal Homo as he rose above the organic level. Probably the search for or the seizure of food, with so simple a type of collaboration as to be directable by configurational means, was the earliest instance. From such humble beginnings to the most complicated interrelations of millions of men over vast territories and long periods of time, requiring directive abilities of the most comprehensive kind, extends an unbroken continuity. Since this progress directly facilitates the rise of Man and indirectly hastens the development of personality by providing more and more new roles for men to fill, its importance justifies a brief elaboration of the idea.

"An institution," said Sumner, "is a concept and a structure," [6] the concept holding the structure together. The concept is in fact the directive influence, even where it is only a configuration. The structure is the network of relations which holds together individuals so that they may act as socii, i.e., combine their energies. Where the needs to be satisfied are permanent, where basic interests are to be served, the fundamental institutions of society come into being. Where they are destroyed, the society deteriorates and degenerates. If they become impaired, the first necessity is to reconstitute them. A new basic need would call a new institution into being.

There is thus a first classification of institutions into primary and secondary: those which are universal because they satisfy basic, usually organic, needs and those which are local or temporary, sometimes serving only the passing desires of a single individual with the aid of an accommodating friend. From another point of view, institutions may arise spontaneously or be constructed systematically. In Sumner's words, they may be crescive or enacted. Institutions grow, i.e., the satisfaction of need and a corresponding structure proceed slowly at first, probably from a configurational starting point. Improvements are made from time to time, providing a slightly better adjustment of socii and increasing the harmony of their relationship, until in the end the process comes clearly to be understood and can be modified systematically. The procedure, once comprehended, can be employed deliberately with reference to a temporary or limited objective.

It is no easy task, this organizing of men, whereby they become members one of another. Hence there is a general tendency in all societies to retain old concentrations of socii and turn them on occasion to new uses.

This transfer of function from one organ to another or the replacement of an old function by a new one is a constant temptation

6. *Folkways*, p. 53.

to those upon whom has devolved the task of societal direction or those who seek to exercise it for their own ends. The army and the school offer especially tempting opportunities. The former particularly, because of the relative perfection of organization to which it has attained, has frequently been used for nonmilitary purpose. It serves likewise and for the same reason as a kind of model for imitation when new interests have to be served. In industry, for example, where organization is imperatively called for, it seems easy to make rapid progress by developing "companies" and putting them under the commands of "captains." But war is no true precedent for industry; here is a new basic interest in the experience of mankind. The corresponding institutions can only be crescive.

In the light then of the foregoing considerations, an institution may be defined as a network of relationships holding individuals together in such a way as to facilitate the effective cumulation of their collective efforts and experience in the satisfaction of an interest. In more technical terms, an institution is a concentration of socii about an interest.

If, now, the organization of men whereby they become socii is not easy, the question at once arises how such concentrations are brought about. A more thorough analysis of the situation than was possible given the ego psychology of the past reveals two sources of societal operations: the configurational and the directed. The first was so limited in possibilities that it was soon superseded (though not completely abandoned) in favor of the second. But the second by its nature had to be primarily individual. An individual human being in a given situation forms in relation to it a project, i.e., under the impulsion of desire he constructs a mental picture to be exteriorized. Such projects will be individual if they are in any degree complicated, since the very characteristics that make men individual work to minimize, though not to negate, the possibility of several individuals forming at the same time mental pictures so similar as to lead to parallel or even converging courses of action.

The outcome, in the primitive world or in any other truly novel situation, i.e., one where no guidance can be had, is a variety of projects, each formulated by individuals who are thus potential centers of societal activities of which they will be the *heads*. Those who help them to realize their visions will become *hands*. This functional difference can be generalized. It seems certain that in every societal operation (and *because* it is societal) there are two distinct functions: that of the *primer* or *mover* and that of the *seconder*, the directive and the operative. Even on the configurational level some individuals are certain to be more alive to the needs of a given situation than others and so are more quick to take the lead in action.

From this point on, the societal aspect of the situation develops. First, the project itself may be inadequate and require to be amended in one or more points. If the amendments are suggested by others than the original author, the project may be beyond the unaided capacities of the author. He may then have to call in others to aid him. At this point the realization of the project becomes a societal phenomenon. Perhaps it would be well to distinguish between these two kinds of collaboration by calling the first subjective and the second objective. To do so is to call attention to the fact that collaboration may extend beyond the life of the original initiator.

The more numerous the individuals with projects which require collaboration, subjective or objective, for their realization, the more numerous are the possible centers of societal energies, the more numerous the concentrations of socii. Individuals who direct these energies develop, and develop into, societal forces. These conditions of cultural development Comte was one of the first to glimpse as a whole. Out of his meditations on the matter he developed, in the fifth chapter of his *Social Statics,* a positive in contrast to either a theological or a metaphysical theory of leadership.

> Every true social force is the result of a more or less extensive co-operation, summated in an individual. This co-operation may be subjective or objective; it is almost always both at once, in proportions varying with the degree in which time or space enters into the matter. The only form of purely personal force is physical force in the strict sense; and even it deserves to be so termed only when it makes no use of those instruments which imply a certain co-operation, either in the past or the present. . . .

But insistence upon the necessity of co-operation for constituting any force whatever in the sociological sense should never cause the second half of the preceding definition, the need of an individual representative," [7]

to be neglected. Although all social functions are essentially collective, their exercise always requires a person as their organ, spontaneously if not systematically. A cooperation which was never summated in a person would remain entirely sterile; indeed, until it has an organ the cooperation would be only apparent. For it always consists in

the more or less durable grouping of several individualities around a single preponderant one. . . .

When this central influence anticipates the readiness of the parts for combination, co-operation is systematic, for it results from the action of the chief over the members. The co-operation is spontaneous, on the other hand, when the tendencies toward convergence show themselves before a common center is found. But in the latter case, which has hitherto been the most frequent, the co-operation and consequently the force, do not really exist until the concentration is brought about. . . . *This essential condition of concentration in a person is the point at which the positive theory of social forces differs radically from the metaphysical theories concerning them.* . . .

The need of being condensed in a person is the decisive character of social collaboration.[8]

In other words for effective collaboration leadership, or better perhaps directorship, is a necessity whether the smallest or the largest associations are in point. Theory or action which neglects this fact is in danger of fostering either illusion on the one extreme—all men indifferently can be leaders—or anarchy—no leadership is required—on the other. But it should be emphasized, especially today, that nothing more is involved in the statement on leadership than the words convey. There are no philosophical overtones. The whole point is that men combine their efforts effectively only under direction. Direction, therefore, is a societal necessity. It must be

7. *Politique,* 2, 265–266.
8. Comte, *Politique,* 2, 266–267.

provided for solely on a positive basis. No divine rights or mystical folk souls are involved.

In any case, leadership is required for the maintenance and furtherance of societal existence. In any advanced societal situation its tasks are arduous, involving particularly the onerous burden of responsibility—the duty, assuming the ability, to give or find the right answers to the questions that a complicated organization of socii may raise. Such heads are not common.

Clear understanding of the sociological nature of their functions should facilitate and even guide the procedure by which they are found. It would seem for example that the chain of choice in a given group should run down rather than up, since otherwise men to exercise super-vision, and therefore possessed of it, would be chosen by men who by definition have little of it. If the former are regarded as the superiors (as they are of course for the particular function in point), then to have the superiors chosen by their inferiors seems to make little sense. Authority in the positive sense should flow, with whatever embankments are necessary, from above downward. It must, if the sociological analysis is valid. To act as if it did not is only to open the way to absolute and mystical claims for the right to exercise without control a function that in any case must be performed because it is essential to societal existence or, at the best, to force leaders, in order to carry out their functions, to use the ruses and so forth which Pareto did so much to bring into the light. The question is of course one of applied sociology and so it is a digression to raise it here; the discussion may be excused on the ground that it helps to bring the phenomena of direction into sharper focus.

Now although the analysis of the kind of facts in question here has not proceeded far and the use of even the limited knowledge that has been acquired is impeded by outmoded conceptions of individuality, it is nevertheless clear that the rise of many spontaneous centers of collaboration, of many concentrations of societal activities involving many directive socii, is bound spontaneously to produce the beginning of a systematization of the functions and organs of direction. It may be that one individual may become superior and dominant with regard to many inferiors, whose vision is limited; it is still more likely that leaders, i.e., directive socii will come into rivalry and even conflict with one another. The outcome of these differences and struggles will be the spontaneous appearance of a societal structure, in which the various groupings and their leaders, victors and vanquished, superiors and inferiors, will tend to become fixed in their relations with one another; and these relations will tend to persist.

That societal organization, with hierarchical relationships, constituting the beginnings of an apparatus of systematization should arise spontaneously out of the clashes of individualities is paradoxical, but no more so than the rise of societal concentrations from the efforts to realize individual fantasies in the first place. Indeed the more complicated result is only an extension and a consequence of the procedures by which the earlier and simpler situation came to be. The relation between the first realizer of a fantasy and his helper gives a result that may be qualified as societal in the first degree. When two directive socii come into organic relation, the outcome is societal in the second degree. As the network of relationships grows, the degree of societal complication increases until the individual beings involved are often completely lost from sight or memory. The consequence is the appearance of a new phenomenon.

This new phenomenon is *power*. It may be defined as the possession of the right to direct the activities of socii. Men with this prerogative become centers of societal activity; they are, and they direct, societal forces. As these forces increase, power augments. How great it may become can be seen particularly well in those cases where collaborators subordinate their organic needs, abandon all personal velleities whatever, and devote themselves *perinde ac cadaver* to becoming socii exclusively. In such cases, numbers alone cease to have the importance that is often mistakenly accorded them. It is the sum of societal efforts that counts; and so a small grouping of socii, concentered wholly upon one objective, directed by a single head, can oppose and overmaster a number of opponents whose only force is their mass and not their direction nor their velocity.

It is the realization of this force and its resultant power that seems to explain the appearance, the aspirations, and the achievements of those contemporary organizations so oddly called parties. No word could be more inaccurately used. What these groups aim to do is to direct and control the whole social life of man. That of course is why there can be only one such party at a time. Their effectiveness needs no emphasis; no more telling proof could be given of the validity of the sociological concepts which explain their existence, their organization, and their power.

There are of course many ways in which power can be gained and exercised. One of them, however, is by general consent adjudged to be the source par excellence of power. It is in the field of government and the kind of power it gives is *political* power.

General agreement as to the primacy of the political among the various forms of power implies the existence of a hierarchy of forces in the societal domain. Why the political holds the first place in this hierarchy is the question next to be considered. The answer involves two inquiries: Why is there a hierarchy of persons? Why is there a hierarchy of interests?

The answer to the first of these questions has already been suggested. Once the configurational stage of direction is passed—and even there some individuals will be first, beginning that is at the point where individual initiative, or more precisely where creative impulsion implemented by adequate imagination, begins to operate—leaders and concentrations of socii come into being and into rivalry. Fixed relations, more or less persistent, develop among them. In other words, an ordination of directive socii comes to pass spontaneously, i.e., with no more conscious purpose than is implied in rivalry for personal domination or the satisfaction of personal interests.

The phenomenon is simple, commonplace, and continuous, as it should be in the case of statical manifestations; so much so in fact that its significance is often unremarked. Once the nature of societal direction has been grasped, it becomes clear that implicit in this element of the universal pattern of culture is a tendency favoring the rise of a single authority in any well differentiated class of activities. As Sumner and Keller say: "Power tends to pass into a single hand as a condition of its being exercised consistently and with some approach to special knowledge and perspective." [9]

The case of monopoly seems to be in point here. It appears from the standpoint of societal direction that monopoly arises not from a desire to maximize profits, as most people believe, nor to minimize

9. *I*, 506.

losses, as others assert, but from the spontaneous exercise of the function of direction. That is to say, the formation of monopolies is, as the etymology of the word suggests, not primarily an economic phenomenon at all, however much it may be affected by strictly economic influences. It is rather an inevitable outcome of the function of vision which, rising to supervision, aims at control and direction not solely for the pecuniary advantage of individuals but for the good of the trade, to which it brings the beauty of smooth operation, arrangement, order—and orders.

Moreover, in the exercise of directive responsibility the point is always reached where hesitation as to the right answers must cease, discussion be ended, and decision made. Only then can the image begin to be externalized through action. Until then uncertainty, doubt, and indecision are likely to exist, especially among subordinate or operative socii, as to the ultimate objective of their cooperative activities; hence the necessity, if the grouping is not to be disorganized, of the rise or recognition of a single agent of concentration on whom shall devolve the function of deciding the *ultimate* aims on which the efforts of socii are to converge. Many directive socii may exist on different levels of a given collaboration but only one can be the *final* maker of decisions. Only in this way can the function of "contenance" and direction be effectively exercised.

This universal need for convergence, contenance, decision, and direction brought it about, especially in the earlier and simpler cultural situations, that the directive hierarchy became incorporate in a single person. "A genuine nature-people can be ruled only by a personality, never by an idea." [10] The positive nature of the need was as yet unguessed, but it was deeply felt that the power which held the sovereign place in the organization of the group should be given a sanction in keeping with the importance of the function it exercised; hence many varieties of theological and metaphysical justifications and explanations.

Somewhere there must exist a final authority. In the absence of a positive insight into the nature of societal phenomena some, *any* justification is defensible if it serves to secure the collaboration without which the group would disappear. No escape from the network of hierarchical relationships is possible for a socius. All that can be done is to move from one sovereign to another, substitute one for

10. Sumner and Keller, *I*, 474.

another, or disguise the facts. The only alternative, even when the positive nature of the facts is known, is to abandon all grouping and all collaboration and live in isolation, i.e., to regress from the societal toward the animal.

It appears then that there is and, from the nature of the phenomena involved, must be a tendency for cultural development to give rise to and be carried on by societal forces. These forces are individuals with initiative. As they arise they enter into rivalry, and from their struggles issue surviving heads in more or less fixed relations of superiority and inferiority. The outcome is a hierarchy among directive socii and the emergence of a final authority to set the ends for which his group of socii will strive.

Expanding the image just visualized into analogous and related domains and utilizing the similarities thus disclosed to construct new mental pictures as guides for further conclusions—i.e., continuing along the line of thought of the preceding paragraph—two ideas take form: first, men with initiative will not merely struggle for dominance in any one region of interest, they will struggle for leadership in the whole range of the cultural pattern; second, if one element of that pattern is conceived to be standing at the head of the interests comprised in the pattern, they will struggle for control therein. The image is clear, and concrete so long as individualities are to be pictured; it becomes less vivid when the effort to substitute interests for individualities is made. But abstraction does not involve unreality; the question still remains, is there a hierarchy of interests? If there is, the hierarchy of men will inevitably correspond to it.

An answer to the question just asked can be reached deductively or inductively. The deductive way was illustrated in presenting the elements of the universal culture pattern. The chapter dealing with material accumulation was given the first place in the ordering of chapters because it dealt with the most general of the phenomena included in the cultural pattern. That is to say, economic phenomena are the least far removed from the organic level on which all animal forms, including the animal Homo, have to live. In this sense it is the first among the conditions which must be met if the human, i.e., societal being is to exist. It is on this ground that

Sumner and Keller base their assertion that in the last analysis the maintenance mores in a society are controlling. "By what stages have men struggled along through untold generations in the effort to get subsistence out of the earth for a larger number, or in larger measure for a given number? This is the question of human history. Other things which have been done or have come to pass are consequential, inferential, incidental or range themselves around this central and absorbing interest." [11] Marx went further, as is well known, asserting that every social phenomenon beyond the means of production is but a kind of superstructure.

These views are tenable; but there is another standpoint from which the facts may be envisaged. Not only is there a scale of generality, there is also a scale of dignity. That is to say, there are degrees of departure from the animal level, degrees of approximation to the human and the personal. From this point of view the phenomena of direction are the most elevated in the societal scale. They have to do with human beings distant enough from the animal Homo to be clearly nascent men. It is with them and not with the materials of the physical world that leaders have to deal.

Even the control of things is exercised through men. Lenin did not contradict Marx in stating and utilizing the fact; he simply thought on a different level. It is at this point that the concept of power comes back into the discussion with greater significance than before. The notion underlies the distinction between the economic system and the political regime. Power, it has been said, is the right to direct socii. The distinction between men and things points the way to discovering why a certain kind of power, political, is supreme and why other types tend to be submerged in or converted into political power. Deduction from the principle of decreasing generality carries the thought further. Inductive conclusions based upon spontaneous collective experience and embodied in language raise the question to a positive level of inquiry.

The point in societal contenance and direction at which activities termed political begin is difficult to locate. It may be doubted indeed whether there is any one such point. The first and simplest

11. *I*, 98, par. 51.

case seems to put the stress upon the extent of the circle within which move the individual beings whose efforts are to be coordinated. Anthropological observation on this point can be summarized as follows: in all societies individuals with different origin rates and capacities for response adjust themselves within the limits of the family institution; political institutions arise when these adjustments take place outside the circle of kindred as well, with the result that one individual will exercise authority over a group not limited to members of his family.

A second set of conditions concerns the nature of the objective at which effort is aimed. It exists when individuals whose cooperation is required for a given end cannot see the outcome of their labors; when, that is, the purpose of their collaboration is not immediately visible to them either because the numbers involved are too great or because the attaining of the goal requires a series of operations, of related partial objectives, each gaining significance from the operation as a whole, without an understanding of which any part would seem to be meaningless. In this situation the individuals with the vision of the whole would, in the words of Sumner and Keller already quoted, exercise supervision over the cooperating members of the grouping.

These two sets of conditions of political behavior seem to provide a foundation upon which a more elaborate structure can be raised. Together they tend to bring into existence societal results of a complicated kind. Family activities need no wide vision to guide them; they may be directed by configurational means; outside them supervision begins to be necessary, and discursive methods are indicated. Together they appear to provide a clue to the explanation of the connection between political and territorial units. It is not that there is any mystical element involved. It is rather that once individuals pass beyond the spontaneous, psychopreferential bonds of the family and so tend to disappear from vision, only the coordinates of space and time can pin them down and fix their positions as collaborators in the larger units arising on the basis of socioexperiential activities over which supervision is necessary.

Still another set of conditions, somewhat more complex, working in the direction of political development is given by Spencer. Cooperation, he says in his chapter on "Political Organization in General," is at once that which cannot exist without a society, and that for which a society exists. It may be a joining of many strengths to effect something which the strength of no single man can effect; or it may be an apportioning of different activities to different persons, who severally participate in the benefits of one another's activities. The motive for acting together, originally the dominant one, may be defense against enemies; or it may be the easier obtainment of food, by the chase or otherwise; or it may be, and commonly is, both of these. In any case, however, the units pass from the state of perfect independence to the state of mutual dependence; and as fast as they do this they become united into a society rightly so-called. But co-operation implies organization. If acts are to be effectually combined, there must be arrangements under which they are adjusted in their times, amounts and characters.[12]

This social organization, Spencer continues, necessary as a means to concerted action, is of two kinds, generally coexisting and more or less interfused but distinct in their origins and natures: "There is a spontaneous co-operation which grows up without thought during the pursuit of private ends; and there is a co-operation which, consciously devised, implies distinct recognition of public ends." [13] The first subserves the welfare of individuals and is without coercive power; the second subserves the welfare of the society as a whole and exercises coercion. Only the second is political.

Spencer's sharp distinction between spontaneous, private, noncoercive and consciously devised, public, and coercive types of cooperation cannot resist analysis. Nevertheless there is an element of general validity in his views. What he calls private ends, looking at them from the standpoint of the individual, may be regarded from another angle. Such activities as he has in mind may in certain cases be considered, in the light of the requirements for group existence, as partial in that they serve only partly and indirectly in the maintenance of that existence. As such, they are in contrast with those activities on which depends the network of relationships that holds individuals together as a group, relations which for that reason may be termed total.

12. *Principles of Sociology*, 2, 244.
13. P. 245.

In these words "partial" and "total" a distinction is emphasized which runs through the whole range of societal existence, beginning with the domestic. Even on this simple cultural level, certain activities and functions are quite indispensable for the family existence. They indirectly or directly involve the welfare of all the members, i.e., they are essential for the continuance of group membership and so they may be thought of as inclusive and total in their scope. Other activities may be relatively limited in their extent and implication, advancing the interests of but one or of several individual beings and not being essential to the preservation of the domestic network.

If the differences denoted by the contrast between the words "partial" and "total" are truly functional, they should have found, more or less quickly according to cultural development, organs correlative to them. They seem in fact to have done so. The need for holding individuals together and within bounds and for directing their efforts may be less acute in the domestic group than elsewhere; it is none the less basic for all that. And if so, then the emergence of some individual points of concentration, systematizing the co-operative activities of individual beings, is implicit in the situation even though the office may not reside permanently in any one member. Too exclusive or too active pursuit of individual or private or partial ends may be disastrous for the family group as a whole. The individuals pursuing these ends will have to be controlled, that is, they will have to be assigned roles, by the organs in whom the public, inclusive, total functions are embodied. Gerontocracy seems to have had no other origin.

When individual beings go beyond the domestic grouping into the cité, they form relationships which have been termed civil to distinguish them from the domestic. It is in reference to the later and larger grouping that the distinction between partial and total becomes more sharp than it was in the case of the domestic society. In fact, the difference between partial and total objectives is here so clearly marked that it has usually been considered to have originated on this cultural level rather than below it. In any case, the need for an apparatus of systematization is more evident on the civil than the domestic level, and its construction was there more nearly conscious and deliberate than elsewhere.

In civil societies too the characteristic differences between partial and total functions, organs and objectives begin to receive distinctive names. Here the word "political" can be introduced with some approach to precision. The word had as its original referent the *polis,* an integrated societal and cultural unit, and this general reference it has never quite lost. It may therefore be applied to those inclusive functions upon which the existence of the cité ultimately depends. "Political" would thus come to mean the total or ultimate or public ends or objectives with which in the last analysis the entire civil grouping is identified, since it is for the obtaining of these objectives that the network of civil relationships exists and by which it is maintained.

There is still another, a fourth, distinction that has been utilized to fix the meaning of the term "political." It is found in the complex of ideas summarized in the word "externality" as applied to group activities. These latter are for the most part carried on within the group itself; but there are occasions when a given group has to deal in a corporate capacity with another. Thus there arise intragroup and intergroup activities. The first named would be internal and the second external. The total nature of the second kind of activities is clear; they are easily recognizable as a distinct class. When such relations have to be carried on, they are usually entrusted to those organs who carry on the total functions inside the group. What results is a new version of the control situation; the totality is redefined, but it is not created for the first time. The resulting responsibilities are simply added to the already existing necessities of control, and the nature of the political becomes more evident than before.

The division of directive phenomena into internal and external reveals clearly a hierarchical relationship between societal activities. It throws light too on the ultimate emergence of certain classes of relationship as the most important of all that cultural existence gives rise to. The total, the external, directive functions are the most important because upon them depends in the last analysis the very existence of the society. The last analysis may require a longer or shorter time; what is involved in the process is the determination of the relative significance to group existence of the various objectives at which societal concentrations aim. There are many such focal points of activity but only relatively few in relation to which all individual members of the group are at some time socii. These activities are total; their extension to the point where they include external relations serves to sharpen the distinction between total and partial functions. The outcome is a hierarchy of societal objectives, at the head of which stand the political.

While the hierarchy of interests is being worked out, a like process is bringing to the fore and ultimately making foremost certain individual beings with "high origin rates," i.e., with directive capacities and desires. Sooner or later it is inevitable that these two lines of hierarchical development converge. They meet in the one individual to whom all questions come at last for answer and from whom all directive and restrictive rulings issue. He is the source of orders and of order. He is the sovereign. In his office as such he controls the activity of all socii. In his hands are the reins of authority. He is the holder of power and of political power.

Now while it is possible that ultimate control over all socii should come to reside in a single sovereign, it is quite impossible that this one directive agency should be able to attend to every detail of its application. Centers of special types of activity have to be brought into relations with one another and with the sovereign. The exercise of power must be effected through subordinates, who in turn must be hierarchized. All the concentrations of socii must be unified, integrated, and systematized so that they will be able to work together with the minimum of friction and conflict. In short an apparatus of systematization comes slowly into existence the name for which is *government*—the term deriving, it is worth noting, from a material trait of culture, the rudder—a directive mechanism par excellence.

At just what point in cultural development political phenomena begin to be systematized in an apparatus recognizable as a government it is difficult to determine. Spencer and many others attribute political phenomena to the effects of war. Only by imperative need for combination in war, they believe, were primitive men led into political cooperation; only by subjection to imperative command was such cooperation made efficient; and only by the cooperation thus initiated were those other forms of cooperation characterizing civilized life made possible.

This conclusion is by no means beyond question. Certain facts point in other directions. The desultory and inconclusive nature of primitive warfare seems so slightly removed as an imperative need from other types of societal activity as to weaken the argument for war as the source of political phenomena. The great hunts, for instance, seem to be quite as total as war and to require as much organization. There is the relation between government and property. There is the hint, hitherto disregarded, which is offered by the etymology of the word "government."

Still more distant from current theories is the position reached by Hocart. "The functions now discharged by king, prime minister, treasury, public works are not the original ones. . . . These were originally part, not of a system of government, but of an organization to promote life, fertility, prosperity . . ." In other words, they were *ritual* to begin with. "It is only by degrees that this organization has enlarged its sphere of action and modified its functions till it has become what it is now, a machinery to coordinate the activities of the community." [14] It is as if the divine king, embodying the total interests of his community, came into relations with an external world of magic. Ritual would be the means of reaching satisfactory relations with such an external influence. "So society must organize itself for ritual." "This ritual organization is vastly older than government . . . When however society increases so much in complexity that a coordinating agency, a kind of nervous system, is required, that ritual organization will gradually take over this task." [15]

In any case, even though it is not yet possible to say how the organized apparatus of systematization comes into being, the essential quality of the phenomena in point seems well established. The nature of the particular control situation will doubtless be decisive as to the origin and method of coordination. It has varied between the extremes of the oriental monarchy and the occidental democracy. Since neither of these solutions has been based upon a positive analysis of the facts but both have arisen empirically in relation to

14. A. M. Hocart, *Kings and Councillors* (Cairo, Barbey, 1936), p. 5.
15. Hocart, p. 34.

immediate needs, other solutions lie in the future. If for instance the exercise of a franchise, operated in the inviolable solitude of a polling booth, rests upon a belief in the individual ruled by a conscience and guided by reason, and if this individual is found to be an inadequate or erroneous picturing of the reality, then the long perspective of time to come will reveal changes to bring the method into closer adjustment with the facts.

One such fact is now clear. Under the conditions of civil society many societal forces arise. They are concentrations of socii about a predominant individuality, a leader. The problem of government thus becomes the problem of the relations of leaders. Whether the basis of government will be despotic, democratic, representative, or quite other, there is yet one point on which all governments agree. Indeed, without this one prerogative they would not be governments in the accurate, i.e., political sense at all. Reference is made of course to the function of final decision. Political phenomena are those that are total with regard to the civil group. Their importance is therefore paramount since they affect the very existence of the cité. Moreover decisions must in the normal case be unequivocal and free from ambiguity, since otherwise they would not be truly directive. The two conditions unite to require that decisions involving group existence be made only by the ultimate source of direction, that all discussion and deliberation be ended before directions are given. Once a total decision is reached, there must be no doubt that it is such. It must, that is, emanate from the final leader of political concentration, and the test of his finality is his complete freedom from veto. No one is above him; when he finally speaks in his official capacity, discussion is ended; action and direction begin. This freedom from interdiction must not be a personal privilege; it must inhere in the office and not in the man. Hence it becomes an abstraction, and from this point of view it becomes known as sovereignty. It implies the right to control all the energies of the civil groupings; it involves also finality of decision.

Now neither sovereign nor government exists in a vacuum; they both exist in, and in large part grow out of, a particular cultural setting. This cultural symplegma is of course more than a mere collection of cultural traits or sum of complexes; it is an organized integration, a true pattern of interwoven cultural elements. It involves interests of an immense variety, economic and other; it has distinct associational characteristics; in the normal case, it possesses a unique language and literature. It is compact of relationships which must be at least tolerable to all those who are formally members of the community and satisfactory to most of them. Under these conditions the citizens will desire to maintain and perpetuate the conditions which are so satisfactory, and the desire will not be least strong among those who have come to be leaders as defined. In fact they will undoubtedly feel that their main function is to protect and consolidate the cultural situation that is so generally satisfactory. Hence with appropriate derivations it will be the duty of the political leaders to defend and eternize the societal situation out of which the political complex existing at a given moment has developed. To this entire societal integration, in the name of which ultimately the government in its sovereign capacity acts, mankind by a subtle irony has given the name state, thus by the very word revealing the consciousness that no power can render permanent what is after all only a phase of culture, fated inevitably to change and to disappear.

It is probably this fact of social change and the consequent effort to oppose its operation in a particular cultural state that have worked together to emphasize the restrictive over the directive functions of government, though both have their place in the societal spectrum. In the Occident for example, where societal change has been so frequent, each new set of leaders has found itself bound or handicapped by existing political restrictions. Government thus became identified with restraint; and those who were contained by it sought logically enough to reduce such activities to the minimum. Still another factor working in the same direction is the tendency for individual initiative to work for partial and private ends. Just because they are so, the public and total organs will often have to interfere to contain these partial internal developments. None of these influences, however, potent as they may be on occasion, are sufficiently strong to conceal completely or permanently the directive forces which in times of peril, emergency, or war must be exercised for the benefit of the community as a whole.

To go further into the analysis of the phenomena called political would quickly bring this discussion into the field of politics as a special social science. Hence it is impossible to penetrate into the details of the specialization and instrumentation of political functions, to observe the workings of law or administration. But it will be necessary before concluding this chapter to analyze more fully the concept of political power and in particular to examine into its source and the methods of gaining it.

If the animal Homo is to reach the human level, certain conditions must be met: material accumulations, forms of association, and means of communication. Each is a necessity for the existence of Man. To these three requisites a fourth has now been added, quite as indispensable to the making of the societal being as any of the others. The first of the reasons why direction is a statical necessity is found in the historical record, abstractly summarized in the preceding section. The second deserves a brief discussion. It concerns the nature of Man. The essence of the matter is that the animal Homo has many unlovely characteristics. Not only is he temperamentally "difficult"; he does not gladly fall into the, kind of continued and collective action to which the word "work" is commonly applied. He does not usually see himself as a worker. In not one of the fantasies of a future or nonearthly state which he has from time to time constructed do the inhabitants, and particularly the hominoids, work. Moreover, as a maker of fantasies he is all too prone to diverge from his fellows and create his own private world. And yet if he is to transcend the limitations of a subjective animal, he *must* come into effective collaboration with other individual beings. The historical facts show that he did; the atomistic tendencies of his individual nature show why he had to. But how was a reluctant laborer changed into an eventual collaborator?

The ultimate source of the convergence of efforts, resulting in collaboration and cooperation, is no mystery. It is nothing more complicated than *force*. "The State is a product of force and exists by force." And not merely the political state; any cultural state rests in the last analysis on the same foundation. In its simplest aspect force takes the purely biological form of superior physical strength. From the vegetable which is uprooted or the animal which is caught or tamed, from the correction of children to the subjection of adults, physical supremacy is the primary means of establishing the superiority of one individual being over another. It too is the final source of those conditions which afford a basis for societal activities by making it possible for men to give orders and so to establish order.

True, there are limitations to the universal use of force and many reservations in regard to its complete effectiveness. Moreover, even though it is both primary and final, it is not the only means of direction to which men have resorted. In fact, they have recognized and followed other forms of leadership, turning to force or recognizing its necessity only reluctantly. Among these alternatives, probably the most important is that known as authority. The essence of the matter here seems to be an awareness on the part of others that a given individual has done and so can do a particular piece of work efficiently. No doubt ritual and magic play a considerable part in such judgments.

Because such an individual can and does take the lead effectively, others will be directed by him even when they do not see the immediate consequences of their actions. They will even grant him the privilege of using force to implement his authority. Its use thus becomes legitimate. Normally it is the adjunction of force to authority that receives social approval. A vague sense of injustice arises when force comes to be the means whereby the function of authority is assumed and exercised. Authority is gained and earned; force, as the term implies, is not associated with such a normal cause-effect sequence.

Nevertheless there are still occasions where force is the final resort, where it is the only way to assure the solidarity on which the existence of society depends. And of course even where it lacks such a sanction, it will be resorted to because it is the nearest way by which individuals can project themselves into positions of control. It holds a prominent place in the making of fantasies; its directness and immediacy recommend it; its exercise is all the more exhilarating in that, far from being dependent upon the willingness of others to conform, it is in fact imposed upon them against their wills.

When the force utilized to obtain collaboration passes the point where it is primarily physical, it does not of course give place at once to willing and conscious motivation. There are other ways than brutal compulsion of making people act together—ways which nevertheless do not require or even imply the assent of the will. In fact, discussion in outmoded terms of the will as an entity distorts the whole problem. The matter is so vital to the sociological position as to demand elaboration.

The simple fact of observation is that men procure the cooperation of other men by a wide variety of means beginning with superior physical strength. The (outward) act of collaboration may be accompanied by any number of (inner) states of mind. The act is the primary objective of societal effort. This act follows the construction of a pictured situation. The image may be made under either of two influences: the objective or the subjective, the societal or the psychical. The first aims to influence what men do; the second is concerned with what they are.

Between these two influences a clear distinction can be drawn by referring to the will as defined in the preceding chapter. There it was said that the will is the final state of desire, once the informative and deliberative processes have duly revealed the alternative implicit in the situation. Implied in this definition are such points as the increase in the intensity of the orectic constants until they become desires, the existence of inherent characteristic regularities underlying their manifestations, and the possibility of a review of the alternatives, limited only by the amount of knowledge, i.e., socioexperiential data existent at the moment.

To influence on this first and psychical level means first of all to abandon all concern with ultimate action, then to present as wide and valid as possible a picture of the situation in which the orectic constants become desires, and finally to deal with all the constants in such a way as to enable each of them to have its due share in the final equilibrium. Once an equilibrium of desire has been reached, then the picturizing faculties can construct an image to be exteriorized in an act. All these requirements are evidently on the psychological plane; they are thus outside the sociological domain. Certain conclusions, nevertheless, can be formulated here; they will serve to point the contrast with the societal phenomena to follow.

In the first place, then, the psychical influence is concerned with the inner, the essential man, whom it regards as an end in himself and not as a means to an end, however august. The end is the development of the man's self, the expansion of the person. The means to this end is *suasion*. In the second place, what is sought is not an objective result but a subjective condition; not an act, however defined, but a state of mind. *Impulsion* then is the goal, but it must be an urge or drive characteristic of the inner man—a resultant, that is, of the inherent nature of the affective motors, the orectic constants. If this impulsion leads to collaboration, good, no doubt; but even so desirable an outcome is not the ulterior objective.

In striking contrast with these psychical occurrents, where man is an end in himself, developed by suasion to follow inner impulsion, are the societal phenomena where man is regarded as a means to an end, where force is used to make him a means and coercion is the result. On this level acts are the objective and men but means thereto. No regard is paid here to presenting as wide a variety of alternatives as possible nor to allowing a free play of desires in reaching an equilibrium. On the contrary, only those orectic constants are roused to activity which will create a particular wish and only those mental pictures will be constructed that can be exteriorized in a given way.

Of vital importance in this connection is the central position of the ideational faculties between the affective motors and the outside world. Because they hold this intermediate place, two possibilities are open: these faculties may operate under the stimulus of the orectics; they may respond to the impressions made by the without. If then either of these influences is prevented from its normal operation, the resulting pictures will be faulty. Particularly critical in this relation is the influence on behavior of the picturing of the outer world: it may narrow, distort, or falsify the alternatives that are necessary to deliberation; it may even prevent the free interplay of the orectic constants.

Whenever either of these conditions is made to exist, the affective balance is not freely struck, that is, the final state of desire is not the result of deliberation resulting in equilibrium; it has been forced. Conditions have been too strong for it. The extraordinary range of these conditions is illustrated by the wide variety of senses which the word "force" assumes. For present purposes it may be thought of as any means of preventing free decision, and from this point of view it may be classified as actual or constructive, i.e., it may be material or ideational; the mental picture may be a faithful representation of a real situation or the picturing of an unrealized situation. In either case, choice is restricted.

Between the two extremes of suasion and force, a transitional and intermediate position is held by the forms of force just termed ideational. They are mental pictures of an as yet unmaterialized situation. They arouse the orectic constants to desire a particular type of exteriorization. In this way they come nearer to deliberation than pictures of an actual, material situation. The latter leave little choice, they result in coercion; the former narrow choice, they result in compulsion. There is thus a series of states ranging from force to suasion. It goes by way of coercion and compulsion; and when the latter is subdivided into imposition and inducement, the road to deliberation and ultimately equilibration is opened.

Into this general scheme the methods of securing collaboration fit without difficulty. The latter is an act or a series of acts comprising a course of action. Actions grow out of states of mind definable as images to be exteriorized. Suasion or force may produce such images. The animal Homo is to be made into a collaborator. As an animal and maker of fantasies, he does not fall easily into that category. Suasion on that early level is difficult. Nevertheless, if the societal mode of being is to be reached, he must be raised to a new level whether his state of mind is or is not favorable. Force is the indicated means.

There are several levels of application. The animal Homo can be regarded and treated simply as a thing. In this case the state of mind is disregarded and what is called brute force is employed. Men are materials, so to speak, and the force used to direct them is material. It can be subdivided into organic or biological, collective or societal. The first of these is nothing more complicated than physical strength, possession of which to a superior degree simplifies so many problems of direction for its possessor, who simply ignores or is ignorant of any problem of wills, however defined. It is mainly exerted by one being against another; it changes the relations between two individuals; it seldom goes further. Against such a force a small coalition or combination can easily prevail. It decides mainly who shall be the center of a societal concentration.

As soon as the collaboration passes the individual stage it comes onto the societal level. Here the force is still material, but it begins to take into account the mental state. What it seeks to do is so to narrow the alternatives that can be pictured that exteriorization, action, can take but one form. It achieves this result by setting up such a situation in the objective world that the practicable choices are reduced to one. Utilization of this kind of force gives material power —the archetype of power—to direct without subterfuge the activities of socii. For it there are two sources.

The first of these two kinds of material force giving power to those who wield it—the foundation, that is, of the political structure—arises from the combination of the physical energies of a number of individual beings around a leader, a head, who concentrates these energies upon the attaining of an objective. Comte, who was among the first to essay a classification of the forms of power, calls this force the force of number. His conception goes beyond the thought of mere plurality; it is the collective aspect of numbers that is in point. Once the energies of a number of individuals are put to societal use, i.e., concentrated under the direction of one of the number, material force results, conferring power upon the director.

Such power is great; but its limitations are evident when the nature of such material force is analyzed. There are, for example, many kinds of achievement that are beyond the energies of number, however concentrated. The cooperation of numbers is difficult to attain and even more difficult to maintain; it is effective in proportion to its permanence. Moreover the cooperation is difficult to direct; it may exceed or fall short of the objective. It is wasteful of energy, too. Contenance, the holding within bounds, is hard to effect; the infinitude of fantasies in numbers shows why. All these limitations and others may be summed up in the judgment that the power given by the force of numbers is limited in that it rests mainly upon only one of the two essential foundations of a societal fact. The force of numbers is mainly collective; it can be made cumulative only with difficulty. It brings into prominence the element of *solidarity* in societal existence.

In the second variety of material force the cumulative element is far stronger than in the first. Here the lever of control extends in the direction of the results of human energies embodied in things. This kind of force inheres in riches or wealth. It can be transmuted into power more easily than number. It is less irresistible at any given moment, but it may become more oppressive than the force of numbers. The latter is expansive in nature; it is dispersed; it requires union to become strong: though difficult to oppose while the union endures, its force is likely to be intermittent. Wealth is concentrated to begin with, often extremely so. It easily becomes oppressive because it may command the materials necessary for life. Its utilization involves none of the difficulties raised by ever-shifting numbers of coworkers. It is a result of human, and it may be animal or even inorganic, energies working through generations, often long after the original directives and operatives have passed from the scene of interaction. It has its main source in cultural *continuity*.

Utilization of force of this kind is relatively easier than that of number in that its concentration is more readily effected and maintained and may even precede the rise of the leader who is to direct its use. On the other hand it is difficult to cumulate; it may require much time to make the initial store; it may be lost to the power of numbers. It is likely to be slow in coming into operation but to persist when once organized, since many interests are likely to be affected by it. The force it exerts in coercing action without willingness seems inferior to that of numbers, where mass exerts great pressure. On a scale of dignity it seems to deserve a higher place than number insofar as it departs further from the animal in the direction of the person.

Still further advance toward the dignity of free collaborators is made when the coercive methods just described are replaced by compulsive ones, when material means give way to ideational. The essence of the distinction here lies in the fact that compulsion depends less than coercion upon the narrowing of possible alternatives to one, and more upon the effort to affect the orectic equilibrium directly by activating some of the affective motors and not others, i.e., to work directly upon the equilibrium by selective activation of the orectics. In other words, at this point it is not so much the deliberative process that is interfered with as it is the freedom of the interplay by which the psychic equilibrium is established. In either case, whether the means used involve interference with the ideational faculties or with the orectic constants, the equilibration is not free and the outcome is therefore forced.

Coercion begins with physical strength presenting so simple a situation that configurational responses are the most frequent; it advances to more complicated situations, real first and then constructive, where discursive methods are required. Compulsion works more subtly and indirectly. Instead of presenting, like coercion, a mental image to be exteriorized as given without essential change and without much concern for motive, compulsion works through setting up images designed to secure permanent influences for selected orectics in the making of the affective equilibrium. The intention is to secure the domination therein of such sentiments that the images stimulated will follow a given pattern of exteriorization. In other words, the emphasis shifts from action to fantasy.

The stages through which compulsion passes to bridge the gap between coercion and suasion are two: imposition and inducement. Between these two forms of compulsion the relations are intimate and for present purposes need not be elaborated. The essential point is that the second is an advance over the first in that it comes closer to the point where the equilibrium of desire is freely established. In this respect the two ideational forms of force are parallel with the two material forms. Number, that is, works well with imposition, wealth with inducement. The first two are direct, they aim at action; the second indirect, they aim at motives. So long as societal order remains normal, it is the second two which are the chief sources of power; but when order is disturbed and in proportion as it is disturbed, there is a regression from compulsion to coercion, ending at last in resort to sheer physical strength.

As to the means mainly employed for the two forms of compulsion, they are two: the symbol and the ideology. Symbols reach their objective by virtue of the fact that they are often so heavily charged with emotion, i.e., so evocative of particular forms of imagery, that when they alone are the stimuli under the influence of which the affective balance is struck, then the action that follows will be the exteriorization of one desire only. In other words, the symbol rouses the psychic constant to the intensity of desire; the mental picture to be exteriorized is designed to satisfy the desire by appropriate action. If only certain constants are aroused so that deliberation is by design prevented, then the resulting action may properly be termed compulsion. The societal aspects of the force involved lie in the fact that the symbol is a collective phenomenon.

Ideologies are the second form of compulsion, and the collective aspect is even more pronounced than in the first. What the term implies is the combining, correlating, synthesizing of a number of concepts so selected and related as to cover a substantial part or even the whole of human existence and thereby to guide or even determine action within the limits set. Here the notion of principles enters, and the thought can be related with an earlier stage of this discussion. Principles, from this point of view, are the guiding lines of action laid down by a prince, i.e., one who takes the lead. What is in question is not the determination of a single act or unrelated acts. These can be induced by the use of symbols; ideologies impose a line of conduct.

If a body of principles—or of concepts synthesized in a myth— can be imposed upon the mind of an individual or if by a selective kind of induction he may be induced to accept it as valid, then that individual's picturizing, his thinking, will be dominated and his actions directed, even to the extent of transforming a scientist, say, into a nationalist. He may or may not like it. Dictation is not necessarily unwelcome. But makers of fantasy are unlikely to be pleased at being mentally coerced. They may have to be browbeaten. They may even reveal the meaning of the couplet which describes them as being of the same opinion still, since they have been convinced against their will.

The intricacies and refinements of coercion and compulsion, extending out into the fields of configurational and discursive logic, are not for elementary treatment. But a word on all the forms of force will not be a digression. It is to begin with an error to condemn force in any form on the ground that it is not moral, i.e., does not allow the orectic equilibrium to be reached freely. True enough, it doesn't; but with relation to a being whose chief characteristic is the making of fantasies, its use is essential for all that. Otherwise the societal level of being, on which alone the moral can rise, would not be or continue.

A wiser distinction is that which classifies the ends for which force may be used. Here the lines already drawn between private and public, partial and total ends come sharply into focus. Many attitudes and judgments of the utmost importance in social life find their ultimate justification in the distinction referred to. Thus on the lower level of material force there is the contrast between kidnapping and gangs on the one hand, conscription and armies on the other; between theft and murder, taxation and war; so, on a higher level, demagogue and dupes as against master and disciples, indoctrination as against instruction. Finally, there is the manipulation of symbols to impose or induce configurations and ideologies exteriorizable in action favorable to private, special, or partial interests, which may be called propaganda. All of the foregoing are partial in nature; as such they contrast with education, which aims at the improvement, elevation, integration of the factors or sources of impulsion, man on this level being considered as an end in himself. But from the viewpoint of the present chapter, the essential point is that men *must* collaborate, that supervision is a societal necessity. All that education can do in this respect is to make men conscious and willing collaborators in a total, public, general objective.

In conclusion, when all these forms of force, material and ideational, acting directly and indirectly for partial or even for total ends, are brought to bear upon men considered as means, the power that results is so mighty that it is easy to see why individuals with high origin rates thirst for it and why efforts to see what is as it is are thwarted by it. And it is equally easy, especially in extreme cases, to realize how crushing is the pressure upon individuals to conform, comply, accede, acquiesce, capitulate, bow, bend, yield utterly, to endure having the person compressed into the socius, whereby men become but unresistant parts in an absorbing totality whose ultimate ends are quite beyond their percipience or their will. The very impotence to which men may be reduced under the pressure of the summated forces of power imposes the consideration, before this chapter is ended, of the problem involved in the question ordinarily formulated in the words, who is to govern the government?

It might at first sight seem that no control were necessary for the organs of control. Power, political and other, is subject to abuse, of course; otherwise it would not truly be power. The statement is but the recognition of a fact; it is no defense of abuses. And so, if abuses are inevitable they will of themselves tend to provide limits to the exercise of power. Many structures of direction, governmental and other, have been erected on the basis of this tendency for power to create its own limits. In the Orient particularly this method of containing power has been utilized. There holders of power have, as de Maistre said, been in effect addressed as follows: "Do what you will; when we are weary of you, we will cut your throat." [16]

In the Occident another road has been followed. There the possibility of excesses on the part of rulers has been guarded against beforehand, at least in theory. The outcome has been the multiplication of limitations, legal and constitutional, often to the point where the leader's initiative and action are all but inhibited—to the great advantage of mediocrities. The oriental method seems but a spontaneous result of necessity combined with societal inexperience, no other choice being open at a given level of culture. Occidental societies have proceeded on an empirical basis but with no permanent success. The future should see the difficulty envisaged as a problem in applied sociology and approached from the starting point of societal statics.

It is clear that direction is indispensable to societal existence. Any attempt to evade the necessity can result at last only in regression to the animal level and at first in the spontaneous appearance of forms of control that are not legitimate, i.e., total ends in the hands of partial agencies. It is also clear that the tendency of directive phenomena is toward concentration and centralization because of the rivalry of leaders, the hierarchizing of interests, and the conflict of sovereignties. Likewise it is clear that the means of direction is force, physical and mental, and its objective is the control of conduct not motive, of action not will. Within such limits abuses of power tend to correct themselves by inciting the use of force as a countermeasure, but these limits are very wide and leave much to be desired.

A more direct way of dealing with the excesses of power is to recognize the facts of direction and by design to restrict the ranges within which power can be exercised. Thus it seems likely that too wide an extension of a single government is likely to favor tyranny in that the uniformity of behavior imposed throughout a wide territory by the agency of force cannot permit the variability of conduct which diversified local cultural backgrounds, past and present, and dissimilar conditions of environment make desirable or even necessary. "Material power," said Comte, "destined above all to regularize special and local operations, can dominate territory

16. De Maistre, *Du Pape* (Paris, G. Charpentier & Cie., 1843).

much less extended even than is today believed. . . . Instead of being enlarged in proportion to the extension of human association, political domination should on the contrary be considerably restricted." [17]

The problem allows of still another and more radical solution. Since societal organization remains imperfect "so long as the force whose preponderance has to regulate the partial activities within it is itself without a control corresponding to its own tendencies toward abuse," could not the imperfection be remedied by "the founding of a more general and more noble society, rising upon the political society as the latter arose at first upon the domestic"? [18] Cultural development seems to provide an answer in the affirmative.

> First there arose spontaneously the most complete but the most restricted association, the domestic society; it furnished the natural element of the political society, vaster though less intimate, having collective activity as its principle, and for its own regulation the material preponderance which results from it. The *cité*, the State, becomes in its turn the normal element of the religious society, the most extensive and the least complete of all, resting upon community of belief and ruled by faith.
>
> Thus the Church freely unites the *cités*, just as each *cité* spontaneously combines the corresponding families, first grouped into classes by virtue of their social offices. So long as social organization could not be completed in this way, the need of binding together the various elementary states caused political society gradually to acquire exorbitant dimensions. But the advent of the universal Church will henceforth allow these provisional expansions little by little to be restricted to the normal limits of the domination without tyranny of which material force directly allows.[19]

Above the state, then, the church: so does the political power find without the disciplinary influence which it possesses so imperfectly within. But a vital distinction must be made at this point. It concerns the nature of the offices which state and church fulfill in the social life of Man. So long as either state or church or both are pic-

17. *Politique*, 2, 320.
18. Comte, *Politique*, 2, pp. 303 ff.
19. Comte, *Politique*, 2, 305.

tured as directive in the societal sense, they will both inevitably manifest the tendency inherent in directive phenomena toward centralization, concentration, and rivalry. Both will tend, in different ways, to become totalitarian, to develop tensions, and to conflict. There is no permanent solution of the problem so long as both organizations are conceived of and built up *as societal structures.*

Insofar as the energies of individuals have to be directed in the pursuit of a common interest, the church is an institution and manifests all the relevant characteristics; it is therefore open to all the temptations that power offers. But there are two safeguards when the problem is approached from the positive point of departure. In the first place, its doctrines are no longer absolute; they possess only the validity common to scientific acquisitions. In the second place, the domain of the church does not overlap that of the state; the two exist on different levels.

Permanent peace between the two institutions develops out of the definitive recognition of a fundamental and irreducible distinction in the nature of their respective activities. What the state deals with and is concerned with is behavior, acts, actions—not motivation, impulsion, wills. What the state works with is socii; beyond them it does not go. But the phenomena manifested by Man are not exhausted by the societal category. Below it is the organic, the biological; above it is the individual, the moral, the personal, the psychological. Sociology envisages individual beings as means; psychology, as ends. The one regulates exteriorizations; the other modifies impulsions. The one works by force, the other by suasion. That is to say, there are two levels of abstraction in question, two irreducible categories of phenomena, two modes of beings, two isolates. Of these the societal is the first in the sense that it lays the groundwork and provides the milieu in which the second, the personal, can develop.

Each of these domains of science is distinct from the other. The moral life, growing out of the energies of the affections, the motivations, the impulsions, is a world of its own. Its data are by nature neither collective nor cumulative; it begins and ends with the personality, which it studies in isolation, using its discoveries for the improvement and integration of that inner world. It leaves the world without to the direction of the state. The interests of the latter are temporal, of the other spiritual. *They are two powers, not one.* Each has its own function. Neither deals with the whole man; hence neither can be totalitarian. Each operates on its own level; hence they cannot be rivals. The second serves as a control for the first in the sense that it points out the ways in which the activities of the first condition the attainment of the objectives at which the second aims. But how the spiritual, as defined above in a positive sense, operates is not here to be discussed. At this point the societal spectrum has been traversed; sociology ends where psychology begins.

CHAPTER 17 : *The Societal System*

Sumner, in dealing with the general characteristics of the folk-ways, points out a fact which has always been more or less stressed by sociologists. The characteristic in question is a strain of consistency. Of it he says that this strain operates because the folkways "all answer their several purposes with less friction and antagonism when they co-operate and support each other." [1] He cites as illustrations of the operation of this strain the two great cultural divisions of the human race, the occidental and the oriental. "Each is consistent throughout; each has its own philosophy and spirit; they are separated from top to bottom by different mores, different standpoints, different ways, and different notions of what societal arrangements are advantageous." [2] The strain begins to operate even on the level of the folkways and becomes all the stronger when the folkways, rising into mores, form the basis for the induction of principles.

These principles, once obtained by reflection upon the doctrines implicit in the mores, are then returned to the mores for which they serve as means of conscious organization, with the result that they seem creative and causative. Thus there is a double source of integrating influence. Not only is there the tendency for societal phenomena to harmonize with one another as they exist on the levels of folkways and mores, but when the stage of principles is reached the strain of consistency is intensified. The intensification results first from the fact that inconsistency on the level of principles is easily discovered and corrected and second from the fact that the corrected principles then go back and down to the mores and serve to bring them into a more conscious relation with one another than was possible in their ascendant phase. Thus there is a continuous movement from folkways to principles and back, whence in time the societal integration of which Sumner speaks.

1. *Folkways,* pp. 5–6.
2. P. 6.

428   DIVISIONING OF THE SOCIETAL DOMAIN

Societal integration—i.e., an experimental and logical adjustment of the mores and the doctrines implicit in them to one another in such a way that a modification of the adjustment at any one point will produce reactions at all other points—such a conception is peculiar to Sumner only in the terms he uses and the degree to which he is conscious of it. Otherwise there is nothing to distinguish his position. From Comte to Pareto, all the writers have been aware of the fact in some degree and have used appropriate though often very different words to express it. In Comte's case the fact was no doubt brought to his attention by Montesquieu and the physiocrats, and biological analogy gave him the word which he employed: "The universal consensus which characterizes all the phenomena whatever of living bodies, and which social life manifests in the highest degree." It calls for the study of "the mutual actions and reactions which are continually exercised one upon the other by all the different parts whatever of the social system." [3] Spencer, as might be expected, speaks also of consensus; and the later sociologists vary in their usage, but everywhere the notion is implicit. Social solidarity is another expression of the general idea. The anthropologists, seeing the fact in the various cultures that came one by one into their ken, speak of cultural integration, ending in a pattern. Pareto, seeing the phenomenon in the social data he was studying, utilized a mathematical term and spoke of the social equilibrium. Still others, and Pareto also belongs to this group, speak of an economic system, the elements of which are, or come to be, in an equilibrium. Historians and others use the phrase "a social system." Still other words might be used, and perhaps it would be wiser for sociologists to drop the use of terms too long employed in nonscientific senses and coin one for themselves, free from the connotations arising from generations of uncritical and analogical usage. In such a case the word "symplegma" is available.

In any case, whatever the word used, it will signify the fact that there is a strain of consistency at work in the mores as a whole and that certain classes of folkways are directly related to other classes in such a way that a change in one will bring about a change in another and so of course ultimately affect the folkways as a whole. In Comte's words, slightly modified, "each of the numerous [societal] elements, ceasing to be envisaged in an absolute and independent

3. *Cours de philosophie positive, 4,* 258.

manner, should always be exclusively conceived of as relative to all the others, with which a fundamental solidarity must without cessation intimately combine it." [4] In sociology as in mechanics, "the communication of movements spontaneously proves the existence of the necessary connections." [5]

Such is the *idée mère* which is the basis of the study of the statical aspect of societal phenomena, whatever the name given it. In Comte's discussion in the *Philosophie,* the concept includes the whole range of social phenomena; it can be restricted with no difficulty to the narrower isolate of societal phenomena. Of course the concept is not any one's personal possession; it is a general sociological doctrine, soundly based upon anthropological observation. Thus Rivers, in his *Melanesian Society:*

> This book shows how hopeless it is to expect to understand human culture if we limit our attention to any one of its component elements. In the more complicated examples of human culture, specialism may be inevitable, though even here it needs to be assisted by the work of those who may lack the completeness and exactness of the specialist, but yet understand the principles of more than one science. In the study of the ruder varieties of human culture, such specialism is far less needed, and is far more prohibitive of progress. The constituent elements of such cultures as those of the Melanesian, Australian or African are so closely interwoven with one another, it is so difficult or impossible to disentangle these elements, that the work of the specialist in social organization, religion, language or technology must be unfruitful and soulless. [6]

Sumner and Keller, raising the anthropological findings to the sociological level, emphasize the same idea in a paragraph with the title "Society a Living Whole":

> It is impossible to get a comprehension of any complex societal structure without taking it to pieces, somewhat as one takes down an automobile. The mind cannot understand either the

4. *Philosophie, 4,* 259.
5. *4,* 261.
6. W. H. R. Rivers, *The History of Melanesian Society* (2 vols. Cambridge, The University Press, 1914), 2, 594.

whole or the interrelation of the parts without the employment of that expedient. Yet it is not always realized that when the analysis is done the results are dead, unreal, and misleading unless the investigator or student frees himself from his categories and, enlightened but not hampered or bound by what analysis has taught him, re-assembles the parts and rises to a view of the intricately interlocking action of all the factors. . . . Similarly with a society: it is not composed of sets of institutions that have been analyzed out and separately examined; it is the whole of them acting together.

"All of these institutions interpenetrate, as do the interests that have summoned them into being." [7]

It is necessary, then, in dealing with the group of phenomena here called statical to keep in mind the complete solidarity of cultural phenomena; it is equally necessary, in order to deal with this solidarity as a societal phenomenon, to classify the collective cumulations with which sociology deals. Thus the discussion is brought back to the elements of the cultural pattern and in particular to the four elements which were selected as universal by the practically unanimous consent of anthropologists and sociologists: capital, family, language, government—maintenance, association, communication and direction—each giving rise to a definite special science, a subisolate in the larger societal isolate, economics, socionomics, semantics, and politics. Within the boundaries of those specialties the sociologist as such does not enter; he is concerned with their phenomena only as they fall within the scope of his own study of the process of collective cumulation; consequently, once the specialist has done his work, the sociologist takes up the inquiry as to the relations of these subisolates with one another.

The reason then for stressing the validity of the concept of societal solidarity is simple. If the concept is valid, the necessity for sociology to go deeply into the nature of the relations between the constituents of the pattern is immediate. The science will have not only to study the nature of the constituents—that is but a preliminary step—it will have chiefly to study their interdependence and be impelled and directed by the desire to obtain such a knowledge of

7. *The Science of Society, 1,* 87, 90.

these relations of interdependence as to be able to rise concerning them to the scientific level of prevision. In other words, the implications of the present chapter for the general task of sociology can be formulated as follows: Given a stated modification of one of the statical elements, to determine the resultant modifications in the others.

It is of course true that the theoretical inquiry just formulated as a general problem has not been completely neglected since Comte first saw its importance. Since his time many men, sociologists and others, have given attention to the matter and some have had an understanding of its sociological importance. Ogburn for example among American sociologists has been distinguished for his work in this connection. "There is a need," he says, "for a sociology which shall be an overall social science to the extent at least of treating in a broad way the interconnections of the various social institutions." [8] On the whole, however, it is true that the general problem has not had the attention it deserves. Most of those who have dealt with the question have done so in a partial manner or from a special or even partisan standpoint. None of them has followed Comte in elevating its consideration to the rank of one of the two major divisions of the science as a whole.

Perhaps one of the reasons for the relative absence of more extensive or more logically comprehensive studies is the fact that such inquiries as have been made have had to be more or less empirical, i.e., have lacked a background of theory. What such efforts need is the basis afforded by a wider structure of thought than has hitherto been envisaged. That is to say, the question as to the effects of a change in one element of the sociological pattern upon all the others should be studied in the light of certain fundamental principles revealed in the analysis of the societal organization as a whole. This organization constitutes a true system, the understanding of which would seem to be a prerequisite for more detailed investigations. This chapter is therefore to be given over to the task of providing a first approximation of a complete analysis of the system of societal order as a whole, in the light of which may then be carried on the tracing of more limited relationships.

8. W. F. Ogburn and M. F. Nimkoff, *Sociology* (Boston, Houghton Mifflin, 1940), p. 755.

The problem raised in the preceding section can be restated in many ways. Perhaps the most suggestive formulation is this: Cannot the conceptions and facts included in the term "consensus" be given a more precise form? Or, in other words, is the biological term "consensus" adequate to express the nature of the relations that exist between the elements of the cultural pattern? That another term more expressive of determinate relationship could be used is certain. For generations the word "system" has been applied to various cultural symplegmas, understood sometimes in a quite general sense, e.g., the medieval system, sometimes in a special sense, e.g., the economic or the political system, the mercantilist or the monarchical system. Certainly in these terms and particularly in the more special uses, there is a clear implication of a structural unity; something more is meant than a simple description. Is there not a place in the sociological scheme for the notion of system, with all the implications of the word? In short, is not the idea of consensus a step on the way to the conception of a societal system?

That these questions should be answered in the affirmative is the position of this chapter, which is thus an effort to give precision to the notion of system and to show that it may be utilized in sociology as it has been elsewhere.

What then is a system? It would be easy to turn to the mathematicians proper for definitions of the term if there were anything to gain from doing so. The notion however is not a difficult one and the mathematical treatment of it, ultimately necessary of course, is here subordinated to the use made of the concept by men who were to say the least capable mathematicians and had the advantage, for present purposes, of more than usual acquaintance with social phenomena, sociological and other. Such men are for example Pareto, whose name is familiar in this connection, and Laffitte, whose work, essentially a continuation of Comte's, has never had the attention it deserves. Laffitte was in fact the first to see the possibilities of a theoretical treatment of a societal system; and it is his work which in the main is here used as a guide.

What then is a system? In brief terms, "a system is composed of inter-connected elements which constantly act and react upon each other." [9] Historically, the concept reached its complete form with

9. Laffitte, *Cours de philosophie première*, 2, 16.

Newton. Since his time, "a system is a totality of inter-connected, inter-related bodies, subjected in other relations to any forces whatever, but within themselves acting and reacting one upon the other according to the law of action equalling reaction." [10] The notion may be restricted or extended; it may apply to or be found in living as well as inert bodies; if the living organism is in point the system aspect is not lost from sight, only something is added to it which does not prevent it from remaining a system. "What characterizes a system is the idea of inter-connectedness; it does not present the idea of a common destination or purpose; there is simply connection between similar or different phenomena." [11]

But is not the use of the term "system" just another case of analogical thought, somewhat akin to the biological or organic analogy? Is anything gained by transferring concepts from mechanics to sociology? Figures of speech have played their part once for all, it is to be hoped, in the upbuilding of sociological theory. The answer is that the concept of system is in no sense a merely or solely mathematical or mechanical concept. In its simplest form, namely, the interdependence of a number of elements constantly acting and reacting upon one another, the notion is applicable through the whole range of nature, inorganic or organic. Indeed it is inaccurate to speak of the notion as being applicable to this or that range of phenomena. The fact is that the various classes of homogeneous data dealt with by the different sciences, inorganic or organic, all show the relationships which by abstraction were reduced to the concept of system, the abstract concept receiving its most systematic treatment in the field of mathematics. There is no analogy in question when a system of societal phenomena is spoken of; sociology is simply one of the domains where certain relationships of phenomena abstractly termed "system" are to be found.

It is worth pointing out in this connection how many terms now consecrated by usage to the mathematical or physical sciences had their origin on the organic or superorganic levels of thought. What happened is that societal induction, acting spontaneously and fash-

10. Laffitte, 2, 109.
11. Laffitte, 2, 170.

ioning language as it developed, seized upon certain phenomena of social or organic life and integrated them under a particular name. Then by a continuing process of abstraction the synthesizing factor within the integration was gradually recognized, stripped of its accessory aspects and isolated. Then the isolate was seen to admit of mathematical treatment. System is such a concept. Thus the recognition of the idea has proceeded from above downward; the mathematical development has moved from below upward. A like instance occurs on the organic level, where the word "evolution" began by being historical and social and ended by becoming biological in its implications.

An objection of greater apparent force may be found in the criticism sure to be made that to introduce mathematical conceptions of this type into sociology is to make or tend to make it mechanical. It will be well to linger a moment on this charge, since it is often made and is implicit in many of the dogmatic assertions that sociology cannot be a science.

What then lies behind the idea that there may be so to speak a mechanics of sociology and to what extent is the idea by its nature inapplicable to sociology? A sociological analysis of the concept in question will serve to answer these questions. It starts, as all such analyses must, with the animal Homo. Its source is in his biological equipment. When Man's ancestor strove to modify the world to his advantage, i.e., to exteriorize an image of desire, every activity of this practical kind involved a muscular contraction and was accompanied by a sensation to which the term "effort" was applied. This notion is the outgrowth of a sensation, as truly distinct and irreducible as the notions of form, color, or sound. It is in fact an image, i.e., the product of a distinct sense, to which various names have been given and to which the term "musculation" will here be applied.

From the sensations attributable to the efforts which men made to modify the world in which they lived came the notion of strength and later of force, a notion which is essentially an intimate combination between the internal sensation of effort and the external modification which that effort effects. Force thus comes to be the term descriptive of the efforts by which man pulls or pushes a body to keep it in place or to move it; it ultimately means any effort of man which produces or tends to produce a movement in another body, or in more general terms a modification in its mechanical state, static or dynamic. There are four things to consider in the conception: the point of application of the force, its direction, its intensity, and the time during which it acts. The intensity might be measured by the sensation of effort, if the sense of musculation were more perfect. Since it is not, the usual procedure in such cases has been followed, namely, the sense of sight has been called upon to supplement the deficiencies of the sense in default by various devices which translate effort into "pointer readings." Rising to an abstract level, men have represented force by a straight line, its extremity indicating the point of application, its direction the direction of force, its length the intensity. It was thus brought within the scope of mathematical treatment.

Carrying abstraction still further and projecting himself into the world as always, man in regard to all communication of movement accomplished among bodies in general, even where he himself does not intervene, has represented it as effected by forces analogous to those described above, extending to them at least by verbal expression the notion of effort despite the fact that it is in strict factual accuracy relative only to sensations of a particular kind. In this manner all the phenomena of communication of movement are represented by forces similar to the original human type. Thus it is possible to represent by the abstract isolate in point all that is fundamental and common to all the varied phenomena where movements are effected, abstraction being made of all special particularities, variable in each case. Moreover, science has not stopped here; its representatives have gone further in the same path. *They have assimilated spontaneous movements to communicated movements* and represented them too by a sum of forces suitably constructed.

How this achievement has been effected, involving the concept of inertia—which consists in supposing that a body has no activity of its own but when it manifests movement is moved by an external action of traction or impulsion analogous to that performed by man, involving the concept of internal and external forces, the first being considered as the action of elements interrelated and connected with one another and the second being the expression of actions that can be considered as distinct and separable from the first, involving the concept in another field of cause, in a positive sense the conception of constant relations—cannot be told here.

To give an account of all these details would require for their full explanation a history not only of mechanics but even of thought as a whole. The essence of the matter, however, as far as the present discussion is concerned is easily stated.

When scientific men speak of mechanical forces and mechanical views of the world, they are not (even when they think otherwise) in a position to pontificate in regard to the nature of the world or the universe, to dogmatize in regard to its intimate or essential being, to penetrate to the thing-in-itself. These matters are for metaphysicians, ignorant by definition and by profession of the long cultural filiation which binds them unknowingly to the animal Homo. The scientific man in resorting to mechanical reasoning is simply utilizing on a high level of generality and abstraction the cumulated results of man's experience in the individual and collective use of his muscular energies to modify the world in which he lives. The basic power and sense involved, the muscular, are primary in the modification of the world; when they are rightly guided, the world is changed to men's desires. It is not enough to see this world or endure it or feel it, much less smell it or taste it; it is necessary to *move* it.

Force and its ultimate effect in *modifying* the world without— here is the motivation for giving these mechanical cultural developments their preferred place in man's thinking, not any value higher or lower of a speculative kind. It is not merely that considerations of the kind lend themselves so perfectly to mathematical representation and manipulation. The fact is important but not basic. The justification for the mechanical point of view is deeper than logic. When the mechanical view penetrates into a given field, power of modification in that field is gained; the mechanical view is the test of complete achievement. It *must* be the goal of scientific effort. Thanks to the sense of musculation it is possible by means of the sensation of effort to construct the idea of force and to represent the regular succession of phenomena as produced by imagined forces. Henceforth the world, i.e., that entire succession of phenomena of which men are a part, appears as an immense mechanism. By learning how this mechanism works men can make it work better. Sociology far from repudiating such a goal must strive toward it and measure its progress by its advances along the road that leads thereto.

The first step then in the making of a mechanical theory of societal phenomena, rendered possible by the fact that those phenomena are related in such a way as to justify the inclusion of them in the concept of system, is to review briefly the chief regularities which a system manifests. These uniformities are the laws of mechanics, where they were first formulated, reduced to abstract statement, and correlated. Three of them because of their fundamental nature are mainly in point in this preliminary survey of the possibilities of a sociological mechanics. If they are found serviceable, others can be used as well. The three are due respectively to Kepler, Galileo, and Newton. They bear various names and they have received various formulations according as one aspect or another of their effects has been brought into relief. Not all of these particularities can here be detailed; only the main points of each law will be set forth, and that with special reference to sociological theory.

In the first place then Kepler's law, the law of mechanical persistence, sometimes called the law of inertia, which says that "every state, statical or dynamical, tends spontaneously to persist without alteration, resisting external perturbation," would seem to have definite sociological implications. Laffitte, who is certainly among the first to see the possibilities for sociology of utilizing the achievements of mechanics, long before Pareto, sets forth the idea as follows: When a number of elements have become interconnected so as to act and react upon each other, they constitute a system. Two possibilities can then be envisaged. Either the elements are ultimately dislocated with the result that their interdependence disappears and they fuse with other systems; or they end by arriving at a state of equilibrium. In the latter case, once the equilibrium is reached the system tends to persist indefinitely and is changed in fact only by the action of an exterior force. It opposes to every change a force of resistance frequently called since Newton a force of inertia. It also constitutes a force of impulsion when it acts upon bodies exterior to it which are obstacles to its movement. These aspects of the force exerted by the system as a whole may be envisaged as the consequence of what might be termed the history of the elements composing it, for the force of the system is the result of all the anterior energy acquired by its elements; and it is this outcome of the past which, tending to persist, becomes the force either of inertia or of impulsion just mentioned. And it should be added, to complete this brief expository statement, that not only does the law hold good for a system as a whole, it holds good also of the elements which compose it. Each of them tends to persist in its own state of equilibrium or action and presents the double phenomenon of resistance or impulsion.

The relevance of the law to sociological phenomena needs little insistence. Consider first the case of the societal system taken as a whole. Such a system arises from the fact that each element of the societal pattern acts upon all the others and undergoes their reaction in determinate ways until an equilibrium is established among them. Once the equilibrium is established it tends to persist and present the phenomenon termed continuity. The internal forces, that is to say, continue to act in the direction determined by their past until an external force comes to disrupt them.

In other terms the law of persistence in sociology means, in relation to the interaction of the societal elements, that the cooperation of anterior generations, i.e., the cumulation of their collective experience has created a situation which persists under all the forms of simultaneous activity which its constituent elements manifest. The law holds good for each element as well as for the system as a whole. Take the case of economics, for example. The mode of action of each socius essentially depends upon the state of the planet as his predecessors established it, the various modes of communication, the capitals acquired, fixed or movable, special knowledge, habits of every kind. Under this enormous weight the system persists in its mode of activity and the individual socius conforms. The same thing is true in regard to language, all the bases of which, created by the work of centuries, always persist at a given moment. The same is true of the family or of the government. It is the law of persistence too which explains why slight disturbances of a societal kind have brief effects and without any special efforts disappear. Pareto mentions the sociological fact and compares it to the biological principle known as the *vis medicatrix naturae*. The study of what anthropologists call survivals, and might better be known as "persistants," belongs here.

The law of persistence manifests itself not only in the normal state of society but in its perturbations also. Take the case of revolution, defined as any brusque change of a certain extent produced in a societal system. If the change besides being brusque is so extensive that the system is disorganized, as may be the case following an intense exterior action especially when facilitated by a determinate inner state, the result is complete chaos and the immediate necessity, if men are not to revert to the animal Homo, is the restoration of some sort of order. In this sense revolutionists of the most extreme kind are simply men who wish to substitute one order for another, and when the replacement is effected the succession of orders is affected with a value judgment and termed progress.

But even in cases of replaced orders, and certainly in all cases of less extensive brusque changes, the law of persistence manifests itself by a tendency, more or less intense and habitually effective to at least a certain degree, to a return to the original or anterior state of equilibrium. It is this force of persistence which in combination with the force which has determined the brusque change produces those oscillations which follow the great revolutions. Thanks however to the law, continuity is much less broken in fact than it at first appears to be. The true gravity of the situation is often unperceived. It lies in the fact that the continuity is broken in conceptions, in thought, rather than in the material modes of societal existence. Hence there is a lack of harmony between the new theories and the reality of the situation; there result a long and continuous agitation and also, though in less subversive conditions, the phenomenon that has been termed social lag.

In short, the law of persistence constitutes a universal law both of the world and of men. It contributes to fixity by coordinating successive states, through the persistence of antecedent states, which in fact constitute forces, either active or virtual. The law is a principle of investigation and a principle of action as well. Every time that notable modifications are produced in a system which has reached a certain state of equilibrium, it will be necessary to seek outside the system for the circumstances that could have produced them. If it is desired to modify the system, then it will be necessary to search for new forces to be applied to it.

The first law, then, that seems to be one of the bases for a sociological mechanics offers as its contribution to the general end the conception of an elementary and distinct force, abstracting it from the whole of phenomena and dealing with it in isolation, giving special attention to its persistency of action. It permits a given system to be considered as a whole in relation to other systems; it allows a given system to be analyzed into a number of independent and elementary forces each persisting in its own action. The second law, attributed to Galileo, studies the combination of two or more of these elementary forces. Laffitte, envisaging the law in its most general sense, calls it the law of coexistence.

The law may be formulated as follows: Any system whatever maintains its constitution, active or passive, when its elements undergo simultaneous mutations, provided the mutations are exactly common to all the elements. The formulation is highly abstract, since it is intended to cover a wide variety of phenomena; but the essence of the conception for present purposes is the possibility it offers of considering as quite independent each of the elements that go to make up the system. Thus the action, simultaneous or successive, of the various elements can be dealt with without complication, since by abstraction the state of the system as a whole, whether at rest or in motion, is disregarded as are the mutual influences, by way of action and reaction, of the various elements upon one another.

The law of coexistence and its implications cover many points, notably the following: the coexistence of independent forces; the equivalence of the simultaneous and the successive action of the independent forces; the composition of forces and the determination of resultants; the conception of equilibrium; the possibility of substituting for one another equivalent systems according to the needs of the situation. Each of these consequences of the general law has significance and use in sociological theory.

In the first place, the independence of simultaneous forces is a conception inherent in the notion of cultural elements. Obviously in any culture all the various traits exist at the same time; yet they have always been distinguished and classified into distinct divisions. The clear inference is that the various classes of traits have always been regarded as essentially independent; the fact is so clear that even the earliest spontaneous classifications revealed in language are built upon the assumption; hence the possibility of considering four distinct classes of societal or cultural constituents: material accumulation, association, communication, direction. Each of these when thought of as a strictly independent force existing in isolation manifests the workings of the first law, the law of persistence. When their simultaneous operation in a system is recognized the second law, the law of coexistence, comes into operation.

The second aspect of the law follows from the first. If the forces in question are independent then their simultaneous action can be analyzed into the respective parts due to each force and thus the effect of the action may be envisaged as due not necessarily to the simultaneous action of all but to the successive action of each. An inference from the equivalence between succession and simultaneity is the rationality of intermittent effort, i.e., the possibility of resuming an effort once begun but later arrested. It is in using this logical device quite spontaneously that historians and others, dealing with a given societal situation, have taken up one after another its economic, political, and other aspects and followed each in its development and in its effect upon the total result. Yet it is quite clear that all these activities however named have been in continuous and simultaneous operation.

From the conception of independent forces, acting simultaneously or successively to produce a given effect, comes the theory of the composition of forces and the notion of resultants. The composition of forces is the logical artifice whereby a simultaneous action is considered to be the result of successive actions. The resultant of their composition is an effect—and it may be that the same effect can be produced by the resultants of the composition of quite distinct forces. The resultant is thus a force which can replace the action of two or more other forces or which is equivalent to them. Obviously the theory of composition leads to the theory of decomposition of forces. It is clear that if two forces can be replaced by one, reciprocally, a single force can be replaced by two others, which may be called component forces; and as the same artifice can be applied to each component, it follows of course that a given force can be replaced by an infinity of others. From the sociological point of view the effects of what is vaguely called social change are illustrations of the operation in societal phenomena of the law of coexistence.

In the fourth place, the law in point gives rise to another concept, that of equilibrium. When two or more forces in composition give a resultant equal to zero, the result is an equilibrium between them.

Thus economic forces may be met by political actions, with the result that the general system of the society remains unmodified. In general, when the preservation of a particular system is desired it will be necessary, if its existence is endangered, to find if possible forces which will act in a direction contrary to the forces endangering it. It should be emphasized in this connection that the geometers have demonstrated as a general fact that *a given system of forces has no single or necessary resultant*. Hence a state of equilibrium is no natural or spontaneous result; and so the securing and maintaining of a desired equilibrium requires much more effort than is usually thought necessary.

Finally there is the possibility of replacing a given system of forces by an infinity of other and different systems; hence a source of indetermination, which offers to logical deduction a vast opportunity, for it raises the vision of the possibility of replacing a given system by another which will arrive more easily at a desired end. The making of utopias could thus be put on a scientific basis.

It would seem, when all the implications of the law of coexistence are weighed, that it offers greater possibilities than either of the other two laws here set forth to those sociologists who are impressed by the need for developing the applied aspects of their science. The law of persistence no doubt has point in this connection; but it would seem to be more useful in sociological explanation than in application. The law of coexistence in contrast seems almost to encourage efforts at societal modification. Given a desired change of a cultural kind, the law in point suggests a whole program of investigation and application. What are the societal forces at work now? How can they be analyzed, i.e., what is their composition? Can their effect be met by other forces in composition and so negatived and the system kept in equilibrium? What forces should be brought into composition to produce a given desired change? Need they act continuously, or can a degree of intermittence be allowed? What equivalent systems could be substituted for the most immediately effective but perhaps unavailable systems? In short, the whole field of societal intervention is opened to theory. No doubt statesmen have always had some sort of intuitive notion of the possibilities, but so indeed had every manual laborer in the days before mechanics became a science.

But once the independent forces have been dealt with and abstraction made of the effects of action and reaction, the latter in their turn must be considered. They are the matter of the third and last law of mechanics here to be cited. This law is attributed to Newton. It runs as follows: There is always equivalence between action and reaction, if their intensity is measured in conformity with the nature of each conflict.

It will be well in beginning the discussion of this law to distinguish between the idea of combination and that of action and reaction. There is action and reaction between two forces when they reciprocally modify their degree of intensity; there is combination when the forces do not modify their intensity and produce only a result which is the outcome of the independent action of each. It is the first of these ideas that is now to be taken up, thus supplementing the deliberate omissions which the process of abstraction accounts for in the establishment of the laws of persistence and coexistence. This third law, since it concerns the equivalence of action and reaction, will here be called the law of equivalence. It applies to a more complicated situation than the second, just as the second deals with a greater complication than the first.

These three laws complement one another. The first represents either the action of a single force or the manner in which a single force is constituted as the final result of the anterior activity of any number whatever of forces acting upon a point or a system. The second governs the action of distinct forces, simultaneous or successive, considered as independent of one another. In the first two, only the action of A upon B was in point; but in fact, there is always a reaction of B upon A. It is this law of reaction, always accompanying action, that must now be studied.

The law of equivalence presents two cases: where the phenomena are of the same nature and where they are of different nature. Actions and reactions between phenomena that are homogeneous or of the same nature are governed by a universal law applying to all distinct orders of phenomena: it is called the law of equality between action and reaction. When the phenomena are of different nature, the successive variations of two distinct phenomena are governed by the law of equivalence. Sociologists, who are by definition limited to societal phenomena exclusively, will be concerned essentially with the first form of the law; social psychologists, who deal with two classes of phenomena, the sociological and the psychological, will be concerned with the second.

Probably the best case in which to observe the working of the law of equivalence in its first form, i.e., where the phenomena are strictly homogeneous, is the field of economics. If the four great economic functions, agriculture, manufacture, commerce, and banking, are considered it will be seen that though each has its individual activity, they are intimately related; and it is in this solidarity that the actions and reactions appear. Agriculture by the nature and quantity of its products acts directly upon manufacture, for which it supplies food and raw materials. But manufacture in its turn reacts upon agriculture, furnishing clothing, housing, and instruments; it modifies the mode of distribution of agricultural workers by attracting a certain number of them or repelling others. It also reacts upon agriculture by providing means for improving the methods of culture. Agriculture acts directly upon commerce and commerce reacts upon it by transmitting materials and instruments and modifying the distribution of the various kinds of agricultural activity. Manufacture in its turn reacts upon commerce in obvious ways. Finally banking is affected by the action of the three other economic functions and in turn modifies them.

Another case of the law can be found in the relations between association and direction. Here the phenomena are still homogeneous though classifiable into separate categories. If the association is the cité or the nation, it acts upon the government by either its approval or disapproval or by the resources, inorganic, organic, or human, that it supplies. In turn the regime reacts upon the socionomy by the decisions it takes or the measures it institutes. It can even to a certain degree isolate itself from the association and thus become for it an exterior force, the capital condition of progress.

It is evident [says Laffitte] that if these actions and reactions could be isolated and each one measured, the result would be to create equivalents, corresponding to each distinct class of phenomena. An extreme precision would thus be introduced into the prevision and modification of social phenomena. We are far from realizing such an ideal, but it is useful all the same to envisage it in a philosophical manner. Yet there is one case in which there has been brought into the phenomena of action and reaction sufficient precision to determine a sort of general equivalent; this is the case of exchange. *Price,* in this case, is a true equivalent which measures at least approximately the actions and reactions that exchanges represent.[12]

It will be seen that if the first law, the law of persistence, is useful for historians and the second suggestive in the highest degree for statesmen, the third will be valuable for reformers, cautioning them that wholesale modifications of this or that class of societal phenomena, proposed and advocated as plans submitted en bloc, are always suspect since they fail to take into account the more remote sequence of action and reaction that these plans would entail throughout the whole range of societal existence. The network of relationships which bind socii together into society is too intricate to be disturbed in such summary fashion.

The extension of the concept of system into the domain of sociology suggests the use therein of mathematics as an aid to inquiry and to the formulation of results. Such an achievement in any science is always regarded as a true advance, not merely because it brings a new means of investigation but also because it marks a notable increase in the precision with which the data of the given science are pictured.

It is indeed the second of these points that is the important one. Merely to transport mathematical concepts and techniques into a given scientific domain is far from being a triumph in itself. A formula can never be anything but the translation into appropriate symbols of the concepts distinctive of a particular body of data. It in no sense implies or necessarily helps the more accurate conceptualizing of the phenomena involved. Indeed it may be a disturbing factor in the development of the science, for if the facts transformed into formulas have not been adequately analyzed the formulas can only disguise or conceal deficiencies.

Conversely, the steady advance in the clarity and precision with which the phenomena are analyzed and expressed is the most effective means for bringing into use the concepts and manipulations of

12. 2, 144.

mathematics. No doubt such advances in theory will at first be reflected in very simple beginnings; but here as elsewhere it is the first steps that count. If despite their simplicity these advances are sound in theory, they will lead to continued development; if they are premature, they will have to be retraced.

Moreover it is clear though not always understood that the use of mathematical aids, making calculation possible as well as the expression of deductive conclusions in formula fashion, always implies the existence of a general frame of reference within which alone do the mathematical expressions have significance. It was, for example, an advantage for medical men to be able to use quantitative instead of qualitative terms in describing the state of a patient: the man has a temperature of 105°. But it is sometimes forgotten that the expression 105°, though highly accurate in both mathematics and physics, has no meaning at all apart from a knowledge of the capacities and limitations of the biological organism. Otherwise it might be regarded as a proof of exceptional energy or disregarded as merely a slight advance toward 200°.

In sum, it is necessary for the phenomena of a given isolate to be analyzed and definite relations established among them before mathematical aids can be utilized without deception. If this line of thought is logical, then the first task of the sociologist who wishes to introduce mathematics into his subject would seem to be the discovery of a way to translate societal concepts into quantitative terms. There would be a beginning, simple no doubt but holding out possibilities for the future. The completely abstract definition of societal phenomena as collective cumulations seems to offer certain possibilities of the kind desired. Two suggestions, accordingly, are here hazarded. Both grow out of the preceding discussions taken as a whole.

The first prospect of introducing quantitative terms into abstract sociology is revealed in the chapter on direction. There it was shown that if individual beings are to be socii, their efforts have to be combined and directed, i.e., concentrated. It would seem possible then to determine the number of such concentrations of socii and so determine the societal forces working for one objective or another. It would seem possible further either to determine the number of the centers about whom efforts converge, i.e., to number the leaders of such concentrations or to discover the number of socii engaged in any particular concentration. To combine both of these sets of data, the number of leaders and the number of cooperators, would seem to provide a means for measuring the effective forces working for a particular societal result. To determine the increase or decrease in time of the numbers of such concentrations would provide a means for the calculation of trends, at least within a given society, and would facilitate the task of direction, especially when regarded from the standpoint of the total interest of the group.

A second possibility seems deducible from the very definition of the abstract societal phenomenon. It differs from the preceding proposal in that it is more general and would seem to be applicable rather to the objects of concentration than to the agents. It consists in utilizing a unit of time as the standard or measure and discovering, in the case of an individual or of a group, how many such units of time are devoted to societal activities. No one gives *all* his time to carrying on his functions as a socius; he must satisfy his biological needs and indulge his personal desires. Hence it would seem possible to determine the number of hours, say, that a given being (not necessarily even human) devotes to collective action. In other words it seems not impossible to determine the number of societal man-hours spent per day or per week by a member of a group and so, ultimately, by the group as a whole. Once such a determination were made and then summarized or averaged for the total number of socii, it would be possible to go further and classify societal man-hours as spent in the furtherance of partial or total interests, in operative or directive functions, in particular activities, industrial or military, economic or religious.

If such determinations of a quantitative kind are feasible, either in terms of societal concentrations or of leaders or of man-hours, then the results could be ultimately extended to calculations related to one or all of the fundamental characteristics of the system which this chapter has sought to show exists among societal phenomena.

To define societal phenomena as collective cumulations not only opens the possibility of a quantitative treatment of sociological data, it also makes opportune new judgments as to the applicability of the societal isolate of certain resources of method hitherto deemed beyond reach. Particularly useful in this connection is the recourse to experiment. Hitherto experimentation has been regarded as outside practical use. With the new definition of societal phenomena, experiment in sociology becomes possible.

A simple example is demonstrative. It is today a scientific commonplace that the energy in the atom can be released and utilized. Moreover, the speed with which this achievement has been attained has increased to a degree once regarded as impossible. What has not been realized is the fact that this scientific triumph is not solely physical; it is sociological as well, if indeed it is not chiefly so. How much time would have been required to tap the energy of the atom if the process had been left to purely spontaneous efforts? No one can even guess; what is known is that once it became evident that efforts of this kind were collective and cumulative it became possible to increase the intensity with which knowledge in this field could be advanced. And once this conclusion was reached, it became possible to experiment in the gathering of knowledge of this kind. Men, that is, could experiment in the sociological domain; they could to some extent heighten the degree to which they could control the rate of speed at which knowledge in a given domain could be brought under control.

They could experiment; and their experiments were successful. Thus it is correct to say that the endeavor to utilize the energy of the atom was a sociological experiment. It can therefore be asserted that sociological experimentation is not only possible, it has been successful to a degree beyond expectation. Never before had so vast and far-reaching an experiment knowingly been entered upon. No doubt, too, the art of experimentation in the new field can be refined and improved. No details can be here entered upon. It is however possible to say that overshadowing the practical successes is the insight which has been gained into the sociological conceptions that Ward had in mind when he made his distinction between genesis and telesis.

CHAPTER 18: *The Nature and the Factors of Societal Change*

Briefly summarized, the line of argument at this point is the following: A societal system exists because there are elements, each with its history, combining in different ways, acting and reacting one upon the other and so forming a set of distinguishable forces which are in equilibrium. These constituents of the societal system are the four subisolates already defined and discussed: material accumulation, association, communication, and direction.

None of these four exists *because* of any of the others; each has its own source and development; but they have come into relations with one another in a functional way. It is these functional relations which make possible, give rise to, or cause societal existence; and these relations *must* continue if societal phenomena are to persist. In other words, there is among the elements of the pattern an inalterable arrangement, a fixed order. Change in any one of them cannot go beyond the point where the interrelationship, the functional connection, ceases; if it does, the system ends and societal existence along with it. The interdependence of the elements is necessary to the preservation of the system.

The consequences of this basic arrangement are two. In the first place, there is a necessity, a fatality, which governs the operation of societal phenomena. The functional interdependence which is the definition and basis of the societal system cannot be altered in essentials without destroying the system. From this necessity there is no alternative and no choice. But in the second place, there is a possibility of modifying the working of the system so long as the ultimate arrangement is not altered. Each or any of the societal forces may operate with varying degrees of intensity or speed; the consequences will be varied. Economic influences will be strong in one society, relatively weak elsewhere. So with the other elements —direction, say. That is, the arrangement cannot be altered but the operation of the constituents of the system can vary. Once the fact becomes known, it can be used to bring variation about. Until then spontaneous variations will occur. The situation can thus be described as a modifiable necessity.

Order there must be if societal phenomena are to result; but the order is not immutable since the fact of change or movement or development or progress is evident. But progress is not illimitable since the necessity of preserving the fundamental arrangement is undeniable. Order can never be wholly fixed; progress tends toward stability. The facts prompt two questions, which in a sense are but one: How far can societal order be modified without making it impossible for the societal process to operate? What are the limits beyond which change cannot go without endangering the interdependence of the forces which compose the system? In either case, it is obvious that an immense variety of societal phenomena must be brought into relationship in order to provide an answer.

This concept of modifiable necessity which runs through the whole domain of law, societal or other, demands expansion at this point. Illustrations can best be found in the simpler levels of abstraction, the geometrical or the mechanical. There is for example a constant, i.e., invariable relation between the diameter of a circle and its circumference. It is precisely the existence of this constant relation that makes it possible for men to move with the utmost confidence from radius to circumference or from circumference to diameter when practical needs require.

It is known that the speed of a falling body accelerates at a fixed, a constant, rate. Calculation on the basis of this fatality shows how impossible it is for men to resist the shock of falling, say, a hundred feet or to raise themselves or an equivalent weight by a single effort to the same height. Yet men are not therefore fated to remain on the level. By means of steps or stairs or ramps they fall or rise by almost imperceptible gradations but never violating the laws of gravity. (So too with the psychic laws that underlie morality.) Men know, for another example, that mechanical work is the product of force by speed by time. This product is inalterable. Yet by means of levers and pulleys it is possible to vary the operation of the system, a decrease in speed for example being compensated for by an increase in force. In fact the notion of law and modification can be generalized into the statement that a determinate function of variables gives a constant. That is, if $xy = A$, then either x or y can be increased. If so, then the other will be decreased and the product will be constant. But the number of variations can be infinite without the law being thereby invalidated. The immense range of possibility open to human option and election need not be emphasized.

It is important however to realize that it is the very fatality, necessity, regularity of law that gives men confidence to undertake modifications of it. Thus fatality does not lead to fatalism; necessity involves no surrender. On the contrary, they lead to activity. The concept of immutable laws multiplies human energy a hundredfold, says Laffitte; and it does so by preventing energy from being exhausted in fruitless efforts and concentrating it in a domain where the production of desired results is sure. Not otherwise is to be explained the energy in action of those who in the past strove to affect the immutable will of the deity or in the present believe most firmly in social laws. Not only, they consider, are their energies being expended in the right direction; they serve also to increase the speed and intensity of the forces which work for the inevitable and desirable ends. In all these cases the essential point is the fact that modifiable necessities provide an infinity of variety within limits; and man can exercise a choice by discovering the ways in which modifications can be brought to pass.

One of the clear inferences of the position just illustrated is the homogeneity of all the consequences attributable to a given fatality or law in operation. The fact slowly became evident on the lower levels of abstraction; but it was not until the work of Broussais that the notion was extended to higher ranges of science. Stemming in theory from Bichat and founding what he called physiological medicine, Broussais established the position that the phenomena of disease are essentially coincident with those of health, differing from them only in intensity. Comte seized upon the idea, combined it with analagous concepts elsewhere, and generalized it into the following statement: "Modifications of the universal order are limited to the intensity of the phenomena, their arrangement remaining inalterable." [1]

Broussais' idea, as will be seen, throws light upon the problem of the nature of social change and the factors which produce it. The

1. *Système de politique positive*, 4, 175.

essence of the idea as extended and generalized by Comte is that in any isolate the whole sum of phenomena, the unusual as well as the usual, are manifestations of the same regularities. That is to say, the normal and the abnormal are both forms of the same essential phenomenon and are separated only by an intellectual operation, effected either for man's convenience or because of his mental limitations or due simply to his ignorance. The same laws, the same uniformities, are observable in both. The normal, that is, is a mean about which societal variations oscillate. "In the eyes of science," says Laffitte, commenting upon Comte, "there no longer exists any distinction between the normal state, or the mean, and the disturbances of that state. There is no longer anything but a universal and inalterable order, whose component phenomena can vary in their intensity or their speed, but never in their arrangement." [2]

When for example it is said that the spaces traversed by a falling body are to each other as the square of the times taken to traverse them, there is no question of normal or abnormal bodies or rates of falling. There is but one law for falling bodies. If the facts observed do not conform to the law, the physicist looks not for a new kind of law but simply for the conditions which account for the anomalies observed.

If the influence of the sun in man's planetary system had been, as men were long able to believe, exerted alone, and to the exclusion of every other influence, the planets would describe a perfect ellipse about the central star. Naturally, then, the movement of the planets was described as elliptical; and it was equally natural that the ellipse should be considered to be the normal orbit of the planets. Later it was observed that the sun's influence is not the only one in operation. It was shown that every planet is subject to the actions of the other planets, and so these influences became for the astronomer just so many disturbing or perturbative elements of a normal movement,—elements which have to be taken into account if the reality is to be approached more closely. As an artifice of logic, and from the subjective point of view, this decomposition of planetary movement into normal and perturbative movements is of capital

2. *Cours de philosophie première, I,* 207.

importance; but absolutely speaking these pretended perturbations are an integral part of the astronomical phenomenon, and are not less essential than the supposedly normal movement. The only difference between the fundamental phenomenon and the disturbing phenomena is that the action of the sun, the cause of the former, is the preponderant element, while the reciprocal actions exerted by the planets upon one another are phenomena of less intensity, but of quite like kind.[3]

And it may be added that the concept of gravitation made it possible to bring all the facts mentioned in the quotation, and many others, into a common framework of thought.

Carrying this idea into the sciences that concern men, Broussais and Comte established the notion that there is no essential difference in theory between health and disease, social order and revolution, sanity and insanity. These contrasted states, which differ so much by their consequences, are in each class never anything but variations of the same abstract phenomenon, differing only in intensity and rate of speed. Between a healthy lung and a diseased one, for example, there is only a slight and measurable degree of nervous and circulatory activity. In both the same elements are in action; only, the activity of these elements differs according to the state of the organism, regarded as healthy or diseased. "To be accurate, the organism differs at every moment of the state of health; but this difference, variation, oscillation, does not then pass certain limits and brings no danger to the habitual situation of the individual beings concerned." [4]

In the same line of thought, revolution differs from order only in the passing exaggeration of some of the factors of society; there enter into the revolution no new elements, no abnormal societal manifestations, no phenomenon which does not obey sociological laws. There is but a temporary disturbance of the regularity of the operation of some one or more of the various societal elements with a resulting dislocation, more or less permanent, of the equilibrium of which they are a part. The same position is now taken in relation to sanity and insanity. For Comte there was no difference in kind

3. Laffitte, *1*, 200–201.
4. Laffitte, *1*, 208.

between these states of mind: no new phenomena are met in passing from one to the other, no possession by spirits, say, but simply unusual manifestations of established psychological regularities.

In short, the science of man, objectively speaking, no more than the science of the world, is divided into two distinct parts, one dealing with the so-called normal and another, quite distinct, comprising perturbations, exceptions, disturbances, abnormalities. All that happens is normal in the sense that it is all an outcome of the operation of observed uniformities. In a scientific sense normal can only signify a mean between variations, plus and minus. That is to say, "normal" is a quantitative and not a qualitative term. No doubt some of these disturbances of regularity are more important to man than others. The relatively indifferent ones, mainly in the natural world, with which man has hitherto been better acquainted, he dismisses as disturbances or perturbations; the important ones, chiefly social, he distinguishes qualitatively by special names, such as disease, revolution, sins, etc., but from the objective viewpoint they are one and all in each case only variations around a normal state.

From this standpoint of science the sociologist regards the data of his isolate. All that happens therein is the outcome of the process of collective cumulation. The regularities of the recurrence of societal phenomena are the object of sociological observation and meditation; from the world mentally so pictured flow inductions. They indicate that the intensity and rate of speed at which the process called societal operates may vary but the underlying structure is inalterable, hence certain inferences which may be stated briefly.

First, societal pathology cannot be separated from societal normality. In theory there is no basic distinction to be made between the phenomena of revolution or maladjustment, etc., and the facts of the normal life of society. Such differences as are established are quantitative and not qualitative, i.e., they differ in "more or less" from the normal. It is natural that the plus variations should in the past have received greater attention than the minus, but now that revolutions have been connected with the normal it should follow that minus variations should come into the picture too. Then there would be a scale of societal phenomena running from stagnation to revolution on a continuous quantitative scale. In any case, the line between the normal and the abnormal becomes dim; the more extreme cases are still valuable for study, not because they are thought still to reveal to observation a different kind of phenomenon, but because, being extreme, they reveal more clearly than normal phenomena do the working of one or another factor of variation.

Second, it becomes possible in theory for sociological statements to take quantitative form. Differences between societal situations of varying kinds being only differences due to variations in the intensity or speed with which the societal process works, qualitative distinctions disappear. "The man has a temperature of 105°. Draw your own conclusions." For sociologists to be able to make comparable pronouncements, what is needed is first a knowledge of the societal system and second a unit of measure. Already something of the kind desired can be done. "For five generations the intensity of cumulation of collective efforts in the societal subisolate termed economic has been very much greater than that in any of the other static elements. Draw your own conclusions." Or: "For five generations the number of societal concentrations has been greater in the subisolate of economics than anywhere else in the societal system." Or, better still, "For y years in a population of p people, m societal man-hours yearly have been spent in industrial activity."

From the foregoing considerations, descriptive of the character of a modifiable necessity, emerges an inductive view of the nature of the phenomena grouped under the term "societal change." They are all seen to be results of the societal process operating under a condition of equilibrium among the various cultural elements. These elements may abstractly be regarded as influencing one another by forces, which thus compose a system. Hence the system, the structure, the arrangement of the elements is inalterable. So long as it endures societal manifestations continue, varying in intensity or speed. If the equilibrium is broken, i.e., dislocated beyond possibility of re-establishment, the system disappears and societal phenomena with it.

In the days when observation of social phenomena was casual and unsystematic, attention was inevitably drawn to those happenings which were unusual and striking. The plus variations were obviously most likely to attract notice. They were considered to be different in kind from those occurring in the ordinary course of events and so were given special names. Continued observation raised to a systematic level disclosed a certain similarity underlying both the usual and the unusual, the regular and the exceptional.

At this stage of social induction the distinction between normal and abnormal was drawn. Analysis on this level revealed the composite nature of the concept social and thus societal phenomena became an authentic isolate. This analytical advance facilitated the replacement of distinctions in kind by differences in degree. Societal phenomena came to form a continuum presenting to observation a mean around which oscillate variations. The quantitative begins to displace the qualitative. Societal phenomena are homogeneous all and vary only with respect to the intensity or rate of speed with which the process that produces them operates. Once this advance had been made, facts of observation long isolated could be correlated, empirical discoveries related and synthesized. The whole body of societal observations thus moves toward that unity of conception which is the mark and the goal of science.

The concept of system throws light not only upon the nature of societal change but also upon the nature of the factors which bring the change about. In a system, the elements which compose it are by definition abstracted from all the other constituents of the universe and thought of as a unit. The influences they exert upon one another, i.e., the forces in play, are all internal therefore in contrast to all other forces elsewhere, which are of course external. Hence there are to begin with two sets of forces which produce changes in the manifestations of a system: those within and those without, the internal and the external. Since the internal forces are intimately concerned with the existence of the system, the influence they exert may be said to be direct. Other—external—forces affect only the sum of the forces already equilibrated in the system and do so only by their relations with the system as a whole. Hence with regard to changes in the system these forces are not only external but also indirect factors of change. Finally, since the internal, direct forces are the immediate source whence flow the phenomena characteristic of the system, the word "cause" seems to be strictly in point in relation to them, and so these forces may be termed *causal*.

The external and indirect forces influence the operation of a given system in two ways. If they are more general than the internal forces and therefore anterior to them in the ascending order of increasing complication, then the internal forces operate in a milieu formed by the more general forces in question. The latter compose the conditions under which the given system must exist and operate. Hence the influence of such external and indirect forces as are more general than those equilibrated in the given system may be described as *conditioning*.

If however these external forces are in some cases less general and more complicated than the forces composing the system and so form a superior class of phenomena in the hierarchy, they still exert influence upon the system, but only in a way to vary the operation of one or more factors of the system, not the equilibrium as a whole. That is to say, these superior, indirect, less general forces do not condition the existence of the system but only modify the operation of one or more of the forces composing it. They may therefore be termed *modifying* influences.

Any system then is subject to change through the action of three kinds of influence: internal, direct, causal; external, indirect, conditioning; external, indirect, modifying. If the internal forces are relatively equal in action and the external forces uniform, then the resulting phenomena will tend to be undiversified in kind and constant in degree and will offer little occasion for distinguishing between them as normal or abnormal. If one of the internal forces is predominant or can be made to be so, a difference at once appears between the manifestations to which it mainly gives rise and those due mainly to other, subordinate, elements of the system. Here the classification of phenomena into normal and abnormal begins to be pertinent, but obviously all the phenomena are characteristic of the system and so do not differ in kind. Finally, if various elements of the system are intermittently predominant or can be made to be so, the outcome will be a variety of phenomena differing considerably from one another. Here the concept of the mean will come into play, and along with it the notion of perturbations. The mean will be the normal and the variants the abnormal; but the essential homogeneity of the phenomena will be no more in question than before. When the variants reach the point of abnormality which threatens the existence of the system, special terms will be utilized to mark their disruptive tendencies; and often the use of these terms conceals the fact that the phenomena so qualified are the same in kind as the others and differ from them only in degree. When scientific advance reveals that only a quantitative difference separates what were once distinguished qualitatively, the discipline in which this advance is made moves toward unity of doctrine. In the case of sociology, as will be seen, a societal system has been shown to exist; the normal and the abnormal, including the pathological, have been united and a place reserved for the appropriate treatment of causal, conditioning, and modifying factors of change.

The doctrines outlined above Comte was the first to apply to sociology, in the last chapter of his *Social Statics*. His main purpose there to begin with was to oppose the opinions—based understandably enough upon the fact of the immense variability of sociological phenomena—that the latter were subject to no natural laws whatever. Implied in such an argument is obviously the question of the limits within which societal change can be effected. And this is indeed the title of the chapter: "The positive theory of the general limits of variation proper to the human order." The discussion was to take him far, as will later be seen.

He began with a brief analysis of the internal forces at work in the sociological system: *"Every class of phenomena has its own laws which would subsist even if all the rest of the economy of nature could disappear."* "Every real order can be changed spontaneously by its own exercise," i.e., by "the spontaneous accomplishment of its distinctive phenomena." [5] The cause of these changes is the operation of the forces composing the system. They act and react upon one another with varying degrees of intensity; the state of the system ceases to be what it was; the successive states differ when compared. In both structure and movement, uniformities are observable. Hence there are two main divisions of sociology: statics, dealing with the structure of the system and concerned mainly with the intensity of the forces involved; and dynamics, devoted to the study of the development that results from the continued operation of the forces composing the system and dealing primarily with the rate of speed of the development and the changes due to variations in the rate of speed. No special treatment of these causes of societal change is possible since they are obviously the foundations, the contents, and the main divisions of the science as an independent and general discipline.

5. *Politique*, 2, 431, 430.

But what of the external forces, and particularly those that are more general than the sociological and therefore condition the manifestations of the less general phenomena? Comte points out the various possibilities that are presented by the hierarchy of isolates leading from the mathematical, the astronomical, etc., to the sociological; but instead of studying each in relation to societal phenomena, he combines the geometrico-mechanical, i.e., astronomical with the physical and chemical into one composite group under the name of "the material milieu." "These influences are the easiest to understand and the first whose systematic study was undertaken by our intellect," [6] i.e., by Hippocrates in his work on *Airs, Waters, and Places*. From a strictly logical point of view, the influence of the material milieu upon the phenomena studied by sociology is mainly exerted mediately through its effects upon the phenomena of vitality; but there are cases where this material influence seems to be, or might be, immediate. Comte cites two such possibilities: "these influences, celestial or terrestrial, continuous or temporary" [7] might act to lengthen or shorten man's life; they might affect population, with regard to either its density or its movements. In each case societal consequences of importance would follow.

The second class of external, conditioning influences is that comprised in the vital order. These are more influential than the material, since the sociological order is immediately subordinate to the biological. Unfortunately, laments Comte, the state of knowledge on this subject is so imperfect as to admit of no useful conclusions. Here would be the place, he says, for a truly scientific investigation of the effects of the milieu upon human differentiation. The nature of race, with all its implications, is involved. Nothing however can be said on the subject, for it has hitherto remained outside scientific discussion. It has been the monopoly of "those pretended thinkers who want to make pronouncements in sociology without knowing arithmetic" and "who now use races, as their predecessors used climate, to give themselves cheaply the appearance of being scientific." [8]

In the absence of acquired knowledge on the subject of change in biological phenomena themselves and so of the nature of bio-

6. *Politique*, 2, 446.
7. *Politique*, 2, 447.
8. *Politique*, 2, 450.

logical influences upon sociological phenomena, Comte turns to another factor of societal change which because of its nature and the attention it has received from later writers, especially the anthropologists, demands consideration here. Since Comte's own words express very clearly how he came to the problem, they will be quoted entire.

Abstract sociology conceives of the formation and development of the true "Great-Being" [i.e., the super-organism Man] as proceeding from a single nucleus. As a matter of fact, *the laws of existence and those of evolution must be essentially the same as regards all possible centers of this immense expansion.* Whichever nucleus may prevail, and whatever the way in which the others may finally rally about it,—these matters can in no wise affect the fundamental conceptions of sociology, as logic must have given my eminent predecessor Condorcet to understand. This double determination will become only an important application of true social science, but without participating in its construction. *Even were the multiplicity of human nuclei destined always to persist in such a fashion as to render impossible the unity of the terrestrial Great-Being, sociology, statical or dynamical, would not thereby be profoundly affected.* Yet when Condorcet with admirable logical instinct instituted his hypothesis of a single people, he certainly felt that such an abstraction, although at first indispensable, would subsequently demand an adequate restitution of *international influences.*[9]

Comte, it will be seen, was raising in his own way and in his own words the question of diffusion.

Although our laws of existence and of evolution everywhere preserve their principal character, and their spontaneous preponderance determines the essential movement of every human nucleus, they cannot preserve it from the reactions of others. *When statical or dynamical explanations are pushed to a certain degree of precision,* the necessity of taking these mutual modifications into consideration for the purpose becomes sensible. Happily negligible for the ordinary purposes of our socio-

9. *Politique,* 2, 451–452.

logical theories, they sometimes become indispensable for certain exceptional cases.[10]

For example, at the beginning of the Middle Ages "the occidental movement was notably affected by political changes coming upon it from afar; so that the general state of Europe was at the time dependent upon that of Asia, even the most oriental part." [11]

There is then another factor of cultural change. It consists in "the reactions, necessary but intermittent, which result from the multiplicity of nuclei." [12] But this factor offers no difficulty from the standpoint of abstract sociology. "The judicious Ferguson was the first to glimpse the true principle of this new source of normal variations. In the present context it falls within the scope of the principle of Broussais, since it consists in regarding all such alterations whatever as never being able to affect anything but the intensity or the speed of the fundamental case." [13] It thus accords with the general principle of modifiability which prescribes that "the examination of all alterations whatever be subordinated to the fundamental appreciation of the normal type." [14] This class of factors of change is obviously related to the principal causes but is always subordinate to them. Hence it constitutes an accessory group. Its importance is great; it may indeed in a particular case overshadow the influence emanating from either the material or the vital orders.

What Comte was doing in the passages quoted can be expressed perhaps more conveniently in the more abstract phraseology of the present volume. So worded, the thought would run as follows: The societal process regarded from the completely abstract point of view is not concerned with any population, single or multiple, nor with any nucleus or nuclei. Yet it may be envisaged as operating in a particular group or groups. Such a group as a part of the concrete reality would exist in a particular location and have its own biological characteristics. Spencer was probably thinking on this line when he said that "every society displays phenomena that are ascrib-

10. *Politique*, 2, 452.
11. *Politique*, 2, 452.
12. Comte, *Politique*, 2, 453.
13. Comte, *Politique*, 2, 453.
14. Comte, *Politique*, 2, 450.

able to the characters of its units and to the conditions under which they exist," [15] i.e., to intrinsic and extrinsic factors.

Collective experience, when cumulated by a particular group in a particular environment, would tend to follow the lines of development inherent in the extrinsic and intrinsic factors of Spencer. A given climate, surface, flora and fauna would inevitably influence the activities of the group and tend to concentrate them on aspects of the reality which would be subordinated or neglected by groups differently situated. In short, these conditions would orient the societal process without altering it in any essential way whatever. Thus with regard to any nucleus of human development a third factor of change would be added to the two basic factors inherent in the process abstractly conceived. That is to say, in addition to the intensity and speed with which the process universally operates a third factor, orientation, must be added when a particular population is in question.

The logical outcome of the addition of the factor of orientation to the factors of intensity and speed is the rise of a number of isolated groups, distinct from one another materially and vitally and for that reason differing culturally. At some point in the life histories of these groups they will come into contact with one another. Because their cultures have developed with different intensities and speeds and in different directions, the groups in question will be able to profit in some degree from one another's experience. Their cultures, that is, will be more or less symplegmatic. Diffusion, the transfer of achieved results from one group to another, will be possible and even influential because after all the phenomena in question are the results of a single process. They are all societal developments and so but variants of a homogeneous class. Intercultural influences, the phenomena of diffusion, will fall into the societal continuum at some point. Hence as in any other case they will be classed as normal or variant and so brought into line with all other societal phenomena, thus making possible still greater unity in the internal structure of sociology.

Comte had thus provided a logical structure for the strictly societal factors of change, i.e., those inherent in the very nature of sociological phenomena. On this level statical and dynamical factors were the principal ones; subordinate to them were the influences

15. *Principles of Sociology, 1*, 8–9.

emanating from international, i.e., intercultural relations. From these direct influences, principal and accessory, constant and intermittent, he passed to the conditioning influences, mediate and immediate, exerted by the material and the vital orders. All that remained was to determine the nature of the second class of indirect influences, those exerted by orders of phenomena higher in the scientific hierarchy than the societal—the class which has been referred to already as the modifying factors of change.

But at this point a crisis in thought is at hand; its dissolution was to have far-reaching consequences. Modifying factors are by definition those operating so to speak from above downward, i.e., from the superior isolates of the scientific encyclopedia to the inferior; conditioning factors exert influence from below upward. The range of phenomena that form the foundation of the hierarchy would not be, could not be conditioned as just defined because there would be no isolates below them; the highest range could not be modified as just defined because there would be no level of abstraction above it. The logic of the position is as simple as it is unassailable.

Now for Comte, and indeed for his successors from the completion of the *Philosophie* onward, sociology was the summit of the hierarchy of the sciences. In most cases it still is. Inevitably, then, there could be with regard to sociology no external, indirect influences acting from above. There is no above for sociology. For this final science, that is, and for the phenomena it isolates, there are therefore *no* modifying factors.

Nevertheless, in the final chapter of the *Social Statics* there is a section dealing with such factors, and in relation to sociological phenomena. Logic says there should be no such section. Comte, faithful to the facts, writes and inserts it. The only possible reconciliation between the facts and the logic is the displacement of sociology as the summit of the hierarchy and its subordination to another, higher level of abstraction. This is the position which Comte takes. From this moment on, the hierarchy no longer consists of six members crowned by sociology, as in the *Philosophie;* it will always hereafter consist of seven members. It remains now to show the nature of the seventh science.

Somewhat special attention must be given Comte's unexpected innovation in theory. Not merely is it an interesting development in logic; its importance is much greater. To begin with it was a critical point in Comte's intellectual growth; then it was a far-reaching change in sociological theory; finally, since Comte was the first to make the advances in a conscious and systematic way, it was a stage in the evolution of human thought. And since in relation to this volume Comte's position is just under the surface of every page, there is another reason to be added to the important ones mentioned for examining somewhat closely into the nature of Comte's achievement. His discovery concerned mainly the individual and his place in theory; hence a departure at this point from the straightforward logic of this chapter to open a parenthesis, to be kept within the most rigid limits, as to the nature of the individual.

What had happened was that Comte after a lifetime of thought had come to realize that Man, so to speak, is not completely analyzed and his constituent phenomena all properly disposed of when the animal and the socius are assigned each to its own science. Clearly enough there is the animal in Man; all Comte had done in this regard was to systematize the work of the biologists. Clearly enough the socius is an essential part of Man; Comte from the beginning of his career had grasped the point when he saw that a new science, social physics, was needed to study the influence of one generation upon another. But he had not, even at the beginning of his *Politique*, realized that there were elements in Man's makeup that are not explainable on the basis of either or both of the two sets of principles and laws just mentioned. Not that any new phenomena were in point; after so many generations of men there was little truly new to be discovered. It was the reference of all human manifestations to either biology or sociology that caused certain facts to be misunderstood or even disregarded. To take a homely illustration, what light can either of the two sciences mentioned throw upon the gloomy feelings that ofttimes follow or accompany a severe case of indigestion? The indigestion is explicable, but the gloomy feelings, expressing themselves intellectually in pessimistic judgments on all things—what about them?

Certainly they are not the result of any collective cumulations. They are, Comte saw more and more clearly, a special case of those individual perturbations which do not sensibly alter collective ex-

NATURE AND FACTORS OF SOCIETAL CHANGE

istence and which are of less and less importance as that existence is more and more developed. Far from being cumulative, "their mutual neutralization among different individuals leaves subsisting, in sociology, only the permanent influence of the truly collective attributes, even when simple objective solidarity only is regarded. But these phenomena must still less affect the study of subjective continuity which prevails more and more as regards the social order. For they neutralize themselves more in the succession of generations than in the combination of individuals or families." [16] But because they are neutralized they are not therefore inexistent; and the insistence upon the sociological, its increasing clarification, makes even more evident than before the existence of a class of phenomena hitherto unrecognized.

Moreover, on another level, Comte after many years of emotional starvation in his personal life had found release for his affections in the person of Clotilde de Vaux. No biological or sociological theories could throw any light upon the reorientation of his mind that followed. There are, there must be sources of human motivation that lie beyond the biological processes however defined and persist through the operations of collective cumulation. There must be what later writers have called an inner series of reality. Here are the ultimate sources of man's activity. Here is the individual as contrasted with the animal or the socius. So there must be a place for a new science. There must be a true anthropology, a science of man in his ultimate reality. Such was the movement of Comte's thought. And because his thought was presently to become a part of the universal development of science, interest in its movement is transmuted from mere biographical record into concern with the growth of human intelligence. For a brief period the man and the scientific movement coincide.

Now what Comte was discovering was the significance in Man's makeup of the *psychical constants*—which would endure through every variety of societal change, simply being connected now with one image or view, now with another as the process of collective cumulation gives rise to them. It was not that Comte had discovered these constants at this moment for the first time. On the contrary, he had been aware of them all through the *Philosophie* and in fact ever since he had read Gall. What he had discovered was the signifi-

16. *Politique, 2, 438.*

cance, the place, the supreme importance of the orectic elements, the factors of affective impulsion, the constituents of the personality —which he and all his contemporaries had considered to be strictly biological in nature. The new point of view was far more difficult for Comte's contemporaries than it is for the generation of Pareto and Freud. It was indeed almost incomprehensible then, and his work passed into obscurity. Yet the fact remains that what later men have sought in their own way was the subject matter of Comte's seventh member of the scientific encyclopedia, namely, the science of the individual phenomenon, based on a new isolate and so laying the basis for a new science, the true science of anthropology. In short Comte was instituting and was the first to institute a positive psychology.

A brief return to a passage quoted at length in an earlier chapter of this volume will give point to the remarks made in the preceding paragraph. Psychoanalysis, it was said there, is a dynamic approach to mental life which it considers as the manifestation and interplay of tendencies and strivings that express themselves in motor behavior. These dynamic forces are conditioned by the energy-consuming processes that constitute the biological phenomenon life; they are oriented by the requirements of collective life as they take shape in a given culture.

Comte's action in establishing a seventh science in the hierarchy brought his thought into essential coincidence with the position just defined. It made possible the distribution of all phenomena above the inorganic into three classes. The concrete realities are three: life, culture, personality. There are three corresponding abstract sciences: biology, sociology, psychology. There are three abstract phenomena forming the respective isolates: the continuous renewal of material substance, the cumulation of collective results, and the nature, relations, and integration of the psychic constants. These three domains Comte was the first to see and more and more clearly to define.

Now Comte as early as the forties of the last century was dealing systematically with the data pertinent to the seventh science of the hierarchy and had been more than casually interested in them long before. As he said later, the seventh science, "like any other, has its own inductions, in the making of which popular instinct or feminine reason never waited upon the indications of philosophers or priesthoods." [17] It was these spontaneous inductions to which his attention had been long turned. He found them in proverbs and language, in the picturing of human nature by poets, dramatists, novelists, in the directing of human motive by priesthoods, in the manifestations of the mystics, and on a somewhat more systematic level in the study of man by philosophers and particularly the Scottish school, in the observation of animals by men like George Leroy, in the connections between the physical and the moral as shown by Cabanis, in the demonstration by cerebral physiologists like Gall that the brain is not a unit but an apparatus, in the efforts made unwittingly by the phrenologists to analyze human nature by an exhaustive allocation of parts of the brain to specific aptitudes and dispositions. On the basis of all this and his own studies of history and observation of men, Comte by 1851 had arrived at his own list of psychical constants. In regard to it he had made but one mistake. He had considered the whole matter as a section, the last and highest, of biology and therefore the immediate antecedent of sociology. It was not until he came in the last chapter of the *Social Statics* to consider the forces which exert a modifying influence upon the working of the societal process that he began to see the essentially individual and psychical nature of the material he was dealing with. The result was the separation from biology of the phenomena, now seen to form a true isolate, their consolidation in a new science, and its installation at the head of the scientific hierarchy.

From this redistribution of phenomena and reallocation of relative position flow all the changes that Comte's later work was to show as compared with his earlier, down to and including the first half of the *Politique,* though it required time for many of the implications of the new position to become clear. Most of these modifications in theory must here be passed over; some of them will be discussed later. One of them only seems to demand attention here because it will serve not only to illustrate the consequences of Comte's new position but also to justify the list of societal elements on which the statical section of the present volume is built.

First among the elements which Comte analyzes in his *Social Statics* is religion. In the fourth volume of the *Politique,* where sociology is once more analyzed, the subject of religion finds no place. Since the indications of the later analysis have guided the

17. *Politique,* 2, 438.

choice of cultural elements in this volume, to justify Comte's shift in opinion will serve a double purpose. The key to the change in attitude toward religion, from regarding it as an essential constituent of sociology to eliminating it from the science altogether, seems (for Comte never explained the excision) clearly to lie in the discovery first, that religion considered as a cultural phenomenon is a composite made up of parts belonging to different isolates and second, that of its component phenomena, sociological and psychological, the essential phenomenon belonged in the psychical and not the societal isolate.

The primary question is of course the nature of religion. Comte, believing at first that religion was an element of statics, i.e., a part of the universal pattern of culture, had gone to the study of cultures, ancient and modern, literate and preliterate, to find what religion was. That is to say, he sought a functional definition of the phenomenon, to be expressed not in terms of its object but in terms of what it did and does for mankind. He found that in all cultures religion serves a double purpose: it unites individuals and it unifies or integrates personalities. Examining religion from this functional standpoint, he saw that it was composed of two main parts: a dogma, i.e., an intellectual part dealing with beliefs, and a cult and a regime which together compose a moral or affective part dealing with feelings and acts. In other words every religion has two main divisions, a domain of faith and a domain of love. In the terms of the present volume, religion has a double basis: collective cumulations on one side and psychic constants on the other.

But Comte was long in discovering the significance of his own analysis. The difficulty was that at the time he was convinced that the psychical aspects were purely biological and as such were antecedent to sociology. They were therefore only conditioning factors for a phenomenon whose root was societal. Yet his treatment of the subject wavers. It is curious to see, in the first chapter of the *Social Statics*—where religion is discussed as the first of the statical elements of sociology—how Comte in spite of his theoretical position at the time constantly follows a spontaneous inclination to invert the order dictated by the logic of his position and make the sociological element subordinate to the psychological. Yet on one point he was definite and unwavering: faith and love are distinct and separable.

But since they are two things and not one, the moment Comte came to see that his psychic constants were not biological in nature but belonged in a separate category, being a true isolate, and to put this category at the head of the encyclopedia, a corresponding change in the evaluation of the constituent elements of religion was inevitable. What had before been a secondary and conditioning factor now became the primary and principal phenomenon. In other words the unity, the harmony, the integration of the many drives and urges, i.e., the psychic constants, now became the central phenomenon and the collective and cumulative, i.e., sociological elements became peripheral and conditioning. Hence the ultimate reapportionment of the constituent phenomena of religion, one part only remaining in the domain of sociology with the other, perhaps the major portion, going to the domain of positive psychology.

Love and faith were still united, but now faith, the sociological factor, was only an antecedent and conditioning influence; the essence of the phenomenon was psychical. In the terms of an earlier chapter of this volume, the process of collective cumulation produces a series of images or views which activate the sources of impulsion; in the religious instance these views take the form of a succession of fantasies, of beliefs and appropriate images, polytheism, say, or monotheism, with the whole body of configurations, symbols, etc., which grows out of them. These views and images stir the psychic constants into feelings and desires which are then exteriorized in acts. Moreover, the stimulation and direction of feelings is a basic interest for men, and around this interest grows an institution, the church.

But the feelings, the orectic elements, are constant; they are the same whatever the doctrines or associations involved; only, some of the latter are better or more important than others in that they are more effective in unifying the constants and so producing a more closely integrated personality. But once more the unifying and integrating effect by whatever means produced, and even more clearly the psychic elements that have to be integrated, are all elements of a psychological, not a sociological, process and so are outside the domain of sociology entirely. In short, religion in the concrete, cultural sense is a composite phenomenon, a phenomenon of social psychology, consisting of a societal element, conditioning, accessory, and secondary, and a psychical element, determinative, principal, and primary. Religion then has no place among the statical elements of sociology; those collective cumulations which are the conditioning factors referred to can be and are adequately treated under the heads of association, communication, and direction. The essence of the matter, being primarily individual and personal, concerned with the springs and sources of affection and impulsion, is for a positive psychology.

The implications of the position so summarily outlined in the digression just closed are too many and far-reaching even to be mentioned here. Only one of them all demands attention at the moment, and that because it answers the question being asked when the logical development of the chapter was suspended. The point is that Comte had found there were factors of an individual nature influencing sociological phenomena *from above*. Hence there *were* modifying factors to be taken into consideration in accounting for all varieties of societal change. From this point of view the fact that the recognition of a modifying factor, introducing variation into the operation of the societal process, demanded the reconstruction of the whole upper half of the scientific hierarchy and the subordination of sociology to a positive psychology is an incidental matter and will here be treated as such.

The essential point is that Comte had come to recognize the existence of a class of phenomena above the sociological in the hierarchical order; and since it *was* above, i.e., less general even than sociology, it could exercise upon the working of the societal process only a modifying influence, as already defined. The words in which the nature of this indirect factor of change was for the first time described are the following: "The human order" must for the purpose of applying to it the general principles of modifiability first be "definitively divided into its two necessary modes: the one collective, the other individual, which constitute respectively social existence and moral existence." And Comte adds, in words which hint at the kind of difficulties which must have turned his mind more and more into the line of thought which was finally to bring him to recognize a seventh science in the hierarchy, that this position "results directly from a last encyclopedic extension of the universal principle of my positive classification, based on decreasing generality and increasing dependence. It can now be seen that this final part of the abstract series has no less importance than those that precede it. If such a series were not carried to this normal termination, concrete notions could not adequately be related to it." [18]

"This irrevocable subdivision of the human order into collective and individual" [19] makes it possible to introduce the influence of an indirect, modifying factor into the discussion of change in the collective order: that of the person.

Its influence, when discussion is limited to the particular aspects of any one nucleus of mankind, can therein become more considerable than any other. Thus the principal attention of the public and even of thinkers, was always turned toward it before the advent of sociology. This puerile irrationality, which represents individual forces as the sovereign arbiters of the human movement, often produced profound and dangerous aberrations, when the pride of chiefs was seconded by the illusion of peoples. Nevertheless, the practical instinct of true statesmen always made them actively feel the necessary limits of their power, constantly subordinated as it is to the whole of each situation. . . .

Only a monstrous pride could have suggested a belief in unlimited power to the retrograde dictator to whose tyranny France was too long subjected. . . . But the very example of this personal influence directly furnishes the best confirmation of the general limits which restrict such modifications, like all the others, to simple differences in intensity or speed. For this retrograde domination, developed during a profound anarchy, —which reduced objective opposition as much as possible,— ended nevertheless only in delaying by a generation at most the spontaneous extension of the occidental revolution.

Today, a later and more tragic example could be cited. "Never can an individual arrest a social movement." [20] *L'homme s'agite et l'humanité le mène.*

In this passage Comte was drawn to make more of the limitations upon individual action than of the modifying influence of individ-

18. *Politique*, 2, 432, 435.
19. *Politique*, 2, 439.
20. *Politique*, 2, 454.

ual upon societal phenomena. Laffitte, developing Comte's thought, puts the matter more positively:

> Every mechanical system can move, by displacing its center of gravity, only under the action of a force exterior to the system itself. This theorem applies to sociology. And in the light of it I have defined a great man: a force exterior to the social [societal] system. For a great progress to be accomplished, it is necessary that the superior man who accomplishes it should be able, in a certain measure to isolate himself from others for a shorter or longer period, to elaborate the actions or the conceptions which will give a new impulsion to the social system. But what is true for the great man is true for all men in different degrees, since many men make certain advances, at least upon a modest scale.[21]

The striking fact that emerges from the foregoing analysis and classification of the factors of societal change is the great number of variables that are involved. It would seem that of all phenomena the societal are among the most unstable and mutable. The conclusion is valid. In the hierarchy of isolates complication increases as generality diminishes. This result is inevitable, given the hierarchical arrangements, since each successive higher level of abstraction is conditioned by all that precede it. The statement is illustrated by the case of the vital order, say; and it is equally valid for the societal order insofar as its development is purely spontaneous, i.e., where it is effected blindly with no awareness of the conditioning factors. In other words, by virtue of its very position in the hierarchy the societal order is characterized by a high degree of imperfection.

There are however two elements in the situation which tend to counteract this tendency toward variability, instability, and imperfection. The first of these compensatory features is the very fact that there are so many variables. Each of them is in effect an opportunity if not an invitation for modification. Societal arrangement for example cannot be altered, but the intensity of this or that societal force can be augmented or diminished. Where the societal

21. *Cours de philosophie première*, 2, 188.

order cannot be changed directly it can be varied to at least some extent if the conditioning factors can be modified. In short, wherever there is a variable there is an occasion or opportunity or possibility of intervention.

The second influence counteracting the tendency toward extreme societal imperfection is the nature of the societal process. It consists in the fact that the cumulation of collective experience gives an ever increasing sum of knowledge concerning the existence and operation of sociological uniformities, both statical and dynamical, and of the various conditioning factors as well. That is to say, the mental picture of the societal reality becomes more and more accurate, or in other words the socioexperiential constituent in ideation increases as collective life lengthens, broadens, and deepens. When this influence is combined with the fact of variability and the existence of so many variables, the outcome is that spontaneous imperfection is more and more counterbalanced and offset by systematic modification.

The position just taken can be elucidated and strengthened by recalling the dismissal of the entities will and intelligence effected in an earlier chapter. The will is a resultant; it is the impulse that becomes dominant after the possibilities of the situation have been pictured by the intellect. As the pictured possibilities vary, the will varies with them. It comes into being when feelings are aroused and become desires. The desires are informed by ideation; they are exteriorized when actions are performed. The consequence is that a clearly pictured socioexperiential synthesis conditions the operation of impulsion and so tends to create the will necessary for its realization.

Obviously the impulsion is not bound to exteriorize itself in a particular way. There may be purely subjective influences at work so strong as to blind the will to the pictured reality; there may be contrasting and alternative pictures. Nevertheless, the normal will is exteriorized in the form of the image constructed from materials emanating from the world without; abnormality is precisely the failure to be so guided; when the mental picture is formed wholly at the behest of the impulsions, madness is near.

Two illustrations of the way in which societal ideation conditions impulsion may be given. One is the set of concepts, biological in nature, symbolized by the term "eugenics." What happened in this instance was that increasing biological knowledge took form in the pictured possibility of improving the human stock by processes of breeding. The possibilities thus presented activated many wills so strongly that the resulting impulsions became forces initiating and maintaining actions composing together a movement. It is true no doubt that the picture as originally constructed was too favorable, i.e., it was an imperfect view of the reality; but the movement was not halted by the discovery. The drive supplied the energy for increasing the accuracy of the picture; the impulsion became more intelligent, i.e., guided by a more accurate view of the conditions requisite for its exteriorization.

Even more to the point of showing how wills may be conditioned is the case of that synthesis of ideas summarized in the term "progress." Here the stimulus to the sources of impulsion was more general and more potent than that given by eugenics. No idea has had greater driving power in modern times; it is indeed one of the most distinctive characteristics of the modern mind. True, once more it was in its initial form too favorable a view of the reality, but discovery of the fact has not destroyed the idea; it has served only to increase the accuracy of the picture. In one form or another it still dominates thinking on social matters; and even in those wills where the picture arouses antagonism, opposition serves only to develop the idea. Its force is immense, though in some cases, where the implementation of the idea is not as yet adequately designed, that force is virtual, as in the case for example of the conception symbolized by the term "an economy of abundance."

Into such questions as that of motivation, involving the phenomena isolated under the name psychology—a level of abstraction above sociology—this volume has no right to penetrate; its concern is solely with the societal. Nevertheless, it has seemed necessary to say enough on the matter to illustrate the relations between the two levels, to make clear the meaning as regards sociology of a modifiable necessity, and to supply a commentary on Comte's summarizing statement: "In the natural hierarchy as a whole, the necessary increase of complication in proportion as generality diminishes, always produces two inverse results, which tend more and more to compensate one another, by opposing modifiability to imperfection." [22]

22. *Politique*, 2, 460.

CHAPTER 19: *The Limits of Societal Modifiability*

To have shown that between normal and abnormal societal phenomena lies only a quantitative difference; to have distinguished between the primary and secondary factors of societal change; to have analyzed and classified these factors so as to make clear how great is the number of variables involved; to have found in these variables the source of societal imperfection; to have revealed these imperfections as so many opportunities and invitations to intervene on the basis of acquired knowledge: to have done so much is to have advanced far toward the constitution of sociology as a science.

Nevertheless, the full range of societal phenomena has not yet been covered, even from the statical point of view. The difficulty is that the concept of the normal is hard to make precise when there are many different cases to be covered. What is normal in relation say to the range of societal phenomena encompassed by the word—for want of a better—"primitive"? Or, in the perspective of time, what among so many historical manifestations is normal? Evidently the analysis of societal phenomena on a statical principle must be pushed one stage further before the consolidation of the science is achievable.

The situation is as if in the astronomical system called solar there had been at first no central sun but a number of suns of nearly equal size. In this circumstance, there would have been so great a complication of phenomena that it is likely either that no order in the heavens would have been discovered or that the discovery of it would have been greatly delayed. And yet order there would have been during the whole period, all the same. But the absence of a dominant group of phenomena with which to contrast a minor group would have made difficult the drawing of a line between the mean and the oscillation. The normal in this case would have been inclusive of a very wide range of phenomena, so wide indeed as to have been well-nigh useless as the basis for the establishment of a law.

Assume, now, the operation among the minor suns of this hypothetical universe of a slow movement toward union and fusion, with the ultimate formation of a central and dominant sun. No new mechanical laws would in this case have come into existence; gravitation would have been as operative before as after. But certain consequences of importance would have followed all the same. In the first place, the tendency toward the formation of a dominant celestial body would at some point have become evident. Then in the second place, as this tendency manifested itself more and more strongly two classes of phenomena would have become observable: a major or normal or mean group and a minor or abnormal or oscillatory or perturbative group.

Study of the normal group would have made possible a first approximation of the celestial order, then a second and a third, until the phenomena had all been accounted for and the existence of regularity and uniformity among the heavenly bodies had been established. Once this advance had been made it would then have been possible to refer the discovered laws back to the earlier multisolar situation and show that the law of gravitation had been in operation all the time. Thus the constant undisturbed operation of the forces composing the system could have been established; and from their uniform working all the phenomena of the system could have been shown to proceed, one stage at a time.

Moreover, in such a system as just imagined, with an ultimately dominant central sun, the normal tends always to increase proportionately to the abnormal; hence an ever greater orderliness observable within the system as the oscillations become smaller compared with the mean. It is not of course that there is greater regularity in fact; the same uniformities are always in operation; the laws do not change. It is only that the relative importance of some phenomena manifested by the system increases in relation to the remaining phenomena of the same kind. With that increase the range of the mean widens and oscillations diminish proportionately. Perturbations, that is, become negligible as the limits of development possible to the system are approached.

The hypothetical astronomical situation just pictured is illuminative of the development of societal theory. In the beginning there were unnumbered nuclei of future societal expansion, each the outcome of all the factors of societal change, causal, conditioning, modifying. Each such center might be thought of as normal with a fringe of abnormality; or, as actually happened, the entire idea of normality could be rejected either as inapplicable or as nonexistent. In such a situation the very notion of uniformity seems irrelevant.

Nevertheless, insofar as these nuclei were societal there was among them an inevitable tendency toward growth and expansion. The process of collective cumulation, the essential societal phenomenon, works to lengthen the societal radius. In some cases all the factors of change, direct and indirect, come into equilibrium and remain so for long periods. But such a situation cannot be permanent. Even the physical milieu has its own changes—ice ages for example, and so for all the other factors. Movement then is inevitable.

In consequence there is a constant tendency toward the increase in size and decrease in number of societal centers. The fact is as certain inductively as it is deductively. An outcome of this situation is a decrease in the number of possible normal cases, a corresponding decrease in the abnormal, and so a clearer conception of the nature of the distinction between the two. The notion of uniformity in societal phenomena thus tends to gain greater support, and the concept of societal law becomes more easily tenable. Moreover the quantitative proportions change. As the range of the normal increases, the range of the abnormal decreases—i.e., the oscillations decrease in relation to the mean. The inference is an ever operative tendency for societal phenomena to attain a degree of regularity that would make the societal system comparable with the solar.

The implications of this concept, societal uniformity in the strict sense, are too profound and far-reaching to be made clear here. One thought however seems so directly an outgrowth of the general discussion and so illustrative of it as to demand inclusion. It concerns the cultural phenomenon usually known as war. Granted the validity of the preceding paragraphs, it is obvious that the search for the causes and still more the cause of war is futile, as indeed the indecisiveness of the enormous mass of material that has been written from the causal point of view makes a priori likely. War has no causes; it is an inevitable outcome of the entire cultural process, varying in nature with the development that process effects.

It is so for three reasons: first, the very nature of the societal process tends to produce fewer but larger and more powerful concentrations; second, the expansion of these centers inevitably brings them ultimately into contact; third, these contacts become conflicts, armed and implemented, so long as the uniformities at work beneath the surface are not understood or even perceived. Each societal nucleus as it expands considers only its own existence, past and present; it regards the foundations on which it is built as absolute; it alone is normal. In this situation any of the elements of the cultural pattern or any combination of them can serve as the occasion for the conflict which is inherent in the working out of the societal process. It may be over the means of maintenance, or the forms of association, or the differences between unifying fantasies, or rivalries of sovereignties that conflict occurs: these are not the causes of war; they are but excuses or occasions. War is a societal phenomenon. It is the outcome of the societal process at a given stage of development. No explanation less cogent could suffice to acquit man of the charges of impotence and stupidity to which his willingness to endure and participate in these conflicts seems to lay him open. Wars are not due to personal, psychical, individual reasons; they are societal and are waged by socii. All the tremendous forces which in other circumstances make men cooperators in societal efforts continue in play to make of them, however reluctantly, warriors. Such influences can be escaped only by withdrawal from the *societas*. The animal, the person—both are overwhelmed. In psychical terms, the will is fixed by the contemplation of a collective representation which limits the satisfaction of orexis to a given form of exergy. Participation in war is at a given moment the form which the action of a socius takes. Wishes, desires, intentions, counsels, plans are of no avail. Nothing can avail but a knowledge of the societal uniformities that underlie the development of culture. And even this knowledge is of avail only to accelerate the advance of societal phenomena to the stage where conflict is no longer the inevitable result of the societal process and so indirectly to hasten the end of war.

Advance toward such understanding of the societal process was made when the analysis of the forces working for societal change distinguished between the direct and the indirect. Still further advance resulted from the study of those historical cases where certain societal centers had become relatively dominant. In the Occident the critical case was the rise of Rome, as is evident from the records of scholarship in the 1500's and 1600's. A centralizing tendency in societal phenomena began then to be observable; a central societal "sun" was taking form. Both concepts quickly became the focal points of observation and theory.

This inductive approach on the basis of history was quickly supplemented by the deductive methods made possible by the rise of rational mechanics and particularly the dynamic aspects of that science associated with the name of D'Alembert. To summarize this development will make clear its historical significance and its relation to sociological theory.

Briefly, then, mechanics had its origin in antiquity and in particular with Archimedes. The latter formulated and developed certain fundamental concepts relating to bodies in equilibrium and so laid the foundations of statics. His ideas languished in antiquity and were not to be resumed until the seventeenth century. At this time his line of thought was followed by Stevin in a way which might have resulted in a complete theory of statics, reached directly. Such a success was not to follow, however. What Archimedes and his successors lacked was any treatment of the phenomena of motion. It was this aspect of mechanics, giving rise to dynamics, that absorbed the attention after Galileo of most thinkers in the field. Thus it was that the study of rest or equilibrium was reached by way of the study of motion rather than by the seemingly more logical line of approach.

The effort of these thinkers of the 1500's and 1600's resulted at first only in a number of unrelated discoveries relatively limited in scope and formulated as particular principles, essentially independent of one another. Throughout the early 1700's there was a general, rather spontaneous effort to bring these unrelated principles into logical relationship as the foundation of a new science, dynamics. The correlating idea which made this unification possible was the contribution of D'Alembert.

In 1749 in his *Traité de Dynamique* appeared the principle which was in effect to make possible the reduction of "every dynamical question to a statical one; and hence, by means of the conditions which connect the possible motions of the system," to "determine what the actual motions must be." [1] In other words, D'Alembert "ended all the earlier isolated investigations by rising to a general conception as to the manner of taking into account the dynamic reactions of the bodies of a system in virtue of their connections, and in establishing later the fundamental equations of the movements of any system whatever. This conception . . . consists essentially in reducing questions of movement to simple questions of equilibrium." [2] But he did this by an essentially dynamic procedure: he dealt with equilibrium as a special case of movement, one in which the forces producing movement were reduced to zero. It was Euler who completed the development of this idea, making it possible to deal with all the transformations of a mechanical system by translating them always into conditions of equilibrium, and so transmuted dynamical into statical questions. LaGrange, combining D'Alembert's principle with the principle of equilibrium of virtual velocities, finally raised mechanics to the logical height of a science deducible in all its aspects from a single fundamental theorem.

It was this theorem, essentially due to D'Alembert, that Comte generalized and extended to all systems, thus reducing questions of dynamics to principles of statics in all fields and so bringing sociology into position as a special case under a general law. In Comte's generalized formulation, the statement reads: "The law of movement is always to be subordinated to the law of existence by conceiving of all progress as the development of the corresponding order, all the conditions whatever of the latter controlling its changes, which taken together are its evolution." [3] It was the central point of this enunciation, progress is the development of order, which was to do even more for the organization of societal theory than did the principle of Broussais.

For this advance to be made however there were historically and are logically two requirements: first the demonstration of the specific nature of societal phenomena and second the recognition that these phenomena are so related as to form a system. Analysis of the

---

1. Quoted in W. Whewell, *The History of the Inductive Sciences* (3d ed. 2 vols. New York, Appleton, 1858), *1*, 365.
2. Comte, *Cours de philosophie positive*, *1*, 555–556.
3. *Système de politique positive*, *4*, 179.

factors of societal change into direct and indirect satisfies the first requirement; analysis of the data into classes, distinct but related, is the fulfillment of the second.

The words of Sumner and Keller express the thought implicitly and explicitly. "Society . . . is not composed of sets of institutions that have been analyzed out and separately examined; it is the whole of them acting together." But there "is no way to portray at once the whole intricacy of society and societal life"; hence classification is indispensable. Fortunately it is readily practicable, too. Societal phenomena "tend to form accretions about nuclei; and the nuclei are interests." All the resulting "institutions interpenetrate, as do the interests that summoned them into being. . . . Each of these interests produces consequences on the domain of the others which are often, indeed, foreign to its own satisfaction," [4] i.e., there is action and reaction among them. In short there are societal phenomena produced by classifiable forces which are related to one another as a system.

Along with the development in sociological theory which formulated and satisfied the two requirements stated above and were so identified with it as to be practically inseparable from it went the gradual transformation of statical into dynamical, and then of dynamical into statical, considerations. The study of societal order, that is, gradually gave rise to the concept of progress; then the latter was in turn reduced to the development of order. These terms were seldom used; most of the changes in theory went on under the guise of history. Nevertheless the transformation of dynamics into statics in sociology paralleled the like development in mechanics, as a brief review of the facts will make clear.

In the beginning was Aristotle, a sociological Archimedes. To him Comte gave the title creator of social statics because in Comte's opinion he had discovered the essential character of every collective organization, namely, the separation of offices and the combination of efforts. The validity of this attribution need not be challenged, even though Aristotle certainly never gave the thought the explicit formulation Comte ascribes to him. In any case, nothing was made of the general principle; and antiquity was satisfied with what has been called a circular or cyclical view of historical events —which was in fact only a sequential view of them, one social or-

4. *The Science of Society, 1*, 87, 88, 90.

ganism succeeding another, each rising and falling. The essentially statical nature of this conception is revealed by the belief in a decline from an ideal, a golden, age working itself out in practice in the necessity of supporting any desired social change as a return to an initial perfection, forever being blemished.

Christian theorists modified the sequential conception of history by dividing the human record into two parts, one of which was a preparation for the other. They thus vaguely introduced the idea of direction into the sequence; and Joachim of Floris sought to extend the idea by dividing man's existence into three parts: the ages respectively of the Father, the Son, and the Holy Spirit. Nothing came of this effort, and the accepted version of history became that represented by Bossuet in which the curve of social development, moving through Egypt, Greece, and Rome into the Christian Era, passed on into a region not of this world.

It was not until the 1500's and 1600's that the existence of a new historical problem began to be manifest. The parallelism between sociology and mechanics is thus double. Not only had a gap of millennia separated the rise of the two aspects of each subject, but in each case when the elaboration was resumed it was the dynamical development with which it began. For sociology the impelling force was the rapid growth of history in the fifteenth, sixteenth, and seventeenth centuries and its outcome in the picturing of a vast historical perspective in which events flowed one into another. Like mechanics, sociology began to study movements.

With the multiplication of data came the inevitable necessity for synthesis. The case of Rome, as has been said above, was the most obvious point of concentration. Here was a unit of observation, a state which lasted a thousand years, which rose and fell, which presented impressive scenes of grandeur and decadence. Moreover there were other states which had preceded it: Greece, Egypt, Babylonia, and still others, emerging slowly from the past. Two consequences were inevitable: the notion of gradual growth and concentration as a constant historical phenomenon; the emergence of a kind of central societal sun, making possible a distinction between mean and oscillatory movements and so initiating the idea of social law. No doubt here was only a first approximation; the data included only a part of the Occident, to the exclusion of all the rest and of the Orient entire; but the omissions were of no consequence. Time would remedy the deficiency.

In all this record was there nothing but a sequence of states, a mere succession of unrelated equilibria? Vico was clearly moving away from this limited conception, but Rome was still too imposing an existence for him; besides, the antecedent, the earlier, the primitive periods were still too undefined. Nevertheless the foundations for an inclusive synthesis were being enlarged. It was evidently not to be long before the historical picture could be seen *as a whole*. The man in whom this general and spontaneous tendency of historical thinking first found adequate explicit expression was Turgot. He conceived of the cultural record *as one*. In it, that is, he saw not merely successive social equilibria, independently reached; he saw them *not as unrelated states but as stages in a movement*. From this time on, man could speak of history in a quite special and synthetic sense: not the record of this or that country or people but the record as a whole, a unit, a synthesis. The dynamics of sociology had arrived.

Condorcet developed the idea by regarding the historical record still more abstractly as the work of a single hypothetical people. Into this concept could be absorbed analogous ideas reached by earlier thinkers in relation to some special aspect of cultural existence. Philoponus was one such example, conceiving of thought as a human characteristic and attributing it to a single ever-living thinker. Pascal meditating upon the continuous growth of science was another. Comte abstracted and generalized all such concepts still further by his insistence upon the influence of one generation upon another. The historical movement was *one;* but since the unity was at first to be discovered only by the study of successive stages, Comte in developing his ideas in the *Philosophie* gave dynamics greater importance than statics.

One advance yet remained; it was made in the *Politique*. It involved the reversal of the position taken in the *Philosophie*. Statics, in the second volume of the *Politique,* is definitively given the precedence over dynamics. In other words, Comte came finally to see movement as an outcome of the initial structural arrangement of the system. The line of thought is clear. The historical record viewed as a whole consists of a series of stages; but in each stage the same process is at work. Each stage is a new equilibrium of the forces composing the system; this succession of equilibria implies and involves no new element in the system. Hence it becomes possible to turn attention to the nature of the system which accounts for all the successive equilibria. Dynamics thus is reduced to statics.

One final influence is inevitable. If dynamical sequences are reducible to statical principles, then the elaboration of statics will account for dynamical phenomena whenever they occur. *Sociology is thus freed from history and becomes a strictly abstract science.* The societal system has an arrangement, an order, of its own. The development of this order produces a related sequence of equilibria; progress is thus inseparable from order. The definition of the societal process, i.e., the essential nature of societal phenomena, as collective cumulation is at once the recognition of the new position and its completely abstract formulation.

When the historical development just sketched was completed and the translation of dynamical questions into statical problems finally achieved, it became possible to go back over the entire societal record and see in it an orderliness, a regularity, that had at first been invisible. Not only had the normal and the abnormal been differentiated and then transformed into oscillation about a mean, but the various societal concretions in both time and space were shown to be so many cases of a single continuing process. In other words, both anthropological and historical data were absorbed into sociology, and as a consequence the latter could be solidly based upon biological foundations.

From the biological point of view it is clear that whenever forms of life reach the stage of evolution at which they become capable of living together, providing for their needs, communicating at least their feelings, and imposing their wills upon others, a new mode of being and a new level of abstraction exist. It is the direct outcome of the combination of the potentialities just enumerated. It begins when these capacities coexist. Evidently no one form of life is in question. To some degree many of the higher forms manifest the requisite characteristics. Possessing them is what makes them higher. Obviously some of these forms will be better endowed than others in respect to the new level of existence, so all the more will they be superior. The essential quality of these superior forms is their capacity to utilize the experiences of one another in meeting the conditions of life. In other words, these favored forms will be capable in varying degree of living collectively.

Inevitably, given the biological conditions, one of the first uses of the new capacity will be the securing of predominance over rivals. It is likely that ultimate dominance will fall to the form best equipped *on the whole* with respect to the new level of achievement. All the differential characteristics of the competing forms will play their parts in determining the ultimate outcome. Certain initial handicaps at first sight insurmountable, like nakedness, prolonged infancy, fantasy making, may in time be overcome and even transmuted into advantage. Dominance will require time; but once gained it will be permanent and will increasingly tend to separate and differentiate the selected form from its onetime rivals, even though they are closely related in a biological sense. To enumerate the organic differentiations which account for ultimate dominance on the new level of existence would be for sociologists a supererogatory task. When done by biologists the result is simply a definition of the animal Homo.

He it was who became the normal case of the operation of the new potentialities. So completely did he achieve dominance that abnormal cases—varieties of societal phenomena produced by other forms—became so few and so limited as to be in effect nonexistent. The mean, in other words, had its fringe of oscillations, but they were so slight as to be imperceptible. Human thus came to be practically synonymous with societal, and the societal became the means whereby the human was differentiated from the animal.

Such a consequence, however, is in no way inevitable in theory. Many forms of vitality are capable of some degree of sociality. Sociology would be but slightly affected if there were several or many close rivals of the animal Homo. Its theories would in such a case be but slightly changed if indeed at all. They would no doubt have been harder to attain, as the astronomical illustration of one sun as against several makes understandable. The predominance of the animal Homo serves but to simplify the sociologist's task. There is no human sociology to be distinguished in kind from animal sociology. Societal phenomena are on one level, biological on another. The latter are never more than secondary with respect to the former.

If, now, the absence of wide oscillations made it easy to recognize the existence of a body of normal societal phenomena and thus facilitated the early and definitive distinction between the animal and the human, the next stage in the development of thought on the subject was extremely late and difficult. The primary societal phenomenon in its earliest human manifestations was slow in operation and weak in intensity; it was conditioned by many varieties of environment; it was modified by many types of personality, especially the abnormal ones, as the anthropologists have demonstrated. The concrete result was the appearance in the early stage of societal development of a great number of nuclei—centers of cultural potentiality—which archaeology and anthropology have revealed and described.

Evidently in such variety of circumstance the existence of fundamental forces, universally operative, was difficult to recognize. Two conditions had to be met before recognition was possible. The first was the cancellation from the problem of the secondary factors of variation. The second was the appearance of a body of normal societal phenomena adequate for the discovery of that regularity in diversity which is the essence of scientific law. The first condition was met by the rise of the natural sciences. The second was satisfied when the societal process gave rise to concentrations of a size so great as to render other concentrations relatively insignificant, i.e., where a mean and its oscillations were distinguishable. The conjunction of these conditions provided the situation in which a science of the societal phenomenon became possible. A first approximation of such a science resulted.

It took the form first of an historical synthesis, picturing man's record as a whole; that is to say, it was dynamical in nature. At the same time an effort was being made to understand the record as the outcome of an influence continuously operating under all historical forms; that is to say, it was analytical and essentially statical. The combination of these two efforts was first to resolve dynamical movements into sequences of equilibria and then to solve questions of equilibrium on the basis of the fixed arrangements of the societal system. Statics thus came to take precedence over dynamics, and the two disciplines finally merged to produce a single abstract science, sociology.

The whole conception can be put in other words than those just used; its importance justifies the effort. The initial societal elements are beings capable of interaction. By virtue of their interaction they become interdependent. They affect and are affected by others. Thus they live collectively and become socii. From this point of view the principle Comte attributed to Aristotle could in all strictness be made the foundation of statics and so of dynamics and so of sociology as a whole: the separation of offices and the combination of efforts. It carries implicitly the full weight of later theory, but it could be made explicit only by generations of societal activity. It implies the existence of socii, beings working together but each in his own way, thus providing for the cumulation of collective effort and experience. Each of these beings affects all the others sooner or later and so can be regarded as a force in relation to them, especially in view of the fact that as individuals these interdependent beings are soon lost from sight. The individual efforts are too numerous to be dealt with separately; they are therefore classified and become the forces which come into relation and then into balance and in this way constitute a societal system isolable from all other forces, which thus become exterior.

The forces composing the system act in relation to one another; otherwise they would not be forces at all. When they interact, the outcome is a process. This process is not something which results from the interaction of the forces, nor is it their consequence. They are not its cause. It is simply the structure of the system in action. Process, in other words, is a name for the interdependent action of the forces exerted by the components of the system. Process does not cause the movement of the system. The movement is caused by interaction of the forces. As the forces increase in intensity the original order develops, the process alters, and change occurs. Thus the statical and the dynamical are revealed as different aspects of the system, at rest and in movement. "Structure, however enduring, exists in terms of process, and process, no matter how slowly or rapidly it operates, always moves through structure. Structure and process are correlative, not opposing, aspects of phenomena." [5]

5. R. Turner, *The Great Cultural Traditions* (2 vols. New York, McGraw-Hill, 1941), 2, 1238.

As an outcome of the whole discussion a picture slowly takes form of a science of societal phenomena divisible into two major parts, one dealing with the nature of the structure which results from the combination of societal forces into a system, the other with the process that is the interrelated activity of components of the system. It is the first of these divisions that is in point here. It is now clear that not only are the normal and the abnormal, the mean and its oscillations, homogeneous phenomena but also that all instances of such phenomena, however they seem to differ, are in fact the outcome of the working of the same uniformities. In short, societal statics in its entirety is a domain of law.

To this conception the analogy with mechanics gives precision and extension. For example, in mechanics the center of gravity is the point where the weight of a body may be thought of as collected, thus making it possible for special purposes to reduce a whole system to its center of gravity. Is not this concept the solution to such still unsettled questions as are involved in economic determinism and the like? Again, could not such questions as the difference between crowds and mobs or the influence of such ideals as democracy be dealt with as examples of virtual forces? Or in the case of the vague notion known in the textbooks as the acceleration of culture, is there not a parallel between the force of gravitation which constantly and equally increases the velocity of a falling body and the collective cumulation which constantly accelerates societal development?

Such special points of inquiry are no doubt important but they are insignificant compared with the possibility of basing societal statics upon a systematic analysis of a unified body of phenomena rather than upon the personal insights of pioneering sociologists. Statics has to study the equilibrium of the forces that compose the societal system. What are these forces? What is their magnitude, i.e., with what degree of intensity do they affect one another? What is their velocity? What is the history of each? What impulsion does each have taken separately? How are they combined, i.e., what are the laws of their composition, decomposition, recomposition? How do they affect one another, i.e., what are the actions and reactions among them? Such are the directive lines of inquiry in a constituted sociological statics.

But what of societal movement? By implication this question has already been answered. Its importance, however, is too great for the answer to remain implicit in what has already been said of a system. To it the next part of this volume is devoted. There only can it be shown how order as it develops gives rise to progress.

But when the word "progress" is inserted in the text, a question at once arises. Is not a subjective coloring being given to the discussion? Is there not, concealed in the word, a value judgment? How can the use of the word be justified? On this point there are three pertinent considerations.

First, the word *need* not be used. Comte, as one of the first to deal with the question, was one of the first to make the point. After showing in the *Philosophie* the subjective and metaphysical implications in the absolute conception of social progress, he continues: "If one did not have to fear falling into a puerile affectation, and above all appearing to elude a pretended fundamental difficulty, it would be easy, in my opinion, to treat of the whole of social physics without once using the word *perfectionnement* by replacing it always with the simply scientific term *développement*, which designates, without any moral appreciation, an incontestable general fact." And he later completes his thought as follows: "It is necessary to set aside all idle and irrational controversies as to the respective merit of different consecutive stages, in order to limit oneself to studying the laws of their effective succession." [6]

In the second place, the word "progress" can be used in sociological discussion with a definite though restricted meaning. Laffitte defines this point of view as follows:

> Progress means a succession of different states coordinated with reference to a given end, with a gradual improvement effected in the succession. There are several elements in this capital conception. First, the idea of progress implies a succession of analogous, and consequently, truly homogeneous states. Second, a new element enters into the conception, namely the idea of the improvement of a determinate state. Each state is evidently characterized by a mode of action. This mode of action can be effected, preserving the same essential characters, within certain

6. *4*, 293. (Italics are Comte's.)

limits,—that is, with more or less facility and more or less inconvenience. Amelioration, i.e. improvement, means augmenting
the maximum of facility or gradually diminishing the minimum
of inconvenience. Finally, progress, although indefinite, can not
grow beyond all limit. Our nature, as well as our situation, imposes a limit, toward which tends the improvement of successive
states.[7]

In this sense the increasing integration of the societal system, for
example, facilitating the cumulation of collective results, would
undoubtedly constitute progress. Probably the word "efficiency"
best expresses the limited conception here in point.

Finally there is a third consideration, much more comprehensive
in its implications than the other two. Both of them are tacitly confined to the societal isolate, and so the notion of progress is restricted.
But what if the idea were to be enlarged to the point of considering
the various abstract isolates with reference to one another? In other
words, how do these isolates rank? Can the concept of progress be
expanded to include judgment as to the relative position of the various isolates *within a larger frame of reference?* Evidently the meaning and nature of classification with reference to the sciences is
involved.

It seems to be the fact that problems of classification arose first
in relation to man's interests and in the domain of sociology. They
appear to have received their first spontaneous solutions in the
ranking of the hominoids to whom agency and causation were
first attributed. These beings were divided and subdivided and
arranged hierarchically according to their power. It may be that
these implicit classifications were the reflection of the organization
of men into forces on a military basis. At any rate, the concealed
principle on which the organization both of men and of hominoids
was based was brought into the light when the head of the military
hierarchy was called "general."

Generality: here is the principle of natural classification in science, applicable to the sciences themselves as well as to their contents. But what does generality mean when taken as the universal
principle of scientific classification? Several notions are combined
and integrated in the term. Generality as applied to phenomena

7. *Cours de philosophie première,* 2, 181.

means first of all the range within which a given phenomenon is observable. The greater the number of existences in which a phenomenon is manifested, the more general it is. Extension, for example, is more general than life, just as life is more general than culture. Such is the central element of the concept; but there are several secondary considerations.

Thus heat seems to be as general as extension when the number of objects in which it may be observed is considered. Nevertheless heat must be classified as less general than extension on the ground that a greater number of conditions are required for its manifestation, among them being the very phenomenon of extension. The reciprocal relation does not exist.

Finally, where these two requirements are not decisive a third may be added. A phenomenon is more general in proportion as it is more constant and less intermittent in its manifestations. Thus thermological phenomena are more general than electrical, for besides needing fewer and less complex conditions they are much less intermittent and act in a more constant manner.

Generality, then, from the objective point of view is constituted by these three characters: the existence of a property in a more or less considerable number of beings; the more or less considerable number of conditions necessary for the production of the phenomenon; the relative degree of constancy or variety manifested in the phenomenon.

When the abstract isolates into which the sum of observable phenomena is divided are classified on the grounds just stated, a hierarchical series results. The earlier members of this series can in logical strictness dispense with those that follow them and can exist without them. Materiality, that is, does not need vitality and does not imply its existence; so vitality does not imply or involve sociality. Each successive term is thus conditioned by those that precede it and can do nothing to affect the essential nature of the phenomena isolated in the earlier groups. The objective order is thus an order of decreasing independence or increasing dependence. Vital phenomena, for example, have their own regularities, but they are dependent for their existence upon all the orders comprised under the term "material," none of which they can alter in essentials. The material is indispensable for the vital; the inverse is not true. The objective order is thus the order of fatality or necessity.

Now the same series of isolates hierarchically arranged in order of decreasing generality can be observed not only from the objective but from the subjective viewpoint as well. Generality now comes to have a different sense. It now means the number of conditions that are involved when the existence of any isolate is in question. Thus sociality, comprising all societal phenomena, implies first vitality and then materiality. Thus subjective generality means traversing the objective classification in inverse order. It means that the higher levels of the hierarchy, being conditioned by all the levels below them, are subject to the action of many variables, the higher the level the greater the possible variability. Hence the subjective order is the order of modifiability.

Here, as once before in this volume, two ideas that seem incompatible and even contradictory are seen to be correlative. As the order of fatality is traversed, the possibility of interposition increases. The abstract level at the summit of the hierarchy is evidently the most variable of all because in addition to its own uniformities it is subject also to the conditioning influences of all the levels below it. That is to say, the number of variables which are associated with it is the maximum; and for the same reason the possibilities of modification and control are the greatest. All the lower levels are so many stages of advance toward the summit; to move toward it is to progress; to reach it is the goal of progress. In this ultimate sense, *the establishment of a scale of values is the task of science.*

It is at this point that the full significance of Comte's separation of the moral, the psychic, the psychological from the social, the societal, the sociological can be most clearly seen. In his original series of six abstract levels, sociology was the science at the summit of the hierarchy. Hence there were no phenomena beyond its domain; the laws of sociology were final and determinative. They were conditioned by the working of the phenomena below the societal on the scale, but their own operation was subject to no modification. They varied only in respect of their own energies. These might vary, but there was no influence beyond the sociological to play upon them as variables. The outcome of this position, where sociology dominates the scientific hierarchy, is in conventional language the theory of cultural determinism.

But if a level of abstraction above the sociological is scientifically established, then the picture changes. Now the societal is no longer the summit of the hierarchy; it becomes one of the series of conditioning influences. It can be modified because there is an isolate above it. It must be modified when such alteration is required for the advantage of the higher level. It is on this higher level that finality comes at last to reside. Consequently the basis of cultural determinism is destroyed; another kind of determinism takes its place. The name given it matters little. The point is that another abstract isolate has finally been recognized. It will obviously be the most delicately balanced, its inherent equilibrium the most subject to disturbance because the operation of its own characteristic uniformities will be conditioned by the existence and manifestations of all the isolates lower in the scale. It will be the most changeable of all classes of phenomena because the number of variables affecting it is here at its maximum. No wonder then that the distinctive nature and operation of psychical laws—i.e., the existence of a purely moral or psychical determinism, which in historical terms is free will—has been so difficult to ascertain, substantiate, and define.

But once the existence of a psychical isolate with its own regularities has been demonstrated, a position is reached from which the whole question of progress can be viewed in a new light. The principle of generality on which the hierarchy of the sciences is based decides not only the relative position of the abstract isolates; it serves also to determine the distribution and allocation of the constituent elements of the isolates themselves. It decides for example that vegetal shall precede animal in biology, or in chemistry that inorganic shall precede organic, just as it places chemistry immediately anterior to biology. It shows why vitality precedes sociality and personality follows it. It thus provides a steady line of advance from the most general to the least general, from the independent to the dependent, from the unmodifiable to the modifiable; and all this without a single gap in the progression. The choice of a word to denote this passage from one level of the hierarchy to another is a secondary matter. To call it "progress" no doubt implies a scale of values. Comte, the first to see the possibilities, speaks of an increase of dignity as the scale is traversed. But the determination of such a scale on scientific principles is as remote from value judgments as the attribution to Nature of an abhorrence of vacuums is from physics.

Progress then is a term which may legitimately be used in sociology, not merely because it involves all that it expressed by the term "development," not merely because it is applicable to more efficient procedures within the isolate, but because both of these meanings are absorbed in the larger sense of progress inclusive of scientific values as above defined. In this sense societal developments may be called progressive when they tend to favor the expansion of phenomena belonging in the isolate above them in the scale of subjective generality. The whole point of the matter in relation to sociology consists in the fact that by the use of the principle of generality societal phenomena can be ranked. Those are higher which tend to provide and perpetuate the conditions which favor the growth and enlargement of personality. And this judgment is based on no subjective preference for this or that form of life. That man holds so prominent a place in the scale of dignity is due to the absence of rivals, not to the preference of the judges. Those changes, within and without sociology, are progressive which favor the expansion of certain qualities. Of these qualities man on an unbiased survey of the facts is seen to possess an effective monopoly, but the fact is not related to the judgment as to the superior nature of the qualities. For all these reasons, growing out of the nature of the scientific hierarchy, when societal order is developed the result is progress.

But the progress which is the development of societal order is no absolute conception. It is no revival of the indefinite perfectibility of Condillac or Condorcet. It is a relative term, defined by the concepts which it combines. It is the development of order, which is the equivalent of saying that progress so defined has definite limits. These limits are the limitations of the system formed by the interaction of the societal elements, manifesting themselves as forces interdependently connected. In other words, given the initial structure, the basic functional arrangement, the universal pattern, the essential order, then the limits of the development are inherent in the system. Could man exist without material goods, propagate his kind asexually, communicate without symbols, or dispense with direction, there would be no societal system. To develop the order arising out of the formation of the system means therefore neither the negation of these elements nor the addition of new ones but the expansion of the primordial ones. Truly radical alteration of the basic structure would mean not its improvement but its disappearance.

The progress then which is the development of societal order implies two consequences. The first is an increase in the intensity and speed of each constituent element of the system as it gains momentum: material goods, more numerous and more varied; more intensive as well as more extensive association; communication facilitating more and more the exchange of both thought and feeling; more effective and more synthetic direction. The second consequence is continuous increase in the interdependence and interaction, the functional interlocking, of the component elements of the system, subject always to the maintenance of the system. Together the two consequences impose an ideal limit toward which progress ever moves: the maximum development of the elements of the system consistent with their maximum integration.

Toward such an ideal, toward such a geometrical limit, ever more nearly to be approached but never quite to be attained, societal progress advances. The movement may be either spontaneous or systematic. In the first case groups survive or disappear more or less haphazardly, guided at times by wiser individuals, abandoned at other times to passions, but in either case little more aware of societal necessities and conditions than they were of the existence of gravitation. Most societies of the past seem to have been on this level. The sheer force of the societal process carried them on, haltingly and deviously. The second type of societal advance becomes possible when it is realized that progress can be *made*—that increasing knowledge of sociological uniformities and their conditioning factors can be utilized to facilitate societal advances, to free the forces generating the societal process for unimpeded operation, to turn in other words (Ward's) from genesis to telesis.

The maximum development of each societal force; the maximum interdependence of the forces: such, expressed in the most abstract form, are the geometrical limits toward which the societal system moves. It does so because the structure of the system reveals itself in action as a process the essence of which is collective cumulation.

This process is operative in relation to each of the elements of which the system is constituted. It is possible therefore to break down the abstract statement of the limits of societal progress into parts corresponding to the elements composing the societal pattern and to indicate the tendencies inherent in the nature of each element as it develops under the stress of the societal process. Once the tendencies of the constituent forces have been revealed, it will be possible to determine the results that will follow when these forces have been integrated. To make such an integration is equivalent to establishing the limits of societal progress.

Such an analysis, intended to reveal these limits, is now to be attempted. In regard to it certain remarks are relevant. To start with, it is a first approximation only. Its value is rather in the effort than in the results. Indeed, the latter can be disregarded provided the logic underlying them is admitted to be sufficiently cogent to stimulate other approximations more inclusive and better informed.

In the second place, the conclusions to be reached are in no sense recommendations as to policy. They are, however, foundations of policy in the sense that they reveal the ends toward which societal phenomena tend ever to move. Even when all conditioning, i.e., secondary factors are operative they cannot change the nature, the inherent tendencies, of the societal structure and process any more than the density of the atmosphere can alter the law governing the acceleration in the rate of speed at which bodies fall. This law is always operative and must always be taken into account. Indeed its very inflexibility is a stimulus and an aid to ingenuity. Steps, ramps, elevators do not suspend the law of gravitation, they use it. The law is a statement of fatality; it is none the less modifiable. To introduce this thought into sociology is to open a vast field for invention.

In the third place, the formulation of societal limits, however imperfect the first approximation may be, is a step toward the ultimate possibility of ranking societies and cultures. The notion evidently absorbs the anthropological concept of the culture base, in which a larger or smaller number of traits becomes the ground for evaluating cultures as advanced or backward. This concept has the merit of translating qualitative into quantitative terms. Increasingly accurate approximations will move in the same direction.

Finally, the approximation to be made, being statical, will have nothing to say as to place and a fortiori as to time of achievement. It deals with geometrical limits, not with bounds set to the operation of the process. *When* they are to be reached is not a statical concern. These limits are simply statements of the *abstractly* inevitable point of arrival of the societal system, given the accuracy of the analysis.

Thus, to begin with that element of the societal system concerned mainly with the accumulation of material goods, i.e., capitals, it is clear that the tendency of the societal process is to make of these accumulations a more and more collective and cumulative product. As each socius adds his energies to those of his contemporaries and still more significantly to those of all his predecessors, the growing sum of cooperative results tends to reach the point where all mankind has had a hand in the ultimate product. And inversely, it is clear that the proportionate share of any socius in the creation of the wealth on which the life of the collectivity depends tends to decrease.

The increasing societalization of wealth makes explicit certain characteristics of property that were to begin with implicit. It destroys the belief that property is absolute and shows that it is neither good nor bad in itself but only a means, among many others, for securing desired or desirable results. It is in fact but one of the creations of the descendants of the animal Homo in response to needs. The tendency is to regard it with complete relativity.

Another tendency of the societal process working in the element of accumulation is to increase the quantity of wealth and concentrate it in ever larger capitals. No great project in either space or time is possible without them. Moreover the concentration of wealth, besides favoring enterprises of wide scope, works for greater and greater division of labor. Here an important qualitative transformation can be observed. Evidently so long as the various processes involved in the fabrication of material goods are regarded as unitary, i.e., as a craft, needing but small capitals, no extensive division of labor is expedient. But when the scope of the operation increases along with capitals required, the whole process is magnified so to speak, whereupon the sum of processes united in the craft tends to be separated into increasingly isolated procedures; hence a fatal tendency toward minuter division of labor, the relative share of each socius becoming smaller as the analysis of the original craft proceeds.

Still another tendency in the economic domain is that which works toward the expansion of the area within which material production is carried on. The tendency is intensified as production is increased, larger stocks of raw materials becoming necessary and wider outlets being sought. The abstract outcome is the inclusion of the globe in a single market—trade, exchange, becoming completely free.

In relation to the societal element called association certain tendencies seem discernible. Beginning with the domestic association, i.e., the family, the societal logic seems definitely to favor the monogamic type of relationship. The societal process, starting with animal mating, seems to work most effectively where pair relationship exists. The geometrical nature of the outcome is very evident however in this instance, for it seems certain that greater understanding of the factors at work will provide for the tolerance of exceptional cases. In other words, the monogamic tendency will persist but will be understood; men will be more free to reject and at the same time more inclined to adopt the monogamic form of domestic socionomy, which will thus become the normal form of the family as the logic of the societal process exerts its steady pressure.

On the civil level of association it is observable that socii began to be such at first in virtue of their connections through a real blood bond but that these involuntary relationships gradually give way to voluntary ones. That is to say, with the expansion of the group, kinship relations weaken. The secondary group tends to dominate the primary. All socii finally become citizens, i.e., members of the cité. Many consciousnesses of kind develop as groupings of various kinds multiply, prominent among them that which arises from like societal activities. Citizenship—functional integration in the total group—tends to become universal both as fact and as feeling.

Socionomic unity works finally toward the inclusion of all mankind, since the radius over which the civic association extends constantly lengthens as the societal process operates to make more and more individuals true socii in expanding activities. Sumner and Keller put the idea as follows, emphasizing at the same time the quality of the results: "The fact is that the stress toward adjustment, even among those tribes that have plenty of spirit for a fight, makes insensibly for peaceful association; there is an ever-present tendency toward the formation and extension of the 'peace-group.' " [8] Moreover, the "tendency is toward enlargement of the peace-group, and those that lag behind are destroyed or incorporated." [9] Two aspects of association are implied here: numbers and nature. The limits are on the one side the universal group and on the other universal peace. In other words, the societal process in its associative aspects continuously works for a universal and pacific socionomy.

With respect to the subisolate of communication, comprising language, science, and art, collective cumulation is ever at work, providing a logic which is revealed by observable tendencies in each of the three elements just mentioned. Thus in language, along with the symbols recalling mental images of the concrete kind there is a continuous development of abstract terms. They arise from the analysis of the concrete and spontaneously develop general ideas which because of their generality are comprehensible by increasing numbers of men. "Abstraction . . . furnishes to men a larger and larger number of common points in relation to which they may group themselves for concerted action." "Abstract properties constitute a mass of common ideas without which there could exist no very extended relations among men." [10] In other words, symbols become increasingly collective and tend toward integration in a single language universally comprehensible.

On the level of science, the gathering of information and its synthesizing in what have been called views, i.e., mental picturizations and configurations, is continuous and ever expanding as new socii appear and add their contributions. Few indeed are the things that men have not looked into. In the case of food, to take a single example, little has escaped notice. Nothing edible on or above or below the surface of the ground seems to have been unknown to the Australian native, no very exalted example of cultural development. And of course mankind did not stop at the level of food but went on to the higher regions where savoring becomes sapience. The tendencies are clear. First, to extend knowledge over the entire range of observation. Man can learn all he needs to know, for he needs to know only what in some way affects him; and the effects

8. *1*, 19.
9. P. 417.
10. Laffitte, *Cours de philosophie première, 1,* 54, 55.

as they affect him serve as the material for the operation of the societal process. Second, to endow all men with the achievements of science, that is, to comprise all the descendants of the animal Homo within the number of those to whom as socii the cumulated sum of universal experience is available.

Art is so evidently a composite of societal and psychical that the aesthetic has not hitherto been susceptible of adequate analysis. On the psychical side it still remains obscure, but on the strictly societal aspects of the phenomenon something can be said. If no great sum of knowledge yet exists as to the source and nature of the activating power of the image, the image itself can now be seen to be a collective representation in which is embodied the experiences and the mental constructs of many socii, cumulated through generations. Such spontaneous societal products as the Buddha or the Christ, or the more systematic constructions of recent days appealing to millions of men widely separated in space and ordinarily in time as well, clearly point to the creation of art forms capable of moving all mankind.

Because of its inherent nature, direction manifests an understandable tendency toward an increase in the power of the individuals with high origin rates. This tendency is observable in both the general and the special forms of direction, i.e., in both management and government. The extent over which control is exerted tends to widen with an increase in the number of socii, that is, the directive function becomes operative on an ever expanding scale. The result is an augmentation of the scope and influence of the director. Leaders, initiators, tend to become masters, to revive an obsolescent term. This intensification of the directive function is particularly observable in the specialized field where the total interest exists in the presence of more and more partial ones. Government, that is, tends to pass from the spontaneous to the systematic phase, in which partial interests have to be prevented from endangering the societal structure by withdrawal or usurpation. Government thus comes to operate more continuously and more extensively.

So much for the tendencies inherent in the nature of the societal process when operative in relation to the elements of the culture pattern taken one by one. But these elements do not in fact work in isolation, they work interdependently and so tend to integrate. The fact of integration intervenes in relation to the free play of tendencies and so provides limits beyond which the development of the elements of the cultural system cannot go without destroying the system—limits toward which in fact they continue to move without ever reaching them.

This integrative tendency manifests itself in several ways. It begins in the cultural unit, however small—i.e., wherever the societal process operates. In each society, that is, the tendency toward integration gives rise to a true cultural pattern. It continues when the smaller units merge into larger ones, and the increase in size of the in-groups accelerates the integrative action. Finally it reaches its limit when all units have been absorbed in a single universal cultural whole. Thus, whether early primitive isolated units are concerned or transitional combinations or a final all-inclusive union, the progress of societies toward the geometrical limit of a universal pacific in-group is constant. As the mass of societal phenomena increases, the mean grows in relation to the oscillations; the abnormal thus becomes less important with time and the normal, increasing in mass, tends toward greater and greater uniformity and regularity.

As the process works itself out, the various cultural elements come to be more interdependent. Thus the inevitable tendency toward division of labor, developing to a point where a craft is analyzed into a succession of practically reflex movements, comes into relation with the development of science. From the relationship comes the possibility and then the tendency to replace men by automatic processes powered by inorganic energy, with its outcome in the qualitative change of laborers into machine tenders and finally into machine supervisors, the limit being the complete replacement of men by machines.

So great a control over material accumulations has an immediate effect upon the whole range of association. It makes possible the full development of the domestic group, providing the material means for the specialization of function which complete monogamy implies; it relieves socii of the constant pressure of labor and gives them leisure for action as citizens; it works toward a universal society and a consciousness of kind inclusive of all humanity.

Both of the preceding tendencies working together combine with the nature of communication to further the development of a universal language and a universal education, the latter based upon a scientific method, homogeneous at all levels of abstraction. Such an intellectual integration provides a global basis of ideas and of ideology whereby a common stock of images, pictures, views becomes the groundwork for a universal art, thus finally integrated with life.

The tendency toward complete integration of societal phenomena brings into special relief the function of direction and in so doing marks a noteworthy reversal in the relative importance of the components of the societal structure. The elements of the culture pattern have usually been ranged according to their objective generality, the economic at the base, the directive at the summit, the economic thus being the center of gravity of the system. But from the subjective point of view the order of importance is reversed. The interdependence of the elements must be safeguarded at all times, else the system will be destroyed. Hence the need of direction becomes more imperative as the integration of the system proceeds. From this point of view the definition of government as an apparatus of systematization becomes particularly significant.

As the societal interdependence grows the scope of government widens, the tendency toward political unity meeting its limit in a global control. The force which it wields becomes irresistible when all men become purely socii. At the same time the extension of mores to the global limit makes the use of force less necessary. The limit is the state in which an irresistible force is arrayed in behalf of ways from which no one wishes to depart. Moreover, force becomes of less avail as the differentiation of function gives rise to a complexity of relationships whose harmony can but poorly be served by forceful methods; hence the ultimate tendency for all societal phenomena to move toward the level where the sociological gives way to the psychological.

The outcome of the whole statical analysis is the picture of a final, normal state in which all men are socii. Economic conditions are in constant equilibrium; wealth is used for societal welfare. Each socius has a public function; labor is the superintendence of machines. Wages are determined by the nature of the function; their purpose is to ensure its fulfillment. Association is monogamic on the primary level, civic on the secondary level, spiritual on the final level. Action is pacific, since there are no rivalries between sovereignties, yet there is emulation and competition between the many partial interests that voluntary activities establish. There is universal communication. One language brings all living beings into relationship; a uniform education revives all the past and directs attention to the future. There is knowledge of the whole range of science and sensitiveness to the whole gamut of emotion. All these elements are kept in harmony and systematically integrated by organization of a political kind, backed by irresistible force and overwhelming accordance of opinion. These conditions will be the normal, the mean; around them will oscillate the abnormal, but the mass of the normal will be so great as to reduce the abnormal to the negligible.

The section just concluded is an effort to draw conclusions from strictly statical principles. The inadequacy of the effort then as a first approximation must be considered to be due to its preliminary nature, not to its ultimate intention. In one sense the societal state just pictured may be described as a utopia; but this utopia is no wishful construction, it is an attempt to build with strict logic upon statical foundations. As such it deliberately omits every consideration other than sociological. It seeks to determine the limits of societal development in themselves. That is to say, all secondary considerations, drawn from the study of conditioning or modifying factors whether material, vital, or psychical have been set aside. The effort has been to show how societal phenomena work when only sociological principles, laws of a statical kind, are in operation.

Evidently the limitations of such an effort are many. In the main they derive from the fact that statical considerations are timeless. Because of this limitation, conclusions drawn from purely statical premises are subject to two dangers. They lead to error by inducing the belief that any societal situation may be created at any time. Hence they encourage the notion that any desired societal condition, whether past or future, may be maintained or brought into being at will. Purely statical reasoning, that is, may and does encourage either retrogression or anarchy.

The omission of the element of time, then, sharply qualifies where it does not vitiate conclusions of a purely statical nature.

Societal phenomena develop. Statical analysis shows the nature and working of the societal structure; it gives no basis for judgment as to the opportuneness of a proposed change. For this purpose study of the process is required. As the process operates, the order is developed and progress is made. Sociology then must comprise two main divisions. The first, the statical, has now been presented in some detail; it remains to define and analyze the second, the dynamical.

PART FIVE: THE DIVISIONING OF THE SOCIETAL DOMAIN

B. Societal Dynamics: Process and Trend

CHAPTER 20: *From Statics to Dynamics*

A societal phenomenon, an isolate, abstract, specific and irre-ducible; within its boundaries a structure, a close interlocking of parts, a functional arrangement, an order and a process, an active interdependence of constituent elements, a development, a prog-ress; forces reaching equilibrium, forces producing motion; bodies at rest, bodies in movement; in short a societal system divisible in logic into statics and dynamics: such is the outcome of the preced-ing pages. It is the ground plan for a positive sociology.

Of the first of the two constituent parts of the science an explora-tory analysis has now been made, adequate to reveal the nature of the data involved and the relations between them. The major classes of societal phenomena have been established and the in-herent tendencies of each, as it operates under the stress of the so-cietal process, ascertained. As the classes of phenomena fall into equilibrium, each so affecting the other that all are subject to what Sumner describes as a strain of consistency, the outcome in a purely abstract view is a symmetrical pattern of elements, no one of them predominating. In the reality, however, the intensity and speed with which the constituent elements operate vary as well as the conditions under which they develop. The result is an almost unlimited diversity of patterns, as anthropological observation of cultures reveals. Since all these multipatterned cultures are ulti-mately analyzable into classes of homogeneous phenomena, all de-finable as collective cumulations, the possibility of accounting for their differences quantitatively comes into sight. That is to say, a varying number of collective cumulations in each of the four basic classes will correspond to or will create a variation in the basic design.

Now the reduction of differences between cultural patterns to a quantitative basis is a principle of wide applicability. For ex-ample, as has been seen, it destroys any distinction in theory be-tween the normal and the so-called pathological cases of societal existence. If there is marked variation in the relative speed with which collective cumulation is carried on in one subisolate as compared with the others, a cultural lag will be manifest. A disturbance in the normal equilibrium of the societal system resulting from the abnormal operation, in excess or deficiency, of a given statical element may give rise to a crisis or a depression. Failure to harmonize one element of a culture pattern with continuous, rapid cumulation in another may give rise to attempts to readjust the equilibrium or even remake it by a sudden, perhaps violent, effort, a revolution being the outcome. A chronic case of disequilibrium constantly impairing the effective cooperation of socii forms the underlying condition of maladjustment. In all these cases the same order comprises the normal and the abnormal, the mean and the oscillation, the distinction between them being quantitative only.

Finally the establishment of societal statics opens to study the whole field of cultural modifiability. This aspect of sociological theory can be viewed from either of two standpoints: the limits within which modifications are producible in the societal order; or the extent to which societal progress is possible. As to the first of these equivalent alternatives, the essential fact is the applicability of the laws of what has here been called societal mechanics. Given the laws of persistence, of coexistence, of equivalence; given the knowledge of the nature of the societal phenomenon in general and of the subisolates in particular; given the knowledge of the conditioning effects of the isolates below and the modifying influence of the isolate above the societal in the abstract hierarchy—notable advance has been made toward the goal where "man can systematize his destinies instead of submitting to them blindly." [1]

To reach that goal, that is to say, in order to make effective efforts to modify societal phenomena by influencing their intensity or speed, it is necessary to know the nature of the tendencies implicit in the continuous operation of the societal process, to know the limits toward which that process moves. Only so can the dissipation of energy that results from the blind opposition to the continuously enlarging mass of societal results be avoided. To discover and state these tendencies, to define these limits either for the process as a whole or for its constituent forces is the final achievement of sociological statics.

1. Comte, *Système de politique positive*, 2, 468.

A first approximation of these requirements for the conscious direction of cultural existence has already been made. But even if it were more nearly complete than it is, even if it were final, one further advance must still be made. If true guidance in practice is to be achieved, it is necessary to have some knowledge of the degree to which at a given moment the statical tendencies have been realized. The difficulty here is that the formulation of the limits of statical tendencies is attained by a process of abstraction which leaves time and place out of consideration. This procedure is justifiable on the level of pure theory, where indeed it is inevitable. But no effort at societal modification—implying of course a particular cultural situation—can be directed by purely statical considerations alone without grave danger. The "what" of societal intervention can never safely be dissociated from the "when."

Statical guidance is one thing, dynamical guidance another in relation to societal modification. To make clear the nature of the distinction between them Comte used a mathematical comparison:

> The best statical theory never suffices to guide social practice, although constantly indispensable for the purpose. Its exclusive or even its too preponderant use would almost always expose us to grave disturbances, by giving to our political tendencies too absolute a character and too vague a course.
>
> The statical guide is equivalent, with respect to social phenomena, to the whole of the rectilinear types on which a geometer bases the study of each curve, especially in determining its asymptotes. When a line has many asymptotes, as is often permitted by a very simple equation, a knowledge of them all at first furnishes precious light as regards its general figure, of which such a construction offers an indispensable approximation. But this rectilinear sketch can never dispense with a direct and special study of the curvilinear orbit, in which it always leaves undecided many important questions. It would be even more so if politics were to systematize its course directly in the light of sociological statics alone, which can furnish it only a vast group of asymptotes, necessarily common to a multitude of very different routes, among which nevertheless it is necessary to chose.
>
> This definitive choice, the only immediate guide of our social

practice, belongs exclusively to dynamical sociology. Although it should always study progress as the simple development of order previously defined, this more precise appreciation can alone tell us what are at each epoch the practicable steps in the direction of such a type and what course is compatible with taking them.[2]

And at the end of the third volume of the *Politique,* after having given a volume each to statics and dynamics, Comte returns to his mathematical comparison: "Statical sociology only determined the general system of asymptotes proper to the orbit of Humanity without deciding anything as to the curve itself, which could be adapted to these fundamental types in diverse fashions. But social dynamics has just fixed its effective course, in virtue of an arc sufficiently extended to permit a prolongation in conformity with the practical purpose of a study wherein previsions should never be exaggerated." [3]

Societal action then should be based upon statical analysis and guided by dynamical determinations: the thought is clear. But it will be well before going further to delimit more narrowly the nature of dynamics as the term is used here. It does not, for example, include such sequences as were presented in an earlier chapter where the stages in the development of a society from folkways to ethos were delineated. These stages, it is now evident, are but the milestones on a route which all societal systems traverse on their way to an equilibrium, to a distinctive order, given all the conditions of their existence, exterior as well as interior.

What is in point here is a different conception. It involves the relation between statics and dynamics in the abstract, not the course of growth of a concrete society. The process of collective cumulation is continuous. As it goes on operating, the number and mass of societal results augment; as they increase and become more closely integrated, they form a series of equilibria, a sequence of orders, which differ qualitatively because they are differentiated quantitatively. In this sense progress is the development of order

2. *Politique,* 2, 470–471.
3. *P.* 623.

and dynamics is dependent upon statics. But the determination of the nature and connection of the changes in successive orders or equilibria is a dynamic problem. To seek for the bond between these successive changes, to strive to determine the direction in which the changes taken as a whole are moving, is to search for the trend in the movement. Sociological dynamics, then, has for its object to study the laws, the regularities, the sequences discoverable in the succession of equilibria, orders, patterns to which the societal process gives rise. To discover the trends in these movements is its major concern.

The task then of the remainder of this volume is primarily to deal with sociological dynamics, to study societal progress, to follow the development of societal order, to reveal the sequence of cultural patterns, to discover what regularities are to be observed in the succession of qualitative changes that result from the quantitative increase in the number and mass of collective cumulations. When this final advance has been made, the fusion of statical and dynamical knowledge can be effected, which will enable men to base their projects for intervention not only upon a general grasp of societal phenomena but also upon an insight into the nature of the intervention required in a particular time and place.

To propose a search for cultural trends as the logical derivative of the concepts of dynamic sociology is certain to raise at once the objection that such an effort is in effect a return to the now discredited philosophy of history. To deal with this objection requires a brief reconsideration of both anthropology and history. A clearer view of the essential task of sociology as a member of the abstract encyclopedia may compensate for the delay in reaching dynamics.

Both anthropology and history have been presented in an earlier chapter as complementary, the two together constituting a descriptive science of Man the cultural being very much as botany and zoology are the descriptive sciences on which general, i.e., abstract biology is constructed. Of the two cultural sciences, the first has been the foundation in the main for the cultural pattern which underlies the statical division of sociology. True, the statical elements are determinable by induction from the historical cultures. Comte for example relied mainly upon them. Nevertheless, the parallel between the statical aspects of societal phenomena and the pattern data of anthropology is too close to be accidental. And in the same way, what is called by the quite unscientific name of history performs a service for the dynamical aspects of sociology. The question is what the nature of this service is and how is it rendered.

It is impossible to conceive of history in any sense in which the word is currently used without thinking of events envisaged as a continuity. Even annals have a consecutiveness in time which at least satisfies the letter of the requirement. Moreover, continuity implies something more than mere sequence; it carries with it some suggestion of relation. *B* not merely follows *A; B* in some way grows out of *A* and is a point of transit between *A* and *C.* History is not merely a record of change, it is a record of related changes running through which there is a thread, a bond, a unity which justifies their being recorded together. Otherwise there is nothing but a series of anecdotes, a collection of *histoires.*

Because this tracing of continuous relations is characteristic of history in the sense of intelligent records, historians of any seriousness inevitably exceed the narrow limits of a mere record and strive more or less deliberately to find the meaning of the facts they set down in sequence. Implied in this effort is an endeavor to determine the direction of an historical movement at a given point and a projection of the lines of development beyond it. That is to say, historians seek to establish and utilize trends. Thus where anthropology tends to emphasize patterns and so is closely allied to societal statics, history tends to emphasize movements and trends and thus aids in the establishment of societal dynamics.

Now the historian, seeking to understand the human record, often went outside the limits of his field, and where he could find little significance on the basis alone of his recorded data he moved to another terrain, the terrain of religion or philosophy, and there sought the means of supplementing his otherwise meager findings. The temptation, always strong, often grew irresistible to treat the record as an illustration of the working out of principles established on entirely nonhistorical grounds. The outcome was the flourishing and then the discrediting of the philosophy of history as an intellectual discipline.

Sociological efforts to determine trends in societal phenomena suffered from the discrediting of the philosophical explanations.

Especially was this the case when certain theorists concentrating attention upon the dynamical aspects of sociology sought to identify the science with the philosophy of history, or at least to base one upon the other. Other investigators by way of reaction sought to deny that sociology was in any way concerned with trends, especially when they seemed to involve the future. It becomes necessary, then, to preface the chapters on societal dynamics by a brief examination of the question: Is dynamical sociology in any sense a philosophy of history?

The answer is no, but with a reservation: such a construction is in theory possible, but sociology is only one of the elements that go to its making. In the first place, sociology is concerned with history only as a source of data. Sociology deals with the societal isolate; history deals with the record of mankind or some portion thereof under all the conditions of existence, material, vital, societal, psychical. Only as all these factors interplay does the historical reality appear. The distinction is basic; it goes back to the difference between concrete and abstract sciences and all the consequences that follow it.

In the second place, if by philosophy is meant an explanation of the historical, concrete reality—the reference of specific instance to general principle—then it is a clear inference from the sociological position that a philosophy of history is possible. Only it must be a positive, scientific philosophy—an explanation, that is, based upon an understanding of all the facts and the relations among them, not a theological or metaphysical explanation: hominoids, concrete or abstract, are the reliance of the magical mentality, not of the scientific. For the latter, explanations must be based upon regularities and sequences found in the phenomena, not imposed upon them.

Such explanations are increasingly within the range of accomplishment. They can be based upon the findings of the environmentalists since Hippocrates, the work of the biologists in all its variants, the analytical study of political and economic factors, of which sociology indeed is largely a derivative, and the increasing comprehension of the nature and interaction of psychic constants. Each of these efforts has to some degree thrown light upon the synthesis called history; but the concrete reality is the whole interrelated sum of phenomena, the interior and exterior factors, the causes, the conditions, and the modifications that underlie social change, and no one set of explanations can cover all the facts. But a combination of them can undertake the task of explaining the composite reality with some prospect of success; and such for the sociologist is the meaning of the phrase "the philosophy of history."

Evidently then such a philosophy, such a positive explanation of history is no exclusively sociological concern. It may be—and doubtless is—the fact that in the composite explanation the sociologist's share will be the largest. If Man is the animal Homo transformed by continued existence in a societal environment formed by an ever increasing sum of collective cumulations, no doubt the general trends of that societal process will be the basis for the complete explanation; but it will be only the basis, nothing more.

It is to establish the general trend of the cultural movement that the dynamical section of sociology has as its essential task. Yet there is nothing metaphysical or transcendental in it. It is but an attempt, based on the whole history of science, to find an appropriate isolate and then discover relations among the phenomena comprised therein. Among such relations sociology endeavors to find the nature of the sequence of equilibria which analysis reveals as existent in the form of societal orders. Its aim is to discover these relations by an inductive study of the phenomena. So will it aid in laying the foundations for a scientific explanation, a positive philosophy, of history.

Granted then that the problems of dynamics are a logical outcome of the sociologist's analysis of the societal isolate, it must be admitted that the solution of those problems is particularly difficult. The nature of the difficulty can be stated briefly. It is this: given the enormous variety of the cultural patterns which anthropology, prehistorical and historical, presents to observation, how is the sociologist to determine *the* sequence of patterns which will as a first approximation decide the general trend on which subsequent and more detailed sequences can be based? Fortunately the principle on which this formidable question can be answered is relatively simple. It is the following: the determination of a general dynamic trend is to be made quite the same as are general statements in any other part of the science; in particular, the general dynamic trend is to be found by the use of the same procedures that led to the construction of the universal culture pattern.

The position just taken deserves enlargement, for not only does it underlie the present section of this volume, it is likewise fundamental to all that has gone before. To summarize this position then will serve to recapitulate in explicit fashion what has often hitherto been implicit; it will also open the way to the indispensable first approximations of sociological dynamics.

When, then, the observer in any field of interest first regards the infinity of variation which the reality presents to him, there is no way in which he can make initial groupings among the phenomena that are the object of his observation. Things are as they are. Usual and unusual, normal and abnormal, have no meaning. There is the universe and in it things happen so and not otherwise. Substances may vary in weight, say; objects fall at an interminable diversity of speeds; the heavenly bodies in their movements follow irregular orbits; sounds and sights take an infinity of forms; bodies are endlessly different in composition; vegetal and animal existences are all unlike; cultures are never two the same; and individuality is a synonym of unlikeness. It might be that mentality of another kind than man's could find some regularity in this disorder as it stands; man, either as the animal Homo or as the societally developed being, cannot.

Nevertheless, there is a saving fact in this otherwise hopeless confusion. Things seem not to be wholly different. Some of them are alike in at least one or two respects and in ways that man could not devise or effect of his own power, as his discomfiture at seeing a cherished similarity or analogy destroyed bears witness. In other words, if things were not to some degree alike, man could not discover them to be so and still less could he make them so in his animal-descended mind. The animal Homo, being an animal, must have found every new thing strange, unique, unrelated. Only the endless series of his descendants communicating with one another and cumulating their experiences has made it possible to transcend the limitations of the ancestral form. Man then and not the animal Homo has found that things are to a certain extent alike, and upon that fact he has built a growing structure of knowledge.

Man has found that things are alike in ways susceptible of a general statement, that they are some of them alike in kind; and each such discovery is an event in his history. He has discovered for example that bodies under certain conditions fall at like rates of speed and he has found what these conditions are. He has learned that the heavenly bodies are like in their movements round the sun. He has ascertained that sights and sounds and sensations in general are but variations of underlying similarities, that substances are composed of a small number of elements which themselves reveal regularities. Vegetal and animal forms have like functions, each in their kind, and the two kinds have basic similarities. Cultures though infinitely varying are yet but variants of a discoverable pattern; and individuals, he seems now on the point of learning, are but combinations in varying degree of ascertainable psychical constants, revealing uniformity. And so man has attained to some power of comprehension of what he calls the reality, the source of those images that become ideas.

To bring within his grasp the infinitude of variant manifestations in which he finds himself and of which he is a part, man has aided himself by an ingenious even though spontaneous device. Beginning with the fact of similarity within limits among the things with which he has to deal, he has established certain degrees of similarity: those which are not too greatly dissimilar are thought of as a class; those which vary beyond those limits are considered to be exceptions. With time this device has become systematized and deliberately applied. Certain cases, the most numerous and least varying, have been made into a mean around which the less numerous and more variable phenomena oscillate as they manifest more or less of the characteristics upon the existence of which the mean depends.

Thus arises the concept of a normal state and an abnormal state—a concept which applies to the whole range of knowledge and is found in every isolate. Thus there are irrational numbers in mathematics, perturbations in the physical world, health and disease in the biological, order and revolution in the societal, virtues and sins in the moral world. In all these cases there is never in question anything but a mean. Never does the actual orbit form a true ellipse; never do two bodies fall at exactly the same rate; never is health always the same, even for the same organism; never is a culture a true order; never is the virtuous man wholly pure. Always in every class of similarities there is a fundamental part which represents the phenomenon in its generality and so is considered as invariable.

This generality, reached by way of abstraction, is an expression of the mean and about it oscillates another part composed of disturbing elements, envisaged as tending to depart from the mean.

Such is the procedure by which man has succeeded in bringing order into one field of his interests after another. From mechanics on to physics and biology examples of the procedure can be drawn. In mechanics movement is regarded as uniform and causes of acceleration and retardation are then introduced. Bodies fall with a regularly increasing rate of speed—except when they do not, and then the influence of disturbing factors is introduced to account for the anomaly. Health is an equilibrium among the constituent elements of the organism, a perfect operation of the consensus which unites them; when it ceases, morbid influences begin to operate. In the static aspects of sociology the same principle is valid. Order is a perfect equilibrium among the societal subisolates; when it is impaired maladjustment begins its deleterious work. So finally it must be with the dynamical aspects of sociology. Its foundation must be the establishment of a mean, normal succession of orders. In such a normal series of normal orders the fundamental regularities in the development of societal phenomena must be sought.

To extend the concept of the mean or normal state to the domain of dynamics is to assert the validity therein of all the consequences that have been drawn elsewhere regarding it. Thus the lack of any clear line of demarcation between the normal and the nonnormal continues. So many collective cumulations of a given kind and the result is normal; so many more or so many fewer and the result is an oscillation. The consequences are qualitative no doubt, but the differences are quantitative. What the would-be modifier of societal phenomena is ultimately endeavoring to bring about is but a quantitative variation.

True, in fields like the societal, where the oscillations mean so much to the individuals concerned, men will no doubt continue to speak of revolutions or maladjustments just as they contrast health with disease. No one speaks of revolutions in astronomy or physics; the changes are known to be quantitative and as such do not deserve such sensational terms. Nevertheless the same regularities and uniformities that apply to the normal apply to the nonnormal. "The phenomena termed 'perturbative' are in the world-order simple complementary phenomena, united to the fundamental phenomena by an intimate and indissoluble bond." [4] It is this concept which is to be utilized in the construction of a sociological dynamics.

Enough has now been said to make intelligible what is now about to be undertaken, namely, the establishing of the course of the mean development of societal phenomena, the normal course of societal progress. It will be the first approximation of an abstraction to serve as the starting point for further search for regularities, uniformities, abstract relations of a societal nature. It will in theory be based upon an inductive study of all cultural developments, past and present, even though the rigor of this requirement may have to be relaxed in favor of the first approximations.

The immensity of the task may make it seem impossible of accomplishment; but it may well be asked how the determination of the normal is more difficult in regard to a sequence of societal orders than in regard to a universal pattern. Indeed the task might seem a priori easier in respect of the dynamic than of the static problem in view of the circumstance that the number of societal orders that must be studied to determine the normal trend is probably much smaller than the number required for isolating the pattern. Moreover, there are already in existence the purely spontaneous efforts that have grown out of the study of the records and become the bases of the conventional historical sequences. The work of the philosophers of history need not be rejected *in toto;* often theological or metaphysical defense has been made for what were in fact shrewd empirical conclusions. Finally there are those who have striven directly to formulate an abstract historical sequence on the basis of their meditations upon the entire record of Man.

In the light of this store of material, the task of discovering a universal cultural trend may not seem so impossible as it at first appears to be. It is no more beyond attainment than once seemed to be the universal culture pattern. No theoretical difficulties are involved in the one that were not involved in the other. It is simply that the concept in the second case is less familiar. To make it more easily comprehensible, an illustration may be hazarded.

Suppose then that a party of men set out from New York in an automobile. One of the group wishes to see what lies to the west

4. Laffitte, *Cours de philosophie première, 1,* 200.

and especially to satisfy a lifelong dream of seeing the Pacific Ocean (if indeed it exists); another is greatly interested in mountains and wishes to see as many as possible; a third desires to visit as many cities as he can; a fourth is given the responsibility of seeing that the consumption of gasoline and oil is kept to the minimum; still another may be going just for the ride. It is clear from these statements of vague general tendencies in each case what the ultimate general destination of the group is; but where its members will be at any given moment of the journey is unpredictable, for no one in the party has at the start any guide but a map of New York City and its environs.

Now even though the itinerary is entirely unplanned, it is clear that Boston for example is eliminated from the first as a point of transit. It is improbable that Philadelphia will be traversed. If the party goes by way of Cleveland, Pittsburgh has very likely been missed and arrival at Chicago rather than St. Louis is indicated. At Chicago, a view in retrospect will show a definite route traversed no stage of which was deliberately planned beforehand. Yet as a whole it will indicate with increasing accuracy the general and even the special destination of the party. By the time Denver is reached there is even less doubt on either of these points. It will be possible then without much hesitation to project the curve of the journey and discover the city of San Francisco at the end of the curve—to the great advantage of all the party and especially of the economizing and coordinating member, who will find himself more and more referred to and deferred to as the journey is prolonged.

The fact worthy of special notice is that every foot of advance from New York has played its part in making more and more definite the ulterior advances. And if the environmental aspects of the journey are kept in mind, especially the mountains, then the course is seen to have been even more narrowly conditioned. Rivers can be crossed only where there are fords, ferries, or bridges available, and of course the car can go only where there are some semblances of a road.

So much for a single expedition of the kind; but now enlarge the illustration to include a hundred, a thousand such enterprises and plot the course of each upon the map. Not every party goes across the continent successfully. One totally errs in direction and lands in Boston. Another finds itself in Atlanta and has no funds to continue. Others fall into unsounded streams or die in the desert, the extent of which was grossly underestimated. Still others find intermediate points so agreeable that the journey is abandoned. An entirely new party takes the car and continues the journey. Long before the final destination is sure, the experiences of individual parties are shared with others and become by diffusion a common stock of guidance. Finally, a great majority or a small minority gets through.

A study of the records upon the map makes possible the determination of a mean or normal route, from which marked deviations will have to be explained. If most of the lines run through Chicago and Denver and only a few others are scattered here and there, then the normal route lies within narrow limits, i.e., the limits of variation are narrow so that even a route by way of St. Louis would be abnormal; but if equal numbers are shown to have gone by way of each of the cities of Chicago, St. Louis, and New Orleans, then the normal limits of variation are wide and a route would have to go by way of Mexico or Canada to be considered abnormal. Yet each party has set out from the same point, has been composed of similar members, and has utilized the same method. In other words, there is no difference of a qualitative kind between the normal and the abnormal; the same regularities are at work in them all; the results vary quantitatively only.

Groups of men have set out on cultural journeys too, and they have arrived at all sorts of destinations by all sorts of routes, the number and variety tending to decline with the diffusion of experience. It would be possible to plot these varied courses upon the cultural map and so obtain the material for determining the normal course of cultural development. Generation after generation, group after group—the records have accumulated. The outcome has been a sequence of ages, of periods, of eras, of epochs, the underlying process never changing. From pattern to pattern, from society to society, from equilibrium to equilibrium there has been movement, change, evolution, development, progress. When the record is envisaged as a continuity, a question arises. What is the general trend effective in this immense social movement? And what is the particular trend observable in it at any given moment? Such is the situation whence arises the central problem of dynamical sociology.

One difficulty however has hitherto precluded any successful attack upon this problem. The nature of this difficulty, once concealed, is now clear. The record is not the simple story it once seemed to be. It is in fact a composite, to the making of which many factors have gone. Analysis of the social, the historical data reveals the complex interplay of elements, of forces, which now begin to be distinguishable. Henceforth it is possible and necessary to speak of material (environmental), vital (organic), societal, and psychical influences as operative in the making of the record. All of these together are in concurrent action in any historical situation taken as a concrete reality.

One by one these forces have been recognized and isolated. The last such decomposition occurred when the social was shown to be a composite and was differentiated into the sociological and the psychological, the collective and the individual, the societal and the personal or psychical, the cultural and the moral. Moreover the relative importance of the various constituents of the reality has been determined. It is now clear that the central point of interest, the focal point of attention, in the historical sequence is the societal element. The other factors are either conditioning or modifying. The collective and cumulative process alone holds all the other elements together and gives meaning to their combination.

An analogous difficulty confronts the investigator when he turns from the historical record to the societal development. It calls for the application of the same rule of method which suggested the breaking down of the historical reality into its constituent elements. The difficulty is the still complicated nature of the societal results even after they have been isolated from the historical record as a whole. The solution is implied in the question prompted by the rule of method in point: Is it necessary to assume the existence of a single law covering the societal development as a whole? Or is it not rather an immediate inference from the rule to ask whether the results of the societal process may not be analyzed and classified? It was done in the case of statics; can it not be done for dynamics also? If the answer is in the affirmative, as the rule suggests, then it will be necessary to seek for several uniformities of a dynamic kind rather than one. Such a conclusion would tend also to suggest a reason for the long delay on the part of sociologists to deal with the dynamic aspects of their science, for it would imply that the apparent assumption that the dynamic construction is impossible is an erroneous opinion based upon the failure to achieve an adequate analysis and consequent simplification of an extremely complicated sum of data.

That the task of searching for societal uniformities of a dynamical kind is part of the responsibility of the sociologist will not be argued further but simply taken for granted, though not without reasons. In the first place, the projected inquiry is the logical outcome of the whole argument of this volume. In the second place, it was indirectly called for by Leibnitz, directly undertaken by Condorcet, and continued by Comte. Third, it is a point of arrival for all the historical investigation of the modern world. Again, it has in fact been undertaken by all the representatives of various revolutionary movements of the time: Saint-Simonians, Fourierists, Marxians, Communists, Fascists, down to the humblest aviatrix. Finally, the only group which has not given the problem its due attention is the very one which by definition at least is the one most competent to deal with it, namely, the sociologists. The anomaly is too tragic to be allowed to continue.

No better way exists for sociology to work for the reclaiming of a domain that is indisputably its own than to continue the line of thought opened in this chapter. Can the results of the societal process, the cumulation of collective efforts, be resolved into distinct classes? The answer is in the affirmative. There are at least two such classes, clearly separable. The fact emerges from advances already made in the development of sociology.

To begin with, there is the distinction made by the anthropologists between material and nonmaterial traits. Of far greater significance is the debate between the advocates of ideas as the guiding influence in history and the proponents of material forces on the other. The second of these groups has made its ground sufficiently secure against the first to justify the assertion that there are two major factors of the societal reality, an intellectual and a material. Even more important is the contrast which appears in the work of the later sociologists and particularly in the cases of Sumner and Durkheim. Sumner, especially in his later work, *Folkways,* constantly insists upon the importance of what he terms acts. Durk-heim, also in his later work, is concerned with representations. In each case the author is at pains to point out that the phenomenon, whether act or representation, begins by being individual and ends by being collective, i.e., it is not at first societal but only becomes so through the process of cumulation. Thus there are collective acts and collective representations. The contrast is sharp and indicative of the existence of two classes of dynamic sociological data. Finally, there is Comte. In his case the division of the dynamic field was a characteristic of his sociology from the beginning. Thought and action were always distinct in his mind and each was given separate treatment. For him there were from the beginning two dynamic laws, one revealing uniformity in the sequence of ideas, the other in the succession of acts. Speculation and action, each cumulative in nature—such were in Comte's analysis of dynamics the basic divi-sions of societal data.

The position he took can be supported inductively and deduc-tively. Inductively, the primary evidence is that offered by language, which as the result of both spontaneous and systematic observation through the ages divides the manifestations of men into thoughts and acts. Whatever conclusions a future psychology may reach as to the essential nature of these psychical functionings, the results are different and belong in categories so distinct as to suggest the existence of distinct psychical sources, centers, or organs to account for such dissimilar societal phenomena.

Deductively, the problem takes this form: which of the mental powers of men allow of cumulation when they are exercised under group conditions? Utilizing the conventional terms feeling, thought, action, which of them allow of cumulation? Feeling, it would seem, does not. Feelings, emotions, sentiments, propensities, passions, whatever the term, do not cumulate; they vary only in intensity. A passion is not a cumulation of emotions; it is an intensi-fication of them, or of one. The point holds good throughout the whole affective range.

But the functioning which results in thought and action, what-ever its inherent psychical nature may ultimately be found to be, does allow of its results being combined or fused or amalgamated—in a word, cumulated—whereas the affective functioning does not. It seems as its intensity augments simply to increase the intensity of the functioning of the other two. It is the latter only which have results, direct and objective; feeling always remains inner and subjective.

There seems then to be a valid basis for distinguishing between two classes of societal data, two kinds of collective cumulations describable in ordinary language, whatever their ultimate psychical differences, as thoughts and acts, speculation and activity. This classification rests upon views held by anthropologists and sociologists, expressed in contrasting form by Sumner and Durkheim, formulated clearly by Comte, and supported inductively by the evidence of language and deductively by a review of the psychical capacities of men. Accordingly there should be two sets, two kinds of regularities, two basic dynamical laws underlying the trend of societal development. Indeed, this trend itself will be the outcome of the combination of the two dynamic sequences. Each of them must therefore be given special discussion.

CHAPTER 21: *The Ends of Action*

If man can predict, with an almost entire assurance, the phenomena whose laws he knows; if even when they are unknown to him, he can, in the light of the experience of the past, foresee with a great probability the events of the future; why should it be regarded as a chimerical enterprise to trace with some color of truth the picture of the future destinies of the human species, drawn according to the results of his history?" [1] In these words Condorcet posed the problem of formulating the theory of the laws of the progressive evolution of Man. He went further: he envisaged the history of mankind as an abstract development consisting of a sequence of related stages.

What Condorcet did can now be stated in terms growing out of D'Alembert's achievements in turning dynamical into statical problems: he resolved history into a succession of orders, stages, or equilibria and revealed it as a sequence of patterns. Sequential changes in pattern: such is the definition of societal progress; i.e., progress is the development of order. Once this concept is clear, the ascendency of statical phenomena over dynamical is evident. In all the historical transformations there is at work the same process, namely, the cumulation of collective results. This progress is the structure of the societal system in action. It is inherent in the basic arrangement of elements of the system and can be observed so long as the system endures. It is therefore possible, turning away from the study of the stages of societal development, to examine into the nature of the changes revealed by the succession of orders and to do so by following directly the process of collective cumulation. Condorcet's advances in theory are thus absorbed into the general body of sociological doctrine.

Still further theoretical advance was suggested when in the preceding chapter it was shown that the difficulty of arriving at dynamic societal laws was in part due to the fact that the data involved

1. Laffitte, *Cours de philosophie première*, 2, 187.

were more complicated than is ordinarily believed. Two classes of societal phenomena, it was asserted, compose the dynamic group: thoughts and acts. Each must now be studied. Moreover, once the distinction is justified, a second question arises: can any hierarchical relation between these two classes be established, or, if a hierarchical sequence cannot be discovered, is there at least a priority? Which of the two classes should be dealt with first? Or is the order of treatment purely facultative? To decide the question in either form, subordination or sequence, a more penetrating examination of the nature of the two classes will be required. What then is an act, to begin with?

All activity whatever of man is reducible finally to muscular contraction. Thanks to this contraction man initiates, maintains, or puts a check on movements. From this general point of view, activity is common to man along with the whole animal species. In proportion as the animal organism rises in the scale, i.e., in the animal series, the contractions are more and more coordinated so as to tend toward some determinate end. For man there are two sorts of activity depending upon whether he acts upon man or upon things. Action upon men consists in the series of contractions of every nature by which man modifies other men by translating the within to the without, i.e., by expressing a state of mind. Action in regard to things consists in displacing or modifying by coordinated contractions all that surrounds man, whether inorganic or living. Thus when man cuts and works wood, digs the ground, or directs the movements of men and animals, he acts upon things. These latter activities it would seem are essentially what Sumner had in mind when he spoke of acts. They are as well the normal referents of the word in everyday English language.

It is more difficult to give a brief statement of what constitutes thought. All that can be done is to give a general description based upon centuries of man's observations of his own and other mental activity. First then the process described as thinking begins, it would seem, with sensations produced by the external world. These sensations result in impressions, which may somewhat loosely be called images. These images become the basis of mental constructions, seemingly by being combined in every possible proportion. The combinations or transformations of images or impressions are then connected and related in such a way as to construct in the mind reproductions or pictures of beings or events, in isolation or in succession. These seem to be the "representations" of Durkheim.

Muscular coordinations and mental constructions, acts and thoughts: such are the bases upon which common knowledge allows the sociologist to work. But these foundations are only the beginnings, the starting points, the "given," the preconditions of sociology. It is only when these activities begin to operate in a collective, i.e., societal setting that the phenomena of the higher science begin.

That is to say, under such societal conditions not only are the muscular contractions coordinated but these coordinations, these acts, are themselves coordinated when the individual in whom they take place combines his efforts with those of others. There is thus a double coordination: that of the animal, resulting in an act, and that of the socius, whose act plays a part in an end which is that of the collectivity to which the coordinating organism belongs. It is the same with mental phenomena. What sensation is, what images are or indeed whether there are any, how they are transformed or fused into pictures or representations: these questions are secondary in importance for the sociologist. The essential point is that the coordinated sense impressions are themselves coordinated by collective existence. In any case all that is being said for present purposes is that men learn from one another, that *interlearning is a reality*.

Turning then to the coordinated muscular contractions which are acts, the sociologist is interested only when these acts are themselves so coordinated as to reveal some group purpose, i.e., when they are performed by socii. "The mammal other than man, acting only *individually*, uses every means to conserve his existence; there is no doubt some variation in the means used, but they have only one end, ever the same. On the contrary, when man acts *collectively* there is not only co-ordination of the movements of each individual but there is also co-ordination of the movements of the various individuals among one another. Hence it is possible to conceive of the collectivity as being organized to attain ends which are not always the same." [2]

In short, and in conclusion, the increase in the number or mass of collective cumulations—in any case a quantitative increase—

2. Laffitte, *1*, 364.

results in qualitative changes in the ultimate nature of the collective activity, giving it at various times various aims in which the member of the group cooperates, perhaps without full awareness on his part. Since there is a single process and but a quantitative result, there is a possibility of making a single general statement which will reveal a regularity in the working of the process. The outcome would be a law governing the succession of societal ends which coordinate the acts of the members of the collectivity. That is to say, societal activity has its distinctive uniformity.

Can the same be said of collective representations? It would seem so. If there is an increase in the number or mass of collectively coordinated acts, so there is an increase in the mass of thoughts. If the quantitative change produces qualitative variations in the one, resulting in a regularity in the succession of collective ends, there seems to be no reason why there should not be a like regularity in the other. Moreover, the existence of the latter would serve to simplify the consideration of the former. Thus for instance any consideration of the means, the tools for example, by which the ends of societal activity are effected will clearly be a part of the intellectual rather than the active development.

Comte saw the point and stated it succinctly. There are two sorts of activity, one theoretical, the other practical. "Both present the same biological character, but they differ sociologically in the light of the purpose and result of the movements accomplished. In effect, the first is limited to manifesting the interior state of the animate being, while in the second, it modifies the exterior world." [3] It is the second of these classes of collective achievement to which the word "activity" is ordinarily applied, both because of its greater intensity and because of the importance of its results. "Speculation" and "thought" are terms applicable to the first. True action, that is, relates to the world without. But accuracy of conception and expression, especially with reference to societal consequences, necessitates a further distinction. "It consists in habitually separating the appreciation of means from that of ends. . . . Whatever be the direction of our activity, we practise in it procedures essentially due to the mind, of which they even compose the principal domain, since speculation is always destined to perfect them." [4] That is to

3. *Système de politique positive, 3,* 54.
4. *Politique, 3,* 55.

say, how an act or coordination of acts should be done is one thing; what it is being done for is another.

And so there will be two related regularities of societal development, one revealed in human collective action and the other in human collective thought. Admitting then the theoretical existence of these two sets of regularities, which it will be the business of the text later to formulate, the question still remains, what is the nature of the relation between them? Which should be discussed first?

This clue to the solution of the problem can be found in Marx, whose work made clear the necessity for discussing the question of the relation between the two classes of societal data by challenging the position held almost universally before his period that the history of man was the history of ideas. In a discussion of the development of the machine from the middle of the sixteenth century on, he points out the subordinate part played by machinery in the early part of the period as compared with the division of labor and then remarks: "Momentous were the scattered applications of machinery in the seventeenth century, for they gave the great mathematicians of those days a practical basis and a stimulus for the creation of the modern science of mechanics." [5]

"A practical basis and a stimulus": here is the key to the relation between the two sets of collective cumulations, acts and thoughts. No one would contend that mathematics or even mechanics was the work of the men of the seventeenth century only. Mechanics alone goes back to Archimedes and mathematics in the larger sense can be traced backward into the abstract number series of prehistoric cultures. All the achievements of earlier centuries were there for the men of the seventeenth century to work with and build upon. But the efforts then being made to increase the production of goods gave to the mathematicians a very real incentive for the expansion of abstract theories to cover the new concrete phenomena that were being multiplied. It will therefore be in point to expand this conception of the relation between act and thought.

"The spontaneous development of our intellect no doubt tends to determine in a gradual way, of itself and without any other motive, the passage of each branch of our knowledge" to the positive stage, said Comte as early as the third volume of the *Philosophie*.

5. K. Marx, *Capital, 1,* 367.

But our speculative faculties have by nature, even in the most eminent minds, too little activity of their own for such a progression to be anything but necessarily and extremely slow, if it had not been happily accelerated by an outside, permanent, though inevitable stimulation. The whole history of the human mind down to the present affords no example of any importance in which this decisive revolution was really accomplished by the way,—the only rational way,—of a simple logical enchainment of our abstract conceptions. Among these auxiliary influences, indispensable in hastening the natural progress of the human reason, there must be carefully pointed out as the most general, the most direct and the most efficacious, the energetic impulsion that results from the needs of application.[6]

Comte goes even further in recognizing the share of the economic element in stimulating mental evolution:

It is above all to modify the natural order that we have need to know its real laws. Thus the positive spirit, principally characterized by rational prevision, everywhere emanates from practical notions. But such an origin would never have allowed it to acquire abstractly a sufficient generality, if human activity had always remained purely personal, for lack of adequate accumulations. *It is then to the gradual institution of capitals that we owe our true theoretical development.* Besides procuring for it special organs by giving rise to existences dispensed from material labor, they alone can furnish it a vast destination by permitting a collective activity often directed toward great and distant results. When these conditions are not filled, practical life hinders scientific expansion by limiting our real discoveries to purely empirical laws, not less incoherent than particular. Thus the powerful theoretical impulsion, emanating from material needs, depends above all upon the formation of great capitals, which more and more directs towards the species an activity destined at first toward the individual. The co-operation of generations being then guaranteed, the true philosophical genius constructs little by little this general conception of the

6. Pp. 216–217.

natural order which, long limited to the first mathematical laws, ends by including all, even the moral and social world.[7]

In the second place the results of action, by affording a practical basis—experiences—for thought are a constant aliment to the process of collective representation. With every effort to subject the exterior world to the needs of man, new impressions, new observations are made and accumulated. The mass of data thus gathered for purely practical purposes gives an ever increasing body of factual information. These results are spontaneous at first but they tend to become systematic, especially when individuals become more or less specialized in their functions, with the result that they each no longer perform the same general round of activity but do different things and so come into contact with different aspects of the external world. The outcome is a great collection, uncoordinated and crude, of items of information which are the materials on which thought operates to give an increasingly accurate picture of the world without.

Finally in the third place the results of activity, collectively produced, form when cumulated a guide for the operations of the thought process. They make it necessary for the mind to recognize that certain facts are related to others since they always recur, either in combination or in succession. The mind, the organ of attention, is thus compelled to advance along certain lines regardless of whatever tendencies it may have to create combinations, fantasies, without regard to the real world. The contrast between dreams and waking is an illustration of what is meant. Classification, or the detection of similarity, is thus not a purely facultative matter. For example, in the case of his fellow animals, similarities and differences must at a very early time have imposed themselves vividly upon the animal Homo as in fact they still do for his descendants.

Thus there is a real relation between the two classes of societal data: those that result from collective action and those that result from collective thinking. The first serves as a stimulus, an aliment, and a guide to the other, and so there is a definite relation between the two which makes of them a true system as already defined— elements intimately interdependent acting and reacting constantly

7. *Politique*, 2, 166.

one upon the other. But they each have their own course: *this point is absolutely fundamental and upon it all the arguments for an economic determinism in whatever form ultimately break.* To stimulate, to aliment, to guide: these are one thing; to determine, in the sense of causation, is another. For the first there is every evidence, for the second none that is not basically reducible to the evidence for the first.

Thought, opinions, collective representations, whatever the term, have their own origin and their own filiation; never do they reach the point when traced backward at which thought becomes act and so loses its identity. The mathematicians of the seventeenth or seventh or twenty-seventh generations have their filiation with the mathematicians of the earliest generations; so with the astronomers, the physicists, the biologists, or the sociologists. The great revival of commerce and trade in the sixteenth and seventeenth and eighteenth centuries of the present era had enormous effect in stimulating thought in every field; but this thought in every case was based upon the thinking of earlier generations. The chemists sprang out of the alchemists as the medical men out of Hippocrates, Galen, and Averroes. In short there are two divisions of collective cumulations and not one, related at every step no doubt but in theory completely separate. However great the influence of one upon the other, the two are radically independent.

Since then they are independent, the question of their relation recurs. It has already been answered inductively. Since action serves as a stimulus, aliment, and guide to thought, it is logical that it be treated first in order. Deductively the same conclusion is reached. What has just been said shows that action is more general than thought, as defined in an earlier chapter. It should therefore be given first consideration.

Moreover the position just reached is supported by anthropological induction insofar as it has been directed to the point at all. Sumner and Keller summarize the data on the subject when they say, for example:

> Borneo natives concern themselves solely with what touches their immediate interests: "The same limitations of their knowledge revealed itself in [their indifference to] the names of animals and plants which they did not use as food or for some other

purpose in their domestic economy." . . . The need of the Shingu natives to find out the nature of a new thing was exhausted by the question whether the traveller had made it and what it was called. The excellent observer [von den Steinen] who reports this maintains repeatedly out of his wide experience of savages that the necessary and useful preceded the reflective and sentimental.[8]

Out of the flood of anthropological anecdote two bits of flotsam may be salvaged. They put the whole argument at this point in an amusing way. The first is told of the Eskimos. " 'Peary once turned to one of his Eskimo hunters who sat pensively outside the skin tupik on a brilliant Arctic summer day and said: "Of what are you thinking, Tauchingwaq?" The brown native shrugged and smiled. "I do not have to think, Pearyaksuak (Great Peary). I have plenty of meat." ' " [9] The other is told by Malinowski: "When moving with savages through any natural milieu, I was often impressed by their tendency to isolate the few objects important to them and to treat the rest as mere background. In a forest, a plant or a tree would strike me, but on inquiry I would be informed—'Oh, that is just "bush." ' " [10]

So there it is in a word. Whatever is not within the range of the practical is outside interest; it is just "bush." "But if on the contrary, the object happened to be useful· in one way or another, it would be named. . . . Everywhere there is the tendency to isolate that which stands in some connection, traditional, ritual, useful to man, and to bundle all the rest into one indiscriminate heap." [11]

Facts which fall outside a given system have not only no significance for the primitive mind; they are not observed at all. The man of today is no different from the native; if fewer things are just bush, it is because the range of societal interests is far greater than it was.

A more elegant statement of the idea of bush can be made, and to do so will bring this section to an appropriate close. The possibility is suggested by one of the contemporary efforts to make logic more positive. "We do not," says one of the writers on the subject,

8. *The Science of Society*, 2, 760.
9. Sumner and Keller, *1*, 99.
10. Related in Stuart Chase, *The Tyranny of Words* (New York, Harcourt Brace, 1938), p. 61.
11. Chase, p. 331.

"ascribe the same importance to all the elements of what is observed. Some of these elements we consider extremely important or essential, while others are quite ignored by us. This does not mean that we consciously make a choice. On the contrary, in the great majority of cases it seems to us that what we observe presents itself to us in such a way that certain of its elements are more dominant or more obtrusive than others." In consequence the logician recognizes the existence of "a convention by which certain elements within what is observed are given a preferential position compared with certain others when the formulation of a protocol statement is decided." To this convention is applied the term "preference principle." "The acceptance of a preference principle is merely the conscious application of something that happens quite spontaneously and as a rule unnoticed every moment of a man's life." [12] The emphasis here is on the individual; the general concept is obviously applicable to the social. So to apply it makes it possible to summarize the present section by saying that societal activity serves to give a preference principle for societal thought.

The way is finally clear for the effort to determine the nature of the regularities discoverable in the first of the two classes of collective cumulations, those that have here been called acts. The objective must be clearly understood. It can be stated as follows: Men *as socii* unite their efforts, i.e., make muscular contractions for the purpose of modifying things. In making these contractions there is a double coordination: that which coordinates the muscles in view of a particular act—this is biological; and that which coordinates the act by making it a part of a number of other acts performed for some purpose advantageous to the collectivity—this is sociological. In the latter case there is a collective result, and these collective results cumulate through time forming a greater and greater mass of societal phenomena.

As this mass increases it more and more narrowly defines succeeding acts, since they have to be performed in relation to the existent mass if they are to have meaning. The cooperating individual, the socius, may be quite unaware or at best only slightly aware of the

12. Bent Schultzer, *Observation and Protocol Statement* (Copenhagen, Levin & Munksgaard, 1938), pp. 30, 26, 29–30, and especially 32–93.

ultimate collective significance of his act. The fact is of no importance; what is important is that the act is performed: the results remain and delimit the next act or coordination of acts. The mass or number of acts increases; with the quantitative increase comes a qualitative difference between the successive purposes or ends of the group, i.e., the collectivity. The ends for which the socii cumulate their efforts change. There is a sequence of such changes historically established. The task is to find the nature of the regularity underlying the sequence of changes.

The problem can be restated as follows. Groups or collectivities, associations of socii, unite their efforts for different ultimate ends; they may be regarded as moving from A to C. What is involved then is the finding of a path from A to C which may be regarded as a normal route, a mean. About it there will be oscillations; from it there will be departures. Both will be regarded as abnormalities with respect to the normal route, i.e., in comparison with the normal results of the operation of the process. But the normal and the abnormal are only quantitatively different, since they both result from the operation of the same process. The whole problem then reduces itself to the task of determining a normal succession of normal societal ends. Parenthetically, it is assumed here in this simplified exposition that there is only one such end discoverable in a given group; such is often not the case, as the existence of extensive military organizations in modern industrial nations shows, but in an elementary discussion the assumption is defensible; it is even indispensable. A first approximation is hardly feasible under other conditions. Besides, it would be difficult to find a case in which a collectivity pursued in permanence several ends of equal importance.

Whence are to come the data on which can be constructed such a normal sequence as that set forth above? The answer is clear. For many generations now the human record as a whole has been in the course of compilation and construction. It has steadily been pushed back into the past; it has steadily been increased in detail in every age and country and epoch; there is now no important culture which has not had attention; the great lines as they now exist are likely to stand forever. Moreover, in the expanding of this record there has been going on a more or less conscious construction of a normal sequence. That is to say, an abstracting process has been spontaneously at work. World histories, outlines of history—with all their weaknesses they bear witness to the slow recognition of what might well be called a normal course of human development. It is a vast and continuing induction. Its results have hitherto been more or less spontaneous; what they now require is to be taken up and continued systematically.

In the attempt to make more systematic the spontaneous induction that the expansion of historical knowledge has been effecting, what is the proper procedure? How shall the course of history be determined? The logical method best applicable in theory is that which prescribes first the determination of the nature of the extremes of the record and then the subordination of an intermediate term to the extremes so established. There is reason, however, to believe that in the case of the search for regularities in the sequence of acts it would be expedient to approximate the mean between the extremes first and turn to the extremes afterwards. The defense for this reversal of the normal use of the method lies in the fact that the histories, however they may differ in regard to the extreme terms and particularly in regard to the latest term in the chronological sequence, are nevertheless practically unanimous in presenting one particular coordinating end of societal activity as always existent at some time in any prolonged collective existence.

This universal activity, found in all the historical records at some time, is war. Now it would certainly be superfluous for this discussion to go into detail to establish the fact that societal activity has in countless instances been coordinated about military action. Indeed, the necessity would almost seem to be that of showing the reality of any other ultimate purpose of societal organization. The difficulty is obviated by precision in definition. When "war" is alluded to here, the term is used only with reference to those cases in which the ultimate coordinating principle in a society is military activity, that is, in which the society is organized for war as its ultimate end. But even with such a restriction there will be little objection to the assertion that war is one of the stages through which passes any advanced society and therefore must be included in any normal societal sequence.

A more penetrating question is this: Is war a middle term between two extremes? The question can be answered only by finding such extremes; and so the discussion must return to the precept of method that every intermediary should normally be subordinated to the two extremes between which it operates a connection. These extremes must now be sought.

Between what societal stages does war serve as an intermediate term? In the first place, then, where does the process of cumulating collective actions begin? The answer is partly deductive, partly inductive. The deductive part is an inevitable inference from biology: that science presents the animal Homo as absolutely dependent, like any other living thing, upon the continued satisfaction of organic needs. Here the animal Homo has the last word. Whatever else his descendants do, they must eat; and so they are not left in bewilderment at the beginning, wondering what a collectively living animal must turn its attention to first. The animal Homo tells them quickly and in no uncertain terms and puts a time limit too on obedience—or else . . . It needs no reliance upon or even reference to anthropology and the primitives to know what the first societal activities were which served to correlate the coordinated muscular contractions of the primitive. The inductive evidence is quite as clear. At the present moment, anyone suddenly removed from the presence of socii reverts almost at once to the animal in respect of food; and collectivities in abnormal circumstances take care in all cases possible of their food supplies. Such activities are first in more senses than one. Both lines of evidence converge to show that the first collective activity was, and had to be, the hunting of food.

Collective hunting then is the beginning of Man's societal activity, and there he would have to begin again if tomorrow he were to be stripped of all the cumulated results of sociological development. The hunt and the chase, or more precisely a hunt and a chase, were his first concerted actions. The purpose of activity was the finding and gathering of food; the word "collection" suggests both the aim and the societal means for attaining it; for the moment then it will be justifiable to throw the hunting stage into the background by calling the first stage of societal coordination the collection stage.

But what is the most advanced phase of the societal process? On this point two lines of reasoning converge. The first is anthropological. It grows out of the concept of the culture base. Of two societies, that is the most advanced where the stock of culture traits is largest, or, in sociological terms, where the mass of collective cumulations is greatest. By this test and not by any subjective preference the Occident is first. The sociological verdict is approved by the historical judgment, for any historian dealing today with mankind as a whole would feel bound to end his record with the West.

Moreover, there is a special advantage which the western phase of the societal movement shares with the earliest: that is that the two are original evolutions. They are both instances of invention, to use anthropological terms, and not of diffusion. The statement is true of the first stage by definition; the animal Homo at that point first began to manifest cultural phenomena, which thus must have had an independent origin since there was no source whence they could have been derived. Essentially the same thing can be said of the Occident, using the word in the cultural sense. Since 1600, say, and indeed earlier, the societal movement there, mainly assimilative up to that time, has become more and more creative. Certainly none of the cultural characteristics that constitute the particular physiognomy of the modern period were diffused into the West; on the contrary, the movement is from within outward.

Taking the Occident then as the latest development of culture, the next question is this: Among the many forms of activity manifested in the West which is the one that ultimately serves to coordinate all societal actions? The normal state of the Occident, the activity which gives ultimate societal significance to individual acts, is some form of industry. That is to say, the collective activity of the Occident is normally cumulated with reference to industrial ends. Here again little objective judgment is required for the decision. Warlike activities in proportion to their scope require in the western world the reorganization of normal societal life; society —the whole complex of relationships holding socii together—has to be reorganized for undertaking extensive warlike activities; or conversely, a war disorganizes the normal life of the community and at its end must be followed by reconversion. No doubt the industrialization is not complete and industry is not yet wholly organized; nevertheless the general statement is valid both as a fact and as a trend. Modern society is essentially industrial.

The two extremes are thus clear: the beginning, where the process of collective cumulation has just started, and the present or latest state of culture, where the mass of collective cumulations is greatest. Between these extremes the intermediate term would be easy to find if it had not already been stated. It is of course war, which requires and obtains for successful results the coordination of all the activities of the socii in a collectivity, and this whether conflict is actually in progress or not.

Here then is a progression from the hunting activities of the primitive to the industrial activity of the most developed society, the intermediate step being clearly martial activity. In short, here is the normal movement of mankind, resulting from the continuous cumulation of the results of coordinated muscular contractions themselves coordinated for collective ends. It leads from the collection stage to the industrial stage, passing through a military stage. The normal succession of ends correlating societal activities is thus established. It has been presented dynamically as a series of stages; it might have been reached statically as a sequence of related equilibria.

As just formulated, the statement of uniformity discoverable in the course of human development is too broad and too far from the reality. It is too much like saying that in going from New York to San Francisco it is necessary to pass through the Middle West. Greater precision is needed; it can be had by increasing the number of terms in the formulation. It is therefore necessary to have recourse once more to the rule of method already employed, checking the conclusions against the historical data.

But before the argument is carried further it will be well to guard against a criticism that might arise from the superficial similarity between the sequence of ends of societal activity as formulated, or as to be enlarged, and the various schemes of inevitable linear cultural evolutions to which the anthropologists have raised such strenuous objections. Their criticisms are sound. There are no such evolutions to be found. But their rejection of such linear schemes does not touch the validity of the effort here being made. A factually existent evolution is one thing; a normal societal development is another. The latter is a generalization and an abstraction. It is an effort to set aside all secondary and modifying factors whatever from the record of man's sociological advance. It strives to determine the course of collective cumulation as if no extraneous factors or influences whatever had been in operation, as if the process had operated under ideal conditions, as if only the inherent tendencies of the process of collective cumulation had been at work.

To turn at this point from the dogmatic to the historical form of exposition will be no obstacle to the straightforward movements of thought. On the contrary it will aid in the expansion of the statement already formulated of the filiation which holds together all stages of societal activity. It will add new terms to the progression: collection, war, industry, by showing how the pioneer in this field —Comte, of course—reached his original position and then elaborated it. His thought begins with the essay of 1822, where the author is concerned primarily with the nature of the social transition going on in the modern period. His immediate effort was to understand and facilitate the passage from the feudal and theological system to the scientific and industrial regime. A first outline of the trend of activity is implicit in the statement that the two great ends of human activity are industry and war. Continued meditation supplied a middle term between these extremes and the essay thus came to the first expression of the trend. War is decomposed into two types of military purpose, conquest and defense. The initial dualism thus becomes a progression; mankind passes through three successive states: conquering, defensive, and industrial.

After this initial progress Comte made no advance until 1839, when in the fourth volume of the *Philosophie* he deals at length with the law and shows its necessity. Not until 1853 in the third volume of the *Politique* does he return to the topic, as a part of the discussion of the theoretical basis on which a philosophy of history must rest. The formulation of the law remains the same, and in the fourth volume of the same work it is still essentially unchanged: "Activity is first conquering, then defensive, and finally industrial." [13] This part of Comte's thought might thus be said to be at once the most original and the least thought through of his major sociological formulations.

These two characteristics are probably interrelated, each being partly due to the other. The originality of the induction can best

13. Comte, *Politique, 4,* chap. 3.

be seen by viewing it in the light of opinion before and after 1800. The turning of swords into plowshares is of course nothing new, nor is the utopia of perpetual peace; but in addition to these generous aspirations of men of good will in all times, there had in the eighteenth century accumulated among the abler thinkers a mass of opinions on which Comte's thought rested and which was to impel him in the direction of his more comprehensive and penetrating generalization. Among these thinkers may be mentioned Quesnay, Adam Smith, and Hume. The latter moved forward a step toward Comte in his essay "On the Population of the Nations of Antiquity" in his *Political Essays*. Here Hume took as one of the indications of the degree of civilization reached by a nation the size of the population it could maintain. Then he compared the military slave-holding states of antiquity with the more pacific and slaveless societies of modern times and showed the superiority of the latter. Still another influence was Condorcet, in whom the revolutionary current toward a regime of peace and harmony found eloquent and reasoned expression even under the shadow of the guillotine. After the turn of the century came the utopians: in 1808 Fourier in his *Theory of the Four Movements and of the General Destinies* planned the organization of an industrial regime; in 1817 Saint-Simon published his *Industry*, with the epigraph "Everything for industry and by industry." And in a more sober way, the economist Dunoyer was maintaining and revealing the superiority of an industrial regime.

"On all sides then the social evolution in the Occident was giving the industrial regime greater and greater preponderance; the conceptions of the thinkers of the time were formulating the phenomenon more or less clearly and giving it both more intensity and more consistency; but they all failed more or less to recognize the necessity of a prior military regime; and *in proclaiming the advent of industry, they could only condemn, in both the past and the present, the regime of conquest.*" [14]

Against these tendencies one man spoke out loudly: Joseph de Maistre. In 1796 in his *Considerations on France* he proclaimed as a great general and fatal fact the necessity of war, which he connected with Buffon's biological law of the destruction of animal species one by another. But he was too greatly dominated by the

14. Laffitte, *Cours de philosophie première, 1,* 376.

biological aspect of the phenomenon and was unable to make out the civilizing role of conquest. "War is the habitual state of the human race. . . . Somewhere or other on the earth, human blood must flow uninterruptedly." [15]

Thus there was no lack of divergent and unrelated analyses of a special and restricted scope. Out of them Comte was to draw the coordinating statement which shows the future to be connected with the past and so to be a consequence of the entire evolution of the species. Perhaps it was the very extent of the advance made by his own formulation over the speculations of his predecessors that accounts for his failure ever to go in essentials beyond his thought of 1822.

His reasoning can best be illustrated from the fifty-first chapter of the *Philosophie*. "All the various general means of rational exploration applicable to political investigations have already spontaneously concurred to show the inevitable primitive tendency of mankind to a life mainly military in nature, and its not less undeniable final destination in an existence essentially industrial." "The invincible antipathy of primitive man for all regular labor leaves him no other kind of sustained activity than that of the warrior, which is besides the simplest means of procuring his subsistence." [16] Habits of regularity and discipline could in early times have been fostered in no other way. Without them no true political regime evidently could have been organized. "This natural ascendancy of the warrior spirit has not only been indispensable to the original consolidation of political societies; it has above all presided over their continuous increase in size, which could otherwise have been brought about only with excessive slowness, as the whole of historical analysis clearly shows." [17]

Hence a long preponderance of military activity was as inevitable as it was indispensable. Nevertheless the very same principles which account for its rise show just as clearly its essentially provisional nature.

Industrial activity spontaneously presents the admirable property that it can be stimulated simultaneously among all individuals and all peoples, without the expansive growth of one being

15. De Maistre, *Considérations sur la France*, p. 33.
16. *4, 569, 571.*
17. *4, 573.*

irreconcilable with that of the others. On the contrary, the full expansion of military life in a notable part of mankind implies and at last determines in all the rest an inevitable compression, —which is even its principal social office as regards the whole of the civilized world. Thus while the industrial epoch has no other general duration than that, as yet not determined, fixed for the progressive existence of the species by the system of natural laws, the military epoch has had of necessity to be essentially limited to the time adequate for a sufficient and gradual accomplishment of the preliminary conditions that it was destined to bring into existence.

This principal end was achieved when the major part of the civilized world found itself at last united under a single domination; it was brought to pass, *in our European series,* by the progressive conquests of Rome. Thereafter, military activity was evidently destined to lack both object and aliment: hence its preponderance, since that inevitable point, has been constantly decreasing. It no longer hides the gradual rise of the industrial spirit, whose progressive advent was thus suitably prepared for.[18]

Yet the radical difference between war and industry makes necessary an intermediate and transitional stage between them:

The total development of the system of conquest proper to antiquity would have been able to determine the *direct* advent of industrial civilization only if it had embraced the whole of our species. Such a plenitude being impossible, military activity continued to prevail among the smaller peoples who had escaped the gradual incorporation. But from this time on, the military activity was especially directed against the dominant population, which was then led, at first spontaneously and then systematically, to change attack into defense. It is thus that *feudal civilization* had to succeed to conquering sociability, so as better to prepare the industrial regime.[19]

In the foregoing analysis of activity certain weaknesses are obvious. They are, however, the sort of inadequacies which follow

18. *4,* 575–576.
19. *3,* 62–63.

from the imperfect use of a right method; they are therefore reparable. Briefly stated, these defects are: too absolute an interpretation of biological data in the direction after Buffon of what will later be called the struggle for life; too much regard for philosophical interpretations of the political developments of history; too great reliance upon a psychology believed to be the highest range of biology and so supplying data for immediate sociological use; too restricted a range of history—"the European series"—and a consequent overemphasis of the medieval record: finally, too little anthropological knowledge of primitive culture. All of these inevitable shortcomings of a first approximation can be corrected; a second approximation will result, to be corrected in its turn.

By implication part of this cumulative improvement has already been made in the progression developed in the first section of this chapter. The three main stages of societal activity are collection, war, industry. The first of these terms gives greater precision to the earliest activities of Man than the state of anthropology in Comte's time allowed him to do. It corrects the direct deductions from biology by reference to cultural data. The collection stage thus is a necessary addition to Comte's formulation.

At the same time Comte's analysis of military activity makes it possible for the second term of the original progression, war, to be decomposed into its two phases, conquest and defense. The progression thus becomes a series: collection, conquest, defense, industry. When this step is once taken, the nature of the method by which the series can be extended is clear. First, any two successive terms of the series must be regarded as extremes and an intermediate term sought for to connect them. Second, the historical basis for this search must be enlarged from the European series to include the whole record of mankind. Thus can the normal course of societal activity be given greater and greater precision.

In utilizing the method just defined to expand the series of four terms given above, the first gap to fill is that between the first two terms, collection and conquest. The first stage hardly reached out to war; conquest hardly extends back to collection. An intermediate stage is needed. Anthropological data as they exist today simplify the task of finding the required intermediate term. Man at an early period of his development ceases to rely mainly upon collection and turns more and more, and finally mainly, to raising the material which provides his sustenance. The products thus obtained may be vegetal or animal in nature—hence perhaps the so-called pastoral and agricultural stages. It seems impossible to show any sequence connecting these two activities. Actually other than strictly sociological factors seem to influence any given collectivity in its choice between the two. It may be that environmental influences, say the flora and fauna of Spencer, will decide. The normal course may therefore go via either of two routes.

Both of them, however, could be embraced easily in a single term. The point of course is that societal activity became creative rather than acceptive in regard to both the vegetal and the animal worlds. "Cultivation" would seem to be such a suitably inclusive term and could serve as an intermediate between "collection" and "conquest." A more revealing term might be found; "production," say. It would have the advantage of carrying the thought beyond the range of food alone. In any case the original series now becomes a sequence: collection, production, conquest, defense, industry.

Even with this addition, the distance between the second and third terms seems too great. An intermediate stage can easily be found. What is involved is control over materials. Both anthropology and history show how easily it may be achieved by seizing products once they have been brought into existence. The seizure of products later gives place to the subjection of producers. The first is more sporadic, unorganized, and temporary than the second; it is also more widespread and enduring. To it may be given the term "predation," and under this name it becomes a true intermediate stage between cultivation and conquest.

If now attention is turned to the later stages of the sequence, a definite gap is revealed between defense and industry. Not only is this true, but it is also true that industry is by no means yet in normal existence. Its place in the sequence results from projecting the filiation of societal activity into the future. An intermediate term is required. To supply one will strengthen the law as a whole by basing it still more solidly on the historical data and at the same time render it more useful by relating it to the present.

Such a term can easily be found by resort to the history of recent generations. What it should denote is clear in the light of economic changes which are now an historical commonplace. Indeed Comte three generations ago had the essential facts, though he failed to carry his insight to the point of expanding his original formulation of the law. In 1853, analyzing the nature of a truly industrial type of active coordination, he drew a distinction which suggests a name for the intermediate stage being sought: "This *social elaboration* of industry had above all to consist in a decisive separation between the workers and the entrepreneurs. On this separation necessarily depended the fundamental transformation of the character of industry which, at first purely individual, could finally become truly collective only by virtue of the normal preponderance of the directives over the operatives." [20]

Here is the key to the definition of an intermediate term between war in its defensive phase and industry. Comte saw the point but, swayed both by the abstract nature of his construction and by the generous anticipations of his predecessors and contemporaries, he overestimated the rapidity and directness of the transition between war and industry. Recurrence to history corrects the error. It shows that the modern period, since say 1600, presents the picture of industrial life, but only in a nascent unorganized form. It is *industrialism* rather than *industry* which has shaped the mores of the present. As a matter of fact, the individuals who were the agents of the early stages of the transition were termed adventurers by those who knew them best; and later they became entrepreneurs. *Enterprise* rather than industry became the dominant societal activity. In this word is the clue to the nature of the activity which served to connect defense with industry in the normal sense.

The difficulty in formulating the later phases of the active sequence is not merely a matter of words. There are two circumstances that complicate the task. In the first place, there is a problem of emphasis or selection. In the making of the formulation which shall receive prominence: the descending phases of war—war as conquest, as defense, as instrument of policy; or the ascending phases of industry—industry as support for war, as individual objective, as societal end? Answers to this question are inconclusive because of a second circumstance, namely, that the societal change now going on is an original evolution. Mankind has never gone this way before, and so the choice of route must be spontaneous. Hence

20. *Politique, 3,* 491.

judgments both as to the choice of new roads to be taken and also as to the very decision to leave the old ones at all will lack finality.

Comte's pioneering words on this topic are in no wise invalidated by the dubiousness of his psychology. All the normal properties of military existence, in his opinion, long form a profound contrast with the tendencies inherent in industrial life. The exercise of the latter begins by being essentially personal or at least purely domestic. This egoistic character persists in it even when industry has taken a great development, as we see too well today. Hence results the principal obstacle to the normal systematization of pacific life, while the moral aptitude of military existence renders it easily susceptible of a full organization. That is why up to the present the natural superiority of the only activity that allows of universal and continuous growth has been neutralized. However great the public utility of industrial services, so long as it is not suitably felt by each private cooperator its principal moral reaction cannot be developed. Despite the superior nobleness of the instinct of construction, the instinct of destruction remains more worthy as well as more energetic if it is exercised habitually in the light of a social destination and the former for personal satisfaction. The very morality inherent in voluntary exchange tends even to be effaced entirely when the contrast between constructive effort and conquest seems reduced to replacing violence by fraud.

What these words show is the indeterminate and equivocal nature of a transitional phase of development. They reveal the uncertainties that are inevitable when a road into the future has to be chosen in a purely spontaneous manner, a road that need never be traversed again once it has led to the destination. What this destination is, is clearly indicated by induction of a dynamical kind and confirmed by the statical findings of an earlier chapter. It is industry, the correlation of the acts of socii by participation in constructive efforts for collective ends. Here then is the equilibrium toward which the societal system is moving, the latest variation in the basic cultural pattern, the next principle of preference for the selection of materials for thought. It completes the formulation which presents the results of the continuous filiation of societal action. This formulation consists of several terms which denote characteristic states when regarded each as a form of order and which are related stages when considered together as the continuing effects of progress: collection, production, predation, conquest, defense, enterprise, industry.

The normal succession of normal equilibria portraying societal progress as the development of a related sequence of orders through the continuous operation of a uniform process has now been depicted with enough detail to make it useful in understanding cultural evolution. The chapter would therefore seem to be at an end. But there are two questions so obviously rising out of the discussion that they cannot be left unanswered without leaving the chapter logically in the air. First: if there is, underlying the terms of the formulation finally reached above and any other terms which it might by expansion come to contain, a single process constantly in operation, cannot a general statement be made concerning the nature of the uniformity revealed in the working of the process? If so, can it be put in the form of a relation between two variables? Second: if the process in question has been operative since the beginning of human society, is it going to cease with the inauguration and systematization of industry? In other words, in what sense is the stage called industrial final?

To the first question above the answer is definitively in the affirmative. A uniform process, cumulating the results of collective action, does continue in operation through all the stages of societal development. Moreover, there is a constant increase in the mass of the results cumulated. Here then is one of the two variables required for the formulation of a law covering any and all stages of the process, however extensive or restricted. The second variable is more difficult to formulate. It concerns the nature of the changes in the ends that coordinate collective actions as they increase in mass. An inductive review of the stages of societal development, from the hunting and gathering pererrations of the animal Homo to the industrial organization of modern Man, shows a continuous decrease in the destructive effects of his acts and a corresponding increase in creative, productive efforts; hence a first approximation of a law of societal activity: The productivity of the ends which correlate societal action varies with the mass of cumulated collective acts.

As to the second question, it is certain that societal activity will continue. But with what result? There are two possibilities in logic. First, the stage of completely organized industry is in the nature of a geometrical limit to which activity will ever tend but never reach. Second, the stage of industry when attained will itself be but the beginning of still another general stage. That is to say, the basic dualism war, industry may require a third term as yet in the obscurity of time. It may well be that the socii of that distant period, having mastered the production of material goods, will once more make a qualitative change and engage in the creation of aesthetic satisfacients. Thus art in the inclusive sense would become the third term in a progression reaching out into a future too distant to be considered here.

CHAPTER 22: *The Bonds of Thought*

One of the two major foundations upon which a universal culture trend must rest has now been laid. One of the two classes of dynamical societal phenomena has been shown to reveal a sequence of normal stages. This class of collective cumulations comprises the results of the activity of men when as socii they combine and direct their efforts to the achievement of a collective aim. These societally coordinated muscular contractions, these acts operating upon things, serve not only to provide the satisfactions required by the basic needs of the animal Homo; they serve also to guide his thinking by providing a principle of preference in the selection of significant material for his thought. What the nature of this thought is has already been partly made clear; it remains to carry the analysis to the point where the words "a normal course" become significant.

To penetrate into the mysteries of thought in the abstract individual sense is the affair of the psychologist. What an image is, in the psychical sense, or whether indeed there are any such things, is no concern of the sociologist. What interests him in his function as student of a different isolate is the fact that thoughts, whatever they are, do cumulate. The cerebration of one human being in some way joins onto the cerebration of another; thought grows; it becomes collective. That this growth is a fact, the unanimous agreement, the universal induction of the race, gives irrefutable testimony.

In the case of the individual being it is obvious that his mental pictures are coordinated sense impressions just as his acts are coordinated muscular contractions. It is not then a digression to inquire, in relation to the sense impressions, what are the sources of the coordination that transforms them into images. Moreover following this line of inquiry will show the point at which the sociologist comes into the picture.

As to the inner means of coordinating sense impressions in the individual, i.e., completely isolated being, there are two. In the

THE BONDS OF THOUGHT

first place, the picturizing faculties—being faculties and not senses and therefore dealing indifferently with the products of all the senses—have their distinctive modes of operation. The sense impressions are materials to be utilized by the mind in its own fashion. Concretion, abstraction, induction, deduction: these are characteristic examples of intellectual cerebration. When Comte saw this point clearly, he was able to amend the Aristotelian dictum "there is nothing in the intellect that was not earlier in the senses" by an addition due to Leibnitz: "nothing, save the intellect itself." The intellect, in other words, is structured. But, said Comte, the distinctive nature of the intellectual faculties can be discovered not by any analysis or observation, however minute, of individual, isolated beings but only by observing the results of their collective operation through the ages. In other words, the structure of the intellect can be discovered only by studying the process to which it gives rise.

The second source of mental coordination consists in the connection between the affective motors—i.e., the orectic constants—and the intellectual or the eidomorphic faculties. The affective elements are interrelated and so give rise to a logic of feeling. They are likewise connected with the intellect. "The wish is father to the thought"; but the proverb is only a loose induction. It is no more a psychological explanation than the statement "the acid eats the metal" is a part of chemical theory. It is nevertheless testimony to the effect that sensory materials are coordinated not only directly by intellectual but also indirectly by affective forces.

Defective as these and similar inductions are, both intellectual and affective, they do nevertheless indicate to the sociologist the point where his investigations should begin. They show that individual sensory materials are doubly coordinated before, or without, the exercise of any collective influences whatever. Only at this point does the societal process begin to have its distinctive materials. Just as true acts are the starting point for societal coordination in the field of what has been called activity, so are the doubly coordinated sense impressions—true thoughts—the starting point for societal coordination in the field of speculation. They compose the domain within which the societal process may operate.

The immensity of this domain should be emphasized. It is in fact the whole world of fantasy. Laffitte has well described it in the following passage:

In truth no one can see what limits to assign to the combining power characteristic of our minds. The most extraordinary, the most bizarre, the most sanguine inventions of the human intellect become easily explicable in its light. The creation of monsters and of angels seems of the same order as that of any personage whatever of drama or romance. The creation of God, even, is no longer inexplicable. What should have brought metaphysics and theology to more just ideas as to the value of their own inventions is the common remark that they have never been able to give the most grandiose, the most majestic, the most venerable of their beings anything but the physical or moral qualities to be found in men and animals. All the divine qualities are equally human qualities; the wing of the angel is found, in principle, on every bird. The combination of images is a synthesis which puts in play all our cerebral functions. The feelings particularly intervene therein, and in two ways. For one thing, the emotions are so bound up with the images that the latter cannot be recalled without at the same time awakening the former, which then by way of reaction arouse new images. For another, feeling intervenes directly to provoke, aid, sustain either the formation or the modification and the combination of images. Unless we call upon the mind for some special and sustained effort—and even then some impelling emotion intervenes at the beginning— the spectacle spontaneously offered by our intellect is that of a succession, more or less incoherent, of images which are born and die under the influence of the passions which do battle in our brains. Dreams are an example of what cerebral spontaneity can do of itself, and our intellectual and moral life would be a perpetual dream if the external world with its own regularities and its terrible exigencies did not intervene as a regulator.[1]

For the individual being, then, conceived of as existing in complete isolation, there are two sources of control in relation to his thinking. The first of these is inner and consists in an increasing integration both of the intellectual faculties on the one hand and of the affective constants on the other, and a more and more complete unity between the two. To this inner spontaneity is to be added

1. *Cours de philosophie première, 1,* 280–281.

the influence of the outer world, exercised through its regularities and uniformities. Utilizing all these factors of mind, the individual learns, i.e., reaches a coordination of thoughts in a strictly individual sense, in the light of which new experiences come for him to be significant, to have meaning. But this meaning may well be strictly personal, as the cases called pathological make clear. It in no sense assures the ability of the individual to cooperate with others. His personal coordination may be so different from theirs as to result in his alienation, in the double sense of the word. Otherwise expressed, an individual may be well integrated innerly without necessarily being sane.

It is at this point that the sociologist begins to be involved. If men are to live and work together it can only be as the result of their having so similar a view of the world without as to enable them to combine their efforts in relation to it; and this result can be attained only when there is a fundamental similarity between the coordinations which give meaning to experiences. Under these conditions individual beings come to have views in common and communication becomes possible; a community begins to exist; the socius is born, society develops.

In other words, not only must the materials afforded by the senses be combined into pictures, views, configurations, images, but these combinations or conceptions must themselves be coordinated in some persisting way if the individual of today is to cooperate with the individual of yesterday and a fortiori if these selves once unified are to be able to work together with other selves.

It is the existence and persistence of similar or quite identical methods of coordinating conceptions that make possible continuing unity of personality in the individual; it is the same factor which is at work in the uniting of individual beings. Similarity of mental structure on the one hand and identity of external situation on the other make the two results, and particularly the second, possible. Only by possessing some common framework of thought can projects be formulated and effected by groups. Only so can like circumstances have like significance for all. In short, only in this way can men become socii in speculation. As soon and as long as they can fit their conceptions into like cadres they can cohere, confer, concord, and cooperate. To do so means simply the coordinating of conceptions by utilizing like principles of coordination—the reference, that is, in the last analysis of thoughts to the same set of structural relationships.

That all men do not utilize or possess the same set of principles whereby to coordinate their conceptions is evident from the observation of cases where agreement is impossible to individuals not pathological. The existence of various methods of coordinating experiences—methods not confined to individuals but characteristic of a group—is obvious. And of course the observation of many systems of thought coordination prompts the inquiry whether there is any relation between these systems and particularly whether there is any sequence between them. Such an inquiry is the purpose of this chapter. It should be emphasized that what is involved is the search not for new experiences but for the ways in which all experiences, old and new, are bound together into meaning. It is not the newness of thoughts nor the difficulty of attaining them that is in point; it is the network of relationships that holds them together.

In other words, the objective of the chapter is the discovery of the sequence of spontaneous cadres or syntheses which have served at various times to correlate the growing sum of collective representations that has resulted from the continuous operation of the societal process. The mass of collective cumulations of thought grows, but as it increases quantitatively, are there qualitative changes in the spontaneous connections that arise to bind together the facts observed? What structures of relationship have successively been pictured into which all observed phenomena, old and new, can normally be fitted and thereby be given meaning? Such principles bind representations together; they are the framework, the web, the ligatures of human reason; they are in a double sense the bonds of thought.

In the preceding chapter, the acts of men as individuals were shown to possess societal meaning only when they were coordinated by some purpose common to the group. Out of the sequence of these societal ends comes a series of principles of preference regulating and directing the choice of phenomena for observation. The phenomena thus preferred to attention have in turn to be coordinated if they are to have meaning, i.e., significant relationship; the various ways in which this coordination is effected compose a sequence of frames of ultimate reference.

What methods, general and special, should be utilized in answering the question just formulated? They have been exemplified in the preceding chapter: the establishment on inductive bases of the extremes of the cultural record and the finding of an intermediate phase whereby a dualism becomes a progression and reveals a movement. But where begin? At which extreme?

Choice need not long be delayed; the latest phase seems best. Not only is it an original evolution and thereby brings into focus the societal situation in which the cumulation of collective representations is at its maximum; it is also the point on which there is the maximum of agreement. It is thereby freed almost entirely of the element of value judgment. Hence the first question to be asked is the following: Taking the Occident as the culture area where collective intellectual cumulations are today at the maximum, how are these societal products there coordinated and synthesized? What, in other terms, is the frame of ultimate reference characteristic of western thinking? What is the dominant bond of modern thought?

The answer is not far to seek. For more than fifteen generations now the growing concern in the domain of knowledge has been the search for law. It became dominant in the age of Newton and has been expanding ever since, reaching into one domain of speculation after another. From this point of view the dominance of law is precisely what makes the intellectual world of today modern. To discover the facts, to analyze, classify, abstract, and isolate them; to establish abstract relations among abstract phenomena; to find the constant and permanent in the midst of the varying and changing; to concentrate attention upon the establishment of regularities and uniformities: such is the goal of modern speculation.

To formulate the synthesizing principle which gave meaning to man's earliest experiences and served to bind into significance his first collective cumulations is more difficult. Induction is less direct; the generations who made the first frame of ultimate reference are lost in the mists of prehistory or the obscurities of geology. They left many indications of their coordinating principles, as language in its etymological aspects so clearly reveals; but the conclusions are inferential. If induction is weak, however, at this point deduction is strong. All it requires is something more than lip service to the doctrines of biology. Men are the descendants of the animal

Homo; their beginnings are those of an animal. No doubt they were the beginnings of a particular animal, the animal Homo, but the general position is not changed by the fact; the differential characteristics were at that moment potential, not actual; as animal, however far that level was later to be transcended, man began.

Both induction, direct and inferential, and deduction, organic and societal, agree that thinking, i.e., the coordination of thoughts began by being psychopreferential. That is to say there was an inner, spontaneous, primordial principle of synthesis. What this means is that the events of the world without, pictured in or by the intellect, were bound together to begin with by virtue of the bonds existing in the world within. In other terms, the first principle of synthesis, the primordial frame of reference, was a psychical, moral, orectic bond supplied spontaneously by the operation of the psychical constants that lie at the foundations of human personality. In them man found the causes of his own activity; in analogous sources he found the causes for the phenomena, the activities, of the world in which he had to live.

The search for causes, a bond of causality: such was the initial intellectual effort of man and such the initial synthesis. The essence of the matter, underlying the wide variety of possible terminology and so dispensing with special and detailed discussion, is expressed in the following words: "During our long infancy, individual or collective, that is to say so long as the search for causes prevails over the study of laws, the progress of human reason consists above all in restraining our interior inspirations more and more in order to make them conform better to exterior impressions. Before observation could unveil to us any analogy capable of guiding our synthetic tendency, we are forced to draw from ourselves all connections; so that *our first step always results from a purely subjective logic,* whose domination is then almost unlimited." [2]

Cause and law, causality and uniformity, the psychopreferential and the socioexperiential, magic and science: such is the initial dualism on the basis of which the normal course of speculation must be established. The evidence for the validity of this basic dualism of thought is the whole of history in the widest extension of the term. It is the outcome of centuries of societal induction. It has been formulated in many ways and by many men. Among them, to choose

2. Comte, *Système de politique positive, 3, 23.*

a single notable example, was Max Weber. Of him it was said: "The growth of the rational habit of thought and of its attendant release of society from magic was for Weber the strand upon which all sociological concepts must be strung, regardless of the religious or the ethical value of that strand." [3] Weber's own words are: "The release of the world from magic and its concomitant rationalization may be good or it may be bad, but it is our destiny." [4]

To set up two contrasting states, however, is not adequate for determining the normal course of thought even though they contrast not only in content, as cause and law, but also in time, as earliest and latest. In such a dualism there is no progression; it may record only opposition and the substitution of one method for the other. A third and intermediate term, leading from one position to the other and connecting them, must be discovered before it is clear that a *movement* is in question. Such a middle term can be supplied by historical induction and supported by logical analysis.

This link between causality and uniformity can be found either by following forward the development of cause or by retracing backward the history of law. Either path leads to a middle ground where the two concepts coalesce. Cause is elevated to the position of the will which is the final orderer of the universe; the order found in the universe is interpreted as the work of an omnipotent will issuing laws. In either view of the matter causality leads to uniformity.

The transition is made by way of a transformation of the initial concept of cause. That is, there are two sorts of causality. The first of these phases of psychopreferential thinking consists in the attribution of subjectivity directly to the things that have to be brought within man's mental grasp. The cause, that is of their manifestations, lies *in the things themselves*. They are active; they cause results directly, as do men and other animals. Causation is concrete. In the framework of concrete reference, natural objects are envisaged as agents in the strict philosophical sense; they are free agents,

3. Cf. Howard Becker, "Historical Sociology," in *The Fields and Methods of Sociology*, L. L. Bernard, ed. (2d ed. New York, Farrar & Rinehart, 1934), p. 26.
4. Max Weber, *Wissenschaft als Beruf Gesamonett aufsatze zur Wissenschaft Lehre*, p. 554, quoted in *ibid.*, p. 26.

like men. They are self-determined. Like men they may be influenced.

The second phase, clearly the result of the cumulation of collective experience, is a more abstract type of mental bond. It consists in regarding things as in themselves passive but moved by powers *outside and above the things moved*, i.e., by fictive personalities. Causation becomes abstract. Thus there are two kinds of causality, direct and indirect. And since the explanation in both cases is made in human terms, the cause takes the form of a will. Hence there are two kinds of will, the indwelling or natural will and the outer or higher or supernatural will. Thus the mental progression which is the normal course of speculation reduced to its lowest terms can be formulated as follows: first or direct causality (agency), second or indirect causality (causality proper), uniformity; natural will, supernatural will, law.

On each of these levels the effects of the societal process can be observed. The mass of collective cumulations augments; the quantitative increase gives rise to a qualitative change. Nascent man first binds his representations into significance by a strictly subjective method; the only thing he knows is the operation of the (conscious) world within. A greater and greater mass of observations, collectively gathered and refined, forces him to modify the utterly naive views with which he must begin his intellectual activity. Abstraction from constantly recurring phenomena produces a modification of the initial naivete. A second and more sophisticated type of causal explanation results. It is superior to the first; it is wider in application; it is more satisfying; it embraces the expanding range of phenomena with which developing activity is making him familiar. A new way of binding representations, themselves more and more collective in nature, is the outcome. In short there is constructed a new frame of ultimate reference.

This second method of intellectual coordination is obviously intermediate between simple or direct causality, pictured as agency, and uniformity. It makes possible the transformation of the dualism of cause and law into a progression, so that the normal course of human thinking may be regarded as established in principle. It rests upon historical and analytical foundations, accessible to all. As a formulation it is obviously very general; it needs to be expanded. Collective experience shows how the expansion can be effected. The method was stated and applied in the chapter preceding. With the historical record as a guide it should be a simple task to insert intermediate terms between successive members of the progression, each pair being regarded for the purpose as extremes. From fantasy through fiction to fact; from direct causality interpreted as indwelling or natural will through indirect causality and supernatural will to regularity, uniformity and law: such is the expansible progression which in substance defines the nature of the intellectual movement which successively supplied principles for the coordination of thought, constructed a series of frames of ultimate reference, and thereby provided the bonds by which to hold together the sum of collective representations existent at any given moment.

Down to the present, the theory of this chapter has been set forth in strictly dogmatic fashion. The dogmatic form of exposition must now give place to the historical, involving a brief survey of the process whereby the preceding formulation was developed. To do so will aid in the necessary expansion of the progression into a form more closely corresponding to the historical reality. It will explain why the second of the two basic dynamical laws of sociology has been for the moment left in progression form. At the same time it will give some notion of the inductions on which the whole conception rests.

No doubt the reader of the section just concluded has been vaguely aware that he was in the presence of Comte's law of the three states: "Every branch of our knowledge passes successively through three different theoretical states: the theological or fictive, the metaphysical or abstract, and the positive or scientific." [5] If his awareness was not intensified into certainty, it was mainly because of the unfamiliarity of the wording. Not entirely so, however; for the formulation of the preceding section brings into the light an aspect of Comte's law that is concealed by the terms usually employed. A change in meaning seems involved in the change in words.

Such is not the case, however. Comte's law does not in fact mean

5. Essay of 1822 ("Plan des travaux scientifiques nécessaires pour réorganiser la société"), Appendix to *Système de politique positive, 4, 77.*

or imply what it is usually construed to mean, namely, that religion and philosophy are things of the past and will ultimately be superseded by science. What Comte had in mind was something other than the platitude that reason tends to prevail over emotion. In fact, he was not thinking of religion or philosophy or science as such at all. He was thinking of the ways in which thoughts are combined and coordinated, how they are given meaning by being fitted into frames of reference, and how the final or ultimate cadres into which conceptions are fitted are articulated.

Religion, philosophy, science: each has its own function in human life; each may be envisaged as a distinctive body of representations combined in different ways and for different ends. The question is how the representations are combined so as to have meaning. There are three ways, Comte is saying in his law, all three of which can be used to colligate phenomena in any domain of thought. To denote these three frames of reference Comte used terms drawn from the instance which seemed to him historically the best to illustrate the respective method of coordinating phenomena. Religion, that is, in its most characteristic historical form, has been theological, philosophy metaphysical, science positive. But they do not always have to be so.

Religion does not give way to philosophy and philosophy to science. As foci of thought they will always exist. Each responds to a basic human need; each has its own body of collective cumulations. But in each case there are three ways of relating and correlating the data. Religion, that is to say, may be theological or metaphysical or positive. And so may philosophy and science.

So convinced was Comte of the validity of his position that he wrote a positive philosophy, strove to raise the science of social phenomena to a positive level, planned and in part organized a positive religion. These three were to be harmonious one with another because they would all three be unified within the framework of the same ultimate reference. It goes without saying that the three conflict when they are coordinated by different cadres of relationship; but once they all utilize an identical frame of reference they come into permanent harmony. And why not? Man's basic needs do not change. What changes is the way in which are correlated the results that come from collective experience in satisfying those needs. The interests to which those needs give rise are universal and perdurable; they are consurgent and coadjutant; how can their conflicts be eternal?

Only a very brief historical review is necessary to support the interpretation just given. Reference to Anaxagoras, Aristotle, and Philoponus is not in point in regard to the initial discovery of the law, though they are certainly included within its scope when it is fully expanded. It was in fact the growth of science that was the starting point of the induction. Pascal was thinking of the growth of science when he said that the whole series of human generations should be regarded as one man, ever living and ever learning. Turgot in 1750 stated that the sciences in their development pass through regular stages. Toward the turn of the century the idea was more or less general, as is shown by the case of the doctor Burdin, who in the entourage of Saint-Simon was saying that the sciences had first been hypothetical and conjectural in their evolution and then positive.

Such statements, however, despite the brilliance of insight that honors their makers, were far indeed from having the universal extension which Comte gave his law as he moved to the terrain first of the development of the intellect in history, i.e., in the race, and then to the recapitulation of that history in the individual. His meditations on the subject continued for more than thirty years, and in six passages in his work—1822, 1825, 1830, 1839, 1853, 1855 —the law is formulated and expanded.

It would in no sense be a digression from the straight line of thought in this volume to trace in detail the germination and growth of Comte's thought in regard to sociology, for in this case the history of the science is for a time coincident with the biography of the man. Space however is lacking for so detailed an exposition as would be required. All that can be done is to trace the general lines of advance and summarize the progress made from time to time.

First and most important of Comte's efforts was the obliteration of the line between natural and moral philosophy. Success here meant the establishment of a series of abstract sciences above or beyond the inorganic. Achievement of this aim resolved itself into the institution of a sociology. Above the inorganic level were four classes of phenomena: the vegetal, the animal, the intellectual and moral, the social. The first three of these Comte assigned to biology, the last to sociology, without realizing that he was in fact following the distinction between the individual and the social, ethics and politics, on which moral philosophy was constructed. He had however instituted a new science; the encyclopedic hierarchy had six members, with sociology at the summit.

But from the beginning there was difficulty with the intellectual and moral data assigned to biology. Did they belong there? If not, then where? To separate them off into a distinctive science—Spencer's solution—was little help, for it did not change the essential sequence of the classes of phenomena; and it was precisely there that the real problem lay. Was this sequence correct? When biology was finally defined as the science of life, abstractly defined, the urgency of a final answer to these questions increased.

If intellectual and moral phenomena were definitively separated from biology, they must belong in the only remaining science of the encyclopedia, sociology. And this is precisely the solution to which logic forced Comte in 1853: "All genuine appreciation of mental laws belongs to the positive study of the whole of human development. But reciprocally sociology is reducible to the true science of the understanding. It is the total study of the intellect of man." [6]

Undoubtedly it seems almost incredible at this distance that a man of Comte's power was so long in distinguishing between the intellect as one of the constituents of psychical life on the one hand and the cumulated result of its collective exercise on the other. But two facts mitigate the severity of the judgment. First, the notion of the collective exercise of the intellect could not be entertained so long as the intellect was equated with reason and attributed to a self-contained ego. Second, there was at the time no science of psychology. Comte had to institute that science and give a new version of the intellect before he could find a definitive place for his sociology. Increasing attention to the nature of psychical unity—the integration of the personality, in terms of today—finally gave him the basis for a positive psychology (for which his name was *la morale*) and showed the existence of a new isolate. Thus the hierarchy came definitively to have seven terms, with sociology between biology and psychology.

6. *Politique, 3,* 47–48. The remainder of this chapter is based on the same volume; quoted passages are taken from pp. 31, 13 (5), 14, 15, 36–37, 37, 81–82, 173, 37, 38, 22, 26 (2).

Sociology thus came to have a fixed position in the abstract hierarchy on both inductive and deductive grounds, the first because of the improved analysis of the data involved and the second because the final solution was in complete accord with the principle of decreasing generality on which the hierarchy is based. The next task was the division of the subject. Here no difficulty arose. From the beginning Comte was familiar with the distinction between statics and dynamics, which he had studied in both mechanics and biology. At first he gave dynamics the precedence, but it was not difficult in the light of D'Alembert's theorem to correct this misconception; hence the reversal in the *Politique* of the position taken in the *Philosophie*.

There remained finally the formulation and expansion of the dynamical uniformity observable in the operation of the human intellect. The importance of this law to Comte's entire sociological construction must be emphasized. It made sociology possible, to begin with, for if one regularity could be found in social phenomena others no doubt could, and so a true science would come into being. Then continued meditation upon the law slowly brought into the light consequences at first only implicit in the idea. For example, the law was clearly dynamical; what then was the statical element of the science? The outcome was the division of the science into two sections.

Obviously there were difficulties in establishing the law. What, for one, was the scope of the regularity observed? To begin with, it was limited to scientific materials. This initial concentration upon science was the source of the original formulation. Science, the point of arrival of thought through the ages, was positive in nature; religion, under whose auspices thinking began, was theological; in between came philosophy, whose method was metaphysical. The use of these terms threw into the background the essential significance of the law and obscured it even in Comte's own mind. Yet it was there all the time, as occasional comments demonstrated: "This purely subjective logic [of the initial state] is then in the beginning as normal as are today the best scientific methods. Furnishing then the only means of binding facts together, it alone allows our observations to be developed." Here is evidently implied the concept of a normal succession of normal bonds of thought.

Gradually the scope of the law was expanded to include, beyond science, the whole body of intellectual activity. With this enlargement of the original scope went a parallel extension of the historical grounds for the induction. To begin with, it was quite as definitely limited to the European series as the law of action. In this series particularly was support to be found for the transition from theological to positive by way of the medieval development. But with time the range of induction was extended until Comte came to be the first to grasp the importance of what is now called the primitive world.

Finally, there was the question of the relation between the law of thought and the law of action. Here Comte faltered. "The real supremacy must be assigned to the least energetic of the three grand divisions of the cerebral system": feeling, thought, and action. Yet "to give first place to the least energetic may seem anomalous; still it has always been usual to make the progress of mankind consist in the advances of the intellect." *"No doubt we can now trace this habit to the metaphysical regime,* which reduced our nature to speculation alone, neglecting affection and even action, because its vain theories could find no distinctive place for them." "Although the intellectual faculties are in themselves weaker than the active, they appear to have greater influence upon man's evolution, especially in the collective aspect." And yet "speculation is always essentially directed by action." "Despite the abstract independence dreamed of by the pride of theorists, all our mental revolutions have been born in turn of the successive exigencies of our practical situation." But finally, "to gain knowledge and to bring men to mutual understanding: such is the double attribute by virtue of which the mind appears to direct the whole of man's evolution. Although its real part therein is only that of a minister of the activity that the feelings determine, its characteristic efforts should receive chief attention in the systematic view of history." And so Comte with the key in his hands—the influence of the metaphysical regime—turned for the time away from the door to a new view of historical causation to follow, no doubt under the guidance of Condorcet, his spiritual father, the conventional paths.

Extending the inductive bases for his law brought Comte, as was said above, into contact with the primitive phase of culture. The consequences were inconsiderable to begin with but soon became momentous. In the primitive world under the guidance of De-Brosses Comte found fetishism. It seemed to him at first only a preliminary and subordinate form of theologism. At most then it would require only a slight amendment of his original formulation, which would now comprise four states: the fetishist, the theological proper, the metaphysical, and the positive.

No sooner however had the original form of his law been modified than Comte began to question the validity of his position. The questioning once begun continued until the initial formulation of the law was replaced by another, the metaphysical disappeared entirely, and the law was so transformed that what was to begin with only a first approximation became quite definitely a second approximation and as such much closer to the reality of cultural development.

Both fetishism and theologism proper are forms of causality, but how do they differ? In the answering of this question Comte began the transformation of his law. "These two general states of the fictive synthesis differ radically in the way in which they conceive of directive wills. In the first and more spontaneous, they belong immediately to the bodies whose phenomena they explain. But the second and more fictive way attributes them to beings independent of the different existences that each of them governs without having any determinate seat."

Despite their necessary succession, these two fictive regimes are almost never entirely separated. Under the preponderance of the one, the accessory existence of the other can usually be perceived. Thus the passage from fetishism to theologism is everywhere operated almost insensibly although *it constitutes the most profound and the most decisive of our preliminary revolutions*. Their affinity results from the fact that the first system is concerned above all with the beings themselves and the second with their diverse common phenomena, in sequence with the natural progress of human contemplative thought, individual or collective. Now the spontaneous preponderance of one of these two modes can never produce the entire desuetude of the other. The mind which is most narrowly limited to concrete contemplation is sometimes absorbed in abstract contemplation . . . ; the inverse disposition is more easily appreciable.

After such a beginning it was no longer possible to continue to think of fetishism as only an initial and subordinate form of theologism. It became a distinct phase of intellectual evolution in its own right, and all Comte's later thought was to make the separation between the two states more and more marked. The decisive step was taken in the second chapter of the *Dynamique* where fetishism is discussed and analyzed at length as a main phase in the filiation of thought. "I need not here set forth again the fundamental distinction between the fetishist mind which forthrightly makes animate all natural beings and the theological mind which subjects them in passiveness to supernatural powers. *Anyone who should today persist in confounding these two ways of conceiving of causes would by that very fact manifest a radical inaptitude for sociological studies.*"

In short, Comte had come finally to challenge the universal assumption that mankind had begun its intellectual evolution with a belief in deities. Fetishes were not deities at all. They were a more primitive form of causality. They *preceded* the deities. The expansion of the new idea continued to the point where fetishism itself as a distinctive mode of thought was subdivided. There was first a spontaneous and then a systematic phase. In the spontaneous phase, the beings or objects in which wills were thought to be actively operative were the accessible ones, immediately under observation. Thus they were mainly terrestrial. The systematic phase began with the gradual reduction in number of fetishes and the concentration upon the smaller number of powers at first more widely attributed. The reduction in number and the concentration of influence were due to the growing cumulation of collective experience, which more and more revealed the inadequacy of the assumed wills. Fetishes of this second type tended to become nonterrestrial, inaccessible, and so celestial and sidereal.

"The first causality, always limited to *beings,* could not give adequate satisfaction to our general desires for prevision, aroused by our needs for action. Under the second, relative chiefly to *happenings,* the universal aspiration was to foresee the working of the directive wills by virtue of an assiduous observation of their various doings." In other words, as man's experiences broaden from the concrete to the abstract he passes from the study of beings to the study of occurrents, and in so doing he transfers to fictive beings

THE BONDS OF THOUGHT

the wills formerly supposed to reside in objects. That is to say that as fantasy evolved under the stress of experience, man was guided by two distinct kinds of hominoids, fetishes and deities, and in that order.

The foregoing development of theory so illuminated Comte's earlier ideas in regard to theologism that it could now be subdivided in its turn.

> When theologism replaces, or rather absorbs, fetishism, it can be developed in two successive modes: the first polytheistic, the second monotheistic, the distinction between the two being undeniable although as a rule it is grossly exaggerated. It consists less in the multiplicity or unity than in the independence or the subordination of the different fictive beings. In the last analysis, they remain very numerous so long as theologism preserves a true activity, especially social or even only intellectual. But the divine hierarchy can leave to each of them its own empire or transform them all into ministers of their supreme head. The spontaneity of the first mode makes it both the most complete and the most lasting; in all respects it constitutes the principal phase of the fictive synthesis.

Monotheism is the final form of the second phase. It is inadequate as a guide for action; it cannot abide, resist, or survive discussion. It is an inevitable stage in the original course of thought, but once it has occurred it need never be repeated.

Thus there are two stages of causality each with its subdivisions; but what has become of the metaphysical state? Once it was a main transitional stage between the other two, theologism and positivism. Now however that the basic progression in the evolution of thought has become fetishism, theologism, positivism, where is the metaphysical? It still exists and in its original position but with vastly diminished importance. Where it was once a main stage in the basic progression is now simply a transitional phase. It now serves to bridge the gap between theologism in general, particularly in its final form of monotheism, and positivism. What has always really led to the passage of the intellect from one phase of its development to another has been the continuous growth of experience in the direction of positivity. At a certain stage in that growth "systematic entities are substituted for spontaneous divinities. The very indetermination of these abstract conceptions becomes the natural source of their fitness to aid in transitions. For each entity in this phase can be envisaged as the spiritualized god whom it replaces and as the general phenomena which it designates, according as the mind is closer to theologism or to positivism." Its chief historical service was to inspire the ontology which accompanied the decline of monotheism. Otherwise it could be omitted from the normal course which was followed by the filiation of thought.

What happened to the metaphysical state is like what happened to the state of defense in the original formulation of the law of active evolution. Comte, having based his first approximations upon occidental development, then turned for further inductive materials to universal history. The result was to enlarge the base of his law in both cases and show that the period he had once considered to be of critical importance, namely, the Middle Ages, was much less important in the larger view; hence the revision of his law, revision which makes possible a return to the dogmatic form of exposition.

Resumption of the dogmatic mode of presentation allows of certain improvements in the formulation of the law of speculative evolution. Several of its original terms are so reminiscent of religion as to misdirect the attention of the reader and thus serve to obscure the real intention of the law. In fact it had from the first no more to do with religion than with any other department of thought. A more abstract phrasing will bring into relief the precise nature of the uniformity which the law seeks to express.

The first state in the intellectual filiation, the first stable equilibrium of thought, is that in which representations and observations are bound together in a framework of causality, which is therefore one of the two members of a basic dualism, uniformity being the other. Now there are two principal modes of causality, the second providing a transition between the first and last members of the dualism, which thus becomes a progression indicative of a true movement of thought.

The first member of this progression—the first state if it is regarded from the static point of view, the first stage if from the dynamic—is centered about the first of the two modes of causality.

This first mode of causality is spontaneous, wholly psychoprefer-ential, inevitable to beings just beginning to live collectively. It is concrete in that it is concerned with the beings, objects, i.e., exist-ences in the world without. It is direct, attributing to these beings and objects causation in the same psychical sense that it has for men. It moves through two stages. In the first it concentrates attention upon existences in the immediate environment, upon accessible and so terrestrial sources of causation. As cumulated experience renders this initial naivete less and less tenable it finds fewer and more powerful sources, more remote, inaccessible, and so celestial and sidereal.

The second phase of causality shows the influence of collective experience; it is indirect and abstract. It relates rather to happen-ings, events, phenomena, and properties than to beings and objects. Its more abstract conceptions are bound together by being attrib-uted, as characters of personality, to fictive beings who control but do not permanently reside in the seats where their powers are normally manifested. The number of these beings grows with the growth of abstraction; and two ways develop of dealing with them. The spontaneous way is to think of them as independent and often unrelated, so that causality is multiple and dispersed in its source; the systematic way is to organize and hierarchize them and finally subordinate them to one chief, whose ministers they become, how-ever degraded or disguised.

The final unified phase of causality easily and readily interprets causation as due rather to entities than to deities. Entities being little more than personified abstractions, they serve conveniently as a bridge over which the passage from cause to law is made. In their systematic aspects they give rise to ontology, a dissolvent of the fic-tive beings and an indirect support of laws.

One question remains. Each of the two stages of causality has been subdivided, thus changing the progression of which they were a part into a sequence. Can a like subdivision of the final member of the progression be made? The answer is yes, and for the following rea-sons. The entities of ontology, shadowy though they are, are yet the direct descendants of the isolated and then concentrated fetishes of concrete causality, absorbed and replaced by the independent and then hierarchized deities of abstract causality. As such their wills are untrammeled and the laws by which they order phenomena are absolute. This quality of absoluteness is transmitted to the regularities and uniformities which science exerts itself to discover. Continued induction, however, makes it more and more clear that never can the within become a completely faithful representation of the without. "Truth in any given case, social or personal, means the degree of approximation that can be reached at the time in our representation of the world without."

When this point of speculation is reached, the effort to attain to absolute doctrines is abandoned. "We freely form hypotheses capable of verification in order to institute laws sufficient for our conduct; we do not aspire either to form a perfect representation of the world or to give full satisfaction to intellectual cravings." "In the normal state it is recognized to begin with that the subjective should always be subordinated to the objective. This fundamental principle is then complemented and completed by conceiving of this subordination as purely relative to our needs, to which our means must be adapted. All objective syntheses having been renounced, a subjective systematization is instituted, whose aims in practice determine its nature in theory."

In conclusion then the normal course of thought traverses a sequence of seven terms: concrete causality, centered first in many accessible usually terrestrial existences and then in fewer inaccessible usually celestial or sidereal beings; abstract causality, attributed to fictive beings at first dispersed and independent and so multiple and then hierarchized and even unified and so single; ontology with its amphibolous and indeterminate entities; and positivity, where uniformities are first objective and absolute and then subjective and relative. In more condensed form, the normal movement of thought is from fiction through abstraction to demonstration; from natural wills through supernatural wills to law; from concrete causality, i.e., agency through abstract causality—causality proper—to uniformity.

To say in objection to the law of the three states in any of its forms that distinctive types of frames of reference coexist, often in the same mind, is to be platitudinous; to imply that so evident a fact escaped the attention of a mind like Comte's is to be absurd. As a matter of fact, the first enunciation of the law was accompanied by a generalization which accounted at once for the observed facts. This complement of the law deals with the order in which the various abstract isolates become positive. Formulated by Comte in response to the evident sociological data and therefore presented at first as a sociological law, it was later expanded into a universal law of classification.

According to this law of classification, isolates become positive with a speed proportionate to their generality. What this latter term means has already been explained in the earlier section of this volume where the positive basis of value judgments was defined. According to this law, the inorganic world is a whole more general than the organic and therefore reached the level of positivity first. Within the realm of the organic the biological is more general than the sociological, the sociological than the psychological. Vital, societal, and psychical phenomena reach the positive level in that order. The historical record reflects the nature of the phenomena. Obviously then the same mind meditating upon isolates of varying generality may refer one to a completely positive frame of reference, another to a metaphysical, and a third to a causal in either of its two forms. The statement holds good not only for isolates but also for composites of phenomena. Philosophy, for example, synthesizing the whole range of phenomena, will be positive in proportion to the degree in which its elements have progressed toward positivity and it will become more and more positive as the various abstract sciences progress. Religion, to take another example, being occupied mainly with psychical and societal phenomena, the most dependent and the least general of all, will be slow in reaching the positive state. Since these isolates have in the past been coordinated mainly on a theological basis, religion has been the slowest of men's major concerns to reach the level of uniformity and law and has necessarily been in conflict with those departments of knowledge that have progressed more rapidly toward positivity.

To bring this chapter to an end, two questions remain to be answered. The first of these is the following: Can the law of intellectual filiation be formulated in a completely general form? The problem thus raised is that of finding the adequate variables. There are three involved, the third being subordinate. The first is the growing number, the mass, of collective cumulations. The second is the nature of the underlying principle by virtue of which all frames of ultimate reference are created. What marks the successive frames of reference is the degree to which the psychopreferential is subordinated to the socioexperiential. What begins by being fictive becomes under the control of the reality more and more positive. Hence a possible formulation: the positivity of the frames of reference which bind ideas into meaning varies with the mass of collective cumulations and with the degree of generality of the phenomena involved.

The second question is this: Is uniformity synonymous with positivity? In other words, in what sense is the third term of the law as formulated to be considered as final? Two answers are possible. Uniformity may be identified with positivity: in this case the third term is to be regarded as a geometrical limit, ever to be approached more closely, never to be reached. But positivity regarded as a way of viewing the reality may in time find still another frame of ultimate reference than uniformity. "Affectivity," for reasons beyond the scope of these pages, may be suggested as such a term. The bonds of thought would then be causality, uniformity, affectivity; and man in his normal course would move from will through law to love.

CHAPTER 23: *The Universal Culture Trend*

Analytical procedures, exemplified in the two chapters preceding, call ultimately for synthesis. Such a synthesis is the purpose of the present chapter. What analysis showed was the existence of two societal forces, elements, or constituents quite distinct from one another and yet interdependent. Between them is an equilibrium which is constantly shifting and on the whole becoming more stable as the component forces are more nearly integrated. In other words, what analysis shows in this case as in other like cases is that the unity it is commonly supposed to destroy is a purely metaphysical conception. It never was. Like the notion of ultimate reality, it is nothing but an inescapable implication of the bond of causality. It is unity which is being made. Complete unity is a final achievement; it is a geometrical limit. It is not a point of departure ever to be lamented; it is a point of arrival ever to be sought.

The societal equilibria here in question result from the interplay of two factors, the active and the speculative, each of which has its distinctive course of normal development. Together they are the outcome of the societal process. *"L'essor collectif constitue l'unique source de l'évolution active et speculative."* The words are Comte's,[1] and they clearly point to the fact that the two evolutions in combination will indicate the normal course of cultural development. To effect this combination is the task of this chapter. Before it is begun, however, it will be well to dispose of certain preliminaries.

First of all, it is to be emphasized that the combination when effected will lie wholly within the abstract isolate proper to sociology. Neither conditioning nor modifying factors of variation are to be considered. The result will take the form of an abstract universal societal movement, the groundwork of all cultural expansion whatever. The two constituent factors are distinct but interrelated. Together they form a system as already defined. Because the two factors are mutually interconnected, the speed of development of both

1. *La Synthèse subjective* (2d ed. Paris, Fonds typographique, 1900), p. 26.

despite their distinct nature can be regarded as the same. Thus the combination to be effected must result from a fusion of equal and parallel expansions of interrelated abstract elements. Since the societal system underlies all cultural development, the sequence of successive equilibria which the fusion of corresponding stages in the two evolutions implies will provide a theoretical basis—but a basis only—for a positive philosophy of history. The formulation of such a sequence, in short, will define the universal culture trend.

How shall this trend be formulated? The general principle was laid down by Comte as a result of his meditations upon the shortcomings of the merely descriptive titles Condorcet gave his ten epochs. What was involved in an effort like Condorcet's was, said Comte, a classification, a coordination of facts; it should therefore have had the merit of presenting a homogeneous series. The example of the naturalists, to whom are due the chief advances in the general method of classification, should have been followed. "The true principle consists in making the order of generality of the different degrees of division conform as far as possible to that of the relations observed between the phenomena to be classified." In accordance with this philosophic principle, "the principal division of epochs should offer the most general view of the history of civilization. The secondary divisions, to whatever degree it may be deemed advisable to carry them, should offer in succession views more and more special of the same history." [2]

Granted the solution in thought of the general problem as just defined, still another question arises, namely, the selection of terms to apply to the divisions established in the classification. The available vocabulary is inadequate. How absurd to speak of a cultural stage as "neolithic"! Other words such as "fetishism" and "theologism" are often unsuitable, either because of disagreement as to their meaning or because of inadequate referents. The need for accurate terms is real. There is guidance and allurement in the art of nomenclature as developed in chemistry; but even here the instance of error embedded in the word "oxygen" warns against premature effort. Even the terminology of a new discipline must be created by the process of successive approximation.

Moreover, even the existence of an adequate terminology would

2. *Système de politique positive*, *4*, Appendix, 110–114.

leave unsolved the problem of the form to be given the universal culture trend. Each of the two evolutions, active and speculative, was originally expressed as a progression growing out of an initial dualism by the identification of an intermediary stage. Utilizing the same method provided a sequence in each case of seven terms. How many terms should there be?

No final answer is possible. Uniformities are not absolute. Societal uniformities like any other can never be an exact reflection of the world they seek to picture in order that it may effectively be modified. Hence the degree of fidelity with which they reflect the observed facts may be varied in accordance with need. If what is required is a general view of the whole societal development, the normal course can be formulated comprehensively. If there is some special need, then the number of phases within a given stage can be multiplied. No misunderstanding can result so long as the trend is not identified with its formulation. Whatever the words, the movement continues. In this chapter, where no special ends are in view, the progression form of the two dynamic societal regularities will with an occasional exception be utilized.

First of the two factors that combine to give the universal culture trend is the active as already defined. Reduced to progression form, its most general stages are food concern, war, industry. For speculation, the corresponding progression reads: agents, causes, laws; concrete causality, abstract causality, uniformity; fetishism, deitism, uniformism. Of these equivalents, the last is the least analytical and abstract but the most amenable to combination with the terms expressive of the stages of activity; hence the following composite formulation in which the foundations of all cultural expansion are put in the form of a basic progression: fetishistic food control, deitistic war, uniformistic industry.

In this completely abstract formulation, the active evolution is a primary principle of preference, its sequential stages bringing varying bodies of factual data concerning things, existences, occurrents, phenomena, to the attention of the beings—animal, humanescent, human—whose lives depend upon action in regard to them. Speculation, thought, cumulating the efforts of the intellect as it operates under collective conditions, forms a sequence of ultimate frames of reference in which the facts preferred to attention are given meaning by being brought into relation.

Abstract though the societal progression is, its validity is assured by the methods whereby its elements were obtained and by which it must therefore continue to be developed. Induction, using the method of filiation, will be the main reliance. It will be supplemented from time to time by recourse to deduction in either of two ways: direct, as when conclusions are based upon biological data, or inferential, as when they are drawn from remaining traces of original cultural phenomena.

To the initial phases of societal expansion attention is now to be turned. The nature of primeval activity calls for first consideration. It can be dealt with briefly, for there is general agreement in regard to its essential phases. Man began as a hunter and gatherer of food. Differences as to this primordial end of action are verbal rather than substantial. Hunting is the animal search for food; collecting is hunting facilitated by some degree of knowledge as to the time and place where food is likely to be found. That is, a greater mass of collective cumulations distinguishes the second phase from the first.

That hunting and gathering were succeeded by some degree of control over food supply, and for the same reason that collecting succeeded hunting, seems clear. That this third phase was a culmination and a revolution in the conditions of life of the animal Homo, marking the point at which on the material side the humanescent became human, seems likewise clear. Since the facts are generally agreed to, it will do no harm in the absence of an appropriate term to subsume all three initial phases of activity under the general term "food control."

With regard to the intellectual evolution, the position is less clear than for the active, primarily because inductive indications are weak. Nevertheless, the weight of deductive reasoning has tended to increase with the development of biology and psychology. More is now known for example of the animal mind than was formerly the case, especially in regard to the species most nearly related to the animal Homo. For this reason, conclusions can now be reached that are much less hazardous than would once have been the case; and so on the directly deductive level the analysis of the speculative evolution in its initial stage will here begin.

Involved in this approach to the intellectual development of man is a thoroughgoing reorientation of earlier positions. Whereas under the influence of the ego philosophy the initial stage of thought was once sought by retracing the mental life of man backward from the present, which was thus consciously or unconsciously erected into a kind of absolute standard, the newer attitude is far less complacent. It strives to see the whole record of thought, past and present, as one, consisting of or divided into related stages each of equal importance and significance. No doubt the beings of the earliest period were on an animal level; but they were capable of collective effort and so the highest thoughts of later times are connected by an unbroken filiation with the lowly notions of those humble ancestors. In consequence the inquirer, instead of facing backward and downward from the eminence and permanence of the present, must now look forward and upward from humble beginnings past a sequence of changes enchained in a developing progression.

It is necessary therefore to start the study of the cultural expansion at a much earlier stage than has hitherto been the case. That is to say the active and the speculative evolutions must both be extended back into the biological past. The necessity has always been felt but rather implicitly than explicitly. Thus Sumner and Keller begin the study of capital at "that inferential past which must of necessity have preceded stages of which we have information, in which man was still performing structural adaptations along with other animals." [3] Such suggestions must be taken more seriously than has usually been the case. True, there are no existing societal relics of the remote periods referred to; but the number of forms of man, extinct and living, and his kinship with the anthropoids bring the latter at once into the mental picture of the initial stage of culture, hence the introduction into these pages of those humble individuals Gua and Panzee.

"Gua, the little chimpanzee who was given the benefits of human nursery, showed some very remarkable reactions to objects that certainly had no direct associations with her past experiences. For instance, the experimenters report that she stood in mortal fear

3. *The Science of Society, I,* 163.

of toadstools. She would run from them, screaming, or if cornered, hide her face as though to escape the sight of them." [4] Her excitement was shown to be a result of visual experiences only; it was not caused by the novelty of the experience; it was not a racial phenomenon, nor was it strictly individual: four apes out of thirteen at the nearby experimental station [5] showed a fear of toadstools similar to Gua's.

"Gua had other objects of unreasonable fear: a pair of blue trousers, of which she was afraid the first time she saw them and ever after; a pair of leather gloves; a flat and rusty tin can which she herself had found during her play outdoors. 'It is difficult,' say her observers, 'to reconcile behavior of this sort with the ape's obvious preference for new toys.' "

Other observers have recorded similarly individual aspects of simian behavior. " 'The causes of fear or apprehension in the chimpanzees were various and sometimes difficult to understand. Thus Panzee stood in dread of a large burlap bag filled with hay, which she was obliged to pass frequently. She would meet the situation bravely, however, holding her head high, stamping her feet, and raising her fur, as she passed with an air of injured dignity.'

"Remembering some of the strange inanimate objects in the world of early childhood, one may wonder what sort of expression the burlap bag was showing to Panzee." [6] And who indeed, on any biological level, would care to be leered at by a toadstool! Moreover, "Not only fear, but also delight or comfort may be inspired in these animals by objects that have no biological significance for them . . ." It seems that a "sense of significance" becomes attached to certain objects, forms, or sounds; a "vague emotional arrest of the mind" is caused "by something that is neither dangerous nor useful in reality," by things that are "merely Gestalten furnished to the senses of a creature ready to give them some diffuse meaning." [7]

The case of the apes makes clear what is meant by calling the initial frame of ultimate reference concrete. It leaves no doubt that

4. S. K. Langer, *Philosophy in a New Key* (Cambridge, Harvard University Press, 1942), pp. 111, 112. Based on W. N. and L. A. Kellogg, *The Ape and the Child* (New York, McGraw-Hill, 1933), pp. 177–179.

5. The present Yerkes Laboratories of Primate Biology, Orange Park, Fla.

6. Langer, p. 112. Quoting R. M. Yerkes and Blanche Learned, *Chimpanzee Intelligence and Its Vocal Expressions* (Williams & Wilkins, 1925), p. 143.

7. Langer, pp. 113, 110.

when the state of mind of the apes was disturbed it was the very thing itself that was the source of fear, delight, or comfort. What reason is there to except the animal Homo, already related biologically to the apes, from the psychological conclusion? No doubt the grounds for judgment are deductive; but does anyone suggest that Panzee was alarmed by a spirit in the burlap enemy? or that the first descendants of the animal Homo saw any spirit in the lightning that strikes, or in the wind that blows, or in the kangaroo, or in the elephant, or in the sun that rises or the planets that wander? In all these cases it is the object itself that arouses fear, inspires delight or comfort, strikes, blows, acts, rises, or wanders.

From the interplay between the two initial states, active and speculative, results the primordial societal equilibrium, the first of the cultural stages whose sequence defines the universal culture trend. On the one hand is collective action, concerned with satisfying the immediate and constant demand for food; on the other are the mental operations, organizing collective experience into meaning in a strictly concrete fashion: a principle of preference which confines attention to the range of action whereby food is ensured; a frame of ultimate reference which embraces objects and actions (not phenomena or properties) and so gives meaning to experience in terms of beings and the relations among them. Such is the double foundation for the structure of human life.

To the details of the societal phenomena that characterize the activity of the earliest human groupings little attention need be given here. The unceasing search for food, the restricted range of action and interests, the coincidence of the in-group with the biological family, specialization on the basis of age and sex, the organization of direction in a gerontocracy, the beginnings of leadership on the hunting expeditions—such matters are adequately covered in the anthropological literature. It is more to the purpose of this chapter to analyze more closely than is usually the case the nature of the thought that provides the mental framework of the epoch.

Given the narrow range of attention permitted by a mode of life closely circumscribed by the satisfaction of food interests, given a mentality on an animal level and so by definition uninfluenced by collective cumulation, the resulting bond of thought can be only psychopreferential. That is to say, the connection between observations has to be provided by the within. Besides, the observations are concrete; they relate to the manifestations of things, beings, existences, objects regarded each as distinct. Hence the bonds that form the ultimate frame of reference for nascent men are and have to be moral, psychical, or more accurately orectic, in nature. In this respect men and animals are alike, and the activity of other beings and objects, when they draw attention to themselves, can easily be placed in the same frame of reference even by men of today. It is not that men project themselves into the world without; it is rather an inclusion of men among other existences, a kind of mutual recognition of basic similarity.

Classification of beings brought to attention on the basis of the principle of preference supplied by primeval activity begins negatively by the tacit exclusion of things in no way related to the food hunt. That is, bush is separated from nonbush, the unimportant from the important. It continues by the separation of the unusual from the usual, the abnormal from the normal, and the paying of particular attention to the former because of the power it manifests. In this world where relations are yet to be discovered, each thing is itself. It has its own motives, that is, for behavior; but like all beings it is motivated and so may be swayed—terrified perhaps but more likely placated.

At this point the conception takes form which defines the fetish as that word is used in these pages. From the analysis above flows a necessary consequence: the theory that fetishism is essentially a matter of possession must be rejected. Possession is precisely what fetishism is *not*. The conclusion is a direct inference from the principle that the initial frame of ultimate reference results from a concrete view of the world, biologically determined, which deals with objects and beings and not with abstractions. The notion demands discussion. It is stated conveniently for present purposes in Sumner and Keller's chapter on "Fetishism," where the authors follow the line of thought developed by Spencer and Lippert and the anthropologists generally.

The savage, so this argument runs, sees in nature and in his fellow men a number of unusual and startling phenomena before which he can but stand aghast; in these circumstances his first thought is of spiritual possession. A fetish, then, is "the abode, permanent or temporary, of a possessing spirit. . . . When fetishes were first described and discussed, they were regarded as the product of the attribution of life to inorganic objects. This misapprehension was exposed by Spencer, who saw in the fetish an indwelling spirit which was, in origin at least, the ghost of a dead man. Lippert carried forward the idea of possession by the ghosts of the dead . . . We . . . think that fetishism rises from possession by a daimon or even an anima, that is, directly out of daimonism or even animism." [8]

That there is a quite different origin for fetishism is apparent from Ellis, from whom Sumner and Keller quote at length. Ellis says:

> That the nature-gods are, as a whole, the product of manes worship . . . is . . . a theory not warranted by the evidence, though apparently supported by the high authority of Mr. Herbert Spencer. It often occurs that a family settles near to some river, lake, or hill, and forthwith commences a cult of the indwelling spirit, without any catastrophe having taken place to initiate it. In fact, it may be said to be the rule that whenever a Tshi group takes up its abode near any remarkable natural feature or object, it worships and seeks to propitiate its indwelling spirit, fearing that otherwise it may do some harm. Many of the nature-gods are non-terrestrial, and it is difficult to see by what process they could ever become confused with dead men. Nobody could be buried in the sky, . . . rainbow, or wind—and if these could be conceived to be animated without the intervention of the souls of the dead, why could not terrestrial objects also? [9]

Williams strengthens the emphasis upon the concrete nature of the conceptions in point in his discussion of the Papuan term *imunu*. It cannot be said that "the real *imunu* is something immaterial and the concrete object merely an earthly tenement for it. It would, indeed, be nearer the mark in most cases to say that the concrete object is essentially *imunu* in itself, but that it has an *a'avaia*—soul, spirit, shadow, or immaterial replica, however it be called—which

8. *The Science of Society*, 2, 980, 982.
9. Quoted in Sumner and Keller, 2, 954–955.

can leave the body just as a man's *a'avaia* can leave his body in dreams."

Williams continues: "If asked, 'What is an *imunu?*' a native informant is, of course, completely nonplussed, but, pointing to this and that—and a perplexingly varied assortment of things they may be—he will say 'This is *imunu.*'" [10] Nothing could show more clearly than these words the strictly concrete nature of the native's thought, which is concerned with the things, objects, existences which are of importance to him. Imunu is at once a noun, an adjective, and an adverb, to use abstract terminology. This thing is "mighty"; that one has "might"; this other one is "mighty strange"; the remaining one is "beyond comprehension": all are imunu.

In short the native mind is thinking in terms of beings, not phenomena; of objects, not properties. Wilken adequately (with reservations as to terms) summarizes the position held in this chapter: "In fetishism the spirit is wholly identified with the object in which it is housed, is not distinguished from it, so that it is really the object which is worshipped as a possessed and powerful being." [11]

The discussion cannot be carried further. Once the concrete nature of the thought in question is comprehended, the conceptions advocated here follow logically. The implications are clear. The primitive mind has been regarded retrospectively and has therefore been interpreted in such terms as spirits, souls, gods, possession, worship, completely inapplicable to the immediate descendants of the animal Homo, whereas it should be approached prospectively from such a point of departure as that offered by Panzee and Gua. Only in this way can the misconceptions be avoided which result from the interpreting of concepts developed in one frame of reference in the light of doctrines arising out of a quite different and later one.

Once the specific, concrete nature of the initial frame of ultimate reference is recognized, the phases of a normal course of development within that frame are identifiable. At one extreme, where the search for food is almost individual and the relation with fetishes personal, stand such groups as are represented by the Mandan, among whom "each individual selects for himself the particular object of his devotion, which is termed his medicine, and is either

10. Quoted in Sumner and Keller, 2, 983.
11. Quoted in Sumner and Keller, 2, 984.

some visible being or more commonly some animal." [12] Ellis points out, for the Tshis, "that everyone worships that from which he has most to fear or to expect, and that this is commonly something with which he is brought daily into contact." [13]

Collective activity tends to produce collective fetishes. "Fishermen pay much attention to the indwelling spirits of the sea and of the shoals and reefs on which their canoes might be wrecked." [14] Clearly the range of influence or power of the collective is greater than that of the individual fetish. The tendency is toward the reduction of the latter to a less and less important place in the total scheme of powers; the widening of the range of action thus loosens the bonds of thought.

"All along the western portion of the Slave Coast, the natives, like those on the Gold Coast, see in the roar and motion of the surf a multitude of gods, each of whom is worshipped in his own proper locality, so that there are two or three local sea-gods to almost every village along the shore; but at Whydah and its neighborhood this is not the case, and Wu appears to be considered the god of the sea generally, and not of some portion only." [15] That here is an example of reduction in number along with an increase in power and extent of influence among fetishes seems evident.

Moreover, there is a constant sifting of fetishes on the basis of efficiency; it is still going on. Where the fetish is accessible, which in most cases means terrestrial, the selecting and testing can proceed easily and continuously, accelerated by the concrete nature of the hominoid and its personal relation to individual men. When activity reaches the point where the cultivation of both animals and plants begins, i.e., where the principle of preference brings the world of agriculture (in particular) into view, the reduction of fetishes in number together with increase in scope and power is intensified. Now the vegetation fetishes come into the focus of attention and with them a sharpening of observation concerning celestial phenomena. Once the importance of these phenomena—atmospheric, lunar, solar, sidereal—is grasped, the ultimate dominance of the celestial fetish is assured. Not only are they withdrawn

12. Sumner and Keller, 2, 977.
13. Quoted in Sumner and Keller, 2, 956.
14. Sumner and Keller, 2, 956.
15. Sumner and Keller, 2, 972.

from the immediacy of test to which terrestrial and hence accessible fetishes are subject; they are (especially the planets and the stars) so aloof, so constant in their movements, so high above man's puny activities that sooner or later they become the controlling influences in his world. Fetishism, that is, in its second phase becomes astralism. Moreover, as the number of fetishes is reduced and the power of the survivors increased there is a tendency toward the concentration of all significant influences in a single dominant fetish. In other words, astralism tends toward a monofetishism.

Even more important for the future of thought is an influence which is particularly evident in relation to the fetishes associated with agriculture, the dominant form of activity. Rain, sun, moon, stars—so intimately connected with growth and seasonal change—are the chief natural phenomena involved here. Powerful as these beings are, they are nevertheless restricted in their influence. But there is neither paradox nor contradiction in the fact. Fetishes are concrete in their nature and attributions. In the frame of concrete reference, natural objects envisaged as controlling beings are active. But being concrete they have special attributes only. They act according to their own natures, i.e., only within the range of certain discovered relations: what the rain fetish does is to bring rain; the wind fetish controls winds. Each natural phenomenon is the domain so to speak of a single agent. Each fetish has his sphere and order of action. The vegetation fetish does not create ears of corn or maize; he does not invert or mingle the seasons; he sees only that the growth requisite for a good harvest shall obtain. In short, under and in fetishism begins the first dim realization of a natural order.

"Men of a lower culture," say Sumner and Keller, "are wont to apply the idea of agency rather than of cause." [16] True enough; but with the notion of agency must be coupled, on the concrete level, the notion of specificity of action. It is from the combination of these two notions arising spontaneously from experience with the regularities of the world without whence come the germs of such conceptions as fatality and necessity, whence ultimately are shaped the figures of Destiny and Fate who are to stand so grimly in the background of the deities when in their turn they come to be.

Finally, in conclusion of this section of the chapter, in fetishism is to be found the explanation for "that curious *localism* from

16. 2, 755.

which few of us are free after three centuries of Copernicanism. . . . Pythagoras had, I believe, started that . . . division of the world which Aristotle adopted and handed on to our own times. The two worlds were those of heaven and earth; the distinction was not between a *sensible* and a *rational* system, but between a higher and a lower in space." "Hence in great part our modern ideas of heaven as a region somewhere aloft, from which notion as from the use of terms like sunset, sunrise, we find it impossible to get free." [17] But far more effective than any Greek philosophy in originating this notion was the immemorial astralism in which the stars—the "divine ancients" even for Aristotle—held their superior place in the hierarchy of fetishism.

If the arguments drawn from the biological ancestry of the animal Homo are decisive against regarding the spirit theory as the initial stage of Man's intellectual evolution, the anthropological grounds for making it the second and central stage of that evolution are no less cogent. They are summarized by Sumner and Keller. In eidolism and the ghost cult appear the germ forms that are to shade into later members of the evolutionary series. The "eidolon" or ghost is the disembodied soul of a particular individual recently dead; and "eidolism passes by almost imperceptible gradations into daimonism" which in its turn is a "broadly transitional form." "The daimons are more powerful and longer-lived ghosts; . . . they are anthropomorphic, have temperament, character, and ways of acting, and are susceptible to influences which man can cause to be exerted." [18]

On the next higher level are the beings denominated deities, who are comparable to "the daimons and the eidola as they could not conceivably have been except by reason of a genetic relationship." [19] In other words, the normal course of conceptual development expressed in terms overcolored by religious notions is through daimonism to deitism, the latter assuming two forms, the typical and the exceptional, i.e., polytheism and monotheism.

17. F. W. Bussell, *Religious Thought and Heresy in the Middle Ages*, pp. 534, 514.
18. Sumner and Keller, 2, 931–932.
19. 2, 975.

Thus there are two sequences, which reduced to dualistic form read: the one, fetishism and astralism; the other, daimonism and deitism. The question of priority for these sequences has already been answered; there remains the problem of filiation. How did the second succeed to the first and finally replace it? The connection seems to have been effected by way of the concept customarily called the spirit; consequently it is necessary to analyze this concept with some care. As the effective factor in a transitional development it can be understood only when the two elements of which it is composed are isolated.

Of the two constituent elements in question, the first seems clearly visible on the fetishistic level. Thus Williams in the passage already quoted from says: "The concrete object has . . . an *a'avaia*—soul, spirit, shadow, or immaterial replica, however it be called—which can leave the body just as a man's *a'avaia* can leave his body in a dream." [20] The concept is a general one, as Sumner and Keller make clear: "The attribution of a soul is not limited to the animal or even the organic being. All things have souls." [21] But to apply to this universal characteristic the term "soul" is one more example of carrying ideas from one frame of reference to another. Williams gives the corrective for this misconception when he speaks of shadow or immaterial replica. In fact it seems more accurate to speak of a separable double.

How the notion arose is difficult to decide. There are so many possibilities; shadows, dreams, reflections in the eye or in water or polished surfaces, breath, illusion, hallucination. Any or all of these may under collective conditions have given rise to the idea. The normal source seems to have been the dream. In any case, the core of the concept was no soul or spirit; it was the notion that all things have doubles. Indeed the word "double" would seem to be exactly what is needed here but for the fact that some subtle meta-fetishians have distinguished as many as seven doubles. Out of respect for logic then as well as to provide a quite neutral term, another word seems necessary. The word "replicate" seems available. Accordingly the thought of the paragraph can be summed up thus: all things have replicates.

Of the replicate two characteristics demand emphasis. For one

20. In Sumner and Keller, 2, 983.
21. 2, 820, par. 214.

thing, the replicate is separable from the object of which it is the immaterial replica (as Williams calls it). It goes and it comes; it wanders about; it has a kind of independence which cannot be summarized, so various are the cases. And yet all the time it remains identified with the original thing, object, or existence of which it is the double. Hence for another thing the replicate always retains the concrete and specific nature of the object of which it is the replicate. In consequence, there is no question at this intellectual stage of a spirit or anything else being in possession of an object. The soul (if the word must be used) of a thing is native to it; the object and its replicate are one, and the immaterial replicate may on occasion be as truly an agent as the material object itself. The distinction between identification and possession may seem small when regarded retrospectively; nevertheless, prospectively viewed, from the standpoint of the animal origin of Man, thought at some time had to make such an advance. The question is, how?

The line of speculative evolution leading to the second of the two elements which combine to produce the spirit which possesses objects starts in the distinction between the concrete and the abstract and thereby effects the filiation between them. When collective experience cumulates to the point where objects are distinguished from happenings, beings from events, things from properties, the need for explanations of a more general kind than fetishism affords begins to be felt. So long as the phenomena preferred to attention by activity are unique and unrelated, the individual fetish is adequate as an explanation. It ceases to be so when phenomena are observed to be recurrent and similar, when they become sequential and related, when in short the order revealed by fetishism begins to be analyzed and classified.

At some point of experience the flowing stream every one of whose bends, shallows, and stretches is known separately suddenly becomes *the* river; at some point the planting, cultivating, harvesting of a crop become sufficiently isolated from accompanying phenomena and related to one another as to be recognizable as a single process. At this point, when relations fuse into a unity, the result is a kind of collective phenomenon which can be explained by reference to a single agent. At a still higher level of experience, similar phenomena are observed in several otherwise quite unrelated objects; the outcome is an abstract phenomenon—redness, swiftness—the forerunner of abstract properties. But how within the framework of causality can the movements of the river, the growth of the corn, or the manifestations of likeness be accounted for?

The separable replicate provides an answer. Since the observed phenomena are like or related, they can be attributed to a single agency operating under varying circumstances or in a number of places. The consequences are two: the replicate becomes entirely separated from the object; it loses its specific and concrete character. The object no longer has a replicate; the replicate now has a "seat" which it may occupy from time to time and which it may use as a means for manifesting the particular phenomena which it controls. The replicate no longer is identified with the concrete object or being; the latter is now possessed by a replicate. Usually though not invariably it is pictured as human. "The daimon reveals his origin in the fact that he is anthropomorphic or, less often, zoomorphic. Even the abstractions were, like the less shadowy daimons, formed by man in his own image." [22] In short, the spirit is the outcome of the combination of a separable replicate, normally human in its attributes, with a collective or an abstract phenomenon. A fictive being is the result. The concrete agent disappears; the abstract cause takes its place. The fetish, that is, gives way to the daimon.

The consequences of this shift from free agent to directing cause are beyond enumeration. The essence of the matter is that a world which once seemed active now becomes passive. The things of that world now yield to the wills of the fictive beings for whom they have become the seats. It is now the separable replicates which are free agents; the objects of which they were once the doubles now become their abodes, their instruments, their means. The fading of fetishes, the accelerated reduction of their numbers, the identification of the high fetishes of astralism with equally elevated spirits, the emergence of daimons and their evolution into deities: these consequences follow logically.

What is implied in the substitution of cause for agent is the release of the fantasy-making faculty of man. True, "the mental operations of the race were largely phantasy until science arose," [23] but

22. Sumner and Keller, 2, 958–959.
23. Sumner and Keller, 2, 747.

the concrete nature of observation had in fetishism set limits to the imagination. The fictive being set the imagination free. The line leading back to and down from Gua and Panzee was finally broken once for all. In this sense, the gods made man.

Not only does man explain the phenomena of the world without by such fictive causes, he proceeds to explain his own actions in the same way: hence the multitude of bas, kas, wills, egos, souls, etc.; hence too by the projection of spirit cause into the world without the entire phantasmagoria of metaphysics. Complete subjectivity would seem to be the only possible result. That it did not follow is due to a paradox. The free imagination was not really free. There was the persisting influence of fetishism; there was the relative stability of the world without; there was the guiding influence of societal development; there was the logic of feeling. All these factors combined to keep fantasy within bounds and so ensured the continuation of the course of speculative development beyond the fetishism, astralism, daimonism, deitism in which the principle of causality took cultural form.

To plot the normal course of activity from the hunting and collecting of food to the control of the food supply by achievements of a pastoral and agricultural kind is easy in the light of the data. Beyond this point there is in the evolution of activity a transition, comparable in importance to the change in speculation from fetishism in its various phases to daimonism. Conflict becomes more prominent than before. Collectivities instead of engaging in the sterile and temporary struggles of an earlier age now organize for purposes of aggression. War, that is, becomes a main stage of normal societal development. Men now become socii by virtue of their participation in the coercion of other groups.

The line of filiation seems easy to trace: resistance to passing aggression, vengeance for wrong done, plundering in time of dire need, plundering as a group activity, conquest as the ultimate end of societal activity coordinating all the energies of socii. There is a distinct separation between the seizure of products and the subjection of producers. If the first type of conflict is called predation, then the normal course of activity runs from food production and control through predation to conquest, where war takes on its distinctive characteristics as the ultimate organizing principle for the coordination of societal energies.

In the transitional cultural phase to which the term "daimonistic predation" can be applied, a common activity tends to unite the efforts of the members of the group and unify them; the results are pictured as the consequence of the guidance and protection of spirit agencies. But in this initial phase of a new societal stage the integration of socii is not highly developed. The societal situation in both the real and the spirit world is disordered. "The world of spirits is just as little organized as the primitive people themselves." [24] Only as this spontaneous development passes into the systematic phase does the disorder diminish and the lineaments of a new societal system become distinguishable, where the daimons become deities and are concentrated and hierarchized and predation becomes conquest.

It goes without saying that the transitional stage here in point should manifest much indetermination and overlapping. The high monofetishes of astralism, for example, lent themselves readily to combination with daimons and deities and no doubt accelerated their ultimate advent. Predation looks both backward and forward. War is slow to take its systematic form. One of the consequences of this wavering is that certain early communities exceptionally situated enter upon roads that ultimately end in societal immobility. These essentially astrolatric groups, under the direction of the interpreters and representatives of the supreme fetishes on high, withstand generation after generation the onset of predatory nomadic populations, yield to them, and finally assimilate them without ever greatly changing in either action or thought since both have been stabilized by having been rendered sacred.

Evidently here is a possible door to the future, but it is narrow and extremely hard to open; closed, it ensures stability at the expense of movement. It is evidently guarded by the priesthoods, the representatives and agents of the intellectual evolution. But man is made more for action than for thought. Hence there is an alternative to astrolatric stability. In this other course it is warriors who dominate rather than thinkers. The door they open leads to a rough road, but it is the high road all the same. As multideitistic conquest it is one of the major stages in the normal course of culture.

24. Sumner and Keller, 2, 960, par. 243.

War, especially in its typical form of conquest, develops particularly the activity of the socii engaged. It gives to all those belonging to the group a common end of action, rising above the essentially domestic forms of union that characterize the earlier cultures. The city comes into being as a new stage in the uniting of men. The civic union, arousing the capacities of socii beyond anything of which the family or the tribe is capable, now becomes more and more the center and end of societal action. As predation gives way to conquest the civic bonds grow stronger.

War for products no doubt requires strenuous exertion and effective leadership; but it is ephemeral or at best intermittent. The organization required for success may lapse during intervals of peace. Domination over producers is on a different level. It is more difficult; it demands sustained effort and closer relations among the participants; when successful it must be maintained and perpetuated. It involves a thoroughgoing reorganization of the factors that go to make society. The new way of life must be continued even when military action is for a time suspended. Once a given group is organized on the new pattern, its neighbors or competitors must follow or go under. Hence conquest becomes the dominant form of war.

Activity as always stimulates, feeds, and guides the speculative evolution. Daimonism, because of its absolute and fictive nature, tends toward dangerous excesses. The one safeguard against such subjectivity—masked as objectivity—is the necessity of effectively conducting practical life. The dispersion of supernatural influences makes it difficult to maintain an habitual association of domestic or kinship groups without a sustained common activity to require and give significance to their collaboration. The existence of the civic union as it gains unity, coherence, and continuity becomes imaginable as a collective phenomenon and is thus attributable to the agency of daimons more and more refined into deities. At the same time, the more highly developed coordination of society due to the demands of war, plus the increasing recognition of abstract properties and their relations, leads to a developed hierarchy among the more and more vividly personalized replicates by whom the achievements of men are integrated. Multideitism thus becomes a main stage in the intellectual evolution.

Between the two societal movements there develops an equilibrium which produces a greater degree of unity—larger numbers of men more closely united—than existed before. Yet the equilibrium is unstable. The priest on the one hand recognizes the warrior to be indispensable for the adequate diffusion of sacerdotal authority. The practical man, on the other hand, cannot afford to disregard or dispense with spiritual consecration. War always demands a strict discipline, increasing in intensity as expeditions and campaigns become more frequent and extensive. Military chieftains have their own material sources of authority, but their personal claims to respect, however great, cannot dispense with a spiritual sanction if they are to exact adequate and lasting obedience. In short there is a fundamental affinity between commands that may not be discussed and beliefs that cannot be demonstrated.

But the balance between the two authorities is delicate and precarious. The warrior and the priest are likely to strive for dominance even though they cannot dispense with one another. Where sacerdotal influence gains the upper hand, the outcome is a tendency toward a static society with the emphasis upon order. Counsel and command are identified; the society becomes conservative. Where the soldier predominates, counsel is subordinated to command. The continuance of warlike activity demands a constantly increasing sum of knowledge if only for the greater effectiveness of military action. Such a society in contrast with the first may be termed progressive. Hence there are two forms of multideitistic activity, the conservative and the progressive. The latter, by virtue of the fact that it favors and intensifies the societal process, becomes a stage in the normal development of culture.

Nevertheless, the continuous operation of collective cumulation brings about change; and so the equilibrium reached in the phase of multicausal conquest is slowly altered. The impelling force in the movement is primarily an extension of military activity. It is in the nature of conquest to expand, but the very process of expansion issues in a paradox. As the radius of conquest lengthens two consequences follow: the number of external foes increases with the increase of the circumference of the conquered area, and the difficulties of internal administration augment still more rapidly. Antagonistic reaction takes several forms: the number of external enemies may become too great to be opposed everywhere with success; they may ally themselves against the dominant power;

a single strong rival may arise to challenge the original conqueror. In any case, the urge to expand gradually weakens and conquest, after first becoming merely precautionary, is ultimately transformed into defense.

Speculation too continues on its course. In the main it moves in the direction of increased abstraction. Just as the dispersion of daimonism gives way to the hierarchies of deitism, so do the latter tend toward concentration into various types of unideitism. For this tendency there are several important reasons. First of all probably is the effect of conquest to produce political systems with a single directive head and for these systems to be reflected in the world of deities. Second is the gradual extension of abstraction and a consequent reduction in the number and increase in the scope of collective phenomena. That is to say, with the multiplication of relations there is constant pressure toward unicausality.

Defensive activity strengthens this tendency and canalizes its consequences. As conquest declines, the welcome to new deities and their incorporation into the divine hierarchy of the conquerors both tend to meet resistance. As activity centers more and more about defense, the defending group gathers more compactly together about its supreme patron and protector. The life of the group can more easily be seen as a unitary phenomenon subject to a single will.

Unideitism becomes a distinctive phase in cultural development. It opens a path which must once be traversed in the spontaneous development of cultural phenomena, however unnecessary it may later become for systematically guided societies. Defense as an ultimate end for the cooperation and integration of socii has less cohesive strength than conquest. Empires, that is to say, tend to fall apart, to disintegrate with the weakening of the dynamic of conquest. Yet the parts into which they fall tend to maintain a spiritual unity through allegiance to the supreme will under whom they were once united. Widening abstraction works for the same end. Thus a new type of integration begins to take form. After the domestic group and the civic union comes the spiritual unity; after the family and the city, the church.

The conception of the one deity undergoes still further refinement as the process of abstraction continues to operate. So long as its effects are limited to the reduction of daimons and deities to more concentrated but essentially like forms, they are given little attention. But when these effects pass from the spontaneous to the systematic phase, i.e., when abstraction begins to operate in a uni-causal frame of ultimate reference, a new situation arises. The directing cause—the human replicate once envisaged as a spirit—now tends to become an entity. When causes refined into entities, definable as personified abstractions, are dealt with systematically the result in a narrow sense is ontology and in a larger philosophical interpretation is metaphysics.

This transformation of course is gradual. The world without comes slowly to be envisaged as a sum of related occurrents, a collective phenomenon in the all-inclusive sense but contrasted all the same with the world within. The distinction is reflected in the attribution of human, i.e., moral phenomena to the direct and exclusive interposition of the supreme spirit and the relegation of control over the physical, i.e., material world to a personified abstraction, the agent of the ultimate cause, the entity nature; hence of course natural and moral philosophy.

But this division of authority cannot be permanent. Metaphysical solutions have only a transient validity; they are provisional; like all intellectual products they are relative. The entity is a double concept. As abstraction it may hold together a variety of verifiable phenomena, as in the case of the vacuum abhorred by Nature. As personification it may stand for the manifestations of inscrutable purpose, as the Hand that writes history, or for a complex of unknown or undifferentiated factors or forces, as the Society that makes criminals. In all these cases, minds in fact at such poles of thought as agency and uniformity may harmonize in capitalized words that serve at the same time both to perpetuate the older doctrines and to screen advances toward the new.

That such advances will be made is certain. They take two forms. First, the speculative bonds in metaphysical guise tend increasingly to emphasize laws and correspondingly to weaken the influence of the unicausal deity. The latter comes in this way to be regarded at last simply as the source of uniformity. Second, war, especially in its defensive form, gradually ceases to provide for the needs of the socii involved. Their energies consequently have to be devoted more and more to productive ends, initially individual in motivation. Defense and unicausality thus tend to give way to an inherently temporary phase in which action is characterized by a nascent spontaneous industrialism best termed enterprise and thought takes the form of reason, i.e., reasoning based upon laws regarded as orders emanating from a divine or metaphysical will.

That is to say, a new societal end gradually develops to fill the gap left by the decline of war. The principle of preference arising from the new situation brings into the foreground of thought the properties of the material world. Thus the speculative evolution is guided toward increased and now quite conscious and systematic concentration upon abstraction. Science, that is, in the relativity of cultural development appears as a societal objective. Where productive activity was once auxiliary to war, war now becomes subordinate to industry; where abstraction was once spontaneous and secondary it is now primary and systematic.

The gradual shift from causality to uniformity as an ultimate frame of intellectual reference, resting finally upon a parallel shift from war to industry as the end of societal action, forms one of the great transitions in the course of cultural evolution. It is comparable only with that which raised human action and thought from fetishism to daimonism, from hunting, collecting, and growing to predation and war. But one great difference between two otherwise analogous developments must be remarked. The first was a purely spontaneous movement. It went on, so far as can now be seen, without the nature of the change that was going on and its significance for human existence ever having reached the level of awareness.

No such calm, however, in either action or thought as characterized the first major transition in the normal course of societal development is possible for the second. The essence of the matter consists in the fact that as the integration between action and thought proceeds, the outcome is a relatively fixed structure of relationships which is the basis of the society corresponding to the stage of war and causality. It is a relatively stable equilibrium which condenses the rights, privileges, and duties of socii and gives them a permanent set. Any change in it involves a corresponding alteration of the position of the individual socii throughout the societal structure.

When such a far-reaching modification of societal relationships is in process or is even threatened, the situation can only be described as revolutionary. Moreover, this transitional societal phase is not only revolutionary; it is anarchical as well. If the changes in progress render uncertain the position of all socii, so do they at the same time unsettle all opinions. The advent of uniformity as an ultimate frame of reference implies the ultimate abandonment of the whole body of doctrines, principles, and philosophies based upon causality. Thus the way is opened to a multitude of rival and competing doctrines, negative and positive, with no dominant direction for the guidance of thought. In the field of activity the replacement of war in all its phases by industrialism and industry implies a like condition of rivalry and disorder. Revolution and anarchy: inevitable as the outgrowth of the entire past, indispensable as the assurance of continued societal development: such are the characteristics of the second great transitional phase of cultural evolution.

No disorder, however, short of destroying the arrangement that makes sociological phenomena possible can do more than delay or impede the operation of the societal process. It is of course on the highest levels of abstraction, the societal and the psychical, in the movement toward productionism and uniformism that the results of the process are most evident. When the influence of these new concepts reaches the upper levels of the scientific hierarchy the ultimate reorganization of the whole structure of institutions which incorporated the notion of cause and the objective of war becomes inevitable. The societal process as usual works at first spontaneously and then systematically. Eventually it brings both thought and action on the upper levels of abstraction into harmony with the principles that have already been reached on the lower levels. The outcome is a homogeneity of method and doctrine that translates itself into an unprecedented societal equilibrium which is the basis of a new stage of culture, the stage of uniformistic industry.

The first spontaneous strivings toward a new societal synthesis are observable in the domain of action. With the alteration of aggressive into defensive warfare goes the necessity of providing for the production which can no longer be supplied by exploitation through conquest. The factors of production are at first regarded as purely individual, but when they are multiplied and expanded it becomes evident that they are in fact collective and collaborative in nature. That is to say, a new principle of societal organization

comes slowly into operation as the directive force in the concentration and organization of socii. The application of this principle involves no determinate set of concrete plans for reorganization. Each major societal grouping is, in full accordance with the
law of persistence, conditioned by its past and its biological and
material setting. But there will necessarily be certain physiognomi-
cal features common to the new societies because the same basic
principle of societal organization is at work in them all.

First among the distinctive features of the industrial stage is
the disappearance or the transformation of the masses, so-called,
upon whom the earlier social structure rested. Their disappearance
is bound up with the emergence of industry as the end of societal
activity. Production, in the complete sense, transforms all men into
active socii participating in the universal task of supplying human
needs. The masses cease to be instruments; they become collaborators in the ultimate societal ends. They become for the first time
truly integrated into society; they are not paid or employed; they
participate in a collective activity and share in its results. They no
longer have to achieve the status of men; they have ascribed to them
at birth the status of citizens.

The process by which this result is attained is to begin with a
spontaneous differentiation on the basis of function. On the one
hand is the operative group: the workers in fabrication and the
laborers in agriculture, the erg-users and the tillers. The urban
worker advances toward the industrial stage far more rapidly than
the rural laborer; but the gap thus created is ultimately filled by
the gradual industrialization of agriculture.

On the other hand are the enterprisers, the employers, the directors of the societal energies that are concentrated in capitals and
embodied in labor forces.

In this basic functional distinction between directive and operative groups is manifested the process which is to bring about an
organization of society meet for an industrial age. From this basic
distinction, purely spontaneous in origin, come all the systematic
developments that characterize the activity of the new age. Its consequences become more visible as industry becomes more abstract
and work tends toward the supervision of the mechanical devices
which more and more utilize the inorganic sources of energy.

Specialization of function continues to develop in the industrial

DIVISIONING OF THE SOCIETAL DOMAIN

process. Midway between the directive group, translating societal needs into policies, and the operative group, producing the goods to satisfy needs, arises an intermediate function, that of the engineers, the managers, translating policy into human terms. Its representatives have a double relationship which varies in intensity as the industrial organization takes form. At first associated with the directive function, they tend with the developing emphasis upon the collective nature of industry as the foundation of societal policy to be intimately connected with the operative group, the workers.

Within the directive group the differentiation follows the lines drawn in an earlier statical chapter where the circulation of wealth was analyzed. The outcome is a series of directive functions to replace what were once individual careers: agricultural, manufacturing, commercial. Finally arises the group now so grotesquely termed bankers, whose function is directive par excellence, for their ultimate societal responsibility, into whatever hands it may fall, is the conservation, apportionment, and allocation of the energies of socii. As administrators of the collective capital of mankind their societal importance is major. In their hands ultimately rests the task of organizing the industrial stage of societal activity.

In close connection with the active evolution the speculative development proceeds. Effective productive activity depends upon a high degree of certainty in the control and expenditure of energy. A knowledge of uniformities gives this certainty; it is thereby favored and therefore encouraged. Limited at first to the lower levels of the abstract scientific hierarchy, it is slowly extended to the higher. The working of the new principle of preference is clear. Productivity depends not alone upon physical science; it is dependent as well upon the knowledge of men, in both the societal and the psychical sense. The extension of uniformity to the moral level is thus motivated and facilitated.

The first advances are on the societal level, as the nature of society is more accurately analyzed. Institutional improvements follow. Prevision in this new domain becomes more and more possible. The outcome is the notion, increasingly definite, that the arrangement of societal phenomena can be so modified as to ensure results planned in advance. Planning, that is to say, is the consequence of the developing power of prevision, itself the outcome of the extension of uniformism to societal phenomena. Hence the industrialist and the scientist come into more intimate and continuous relationship.

Arising from this closer integration of the elements of the new societal equilibrium is that form of progress termed efficiency in an earlier passage. Efficiency and its concomitant, planning, although they make possible advantages that are otherwise beyond attainment, nevertheless fall short of progress in the complete sense in that they fail to deal directly with the phenomena on the highest, the psychical, level. But societal phenomena work toward such a goal indirectly by bringing into sharp relief in relation to industrial activity the need of extending the concept of uniformity to the psychical domain. In other terms, the principle of preference inherent in industrial activity inevitably leads to the study of the inner sources of human motivation.

At this point in the evolution of the third major stage of cultural development, where abstraction passes from the societal to the psychical level, the spontaneous phase of the new equilibrium may be said to give way to the systematic. What is involved here is the acquisition of new knowledge, i.e., the extension of the concept of uniformity to the study of Man in his psychical, ultimate reality. Here the socioexperiential at last closes with the psychopreferential. The former, rising in its sociological aspects to the point where control over the institutional basis of man's life becomes plannable, provides the means for effecting such concentrations of socii as are defined or desired. Yet there are certain limitations. On the strictly societal plane the ultimate means for attaining ends is force. Moreover, on this level no knowledge is reached as to what those ends should be. It is only the psychopreferential, organized on a systematic basis of uniformity and thus reduced to a province of the socioexperiential, that can answer such questions. In other words man comes at last to study men's nature.

Two achievements are involved in the attainment of such knowledge. The first is negative. It consists in the dismissal of the replicate, refined into an entity and concealed behind the phrase "human nature," and the analysis of the collective phenomenon that causality in its metaphysical phase entifies as an ego. The second is positive. It implies the establishment of the constituent elements of the psychical equilibrium and the discovery of the uniformities those factors manifest taken singly and in combination—in short, a positive science of psychology. Such a science, revealing the factors which when adequately equilibrated produce the balance that characterizes and defines the normal personality, provides a positive answer to the question: What is moral, i.e., true progress? It can do so because the societal process, working on the basis of abstraction, reaches at least the point where the uniformities revealed by biological and sociological investigation can be eliminated from the scientific problem, thus leaving only a single body of specific and homogeneous data, the psychical, to be dealt with in isolation.

In consequence these data come not only to be adequately analyzed but also classified and hierarchized. They are to begin with divisible on the basis of sociological induction into orexis, ideation, and exergy. Of these the orectic constants, being the sources of impulsion, are clearly on the highest level of importance. Moreover, when they are surveyed in the light of man's evolution as a whole it becomes possible to subdivide them on the basis of their contribution to the continuance of the societal relationship and thus to evaluate them. It is through the societal, not the organic, process that the animal Homo is made Man; the forces or drives that ensure the continuance of that process are therefore superior to those that work primarily for the perpetuation of the organism. Hence there are higher and lower classes among the orectic constants, and progress in this final analysis means the increasing influence in the psychical equilibrium of the higher orectic constants.

The picturing of the results that follow the utilization of a developing psychical science ensure that it will be utilized. The very sources of impulsion that were strong in creating the conditions which gave rise to the development of science as a whole are also the very ones most strongly stimulated by the fantasied future; hence the will to translate those fantasies into reality and the certainty that the knowledge of the higher psychical constants will be applied, and increasingly; hence also the passage of the new societal stage into a systematic phase.

The first reason for the coming of a systematic phase of cultural development on the basis of productionism and uniformism lies in the increased possibility of control over societal phenomena that a sociological science allows. The extension of prevision from the natural to the social level is the chief factor here. It makes possible a degree of planning hitherto unprecedented. It results first in that form of progress termed efficiency. But the criticism of efficiency that was valid at an earlier cultural period is valid no longer. The change in the situation is the consequence of the advance in psychology. With the establishment of the distinction between the higher and the lower orectic constants, it is now clear what should be the objectives toward which sociological efforts are to be directed. The greater the efficiency the more effective the results and the more certain that desirable ends shall be reached. That is to say the conflict between efficiency and morality ceases. Insofar as the higher psychical impulsions can be freely operative only in a suitable institutional framework, *efficiency becomes the very condition of high morality*. In other words, given a knowledge of the desirable moral consequences on the one hand, and on the other the knowledge of how to create the conditions most favorable to those consequences, the stage of planning can be transcended; man begins to live in a world designed to meet his deepest needs.

The second reason for systematic approach to a world where design holds an ever larger place lies in the possibility that results from the development of uniformity in relation to the moral world. Once the factors of morality are analyzed and classified, the way is open to the direct development of the orectic constants involved. Instead of the spontaneous culture that was inevitable in the past, the systematic exercise and development of the higher constants becomes a practical objective. All the empirical developments that occurred under the regime of agency and causality are now susceptible of inclusion in a true science. In this situation men can will effectively toward a higher moral level, not only because they are impelled to exteriorize pictured results in harmony with the urges of their real nature, not only because they live in a world designed to condition favorably the development of the very constants that are willing the advance, but also because they are able to intensify that will by cultivating directly the very sources of morality.

The formation of a societal equilibrium in which industry and uniformity are integrated—the appearance, that is, of a third major stage in the normal course of cumulating man's collective experience—makes it possible to view as a whole the progression which the successive stages compose and so to ascertain the direction of that movement. To do so is to determine in the form of a first approximation the universal culture trend.

In the first place then societal activity begins with the efforts of small groups to supply their needs by hunting and extends to the point where all men may be conceived to be cooperating in production to satisfy human needs. That is to say, considering the nature of the activity involved, the trend of societal action is toward an ever increasing synergy whereby all men will be socii with relation to a common end. In a similar way the trend of speculation is from individual representations toward a universally accepted view of the world, including man himself, in which a common frame of ultimate reference is the basis for an increasingly accepted synthesis, unifying the individual's thought and uniting it with the thought of others. In other words, the increase of collective cumulations tends to intensify both synergy and synthesis.

With the combination of the two societal trends that this chapter effects, the work of a strictly abstract sociological dynamics comes to an end. And since the conclusions reached here are in accord with those reached in the study of sociological statics, the two divisions of the science harmonize and the science itself becomes a constituted unity. Upon the foundation thus laid, efforts looking toward societal guidance may begin. They will begin in the next chapter, which purports to place the present epoch in the perspective afforded by the entire societal movement.

Even more however can be done. If the present chapter is to end as it began, with a reference to the positive philosophy of history, one further advance must be made. It concerns the emotional or affective aspects of man's life, without which no sociography would be practicable. With the development of synergy and synthesis the size of the in-group constantly increases. In consequence the range within which the sympathies are exercised tends to equal and then absorb the out-group; hence ultimately a maximum of synergy, synthesis, and sympathy completely integrated. Translated into more concrete terms, the trend of the universal societal movement is toward universal collaboration, freely accepted on a basis of universal opinion and maintained by a universal sympathy.

CONCLUSION: TOWARD REALITY

CHAPTER 24: *The Great Transition: the Age of Rationalistic Enterprise*

Constructing a normal course of societal movement, the basis for the determination of the universal culture trend, is the last task of sociological dynamics; and so, since it assumes the existence of statics, it is the last concern of abstract sociology. Beyond the latter lies another isolate, the phenomena of which can only modify the societal movement, never fundamentally alter it. Below it are the conditioning factors of biology and the physical environment. All these elements go to make up the equilibrium which is the social reality; and it is to them all, not one alone, that attention must be turned when history, i.e., sociography is in question.

Nevertheless, even though all the elements in a given historical situation are important, there is a hierarchical relation among them. The basis of the historical record is the societal element. The sociographer must have the cultural development as the background of his work whether he deals with the record as a whole or with only a part of it. Just so the statesman in constructing a policy must see the general view and his special problem in relation to it. Both theory and practice are subject to the principle laid down by Bather for the direction of geologists: "Again and again it must be hammered into the minds of geologists that two distinct sets of names are required: the one consisting of local names for local rocks, the other of universal names, not for rocks but for periods of time. Thus is constructed a time scale against which the local rocks can be placed." [1]

Translated into terms applicable to social phenomena, this principle reads that for the sociographer two sets of ideas are necessary: one concrete, i.e., local and special—the events that occurred within a given period and place; and one abstract, i.e., universal and gen-

1. F. A. Bather, "Address on William Smith" (pamphlet, Bath, England, 1926), p. 6.

eral—a time scale, a normal course of societal movement against which the local events can be placed. Since the former can never in fact be separated from the latter, the analysis of the one must be subordinated to the synthesis supplied by the other. No partial systematization can be adequate which is made without reference to an appropriate total synthesis. And since no limited association can ever be completely severed from the all-inclusive association of mankind, no period, age, or epoch can be adequately pictured without a background drawn to represent the whole cultural sequence.

It is with the foregoing principle in mind that the present chapter has been written. It consists of an analysis, moving from the abstract toward the concrete and so toward reality, of the period usually termed modern. The word of course means nothing in itself. At any period the people of the time might consider themselves modern with respect to their ancestors. To discover the content of the word in the present historical context is precisely one of the objectives aimed at. To attain this end, local events must be placed against the time scale. The outcome, even in the form of a first approximation, should give both theoretical and practical results: it should throw light upon certain subordinate phases of the normal course of cultural development; it should reveal the direction of the modern societal movement.

Adequately to picture in perspective the time period in point here requires a return to the historical survey which underlies the first section of this volume. There it was shown how the Mediterranean culture succeeded the theocratic cultures of Egypt and Mesopotamia. Taking its first characteristic form in Greece, it gradually developed and spread over the entire Mediterranean area through the agency of Rome. The essential characteristics of this culture were two: conquest in the domain of action and multideitism in the domain of thought. With the continued operation of the societal process through generations, both of these characteristics changed. Conquest reached the limits of exploitation, both geographically and administratively, and slowly turned into defense; multideitism gradually gave way to unideitism. The coincidence of these epochal transformations brought with it the "fall" of Rome.

In the disorganization that preceded and accompanied the establishment of a new societal equilibrium on the basis of monotheism and defense, the northwestern area of the Empire fell away from close contact with the remainder of the Mediterranean culture area. While the organized culture of the area was being conserved and defended in Byzantium and then modified and developed under the Arabs, the West went through a period of disintegration within and migration from without. It was followed by a period of cultural isolation and religious conversion. Only about the tenth century did a new societal integration begin to take form, characterized by a feudal political organization and a western Catholic Christian pattern of monotheism. The stabilizing of the new societal equilibrium was made easier and more rapid by the transmission into the hitherto isolated region of the original but forgotten achievements of the Greco-Roman world plus the later developments due to the Arabic civilization, east and west. The consequence was a period of intense assimilation which, at whatever danger to the existent integration, continued until the West had made its own all the cultural acquisitions of the entire Mediterranean.

At some point in say the 1400's, the outcome of several centuries of assimilation began to manifest itself in modifications of the Mediterranean foundations or in entirely new structures based upon them. From this time on there is a period of origination extending down into the present. When finally men over the whole range of both action and thought began to challenge and then replace the millennial accumulations that dated back to the early Greeks, the coming of a new cultural epoch was evident. The lineaments of a new cultural order were distinguishable. An ancient and an intermediate world were being destroyed in the one effective and permanent fashion, namely, by being replaced. The modern world was rapidly taking form.

To give definite dates to the significant periods or events in this societal transformation is difficult; and sometimes to say what is significant is more difficult still. It is in the nature of the quantitative changes that produce qualitative results that they proceed from imperceptible beginnings and are remarked only when suddenly the consequences become visible; hence the difficulty of accurately delimiting the time period of even basic societal changes. In the centuries after the thirteenth there was in progress a continuous spontaneous modification of the conditions of life in the West. As

the facts were perceived by observers of one particular aspect of
society or another and the extent of the continuing alterations
realized, the inevitable tendency has been to write the history of the
period in terms of revolutions. And this statement is valid for both
the active and the speculative developments of western society.
Some writers however have seen more deeply into the nature of
the changes in process and especially the relation among them, so
they have been led to describe the epoch in general terms. Sumner
for example says: "All the changes in the conditions of life in the
last four hundred years have refashioned the mores and given modern society new ideas, standards, codes, philosophies, and religions." [2] But most historians, having no sociological foundations,
have satisfied themselves with serial arrangements of facts and events
summated in terms of revolution.

To begin with the humbler quantitative changes in the domain
of societal activity, the coming of new goals for achievement, binding socii together in new ways, was observable well before the dissolution of the catholic-feudal integration in such phenomena as
the expansion of agriculture, the widening of the economic horizon
beyond the manorial domain, the extension of markets, the development of fabrication first on the basis of the millennial craft skills
and then of the slowly evolving division of labor in the economic
and technical senses. On these coral depths arose the visible qualitative growths that received the attention of historians. First the Commercial Revolution, with the Agricultural Revolution contempo-
raneous with it; both were followed by an even more striking
qualitative departure from the earlier culture, namely, the fabrication of goods first for the factor and then in the factory where the
new means of production, the machines, were installed. To the
factories came the laborers, the tillers who were becoming superfluous in the new agriculture, to become workers. With them came
the Industrial Revolution. It once seemed an epochal culmination
of developing economic forces; it now appears to have been grossly
overemphasized by historians with little cultural perspective and
is regarded as the beginning rather than the end of technical achievement. It becomes still less predominant in perspective when seen
in the midst of such other cultural features as the new navigation,
the new trade routes, the new commercial centers, the new trading

2. *Folkways*, p. 163.

methods, the new banking; all of these and all the others together make the new order, affecting all the factors of the societal equilibrium.

To turn attention to the speculative changes during the period is to perceive a parallel movement. Just as socii were given new ends for action, so were new bonds of thought coming into being. Here too there was a gradual destruction of an earlier equilibrium. The medieval synthesis began to be questioned even in the 1300's. Particularly did the method by which it had been established come under attack. Reasoning of an essentially deductive kind came to be suspected and then rejected along with the authority upon which the reasoning rested. The process of assimilation, continuing into the 1400's, brought new ideas into currency. Scholasticism lost prestige, even at last in the field of education. The intellectual renaissance of the 1200's and 1300's was succeeded by the literary and aesthetic renaissance of the 1400's and 1500's. It revived for a limited class certain selected aspects of the ancient world; and though it little touched the mass of people, it did encourage in those whom it reached the individualism that was being fostered elsewhere in other ways.

Origination on the basis of assimilation rose from one level of abstraction to another. As the implications of the Copernican revolution became explicit, interest in the physical sciences grew, leading to the systematic use of the experimental method which in the Arabic culture had arisen spontaneously and inevitably as the only way in which to investigate effectively the nature of the material world. Galileo is the name that marks the advent of the new method, and from his time to Newton's a new synthesis was in course of construction. The Newtonian revolution was influential beyond calculation, involving as it did directly and by implication the recognition of law in the entire range of subsocial phenomena.

To this period, with its distinctive coordination of knowledge, general agreement has given the name "the age of reason." Characteristic of it was the search for the laws of nature, the main instrument for the search being the reasoning powers of the individual conceived of as an essential part of his ego. "Rationalism" came to be the term descriptive of the mental operations involved. It is now clear that reason defined as an individual possession is in fact a replicate refined into an entity. If it was not itself deified it was at least identified with the supreme cause, who at the same time and by the same metaphysical dissolvent was approaching the time when he too would become an entity. The consequences were all the more readily accepted in that the advance of science had not reached the social domain. Consequently the divine entity was left in full possession of the moral world which by definition was excluded from the material, physical world where science, itself an entity, was in full possession, reason there being under the guidance of nature.

But the dissolvent power of entitism is too great to be halted at any one point. The value of the entity is precisely that it affords an easy transition from the supernatural to the natural by way of the concept of laws which once regarded as the decrees of the all-mighty come then to be regarded as the regularities of nature. Hence the way was soon to be opened which led to the inclusion within the realm of uniformity of even those phenomena which had once been regarded as the personal prerogative of the lawgiver. The inevitable consequence was the extension of the rationalistic point of view to the whole sum of phenomena observable by Man: in short, an Intellectual Revolution.

To this summary of the intellectual advances of the period of origination it is not difficult to add a similar characterization of the activity of the time. First, there was a continuous decline of war, *envisaged as a societal goal*, for either conquest or defense. War, from being an end of societal organization, became more and more a means. Second, the importance of the merchant and the nascent industrialist grew despite all opposition. Not only did they become wealthier—this was no new phenomenon—but they became functionally more important in the new societal equilibrium that was being established. Third, the crescent groups, because of the conditions under which they arose and came to power, were highly individualistic. They failed quite to see what was at first hardly discernible, namely, the collective nature of the achievements through the centuries which alone made their triumphs possible. Moreover they arose in opposition to dominant forces; hence their continuous resistance to any discipline defensible on a collective basis. They relied only on themselves; they were "self-made." Government was the enemy. Lastly, they had constantly to concern themselves with increasing the wealth whose concentration alone made possible the ever expanding scope of their undertakings. Only later did the instrument and means of enterprise become an objective in itself as an end, the gaining of power. What men under the new conditions of life were impelled to do was enter upon undertakings for the successful execution of which larger and larger funds were required. To bring these points into clear focus, the term most suitable is the age of the entrepreneurs, "the age of enterprise."

It is not difficult then to find a phrase to characterize as a whole the period when the modern world was being shaped. The essential feature of the active evolution was individual initiative of a pre-industrial kind; the characteristic aspect of thought was the attribution to an individual entity termed reason of the mental achievements of mankind. There is an evident harmony between the two points of view. The success of the individual enterpriser depended upon his own energy and effort; it demanded that all the elements of each undertaking and all the conditions of each venture should be reasoned out beforehand as far as possible. On the other hand the reasoner, following the rational approach to the material world, discovering regularities and thus making prevision possible, afforded precisely the kind of knowledge useful for enterprise. Indeed it was not to be long before the whole industrial process was to be rationalized. No wonder that the steps even in the scientific process were regarded as individual enterprises. In brief all the motives accord to justify the choice, as descriptive of the initial period of the modern phase of the cultural movement, of the term "the age of rationalistic enterprise." As such the age was an inevitable and indispensable phase of societal development: inevitable because it grew out of the past, indispensable because it was a requisite preparation for the future.

Already on the basis of the outline just sketched it would be possible to place the historical reality against the abstract development in an appropriate position upon the curve representing the societal movement. But to do so without further analysis of the situation would be to open the conclusion to criticism from the logical point of view at least if from no other. It could be said that there was no evidence inherent in the picture already drawn as to the direction in which the historical facts were facing, so to speak. They might in this view of the matter be only an oscillation or a fluctuation, an extreme from which a return to the original starting point might be anticipated. The point is logically well taken. It reveals the necessity of reviewing the period under discussion from the negative as well as the positive viewpoint. So only can the direction of the movement be ascertained.

No great difficulty is involved in the decision. The histories are as full of details on the descendant phase of the cultural development of the period as they are on the ascendant, though for obvious reasons they emphasize the latter. Only a brief account then is required to make clear the point of departure from which the changes already listed proceeded. The record here is written in terms of decline: first, the decline of the feudal relationship as the power of the kings increased, as towns came into independence, as money became the basis of a new economy, as military tactics changed with the coming of firearms; then the decline of the manor with the growth of agricultural specialization, the appearance of the market, the weakening of serfdom, the payment of wages; then the decline of the guilds when the wage earning group was distinguished from the masters, who went on to acquire the dignity of employers and enterprisers; finally the decline of the church through the schisms, heresies, quarrels, politics, venality, and immorality that intensified the consequences of skeptical inquiry, growth of nationalism, study of Roman law, spread of learning through printing, and in general the change in economic and social conditions.

Here then it is clear that a notable local event has occurred which must be set against the general cultural time scheme. Only one point yet must be considered before the place of the first against the second can be determined: What was the general direction of the changes recorded? Evidently the world called medieval was being greatly altered; were these alterations pointing to a quite new situation or only a variant of the old? To discover the trend within the local events is the last requirement for fitting the smaller movement into the larger.

The task is easy on any level: from the medieval army of knights to the mercenary army used for the enforcement of policy; from the self-subsistent manor to the farm supplying the market; from the guild master to the entrepreneur; from the serf to the worker; from the craft to the factory; from the deity through protestantism and deism to the entity; from supernaturalism through humanism to naturalism; from theology to science; from authority to experiment; the list need not be widened nor extended. In any interpretation it is impossible to see it as simply a variation on an existent equilibrium; it is clearly a movement toward a new societal integration. It is at once the end of one era and the beginning of another.

Clear recognition of the transitional nature of the period makes it easy to find the appropriate place on the universal time scale of the local events that constitute the end of the medieval and the beginning of the modern world. In the light of their nature and direction they fall inevitably into that section of the universal cultural movement where causality and war begin to yield to uniformity and industry. Such particularities as they present are due of course to the working of the law of persistence dealt with in an earlier chapter; but the underlying tendencies are independent of the superficial differences. As a matter of fact each national group has its own distinctive traits, but they are all describable in terms of the same general definitions. They are all evidences of transition whether viewed from the local or the general point of view. To them all apply the terms "decline" and "revolution" as indicative of the passage from the medieval to the modern.

Not only is the place of the local events fixed, however. When the lines of direction that traverse them are regarded, they are seen to coincide with the far longer lines of the abstract movement. The coincidence of the two sets of indications—the drift and the trend— gives to the special historical facts the significance of general cultural developments. Particularly telling is it when the conjunction of the two is at a point of transition in the normal course of societal movement. The implication then is that the local group is a representative of mankind and that its departure from the past marks the route along which the other collectivities will proceed. Moreover, the coincidence of the two directions will serve to indicate the lines along which the later development of the local society will follow, thus introducing the idea of prevision into the hitherto solely historical discussion and in this way bringing the dynamical concepts of sociology into relevance.

Now all these lines of thought lead straight to a reassessment of the importance of the transitional development which made the medieval into the modern. This historical change coincides with a societal advance of the first order. Not only is a transition in point; *it is one of the truly epochal transitions in the normal societal move-*

ment. The early change from agency to cause, from collection and cultivation to predation and war was critical enough; but it is dwarfed by the immensity of the later transformation which brings mankind to maturity in the stage of uniformity and industry. It is precisely this advance which is made clear when the medieval decline and the modern revolution are viewed in the perspective of the cultural movement as a whole. For this reason an episode that seemed at first local to the West becomes a matter of concern to mankind. For all these reasons, what this chapter deals with may well be called the Great Transition.

To join the past on to the future as is done when the present is envisaged as a continuing transition between major cultural epochs involves far-reaching revision of many conventionally defined concepts and doctrines. The statement holds true of all the societal subisolates as well as of the general doctrines on which sociology is founded. To effect the necessary modifications of both a general and a special nature amounts in many cases to wholesale alterations of accepted theories.

Take for example the subisolate usually termed economic. Its central element, it is now clear, is the cumulation of the material products upon which the cultural development of man primarily rests, whatever may be the psychical or other accretions that have come historically to be embodied in the conventional term. When the concepts comprised within the economic range are viewed as parts of a continuous cultural development, running back through the Neolithic, they acquire an unusual degree of generality. Thus they become visibly dependent upon the course of cultural evolution. Such concepts as the market become obvious cultural phenomena and as such have only a relative validity. They are revealed as statical abstractions, characteristic of a given or a particular phase of culture. The attempt to make of them universally applicable concepts lacks cogency.

In another aspect, hitherto unsuspected complications may be revealed. Thus the circulation of wealth as described in an earlier chapter may by the very nature of its operations involve a cyclical recurrence of good times and bad or a regular oscillation about an advancing mean. But the existence of such regularities is obviously difficult to determine when the whole circulatory movement is disturbed by being subjected to the influences arising from the sequence of stages which mark the transition from industrialism to industry.

On a still larger scale the same line of thought holds. Thus what were once conceived to be diametrical and hostile opposites, capitalism and socialism, can now be seen to be but aspects of a fundamental transition, both undergoing continuous modification and losing their sharpness of opposition when they are seen to be but parts of a transitional development. Finally there is the case of the isolation of the economic. It was once effected abstractly for the sake of intellectual clarity. Next it was elevated to the level of reality and later to the level of the ideal. Then the economic isolate came to be regarded from the point of view of society as a whole; and now the enormous possibilities of economic development are in evident need of being brought under societal control. Thus the statical abstract is brought back into relation with the concrete reality.

Association, no less than material accumulation, is revealed in a new light when the fact of fundamental societal change is kept in mind. What is going on is the gradual extension of societal influences over increasing numbers. The outcome is manifestly intensive as well as extensive. One result is the disappearance of the distinction between masses and classes in the old absolute sense. In its place is the growing recognition of the fact that an individual may be mass in one respect and class in another, according to the criteria in effect at a given time or place.

Accompanying this change is the tendency toward the recognition of increasingly spiritual bonds between larger and larger numbers of men. The size of the association, that is, tends to increase. It grows from family to city and with the sharpening recognition of each there is strengthened the tendency toward the inclusion of increasing numbers and the willingness to cooperate with them. This growth is effected less and less by force and more and more by suasion. The church thus comes into increasing prominence, whether the bond of union be political, religious, or other.

With regard to communication little need be said, so clear is the influence of the transitional forces. Obviously there is no point in elaborating the consequences of the material, i.e., technical devices which have brought increasing numbers of human beings into more or less intimate relations. What deserves less summary dismissal is the development that has been in process whereby the range of common conceptions has been enlarged at the same time that individuals involved have been intensively cultivated by the extension to them of the growing sum of achievement due to humanity as a whole.

Obviously this cultivation of the human being is both a result and a condition of societal growth, particularly if the movement toward uniformity and industry is to continue: hence indeed the gradual enlargement of the term "education." Once it was essentially nothing but imitation; then it became schooling; now it tends to comprise the entire span of life, each characteristic stage of it receiving its appropriate mental and physical regimen. The result is not only the expansion, the broadening and deepening of personality; the time is brought nearer when the control and guidance of mankind, after having passed from Age to Birth, is given over to Merit.

It is probable that the factor of societal existence most likely to be affected by the movement toward uniformity and industry— and the one most difficult therefore to be dealt with from the point of view of prevision—is that which has in this volume been termed direction. The reason is that direction has most to gain from the development of the psychical level of abstraction. Hitherto the phenomena at the summit of the hierarchy have been so closely interactive that their independence has been a matter of doubt. Now it seems clear that there are two levels: the societal and the psychical. Behind the first is force; beneath the second is suasion.

Continuing analysis of the phenomena on these upper levels is bound to make the distinction between the two more decisive. The outcome will be the clarification and use of the two powers, as they have hitherto been called, namely, the spiritual and the temporal. The use and development of both will be facilitated by the realization that neither is based on anything more than the normal basis of uniformity, all notions of revelation, absoluteness, etc., being set aside once for all. It may even be that the limitation of force will be so well understood as to work for the weakening of the bonds which have in the past held under a single sovereignty masses of men so large and so widely varying that all delicate cultural distinctions have had to be ignored. Government has thus rested on a purely societal foundation of force, with all the crudity inevitable under such conditions. The future development may well turn in the direction of the breakup of these immense societal sovereignties and the substitution of smaller units where cultural differences may find freer expression at the same time that government will be more effective.

It need not be said that no selection of detail from any or all of the societal subisolates could be anything more than illustrative concerning the nature of the Great Transition in progress. What is required here is something at once more inclusive and more probative. What is sought at this point is a general concept arising out of and therefore organically connected with the entire sum of societal phenomena.

Fortunately such a concept exists. It has steadily been emerging from the work of the historians; and it has finally come to be the symbol of the whole urban societal integration. It recalls for the sociologist the two senses of the word "order"—command and arrangement—which in an earlier connection were defined with relation to the physical world. In its customary formulation the idea here in point is expressed in terms so socionomic in reference as to be misleading. It seems to be concerned only with the relationship of men envisaged as classes; in fact the concept involves the whole range of social existence—wealth, place, learning, power— since they all contribute to and are integrated into what has come to be called *the social pyramid*.

This inclusive societal integration had its origin in the ancient oriental urban cultures. There in the beginnings of a new order arose and took their place at the summit of the social structure a priestly class and a military aristocracy. In later days and in rather exceptional instances appeared a merchant or business element. Beneath all of these levels were the masses: the workers (mainly craftsmen and slaves) and the tillers of the soil (mainly peasants and serfs). Little or no recognition of kinship or fellowship with others showed itself in those who looked down upon those who looked up to them. Indeed, with the passage of time the gap between even the workers and the tillers tended to widen.

Never did the essential order implied in the pyramidal structure disappear. "Each of the Asiatic and European urban cultures developed class structures which, however differing in detail from one another, duplicated the fundamental pattern of the ancient-oriental social pyramid." [3] It was modified from time to time as the different levels of which it consisted gained or lost proportional influence. Often there were redistributions of number and power; often there were disputes leading to conflict; but at their end the basic order of society persisted. "Aristocratic orders and priestly groups were often rivals for supreme power, although they commonly found ways to share it."

Inevitably, given the stage of societal development then attained, the attitude of the upper levels toward the masses was expressed in the concept of subject, "which derived most of its meaning from the belief that man is dependent upon the daimonic universe for well being." The hominoids expected men to serve them; the upper levels of men demanded service from the lower. The effect of such beliefs was usually "to make the well being of common men a condition to be gained in the other world only through the performance in this world of duties which actually assured priests and princes of whatever well being there was attainable" here—this well being definable not necessarily in terms of wealth but of power.

The lower levels of the pyramid were in no condition to enable them to do more than protest against the hardships that were their lot; they could often not even do so much with vigor and effect. "The failure of the masses to rise above destructiveness in their struggles was caused largely by the fact that they never possessed either the political experience or the intellectual training necessary to develop a regime in terms of their own interests." Moreover, "in spite of changes in the basic population and in the ruling classes, the cultural tradition persisted, *for indeed the interaction that produced these phenomena was organized in its forms,* and the new groups were bound by them quite as had been their predecessors." In short, there were innumerable revolts; there were no genuine revolutions.

Against this fact the theory of class struggle as a societal constant breaks. Classes—societal stratifications—persisted throughout the whole urban culture, whatever its forms, since the underlying conditions of life, of which they were a resultant, underwent no fundamental alteration. It was not indeed until the beginning of the modern period that the societal situation, in the adjustment to which

3. Turner, *The Great Cultural Traditions,* 2, 1254–1255. Quotations below are from Turner, 2, 1257, 305, 302, 304.

hierarchical levels of society arose, began to undergo fundamental change. What men up to that time had been trying to do was to strive to occupy the advantageous levels of the pyramid and not to undermine or demolish it. Class conflicts, yes; social revolution, no.

Only when basic conditions began to foreshadow the coming of a new societal situation did revolt pass into revolution. The immediate and apparent manifestations of the will to create a new order took the form of new doctrines with the tendency and power to challenge and replace the old. In fact, the first clear signs of a new situation took the form of the revolt; but they were soon to become revolutionary. Sumner's words, quoted above, here become especially significant: All the changes in the conditions of life in the last four hundred years have refashioned the mores and given modern society new ideas, standards, codes, philosophies, and religions. But the point here is that the men, the new estate, in whom these new conditions gave rise to new ideas thought at first in the old pyramidal class forms. They were members of a middle class, whose middle position was a simple deduction from their historical location between the upper and the lower levels of the pyramid.

To date or even to define the emerging new societal situation is difficult. When did the numbers involved increase to the point where a qualitative change was evident or imminent? It may have been in Britain in the seventeenth century; certainly it had come to pass in the France of the eighteenth. What distinguishes the disorders that marked the new situation in France is the nature of the claims that were being made by and for the ascendant groups. The essential points here are two: the rise of a class so changed as to be a new social phenomenon, and the claim of this class to dominance in the social hierarchy. These two characteristics combine to make the revolt in France a revolution.

That is to say that the French Revolution was not just another example of a constant societal phenomenon; it was on the contrary the first truly revolutionary class movement in history. For this reason the judgment is valid and necessary that the movement in France was more than a merely local event. Or, to put the thought in another form, it was a local movement the significance of which can be adequately defined only in the light of the societal movement as a whole. When placed against this time scale the local event becomes a world event. In this context, the unprecedented movement in France becomes the most striking occurrent in the Great Transition, the ultimate end of which is to destroy and replace the whole social pyramid.

It must be said emphatically that the members of the bourgeoisie did not conceive of their movement as anything more than a fundamental remaking of the pyramid. True enough, they talked and even in some cases thought of the freeing, the liberating of mankind. They badly needed the material support of the lower orders to effect their purposes; but the success of their efforts, however liberalizing, was always to be measured in limited terms. That they might be overturning social order was soon realized; stop was quickly put to the extreme revolutionary consequences thus implied.

Now the lowest orders—still the lowest after the rise of the bourgeoisie—had heard and taken to heart the gusty ideas formulated in the revolutionary attacks upon altar and throne, upon deity and king. They in their turn, and very soon afterward, began their own revolutionary efforts. What is in point with reference to the thought here being set forth is the fact that even in their formulations of their aspirations and intentions the new revolutionaries tended to reflect and utilize the concepts on which the pyramidal structure rested. True, they saw that the old structure would be profoundly modified; but both the new hopes and the new projects were formulated in pyramidal terms. The bourgeoisie would free men by destroying and remaking certain privileged levels; the workers would free men by identifying one class with the entire pyramid, i.e., by making all men workers; hence in both cases, and particularly the second, the necessity to attack and liquidate rulers or nonworkers.

Neither proposal derives from a scientific view of the societal process. Illuminative at this point is the first and natural reaction of men when subjected to oppression and frustration, to find or seek relief by constructing an ideal world, a pictured situation in which the repressive conditions are simply negated and omitted. Such a procedure has no relation of course to scientific methods. The latter, with reference to the future, dictate recourse to prevision, for which likes and dislikes, desires or aversions, are alike irrelevant. They dictate the asking of the question: Given the conditions and the uniformities, what are the consequences? Should the conclusions be unwelcome, then it can be asked whether the consequences can be modified, and to what degree; or if they cannot be modified, shall the victims be indemnified, and if so how? In other words, utopias in the nonsociological past have been creations of desire; they should now become constructions of science. Increasing the intensity of the orectic constants gives great energy but it cannot decide the form to be given the resultant exergy. This can grow only out of the continuous operation of societal uniformities.

It is not enough then simply to negate class conditions by an effort to reduce all classes to one, destroying if necessary all recalcitrants. What is required is to place the local movement—the unique eighteenth-century class revolution—in its proper perspective on the time scale, i.e., the normal movement of societal development. Only so can the significance of the event be determined. When this imposition is effected the vision of the past becomes a prominent feature of the prevision of the future. What has been going on, and continues, is no class movement at all. It is the beginning of the destruction of the pyramidal order—hence the class terms in which it has been defined—and the integration of a new order which will replace it. There is to be no dominant class, no class at all in the old sense. Both the bourgeoisie and the workers are products of a single and now dissolving integration; hence the inapplicability of the whole terminology of the past. A world in which all are workers has no meaning for a period in which the concept of work is falling apart. Once man quite literally did not know enough to work. The time is near when it will be possible to accuse him of not knowing enough not to.

In short, civilization, defined as the societal equilibrium developed from the interplay of the cultural factors which made and constituted the urban revolution of the anthropologists, is now quite obviously in process of dislocation. What this change means in the cultural perspective is the ultimate disappearance, first in their primary consequences and then in their secondary implication, of the ultimate end of action known as war and the ultimate frame of reference known as causality. Since it is upon the interplay of these societal forces, deitism and conquest, that the period of urban imperialism in all its variants has been based, the clear inference is that all the phenomena sequent upon the change of conditions that put an end to primitive life by raising men from the domestic to the civic association are being fundamentally altered or replaced. Everything from folkways to philosophies will accordingly be affected. It is in effect beyond the power of conception to envisage all the ensuing consequences. Time alone can make all the transformations possible or conceivable. But nothing less than the gradual remaking of the entire societal symplegma is inevitably involved in the statement that civilization is being destroyed.

Nothing sensational is implied in these formulations of the nature of the cultural transformation in progress. All that is meant is that the old cultural symplegma is being raveled out and a new one is being woven. Neither need the figure of the social pyramid be taken too literally. However aptly it may picture the facts, all that its destruction implies is the disappearance of the hierarchical societal stratifications that accompanied the transition from a domestic to a civic type of association and their replacement by the functional relationships that are required by the new conditions. Socii in other words are being allied in a new way; hence a new society.

When the age of rationalistic enterprise is placed against its appropriate cultural background, the changes in process are clearly seen to be moving in the direction of a truly industrial regime guided by scientific knowledge. The new end of action, that is, becomes industry, in the full sense as defined earlier in these pages; the new bond of thought, uniformity. It is with relation to these developing conditions that concepts and projects both old and new must be evaluated.

Here for example is the synthetic intellectual product called philosophy. For millennia the coordinating principle of philosophic thought has been causality—when it has not been agency. But what relevance or even meaning can this principle continue to have in the face of a sidereal universe where distances are inconceivable and conditions unimaginable? No one can even say that it *is* a universe that is in question. The very word reveals the presence of a philosophical principle that was evolved in an earlier stage of knowledge. How can the concept of cause, first or last, multiple or single, retain its validity in the light however dim of the fixed stars?

Here, to take a positive rather than a negative case, is the achievement hailed as the greatest scientific triumph of all time, namely, the release of the energy in the atom. It is quite clear that in the movement of thought that led to the final result there is not the slightest hint that it was due to the assistance, direct or indirect, or the presence, far or near, of any hominoid whatever, fetishistic or deitistic, multiple or single. From the first to the last the investigation of the atom was carried on in the ultimate frame of reference supplied by uniformity alone.

Here from another point of view is the vaunted wisdom of the ages and particularly in recent days the wisdom of the East. Beneath the laudation of these wisdoms is the tacit or overt assumption that somewhere, presumably in the revelations to or by some sage or preferably some seer, the more ancient the better, is to be found all the guidance necessary to direct the social behavior of men. They have the knowledge, in other words; all that need be done is to follow the light.

But now that men have slowly come to the study of the sources whence these wisdoms have been drawn, a surprising situation is disclosed. The wise men are found to have been evolving their theories while they have been occupying advantageous positions on the upper and often the highest levels of the social pyramid. Beneath them and supplying all the needs of the superior men above through untold generations are the millions upon millions of inferior beings who compose the foundations of the pyramid, starvation racked, disease ridden, infested with trillions of intestinal parasites, enjoying a life expectancy of some twenty-five or thirty years and justifying their very existence by virtue of some service to the superior wise. Such wisdom is suspect, rightly. It may be, it may well be hoped, that there are in this wisdom some valid inductions as to man and his motives, thoughts, and actions. But it is only after its pronouncements have been subjected to the test of scientific method that their worth and validity will be confidently assessed.

Nothing can be clearer, in the light of the changes to which the Great Transition is leading, than the inevitability of subjecting to reexamination and redefinition all the conclusions of the past. Liberty, for instance, and freedom and all such notable conceptions will be certain to be reformulated when they are analyzed in the ultimate frame of reference supplied by industrial activity organized functionally and scientific uniformity extended to the moral world. The work of those who embody or defend the older framework of thought may be impassioned statements of belief or the arguments of advocates, but they are irrelevant to the major issue. The abiding place of wisdom is no longer the superior realm of the spirit; it is only the higher levels of the pyramid.

Analogous conclusions can be reached in relation to the cultural factor called religion. There is to begin with no question as to its existence and influence. "No society without a religion" is the sociological verdict supported by a vast accumulation of anthropological data. But the notion that religion is a supercultural influence emanating from a nonsocietal source is baseless. The very existence of the religious element of culture is the outcome of the fact that Man is the animal Homo continuously being transformed by collective cumulation. Thus the inductive evidence is complemented and even strengthened by deductive conclusions. *Because* Man is a social being and not an isolated animal there must be the recognition of some power or influence beyond or above the organic individual to which his activities as a socius can be referred so that the value of these activities can be decided. The source of these bases for value judgments are obviously outside the individual being. But to take this position is to say at the same time that religion is but one of the interdependent elements which are integrated or equilibrated in a given cultural symplegma.

No other position seems possible in the light of historical knowledge or sociological analysis. Inductive support is hard to bring to bear on the point simply because of its immensity. Perhaps one case only may be cited because it is illuminative and decisive. It is that of Robert Owen. With all his ability and moral earnestness, he was unable to operate his mills on obviously Christian principles even with the added inducement of a ten per cent dividend. The difficulty is that religion has a double basis. It is both societal and psychical in its makeup. It was the discovery of this fact that made Comte, in his final revision of his work, cease to count religion as one of the societal subisolates. Not only must the activities of the socius be integrated with those of other socii (or else they are not socii); the orectic constants of the person have to be integrated as well (or else he fails to be a person). The social instrument for integrating personality and uniting personalities is religion.

Of the Bakongo in Africa, for example, it is said that their worship of the good ancestral spirits gives the tribe cohesion and the individual a sense of purpose; hence a sense of continuity and of unity with both nature and the unseen world. But men do not remain on the primitive level of culture; their concepts of the unseen world vary with time as the process of collective cumulation carries them on to new views of the unseen. It may well happen that the new views, resulting from continued ideation, may not stimulate strongly or may even diminish the proportional influence in the orectic equilibration of certain of the psychic constants. In other words, the orectic integration that is effected by a given societal situation may fail to meet the standards of an integration which on some absolute basis has come to be regarded as ideal. In such a case preaching, however defined, is without effect. Man remains sinful (or some of its synonyms, such as sensate) and falls below the ideal. But to make such judgments is completely futile. It is precisely the existence and nature of sinfulness that requires explanation. The first step in this explanation is the recognition of the operation of the societal factor.

The case of the Thomistic doctrines is illustrative here. First, there is the selective treatment of a body of thought which in other connections is held to be a remarkable example of intellectual unity. Thomas, for example, demonstrates the existence of angels and goes on to prove that each human being has an angel as guardian. The proof is at least as cogent logically as the more noted demonstration of the existence of a single deity. Yet for evident cultural motives the first position is kept in the background and the second emphasized. It is as if a single original garment were to be cut into pieces and a new one fashioned from selected fragments. But second, insofar as objective validity is concerned, even the selected arguments are valueless. What they do show, with finality, is why men at a particular stage in their cultural development held so firmly to a particular doctrine. Any other conclusion is invalidated by the simple fact that the animal Homo as he arose from the animal level was possessed of no doctrines whatever. They have all been developed on the societal level in virtue of the operation of psychical and societal uniformities which are now the subject of investigation.

It is with little surprise then that the sociologist has observed the falling away of literally tens of millions of men from their ancient beliefs within a time period to the brevity of which history presents no parallel. They will not return; love in these matters is irreversible. Still other consequences in this line of development are in process. The institutions by which beliefs are implemented —the churches—losing the vigor which comes when the beliefs they hold are living tend more and more to emphasize the institutional aspects of their existence, whereby they can retain the power that may for a time take the place of suasion. There are secondary consequences too. The first is the decline in the level of the ability of the men who compose the institutional framework as the emphasis slowly moves from suasion to power. The second is the inevitable tendency, where a necessity is felt to set a limit to the bounds of a continuing movement, toward passivity and obscurantism or both.

On the side of positive gain one thought, derived from an inductive view of the phenomena called religious, should be listed. It arises from meditation upon the fact that holy men, saints in general, insist upon separation from the world in order to find the conditions under which their sanctity may be developed to the utmost. The innumerable forms which this isolation takes need not here be listed. What is important is to see how this insistence supports the sociological position. Nothing whatever but the difference of vocabulary—one developed in a frame of reference of causality, the other in that of uniformity—prevents the immediate recognition of the fact that the saint and the sociologist are in complete agreement. The latter insists upon the distinction between the societal and the psychical, the saint upon the separation of the spirit from the world; the sociologist insists upon the fact that the societal conditions the psychical, the saint upon the necessity of leaving the world in order to have the proper conditions in which to perfect his spirit. There is no disagreement in theory; it is only in words. The time may well come when, after each has been subjected to scientific analysis, both the saint and the world will be so modified as to allow of a truly functional relationship between them.

In the gradual movement toward a new ultimate frame of reference, the growth of science too has been affected. It is, as might be expected, in the development of the social rather than the physical sciences that these influences can be seen. In this connection a bit of historical detail dating from the beginning of the nineteenth century will be relevant.

Sumner's words form a fitting introduction: "The middle class in Europe has been formed out of the labor class within seven hundred years. The whole middle class, therefore, represented the successful rise of the serfs." [4] These new men with the vision of a new world rose as individuals. There were for them no accepted norms; each did what he pictured his situation to require. The appeal to inner urge and to consequent action was so immediate and strong that an intensification of human energy resulted, with an output of exergy probably unique in history. No labors seemed too great, no sacrifices too severe. Inevitably the qualities that made men able to realize their desires were elevated into universal virtues and incorporated into religion. Especially loud was the outcry against all restrictions that seemed to handicap the protesters. It finally reached the level of systematic formulation and was embodied in a philosophy, the creed of individualism.

But the very intensity of the singleminded will to succeed, i.e., come up from below and replace aroused opposing forces which grew strong as the consequences of unrestrained freedom grew clear. The new men came from classes with no ideals that could control the rising group; such virtues as they had were the virtues of the dominated. Their success was individual; those who did not succeed were therefore inferior and deserved no consideration. To them work might be given, but nothing was owed to them. The notion that the successful individuals were themselves the products of cultural advances, especially in technology and science, could not occur to them. It could to others, however, and to their theories was added the fact of the cooperative, social nature of the factory and of industry in general. And so at the very moment of its greatest triumphs and because of them the individualism of the period was faced by an opposing doctrine, the philosophy of socialism.

No adequate definition of the term has ever been formulated, as Pareto showed; but it was never susceptible of formal statement. It was first a negation of individualism and second a vision of a better future. Hence it could be implemented, in theory, in as many ways as there were minds. It needed above all to be made sci-

4. *Folkways*, p. 166.

entific; and Marx gave his energies to the task. But he was not, as is generally believed, the first to do so. The line between generous aspiration and scientific direction was first drawn when Comte quarrelled with Saint-Simon and parted from him. The ground of their disagreement was Comte's insistence that only a *science* of social phenomena could serve as an adequate guide for the changes that society evidently needed; no improvisations, however brilliant, could suffice. And so in 1824, in the persons of Saint-Simon and Comte, socialism and sociology took divergent though not opposite paths. Marx, twenty years later, rightly saw the need of scientific guidance for societal change, but he was handicapped by his metaphysical background, his unavoidable ignorance of psychology (so general in 1848), and his insistence upon the economic as the sole motive force in societal development. Hence despite his righteous indignation at seeing the gifts of humanity monopolized for individual advantage, his work hardened into a body of quasi-sacred *doctrine* which can be adapted to meet new knowledge only by a pretense of restoring or discovering the true meaning of the ancient texts. Comte, on the other hand, put his reliance upon scientific *method,* which led him far beyond his contemporaries but made him surprisingly accordant with later thought. If there is any validity in the dictum that in science it is the method rather than the doctrine which counts, his example is the safer guide.

It will be well here to observe some of the consequences of the insistence upon doctrine rather than method. Marx, for example, not carrying his historical analysis far enough, failed to see that his work involved not only the destruction of the social pyramid but its replacement. Hence he always thought in pyramidal terms. Again he seems not to have advanced far beyond causality in the direction of uniformity as an ultimate frame of reference. Some of the resulting limitations upon his thought may be mentioned, always with due recognition however of the part it played in raising fundamental questions that still demand scientific answer.

There is to begin with the failure to advance beyond the Hegelian dialectic toward the recognition of the fact that social progress occurs in the form of oscillations about a constantly advancing societal point. There is a failure to see the class movement in its cultural perspective, which makes of it not a societal constant but only the effective historical agent in the final destruction of the structure characteristic of civilization, and consequently the inability to rise beyond the conception of class toward that of function. Coupled with this weakness is the inadequacy of the treatment of those cultural epochs which preceded and which are to follow the epoch of class struggle. From another point of view there is the tendency which Marx shared with Spencer and even with Sumner to regard Man once for all as a reasoning being *per se* rather than to move toward regarding him as an emotional being guided by the experience of the race. Again, in his conception of scientific law, Marx like so many of his contemporaries stressed strongly the inevitability or fatality aspects of the concept rather than the possibilities of modification. Rarely indeed do uniformities dictate as a necessity a single line of action. Again, there was the rejection of societal continuity in favor of the concept of solidarity and its outcome in the need to isolate the new movement from other cultural influences, at least for all the time—obviously incalculable— which would be required to solidify the new symplegma beyond danger of extraneous influences. Finally, there may be mentioned the almost exclusive utilization of appeal to interest as the driving force in determining the will to create a new situation. Here no doubt is the explanation of the tremendous rapidity with which the new doctrines were advanced. But interests are the source of conflicts. Comte, in contrast, made his appeal to the sympathies. It may well be that time will approve his choice.

In the elevation to doctrinal level of theories that method was to weaken with scientific advance, especially in the domains of sociology and psychology, it is clear that Marx in his construction mingles utopian elements with positive ones. With the passage of time and particularly with the attempts to translate doctrine into action, the utopian elements have tended to reveal themselves. Hence there has been a necessity to move away from utopia toward a reality which of course fails to meet the utopian standards. The outcome has been the rise of an insistence upon a distinction between two stages in the new social movement: one the true, pure communism relegated to an undefined future, and the other a socialism which is being temporarily and experimentally constructed today. The distinction has its usefulness, obviously; but its disadvantages are great. On the one hand it restricts and distorts and discounts the present; on the other, though it may silence many of the utopians, it repels and rejects and antagonizes the more doctrinaire, emotional, ambitious, and illiterate. Moreover it tends to split the forces making, and making for, the future and compels unwilling choice often where no final decision is in fact required.

A larger view dispels many of these difficulties. When the present is viewed in the light of the universal culture trend, it becomes simply a moving point of transition separating and connecting the past and the future. The situation that ensues can be regarded from several points of view. It may be and usually has been regarded as a mere change in societal phenomena with no special meaning either prospective or retrospective. From this point of view, what has been occurring is a transformation more or less profound of the cultural equilibrium that characterized the Mediterranean world for some five or six thousand years. Inevitably, then, the changes that have occurred or been proposed have been formulated in terms of the pyramidal structure described above. Even the most revolutionary proposals have been expressed in language descriptive of a rejected past in which class relations were regarded as an historical constant and so the projected future was pictured in class terms even when classes were to be destroyed.

From the point of view of those who had some inclination to contrast the new societal phenomena with the old, there was another possibility. It consisted in striving to find terms adequate to mark the difference between the old established structures and the newer emergent ones. Such words as "adventurer" and "enterpriser" began to appear. As these efforts gradually gave way to more systematic developments and the industrial aspects of the time became more apparent, there came the possibility of contrasting the old and the new by way of a distinction between the status relationship of the pyramid and the increasingly functional relationships coming into being with the rise of industrialism. It is this contrast which has been in point in these pages when the words "pyramidal" and "functional" have been used. No doubt they are inadequate, but they have served to indicate a basic distinction between the newer and the older societal phenomena.

There is still another way to describe the facts in point. It grows out of Sumner's ideas and fits accurately into a vocabulary that has developed during the past century. In these terms what has been going on for twelve or fifteen generations is the development of a new culture out of an older one. All of Sumner's description of an emergent body of folkways and mores, growing without conscious encouragement or even knowledge and spreading in the same way until now the process has begun to reach the systematic stage where a scientific formulation becomes possible, is now a reality. In the terms of anthropology there is a new culture in process of growth.

It is likely that anthropology provides the vocabulary most fitting to give precision to the description of the cultural transformation now in process. For this new science the making of a new culture and its spread is no new phenomenon. The vocabulary and the basic concepts required to describe and understand the current changes are already in existence. It seems almost certain that the sociographer of the future will see the present in this anthropological light.

The present situation is complicated, however, by two unprecedented factors. The first is the fact that history seems to record no case in which a new cultural symplegma has ever developed in the midst of a preexisting culture which it then replaces. Cultural change of such extent has in the past involved a transfer from one group to another. That is to say, the sociological line of descent has seldom been identical with the biological.

The second complicating factor is of another order of difficulty. It is strictly sociological in nature. It becomes significant only when viewed in the perspective of the universal culture trend. According to this concept, the new culture in process involves one of the profound transformations of human society. The change from agency to causality, from collecting to predation and war, was no doubt far-reaching but it is not to be compared with the fundamental alterations in both the ends of action and the bonds of thought involved in the cultural movement into uniformity and industry.

Exactly what this change implies cannot as yet be made the subject of prevision. Sociological science has gone as far as present knowledge allows when it states the nature and general objective of the movement now going on. More detailed consequences must await further inductive examination of societal phenomena. Nevertheless, if specific changes are beyond present calculation it is quite possible to speak generally. From this viewpoint, what the future is bringing with it is a complete change in the fundamental relations of men. It has been proceeding for some generations already; it will certainly continue. Involved ultimately is a transformation of all cultural relations and the rise of new societal structures on the basis of new conditions of life, leading from new folkways on to institutions and philosophies.

The contemporary outcome is the anarchy of idea that now characterizes the thought of Man in the western world, which is the center where both the old and the new are existent. Sumner makes it clear why all the doctrines that emanate from the Mediterranean world are in dissolution and dispute. New philosophies, new deductions from new societal life conditions claim greater and greater authority. Old concepts become increasingly inapplicable under new conditions. To take but a single example, that of liberty, with its connections with leadership: retention of the word conceals the divergence of meaning inherent in the difference between a definition based upon military activity envisaged in a framework of causality and one formulated in terms of a functional relationship in industrial activity developing in a framework of uniformity.

Not only is there an intellectual transformation in process going back at least to the Greeks, there is also a shifting of the whole foundation of power relationships. Every element of the old pyramidal structure is being displaced as a new structural relationship slowly arises out of the new conditions of life. The masses are integrated into the body of citizens, the classes disappear or become functional directors of industrial activity, their control dependent upon their services to society.

If then the historian of the future sees the present as the record of an emerging culture, he is certain to see it also as the age of conflict between the old and the new worlds. In this conflict all who in any way benefit, whether materially or spiritually, from the pyramidal structure will be more or less consciously arrayed against those who move spontaneously toward the new. He will see, in short, a situation in which the forces that work against societal development will be actively in operation.

Long ago Briffault described and defined these forces when he called them custom-thought and power-thought. The first of these works mainly on the intellectual plane, defending by whatever means of advocacy the thought structures of the past, where sages and seers of various origins have propounded answers to Man's

problems. That none of them ever for a moment could envisage
an industrial world based on uniformities is irrelevant; what is new
must therefore be bad. Far more dangerous is the influence of
power-thought. Not only is the use of material means certain to
take all the imaginable forms of force against the new; no nuance
of the lie will be left undeveloped or untried. And no combination of the two forces will be left unmade, no matter how incompatible they are or have been nor how temporary the union. Nothing but the continued replacement of the old by the new will defeat
these forces of obstruction.

The period is thus bound to be a time of anarchy and violence.
It seems to develop conditions which favor the workers and the
scientists. But even these terms are vague and point to the past as
much as to the future. What is a worker when the nature of work
is being revolutionized? What is a scientist when science comes
to be concerned more and more with the uppermost levels of the
abstract hierarchy? In such a time, when consent, however defined,
favors no dominant group, the reliance upon force is bound to be
constant. Some will strive to maintain or revive a past regarded
as ideal; some will work mainly to conserve an order adequate for
the normal business of society; some will be roused by the weakening of order to use power, however gained, for the satisfaction of
inordinate ambition; still others will seek to hasten the transition
to a scientifically guided future. All inevitably tend toward some
form of dictature.

In these troubled conditions there will be no opportunity for
the rise of ridiculous pedantocratic philosopher-kings. Man in the
cultural sense should by now have relegated such notions to oblivion. What is occurring seems to encourage ideal mongers and
fantasy makers. They arise only because of the disorder that the
clash of cultures produces, disorder which helps to make clear why
a new culture has usually needed a new population for its development. What is in fact going on is the gradual spread of new societal
conditions out of which new traits will be produced. They will not
be the result of wishes, desires, dreams, or fantasies; they are the
outcome of the whole societal past, developing in accordance with
the nature of societal phenomena by which men's personal, affective, psychical life must be conditioned if it is to endure.

What is needed, then, for the direction of societal life is the sort of man who can guide the life of his group in ways convergent with the course of societal development. In the past, such types were given the name of statesmen. The term should be retained no doubt when such men pass from the spontaneous to the systematic level. The time seems near when they can make this advance, for the possibility of conscious direction of society seems greater then ever before. Today the statesmen can be guided by the general knowledge of cultural uniformities, both static and dynamic. In addition there are the three uniformities defined in the chapter on social change. The first of these, the law of persistence, can serve as a guide in harmonizing the cultural past of a given group with the developments inherent in the growth of a new culture. The second, the law of coexistence, opens the way to applications of a kind unprecedented in the government of societies. The third, the law of equivalence, serves as a safeguard against one-sided schemes of societal reform. All together they raise the possibilities of societal direction to a new level.

These possibilities however point to no utopia. What is going on is the emergence of a new culture, a new societal state. Sociological phenomena are no more and no less subject to the uniformities that result from their structure, their inalterable arrangement, than they ever were. As the new conditions of life direct the action and thought of men, the ideals, the imaginary commonwealths that arose mainly from a desire to negate the evils of the past, will be set aside and no doubt transformed. Already the sharpness of the lines that separated say capitalism and socialism are blurred, as each is envisaged as a correlative aspect of a new culture.

There will be no utopias. Even when uniformism and industry have become the bases of a new society there will still be sources of difficulty. The functional relations between the operative and the directive agencies of society can degenerate into strife between numbers and wealth. Fortunately situated groups may strive to monopolize the advantages from which they profit. And finally the psychical organization of men, fixed as it was through uncounted millennia of animal existence, will always present obstacles to the harmonizing of the orectic constants with the societal conditions in which desires will have to be exteriorized. Too much must not be expected from the sons and daughters of the animal Homo.

CHAPTER 25: *Beyond Sociology: the Whole Man*

From the simplest to the most complicated phenomena, from the lowest to the highest levels of abstraction, from one isolate to another the thought of mankind has steadily made its way. Through the entire encyclopedia of the sciences from mathematics to physics, from physics to biology and then to sociology, from the isolates underlying geometry and mechanics to those underlying the sciences of life and culture the ascent has continued. Only one higher level remains: there at the summit of the hierarchy the inquirer is face to face with the spiritual.

Contrary to what is often insinuated, the scientific investigator is by no means disconcerted at finding himself in the presence of the spiritual. He has had the experience so often before that it is no longer novel. Indeed he should soon be writing a natural history of spirits now that sociology has accounted for their origin. They met him before any science had yet come into being and they have had to be driven from one field of induction after another. In mathematics they were behind the *phusis* which, as number, was the source of all things. They were in the stars; they *were* the stars. They were in the wind and the rain, in the amber and the lodestone. They appeared in wine and turpentine and alcohol. Expelled thence they reappeared in the natural, vital, animal spirits of biology. Their next home was in sociology, where the spirit of France, the mind of England, the soul of America served for a brief time to lend deceptive ease to cultural explanations. Their final lodgment is the psyche of man. The inference is clear. If psychology is to become a science and in proportion as it does become a science, the spirits must and will be driven from the spiritual.

The little man who has served as pilot on the spiritual plane under the name of Will, the little man who has laid out the course as navigator under the name of Intellect alias Reason—both of them and all their kind must be thanked for their services, which need by no means be underestimated, and retired. Man in short must resolve one more paradox and drive from his own brain, which created them, the last of the hominoids. The study of the psyche, the spirit of man, must be transformed into the study of personality, envisaged not as an entity but as a product, an equilibrium, of many factors. To this end the study of the pertinent data, instead of being carried on in the now outmoded frame of reference resting upon causality, concrete or abstract, multiple or single, must henceforth be transferred to the level where the bond of thought is uniformity.

Such a transfer means the final achievement of science—that term being understood to refer to no entity but simply to the continuous systematic cumulation, for human guidance, of the results of collective experience, issuing both in doctrines and more importantly in methods. Toward such a culmination of complete homogeneity in thought the societal process has always been moving. Long ago the basic form of the ultimate hierarchy of knowledge ceased to be in doubt. The inorganic precedes the organic: on the first the second depends and by it is conditioned; by the second the first is modified but never altered in its essential arrangement. Once this critical position had been firmly established, its implications needed only to be worked out and the subdivisioning of the inorganic followed. Physics, celestial and terrestrial, leads to chemistry. Mathematics, as tool and as logic, underlies them all.

Difficulties abounded however when the analyzing, classifying, and isolating of the ranges of phenomena above the inorganic, the inert, the nonliving were undertaken. Such efforts were at a disadvantage because they were and had for so long been integrated in a causal frame of reference. Even when some advance had been made the distinction between natural and moral philosophy was obstructive, since it tended to favor the inclusion of all phenomena beyond the inorganic in one all-inclusive category, living, and to exclude many varieties of data, especially on the human level, from the domain of science entirely.

To this confusion of thought sociology puts an end by dissecting out from the entire body of organic phenomena a single class by isolating it and discovering uniformities, through the use of an appropriate method, within the isolate thus abstracted. Two consequences follow. First, "living" as a term applied indiscrimi-

nately to all phenomena beyond the inorganic ceases to have perti-
nence. Life, that is to say, ceases to be an entity. The phenomena
cease to be personified, they revert to the status of a collective phenomenon and as such become the subject of analysis. If in this
hitherto collective group there are sociological phenomena, then
there must be other classes as well, since sociology by definition
deals with only one specific class. Hence the task of distinguishing
and delimiting all the classes once dealt with as a unified group
becomes imperative. Beings, or some of them, live sociologically—
how else do they live? The expansion of the hierarchy above the
inorganic becomes inevitable.

In this scientific development sociology soon comes to hold an
intermediate place and so to be in a key position. Once it is established as a specific and irreducible isolate, other specific classes are
soon determined. Thus beings must live biologically before they
can live societally. Biologists in the persons of Bichat and Blainville met the sociologist in the person of Comte; the outcome was
a completely abstract definition of life in a biological sense. Sociology thus was delimited from below. As a body of phenomena
it tended still to be fused and confused with another class of data,
the psychical. Gradually, however, it was seen that beings must
live societally before they can live psychically; hence the delimitation of sociology from above. Its independence was declared by
Sumner. To the isolate that remained after biology and sociology
had claimed their own, an old term rescued from metaphysical
obsolescence was applied. No doubt it is as yet impossible to give
a strictly abstract definition of the psychical fact; as yet it can be defined only by exclusion so to speak, that is to say, it is what is left
of the organic after the vital and the societal have been analyzed
away. Nevertheless, for centuries mankind has been assembling a
mass of observations which now are being systematically organized
as the basis for the study of personality. Hence it is not premature
to declare that the preparatory stage of scientific exploration has
been concluded. The whole sum of phenomena observable by man
has been brought within the framework of uniformity in an encyclopedic hierarchy extending from mathematics through psychology. For the first time scientific development has reached the point
where it can deal with the whole man.

When all the sciences are included within the uniformistic frame of ultimate reference, the outcome is a homogeneity which makes possible certain general statements concerning all of them. One such statement grows out of the fact that as hierarchical relations were established among classes of abstract phenomena, the principle spontaneously directing the ordering of the slowly recognized isolates became clear. Phenomena, it came to be seen, differed as regards generality and complexity. Here then was a way which if systematically followed would lead to the construction of an encyclopedic hierarchy of the sciences. In it the various levels of abstraction would be arranged in accordance with the general principle that had spontaneously appeared.

On this basis, when utilized systematically, the first clear and irrefutable division was that which separated the inorganic from the organic. In this case the second phenomenon is not only less general and more complicated than the first, it is dependent upon the first and is conditioned by it. Here then was a general principle deriving from the principle of classification. It was found to be valid whenever a new abstract isolate was recognized. On all levels of the hierarchy, the less general isolates were dissociated from the more general and were seen to be dependent upon them. Thus the biological is less general than the chemical, i.e., the molecular than the atomic. Only from the biological can come the societal, and only from the latter the personal. In short, throughout the entire realm of scientific observation the higher or less general level is dependent upon and conditioned by the lower or more general.

Objectively, this principle is universal; it is just as widely valid subjectively. The hierarchy of isolates is also a scale of values. The organic is on a higher level of dignity than the inorganic. Only where there is vitality can the still greater worth of sociality be reached, and the value of personality arises only from a level of sociality. That is to say, the higher values are always dependent upon the lower; they are conditioned by the lower; and, as Sumner saw in a special case, they can come into being only as the lower values give them a basis for existence.

A second general statement, universally valid, is based like the first on the homogeneity of the sciences. It carries implications for action even clearer than those just under the surface of the first statement formulated above. The lower levels of abstraction condition the higher; in what way can the higher affect the lower? Only by way of modification, it was said in an earlier chapter. But in what does this modification consist? The answer is that the basic structure, the essential arrangement of an isolate cannot be altered: not that change is impossible, but that it cannot be carried beyond limits. Biological phenomena, for example, can be modified up to any point short of producing the conditions where renewal of substance ceases; past that point they cease to be living. Societal phenomena cease when collective cumulation ceases. The underlying idea here is that which is usually expressed in terms of causality as follows: Man must submit to the laws of nature; only by complying with them can he master the phenomena.

What is meant by these causal expressions is that the arrangement of each specific group of phenomena cannot be altered beyond a given fixed point. If it is, then the structure, the arrangement, ceases to exist. Under such conditions all that can be done within a given isolate is to modify the intensity of the phenomena to be altered, that is to say, change them quantitatively. This condition is what might be called a statical limitation to modification. There is another, of a dynamical kind. Wherever structure manifests itself in action there is process; and process means a succession of phenomena. Hence there are two restrictions upon modification: first, only the intensity of the phenomena can be modified; second, in modifying them regard must be paid to their nature and their succession. The principle is valid throughout the scientific hierarchy.

Still another consequence of bringing all phenomena within the framework of uniformity is the termination of an old philosophical dispute, inherent in the causal frame of reference, namely, the quarrel between materialism and idealism. Materialism, in the positive sense of the word, is an attempt to account for the phenomena isolated on a given level as due to the influence, action, operation, or existence of the phenomena on a lower level: thus it is materialism to attempt to reduce biological or sociological or psychological phenomena or all of them together, i.e., the whole range of the organic, to phases of the operation of inorganic factors, physical or chemical or both. It is materialism to reduce sociological or psychological facts to a purely biological basis. It is materialism to explain personality solely on the basis of societal phenomena and their laws. As the recognition of isolates has risen from one level of abstraction to another there has followed, in the causal interpretation, a succession of "determinisms," the latest of which is cultural determinism. The holders of these theories are materialists all. The one sound support for their position is the fact that the lower isolates condition the operation of the higher.

Idealism is the inverse of materialism. It traverses the hierarchy from the top downwards. Thus it is idealism to attribute societal phenomena to the sole operation of the factors of personality. In strict logic it would be idealism to explain biological or physical phenomena as due to psychological factors, after the fashion of the fairy tales. So too it would be idealism to account for biological phenomena by sociological laws or physicochemical facts by biological explanations. Putting these positions in plain words shows why there is so little idealism outside the psychological domain. It is so patently absurd today to propose explanations of this kind anywhere outside the range of the societal or the psychical that no one entertains the thought of doing so. "The moving of mountains" is now known to be a purely metaphorical expression; but it has not always been so, as the mythologies make clear. Such are now completely discredited, with one exception: idealistic explanations of societal phenomena are still numerous in the absence, or the ignorance, of the sciences supplying a knowledge of the uniformities observable in the two isolates involved. But this situation is only transitory; it can be disregarded. Idealism has its only basis in the fact that phenomena on a given level can be modified by those belonging on a higher.

Between these two opposed philosophies the distinction can endure only so long as all the various classes of phenomena are not reduced to law. With the extension of the concept of uniformity to one isolate after another, the situation changes. As materialism ascends the scale of the sciences it passes in due course from the old to the new: from biology, where for example racial causes are given for societal phenomena, to sociology, where societal phenomena are called on to account for the orectic constants. It is still materialism at this point since the higher level of data, the personal, is accounted for on the basis of a lower, older, and better known isolate, the societal. But when the last level is reached—when the scientific inquirer passes from the societal to the psychical—materialism is suddenly transformed into idealism since there is now nothing higher to be observed and accounted for. At the same time idealism disappears too since the data that comprised it are now dealt with on a basis of positive science, not of metaphysical philosophy; i.e., they are transferred from the jurisdiction of causality to that of uniformity. In short, by virtue of a gradual extension of a positive frame of reference materialism becomes idealism and idealism is transformed into science.

Still other difficulties are resolved or dissipated by the extension of uniformity to the highest levels of the encyclopedia. For example, the perennial conundrum concerning the relations between the individual and society disappears as the pseudo problem it always was. Insofar as the old formulation had a meaning it dealt with a correlation as inseparable as that which connects hills with valleys. But now it is clear that the individual is a complex of animal, socius, and person, each element belonging to a specific class of phenomena; that society is only the resultant of the integration of many factors. The individual does not make society nor does society make the individual. The whole conception is but a reflection of the obsolete division of philosophy into natural and moral. What is involved is the relation among three irreducible isolates, the vital, the societal, the psychical, and the way in which the phenomena in these three categories are mutually modified or conditioned.

So too does the old problem of free will find a reformulation when the ultimate basis of interpretation is shifted from causality to uniformity. It is evident to begin with that a question so formulated can arise only in a nexus of causality. Once the notion of the will as an entity with a causative influence is set aside in favor of the concept that makes the will the final state of desire, the whole problem of freedom in this connection has to be restated. Such positive data as remain after the entity is gone must be given a new interpretation.

In this new formulation what is important is the recognition of the fact that psychical phenomena form an isolate of their own, specific and irreducible. They have an unalterable arrangement, resulting in a distinctive structure and process. In other terms, there are uniformities which are operative throughout the whole domain of the psychical. Particularly is the statement true of the orectic constants which are the source of impulsion. In this abstract sense the will is free, that is to say the operation of the psychical elements in reaching an equilibrium is subject only to the uniformities existent within the psychical isolate. Like the phenomena of any other isolate, they may be conditioned by other and lower uniformities, but in any normal case the essential quality of psychical functioning is unaltered. In other words, there is a moral determinism; the factors of personality function according to their own laws. In still other terms, in the framework of uniformity the metaphysical concept called freedom of the will becomes transmuted into the positive concept of the irreducibility of the phenomena comprised within the psychical isolate.

Finally, in concluding this inadequate review of the consequences of the rise of uniformism as an ultimate frame of reference, the inclusion of the highest ranges of observation within the domain of law makes possible an approach to the question, What is the nature of Man? He has long been authoritatively declared to be a reasoning, rational being. It is seldom recalled, however, that positive science has had nothing whatever to do with this pronouncement. It rests wholly upon data gathered, colligated, and interpreted in the framework of agency and causality. Science has never been in a position to speak on the subject. Only since the rise of sociology and psychology has it been possible to envisage a positive answer to questions of the kind here in point. Hitherto a group of phenomena obviously associated in some functional fashion has been observed in the behavior of men. It was denominated the mind—the organ of attention—and its operations were considered as a unit. It forms the perfect example of a collective phenomenon. Just what the operations involved were, into what classes they might be divided, how each class was related to the others—such questions were beyond the asking. It was sufficient to attribute the whole complex to the work of an entity reason, with which Nature, the agent of the final cause, had endowed mankind.

Discovery of a societal phenomenon and an appropriate method for dealing with it destroyed the causal hypothesis of mind and turned analysis to the search for uniformities. The separation of collective cumulation from the sum total of mental phenomena was the work of sociology. It showed that through generations of collective existence experiences had been accumulating which put at the disposal of new members of the human stock the knowledge that earlier men had acquired. Here, it came to be seen, was the guide for individual descendants of the animal Homo, not any endowment of the race as such. Reason, in short, is a societal product; the animal Homo and his descendants are not reasoning beings at all.

Moreover it was discovered as a part of the same inductive achievement to which sociology is due that societal facts were the *results* of mental, i.e., psychical factors distinguishable as sources and destinations. Continuation of inductive analysis revealed behind results the operations of functional elements to which the spontaneous cumulations of experience summarized in language had long given the designations feeling, thought, action. These terms were found to be descriptive of such distinctive and separable functions as impulsion, i.e., orexis, as the picturing of existent or desired conditions through the operation of the eidomorphic faculties upon the impressions made by the senses, i.e., ideation, as the exteriorization of images, i.e., exergy. These three divisions of the mind are components of an apparatus, each capable of independent exercise but normally working interdependently with the others. Hence they may be considered as a system and the outcome of their combined operation an equilibrium.

It was discovered in addition that both ideation and exergy gave results that could be cumulated; and thus the inductive distinction between results on the one hand and sources and destinations on the other was deductively validated. The *source* of psychical operations was found to be impulsion, the functioning of the orectic constants; the *destination* was the satisfaction of the impulses, an end to which both ideation and exergy were subordinated. That both ideation and exergy produced results that could be cumulated in the course of generations of collective experience was a quite secondary matter from the psychical point of view. It could provide a basis for sociology, no doubt, but it could not alter the fact that the animal Homo was a creature of impulse, the satisfaction of which is his chief end. His action is the outcome of the desire to make real the pictures that impulsion stimulates; his ideation is the picturing of the conditions that satisfy impulsion. Thinking—ideation—is ideally a pleasant reverie; and men do not voluntarily reason. They are compelled by dire necessity to be guided by the facts of the world without as they have been discovered by millennia of experience; fundamentally they, as individual descendants of the animal Homo, are makers of fantasies.

With the division of psychical phenomena into three classes, orexis, ideation, and exergy, the construction of a scientific scale of values already begun can be resumed and completed. Its relation to the nature of man as just defined will immediately be apparent. Just as the psychical isolate holds the place at the summit of the hierarchic scale of the sciences, so the orectic constants are the highest in the domain of the psychical. Both ideation and exergy are their ministers and on occasion even their slaves. As the ultimate source of impulsion they are the center or seat of complete subjectivity. Both ideation and exergy are in this regard objective with respect to orexis. No doubt the three compose an apparatus, but the central element of the equilibrium that results is orexis. It is therefore the ultimate source of morality and so its predominance in the scale of values is deductively justified.

Sociological induction enables the scientific investigator into psychical phenomena to go still further. Orexis itself is but a general name for the psychical constants which are the subjective sources of impulsion. It is itself a composite, in which drives of various kinds come into an equilibrium. Societal observation through the centuries has distinguished several varieties of impulsion classifiable in a series. The extremes of this series are those urges that concern the existence of the individual, isolated being and those that motivate the group member. Impulsion, that is to say, gives rise to two classes of orectic forces, the interests and the sympathies. Intermediate between the two stand those individual urges that find satisfaction in activities that benefit the collectivity. The result is the analysis of the orectic constants into three divisions: interest, ambition, sympathy. The will in all normal cases is an equilibrium of these three forces.

In regard to them two remarks may be made. In the first place, they are innate. In the words of Alexander, ambition, competitiveness, and the urge for accomplishment are not imposed upon the individual by external cultural conditions; the latter may encourage and strengthen one attitude rather than another, but culture does not introduce anything into the organism that is not already there. Sociology confirms this opinion by revealing the difference between results and sources, the latter being the essential motivations of the individual. In addition, sympathy cannot be reduced to enlightened self-interest since rational effort of this kind is quite impossible in the absence initially of the knowledge that would guide action. Moreover, on the animal level, action on behalf of others may lead even to the destruction of the animal so motivated. Gall in fact long ago demonstrated the innateness of the propensities, and Comte was led by his influence plus the study of the effect of one generation upon another to generalize the position: societal phenomena, he said, "determine the fundamental direction of all our tendencies whatever," [1] but that is all; the tendencies are innate.

In the second place, the spontaneous inductions of mankind systematized by sociological analysis lead to an evaluation of the three classes of orectic constants. Deductively, the same principle of decreasing generality and increasing complexity that served to construct the scientific hierarchy serves also to determine the place within each isolate of the elements comprised by it. From this point of view the sympathies are undoubtedly the highest level of psychical phenomena. Inductively, the same conclusion is reached. The interests plus their annexes the ambitions are far stronger and more numerous than the sympathies, but their ultimate effect is to isolate the beings that are so motivated and thus to atomize the societies they might tend to form. Individual impulsions work to bring their possessors into conflict and at the best to negate one another in action. It is only the sympathies that finally serve to hold beings together and thus to make possible the societal exist-

1. *Système de politique positive*, 4, 3; 3, 9–10.

ence that increasingly multiplies contacts, combines and recombines impulsions, and so exercises continuously the constituent elements of the psyche whereby personality is developed. Only the sympathies can finally serve to integrate the orectic constants as a whole. They thus come to hold the highest place in the scale of values.

Solution of the problem of values makes it possible for the first time to put the problem of moral progress on a scientific basis, to shift it from the framework of causality to that of uniformity. Man, it has been seen, is a maker of fantasies, prompted by three varieties of impulsion: interest, ambition, sympathy. Of these three classes of orexis the sympathies hold the highest place in the scale of values. What is needed then to secure the improvement, the true progress of Man is to obtain in the psychical equilibrium a greater share of influence for the sympathies. What is required is to raise to a maximum or an optimum the intensity of the operation of the sympathetic orectic constants. Raising Man to a higher moral level and holding him there means permanently increasing the intensity of the sympathies.

Implied in this formulation of the ultimate problem of science are certain conclusions that should be made explicit. The first and most evident of these implications is the positive view of personality as a product, an integration, an equilibrium to the making of which many factors have gone. Both the validity and the significance of the facts have constantly increased since the days when Comte made the unity, the harmony of the inner life the central point of his meditations. Later schools have strengthened the position. In the words of Alexander, what most impresses the psychoanalytic observer is the internal heterogeneity of personality.

The second implication of the positive view of personality is a consequence of the first. If heterogeneity is a characteristic of the factors involved, then there are many variables in play in producing the final result. And if there are many variables then there are many ways in which to bring about changes in the results of their interaction. Psychical phenomena, being at the summit of the scientific hierarchy, are particularly subject to factors of variation. They are the highest and noblest of all the isolates and as such are conditioned by all the lower levels of phenomena: societal, vital, physical. Change in any of them will have its ultimate repercussion upon the psychical. Not only is this source of variability constantly open, but within the psychic isolate itself there are many variables: the several classes of orectics, the different eidomorphic faculties, the degrees of exergy. Here then are many opportunities for influencing personality.

Dominant among these variables are the sympathies. Their importance is unique. Not only do they as the bearers of the highest values have a special function in serving as the center about which all lower impulsions may be gathered and reconciled; they are also the constant forces that work to bring personalities together in harmonious relations. Because these orectics exist and are innate, the ultimate moral problem of Man can be formulated in the framework of uniformism: By what means can the unity of personality and the union of personalities be secured and so the continuity of generations? The innateness of the sympathies makes it possible to propose the problem just formulated for scientific solution; indeed unless they were innate it could not be propounded at all. It was after seeing the significance of these facts that Comte declared: *"The innateness of the benevolent propensities and the movement of the earth constitute the principal results of modern science,* since they lay the essential foundations, one subjective, the other objective, of true relativity." [2]

Concealed within the second implication is a third, the most subtle and obscure of all. Manipulation of variables in accordance with a knowledge of the uniformities involved may produce results of value, but it has one serious limitation. It may for example secure for the sympathies a greater share in the making of the psychical equilibrium than they would otherwise have, but it does not for that reason effect a permanent increase in the intensity of operation of the orectics in question. There remains then a final question for scientific discussion. How can the sympathetic orectics, the most profoundly subjective element of man's nature, be *directly* reached so as to give them an absolutely greater share in the making of personality? The question seems to resolve itself into another: How can the subjective be dealt with objectively? Evidently here is a question for the psychologist in the strictest sense. It is not for the sociologist, utilizing only descriptive and empirical cumulations of experience, to deal with. All he can say is that once the

2. *Politique, 4,* 20.

answer is obtained the descendants of the animal Homo will at last be able to transcend their ancestor and become Men.

It need not be said that phenomena of such importance to Man as those in point here have not gone unregarded in the past. They have of course always been observed, but they have been synthesized and given meaning in cadres of causality or even of agency. Within these limits the interpretations and conclusions have widely differed. In some cases the very existence of personality has been unfavorably viewed in the belief that it was an obstacle to Man's union with a greater whole. In other cases the factors of personality, particularly the orectics, were regarded as sources of unrest and so attempts were made to subdue and control them. Internal calm through the extinction of desire was the objective. Historically such absolute views seem to have been the product of India, where deitism flourished in all its forms from daimonism to entitism, just as fetishism reached its maximum of development in China.

In the West such absolutes were not reached, and when their influence began to permeate that region the extension of uniformity to the lower levels of the scientific hierarchy had already proceeded to the point where causality was being more and more restricted to the higher isolates; hence the more nearly relative conceptions that gained currency there. In its most typical western form the essential problem of personality was formulated by Paul, in whose mind the conflict between the higher and the lower tendencies of Man took a particularly vivid form. Man unaided was helpless in this struggle. The natural Man born in sin could not strive against his own nature. Only help from above and without could avail, and this help had to be asked for. It might not be granted. Only, that is, by grace could the higher triumph over the lower in the conflict between the forces of good and evil; and no one could assure to himself the indispensable aid. It was a matter of choice exercised from on high inscrutably.

Gratia sive dilectio: back of these words is the solution that was reached in terms of causality to the problem of securing in the personal equilibrium the dominance of sympathies over interests. This moral gift was free—how it came was unknown; it was inexplicable—why it was bestowed was unknown also. Nevertheless men might make themselves worthy of being chosen as the recipients of grace. They could, if not obtain it, at least try to merit it. They might thus become vessels of election. There were, they not too confidently believed, some inductive hints as to the connection between behavior and election, but that was all. So men set out to use what had to be purely empirical methods of psychical training to effect what was in fact the restoration or the establishment of an orectic equilibrium centered about the sympathies. To these efforts, east or west, whether aimed at absorption into the Luminous All or the attainment of an Ineffable Peace or submission to an Inscrutable Will, the name that has been given is mysticism.

In the future the assemblage of purely empirical data gained by a long course of spontaneous psychical experimentation collected under the term "mysticism" must be subjected to scientific analysis and the surviving facts synthesized in the framework of uniformity. Here as elsewhere the continued orchestration of sonorous phonemes without referents cannot take the place of positive inductions. The existence and operation of the sympathetic orectic constants—whatever the refinement and ultimate definition a scientific psychology may give to these descriptive terms—opens the whole domain of personality and its factors to the search for regularities and the control of laws. No longer are daimons, deities, entities, replicates or hominoids, agents or causes, multiple or single, the appropriate frame of reference for the interpretation of human behavior in its spiritual aspects. In consequence all the empirical devices of the past—rites, rituals, invocations, appeals, prayers, incantations, offerings, sacrifices, sufferings, fastings, mutilations, asceticism, dreams, dances, drugs—must be subjected to critical analysis with the object of increasing the knowledge which will lead to the control of the orectics and in particular of the sympathies. In short, the mystic must become scientific.

The first step toward this goal is to view the facts relatively and not absolutely. To say that psychical phenomena form an abstract isolate is one thing; to say that spiritual phenomena can be isolated from all other human concerns is something else. The second statement cannot even be formulated intelligibly for it means that the person has no relation with the socius or the animal; hence of course the relegation to a heaven of such unconditioned and unrelated replicates. It may well be that a certain withdrawal from the world is necessary for the attainment of a certain degree of moral purity; that is to say, in positive terms, the conditioning effect of societal and vital and physical phenomena upon the moral may inhibit certain types of behavior. But to cut off entirely the conditioning influences of the lower isolates is to extinguish the higher completely. Of course it is never done. The beggar's bowl binds him to all mankind. Wisdom of this variety may ensure the calm that comes from the extinction of desire; it ensures as well the extinction of the species. To such lengths it never goes; but what of the effect upon the race of the continuous extirpation of those who are presumably so superior as to be capable of reaching the highest levels of morality and remaining there?

Moreover, upon the most favorable interpretation, the isolation that comes from withdrawal from the world is fraught with danger. All the spiritual advisers agree in warning the mystic against the tendencies toward vanity and inaction which threaten him, dangers that easily become conceit and indolence to end in arrogance and passivity. Evident enough among the saints, they are all the more conspicuous among those smaller souls who single out from among the mystical phenomena those that tend to favor ideational creativity and then as litterateurs, poetasters, and fantasists of all kinds transmute into a right and a superiority what is at best but a privilege and a responsibility. The saints did no such thing; but even in regard to them the question must be asked whether their superiority, transferred from a causal into a uniformistic frame of reference, can retain the absolute values attributed to it. Of what value is an achievement which demands withdrawal from human kind to be consummated?

From a relative standpoint based on a positive psychology, what is ultimately involved in these profound questions is the nature and relation of the orectics, the sources of human behavior, and particularly the part played therein by the sympathetic constants. No doubt the sum of positive knowledge on these high matters is small; the psychologist is still as far distant from his essential data as the physicist of the 1800's was from the atom. No doubt the difficulties to be overcome are formidable. If a warning were needed against overconfidence it could be found in the fact that observers in the past, despite their all-surpassing motivation, could never gain inductively more than mere hints as to the causes of the conversions, often sudden, by which men were born again. That is to say there are few or no empirical guides for effecting a transfer of dominance in the personal equilibrium from the interests to the sympathies. In regard to the plan of Providence in the bestowal of graces, says Poulain, "God has not willed to reveal all his secrets to us." He "has committed himself to nothing, and he makes it clear." [3] But in another frame of reference, it may well be when all the implications are grasped that the problem of grace will become the very center of psychological research.

No doubt too the deeper problems, going perhaps to the root of the spontaneity that underlies orexis, are still to be attacked. The point is that the road to the future is open. Hominoids and replicates no longer serve to supply illusory agencies and causes. Within the uniformistic frame of reference the societal process whereby inductive procedures in the past have led from one acquisition to another will continue to operate, even more effectively than before. It will take time; but the critical point has been passed. No doubt finally such an attitude asks much of these upon whom it is incumbent. "Few indeed," said Comte, "are the intellects, especially if cultivated, who are able to wait patiently in doubt, and while doubting to prepare." [4] For these impatient souls the spirits are always at hand to lend solace.

Ascending from one level of abstraction to another, the thought of this volume, mirroring the advance of scientific speculation, has reached the least general and most complicated of all the isolates. It has moved steadily from the objective to the subjective until it has met the highest phenomena observable by man. Here in the realm of the highest values, where the inner spontaneity manifests itself in the form of orexis, lie those sources which give rise to desires that must be satisfied and so to results wherein the sociologist finds the material for his inductions. The place of sociology in the encyclopedic hierarchy of the sciences and its relations with its adjacent isolates is thus fixed. It remains only to solidify this position by a rapid review of the ground already traversed, but moving this time from the subjective to the objective.

Such a review, conducted within the frame of reference of uniformity, begins with personality. And here at once a distinction

3. A. Poulain, *Des Grâces d'oraison* (9th ed. Paris, Beauchesne, 1902), p. 561.
4. *Politique, 3,* 513.

must be made. Personality is in no sense a synonym for individuality. The latter is simply a term for the sum of the factors which distinguish one being from another. To encourage individuality is all too often to foster oddity and eccentricity, to bring the individual into opposition rather than harmony with his kind, to isolate him from them. Personality implies the balance, the integration of all the orectic constants; and this in turn implies an equilibrium about the sympathies, for they alone can secure the subordination (not the extinction) of the interests and discipline (not destroy) the exergy which characterizes them.

Personality then is an equilibrium more or less complete and stable, into the making of which many variables enter. As yet only empirical measures have been discovered for conscious control of these factors of variation. Particularly difficult is the task of directly increasing the intensity of operation of the sympathies. Certain advantages seem to follow ascetic practices aimed at diminishing the energy of the interests so that the sympathies may be relatively stronger. Isolation too has its value: harmful when carried to the extent of cutting men off from their fellows; useful when it allows them to separate themselves sufficiently from their culture to enable them on their return to it to become an exterior force capable of modifying it.

On a somewhat lower level, both ideation and exergy can be used as variables in the alteration of personality. The first can supply stimuli for the orectics by creating mental pictures designed to arouse emotions of a particular kind. Common enough in a spontaneous way, the systematic use of ideation has great possibilities as can be seen from such cases as that of Loyola and the spiritual exercises he employed to form his disciples. Ideation itself may be improved too by submitting it to the discipline that experience has shown to be necessary if thought is to be a valid guide for behavior, that is, by subordinating fantasy-thinking to reality-thinking. In regard to exergy little need be said, for the essential point here has long been known, namely, the usefulness of good deeds to stimulate and strengthen good motives.

What may be accomplished by a psychology expanded in the framework of uniformity cannot now be foretold. Already it is developing a therapeutic whereby in Dante's phrase "to straighten those whom the world made crooked." Presently it will move on to a hygiene, for the community as well as the individual. The sociologist can confidently anticipate such information as the breaking point of moral resistance, whereby the social engineer in the building of institutions will be as greatly aided as is the civil engineer by studies in the strength of materials.

Yet when all is said for the psychological level of abstraction, it still remains true that the person is incomplete. The very word suggests the fact. Who or what is speaking through the person? For the Greeks it was *nous,* the active intellect, for the medieval world *Deus nos personat.* Transposing the question into the frame of reference of uniformity answers it in a positive fashion and at the same time explains the meaning now given to the term "personality." What is speaking through the individual being is the sum total of the results of the societal process which in the course of time has subjected the innate psychical constants to an infinity of stimuli, developed each of them, and combined them in countless ways. The result has been the transformation of animality into humanity; and it is Humanity which speaks through the animal Homo and converts him into the human person, the Man.

Beneath the person then is the socius; and in the distinction lies the solution of one of the essential problems of human development, namely, the relation between the spiritual and the temporal. This age-old conflict, absolute in a framework of causality, becomes collaboration in a relative world of uniformity. The two powers are separate; both are necessary; neither is supreme. The only authority either possesses is that which comes from scientific knowledge duly validated. Each has a place, for the man is not only a person but a socius, not only a socius but a person; and in any normal situation both aspects of his nature must be respected. "The separation of the powers": in this phrase the psychical isolate and the societal isolate find recognition. The mystic, having become scientific, must take his stand in the real world beside the ruler; both spiritual and temporal directors are required. The yogi and the commissar are not rivals or opponents but coadjutors.

At this point in the descent of the hierarchy the variety of progress termed efficiency in an earlier passage comes into relevance. On a basis of sociological science it becomes possible to modify the conditions of life in such a way as to favor the production of folkways designed to promote the mores and prompt the actions which will facilitate an integration of the orectics about the sympathies. Preaching, i.e., the appeal to sentiments, will not avail here. It proceeds in a kind of idealistic vacuum in which the person beats his luminous wings in vain and may even die, like Ruskin, from what should be called the Platonic disease. No wonder the mystic withdraws from such a world.

Under a positive synthesis the situation changes. The mystic returns to earth and in a relative frame of reference directs the attention of the statesman to the human qualities which societal conditions should favor. To this end the whole field of interposition lies open, mapped by sociological induction: economic, socionomic, semantic, political. Even more is in prospect when such composite sciences as social psychology arise to bridge the gap between the completely abstract and the entirely concrete. Enterprises of hitherto unimagined range and scope come within the clear bounds of possibility. The pictured prospects which ideation under such stimulus creates raises the intensity of the appropriate orectics to the point where they become the dominant drives and thus determine the will to exteriorize the image of desire.

All the traditional and sanctified societal institutions come under scrutiny. They are recognized for what they are, namely, the spontaneous and empirical efforts of mankind to meet the needs of societal existence; and they are judged on their capacity to fit into a society where the sympathies are encouraged by institutional means. Such absolutes as property, individual initiative, government become purely relative and are limited, extended, or transformed on scientific grounds. A scientific morality adequate to meet the requirements of men at a given stage of development can be formulated and modified as they advance.

Religion is no more exempt from such remaking than any other product of the societal process. Its human and relative function is twofold: to create and maintain harmony among the factors of personality and to foster a union of such integrated personalities, thus ensuring the continuity of their collective existence. Expressed in such terms the problem of inventing a religion is a problem of applied social psychology, the requisite materials for which already exist. It becomes a rational proposal to suggest the making of a religion designed to meet the needs of a given collectivity—tribe or people—and raise it to the cultural stage of uniformity without the need for it to pass through such intermediate stages as monotheism. Just so in a parallel case is it possible for a group to enter upon the stage of industry without passing through the difficulties of industrialism.

Descent to the next lower level brings into view the animal, who must be ministered to as well as the socius and the person. He must be nourished, clothed, and housed. The biological knowledge already available for the favorable conditioning of the higher levels now extends to the point where plants can be modified, or even made, to order; tomorrow it will be the turn of the animals. And ultimately the eugenist, supplied with the knowledge that the animal Homo in order to lead a societal and psychical existence must be characterized by health, probity, intelligence, and industry and equipped with the knowledge of the biological conditions required for the manifestation of those qualities, will be able to raise his eyes from the melancholy contemplation of pedigreed pigs and horses to the vision of man regenerated.

On the physical level, the advances already made on the exclusive basis of complete uniformity, such as the creation of designed substances or the supplying of inexhaustible sources of energy, are already almost commonplace. Still further achievements await the stimulus of the needs that an advancing society may feel. But no one today knows better than the physicist that the crest of scientific inquiry has moved on to higher ground.

The synthesis just traversed, homogeneous in concept and method from top to bottom, is of course subjective. In a framework of uniformity what else could it be? Its values are human values. What reason is there to think that the very concept of values has any other than a human source and relevance? But the human is not the individual descendant of the animal Homo; it is the cumulated product of collective experience through the ages. It has been made by Man for men. Hence it is homogeneous in a double sense, logically and psychologically. It obviates once for all the confusions and dangers of the transitional past. It makes an end of the schizophrenia that sincere minds are threatened with when they have to change methods in passing from one level of abstraction to another. It saves clever minds from the cynicism which comes from seeing demoded methods and doctrines defended from motives of interest. It keeps mediocre minds from falling into indifference to all higher motivations because of endless quarrels over doctrines and methods. Finally, in a positive fashion, it guides the individual member of society. As a person he is responsible for the development of his own inner life, doing what he can to balance his personality about the sympathies. As a socius he lives by and through the societal groupings: family, country, humanity. Modest success in living for these collective existences is possible for all normal beings, in contrast to an individual competitive struggle where failure is by necessity the common lot. If in addition as citizen he wishes to advance the day when progress is made by his group, then he must join his efforts under appropriate leadership with those of others for the desired end.

In short, men are guided by Humanity. Hence they can work with confidence. From confidence comes courage; from courage, energy. Both Comte and Spencer saw the possibilities and the spirit in which they should be realized. The words which both approved as expressing the guidance that comes from the study of sociology are therefore appropriate in bringing this volume to a close:

Calm and Activity.

BIBLIOGRAPHICAL NOTE

For a volume like the present, which strives to effect a synthesis, the adjunction of long lists of books presumably in support of the positions taken is mere vanity and even a kind of eruditional exhibitionism. Bibliographies abound in both general and special treatises which are known to all. Moreover, it should be remarked that often a particular volume gains rather than lends authority by being fitted into a synthetic context. The only exceptions are those that contain only the raw facts.

Hence there is no bibliography here. Yet it would be unpardonable not to mention the main begetters of the views expressed herein. They are two. For the general structure of thought which takes uniformity as the final frame of reference, Auguste Comte of course is the source, especially in

Cours de philosophie positive (1830-42), the second half in particular and above all the final chapters, which are a sort of discourse on method.

Système de politique positive (1851–54), the four volumes entire.

La Synthese subjective (1856), particularly the introduction to Vol. *I*, the only one written out of four planned.

For material more narrowly concerning sociology, W. G. Sumner is the source, in

Folkways (1906)

Finally, two works have been influential although they were never written:

Comte, *La Morale théorique, instituant la connaissance de la nature humaine.* (Nothing but the barest outline of the volume remains, dated 1857.)

Sumner, the sociology to which he refers in the Preface to *Folkways,* p. v.: "My next task is to finish the sociology." Keller, in the Preface to Sumner and Keller, *The Science of Society,* p. xxiv, wrote: "He said that all he had written on the general treatise must now be done all over again in the light of *Folkways,* and that he could never rise to the task."

INDEX